To my friend
Jim Valentine

J. I. Mane

12/95

Mack's mother writes
about a way of life you
and I missed in more
ways than one!
This book is a
biography, autobiography,
and a book of poems!

TIME REMEMBERED

Elizabeth Braswell Pearsall

TIME REMEMBERED

*With Sketches
From
Eastern Carolina
and·
Captiva Island*

A Memoir

Elizabeth Braswell Pearsall

North Carolina Wesleyan College Press
Rocky Mount
1995

LC 95-67938
ISBN 0-933598-55-6

Published by
North Carolina Wesleyan College Press
3400 North Wesleyan Boulevard
Rocky Mount, North Carolina
27804

Table Of Contents

Foreward   Letter to the Reader i

Part I: Village Bells, Country Bells 1

Part II: At the Falls of the Tar 130

Part III: Beyond the Sea Grapes 277

Part IV: Life Within the Compound 309

Part V: An Evening at Bellemonte 399

PartVI: The Homing Instinct 487

Part VII: A Moonless Sea 503

Part VIII: The North Star 517

Part IX: The Quiet Eye, The Quiet Things 529

Afterword 559

Appendix   Braswell Family data from *The Book of Rocky
            Mount*, published around 1910 564
            Note on Robert Bracewell, the original
            Braswell American Ancestor 568

Pencil Drawings

Drawings   Page

I: Shadowlawn . . . . cover

II: Melissy's Tobacco Twine Trellis and its
      Morning Glory Vine 8

III: My Grandmother Bryan's Key Basket 16

IV: A Walk to the Spring at Panacea 38

V: St. John's Episcopal Church in the Village 45

VI: Our Own Gateway In The Snow 163

VII: The Well at Chapel Hill 180

VIII: The State Capitol. Its Construction
      Begun in 1833, Completed in 1840 239

IX: Captiva: The Pier Over the Shallows Near
      Blind Pass 291

X: A Small Square of Needlepoint Becomes
      A Connector 494

XI: The Steps From the Upper Terrace Into the
      Dooryard Garden of My Present Home 543

*Life is a continuous
process of endings and beginnings,
all flowing together*

James J. Kilpatrick
Fox's Union

The past is forever in the present, even when it is forgotten.

George P. Garrett
A Selecton of Literary Essays and Reviews

Dear Reader,

There are three persons who have been vital to bringing these reminiscences to the light of day: Rosa Leonard, Louisa Messenbrink, and Marybeth Sutton Wallace.

There has been a fourth. For it was Terry Smith – and here I use the shorter version of his given name, Leverett – Professor of English and former Associate Dean of our local North Carolina Wesleyan College, who, on a certain Founder's Day, when I was, as usual, in attendance, suggested my writing something about my family to be placed in the college library. This would, of course, include information concerning my husband, Thomas Pearsall, and his life of public service to our state.

Neither of these four persons, neither Rosa, nor Terry, nor Louisa, nor Marybeth has been a part of my past. For one thing, I am of a far earlier generation. Their own ages differ, as do their backgrounds. Louisa is in her early thirties and is the latest to come to live in our community. Terry, originally from New York State, is now in his twenty-second year at North Carolina Wesleyan College. Marybeth Wallace, a young Kentuckian, came into our community six years ago when her husband joined a local law firm, and was to become Director of the North Carolina Wesleyan Press. It is in that capacity that she has kindly done my editing. Only Rosa's background and mine are similar.

When the invitation to do the writing was extended, I wondered – aloud – if my casual, homespun style would be up to the mark. With the assurance that it need not be any literary gem, that it would be classified as regional writing, I accepted. Considered in that light, in a sense, it was already written. For I had, for some time, been at work on the story of my life: where it had begun and where it had led. Naturally, it was the story of my family as well, and since I had always felt that my real life began when Tom came into it, unmistakably, it was our story. Its function, I assumed, would be to lie, handwritten, in that "bottom drawer" of keepsakes, which, over the years, from the milestones of her life, the woman of sentiment slowly fills. Since Tom's death, I had found comfort in writing, for to pour out my grief was to feel his presence, that feeling which I clung to with all I had. I can see, now, that it was a cry into my search for meaning, an attempt to strengthen my faith in our ultimately being together again, without which, I felt I could hardly go on.

Slowly, I came to write of brighter things. Penning a few daily paragraphs became a habit. The only subject I had, was, of course, life, life in general, my own in particular. And, since the diaries and old letters on both sides of my family had meant so much to me, I felt some sense of obligation to glean from them enough to link the generations, those earlier, my own, and those yet to come. I could envision a day when, on opening that hypothetical "bottom drawer" to the discovery of the result of my effort, there might be the tender exclamation from a loved one, as a witty friend of mine predicted would no doubt be true of her own, "Oh! Bless her little heart!"

But, having had no office training, as I wrote, I found my filing system, or lack of such, a perpetual source of woe. In an earlier effort, I had taken action on an article by a professional writer in which he confessed to a weakness similar to mine. In all seriousness, he told how he had overcome this handicap by taking a spare room in his house, by stringing innumerable clotheslines across it, and by laying in a supply of clothespins. These he used, literally – and the pun is mine – to hang his thoughts on. He had found this system entirely effective, and I could hardly wait to duplicate it.

Taking the largest bedroom in the house, I spent a day devising the rigging. The solution to transporting my assortment of notebooks and other writing paraphernalia upstairs to that room seemed to lie in the use of a large laundry basket. So with a plastic one of bright yellow, I climbed the stairs to the now unused master bedroom. It took portions of several days to fasten the papers, in random fashion, in place. That done, I was ready.

But the system had its drawbacks. As I made my way up and down the aisles, scanning for a desired item, it was only when I was fully upright – and even then my elbows must be held close to my sides – that I was halfway comfortable. When not in that rigid position, the only way to give my attention to the papers on the lowest line was to move down the aisles on my knees. The middle lines required a bent-over position. At those times when the phone rang, I would come charging out of this network in a frenzy; the scramble wreaking havoc with my hair.

For obvious reasons, I was not planning to give my methods any publicity. But then, one day, my cousin, Peggy Perry, came by. When I came downstairs to let her in, my wild hair required some explanation. Peggy has a keen sense of humor, and when I showed her my setup, she all but died laughing, could hardly stop long enough to say, "Well, now you have the perfect title for your book: *From the Clothesline.*"

It was, indeed, a perfect fit, as I laughingly agreed. And assuring Peggy that I was in need of a break, we made our way to the kitchen to brew a pot of tea.

As often happened in those days, however, our friends from farther North, in driving down to Captiva, an island where for twenty-three years our family had a second home, a story to be told later, would stop overnight with us. Our system had always been to assure them that the latch-string would be out. All that would be needed would be a phone call the night before they were to pass through. And since life is, if anything, unpredictable, there came a call that night from Libby Bennett of Boston, a proper Bostonian if there ever was, who was motoring down to Captiva with her son, his wife, and their son and daughter. This mixture of ages and sexes meant that my three extra bedrooms must be put to use. Down must and did come the clotheslines. There was no time to unfasten the clothespins, so lines, clothespins, and assorted pages were dumped helter-skelter back into the laundry basket. And in this state of defeat, for a very long time, the basket sat in the attic, unattended.

Yet, when several years had gone by, hope sprang again. Mainly because I had arrived at what seemed another inspired filing system: that of using my dining room chairs. That I happened to have ten chairs suggested that by poring over what I'd already written, and sorting it into ten chapters, one for each chair, and contriving a reasonable facsimile of a table of contents as to chairs and their chapters, or chapters and their chairs, I might seem to have something going, and would begin to feel a measure of composure. Yes, this was it. Why had it taken me so long to think of it?

Somewhere in this procedure, I stopped to read a page I hadn't seen in a long time, and, as once in a while I'm told will happen to a writer – and I was now easily thinking of myself in that pleasing category – the page seemed rather good. It seemed to say what I meant to say. My pleasure was short-lived, however, for in the same breath I recalled the admonition given by professionals to amateurs: when you've written something that affects you that way, throw it out! The inference, I suppose, being that you've probably tried too hard, and in so doing, have lost your identity. With this in mind, I decided to make Laura, my housekeeper, my sounding board. Calling upstairs, I asked, "Laura, how about coming down and bringing two

of those folding chairs from the sun room into the dining room for me?"
For the other chairs, now lined up against the dining room walls, were laden.
"With the table between us, we'll sit opposite each other for an experiment.
I want to read something to you. Tell me if you find it interesting."

When I had read it, I asked, "What about it? Is it interesting?"

And she answered with due politeness, "Yes'um."

Then, inquiring more specifically, I went too far, "But had you never
seen nor heard of me, would it be interesting?"

The question gave Laura pause, for it was against her principles not
to be honest. After a slight hesitation, she came out with another
"Yes'um," slowly adding, "It might would!" We laughed together, and I
decided to let the question lie.

It had only been a few months since Terry's suggestion about writing
something for the library that I had met Rosa Leonard, the highly regarded
teacher of English and Journalism in our local high school. In the
succeeding months, through a shared interest in writing, Rosa and I
became friends. She expressed interest in seeing some of my own, and so
one afternoon after school, she sat in my sun room surrounded by a welter
of notebooks.

When Rosa told me that she was undergoing the deep sorrow of
knowing that her son, Pat, a young man of twenty-eight, was slowly dying
of AIDS, that at such a time she should take an interest in my writing, was
the measure of Rosa's thoughtfulness of others. For eight years she had been
making the flight of three-thousand miles, at intervals, to comfort her son,
and to urge him to come home. When he finally made up his mind to do
that, he called his mother on the phone, and broke her heart with this
simple statement, "Mother, I want to come home to die, and I want one
of those nice Episcopal funerals."

During the few months that Pat had to live, I saw him several times.
I knew that he liked books and enjoyed writing and that he had served in
the armed forces on the *Stars & Stripes*. When the end came for Pat, he
was buried with military honors. Soon after his death, Rosa brought me
a letter that he had written and left in his computer. In his letter Pat
thanked me for the use of the books I had lent him, adding, "Mother will
return them." He also mentioned how he had enjoyed our visits together
in my home and how he liked hearing about Captiva: "I enjoyed the things
you read to me that you had written. I hope you will keep on." This

unselfish encouragement from a young man whose own life was being cut so short has made me value the time that I've been allowed, and has indirectly given my own writing more purpose.

As Rosa sat in my sun room that day, making her way through what, no doubt, she had hoped would be a glance at my notebooks, I watched the furrowing of her brow without surprise. For my handwriting has long had a bad reputation. Even the most long-suffering of my friends have always complained that it is only on the third reading that the gist of my letters will come through. It might even require a few days. And, worse still, I'm that period piece, that anachronism, who has never had a romance with a typewriter, nor a word processor, nor any other kind of computer.

As heavy as the going was though, Rosa ploughed on through my pages long enough to say, as she looked up, "There's something here. It would be worth preserving. You might even want to consider publishing. If you did, I'd be glad to do your editing."

At that, my ears pinked; then paled again, as she followed with, "But of course, nobody can or ever will read it in its present form. It's all but impossible. Somehow you must get it typed."

From then on, she peppered her conversation with publishing terms, and my head began to swim, for she even tossed in the word, "manuscript." But, of course, there was the stumbling block of my not typing. Where could I find somebody with a talent for decoding and the necessary amount of patience to do my transcribing? As sometimes happens, however, fate stepped in. Earlier than I dared expect, there came a stroke of fortune. Almost overnight, as my beloved friend, Julia Black, of Pittsburgh, Port Hope, Ontario, and Captiva would have said, "as if it were meant," into my life came Louisa. It was in this way:

Urged on in my writing life now by both Terry and Rosa, one morning I was scribbling away when both of my sons, now middle-aged, Tom, named for his father, and Mack, named for mine, came by together, with papers for me to sign, and business affairs to be discussed. Where my writing was concerned, the two had always been supportive. Yet, to make sure that they understood my zest for the pen, even if it led nowhere, as apparently it was doing, I had once quoted to them the Latin poet Juvenal, who, as early as the second century, made the observation that "an incurable itch for scribbling takes possession of some and lives on in their insane hearts." "Insane or not," I had added, "Who knows?" For I knew that before the visit ended that day there would be, from one or the other of the sons, the polite inquiry, "How's your writing going, Mother?" And, true to form, one of them did ask. I was ready for the question for, for some time I had been giving thought to my handwriting dilemma, and thought that I just might have found a way around it.

My answer was, in part, a question. To give it importance, I began, airily, "Oh, I've written quite a lot lately," and then went on to tell them what Rosa had said. "What would you think," I asked, "of my taking some of my writing down to the office for typing? Those girls are so nice and seem so fond of me." There were eight of those young women there at the office, all amiable and snappily dressed; seemingly equal to anything that might come.

My sons flew up in alarm. "Oh, Mother, please, no!" began Mack. "It will mean mass confusion. There's not a person alive who can read your handwriting. All those letters you used to send to us at Asheville School and Chapel Hill we could never make heads nor tails of. I hate to tell you, but we would sometimes meet on the campus and say, 'Have you heard from home?' and nine times out of ten the answer would have to be, 'Yes, a letter from Mother, but I couldn't read it.' "

"Well, you at least knew that I was alive. That was something." And I was beginning to get a little up on my haunches. For by this time in life, having read innumerable biographies and autobiographies, I knew that I was not the only one with this flaw. As impossible as my handwriting is, it helps to read what has been said by one of her friends in regard to the illegibility of the handwriting of Lady Sybil Colfax: "The only hope of deciphering her invitations was to pin them up on the wall and run past them!"

"But we do want you to finish those memories that you're writing," interjected Tom. "They will be our legacy. Let's just try to think of a better way than the office. Can't you take it to a public office service?"

But I had already tried that, without success. Sitting that day at the elbow of a bright young thing, my literary offering lying forlornly on the desk before her, one in a row of other secretaries, who, all at their desks were going full speed ahead, I watched this poor lamb attempting to read my first page. Obviously, it was going to be a matter of pushing water uphill. I had a sure feeling that she'd never make it. And I gave it all up.

A much earlier suggestion from my sons had been, "Let us get you a tape-recorder." I had tried that. That too, was a failure. My voice was a horror. My diction came out in something of the way I imagine a catfish would talk. If I had thought that I sounded like that in real life, I would never have opened my mouth again. I knew that the only thing my writing might have going for it, was and is, perhaps a measure of spontaneity, and that, talking into a tape, that small spark might easily be snuffed out.

When these two attempts of mine at finding a solution came into the conversation that morning, my sons laughed at my dilemma, as I did myself. It was impossible not to.

Mack spoke up, "Well, then, let us get you a part-time secretary to come to you at home."

"Oh," I replied. "That would seem too pompous; my work isn't all that important."

"You're wrong there, Mother," said Tom. "If it's important to you, it's important to us."

But I still held out, which led Mack to conclude, "I think you're just having one of your economy spells, Mother. Forget expense. What's money for? And anyway, you have enough. We'll certainly see that your lifestyle never has to change."

"And you must remember that you don't take long trips anymore," Tom pointed out.

"I don't really want to," I said. "As you get older, travel becomes arduous. And do you remember that story I used to read to you about the little wandering mouse who always said when he came back, 'Home is best'?" They did remember.

Continuing, Mack felt constrained to remind me of my propensity to hang on to my cars. "You know you drive your cars for ten years."

"That's because I like them better after we get used to each other," I replied. "You know Vivian (my sister, their aunt) used to say, at the end of ten years when she had ordered a new car, 'When the new one comes, they're going to have to tranquilize me to get the old one out of the yard.' That's the way I feel."

Bringing up another angle, Tom pointed out, "You know you do share what you have."

"Sharing is life's greatest pleasure," was my comment, and they agreed.

"Then why do you balk at having a part-time secretary?" one of them wanted to know.

"I'm not balking," I said, with some dignity, but relenting a little. "I'm just getting used to the idea. Now I've decided. Let's get one."

With that, they left for the office, Mack, who manages the family's business affairs, saying, "I'll put Pauline on it right away. She'll call you."

And Tom, who lives in New York, but comes home often on business, said, "This is going to be wonderful, Mother. The other was an exercise in futility."

At that point, feeling that I should make some kind of statement that would sound as if I were in control of things, I answered vaguely, "Not entirely." My voice trailed off, and the three of us moved through the hall to the front door.

But there was no time for further conversation. Briefly, Juvenal returned to flit through my mind; yet on his heels came that much later figure on the literary scene, Thackeray, whose perception of a writer's motivation for writing was far more flattering. For this novelist, who gave us *Vanity Fair* and thereby made Becky Sharp into a household word, says companionably, "There are a thousand thoughts lying within a man which he does not know until he picks up his pen and writes." It is a point of view I find easy to accept.

Standing on the front stoop, we said goodbye. As they drove away, birds fluttered across the lawn, squirrels scampered up and down the tall old pines with nesting material in their mouths, for it was spring. Turning my head, I could see where a baby rabbit might have been nibbling at the shoots of my lily-of-the-valley where it grows under the dining room window. I could look to the side across the lawn and over the low rock wall into the garden that is basically the one that Tom and I began early in our marriage, and that now belongs to someone else. Some of the flowering shrubs have been there that long: camellias brought from my Mother's garden, lace-cap hydrangea brought from the Elizabethan Gardens on Roanoke Island, among others.

Near the gateway, between the two gardens – that of the Feasel family and mine – growing against the rock wall on my side, are foxgloves that have been planted by the birds. I see them from my dining room window, and it's like a lovely poem, written for my special benefit. On the other side of my present house, from the back of its living room through its large window of colonial-size panes, and across the terrace, I see some of the perennials from our old garden as well. I love the names of some of the other plants that grow there, and in the dooryard garden, reached through the sunroom: the shrub called poet's laurel, graceful and waxy, and evergreen, and lovely for bringing indoors; the low-growing Daphne which blooms through the snow, and placed in bowls over the house, makes every room as fragrant in January as would a bowl of lilacs in April or a single magnolia blossom from my old garden in June. In that intimate area of the garden, the Daphne and the Carolina winter jasmine, or jessamine, would have preceded the snowdrops that come in February; the snowdrops would have led into the jonquils. And at a distance, among a scattering of trees, these winter-blooming plants would have given way to a canopy of dogwood, which sometimes, at Easter, is at its peak, the whole enclosed by a split-rail fence.

For the grounds of the second, like those of my earlier home, are naturalistic. It brings me pleasure to keep them in that spirit, not only for myself, but because my sister, Vivian, had put so much of herself into making beautiful a combination of the rustic and the more sophisticated when it was her home. At her death ten years ago, the house became young Tom's, for she wanted him to feel that he would always have a home in North Carolina. It was in that way that I came to occupy the smaller of the two houses, which as long as I live, is virtually mine.

The Feasels, who now own my old house, have made the garden there beautiful in a different way, but they have left the statue of Hebe, goddess of happiness and mirth, where she stands at the lower end of the slope. Her presence seems especially fitting for this growing family, who, in one short year have made me feel that they are part of my own.

Mattie, the little four-year-old girl, when she comes back at noon from play school, is sure to run through the gateway to ask, "Do you have any more of those cookies?" or to borrow another from my collection of Beatrix Potter books, or perhaps to ask to be read to. On an average day, it might be to announce that John has been cross and is having to be put down early for his nap. On one particular spring day, Mattie came running over, breathless, her cheeks flushed with excitement, to tell me that the bluebirds in the bluebird nesting box that we had been watching daily had hatched.

I could counter Mattie's exciting news with a bit of my own. "Now, let me tell you something," I began. "A tiny house wren has built her nest in our garage on the ledge above the roll-up doors. And whenever people come and go there, she flies up, frightened within an inch of her life for the safety of her eggs. And from a dogwood bough, she loudly scolds us. For the period of the nesting, we leave the cars outside. Now let's go and find out how long that will take."

She liked the idea and very soon we were settled, side by side, on the sofa in the living room, the *Birds of Carolina* book open on my lap. Mattie sat as close to me as if we had been knit by a single thread. We began to read about the call, the shape, the size, and the habits of the Carolina wren. We were delighted to find that the hatching period was only thirteen days, and we knew that we would soon have five tiny fledglings, their heads thrown back, their little yellow mouths wide open, cheeping for their Mother and for her return with food.

Recounting these pleasures to my sons the morning of their visit, as we stood on the stoop saying goodbye, I could say to them, "How sweet it all is. And I hope Tom knows."

The following day, Pauline Johnson, the wonderful head secretary at the family office, called to say that she had talked to a lady at the agency for temporary help and had found that a number of part-time secretaries were available. She gave me the telephone number of the agency.

My call there was, perhaps, one of the briefest on its records. Explaining who I was, the lady to whom I was speaking answered, "Oh, yes, Mrs. Pearsall, I was expecting your call. I have several secretaries available at the moment. There's one young woman who, with her husband, has come down from New Jersey to live out in the county. They've bought eleven acres on which to live and to start their plant nursery. Her name is Louisa Messenbrink."

"Oh, that's the one I want," I said in a burst of delight. "They're probably Dutch and grow tulips!" How could they *not* be, with that name?

We both laughed, but I was sure of my choice, for I had long ago learned to trust my hunches. And the practice was never more justified than in this case. From the very outset, Louisa and I have enjoyed a unique congeniality. When she told me, in the beginning, that she liked books so much that if nothing else were available, she would read the information on a tube of toothpaste, I knew that we were halfway home. Intelligent, warm, perceptive and fun-loving, our sessions of fifteen-or-so hours a week all winter have been hours we've both looked forward to. Now, in the growing season, so important a time for Mark and Louisa, our sessions have been reduced to only two hours a week. As time went on, I expressed to Louisa that I was not planning to use photographs in the story, but a few pencil drawings, their subjects already coming to mind; indeed, though I have no talent for drawing, I had done a number as an example, and since I knew that she had been an art major in college and was at home in that medium I asked her to try a few sketches. She had not the slightest trouble catching on to my ideas. I gave her the details, and there was one more answer to my endeavor, one more bond between the two of us. As time went on, the bonds increased. So much so that, by the day I took the manuscript to Marybeth for editing I could write this little poem:

To Louisa With Love

For all the chapters
and the pages that
we shared,

For the commas
and the colons
that we ensnared,

For the italics and
quotations on which
we fared,
for digressions for
which the reader
must be prepared

For, as we wrote, together,
day to day,
our concerns for syntax
went astray
and left us with a
freedom in the air
to tell a story
that had fallen in our care.

Before I begin this story, may I express my appreciation to two librarians in particular, Anne Wilgus of Wesleyan College, and Susan Reese, of Braswell Memorial, whose sustaining powers throughout this endeavor have given me the comfortable feeling that they were always at the other end of the telephone.

When the news made the rounds, however, as everything does in a small town, that I was writing a book, I had the feeling described in one of Montaigne's essays when he had given up the practice of law in the city and had gone to live in the country to write. "The people in my region of Gascony," he said, "think it funny to see me in print." As high flown as the analogy is, it was pleasant to feel I might have something in common with so great a mind.

So that, all things considered, things in my writing life seemed – at long last – to be falling into place. And in that sailing language that Tom so much loved, which, whenever I now use makes me feel that he is near, I felt that I might now have "a fair wind and a following sea."

To the memory of
Tom,
in whose circle of light during our long marriage I was
to spend the major portion of my life,
and from whose wisdom and patience I was to learn
the truth of his philosophy, that, "Things have to evolve."
And to the memory of my sister,
Alice Bryan,
a cripple from the age of eight until her death at thirty-two,
and to the members of my family,
especially to my grandson,
Brad.

And to Buffie, more formerly, Elizabeth Stevenson Ives, who brought
Captiva Island into my life, and into that of my family.

And to those others of my friends, old and new, of whose affection and
support I have been conscious all the while, when, in order to have time
for putting down these reminiscences, I have been deprived of their
companionship. And to James Bruce Ross, Professor of History at Vassar
College and author in the field of medieval history. As the fifth daughter
in a large Missouri family, this remarkable woman was given her father's
name, but was known to her friends and relatives simply as "J.B." or "Jay."

And to the memory of Helen Ross, the psychoanalyst, recognized
nationally and internationally for her work among disturbed children,
including those who had undergone the horrors of the Blitz in England, and
known nonprofessionally as "Hie," a nickname derived by her siblings from
the word, "highbrow."

It was in 1954 that Tom and I came to know the two sisters, Hie and
Jay. We had reached our fifties, as had Jay; Hie was in her late sixties. I
was the youngest of the four. While the Rosses had been going to the island
since the early twenties, it was new to Tom and me. Through a hastily made
decision we went to Captiva, only a name to us at that time, a roundabout
tale to be told later. It would be three years, however, before we would get
to know the Rosses, for they had not as yet retired. By that time, we no
longer rented the small guest house in which we'd started out, but had
bought a cottage that happened to be next to that of the Ross house. And
if we had loved Captiva before they came, with Hie and Jay and their

retirement, and our family-style friendship – one that would last for two decades and that still goes on between Jay and me – the island held, for us, not only all the other things we'd come to love, but a close-at-hand intellectual stimulus that was the proverbial "pearl beyond price."

When the Ross family first came, their family was larger. The island, then, had to be reached by ferry, a condition that carried over far into our own years there, at the beginning of which, there were only around thirty houses. Each house was hidden, as was ours, by such a density of vegetation that there was a pervasive Robinson Crusoe air. In keeping with the emphasis on the natural world, houses, though far from being huts made of thatched palms and palmettos, were simple. In summer, they sat closed and shuttered; in winter, year after year, like migratory birds, their owners returned, returned to renew old friendships, to engage in interests peculiarly their own, and to be joined in affection for, and protection of, what was spoken of affectionately as "Our Island."

It was like the Rosses to have chosen for their winter home a then little known island, one where life would be simple, almost rugged, for in summer, they went to one even smaller. Indeed, there was nothing on Footprint Island but the print of a foot in a boulder, and their crude, wooden house with its primitive wooden shutters which served for windows and were rarely closed, for the family believed firmly in the healthful and simple life. So resourceful were they in combining this philosophy with a daily balance of the amenities, that to observe them day to day as intimate neighbors was to feel they had found some golden secret, some answer that might be applied to our own way of life. As Earl Groves, a friend and frequent houseguest of theirs, and head of the music department at Vassar College, and of whom, when the two had met, Tom was to say, "Earl may be a music teacher, but he's a man's man," said, reflectively, one day, "Of all the people I've ever known, I think the Rosses know best how to live." There would hardly have been room for argument. And for a part of each year, Tom and I were in a stone's throw of this example. It was there, as next door neighbors for intervals in winter, that the deep friendship between the four of us began; there that, aware of my love for books, and always looking for another mind to stretch, no matter its caliber, or its age, Jay said to me with enthusiasm one day, when our friendship was new, "Elizabeth, I shall start right away feeding you things to refine your reading taste." For to her scholarly mind, best sellers were often looked at askance, to some degree suspected of being only pot-boilers. And I could not have known – at that point – that it would be Hie who, on a later day, would urge me to write.

≈ ≈ ≈

Seven years later, with the realization that a sudden illness of Tom's would be terminal, life, for us, reached its lowest point. We both knew that we were slowly slipping away from each other, yet it went unvoiced, for that was our way of protecting each other. As refuge from pain and reality, Tom was being given sedatives. My own refuge, day after day, as I sat quietly in his room waiting for the approach of final separation, was to return, silently, to the past, for it had brought me more than my share of happiness.

Hie's lingering illness and subsequent death had come a year before the failure of Tom's health. With less than a year to prepare, emotionally, for the inevitability of Tom's approaching death, for one of the doctors had confidentially likened the progress of his illness from lymphoma, and lymphoma in its rarest form, to a prairie fire, when the end came, except for being thankful that it had brought Tom release, my grief was almost more than I thought I could bear. At night I would take off the bright mask I had worn by day, among people, and write the things I felt. With the world about me asleep, Tom seemed near. Just to have words fall onto paper was to be taken out of time, and into a world where there was no need to think. And since writing had supported me through that first pain of grief, I gradually came to feel that for me, a day without writing was a day wasted. As the days went by – I suppose because I so much needed something to tie to – I seemed sometimes to hear Hie asking, "Elizabeth, did you ever get around to that writing?"

And I realized, that in my sorrow, I had been doing that. I was using it to ease my heart.

Time remembered
is grief forgotten
Frosts are slain
And flowers begotten

Swineburne

Now, looking back over my life, as with age we do more and more, I can see that mine falls loosely into four parts. First the early years, when our family of four daughters, of which I was the youngest, my sisters and I were coming under the influence of family attitudes, when we were being given responsibilities which would include those related to our education.

Second, the beginning of the fulfillment of which I had always dreamed, that of having found my alter ego; our marriage, the joy of the births and bringing up of our children, a time in which outside influences, some of them major, would enter our life, requiring searching decisions.

Third, the years when, the nest again empty, Tom and I would decide to have a second home. This period I think of now as the Captiva years, twenty-three in all.

The last ten years would be those of my being alone, days and months of finding out about myself and of coming slowly to feel that I could deal with the story of my life, so much of it bound up with Tom. With time, I find that I can tell the story in the way that he would have wanted it told, with laughter and joy, for it seems – in retrospect – almost unbelievable that we had so much. I write in an effort to hold something of what we had, wondering as I do, if there might be things worth passing on.

From the beginning, I knew that if the story were to be told at all, it would have to be done in my own way – that its style, if any, would necessarily be relaxed, informal, almost conversational. That it would run to digressions was a foregone conclusion, for that has always been the narrative style of the South; for some of us, the habit is second nature. Time and observation have taught me that it is when we try to be other than as we are that we become an empty vessel.

As for memory, since few of us are Einsteinien, or born to appear on Jeopardy's quiz programs, I should imagine that most of us would greet with enthusiasm that opinion of the Irish-born writer Elizabeth Bowen who at eighty-eight, and with apparent gratitude, could say, and here slightly paraphrased: The charm, one might say, the genius of memory, is that it is choosy, and chancy, and unpredictable; in the photography of the mind, rejecting the edifying cathedral in favor of the small boy chewing a hunk of melon in the dust.

That this well-known novelist has memory choose the boy over the cathedral seems to say that it is in those indefinable bonds between us as human beings that our contacts with each other, whether they are intimate and long-lasting, or only casual and brief, will each leave their imprint: a less succinct way of expressing Emerson's philosophy, "I am a part of all I have met."

Certainly, the story of my own life could never, to my own ears, ring true, unless it reflected – in part – some of the relationships that have been mine. For it is in those that lie the story's thread.

TIME REMEMBERED

VILLAGE BELLS, COUNTRY BELLS

≈ ≈ ≈

*I*n a country village of the South, of a time that might have been anywhere between nineteen hundred and the 1930s, there was a character who, described to me by verbal account, might easily have been one of my own village and my own time, and who – to me – is so unforgettable that, as a matter of southern folklore, I feel he should be recorded. The story runs this way:

There was an old countryman who, with the coming of autumn, would begin to go around selling firewood. From his mule-drawn wagon, his dog riding beside him on the wagon seat, the wagon now loaded with bundles of lightw'd, the regional name for kindling, with lengths of oak for the village fireplaces, and pine for the kitchen "ranges," the old man would call out, in a singsong voice:

> *My name is Joe Byna.*
> *I live in Callina.*
> *My fie-wood is good'n dry.*
> *If you don't believe me,*
> *Jus' buy some and try me,*
> *I'm tryin' hahd to get by.*

As the days and nights grew cooler, the wagon would come round more often. With December, the sunny skies might, for a day or two, give way to gray; this would make the old man think of snow, and though it would not often happen, there were those years when he might waken to an all-white world. Then, out early, as usual, his dog and his mule sharing the excitement, the old man's voice would have a different sound. Cheery and full, it would ring out with:

> *Simmon beer and cydah,*
> *red bird in de snow,*
> *Christmas be a comin'*
> *Be heah fo'e you know.*

By late afternoon, tired, but happy, he would be back again in the country. His mule fed, he and the dog would go into his simple house to have their supper by the fireside. Then, no doubt, it would be important to sample the simmin' beer to be sure it was aging well for Christmas, and, with a swig or two from the jug, the old man and the now drowsy dog would settle down again, to dream by the fire. And their dreams would have been those of the woods and the fields.

In another part of the world, a generation or so earlier than that of Joe Byna, there lived another man who loved the quiet of the country. He was, however, many things that Joe Byna was not: high born, owner of vast estates, and a writer. In a beautiful passage from one of his novels, he evokes that almost spiritual element that is to be found in the tranquility and the silence of the countryside:

And once again, he began to listen to the silence, awaiting nothing – and yet at the same time expectant. The silence engulfed him on every side; the sun ran its course against the tranquil blue of the sky and the clouds floated silently upon it; it seemed as if they knew why and where they were going. At that very time, in other places on earth, life was seething, hurrying, roaring on its way; here, the same life floated by inaudibly, like water through marsh grass.

Turgenev, Home of the Gentry

≈ ≈ ≈

The warm breezes of afternoon blew over the fields, fields that were among those I'd known as a child. These were those on my Grandmother Bryan's farm. The crops – in the main – were the same. But the methods of planting and harvesting were a far cry from the days of my childhood, those of the mule and the plow. I, myself, had changed as much, for I was now a grandmother, and as such, I was beginning to find pleasure in delving into the past.

For a link with that, there was Melissy, the only remaining person who had known Grandma from the time when she was a young widow of thirty-six, bringing up her seven children, and as mistress of the plantation, meeting the daily challenges that went with those dual responsibilities. Sitting on the porch of Melissy's cottage that afternoon, the grove surrounding the "gret house" in sight, I knew that I could do no better than to begin the story of my life with that fine old woman, who was then in her late nineties.

No doubt at Melissy's birth, she had been given the original form of her name, Melissa. For old Dr. Phillips, when he was not driving about in his buggy, visiting the sick or practicing medicine in his one-room wooden office that sat in the side-yard of his home, Mt. Mariah, a mile down the road from Grandma Bryan's, spent his time delivering babies around the countryside and was often asked to name them. And since Dr. Phillips was well-read, on these occasions he was never at a loss. For Melissa was not a country name. In the free and easy way of plantation life it would not, in that form, long survive. And certainly "Melissy" seemed to suit this farm woman. Some twenty-five years older than I, our lives had overlapped, and this was our mutual good fortune.

Born on my Grandmother Bryan's farm, Melissy would remain there the rest of her life. As housegirl, in plantation language, in the "gret house," the relationship between the two would be a close one. Grandma was to die when I was a freshman in college, so that it was in the years of my childhood and young girlhood that I had known Melissy best. Those were the years when Uncle Hugh, Grandma's son, still a bachelor, was a kindly, slightly literary figure in my life. When Grandma had died, Uncle Hugh married and had the joy of having a family of his own, two sons and a daughter. Melissy stayed on as house-help, gradually reaching the age of retirement. It was in her own cottage on the farm, where she had been born and would live out her life, that on summer afternoons in my own later life, I would often go for a visit.

She was a fine-looking old woman. Although her brown skin was dry and wrinkled, her hair, gray and thin, her fingers were still straight and strong. Her health was such, that in spite of the heat of southern summer afternoons, I might find her chopping around her flowers. I once asked, "Melissy, I wonder why it is that country flowers always seem to do better than those grown in town?"

"Lawdy, honey, it's because we wucks 'em," she said. And that was what she had been doing with her hoe that afternoon, scratching lightly around each plant.

Sitting on one end of her narrow porch, shielded from the sun by morning-glory vines that grew in a network of tobacco twine that allowed the warm breezes to blow through from the fields, the two of us would begin a lazy conversation, one that always led into the past.

Melissy's porch at that shaded end held three rocking chairs. The other end, with its assortment of containers – mostly coffee cans and old lunch pails, anything that would hold a little earth – was bright with flowers. With these and the morning-glories, her simple house and its surroundings became a thing of charm. And always when I was there, I was again impressed with the fact that no matter how humble the home, no matter how small, no matter how badly it may be in need of a coat of paint, there is, in every human being, that innate longing for beauty which will come to the surface. For, in his search for meaning in his life, man often finds it in creating something which, to him, is beautiful.

In the yard about the house, there was a flourishing fig tree, and a peach tree, old and gnarled but still bearing very sweet fruit, though its peaches were growing smaller each year. There was an apple tree, still hardy and bearing. In her vegetable garden there was a long row of sunflowers. As a child I had seen these large yellow faces on their tall sturdy stems in everybody's garden, including ours, and I had always loved watching their heads turn with the sun. In those days we had no idea that this commonest of all flowers in country gardens would come to be used commercially as a favorite food of the cardinals. Our cardinals had them for the taking.

Those little summer visits to Melissy would come about through Tom's having called me some long summer afternoon from the office to

say, "I've decided to spend the rest of the afternoon on the farms. Would you like to go?" He knew that if I had no plans, I would.

Now and then, as we started out, I would suggest, "If you're going to the farms in Edgecombe," one of the three counties in which our farms lay – the other two were Halifax and Nash – "I think I'll let you drop me off at Melissy's, if you could pick me up after about half an hour."

These half hours were delightfully restful. There was about them a gentleness and a mellow wisdom. Even Melissy's name, when spoken slowly, seemed to have a soft southern air. These quiet visits helped me to place the busyness of life in perspective, and in something of the way that I, myself, enjoyed being with Melissy, Tom, when he came back for me, would find pleasure in sitting for an interval in that rare timelessness.

Sometimes my visits might fall on Sunday afternoon instead of that of a day during the week, and this brought me an even deeper nostalgia. For, with the slanting sun of late afternoon, from beyond the woods in the direction of the swamp which was referred to as "The Islands" or as "The Road of the Seven Bridges," for, indeed, crossing the swamp required going over seven simple, wooden bridges, would come the sound of the church bell from "Mawnin' Stah," the church that Melissy and the other domestics at Grandma's and at our house, and that the tenants in the area attended. Listening, Melissy and I would be momentarily silent, each of us picturing the church members standing about outside the church, quietly talking and fanning, waiting to go in.

My mind followed the road through The Islands and the Seven Bridges. They were less than ten miles from our village, and our family owned land on the other side of that low area. In the way of the time, landlords often spent Sunday afternoons visiting their farms and their farm families, so that, on some Sundays, after we had been to Sunday school – there was a church service at St. John's only once a month – and after a large midday meal and Father's nap, we would all pile into our car, the Overland, later, the Hudson, and after that, the Franklin, for that Sunday afternoon ritual of going to the country. Robert, the driver would be at the wheel, the top of the car would be down. The youngest member of the family, I would sit in one of the jump seats, this riding backward giving me a long, lovely view of everything. My favorite of those excursions was the one where the road led through The Islands.

Once inside the swamp, for a mile or so there would be cypress trees, and near the parent trees, "their knees." Standing in the dark, still water and reflected, the two became twice beautiful, and the road itself was shadowed; at points, it was under water, and with the water swishing up to the running boards of the car, we would be sprinkled to laughter, wondering as we laughed, if our motor would stall.

There were, indeed, seven narrow, wooden bridges. With the weight of a vehicle, they rattled alarmingly, an enormous improvement to the adventure. To make things complete, if it were spring or summer, there would nearly always be a more than graphic approximation of the Garden of Eden, where, an arm's length away from the bridge we were crossing, from the bough of an overhanging beech or river birch, and reflected in the water to make two of them, would be the dangle of a long, wriggly snake.

As exciting as it had all been, however, with *that*, to return to the openness of sunny fields of cotton, corn, peanuts, and tobacco was not a bad exchange.

But Melissy was returning to the present, with, "Lawd, Miss 'lizabeth, I do declare, you is good faw de so' eyes. How cum you stay so little?" Meaning not especially fat.

Then, without waiting for an answer, "Dis sheah poach be nice and shady uv a moanin', but in de eeb'n de sun make it hot, lessen I plant dem moanin' glory vines."

One of the stories that Melissy liked to bring into conversation was that of how Aunt Lucy, who had been mammy to Grandma's children and almost that to the grandchildren, had come to be there in Grandma's home.

"Yes Ma'am," she would say. "Sho as you bawn, yo' Grandmama was a good 'oman. She never tunned nobody away if dey was in need. An' dat day, when Lucy wont no mor'n sixteen yez old, an' come up to de gret house, knocking on dat side do' an' say, 'Miss Bettie, dey dun *tunned me out*,' Miss Bettie tuk her in." Obviously, Lucy was pregnant.

Melissy set the scene by saying, "Miss Bettie an' Miss Livvy an' Lizzie Dozier was settin' in de *Little Room* cuttin' out an' using de sewin' machine to make dem long heavy sacks dat de hands used for pickin' cot'n."

I knew how heavy those sacks were, even when empty, for I had once asked Grandma to let Aunt Livvy make a small one for me. I wanted the experience of moving bent over, down the long white rows and of finding out how long it would take to fill my sack. At first, it was fun, but my enthusiasm soon waned. The cotton bolls were prickly, my small fingers could, in no way, compete with the long practiced hands of the women, and I regret to say that I gave up early in the day. I had heard so many of the farmhands – and the hands who were cotton pickers always seemed to be women – brag about being able to pick a hundred pounds a day that for ever after I would marvel at both their perseverance and their skill.

With Melissy's description of the making of the cotton sacks I had the scene firmly in mind. It would have been a winter day when Grandma had Aunt Livvy, the woman on the farm who did the best sewing, come to the house to begin a two weeks' period to get the cotton sacks made and ready for the next crop. Lizzie, one of the twin housegirls, would have been there to help and to learn from Aunt Livvy. This would have been going on in what was spoken of in Grandma's house as the "Little Room." It had a large fireplace, and in winter that would have been glowing with heavy logs.

And here, my mind plays over the fact that in three generations, Grandma's, Mother's and mine, we each had a certain room that because of the activities therein seemed especially colorful. In Grandma's house it was the "Little Room." In Mother's and Father's first home, spoken of as "The Cottage," it was the "Long Room" where my sisters and their governesses had their lessons. In the newer and larger house into which we moved when I was three, there was the "Linen Room." This was upstairs. It was large and light, full of shelves and cupboards, and was where the ironing went on.

It was here that Rhody and I shared many hours as she ironed, which she did everyday after lunch, when the preparation of the largest meal of the day was out of the way and Julette, the cook, no longer needed her help in the kitchen. Rhody's tales were different from those told in the kitchen; not so exciting, but she made up escapades in which animals took on human characteristics. In a sort of mish-mash of Uncle Remus and Aesop, they talked, were sly, played tricks on each other, and got their come-uppance, all of it much to my liking.

But the most colorful stories were those that went on in the kitchen when several of the domestics were there together. I was enthralled with the way one or another of them was always priming the pump to keep the tale going. There were a number of ways to do this: "Ain't it *so!*" "Sho' *do!*" "Sho' *nuf?*" "Sho's you *bawn!*" "I'm a *tellin'* yeh!" "Ain't it the trufe!" "Lawdy, *Lawdy!*" and "Lawdy *mussy!*" And now and then, the ultimate in appreciation of the story under way, especially if it were a horrible one:

11

"Sweet *Jesus!*" Not a fragment of the tale was left out. Each detail had to be carefully worked over, and although my own method of appreciation was one of silence as I sat wide-eyed on a stool – one of several that surrounded the large trestle table where the domestics had their meals – it was no less ardent than that of the other listeners.

For the years of bringing up my own family, in our home, it was the breakfast room that became my favorite. This large, rectangular room had three wide windows with heavy mullions; its floor was of dark-green rubber tile. The large window at the end of the room was deeply recessed between twin cupboards of arching doors. All the hinges in the room were "H" and "L" and were made of dull black metal. There was a heavy cornice and a chair rail. The long table was of pine, and seated as many as ten.

Tom and I had planned that house. For its floor plan, we enlarged and elaborated on the Raleigh Tavern in Williamsburg. When you stood in the entrance hall, you looked immediately through a distant archway to the focal point of a fireplace in the paneled den. To the left you looked through double doors into the living room, its fireplace at the end as well. The vista extended into the sun room. From the same point in the hall, looking to the right, there was a vista through the eighteen foot long dining room, and on through the twelve feet of the breakfast room to the commanding point of the recessed window. The house was indeed, a house of vistas.

In the breakfast room there was nearly always a cheerful hubbub of some kind. The children would be bringing their friends home for meals, or doing their lessons at night. In the morning I would be telephoning the grocery order, for in those days, groceries were delivered. In this, the worst place in the world to concentrate, I would sometimes sit down to indulge my penchant for writing. No wonder nothing came to light. I see this, now, however, as just one more characteristic proof of my choice of the fragmented self. Perhaps I felt that I might miss something if I shut myself away in another room, because I've always had a strong feeling that all of life's moments are to be lived, even those of little consequence, for they all add up to something. Certainly the world wasn't panting for anything I might have to say. In essence, I suppose I felt that since I didn't know anybody else who was under a similar compulsion, my writing wasn't important. Indeed, when the children had grown up and I had once been slightly immobilized from a fall and was wearing a cast, a friend who found me lying contentedly on the sofa with a yellow pad and a ballpoint, commented, "I think it's perfectly remarkable that you can be so happy here with nothing but pen and paper."

No doubt my oldest and dearest friends still feel that way about me. But neither do I understand their overwhelming commitment to some of the wide assortment of interests in which others engage, and into which, over time, I have, indeed, allowed my own powers to be drawn; such things as knitting sweaters, doing watercolors, such things as getting mythology straightened out in my mind (a failure), as pledging myself, intermittently, to creative cookery, and to dedicated gardening, always, in the end, returning to my first love, writing, and to its twin, reading.

The center of activity in my present home – living as I now do, alone – is a room I speak of as though it were the bridge of a ship, referring to it as "the Key Room." Originally designed as a breakfast room, it is now a combination of breakfast room and work room, the one in which I just happen to keep keys to things. Fancifully, I think of it as the "Morning Room," that room that seemed to have been used by Edwardian ladies so picturesquely in many novels of English country life.

In truth, in the years of my teens when life, for me, was nothing if not romantic, I found it hard to decide which of two roles, once Prince Charming had come to claim me, would be mine. I had gradually abandoned the youthful question of whether to become a missionary or a dancer. I had come to know that my own happiness would lie in making a home for the one to whom I would give my heart: in bringing up our children, in my being something of a "fixed point" for the family; to be there to cheer them on, to bind their wounds, those either of the body or the spirit; a home where, in days of joy, we would form the bonds of unity and happiness. Serenely sure that fate had this in store for me, I had now only to decide which of two roles had the deeper appeal: whether to be the Lady of the Manor, sitting at the desk in her morning room doing her accounts, composing her menus, and lining up her staff in preparation for their duties of the day, or would I be happier as a motherly figure in an apron, cheeks flushed from the oven, standing inside the doorway of her rose-trimmed cottage where hollyhocks nod in the sun. In this happy state, she awaits the arrival of her rosy-cheeked children and her husband, the latter who, approaching the cottage with long strides, leaps over the fence in his joy at being home. It was such a difficult choice to make, that I decided to wait and let life make it for me. Ultimately, in a more realistic sense, one not so given to extremes, I was to play a watered-down version of both roles. And like everything else in life, it would be found that each of the roles had its pluses and its minuses.

Melissy, continuing her reminiscences about Grandma, said, "Miss Bettie say," for that was the way all plantation hands addressed Grandma, " 'Lizzie, you go to de kitchen an' tell yo' Mama and yo' Grandmama dat we gonna take Lucy Davis in to live wid us.' "

The rest of the message was borne by Helen, the twin daughter of Aunt Mary the cook, who was the daughter of Aunt Caroline. Aunt Mary and Aunt Caroline spent their days in the kitchen when they were not in their own houses which sat behind the vegetable garden. There was a third house which belonged to Flonnie, who did the laundry. Grandma had said to Helen, "Tell Aunt Caroline to let Lucy stay in her house with her now. When the baby comes, her mama and papa will get over being upset. They'll want to take it and raise it with their other young children. And it will have a good home. I'm going to take Lucy in the house to help me with my own children." As it turned out, Lucy's baby was a son. He grew up to marry a girl on the farm, and to have a lifelong devotion to his mother.

I guess it tells something about Grandma's judgment of human nature for her to have selected that particular girl to live in the house with her, which Aunt Lucy would do for the next forty years, to influence Grandma's own children and grandchildren. (The account of Aunt Lucy's tragic death by fire comes later.) I was to know her for the first six years of my own life, to come under her influence almost as much as Grandma's, and to weep inconsolably at her death.

Melissy liked to talk about Grandma and plantation life. She would go on: "Won't no finer plantation mistiss no-wheah dan Miss Bettie. Whenever somebody say, 'Wheh you stay?' and I say, 'Wid Miss Bettie Bryan,' dey say, 'You got a good place,' " for Grandma was widely known and respected.

I remember asking Melissy, "You never did know Grandpa Bryan, did you Melissy?"

"No'm, but we heard tell he was a stujious man, an' everybody laked him. Miss Bettie had all dem chullun to bring up by herself. Seven on 'em, when yo' Grandpa had de gallopin' consumption an' had to go way out West for de dry air, but he couldn't get kyude, so he come home to die. And when yo' mama was three month old, he died. Mr. Charlie and Mr. Hugh was yo' Grandmama's oldest chullun. Dey was jes' fo'teen an' fifteen. But Miss Bettie sent dem off to school, an' she took keer of everythin' herself."

"You know, Melissy, that Grandpa Bryan's brother, our Great Uncle Harry of Oak Grove Plantation, died young, too, so that at the same time, the two Bryan families were growing up fatherless, not many miles apart." The two sisters-in-law continued to have a close relationship, so much so, that Grandma had given my mother Great Aunt Sue Bryan's name, "Alice Susan." "But it's strange that Grandma didn't remarry, Melissy. She must have had chances."

"Y'ebm, she sho' did. Deah was a lot of dem nice mens roun', but she don' pay 'em no mind. Seem lak a wido' 'oman wid all dem chullun need a husband doe."

"That's true, but Grandma said one time when I asked her about it, 'When you've had the best, you can accept life on its own terms.' And you know, Melissy, Grandma was lucky in that she had two brothers that she could lean on." Uncle William Sherrod still lived down on the Roanoke at Rainbow Banks. "You remember the name of that plantation, don't you? And Uncle John Sherrod, who was a doctor, was not so far away. He lived down below Tarboro. So I guess you could say that Grandma was only forty miles from each of her brothers." My great uncle John Sherrod had served in the Civil War as a surgeon; his health was never very good after that. Still, if Grandma sent him a message that one of the children was critically sick, he would come right away.

"And then down the road," I continued, "you remember Dr. Phillips? He lived at Mount Mariah? And then, Battleboro had a doctor, too, Dr. Whitehead, so Grandma could always get medical help when the children were sick. Uncle William was a businessman and a farmer as well. He helped her hire her overseers and advised the overseers as to how many acres of the different crops to plant. And, too, Grandma knew that she could always ask her unmarried sister, Great Aunt Anne, to come for long stays, and she sometimes did. Aunt Anne would come from Rainbow Banks, the Sherrod house, with its hand-painted parlor ceiling, which is still in family hands. So in some ways, Grandma was lucky."

And then I would ask, "How did Grandma dress, Melissy?"

"Well, 'round de house, she wo' her gray clothes o' her pupple. I reckon

you 'members dat in dem days, widows never wo' no mo' bright colors. Miss Bettie, when she dress up, always wo' black for bein' in mo'nin', but she say gray an' pupple was de colors fo' second mo'nin'. In de daytime when she seein' bout things round de house and yard, you know, lak de smokehouse, and de wash-house and de pantry, she always carried her little keybasket." *How well I remember that small boat-shaped basket, covered in black leather and studded with brass nail heads, which now sits on my desk.* The basket is lined with a dark-red silk, now faded, on the bottom of which is embroidered a large tan-colored key, as though it were one lying in the basket. It gives me a graphic picture of the plantation mistress in the days of reconstruction, who, as one southern writer says, "was always locking and unlocking her stores."

"She stay busy all de time, but she don't do no hahd wuk. Her hands dey always jes as white as snow. An' lawsy mussy! When Miss Bettie dress up when company coming, or when she goin' somewhere, she wuz somethin' to see."

"And what would she wear then, Melissy?"

"Well, when she would go to Tahbruh she would put on her black silk dress, an' her black bonnet dat had dat long black veil dat hung down in de back an' had a little narro' white ruffle 'round her face."

"I've seen that bonnet, Melissy, and that little ruffle you're talking about was called ruching. You know, there was a queen who lived in England during Grandma's early life and her name was Queen Victoria. We had a book when I was a child that told all about that queen, and on the front of the book was a picture of her that looked exactly like Grandma. They were dressed entirely alike, the same little bonnet, the same little black silk gloves, their hands folded in exactly the same way, over their stomachs."

"Y'ebm. Miss Bettie love to go to Tahbruh. She had so many kinfolks deah besides yo' Aunt Annie an' yo' Aunt Nellie. Miss Nellie, she live on de commons. Roun' de cawnah from Miss Nellie was some mo' kinfolks, de Clarks, an' de Penders, an' de Peters, an' de Harts, an' de Basses, an' de Browns. I went wid her one time."

"Oh, yes," I interrupted, "I only dimly remember all those people. Except Aunt Nellie and Aunt Annie, everybody else was called "Cousin" somebody: Cousin Sue Hart, Cousin Lossie Clark, Cousin Anne Brown, Cousin Ada Bass, Cousin Cora Johnson. Cousin Benjamin Mayo was Aunt Annie Mayo's oldest son. He lived in the country on a plantation he had inherited from his Uncle Jones Mayo. Aunt Annie and her family lived in the country too. Melissy, you must remember all about Aunt Annie's fire, don't you?"

"Dat I do. Dey say it come in de middle o' de night. Somebody come knocking on de side do' an' Miss Annie run to see who wuz it. It wuz de hoss-feeder come to tell her dat de stables wuz on fie, so she run back to tell her husband. He won't so well, and he couldn't move in a hurry, an' when she told him 'bout de fie, it give him a heart-attack and he died. Dey say it wuz somep'n tubble, wid de fahm bell ringin' out in de night fuh de han's to cum runnin', and de overseeah an de hosses cum out an' dey a-rarin' up an' a-screamin'. Lawd a mussy!"

"Mother said Aunt Annie hardly smiled for the next twenty-five years," I added, "But when she moved into town, to Tarboro, she began to get better." The Aunt Annie I knew was sweet and jolly. Tom and I used to go to see her often, and she came to love him so much that she wanted him to have two of her special blankets, those that had been woven from the most recent shearing of her own sheep, for she still held the farm, and she gave the blankets to him one Christmas.

It was sad to see Aunt Annie's mind slipping away. Like all Grandma's daughters, she enjoyed playing the piano, and even when she had lost the ability to read the notes, she would make her way to the piano and in the semi-darkness, sit down and play. With the coming of television, every morning, after her bath, Aunt Annie would be placed in an easy chair to watch the motion of the figures on the screen. She seemed fascinated, and still mobile enough to be able to walk to the dining room for meals, when the nurse would say, "Mrs. Mayo, lunch is ready," Aunt Annie would get up and go over to the television, and in her gentle way, would say, "Will you excuse me now? I have to go to lunch." And then, "Won't you have some with me?"

When you've lived a long time and have seen a lot of life, you may conclude, as I have, that a person's manners are with him to the very end. A far more recent example of this came from the other side of my family, my father's. Dail Holderness married my first cousin, Nancy Braswell, Uncle Jim's daughter, and they had spent their long married life in Tarboro, where Dail was president of a large telephone company. They had brought up a wonderful family, two of whom had become Presbyterian ministers. Of all the people I've ever known, I consider Dail and Nancy the most hospitable, but in Dail, age took its toll, in the form of Alzheimer's.

For three, maybe four years, the decline was steady. Ultimately a full-time male attendant was necessary, but Dail, who, in nature's way, had resisted giving up driving the car, resisted having an attendant. Every time Jim Bishop, the perceptive black male nurse, came on duty, Dail would send him home. This presented a real problem, which the understanding attendant finally solved.

At the time, Nancy was having some interior house-painting done. The painters, as is the custom, appeared in their white clothes and their white baseball caps. In his characteristic way, Dail would greet them with utmost cordiality and insist that they have a cup of coffee or a drink of some kind. Knowing the situation, they never did, but it made Dail happy to have offered hospitality. After many days of arriving and being told to go home, that he wasn't needed, the intuitive attendant, Jim, thought of a ruse. The next morning when he came into Dail's room, he had on white coveralls and a white painter's cap and was carrying a paint bucket. Immediately Dail rose to the occasion, insisting that he have a Coca-Cola. From then on it was smooth sailing, and the two became very fond of each other.

Dail's manners never deserted him. His sweetness was unforgettable, which leads me to another digression. Two years after Dail's death, on a night in April, a dinner party was being held. The scene was at our Benvenue Country Club. An unusually quiet night for the club, we had the dining room virtually to ourselves. At tables for eight, all members of the Holderness and Braswell clans, if not by blood, by connection, which in the South is almost as important, were seated. There were seventy of us; the occasion was Nancy's seventy-fifth birthday. Her five children were present, as were their children. Her blood kin, and those of her late husband, Dail's, who lived in driving distance were there. In the soft glow of pale pink tablecloths and pale pink roses, the youthful grandmother being honored was at her most radiant.

After the first course, her three daughters-in-law stood together and chanted a little ditty of their own composing. At the end of the second course, the grandchildren, with a ratio of more boys than girls, all of them dressed in the way that little boys and girls would be for such an occasion, sang a song, and when the song was over, they each came over to their grandmother and gave her a long-stemmed, pink rose. Naturally,

Nancy had to wipe her eyes, but she was smiling her beautiful smile all the while. Then came the more serious toasts, one by one, from each of her three wonderful sons. One toast, in its simplicity and its truth, was especially beautiful: "As we were growing up, Father always said to us, 'Try to be as much like your mother as possible. She brings out the best in everybody.' "

Since the Braswell clan has dwindled, Nancy and I are two of three remaining first cousins – Lillian, Nancy's sister, lives in Atlanta – and in that we are friends as well as cousins, we spend time together whenever we can. There was a fourth cousin in this age bracket, Emily Braswell, who was to marry Bill Perry, head of the Education Department at Chapel Hill. Emily had a bright mind; the other three of us were impressed that at Sweetbriar she studied Greek. The rest of us were doing well just to accommodate ourselves to Latin and French. Between college and marriage, Emily travelled widely. On one of her trips to the Orient, she spent some time visiting Lillian, who, as a bride, had gone to China to live. Six months later I was to be Lillian's houseguest in Tientsin. A year later, Nancy and her mother and father, my Uncle Jim, were there for a long stay.

Lillian's husband, Bingham Owens, had grown up in Rocky Mount where his father had been rector of The Church of The Good Shepherd in Rocky Mount, serving our village church, St. John's, in Battleboro, as well. Lillian was some years younger than Bingham, but he must have had his eye on her for a long time, for after several years in Tientsin with Du Pont, he came back to Rocky Mount, and in a whirlwind courtship, the two became engaged. In three months, Bingham would return from China for their large wedding, in which the cousins were all bridesmaids. We wore long, coppery-gold, satin dresses, and carried flowers in autumn colors. In a month, I would be packing that gold evening dress with three others that I was taking with me on a seven month voyage around the world. On shipboard between ports, there would be long intervals of days at sea, and on an ocean liner, it was understood that passengers dress formally for dinner and dancing. The gold dress would be the one I wore on the night when I was in Tientsin, when Lillian and Bingham gave a dinner party for me at their home. And thereby hangs a tale.

From the time when we sailed out of the New York harbor, that Lillian now lived in China, and that we were to see her there made reaching that country seem the high point of the trip. It must have been in February that we finally docked at one of the mainland of China's southern ports. Early that morning, passengers disembarked and boarded a special train for what I now recall as an all day ride to Peking. Our stay in that city was to be one of five days; as it turned out, mine was only four. By letter, I had given Lillian the date and hour of our passing through the city of Tientsin, inviting her to be ready to join us when the train should pass through. Without having received an answer, that was what I expected. And indeed, when our train pulled up to the Tientsin railway station on that clear cold morning, I could see through the window, that among the crowd of Chinese in their native quilted garments, their breath smoking as they talked, stood Lillian and Bingham. Quickly they explained that they were substituting a better plan for mine. They were giving a dinner that night in their home in my honor. A bearer would accompany me the following day to Peking. They felt that seeing how life in a British-American colony in China was conducted would be, for me, a nice experience.

That stop for our train was to be only fifteen minutes, barely time for two of the ship's officers to hurry into the baggage car and find my bags. As I stood on the platform, I wondered if, in so little time, among the bags of the four-hundred-and-fifty passengers, they could find mine. But they did, and the train pulled out on its way.

The Owens' home was an attractive blend of English and Chinese architecture; thoroughly comfortable, and best of all, warm. Their property was walled and entered by a heavy door on the street. As soon as we had lunch – with no worries about her approaching dinner party – Lillian took me to the silver quarter of the city. It was teaming with people; the shops were small, and filled with silver to the ceilings; busy silversmiths were engraving intricate designs on silver trays, teapots, coffeepots. I don't recall seeing any flat silver, which in a country that uses chopsticks would not – to a native – seem strange. Lillian and I made no major purchases, and by teatime were back at home, with plenty of time left to dress for dinner.

Although Mother and Father had said they hoped that none of their daughters would smoke – and it was at a time too early to have health reasons for this approach – they did not mind our having highballs. Father had died suddenly when I was fifteen, but Uncle Mark and Uncle Jim, who felt a responsibility toward the four daughters of their eldest brother, Mack, had kept a fatherly eye on us and were broad-minded as well. Having grown up with the feeling that among the other good things in life, alcohol has its place, my sisters and I, throughout life, could take it or leave it, but on that one night in Tientsin, although I was no stranger to the enhancing of occasions with spirits, I was hardly prepared for the way of life in the British-American colony of Tientsin.

There were sixteen at dinner that night in the Owens' home. As the guest of honor, I was seated on Bingham's right. There were five graduated wine glasses at each place. After the first toast was drunk – and I can't remember to whom it was proposed, perhaps to the Emperor, for indeed, as the evening wore on, I had the sensation that we were toasting everybody in China, from His Imperial Majesty down to the lowliest coolie – my eyes began to glow. As I chattered happily, Bingham decided to have a little fun at the expense of his country cousin. A Chinese houseboy stood behind each chair, and for the first time I realized the origin of the terms "eight boy curry" or "seven boy," or whatever. Ours, that night, was seven boy, and quietly and smoothly, seven chinamen passed seven ingredients for the delectable mixture known as chicken curry. First the rice, then the diced curried chicken, then the raisins, and the shredded coconut, and the sliced bananas, and the peanuts, and the chutney; and in between all this waltzing around, in preparation for the next toast, an arm was leaning dutifully over the shoulder of each guest, refilling each wine glass as soon as it was emptied. For each toast, the guests rose to say the Chinese word for "Bottoms up!" which is "Gam-bei!", pronounced, "Gam-bye."

Toward the end of the meal, feeling no pain, and wondering how many more wine glasses must be emptied, I heard the chairs scraping back, and as the guests got to their feet, heard myself – from my southern background – saying in a ringing voice, very slowly and very clearly, "Oh, Lord, do we have to *Gumbo* again?" The guests doubled up with laughter, and I became the pet of Tientsin. I'm told the story still survives.

The dinner over, the ladies went upstairs to get ready to go to the club for dancing. As I started up the long flight, my head was as light as my feet, but not too light to have running through it over and over, the one pleading thought, *Oh, Lord, let me be a lady!*

By clutching tight to the rail I made it to the second floor. Coming down, my dinner partner, a fine, distinguished-looking man, met me at the foot of the stairs. Later, a few miles away at a British-American club, we were joined by the other members of the dinner party who were scattered about small tables for brandy. Although by this time I had been accepted as the life of the party, Bingham read my mind and became remorseful. He had black coffee brought in, and in a little while I was myself again, ready to dance away the night. Everybody had found out that I was engaged to be married, and I felt protected. It was really very warm and sweet.

At nine the next morning, Lillian and Bingham and I were back at the railway station, and I was introduced to the bearer Bingham had chosen for me. He was Chinese and elderly; he was in native costume. From his small black silk cap hung his long queue. The English words he knew were no more than six or seven, but facing each other on single seats, we rode for several hours in smiles and companionable silence. When we'd arrived in Peking and had gone by two rickshaws to my hotel, this dear little man bowed and left. It had indeed been a fine experience, even if I was now rather sleepy, for Lillian and I had talked all night. I had been twenty-four hours without closing my eyes.

On reflection, the life of each of the three surviving Braswell first cousins has truly been filled with interesting experiences and enriching friendships. The accruing of these may then have seemed only a part of the natural order of things, yet possibly we knew from the beginning that chance was playing a part – not pure chance, but chance influenced in some measure by the choice of being at a given time, at a given place, and always aware of our backgrounds. In that last, we were, indeed, favored by the gods. For we came from a sensible line of people, not easily swayed to extremes.

One day, six decades later, living out our lives in Eastern Carolina, a month after her seventy-fifth birthday party, Nancy and her sister-in-law of Richmond stood in my driveway. They were going back to Tarboro. Nancy's lovely daughter-in-law, Mary Ann, was the driver. They had been over for lunch, and we were saying prolonged goodbyes because Nancy and Pat were leaving the next day to go to Germany for the Passion Play. Since I had seen the Passion Play twice, thirty years apart, I was not going. Knowing that they planned to visit other places as well, it seemed in order to say, jocularly, before they got into the car, "Don't take up with any gigolos over there!"

"Oh, but we will," said Nancy. "We already have them engaged. Do you want us to bring you one?"

"Please do," I answered. And then, "Oh! Bring a lot of them, one for everybody." At that we erupted in laughter.

Gentle Mary Ann, who was standing with the keys to the car in her hand, added smilingly, "I *never* know what you Braswell women are going to say!"

I'm sure Mary Ann doesn't, nor do other people, for the women in our family have been given to that kind of bubbly exaggeration. Down the years, our husbands put up with the tendency good-naturedly, only occasionally bringing us back to earth. Had we suddenly changed, they might have wondered. At any rate, I can now see that it has been our stripe. Whether this proclivity for banter is peculiarly southern or not, I don't know. A friend of mine from Vermont expressed that as her opinion. She had known many southern women, and to her, they each had been a composite of what she called "gaiety, grace, and charm." Perhaps she was referring to our collective openness as a region. In that our climate is not severe, are we less tense about things? Does it lead us to enjoy conversation more, and to share the small things in life that often make for laughter? In cities you would be thought weak in the head if you started up a conversation with a stranger just for the sake of talking. There would need to be a reason.

But I have found friendliness in people from all areas, and not only in women, but in men. Two of my friends of long-standing, the Putzels, who now live in New Hampshire, formerly lived in the city of Washington. We came to know them at Captiva. Usually they motored down for their stays on the island, and when they returned, on their way back north, stopped to stay with Tom and me, for by that time, we would have been back in Carolina for spring. Henry and Nory are as much filled with the wine of life as any I know. Nory, a Vassar alumna, for many years, had charge of the Vassar Book Sale in Washington, where the Vassar women made impressive amounts of money, starting at fifty thousand.

On the morning after the Putzels' first stop-over with us, since by that time I had learned to cook and enjoyed it – and more on that subject is to come – I invited everybody into the kitchen to help me with getting breakfast (and I almost said, "to *fix* breakfast," in the southern way, but my Captiva friends always laughed when I used that term, their preference being the words "to make," which to me, is equally laughable). Later, back in Washington, Nory wrote, in her bread-and-butter note, "I have never seen anybody operate in the kitchen with such élan as you." She referred to my method of saying, "All right, Nory, you sit here in this chair and watch the toast in the oven," for our family has always preferred very hard, oven-made toast, and, "Henry, you squeeze the oranges. Tom, you cook the bacon, I'll scramble the eggs," for I like things that have to do with scrambling.

Henry Putzel wrote a thank-you note as well. He urged us to come to Washington, to be their guests, and his closing was as full of malarkey as any when he said, "Please remember that we offer bed and bedlam anytime." And this, from a highly respected barrister, as they say in England, who, for many years had the grave responsibility of editing Supreme Court opinions, in which, "even a comma makes a difference."

We did go for "bed and bedlam" several times. Everything about those stays was delightful – meeting their friends, having meals at the Cosmopolitan Club – but most meaningful of all, being taken by Henry through his impressively quiet, very large suite of offices – a place where so much of consequence that affects the lives of millions is always being weighed. Henry went with us into the inner sanctum, and as he spoke in a softened tone, we could envision the Court in session. Having been married to a lawyer, and having had lawyers in the family, I was accustomed to that recurring phrase, "Our system of jurisprudence is based on that of England." I could relate this to an imaginary scene in "Old Bailey" in London. In that way of holding on to the good of the old, and at the same time, bringing in the new, our own august body of nine justices would not have been wearing wigs, but the attorneys before them might have been wearing the customary morning dress, the air heavy with dignity.

My mind goes back farther still to that time when, in early Greece, on the day of voting, as the day wore on, some of the citizens not having taken the trouble to climb to the Acropolis to vote, officials were sent to round up the slackers. In a city where the inhabitants were usually clothed in white, holding a rope that had been dipped in tar, a number of officials were deputized to encircle and stain the garments of those shirkers of civic duty.

And I chuckle at the old lady in Maine, whose attitude toward the ballot box she expressed in this way: "I don't intend to vote, it only encourages them."

And jumping around again: My mind often leaps back to the time when, under an oak tree in England, among twelve men, "good and true," our system of justice – its jury system –was born. I like to recall that on one of her visits to Africa, Queen Elizabeth II said in her address, "Although

25

our democratic form of government is not perfect, it is the best that, by trial-and-error, has been hammered out in seven-hundred years."

But to return to Melissy.

Sitting on Melissy's porch that summer afternoon, it was nice to hear Melissy recall Grandma with such pride: "Miss Bettie, when she get settled in de Rockaway, an' one o' two of de chullun, and Green Phillips – you 'member, him, don't you Miss 'lizabeth? He was de hoss-feedah – to go to Tarbruh, dey be sumpin' to see. Green, he be all dressed up, settin' on de outside to drive, and Miss Bettie and de chillun, inside dat part o' de Rockaway dat was lak a little house, wid de do' half glass, an' a sho' nuf little doorknob, so Miss Bettie an' de chillun could be lookin' out. It won't lak nothin' else I ever see'd. An' under de seat of de Rockaway, Miss Bettie be carryin' maybe two hams, one for Miss Nellie, an' one for Miss Annie, an' fo' de other kin folks where she be goin' to spend de day, a bottle o' two of homemade wine, which we done made from her scuppernong vine, an' 'tween de shafts wuz dem two matched bays her brother Mr. William Shudd bought for her in Baltimo'. Miss Bettie, she be sump 'n to see. And she be laughin' an' talkin' like anything, 'cause Miss Betty love to laugh, and she love to have a good time."

It was easy to conjure up this picture, for as late as the 1970s I had heard a much older cousin, Isabel Clark James, reminisce about Grandma. Cousin Isabel had grown up in Tarboro, but spent her married life in Wilmington, where she lived to be a hundred-and-three and was honored by the city. "Cousin Bettie," she said, "visiting around Tarboro in her Rockaway was exquisite."

It pleased me to recall Grandma's innate pride, yet to recall with equal clarity how she could assume the role of plantation mistress, struggling alone with the multiplicity of its duties, and could be at home in either sphere. In summer she would be giving hospitality to those town relatives, some of whom would come for a month at a time, bringing their children, the children's nurse, and the driver who would take care of their horses.

"Miss Bettie tuk keer o' de plantation chullun jes' like she dun hern, when dey be sick. She be deah wrappin' hot wet blankets 'roun 'em to bring down de fever, givin' 'em castah oil for hookworm, o' sulfah an' 'lasses in de spring to keep off de chills."

"Those chills were, of course, coming from malaria, but nobody had then found the cause of it," I said.

"Y'ebm," Melissy agreed, and the conversation would drift on into the afternoon.

These were only some of the tales Melissa used to like to tell me. Which of the two of us derived the more pleasure I don't know. And always, as I left, Melissy would say appealingly and endearingly, "Come back ag'in soon, Miss 'lizabeth. Ain't nobody else to talk back with."

≈ ≈ ≈

The village was one of large old trees and streets that had the look of a country road. Houses sat far back, but not so far as to preclude the exchange of greetings and bits of casual conversation between those who would be sitting on their wide, comfortable front porches, and those who would be passing by.

Behind each house would be the garden, its long straight rows given to both vegetables and flowers; beyond the garden there would usually be some semblance of an orchard, there might even be a stable. And if there were a family with a cow, early every morning she would be led out and staked in a grassy area nearby to graze peacefully through the day.

Of village churches there were four; the two largest were Baptist, next in size came the Methodist, the smallest, the Episcopal, St. John's. That the Baptists, as a sect were many, and that their "colored" members worshipped in their own church seemed no more odd to me than that each denomination had its own form of worship. For, since St. John's had a service only once a month, its members often visited among the other churches. White people of all denominations often attended the church-funerals of their colored friends, and vice-versa. And sometimes, during my early childhood, when a revival of several days was being held at "the colored church," my nurse, Koosa, with Mother's permission, would take me with her to one of its weekday afternoon services. For those services I usually sat on Koosa's lap for the sudden outbursts of "shouting" from first one "Sister" and then another, and another, until, among half a dozen or more, in their mounting fervor, one of them would "fall-out" and would have to be revived by fanning and the sniffing of camphor, done in conjunction with the application of cold cloths to the forehead, and although all this was puzzling to me, I felt no sense of alarm. And although Koosa would keep asking me if I were ready to go home, I would vigorously shake my head.

This was so different from the restrained atmosphere of my own church that – at the time – I had no way of fitting this expression of faith into my thinking. Now I see it as having given me an incipient respect for other beliefs.

In the village everybody knew everybody, and, in summer, there was much sharing of fruits and vegetables and flowers. Most families had a farm, one with several pigs, and in winter, the sharing took the form of the more hearty edibles, tenderloins, sausages, and sweetbreads. If there were illness in a family, you might be sure that a bowl of "boiled custard," or one of "floating island," or a large tumbler of egg nog, in every case, suitably covered with a large damask napkin, would soon be on its way.

A believer in all this altruism, heart and soul, and a regular participant, to indulge the fun-loving side of her nature, Mother would – now and then – on April Fool's Day, break over the traces. Early that morning, she would dispatch to her neighbor a tray covered by a square of her snowy monogrammed linen on which would sit her Haviland soup tureen and her silver soup ladle. On the arrival of the tray, the unsuspecting neighbor would find herself receiving a tureen of sand.

All in all, it was a lovely place in which to be born and brought up. Among many other good things, its life was giving us lessons in contentment.

Since Battleboro lies in an agricultural community, a planter usually went, or sent, to its tiny post office for the daily mail. And it was there, one day, that Father had suddenly and overwhelmingly and forever, fallen in love with Mother. It was a little story, that, as a child, I used to get Father to tell me, time and again, for he made it sound beautifully romantic. And it was. It went this way:

The Bryans lived a few miles to the east of the village, the Braswells, a few miles to the west, one in one county, one in the other, nevertheless, only a few miles apart. And the Braswell family, with four young sons, and the Bryan family, with three young daughters, and another, much younger one, were friends.

Apparently there was a reasonable amount of social activity in the community, with Tarboro as its center. Nearly everybody who lived in the country had relatives in town, and when invitations to dances came, the young ladies – as they were called – stayed overnight with cousins, and, of course, in the South, cousins, were, and are, innumerable; once, twice, thrice removed, no matter, the tie is still there. However, after the dances, the ladies' escorts would either drive or be driven back to their plantations for the night.

Often the young men, along with others, "called on" the young ladies for an evening of making pulled candy and singing around the piano, those "parlor songs" of the Victorian era. But the older of the Bryan young ladies, since they finished their years at Salem earlier than did the Braswell young men theirs at their respective universities, soon married among the older of the community's eligibles. Two Bryan sisters went to live in Tarboro, one on the Roanoke near Hamilton. Alice, the youngest, was still at Salem.

I had often wondered how Father, since he had gone to a North Carolina military preparatory school in Oxford, happened to go to the University of Virginia instead of the University of North Carolina. The answer came only recently when Dr. Allen Whitaker, now retired and spending a warm summer afternoon going through old papers, telephoned me to say that the reason his father and mine, who were country neighbors in Nash County, and best friends, chose to go to the Virginia University was a matter of transportation.

At the time, unless the hundred-and-ninety mile distance from Battleboro to Chapel Hill was covered by horse-drawn vehicle, it required a round-about system of frequent changing of trains with long waits between. The first lap of the journey was to Selma to make connection with the westbound train for Raleigh. From Raleigh, you would have boarded another train for the twenty-five mile trip to Durham. And in Durham, you would have changed to two cars and an engine for covering the short distance to Hillsborough. The last twelve miles of the journey would be made by yet another short train, which would have sped you on to the village of Chapel Hill.

By contrast, the Atlantic Coastline Railroad northbound train for Richmond would, in a few hours, make connection with one from the Chesapeake and Ohio railroad from Norfolk, which, on its way to Cleveland, would soon deposit passengers in Charlottesville, Virginia. In that easier journey lay the young men's choice.

After three years at the University of Virginia, Father changed his plans by going for a year to a business school in Poughkeepsie, New York. He had decided to follow in his father's footsteps as a planter, combining this with marketing and a variety of business enterprises.

A number of years went by, and Father did not know that Alice, the little sister at the Bryan home, had grown up, until one day, back at home, he went to the village post office for the daily mail. From inside, through the window, he saw the attractive form of a young woman riding sidesaddle come galloping up, on her mare. Her dark green riding habit matched the blue-green of her eyes, a few dark curls spilled from her black velvet cap, and when she alighted from her mare, as Father said, "She had the grace of a gazelle."

And that is how it all began. In a year they were married. They chose to live in the village, and were to have twenty-eight happy years together. When they had been married fifteen years, and the ages of my sisters were eight, ten, and twelve, my birth would complete their family of four daughters. As I grew, my sisters and I were often likened to the book *Little Women*. And although in time, each of us would read the book, it was not one that we dwelled upon. The parallel of the sick daughter who would die young was too close to the fear under which we lived in regard to Alice Bryan.

≈ ≈ ≈

Five wide wooden steps led up to our front porch where, immediately, on either side stood a cluster of three large Corinthian columns. On either side of the steps were what we spoke of as the "stone guards," those areas of brick covered by a slab of granite. And in memory, those granite slabs are very real. For to a child, who, in summer had been "jumping the rope" a hundred times, or bobbing vigorously in a long rope swing, it was cooling to lie there, flat on the back and, while cooling, by turns, to gaze up into the sky or to look idly at the curl of the acanthus leaves at the top of the columns. From the parlor, there might be the sounds of some piece that one of my sisters was practicing, and in those intervals when that stopped, the music would be taken up by the twitter of birds in the tall old elms that shaded the lawn.

≈ ≈ ≈

In the memories of my early life, I'm forever hearing the endless flow of family conversation. For between Mother and her three sisters there was a close relationship, and since the four of them lived within a twenty-five or thirty mile radius, visits among these daughters of Grandma Bryan's were often exchanged. When these visits happened to come in winter, and at our house, the aunts came without their children. I might, at times, be in the room where these conversations were going on, and as I sat, playing with my dolls in front of the fire, might sometimes be included in the general flow.

Aunt Annie, the least talkative of the sisters, would turn to me – to be sure that I was paying attention – and say, "And Elizabeth, down at Rainbow Banks, a thousand Yankees once camped in your Great-Grandfather Sherrod's grove."

I had already been taken to see the house at Rainbow Banks with the hand-painted ceiling in its parlour. That parlor was the room in which the rosewood piano that had brought the family so much pleasure was spared from destruction by the Yankee soldiers when Great-Grandfather Sherrod told them how much it meant to his three daughters, Anne, Nancy, and Elizabeth, who was to become my grandmother, who had taken refuge to Ringwood, or had "refugeed" as they would have said, with the family silver and loyal servants upcountry. I had been shown, as well, the house in which they had spent the night on their way. I had been taken to its cellar to see the fireplace, bricks from the hearth of which had been taken up for concealing the ten thousand dollars in gold which their father had given them to last out the war.

Apparently my Great-Grandmother Sherrod's death had come earlier, and must have been sudden, for a messenger was hurriedly dispatched the twelve miles to Williamston for yardage of black taffeta and gray calico in order that her three young daughters might be appropriately clothed for mourning.

On another day, Aunt Nellie, always thrilled over something, the one I was said to be most like in disposition, would chime in, "And when Lafayette came through, he spoke from your Aunt Lizzie's balcony! Because when she and your Uncle Jack left the malarial country on the Roanoke to move to Enfield, they bought Cellar Plantation. As you know, your Aunt Lizzie's house sits on a hill, is very tall, and the balcony above the front porch was a good place for Lafayette to speak."

With this they would turn again to talking among themselves, but they had not missed the opportunity to create, in a member of the next generation, an interest in the past.

At the time I had no inkling as to what the aunts were talking about. It would require years for these giblets of information, dropped here and there, to arouse my curiosity. With maturity, I came to understand why the Yankees were camping in my great grandfather's yard. The marker at the roadside says:

> Fort Branch
> Confederate fort built at Rainbow Banks.
> Built to protect railroads and the upper
> Roanoke River Valley.
> Earthworks remain three miles northeast.

The Confederate soldiers, knowing that the Yankees were approaching the bend of the river on which their own enormous cannons were mounted, foreseeing defeat, rolled their cannons to the steep banks, and giving them a shove, scuttled them. The cannons, when I came to see them with Tom and our small sons, had been dredged up and appeared at least fifteen feet long. They were later taken away for several years for restoration. Recently the cannons, now rust-free, housed, and on display, have been returned, permanently, to Fort Branch.

Hyacinths, jessamine, the briar rose,
steep through the night, nor close.
Time through them, with gentleness flows.

Walter de la Mare

All night have the roses heard,
the flute, violin, bassoon.
All night have the casements stirred,
to the dancers, dancing in tune,
'Til a silence fell with the waking bird,
and a hush with the setting moon.

Tennyson

≈ ≈ ≈

In the years of the late 1920s, among the social highlights of our community were the Saturday night dances at Benvenue Country Club. Although we would not, of course, have attended without an escort, we would not have used that stilted term, for, by our time, it had given way to the less formal word, "date." In that beneficence of providence, stags were always plentiful, which assured every girl of a wonderful evening.

Mr. Jim Bunn, our family lawyer, a much beloved local older individual, was always there making the rounds. His love of dancing itself was contagious. Among the young girls on the dance floor would have been his daughter, Jamieson, who received from her father the same flattering treatment as the other young girls. Incidentally, Jamieson was the only person I've ever known who was at Bryn Mawr with Katherine Hepburn. Jamieson's mother, spoken of in the southern way as "Miss Ella Lee," did not enjoy dancing, but sent her family out with her blessing.

For as long as I can remember, more than anything I could think of, I had loved to dance. As a very young child, when a storm was brewing, the wind rising, and the clouds gathering, I would beg to be allowed to stay out until the last minute in order to whirl with the wind for "dancing." The dancing lessons that took place every summer at a resort called Panacea, to which our family went, were my delight. Later, when we began our foreign travels, I considered dancing on shipboard one of its greatest pleasures. The ship's officers were usually good dancers, and wherever I was, in port or out, dancing was a part of my life.

Memories of those years come surging back. One from a South American/African cruise of five months stands out. We were on a boat trip of a day from Buenos Aires down the Tigre river. It was a rather large boat for a river, one commandeered that day for our cruise passengers, and it had an orchestra. There were several guides to explain to us what we were seeing and to take us ashore at certain points. These young men were well-educated, seemingly aristocratic, and of Spanish descent. Of course, their favorite dance was the Tango, which was new to me. Yet when pressed into learning it became easy, and by default, I became a dancing partner for these young men, who, without one, would have been unable to show off their grace. And from my loyal fellow cruise members, there was supportive applause.

This was a far cry, however, from Miss Liza Leach's dancing class for children at Panacea. And to Eastern Carolinians, Panacea meant a large summer resort three miles from the town of Littleton. When I was too small to remember, Father bought a half interest in that property, and the family started spending parts of the summer there. In the years before Panacea, the family had gone regularly to Roaring Gap, a North Carolina mountain resort where the three Braswell brothers usually sent their families to get away from the heat. Those were the years before I was born.

Panacea was surrounded by a wooded area, in the center of which, sat the large hotel. The hotel closed during World War I, and never reopened. Eventually it was torn down and sold at auction. At its heyday, the resort was featured in a Littleton newspaper article from which this excerpt is taken:

> The framed structure had a columned porch three hundred feet long and ten feet wide. It was painted yellow with green blinds and had its own electric plant. The huge entrance lobby with its thick red carpet was adorned with a large, open fireplace and handsome late-Victorian upholstered furniture. A landscape gardener from Richmond was hired to design picturesque walks and gardens and the bridges for which the hotel would become famous. During the first season, which opened in June 1907, the hotel averaged one hundred and fifty guests at a time. Many of these people arrived on a stretcher and were miraculously "cured" by the water; indeed, it was a popular heresay among local inhabitants that Panacea guests "came on a stretcher and left eating ham at night."

Mr. Eugene Johnson of Littleton was the other owner. The handsomest doll I was ever to have was given to me by this genial, fatherly man. The doll's name became Gene, and she could have been a little girl my age. But I'll have to say that I did not love that doll very much; a doll to me meant a baby-doll. I saw no reason for having a doll at all unless I could sing it to sleep as I rocked it, or change its clothes for the afternoon at the time mine were being changed so that I could roll its little carriage around with Velma and Margaret, my two playmates who would be doing the same with their dolls. No matter if a doll *did* have eyes that would close and long curls and pretty slippers. I wanted it to be a *baby*.

The hotel at Panacea was painted a soft yellow. On its porch sat innumerable white rocking chairs and there, for a part of the day, sat the hotel guests. The ladies would have been wearing dainty white shirt-waists and long white skirts; their gold watches carefully closed, were pinned to their sometimes hand-embroidered shirt-waists, near the left shoulder. The men would have been wearing white linen suits, the chains of their watches crossing from one vest pocket to another. These chains would usually display an ornament or two called "watch-fobs," something akin to the charms worn on bracelets by women of a later time. Neckties would hold a stick-pin, often in the shape of a horseshoe. Sometimes the horseshoe itself was made of diamonds, and some men even wore diamond rings. Father leaned to neither; he always wore a white shirt with gold cufflinks, and a small black bow tie. A straw hat with its streaked band was part of a man's summer wear, and these were often convenient for fanning, which, because of the way the men were groomed, proved merciful.

From the porch, hotel guests amused themselves by watching the arrival of new guests who had come by hack, an elongated carriage drawn by several horses. Suitcases and trunks followed by wagon. The people on the porch in their rocking chairs also had the diversion of watching the return of those who had already made the morning trip to the spring.

These trips to the spring were a career in themselves. In the first place, you would have to prove your ruggedness by walking, instead of riding, downhill. In this, you followed either of the two boxwood-enclosed paths that were planted in the shape of a horse-shoe. On the way to the spring, you would pass the bowling alley, but you would not think of stopping to bowl until you had begun to drink the day's quota of the health-giving waters. By the time the morning was over, you could boast of the number of glasses you had downed. Two were considered half-hearted. A consumption of three or more tumblers before lunch was nearer the order of the day.

The spring itself gushed from an old, smooth, orange-colored boulder. A male attendant in a white coat stood by to fill your glass. That the water was a little murky was to its advantage, for therein lay its curative qualities. Were the filled glasses allowed to stand for a few moments, the orange-colored sediment would settle at the bottom. This was the concentration of valuable minerals that provided the baths that were supposedly the cure, or at least the palliative, for eczema and other skin diseases. A small bathhouse for that purpose stood near the spring.

When you had drunk possibly three glasses to get you going, you

climbed the stairs to what was called the "Springhouse," a gazebo built over the rock. Inside the gazebo, on its circular bench, which went all the way around, there was the hum of conversation. No matter how hot it was, the men never took off their coats, let alone their ties. Occasionally, they would fan themselves with their stiff straw hats, but in no way did they seem to wilt.

Indeed, manners and decorum were all. At some point during the morning, the men might absent themselves to bowl. The ladies would continue to drink the elixir and to see that their children did so as well. If a mother failed to urge the fifth or sixth glass on her child, some well-intentioned aunt would say, as was always being done in my case, something like, "Sister Alice, you must make Elizabeth drink more of the water. She looks peaked." For I was a skinny child and fair of skin.

For excitement in this rather dull routine, the children had the fun of wading near the bridge where the waters from the lake tumbled between smooth boulders. We knew that in the afternoon we would be allowed to swim in the lake and to canoe. By the time the morning was over, all ages were waterlogged, and many of the grownups chose to make the trip back up the hill by hack. Children seemed unaffected, often racing up on one side or the other of the enormous boxwood enclosed horseshoe.

Although in Eastern Carolina we would never have thought of calling Panacea a spa, that is just what it was. At one end of its dining room there was a small gold-trimmed balcony. From there, music from the harp, the violin and the flute drifted down to the diners. Windows were always open, their simple straight white curtains of scrim, a popular sheer cotton material of the time, blew out gently. Water glasses were filled and refilled with either water or iced tea poured from well-designed, quart-size ironstone pitchers, of which I still have two in my kitchen cabinet. Banana fritters were nearly always on the menu. That in itself would have made Panacea memorable, but in addition, there was the ballroom. This was large and many-windowed. Its hardwood floor shone, and it was there that Miss Liza Leach gave her dancing lessons.

Miss Liza had come from Raleigh, something that enhanced her in the eyes of the children, and early in the mornings as we counted out loud to the pounding on the piano, we stepped purposefully, this way and that. For Miss Liza was bent on adding this social grace to the lives of her charges. As this was going on, our mothers would be in the writing room, writing to our fathers who would come "up country" for the weekends.

By the time I was three, automobiles had come to our area, and Father and his driver, Robert, would take us on the thirty-five mile trip to Panacea in our Overland, with its top down. There would be some forced stops: an overheated engine with water boiling up out of the radiator, making it dangerous to remove the cap for adding the cool water, which for the purpose you'd brought along, or there might be a puncture or a blowout and no service stations to resort to. These stops seemed interminable. Even so, this mode of travel to Panacea was preferable to making the thirty-five mile trip by train with a long wait for train connections in Weldon.

One of Miss Liza's mandates was that for the first part of every evening, the children be allowed to dance along with the adults. And so, dressed in our best, and after our banana fritters, everybody would go to the ballroom and the orchestra would strike up. The little boys often rebelled; the little girls, not to be deterred, danced with each other. With large stiff hair-bows and matching sashes tied in even larger and stiffer bows over our long-waisted, short-skirted dresses, and with our chubby knees and our one strap slippers called "Mary Janes," bobbing to keep time, and with a great deal of see-sawing of arms, to the admiring eyes of the ring of mothers seated around the walls, we made this elevating circuit. By comparison, all those years later, floating down the Tigre on the arms of one handsome Spaniard after another would be as naught.

I don't know whether I liked to dance because Miss Liza gave me the feeling that dancing was joyous participation in life or whether it was as inborn as my love of the wind and the swaying trees which I tried to emulate. Whatever it was, dancing became my great love. So much so, that in those years in a young girl's life, perhaps between the ages of twelve and fifteen, I was torn between the decision of whether to become a missionary to foreign lands – St. Luke's Hospital in Tokyo, supported by the money we put into our mite-boxes, exerted a heavy pull – or to devote my life to the dance. For of such juxtaposition is a young girl's life made. With time and circumstances, however, neither of these options presented themselves.

All of this is to say that one night – and I was twenty-one at the time – at our country club at home, in the middle of a dance number, my life changed. Mr. Jim Bunn tapped my partner on the shoulder, asking permission to cut in to present a tall, dark-haired, blue-eyed young man with a strong face made soft by a cleft in the chin. Mr. Bunn withdrew, and Tom and I, dancing off slowly, began to get to know each other.

With the strong arm of this stranger to guide me, I felt something that I had never felt before. How, I don't know, but I could sense in Tom's nature, something of that combination of strength and tenderness which had been characteristic of the men in my family, especially Father. And the cleft in the chin caught my heart. I could soon see, too, that Tom loved to dance; as he did everything else, he danced with verve. So that, before long, although the other couples on the floor might be moving in slow rhythm, not us. Tom's favorite was the waltz, as was mine. He especially loved the liveliness and grace of movement that went with a Viennese. They so lent themselves to dips and curves – not exaggerated – but light-hearted and free. And, down the years, wherever we were, if the orchestra played a waltz at dinner, Tom would fold a tip very small, and slip it into the hand of our waiter for the orchestra leader with a request for one of the other of my three favorites, "Greensleeves," "Smoke Gets in Your Eyes," or the waltz from "The Merry Widow." Sometimes we danced, sometimes not.

With that intuitiveness that would come into our lives twenty-five years later at the discovery of Captiva, I was quietly aware of something new in my life. The feeling that I could have danced into eternity was literally mine. During the rest of the evening, Tom came back several times. As we danced, we chatted. There were many things to find out about each other. For somehow, with the difference of four years in our ages, although we knew the same people, we had been only names to each other. With Tom away at prep school, college, and summers spent in mountain resorts as combination desk clerk, tennis and swimming instructor, and with me at summer camps, school, and travel, we had never before been in the same room.

By the time the orchestra played "Good Night, Ladies," I moved in a dream. It hardly occurred to me to wonder if Tom could be having the same feeling. Had I given it any thought, I suppose I might have surmised that in order for me to feel that way, he must.

I knew that my heart had come home. Strangely, I felt no sense of hurry, and, an hour later, drifting off to sleep in a quiet happiness, I slept in the serenity of feeling that it would all unfold.

Those three hours of the dance that were so to shape my life happened to fall on a weekend when the Bishop of our diocese was making a visitation to the Church of the Good Shepherd in town. And the next morning, my sister, Vivian, and I went to the service of morning prayer. The service ended with a familiar recessional hymn, and who should be marching along in the choir on my side of the aisle, and making his own joyful noise, but Tom. There was no way to communicate our mutual surprise. It was only an instant, but it was long enough for Tom to do something wholly in character; he gave me a big wink. After church, he went home and called me.

By late summer we would be engaged, but first we each had to disentangle ourselves from a romantic interest in a distant state. For every day there was our growing certainty that what we had found would last forever.

My heart is like a singing bird and a watered shoot.

Christina Georgina Rossetti

≈ ≈ ≈

This morning, a slender booklet lies before me. Once white, it has now mellowed to a soft cream, the gold of its Olde English lettering has deepened, as well. The letters combine into three simple words, *The Marriage Service*.

Inside the book lies an illuminated column of six lines:

The form of
Solemnization
Of Matrimony
As Contained in
The Book of
Common Prayer

Among the prayers and the exhortations of this small, slender book are the vows, and in appropriate places left for them, appear two hand-written names, Thomas and Elizabeth. At the back of the book are the signatures of the eleven witnesses to the ceremony, and last, covering two pages, is the marriage certificate.

It contains the names of those being united and the date: October 28th, 1930; the place, St. John's Church, Battleboro, North Carolina, in the Diocese of North Carolina; and the name of the rector officiating, the Reverend Francis H. Craighill.

This is the record of our wedding, Tom's and mine.

≈ ≈ ≈

Over the state of North Carolina, the term "Eastern Carolina" evokes a land of broad, flat fields, of long stretches of pine, of lazy rivers often colored by the red-brown clay of the up-lands, and of dark-watered creeks that, joining the rivers, make their slow way to the sea.

The days of late October may be those of summer, and the day of our wedding, fifteen months after we'd met, was one of them. In the village at twilight, people in the village began early winding up the hill to St. John's.

At the home of the bride, things were stirring. Preparations for the reception were underway. And here, I speak in the third person. For that day, and indeed, the wedding, itself, now both seem to have been beautiful

little scenes in a play. Extra help, both male and female, had been brought in from the farms, and as the afternoon waned, they stood about on the long back porch. This was one of the many porches that, on the first floor, all but wrapped our house. Only the octagonal windows in the dining room, and they faced north, were not shaded by one of those wide, comfortable "verandas," on which, for five months of the year, life could and did go on.

On the second floor, there were two more porches, a large balcony that rose behind the Corinthian columns that flanked the front steps, and a utilitarian back porch for airing blankets and winter clothes. It was there that the woodbox that held the firewood for the open fires of the five bedrooms on the second floor was kept. The woodbox was refilled every day by Henry, the yardman, who built the downstairs fires. Rhody, the housegirl, built those upstairs in the rooms of the girls.

The attic covered the third floor, and it opened on to another large, balustraded porch which we spoke of as "the attic balcony." It was uncovered, and less ornamental than the one below. Approached from the middle of the attic by a single stairway, a trap door opened onto a Captain's Walk.

As a child, high above the old elms, their graceful branches always moving in the stir of air, this was my favorite spot. But I was rarely able to enjoy it for long at a time, since I had to have a grown person lift the heavy trap door and go up and out with me, and whoever it happened to be, one of my three sisters, all some years older, or my nurse, or the cook would begin to complain of the heat or the cold, according to the season, and there would hardly be time for being fanciful. For imagining, or probably actually hearing Grandma Bryan's farm bell two miles away, the dogs barking as it rang, or the bells from the country church "Mawnin' Stah," the same distance in another direction. And I have always been drawn to the sound of country bells. To me, they are one of life's most beautiful, half-melancholy sounds. I'm not alone in this, of course. I remember hearing a friend say once, in the countryside of France, as he heard a faraway churchbell, "It's so beautiful, it makes you weep."

The tinge of sadness that *I* heard in faraway bells was probably due to my sister, Alice Bryan's, chronic illness, her frequent long bouts with pain from the incurable bone disease known as osteomyelitis. It was an early lesson for me in the pathos of life.

On the day of our wedding, the back porch where the farm men and women, both dressed in white – the women in their starched white caps – were all standing around ready to serve, two long tables had been set up. They held a stack of silver trays on which the petit fours were to be spread. Cole's in Richmond had sent one of its trucks down with ice cream in fancy shapes as well as those small, beautifully decorated cakes. For even though we were a country family, we could furnish airs and graces on demand. In Mother's desk there lay an invitation to her own mother's wedding, kept through the years, and one to her own. The invitation to my older sister's was there, as well. Though the two earlier invitations bore no stationer's mark, on Sister's there was the word "Tiffany." When the time came, mine would follow suit.

In those years, at every wedding reception, two things were served: hard, frozen ice-cream shaped into slippers and bells. The slippers were pale pink; the bells, white. They came in boxes, each one separately wrapped, and even after having been exposed to the air for some time, they could sometimes be as hard as granite. This called for precision timing. More than would have been believed necessary for softening was nearly always required, with the result that guests were invariably having a slipper or a bell hop off the plate as they tried to pierce it with a fork or a spoon, or that hybrid of flat silver designed for the purpose, an ice cream fork, a combination of prongs and spoon, which, even so, would prove ineffective if timing had not been right. A bride's chest of silver usually contained some of those ice-cream forks. That there should be a dozen or so of these to lie unused except for weddings, and for home weddings, at that, was a pity. The pity is doubled in that now there is never any granite-like ice cream to be dealt with. And I have never found a suitable use for mine, except for tarts.

But the petit fours, ready to be placed on trays, were a dream, and the bride could not resist getting into the thick of things, in spite of repeated warning messages brought from upstairs from her sisters, by both Erdie and Lethy, the housegirls, "Ask Miss Elizabeth, why in the world she doesn't come on and get ready?"

Having such a wonderful time helping to arrange this rainbow of cakes, I would send back the message, "Tell them not to worry. I'll be there in a minute!" But it was typical of my sisters to worry about many things which I didn't.

I knew that my wedding dress was in readiness, as was my veil. The veil had been in the house for three months since it had arrived from Florence where I had bought it earlier that year on a trip around the world with my mother and my two single sisters. Into my bags had gone the lingerie I'd had made in China. Since I'd never been much of a primper, anyway, all I would need would be time to sing through my bath one song, that perennial favorite from my repertoire of high "C's," "From the Land of the Sky Blue Water":

> From the Land of the sky blue water,
> They brought a captive ma-yade
> her eyes were sad with longing,
> her heart was sore afra-ayde.

That poor Indian girl was to remain a part of my life for a long time, for nothing so elevates a reedy, little soprano to the operatic as the hollow tile of bathroom walls. And in those years, I always warbled at my bath. Running neck and neck with the lament of the Indian maiden as a favorite selection, however, was that of another sorrowful maid who grieved for her lost love in her native French. And, of course, trilling in a foreign tongue added remarkably to the dramatic effect.

But October twilight was falling. I was ready to follow Tom to the ends of the earth, and it would soon be the time of our commitment. Yet, I delayed a little longer in getting dressed for my wedding than might have been expected. Even so, when Uncle Mark arrived, tall and dressed in tails and handsome, for, as the older of the two of Father's brothers, he was to give me away, I was in the hall, dressed and serenely waiting. Rhody, like a mother-hen, was standing carefully guarding my train. The three of us left the house by way of the porte-cochere. The other domestics, and those brought in from the farm to help with the reception were standing around, each of them anxious to serve in some small way.

It took practically no time to reach the hill and drive up to the door of the church. The groomsmen and the attendants were waiting in the vestibule, the church, filled. In that my oldest sister, Mattie May, affectionately known to us throughout her life as "Sister," was married – her wedding had come nine years earlier – she was dame of honor. Vivian, as she had been for Sister, was bridesmaid; Velma Harrison, my lifelong friend, was the other attendant. Margaret Bunn, my other closest lifelong friend, had married, and was now looking forward to motherhood. And in the way of the times, an expectant mother usually refrained from situations in which she might feel conspicuous.

At the time, because my favorite colors were a soft shade of blue and jonquil yellow, all attendants wore long blue satin dresses and carried yellow rosebuds. The flower that I love best next to a yellow rose is lily-of-the-valley, and my bridal bouquet was made up of those.

The sad note was that with Alice Bryan's declining health, she was not able to take part as maid of honor as she had done for Sister. Since Sister's wedding took place only seven months after Father's death, it was small, and quiet, and all in white, for in those days, during a period of mourning, it was the custom to observe certain codes of dress. For the men, it was a two-inch black arm-band, made of dull crepe, and sewn on the upper part of his left coat sleeve, near his heart. The women dressed in four stages: black, purple, gray and finally, white. There was no time set for these progressions in the stages of mourning; the length of each was left to the feelings of the individual.

In Sister's wedding, Vivian and I were bridesmaids, four-year-old Sarah Mae, daughter of the Viverett family, with whom our family had long had ties, was ring-bearer. The ring, itself, was borne on the same small white satin pillow that had been used at Mother's and Father's wedding. Since it was May, we wore garden dresses of white chiffon, our wide-brimmed white hats were of that popular material of the time known as Meline. Our flowers were loose sprays of white lilacs; Sister's bouquet was of lily-of-the-valley, a few of their clusters cascading down her shimmering dress. Everything reflected Sister's love of the beautiful, and her exquisite taste.

But that afternoon, in that little church, there must have been a catch in many throats as Alice Bryan, slowly limping, but smiling, an angel with a broken wing, made her slow way down the aisle.

Mother must have wept inside, and have longed for the sustaining presence of Father. Perhaps she felt that it was there, as, the lady she was, wearing lace in a pale shade of lavender, she sat, composed. Soon, however, over the village and the countryside, there was the happy peal of the wedding bell.

Nine years later, that same bell rang for Tom and me as it had done thirty-seven years before for Mother and Father. With our wedding ceremony over, Tom and I were the first to arrive from the church, and as we came into the house that I would be leaving forever, I wept. The sadness of leaving Mother and my two sisters came over me; Alice Bryan, crippled, and Vivian, the next sister, unmarried, for she had had an early unhappy romance which seemed to have left its mark. From the age of sixteen to nineteen, she had been in love with a second cousin, but marriage between blood relations was discouraged since it was thought that the children of such a marriage might suffer mental weakness.

The sadness of it all swept over me, but Tom understood, as Tom would. And my tears lasted only a second, for the bridesmaids and the groomsmen were arriving from the church in peals of laughter. The groomsmen had come from all over and were being quartered at the hotel in town. In the hurry of dressing, grappling with collar buttons, and studs, cufflinks and boutonnieres, two men had gotten their shoes mixed. Bob Huffines, short, and wearing a size nine shoe, and "Big Mac MacKeever," the tall, heavy-set son of the president of the Greensboro branch of UNC who had coined the phrase "when you educate a man, you educate one person, when you educate a woman, you educate a family," wore a size thirteen, with the result that one of the six groomsmen limped, and another shuffled down the aisle.

The reception about half over, the tossing of the bridal bouquet done, I went upstairs, and soon came down dressed in travelling clothes. I was wearing my new full length caracul coat with its mink collar, for we were going to New York. Very popular at that time, caracul was a coppery-colored fur from the lynx. Since these were the days of the depression, Tom's small blue Ford coupe of some years had been re-painted for the trip, and now sat under the porte-cochere, waiting. Tom had been practicing law for three years, but it was a time when legal and medical fees were apt to be paid in hams, turkeys, and chickens. All he really had to count on was a meager salary from the city as prosecuting attorney. But we had faith, and faith in each other.

It was the beginning of a new life for me in many ways. I knew that, as a matter of pride, Tom would want us to live on what he made. I knew that this was something he felt deeply, and I had made up my mind to honor it.

Down the years, we would laugh over what I had been told was Mother's remark when Tom asked for my hand. At first, I wondered how Mother could have asked such a question. Then I remembered that throughout my oldest sister's young womanhood – and Sister had had a flock

50

of beaux, for she was beautiful and attractive and interesting – Father had used that same question in talking to whichever of the swains had come to talk to him seriously about the question of matrimony. He would bring up short any of those whom he suspected of being fortune-hunters, as he quickly asked of John or Joe or Richard, "Do you have any life insurance?"

This was Father's canny way of taking care of the situation, and Sister, while in some cases might have fumed momentarily, would, with basic good sense, soon see the light, and would go on to be happily married to a wonderful man, Robert Diggs Gorham. Together they would have a long and good life. Sister's artistic nature was revealed when she studied art and china painting in prep school and college. It was further revealed when she and her husband built what was to be their permanent home. They surprised us by choosing the architectural style of the Mediterranean. Sister had in mind just what she wanted; an Atlanta architect drew the plan.

The house turned out to be a gem of the Italian; its interior and its furnishings within the bounds of reasonable family life – very nearly perfect. Not only that, in Sister's love of gardens, she created a beautiful one of her own. Maintaining it was her great interest, and sharing both the house and the garden for the public good and church causes was her pleasure. Sister and Bob were to have one son, Robert Diggs Gorham, Jr. He would grow up to become president of Student Government at Chapel Hill, and as a successful entrepreneur, would build our town's first shopping center, Tarrytown Mall, taking its name from our river, the Tar.

I was not present when Mother and Tom were having this crucial talk about my future. If I had been, I would have been doubly embarrassed at the second question that came at the end of this apparently amicable, even affectionate conversation.

Mother had sensed, by that time, that in having Tom in my life, I would have the same kind of happiness which had been hers in her life with Father, and was delighted. Nevertheless, as the interchange went on, she came out with something that in this age would seem altogether outlandish, when she said placidly, toward the end of the visit, "I do hope Elizabeth won't have to cook."

In Mother's defense, I will have to say that in the South of her time, among so-called "gentlewomen," an abundance of help was the norm. Although Mother's mother, Grandma Bryan, had indeed died when I was sixteen, it was not too early even for me to have come under her counseling (the only piece of poor, and not to say confusing advice that Grandma was ever to give to any of her daughters and their daughters), "If you never learn to cook, you'll never have to cook." As archaic as it seems, both Grandma and Mother just happened to be the products of their times and its customs. Times of larger families, larger houses, of larger meals prepared from home-grown products and cooked in a wood-burning stove. It was, literally, and figuratively, an entirely different kettle of fish.

≈ ≈ ≈

Not only was Grandma a stranger to the kitchen, but as though to forestall the temptation to take part in its activities, her own sat far in the backyard, at least fifty feet from the house. More seriously, this custom of placing the kitchen away from the house was, of course, a precaution against fire. It meant, however, that every morsel of food had to be brought across the yard, rain or shine, hail or snow or sleet.

The food was brought first into the buttery, where there were two large tables. In that room there was also a commodious pie safe, one of those tall cupboards made of wood and pierced tin. There were three wide shelves inside on which sat the fruit pies – mainly blackberry and huckleberry and apple, and, since this was the room where the butter was churned – in England it would have been called "the buttery" – the wide, shallow pans of milk were placed there for the cream to rise. The milk for drinking, like butter, was kept in a bucket that hung down in the cool of the well. In summer, when we heard that chain squeak, we knew that somebody was at the well, and that the meal under preparation would soon be served.

During the months of crop cultivation, on the dot at noon, the farm bell rang. That, also, stood far back from the house. This was a signal for the hands to leave the fields to go to their cottages for their "dinner." For "taking out," the horses and mules were first brought to that area distant from the "gret house" called "the lot." There, relieved of their harness and plough lines, they made straight for the shaded trough made from a large old log, and when I happened to be at Grandma's, I always loved sitting on the fence at that time for the pleasure of listening to their long, cooling swigs.

A door from the buttery led into the pantry, that room with the wonderful aroma of ginger cakes and apples. It was also where staple groceries were stored: a barrel of flour, a barrel of cornmeal, a barrel of sugar, and a stand-of-lard. The term, "lard-stand" was one in everyday use in country life. For these large, covered tin containers of either twenty-five or fifty pound capacity had a variety of uses. An important use for these commodious and inexpensive containers was for the boiling of a ham. There was an additional container in Grandma's pantry. It was oblong, made of tin, had its own cover, and was large enough to hold three cakes of four or five-layers each. There was always an apple in this "cake-box" to keep them fresh.

In a carry-over from Civil War days and their scarcities, staples for the day were carefully measured. According to custom, for the first of her duties of the day, the mistress of the plantation would engage herself in what was known as "giving out." At Grandma's, for this morning ritual, Aunt Caroline and Aunt Mary – mother and daughter domestics – would come across the yard from the kitchen into the buttery where meals for the day would be planned. Until lunchtime, the mistress of the plantation wore a large, bibless white apron; a bunch of keys hung from her belt. The larger keys were carried around in a small basket. Among these large keys were the ones to the smokehouse and the pantry. Either Aunt Mary or Aunt Caroline would bring a large, enamelled pan from the kitchen into the buttery. The pan held several tin quart-size containers, one to be filled with cornmeal, one with flour, one for sugar, and another, lard, for no matter what form the meal would take, there would always be two hot breads: cornbread, and either biscuits or muffins. Not to have served cornbread or cornsticks with vegetables or with fish would have been considered downright immoral. This giving out taken care of, the pantry was locked. Relieved of the responsibility of meals, Grandma could turn her attention to her other duties. And she was never idle.

By that time of day, Green, the horse-feeder, would have fed and watered the horses and gathered the vegetables from the garden. Well water was used only for the horses and mules. The water for the house was drawn by hand-pump from an artesian well that, protected from the weather by its shingle roof, stood near the house. A wooden bucket and a dipper always stood on a table on the side porch near the artesian well. On this porch Grandma would make her own contribution to the noon meal; she would slice and season cucumbers paper thin, into a glass bowl, slice and season tomatoes into another. The last thing she would do would be to season a wooden bowl of garden lettuce and sliced hard-boiled eggs. For this she would use vinegar, salt, and sugar, and sometimes a pinch of dried mustard, a treatment for garden lettuce that Mother used throughout life for our family as well. Having carried these things to the dining room table, Grandma would return to the front porch to await the dinner bell. This makes her sound frivolous, but she was anything but that.

Grandma made at least one trip a day to the garden to see what was "bearing," and in that way of the South of the time, every vegetable that was bearing appeared on the table every day. If there were seven, seven were prepared, cooked, served, and in small or large portions, consumed. Since this meal required many hours for preparation, it came early in the afternoon. It would have been unheard of for this, the main meal of the day, not to have had a platter of thin slices of home-cured-ham at one end of the table, and, of course, neither ham nor country vegetables could be served without hot corn sticks and small, thin, hot biscuits. For those not yet satiated, there would still be a slice of pie and a glass of milk at the end. Naturally, after such a meal, the ladies lazed away the next two hours.

In a mixture of the utilitarian and the aesthetic, on Grandma's premises were thirteen cats. These were correctly called "mousers"; in fact, that was Grandma's term for all cats, for keeping the rats out of the corn crib was an important part of farm life. Equally as prominent in Grandma's plantation life were her two ornamental fowls, the peacock and the peahen. Every afternoon at four – and how the peacock knew it was four, I don't know – the peacock would spread his tail and strut about under the trees. To be sure that nobody missed this fine display, he would screech. The ignominious peahen would follow at a distance. Sometimes, as this afternoon show was going on, Aunt Caroline or Aunt Mary would be coming out of the doorway of the kitchen with a large pan of milk, calling "Kitty, Kitty, Kitty," and the show of thirteen cats gathered around a large pan, their tails raised as their little pink tongues lapped the milk, would all but upstage the peacock.

Grandma's windmill, which sat far back near the stables, held a peculiar fascination for me. Interesting enough to watch, there was always in the background its dry little rhythmic clucking that could be heard all over the yard. Then there was the wash house. This sat near the kitchen, and through the long summer afternoons, there was the smell of hot linen being ironed. Lottie and Melissy, their heads wrapped in close-fitting, white cotton cloth, would exchange a cooling flat iron for a hot one from the stove, all the while, in spite of the heat, singing at their work.

In winter there was nobody at Grandma's house but Grandma and Uncle Hugh, her bachelor son, who, after his return from the University, took over management of the farm. And as happy as I was in summer at Grandma's when all the other grandchildren and the aunts were there, the memories of my winter visits, when all the other children were back at their homes, are almost more vivid to me than those of summer, for it was then that at night, the three of us, Grandma, Uncle Hugh, and I, sat by the fire.

Although we had gaslights at home, Grandma and Uncle Hugh still used lamps, and the sitting room was filled with that bright white light from what was called an "acetylene lamp." It was so bright that Grandma could even see to darn, and she taught me that art the Salem way. While darning is no longer necessary – with a mild aptitude for tatting, and for crocheting a trimming much in use at the time for lingerie, an edging called "mile-a-minute," it is the only needlecraft in which I was ever to feel a sense of accomplishment. I had my own little workbasket, my own small silver thimble, and my own milk glass darning egg over which I wove the threads to fill the hole.

As we darned, Uncle Hugh would read aloud from Dickens, O'Henry, Zane Grey, or Bret Harte. Dan, the large old brown dog, would be stretched on his side in front of the hearth, asleep. Sometimes his tail would thump in his sleep, his nose would twitch, and Uncle Hugh would look up and say, quietly, so as not to disturb Dan, "A rabbit's running across his nose."

I suppose Grandma thought it too complicated to try to teach me to knit place mats with steel needles. That task she had set for herself, a dozen place mats for each of her daughters. I was glad to be excused from those lessons, for they included a small round mat for the water glass, another for the cup and saucer, another for the bone dish, and a very small one that would hold the tiny round dish for a pat of butter. For Grandma believed that all dining room tables should be protected.

It was only after Grandma's death that Uncle Hugh married. Since Belle Melton had been Uncle Hugh's ward, there was a difference in ages, but it was the happiest of marriages. As often happened during the 1918 flu epidemic, Belle lost both parents. When asked by his friend, Belle's

Uncle, to become her guardian, Uncle Hugh accepted the responsibility. When Belle finished college, to the family's surprise and great joy, they were immediately married.

Uncle Hugh and Belle were to have two sons and a daughter. Hugh B. married a lovely Raleigh girl, and they live and have brought up their family at their farm, Bryan Acres, near Whitakers. Blair, who married Nell Phillips of the Battleboro community, became a pediatrician, and they have had a happy life, bringing up their children in Charlotte. Bettie Bryan Rierson, the oldest, and another of Grandma's namesakes, still lives at the homeplace. She was to have the tragedy of losing her husband, Bob, in a hang-gliding accident on the farm. It was on a Sunday afternoon when this fine, able Minnesotan and graduate of West Point, who became a successful North Carolina farmer, indulging his interest in hang gliding, met his death in one of the fields.

I had grown used to seeing Bob's plane sit far back behind the stables, but it seemed strange, now, to me, that this kind of accident should have occurred in one of these quiet fields, which I had so long known as they followed the seasons with the same crops. Then I reminded myself that cars now sit in what was Grandma's carriage driveway, that grandchildren now swim in a pool where the carriage house was, and that most of the other outbuildings that related to a far-back time and way of life are now gone.

Bettie has continued to live there and to make a wonderful gathering place for her children and their children. Although far-flung, the present generation feels that life would not be complete without intermittent stays there. Although Uncle Hugh's office in the side yard, where, on "First Saturday," he used to settle with the hands, has been moved to make room for a bath house, it still sits adjacent to the side porch of the "gret house." Now unused, it contains old papers that go back as far as 1856. That was the date of Grandma Bryan's – at that time, Bettie Sherrod's – leatherbound friendship book, one of those sentimental things that go on in the lives of young girls away at school. The book itself is lovely on the outside; it's a beautiful shade of red with a floral border engraved in gold. Its title: *Flowers of Loveliness.* Inside, on the flyleaf, in decorative Olde English, it says, simply, *Bettie Sherrod.* Underneath that, over to the side, Salem, *June 14, 1856.*

Whoever the poetry teacher at Salem was at that time, she appears to have made an impression on her young ladies. For each page carries an original poem of one or two verses declaring undying friendship. Practically every state in the South is represented in Grandma's book. In between these pages are lithographs in which young ladies are depicted in the form of individual flowers. Underneath each illustration, the flower is identified with a descriptive phrase.

In each case, the gowns of these ethereal creatures are fairy-like creations of fanciful leaves that are twined and intertwined up to the lovely, gentle, human face that peeps from its petals. There is one flower to each page. The first of these is a water lily. Draped with the leaves of the lilypad which forms her habit, is the nun, representing "Purity of Heart." There is a page to eglantine, in everyday language, the "sweetbriar." Clothed in vines, she represents "Poetry." There is one to the pansy – and the word "pansy," of course, comes from the French word *penser*, to think – for "Pleasant Thoughts." There is the less romantic combination of a white and red carnation for "Pride." The last plate is given to the white lily, for "Modesty." It depicts a bride with a lovely, gossamer veil, floating off in what can only be thought of as a zephyr.

With this little gem of Victoriana in mind, I chuckle as I try to imagine what the reaction of Grandma and the other ladies of her time would have been to something that took place in our town once Habitat for Humanity was in full swing among us. The account of the incident is lifted from the Church of the Good Shepherd's newsletter, where it appeared after it had been published in the *Reader's Digest*, under

Parish the Thought

A friendly rivalry developed between Methodist and Episcopal church groups in Rocky Mount, N.C., when both broke ground on Habitat for Humanity houses within weeks of one another. One Saturday, a Methodist churchgoer helped his Episcopalian brethren frame their house. At noon he couldn't resist bragging, "About this time on the Methodist project, the women arrive with chicken, sandwiches, chips and tea."

Not to be outdone, an Episcopal minister spoke up, "On this project," she said, "the women are too busy nailing."

To those of Grandma's generation, I doubt that there would have been enough smelling salts *in the world* to have revived them.

Sadly, along with other things found in Uncle Hugh's office, there was included, as well, receipts for the buying and selling of slaves. Bettie Rierson, describing the feeling she had when she came upon these, said, "When I saw those, it went all over me." Later, when she handed them to me, my reaction was the same. To make it even more poignant, however, these human beings being bought and sold – and they were usually in their teens – were being designated only by their given names. Nothing more than their age and the current state of their health was stated on the receipt. The prices for these slaves ranged from seven hundred to a thousand dollars. In some cases, as many as five or six were bought and sold at a time.

The discovery of the evidence of slave buying and selling in my own background sent me to the library to find out more about slave trading, per se. Although it was heartbreaking to find that African family members sold their own, and that human beings were kidnapped for the slave trade, I did find one thing to lessen the sadness. From the *Horizon History of Africa*, by A. Adu Boahen, comes this:

> In the case of slaves, early forays made by the Portuguese were soon abandoned as a method of acquisition. From about 1500 onward, apart from a few kidnapping attempts, it was the Africans, themselves, who delivered slaves to the Europeans for sale: these slaves were obtained in four primary ways: criminals sold as punishment by their rulers; domestic slaves who were resold; prisoners obtained from raids upon neighboring states; and prisoners of full-scale wars.

That, at the time, slavery was recognized as a commercial enterprise now seems incredible to us. This trafficking in human life involved shipbuilding and investors in shipbuilding to name a few, and was considered among nations a necessity for economic development. Yet slavery, as we know, has existed, in one country or another since the beginning of time. Historians tell us that those marvelously straight and practically indestructable roads which were built by the Romans during their occupation of Britain, and which are still in existence to this day, were built by slaves, as were the pyramids, though now the scholars argue that latter point. And although slave-ownership did exist in Africa as well, in tribal communities, we're told that the practice was not associated with inhumanity. That, in a loose sense, African slaves were considered members of the family, allowed to own property, and marry, and have children, and in many cases, carried a title. So that, when the effects of the slave trade in Europe and the New World were universally disclosed, measures were taken in some parts of Africa to place embargoes on the sale of male slaves. But it was in that weakness in human nature that certain of the African rulers succumbed to the temptation of alcohol and material possessions that the more honorable code was sacrificed. The trade subsequently carried on in a less-humane way.

But the hum of activity at Grandma's is a thing of the past. The grounds at the end of Bettie's beautiful garden have been brought up to date with a swimming pool and a bathhouse. Although Bettie's life has not been that of the old-time plantation mistress, she still carries a certain amount of responsibility. Each of her daughters had grown up with her own saddle horse, and for a while after their marriages, Bettie continued keeping the horses. This ended abruptly with a trauma a few years ago when all seven of the saddle horses suddenly died of poisoning. That they had eaten a kind of poisonous wild cherry that grew over the pasture fence was suspected, though it was never proven. Later it was thought that some condition in their feed had brought about their deaths. In any event, that was the end of the old way of life on Grandma's farm.

≈ ≈ ≈

Sifting these customs of Grandma's time, and of my mother's, I now see that to the southern plantation woman, it was not only important to have a cook, but someone to wait on the table, as well. Even as late as my own time, when I was a bride living in a small apartment, Uncle Jim, Father's brother, asked me one day how much help I had. I said that my help consisted of a cook, and he asked, "But who waits on the table?" This was my background when, years later, I landed on an island among northern and western women, who, with their preconceived notions of southern women, would quite literally not expect me to know how to boil water. They were wrong. By that time I had – in a manner of speaking – learned my way around the kitchen.

Gradually, I was able to provide these women with a more flattering image of the so-called "southern gentlewoman." Yet, although I was not half as helpless as they thought, I was far from being able to cook as well as they. On that "do-it-yourself" little island, my pride was at stake. Not that I ever achieved any great heights, but I did learn a few tricks. I could invite six people for lunch and stay out in the boat until the last thirty minutes, confident that things would fall into place, for I had thought ahead. This happy-go-lucky attitude would sometimes cause Tom concern. If it were late in the afternoon, and guests were coming for drinks and dinner, he would say, "You know, I'd rather die than leave the water at this hour when it's so beautiful, but don't you think we'd better go back and get things going?"

And I could answer, easily, "It will all come out all right." Besides, I wanted to be on the water myself. I could not bear to sacrifice any of these perfect moments that Tom and I had together. I had made my peace with housekeeping. Cooking was more to sustain life than to show off. But in a pinch, I could perform. Yet in that sentence, I am being facetious. For my Captiva years in the kitchen had given me self-confidence. So much so, that when we came back one spring from the island, and our beloved Ella told us that she wanted to go to take a sleep-in job in Las Vegas where she would have the care of the two young children of a couple who owned a nightclub and would come home at four in the morning and have their swims, we gave her our blessing, and I suggested to Tom that I wanted to face the challenge of the kitchen myself. He thought it very strange that this should come over me so late in life, and warned me by saying, "Don't you think you're too old to take on such hard work?" And I could answer with complete aplomb, "No," and go on to explain that cooking was not what it used to be. That I would enjoy feeling independent. And that it would bring a pleasant flexibility into our life. This was the pattern for us for the last twenty years we were to have together. How could I have foreseen the truth of Kilpatrick's statement that "life is a series of beginnings and endings, all flowing together"?

≈ ≈ ≈

But to return to Grandma's time. When she was a bride, wooden ranges had begun to replace fireplace cooking. The large brick fireplace at the end of her kitchen was now rarely used. In this one room white-washed structure, Aunt Caroline and Aunt Mary held sway. The third generation of these helpers was represented by Aunt Mary's eighteen-year-old twins, Lizzie and Helen, who cleaned the house and waited on the table.

Lizzie and Helen also took care of the retired family mammy, Aunt Lucy.

Aunt Lucy had a small room on the first floor of Grandma's house. In my time, Aunt Lucy was too old to do more than sit by the fire in her room. Her teeth were gone, and all day long, between sipping a mixture of coffee and milk with biscuits crumbled into it, which she kept in a brown mug, warming on the hearth all the time, she would tell absorbing country tales. Just as in our kitchen at home, I enjoyed being in the companionship of those good-natured, colorful, imaginative people that the domestics were. I loved to sit in a little chair on the other side of the fireplace in Aunt Lucy's room and listen to her as she made up her tales, or told real ones about harrowing things that had happened on the farm.

Sadly, when I was about seven, Aunt Lucy's skirts, of which there were many – one of her petticoats was always of flannel to help her rheumatism – caught on fire, and she was so badly burned that after a few days she died. This is the first death that I remember. The day of the burial was bleak and gray. The fields, except for the swallows and swifts, empty. I had a sore throat and cold, and couldn't go, but I remember standing at the bay window in Grandma's sitting room, watching the cortege as it went through the wintery fields on its way to the plantation graveyard. Many times in summer, on the way to the pond, I had passed that peacefully shaded spot, surrounded as it was by the broad, flat fields which had been the only world that those lying under the stones had known. One of my grownup cousins, Cousin Lina, short for "Evelina," didn't attend the funeral either, and we wept together.

This country procession, in its mixture of carriages, buggies, a few cars (for every one of Grandma's children and grandchildren came), wagons, what we called "dump-carts," and people walking in this gray world, was for me, another lesson in sorrow. Alice Bryan's osteomyelitis since I was a year old had been the first. But the sorrowful impression of Aunt Lucy's funeral was, for me, fleeting, for Lizzie and Helen were soon back with their ready laughter and their great good-nature, and I soon no longer felt grief for Aunt Lucy.

During my early life, whenever I was visiting Grandma, it was the duty of Lizzie and Helen to take care of me, not in an overprotective way, but just to keep up with me. They often took me fishing in Grandma's pond. This spot was made picturesque with cypress trees and cypress knees growing in the dark brown water; dragonflies flitting back and forth down close to the water, and I thought I had never seen anything so beautiful as their iridescent wings in the dappled sunlight. Now and then, something called "mellow-bugs" scooted across the surface of the water and set up tiny ripples. At most, we could hope to catch only a small perch or a catfish. Lizzie and Helen were eager for the catfish, but the only things Grandma would use from the pond were perch. Usually by the end of the afternoon we had a small forked twig with one or two of each kind.

Once, we had the horrible experience of having a water moccasin slither out of his hole and grab my perch which was lying on its twig in the edge of the water. It nearly scared us to death, and the worst part was that we had been fishing from a small island to which we had had to wade, and now we would either have to wade back, or spend the rest of our lives there. I have to admit that I chickened out, that Lizzie had to carry me piggyback.

While the brush with the snake added spice to our excursions to the pond, there were lesser things to make those afternoons interesting. It was always my job to carry the egg basket and its long-handled spoon for gathering the eggs of the guinea and the goose on our way home. Ostensibly hidden, the nests were easy to find; the guinea built hers in the honeysuckle along the pasture fence, the goose chose a clump of pine straw, and was temperamental, hence the long-handled spoon. If, returning to the nest, she sensed that it had been in contact with the human hand, her nest would be immediately abandoned and never returned to. That this was the habit of the goose, per se, made her seem to me rather intelligent; made me wonder at the reputation of the breed for being silly.

With this kind of life at Grandma's, I was a ripe plum for *The Girl of the Limber Lost* when a copy of that book for young girls was given me on my eleventh birthday. After that, when Lizzie and Helen and I went fishing, I spent much of my time searching – without success – for what had been the heroine of that book's daily discovery of watercress, but I found other ways to be poetically woodsy.

In the fall, at home in the village, I would roam the briery ditchbanks – and how I do yearn, here, to use the more poetically British term, "brambled hedgerows." These ran through the orchard and the fields; lovely in summer with Queen Anne's lace and reeds and pokeberries, in winter they were an assortment of tall, stalky plants, of which two were cattails, and the aromatic, grey-leafed rabbit tobacco. It was these two that, every fall, I gathered by the armful for the house, to enhance our hall. By the time my arms were full, my short woolen pleated skirt, my sweater, my middy blouse with its sailor collar and tie – almost the uniform for young schoolgirls of that era – my stockings and my beret would be a network of cockleburs. I had always liked the large, heavy brass umbrella stand, that, with its lion's head on either side and a ring through its nose sat just inside the front door. And by appropriating this for my wild armful the effect would be impressive.

There was, however, one drawback. Left where nature intended it to grow, the odor of the rabbit tobacco was not offensive. Brought inside, its sourness was overwhelming. It permeated the house, and the family would beg for mercy. So that – and truth to tell, my own nostrils would be gradually undergoing a change of heart – by the second day, I could bring myself to take it out. I would, however, leave the cattails in until I could overhear somebody in the hall, saying, a little crossly, "What *can* Elizabeth have done with the umbrellas?"

A few years later, some experiences would almost be *too* woodsy. In the warm, humid, summer afternoons, I would go with a group of other young girls and an equal number of boys to swim in Swift Creek. The girls were always much more interested in watching out for a snake that might be dangling from an overhanging bough than in the fact that during the Revolution, as he led his men toward Virginia, it was at that point in the creek that Cornwallis had crossed, a historical point which seemed to interest the boys.

I, for one, have a phobia about crawly things. Truthfully, I would rather be in a room with a hungry lion than to have to pick up a worm or to have what we used to call a "measuring worm" crawl on my arm. If somebody should say, "You're going to have a new dress. A measuring worm is on your back," I would jump and plead, "Get it off! Get it off!"

Yet, I have always had a kind of daring side to my nature. At Grandma's, in order to get to and from the pond, Lizzie and Helen, my companionable older protectors, and I had to walk a long way down a cart path through the fields. On one side the fields gave way to a pasture that was the domain of the bull. The cartpath went around. We had been cautioned never to wear red when we went fishing even though the bull was always penned. Just the same, if the bull were at the other end of the pasture, I could never miss the opportunity to annoy him by climbing the fence and taking the shortcut, knowing as I did, that he was going to see me and come charging at a gallop to do me in. Lizzie and Helen always did their best to keep me from doing this, but I was not going to give up this best part of the fishing excursion. Scrambling over the fence was wonderful. They secretly understood, and never did tell on me.

In another situation, however, they did. I had always loved to climb up on things and leap off. Grandma had the perfect set-up. The stable was large and tall. You could go up the ladder to the loft, climb out on the roof to its edge, and then shut your eyes and jump to the ground. Round and round and round, this was a thrilling experience. But again, Lizzie and Helen tried to dissuade me, and again, I wouldn't listen. Then one day, as I landed from my leap, Helen was not there. She could be seen hurrying through the gate, bringing that classic vital disclosure from Grandma, "Miss Betty say, 'Stop jumping off'n de bahn. You'll make your feets big.'" Could anything have been more southern? After all, Grandma herself had small feet, for the little white satin bag that had held her dancing slippers still hung on one of the posts of a bed that sat unused in the plunder room. The slippers were so small as to be hardly believable.

To her way of thinking, a lady must take care of her hands, as well. They must never be exposed to strong soap. Several times a day, a homemade lotion of rose water and glycerin was applied. A lady's hair was always washed in rainwater, and a large barrel, like a wine barrel, for this purpose sat on the back porch. This custom carried over into my mother's life. We, too, always had a rain barrel on our back porch.

I could go along with the rainwater, but having your hair shampoo'd with the eggy-smelling raw egg was not an aesthetic experience, however well it cleansed the hair. The hair was rinsed until it squeaked, wrapped in a towel, and then rescued from the scent of egg with bay rum, that pleasantly scented liquid that was used by men as well as women, sprinkled freely about the head. For sweet scent, a lady kept lavender in the drawers of her dresser, and when she dressed she used toilet water, usually Hudnut's Violet Toilet Water, a lovely amethyst-colored liquid. I loved the way I was sometimes allowed to shake the bottle upside down in order to apply the little droplets to the underside of my forearms and my wrists. Ladies always used this in the afternoon when they rose from their naps and put on their cool lawn dresses.

Grandma's reticule, a small, dark-brown round satchel that opened from the top, with its round handle, seemed to suggest the roundness of Grandma herself. The reticule always had smelling salts in it. In her medicine chest and in Mother's as well, there was always a bottle of camphor to sniff for headaches; there was iodine for cuts and something for scratches called "healing oil." There was castor oil, an obnoxious dose given when you had a cold. The other treatment for colds in children was to rub tallow on the bottoms of their feet at bedtime. Sitting on somebody's lap, you would hold your feet as close to the fire as you could bear, then you were lifted by this grown person into your bed. At Grandma's it would have been a feather bed.

When I had a cold and happened to be at Grandma's, this tender treatment would change abruptly in the morning. Snuggled in a feather bed, hearing the first farm bell and the dogs barking only made snuggling the more sweet, for the bell rang very early; it was a signal for the hands to go to the field. Fleetingly, the difference between their lot and mine would cross my mind. At six-thirty, Aunt Mary, who, except for Uncle Hugh's which was taken care of by Green, came in to light the fires. At seven, she left the kitchen routine to Aunt Caroline to go through the house ringing the rising bell. There were two double beds in Grandma's room. I slept in one, she in the other. With the first clang of that bell, Grandma's little feet would hit the floor. Mine were expected to do the same. No matter that I was born on her birthday and became her namesake. I came in for no preferential treatment.

At times, the house would be filled with other grandchildren. In summer, we might even be sleeping on the upstairs porch on pallets, but nobody could lie in bed a half second after the rising bell. In Grandma's part of the world, sometimes for a month at a time, a cousin would come with her children and her driver, the latter, called a "horse-feeder." Grandma, with her understanding of children, and with her jolly personality, never felt that one child more would be too many. However, children were not born to be indulged. Though generous with her hospitality, she had been a young woman at the time of the Civil War. She had known hardship, and she felt that younger generations should be brought up to face reality.

On the other hand, Grandma believed that women should be protected from life's harshness. And since, in order for food to appear on the table three times a day, this growing and gathering and preparing ever-present, this facet of life was to be delegated to others. In her case, the kitchen was the domain of Aunt Caroline and Aunt Mary. These things make

Grandma's warning to her daughters and their daughters about not learning to cook more understandable.

≈ ≈ ≈

In the two questions that Mother asked Tom when he came for his serious conversation, lay overtones of Grandma's contrasting philosophies. I've given a lot of thought to the southern gentlewoman's having stayed aloof from or having been so frightened of the kitchen. It was not that she was lazy, not that she was idle, not that she shirked responsibility. It was, simply, that from lack of practice, there was a lack of self-confidence.

Not having "somebody in the kitchen" was a daily fear. It did not matter how inept the person was. If there were somebody in there, life for the lady of the house could go on; otherwise, it could not. Indeed, in my own childhood, I remember hearing one of Mother's friends saying jokingly, "Your mental, moral, and spiritual welfare depends on your cook." For even as late as when I was married, ours was still a wooden range. Just keeping the fire going was an undertaking.

This was the prevailing attitude, even in 1930, when my own time came to assume housekeeping responsibilities; although we had a gas stove, I started out with a cook. The cook, however, didn't come on weekends. Back home from our wedding trip to New York, and settled in our small apartment, on a certain Saturday morning there came a crisis. With high heart, I was in the kitchen early, but coming to grips with a gas stove was something new to me. Although electric toasters had come by that time, somehow, Tom and I had not been given one as a wedding present. Anyway, I was used to seeing toast made in the oven when we had it, which was seldom, because we still had hot biscuits, hot cornbread, pancakes and waffles, and now and then, beaten biscuits. Toast was if you couldn't do any better. So that on that morning, simultaneously, I had toast browning in the oven at a gallop while bacon fried, eggs scrambled, and coffee perked. The ringmaster of a circus was never busier. Naturally, my performance was flawed.

Although with time I did learn to cook, I can't say that it was to become my most pleasurable pastime. I've been able to get by, however, even now and then to the point of impressing people, to their surprise. I still think that more dexterity, more real coordination is required in getting a hot meal prepared, all of it coming out right at a given minute, than anything I can think of, except, perhaps, the countdown on a launching pad.

That Saturday morning in our apartment, the toast burned, the apartment filled with smoke, and the smell of burnt toast permeated the air. I hurriedly threw all of the first blackened batch out the back door, for ours was a first floor apartment, then started with the second pan.

Poor Tom, shaving, sensing what was going on, and trying to decide what, if anything, would be the diplomatic thing to do, the smoke worsening, soon knew that he had to take action. With lather on his face, he appeared in the kitchen, trying to say, in a soothing voice, "Let me handle the stove for you."

By that time I was pitching the second pan of toast out and he was turning down all the flames. The only thing I have to say for myself in that situation is that I did not turn into a weeping bride. I just said, "Dern. I belong in the *country*." Tom laughed, as he would down the years when I would rarely come out with something to let off steam. He thought that, in my case, it seemed incongruous. We flung the windows and doors open to get rid of the smoke, and together, managed to get the third pan of toast in the oven, and by that time, I was laughing, too.

The furnishings in our tiny apartment can best be described as "early attic," or "porch." Our budget was so close for a while, that one day when Tom came in and said that he had ordered the Encyclopedia Britannica, including its two-shelf cabinet, "on time" for five dollars a month, without letting it show, I thought he'd lost his mind.

There were many of these adjustments, which, in one form or another, all young marriages face. However, we survived those lean years, for everybody was in the same boat. Occasionally, on Saturday nights, we would get together with our friends. There were twelve couples, and throughout life the twelve of us have commented on the fact that there was not to be a divorce in the whole group. We have wondered if having started out in the years of the depression, when our marital ties were being firmly cemented through interdependence and joint self-denial, might have had something to do with it. Was it something to do with having been tested right away and not found wanting that gave us confidence in each other?

≈ ≈ ≈

Our wedding trip to New York had included an overnight stay in Richmond at The Jefferson. As children, Tom and I had each been there, over and over, as we went to the Richmond specialists, and had had the pleasant excitement of seeing the live alligator in a pool in the lobby of that grand old hotel. For sentimental reasons, we wanted to return. Tom loved the city of Washington as well, and from having gone to school there, so did I. Since The Willard there was famous for its Peacock Ally, that was another choice.

For the New York stay we had chosen The Astor. Nothing but Broadway and Times Square would be equal to our happiness. We long chuckled over the events of our first day in that metropolis, each of us deferring to what the other one would like to do. I insisted that Tom make the choice. To my surprise, he came out with what seemed the strangest notion in the world: "Well, I've always wanted to see Grant's Tomb." So we boarded a double-decker bus, climbed to the top, and there, in three-inch heels, the rest of my getup worthy of Buckingham Palace, we rode the long way uptown for Tom to see that Grant was safely buried. Tom was a great reader of Civil War stories, the battles, in particular. His maternal Grandmother, Rachel Middleton Pearsall, had written a little book called *Women of the Confederacy*. On that subject, Penelope Jenkins Harris of Kinston, a first cousin of Tom's on the maternal side of his family, now has a copy of a cookbook which their grandmother was using in 1871. Deprivations of the Civil War were still there. Plantation mistresses had come to a different way of life, one that required ingenuity.

Help for these struggling women was furnished in this small book, entitled *The Young Housewife's Counselor and Friend, (The Duties of Wife and Mother)* by a certain Mrs. Mary Mason. To be sure that they understood, Mrs. Mason had added on the outside of her book, *Prov. xxx.i.27.: She looketh well to the ways of her household, and eateth not the bread of idleness.* Her publisher had been Lippincott of Philadelphia. There were "receipts" – the term in use at that time for "recipe" – for making black dye, for cedar dye, for scarlet, and for something called brazilwood dye. There were variations for dying cotton black and for dying wool brown. These required the use of alum, lye, vinegar, the leaves from the chinquapin, the alder, the sourwood, the sumach, and for some reason, parsley!

In suggesting copperas for brown wool, Mrs. Mason recommended at the very last, as the housekeeper stood stirring the pot: *Add article to be dyed. Boil an hour or so; ring out and dip in strong, cold lye. When dry, rinse in cold water. This gives a genuine, bright brown, which is the prettiest contrast for blue; and when checked in together, makes a dress becoming enough for the proudest Southern Dame or Belle. Ladies, try it.* We can see, as some sage has said, "Situations change, emotions do not."

With the trip to Grant's tomb, I learned quickly how Tom liked to "do a city." His philosophy was that you could never get to know one unless you walked about in its streets. In my travels, I had gained the same knowledge and had formed the habit of always being prepared. To that end, I had bought a shoe-bag. These so-called "shoe-totes" came out in Europe before they reached America. Mine was, and still is, one of dark-brown snakeskin with a shoulder strap. With a lady-like pair of shoes inside, I could start out in my flat-heeled walking shoes, knowing that I would have that blissful feeling of being, at one and the same time, mobile and comfortable; a rule of thumb that would enable me, on short notice, and in a hotel lady's room to become a lady, ready for whatever was required. If I had one recommendation to make to younger women, it would be doing this. It will keep the man in your life happy and will free you from trips to the podiatrist. More than that, you will have been given experiences to draw on throughout life, which in no other way could have been yours.

The Boy Scott motto, "Be Prepared," is worth remembering. For there will be times in every woman's life when she will be required to fill a multiplicity of roles, and in a short span of time, to be by turns, a lady and a foot-soldier. This should be learned early in marriage. And woefully, since the situation in each woman's life is peculiarly her own, it usually has to be worked out in her own way. In a thousand ways, a woman's life has been and always will be fragmented. However difficult, as she goes through this fragmentation, she will keep her patience, and her courage, and her self-respect, knowing that things will not always have to be this difficult. At times, she will hardly know who or where she is. But she will be undergirded by the knowledge that she has committed her life to the one whom from all the world she has chosen to spend it with, even if the choice requires times of submerging of her own aspirations, those things which lie deep within her.

No matter how much has been said or written to the contrary, I will always believe that there is not a man in the world who does not, even if only secretly, want the woman he loves to occupy a pedestal. We may not consider ourselves worthy, but we recognize the value of the illusion. At times, our pedestals may be rocky, but, with the application of Virginia Woolf's theory that "the person one lives with should keep one at one's best," our pedestals will usually right themselves. Emblazoned in a woman's sky must eternally be the word "flexibility." But, as Mary McCarthy said, I digress within digression.

My snakeskin shoe-tote was a far cry from my Grandmother Bryan's satin slipper bag which held her satin dancing shoes. At the time, she and her sister, Great Aunt Nancy, were often being driven in their Rockaway from their plantation home on the Roanoke, "Rainbow Banks," to Tarboro, the county seat of Edgecombe, or to Williamston, in Martin, twelve miles away, for dances. In each town they had relatives whom they visited.

This Rockaway of Grandma and Grandpa Sherrod's was a two-seated vehicle pulled by two horses, with a seat in front for the driver. It was a mode of travel that carried over briefly into my early life when I was at Grandma's. Even after her Rockaway was no longer used, it sat at one end of the stables gathering dust. Among the old letters that I have is one from Grandma's brother, my Great Uncle William Sherrod, a planter and banker, who, every spring, as planters did, went to Baltimore to buy horses and mules. Uncle William writes to Grandma, "Today I've bought the two matched bays you wanted for your Rockaway." That custom of buying carloads of horses and mules went on during my lifetime until automation had arrived. The shipment would come in by rail, and the whole village would go down to see the unloading. That my father sometimes had as many as two boxcars of these animals made it doubly exciting.

With the opening of the boxcar door, the men from the farms going inside to put halters on the animals, the frightened horses and mules would go wild with kicking and shrieking as they were led down the ramp. Even at a distance, this part of farming was frightening to a child, but was recognized as an important preliminary to spring planting. Tobacco plants would have been started in beds in winter, and covered with cheesecloth for protection against cold freezes. Then, in April, the plants would go into the tobacco fields, one by one, into a hole made with a stick and filled with a dipper of water from a bucket. Often children would be kept out of school to do this. Therefore, year in and year out, in this agricultural area, life went on within the framework of the seasons. Two months after planting, the fields would be greening, for it is in that combination of the increasing heat and humidity of spring and summer that Eastern Carolina becomes a veritable Garden of Eden.

But to return to our wedding trip. Tom's earlier trips to New York had usually been made with a bunch of Dekes, members of his Delta Kappa Epsilon fraternity. While not all the fraternity members came from wealthy families, there were some of that kind from the Piedmont section of the state. Tom, however, as soon as he entered college, began to work during the summer and at the Christmas holiday. This provided him with spending money, which, to most of his fraternity brothers, came easily. His trips to New York would usually have been combined with house parties at the homes of Sarah Lawrence and Bryn Mawr girls.

My own earlier New York stays had been with my family for shopping and for seeing plays, but on this, our wedding trip, there would be no shopping. In the first place, I had my trousseau. I would not need any new clothes for a long time. I was saying goodbye to my charge accounts. In those days, before charge cards, you would give your name and address to the salesgirls over the counter at the time of purchase, and I never knew one of them not to almost faint with delight and romance as I said "The Planter's Bank, Rocky Mount, North Carolina." Swept away, their pencils would come to a stop in mid-air, with, as you could tell, visions of moonlight and magnolias, of crinoline, and flunkies fanning dining room tables with long-tailed peacock feathers. I would have hated to deprive them of their illusions by confessing that we, too, ate, worked, went to bed, and slept just like other people. So deeply imbedded in their minds was this romantic attitude that it would take a long time for it to be dispelled. It was a notion intensified, of course, a hundred-fold, a few years later, with the publication of *Gone with the Wind*.

In that Tom was four years older than I, although we had grown up eight miles apart, we had not actually met until after our college days. While he was enjoying his youthful fling at Chapel Hill, and all the things that stemmed from that, I was enjoying mine in Washington and Richmond. In Washington, I had developed friendships in the diplomatic circles; within those circles there was a great deal of socializing. On Mother's side, I had relatives in Richmond. Their homes were always open to us when some member of the family had to stay in the hospital, and at other times, as well.

It was one of those delightful times in a young girl's life when there are more young men than young women, many of these students at the Medical College of Virginia, or those ready to do their internships in other areas. Proposals came, right and left.

This favored life, combined with travel, filled my years from nineteen until twenty-one; the years when it was of major significance who wore whose fraternity pin. Later, when Tom and I had become engaged, since there was no money for an engagement ring, Tom's fraternity pin sufficed. In its black-and-gold simplicity, it was not too overdone nor too underdone to be worn at all times; and during those seven months when we were separated, as I went around the world, sometimes as far away as ten thousand miles, I always wore this symbol of our commitment. It served the double purpose of letting it be known to the many attractive men I was meeting, one after another, that I was, in that old phrase which I like, "bespoken." My heart had found what it needed. I knew that Tom had put up his little car and was walking to work, using it only to drive to the county seats or to Raleigh or to Chapel Hill, and this, to save for our future. He knew that I always wore his pin.

Without any promises, we wrote everyday. The only promise we had made was to cable each other once a month. With cabled words five dollars each, we had worked out a code which meant three things: I love you, I miss you, I long for our future. On those long stretches at sea, my letters were long, and I never failed to write. Mailbags containing the letters for the four-hundred-and-fifty passengers and the three-hundred-and-fifty member crew would be brought out early by the pilot boat, lifted up by a hook, quickly sorted and put into our mailboxes, enabling us to read our letters before reaching the mainland. If the port happened to be too shallow for our liner, we reached the mainland by launch, and often, in a high gale, in the back of some small boat chopping its way across a rough sea, I would be trying to keep the pages from Tom's letters from blowing overboard as I read them.

Sometimes the letters brought my tears, especially the one that told me that our dog, Mike, had died. Mike was being kept by my married sister and her husband in their apartment in Rocky Mount. He was old and stiff, and could hardly see, but we loved him, of course, and Tom would often go to see him while I was away. But my tears were brief. For there was much to be happy about. Alice Bryan was staying relatively well, was able to take

72

part in most of what we were seeing and doing on the cruise. In a short while, we would be in one more port on what was, to us, "the other side of the world," ten thousand miles from home. Those moments were always thrilling, something like the ones before a curtain rises in play. I knew that, figuratively, Tom was following us on our long journey, almost mile by mile, and that, as the days passed, he was marking them off, one by one. And I wondered that I could be so blessed.

It was not to be expected, however, nor had it been true of the trip up to that point, that all we were to see would be joyous. There would be the heart-wrenching experience in India, of being in attendance at one of what was called the "Burning Ghats," the scene of a Hindu cremation. It now seems callous of our guide to have taken us to intrude on the grief of the family, unfeeling of us to have gone. I recall none of the ins and outs, except that, suddenly, we, a small party of about eight, were standing inside a high, white stucco enclosure of perhaps forty feet by thirty, one open to the sky, in which a father was placing the cloth-wrapped body of a five-year-old son on the funeral pyre. In memory, the pyre was shoulder high, its wood neatly arranged, its shape, oblong. The members of the family watched, dry-eyed and silent as the father lighted the fire. The tears were ours, and we soon quietly left. We knew that, on the other side of those high, white walls, lay, bleached by the sun, the bones of countless human beings of that faith who had gone before, and that, by tomorrow, those of the small child who had been granted so little time on earth would have joined them.

But now we are back at Grant's tomb. Having been assured that the great general was satisfactorily entombed, Tom could then turn his attention to the Metropolitan Museum. During the next five days we would visit the Museum of Natural History, the Aquarium, the Library, and see as many plays as we could. We had both been in New York seven months earlier when I had returned from my long sea trip. Tom had seen me off from New York as I left, and would be standing on the dock when our ocean-liner, returning, came slowly into her slip. I knew that he would be there; I did not know that he had come up a round-about way. He had gone by train to Norfolk and by boat from there to New York in order to save money. At all costs, he would have been there, however, for he was a gentleman, through and through.

≈ ≈ ≈

What was I bringing to this marriage? In retrospect, the one thing that stands out in my mind is that, although born to advantages – and up to this point there had been no testing of my mettle – from these very advantages I had been given a reasonably positive outlook, one that would rarely desert me. How could a little girl, by a wide margin, the youngest of four daughters in a loving family, and in that favored spot, somehow treasured, not have begun to develop a happy approach to life; one who, down the years, could close her eyes and go back to those times, when, under some minor illness, she might lie all day on the daybed in her mother's sitting room, and to the sounds of the ticking of the clock and a singing fire, have fairy tales read to her? Even Gyp, our short-haired black terrier with the large white spot on his chest, but graying around his mouth, might have been lured away from the fire to join me and to snuggle under the warm Scottish throw with which I was covered. But it was only when I was sick that I thus was cosseted. For that too, I am grateful.

≈ ≈ ≈

Born on my Grandmother Bryan's birthday – and this was the only grandparent I was to know – and becoming her namesake, no doubt it was natural that among her grandchildren, I should hold a certain place in her heart. Certainly, she held one in mine. This was increased by the fact that Mother was the one of her children who lived nearest to Grandma in the country, giving me two homes; a perfect situation in which to grow up. Yet Grandma, like Mother and Father, was not one for over-indulgence. Her affection was expressed, in part, by discipline.

There were, for me, other than Grandma's, many sources of affection. Always addressed by Mother in letters and on postcards as "Precious," this wealth of affection, did, however, have its dark side, for it meant that I grew up under a lot of bosses. Everybody around me, including the domestics, seemed to have a vested interest in bending the twig. Although this might, at times, have been bothersome, it just might have saved me from the sad fate of becoming one of those spoiled little creatures whose chances of true happiness begin early to erode.

One thing I knew. If I wanted to do a certain thing, I'd better not talk too much about it; it would inevitably be subject to a variety of opinions. It probably – whether for good or ill – built up in me a trait that I now recognize: if I want to do something, I think it through carefully before subjecting the idea to what might turn out to be conflicting opinions. Having done that, unless I have run into serious opposition, more than likely, I will stand my ground. This, however, is not to discount those checks and balances which are a necessary part of life, which, I was to find, that as much as any other single thing, go to make *marriage* the wonderful institution it is.

≈ ≈ ≈

The poet Shelley once wrote an especially beautiful paragraph on childhood:

> *Know you what it is to be a child, he asked? It is to have a spirit still streaming from the water of Baptism, it is to believe in love, to believe in loveliness, to believe in belief. It is to be so little that the elves can reach to whisper in your ear. It is to turn pumpkins into coaches, and mice into horses, lowness into loftiness, and nothing into everything. For each child has its Fairy Godmother in its soul.*

From an old, yellowed clipping I
found in one of Mother's books.
It was taken from the
Dublin Review of July 1908.

At the time when Shelley's thoughts on childhood were originally published – I assume –in an Irish newspaper, I was a child of two. Mother's clipping – and I suppose she had come across it as it was quoted in some American newspaper – might have fortold the happiness that would be there for me at birth, for born into the security of family affection, to means and position, from earliest life, I must have felt the presence of a fairy godmother. These blessings which neither my sisters nor I had done anything to deserve, would, nevertheless, slowly provide us certain positive attitudes which would stay with us forever. There was the added blessing of having parents who, in bringing up their young, kept to the middle of the road. Neither too lenient nor too strict, they counted on examples of love, given and received, of trust in fellow human beings, and on examples of not being "censorious" – a word rarely used now, but one of Father's and Mother's favorites – synonym for the more commonly used word, "judgmental" – to guide us. The phrase, "Don't bear malice" was often heard. We were given the gift of laughter, as well, and since we had more of the world's goods than the average, there was the example of sharing.

Now that I am the only surviving member of our family, my thoughts much in the past, looking back, I can see that in no better way could our parents have prepared my sisters and me for life, life as we would come to know it.

≈ ≈ ≈

Since there is no order in memory, it may be that, in autobiographical writing, one memory will serve as well as another for taking us back through the maze to our earliest. For me, earliest memory begins with sounds; the sound of certain voices, the timbre and the rhythms of their speech. With the voices go certain scenes. Seeing the figures is as though I were looking through the wrong end of a telescope; I can see them, but dimly. At first, they move about in silence. Then, slowly, through their voices, each voice as distinct as though it were yesterday, the figures begin to come to life.

The voices that come to me as the earliest in my life are naturally those of my family, and in memory, in that first little scene, I often hear first one voice, and then another, but sometimes there are several in unison. The picture that comes most often is the one in our house, in which the gong that called us to meals has just rung. Why we called it a "gong" I don't know. It was more like a small xylophone. It hung on the wall in the back hall, where, under Julette's strong, dark, capable hands, the small padded hammer played a cheerful little do-re-me-fa-so-la-te-do! For although Julette had never had a music lesson, she could not have escaped hearing my sisters practice their scales on the piano in the parlor, especially in summer, when not only the parlor doors into the hall were open, but the doors and windows all over the house.

Julette's name had early evolved from the classical "Juliet" to the simpler country version. Doctor Marriott, our family doctor and Father's best friend, when called on at times of delivery to name new babies, would often resort to the classical. Among the farmhands and the domestics there would, now and then, be "Octavius," which would immediately become "Tave," "Theophalous" would become "Awfy," "Drusilla," "Dru," and "Beatrice," which would become "Bee-AT-trice," the emphasis on the "AT." Mother drew the line at making the lovely name Beatrice, the name of a later cook, into that form, and would not allow us to. It is, indeed, a beautiful name.

At the sound of the gong, wherever I was – in the dollhouse under the pear trees, or lying on the low limb of the locust tree that grew near the stables, or "skinning the cat" a hundred times in the swing that hung from the cottonwood tree – I would start running toward the dining room, and usually the last to arrive, everybody else in place, would flop into my own chair in song, to be told instantly by one, two, or three others, "Don't sing at the table!"

Even Julette, coming in with hot biscuits would say, "Hush your singin', chile', wheah' yo' mannas? Your pappy can't eeb'n ask de blessin'."

≈ ≈ ≈

It was probably inevitable that I should be a singing child. In a country way of life, in a large house, and one built in the southern way, with emphasis on summer breezes, there were high ceilings, none under fourteen feet, and many windows and doors. Singing going on in one part or another of the house during the day was pleasant, and with so much space, it didn't bother anybody.

The help sang at their work, and in addition to my sisters' singing, and those gatherings around the piano when their suitors came, Mother would often go into the parlor at night, and as she played, undergirding the trills of our sopranos with the balance of her own firm alto, we would all happily harmonize. Mother was only five-feet-four and slender, and the strength of her singing voice always surprised me.

On those nights, Father might be sitting on the front porch at the parlor end, and while he himself didn't sing except at church or at home occasionally in something like a barbershop quartet, he seemed to enjoy our little concerts. Sometimes, when he sat there in the darkness, I would go outside and sit with him, finding him by the glow of his cigar and from the half-light of the parlor. Aware that I was coming, he would say in his gentle way, "Come on out, Babe."

Sitting in the large, old rockers, although we might not talk much, these times were lovely and companionable. If it were a Sunday night, we could easily hear coming across the fields from the tent revival, the hymns and shouting of a congregation caught in a frenzy of religious fervor. At a distance, it was beautiful, part of a familiar night scene in summer. Father would often share his thoughts, "The hands have worked so hard in the heat that they've earned this hour of freedom." And I knew that they were rejoicing in the thought of a better world to come, a world in which they firmly believed.

It was the words to the songs that troubled me. I knew those to many of them, and they were hauntingly beautiful and poignant, for they conveyed a sad resignation to their lot. They were the songs that the domestics sang around me, and although I knew that the words brought them comfort, that their hope lay in a future world gave me a feeling of sadness. As I grew older, that feeling was to prevail.

I looked over Jordan and what did I see,
coming for to carry me home?
A band of angels coming after me,
coming for to carry me home.

Swing low, sweet chariot,
coming for to carry me home.

If you get there before I do,
coming for to carry me home,
Tell all my friends I'm coming too,
coming for to carry me home.

Swing low, sweet chariot
coming for to carry me home.

I recently came across information on spirituals in a publication of *Literary Sketches*, a unique newsletter published in Dallas, Texas, to which I subscribe for the small sum of seven dollars a year. This informal four-page treatment of things and persons of interest to book lovers is a literary bargain and a delight. In the article, "The Spirit of the Spiritual," the Editor, Olivia Murray Nichols, explains the origin of the Negro Spiritual and tells of its current standing in American literature:

Early in the nineteenth century, Ralph Waldo Emerson pressed for an indigenous American literature free from European form and idiom. He felt rewarded when "Leaves of Grass" appeared. Innovative as Whitman's poetry was, however, it was not the first identifiable literary art form born in the USA. Negro Spirituals were older and as uniquely "American," but because they evolved from folk tradition without benefit of publication, recognition of them as Literature was slow in developing.

Traditional songs and stories, as well as customs, remain closer to an "original" within strong family communities. One of the tragedies of slavery was that too often families were separated. What endured of a "collective consciousness," to use Jung's term, underwent alterations within the historical boundaries of American slavery. Traditions retained form an African past adapted to American influences and associations, both northern and southern. As a result, slaves developed rich ethnic distinctions no other peoples in the world can claim. One manifestation of this unique culture was the Spiritual, which emerged from the one element of "white culture" available to almost everyone - the Bible.

In "All God's Chillun," J. Garfield Owens says:

[Spirituals] expressed...a way of life, a philosophy of life. They represent the unconscious efforts of the Negro slaves to make sense of their shattering life situations. They represent the rare genius with which slaves distilled the best from their own tradition and way of life and blended it with their newly found Hebrew-Christian tradition. In their songs the slaves tell in words, nuances, and music of their struggles, weariness, loneliness, sorrow, determination, and assurance.

Our own songs on those nights around the piano were of a different kind. After a while I would go back into the parlor and join in those Irish songs Mother loved so much: "Mother MacCree," "The Rosary," and "When Irish Eyes Are Smiling."

Our repertoire was practically unlimited; our music cabinet, filled to the brim. To prolong the pleasure of the concert, sometimes Mother would stand up and raise the top of the piano bench and we would make additional selections. We might have chosen one of the popular wedding songs of the time: "Love Divine," "I Love You Truly," "Until," or, my favorite, the one that I knew that when the time came, I would want sung at my own wedding, "Because."

Because you come to me with naught
save love, And hold my hand and lift

mine eyes above, A wider world of hope
and joy I see, Because you come to me.

Because you speak to me in accents sweet,
I find the roses waking round my feet, And
I am led through tears and joy to thee,
Because you speak to me.

Because God made thee mine, I'll cherish
thee, through light and darkness, through all
time to be, And pray this love may make
our love divine. Because God made thee mine.

In winter, the doors between rooms were always closed. This made it possible for the domestics to continue their singing with freedom. And the reason that the inside doors were closed in winter was that Father thought steam heat was not healthful. He said that whenever he went to his meetings in town, the bank board meetings, stockholders' meetings, or whenever he sat in his lawyer's office – any of those things that went on in town – it stopped up his nose. So that our life in winter went on with open fires in practically every room, while our halls were frigid.

It was a family custom after meals for women to back up to the fireplace to get warm. Their skirts were woolen, and many times, this combination of wool and a bright fire resulted in the tragedy of a skirt shrunken to two or three inches shorter in the back. My sisters had several of their best dresses ruined in this way. But now to go back even further in time.

≈ ≈ ≈

It was in 1907, that in the village of Battleboro, where I was born, grew up, and married, on a summer afternoon, a small assortment of vehicles was turning into our driveway. It was the occasion of my first birthday, and Mother, always imaginative and playful, was entertaining in her own way. For in addition to the arrival of carriages, surreys, and one or two buggies, there might have been a sulky, as well, for Cousin Benjamin Mayo, from below Tarboro, liked horses. He had some that raced, and some for home use.

Father had a sulky as well, but it usually sat in the stable gathering dust.

For as Father grew older, his interest went more to baseball. He never missed going to the World Series, always taking a few male friends along, and although he still loved a pretty horse for driving over the farms, he usually went in the buggy with Henry, his driver, at the reins, freeing him for talking with his overseers and tenants.

Cars had not as yet come to our part of the world, but they were on their way, and when I was three, our family owned that marvel of transportation and the open breeze, an Overland. This new mode of getting around, of course, required the proper equipment: goggles, caps, and dustcoats for the men, and for the ladies, dustcoats, goggles, and large straw hats with gauze-like veils that tied under the chin.

With no telephones as yet, and living within driving distance of relatives on both sides of the family, invitations to the birthday party had gone by mail to our nearest of kin: those of the village, those of the countryside, and those of the larger town, Rocky Mount, eight miles away, where two of Father's brothers, Uncle Mark and Uncle Jim, and their families lived, and where most of our social life went on.

Mother was a sentimental "saver," and when I had become a Grandmother, I found one of these invitations among her keepsakes. The invitations themselves were tiny, each enclosed in a larger envelope. The small card in Mother's beautiful Spencerian read:

> *Emily Elizabeth Braswell*
> *at home*
> *June 4*
> *at 4:00 in the afternoon*

For the party, refreshments would have been served on one of our porches. No doubt there was that day strawberry ice-cream, hand-churned, and Mother's Lady Baltimore cake. In Eastern Carolina it would have been too early for peaches, our favorite flavor for ice cream, but the long rows of strawberries in the garden stretched endlessly between those of the flowers: the roses, the Pinks, the Ragged Robin, the Cosmos, the Black-Eyed Susans, and the Larkspur. There were the sunflowers as well, to say nothing of the long rows of sweet peas, which, when I was a child of perhaps nine or ten, it was my responsibility to cut every morning or they would stop blooming and we would have none for the bowls which were kept filled with them on the porches, and which, in the absence of roses, would fill a glass and silver bowl which, in summer, always sat on the dining room table.

In the garden, with the coming of May, between all those flowers, the long, flat rows of strawberries would have ripened to red, and for weeks we would have them with sugar and cream, or for shortcake, and, especially, for the ever delightful strawberry ice cream. And there were plenty of domestics to turn the freezer, to take out the dasher, to pour off the salt water, and then to pack everything down tight until mealtime, or to whatever the hour of its grand opening. No ambling to the refrigerator as we do today, to open a carton of something frozen goodness knows where, flavored with fruit possibly grown out of season, hastened to maturity by chemicals, and ripened under glass and artificial light. But then, I'm as glad as the next one for the easy life. It just seems in order – once in a while – to remember.

Our Jersey cow gave the world's richest milk, the cream unbelievably thick, and since we always had quantities of this left over from making butter, with this small birthday gathering of Mother's to open the season, the regularity of making ice cream would have begun. Yet, strangely, nobody was fat.

Had I been a winter child, Mother would have gathered us around the table in the dining room. From her own end in front of the fireplace, with Father at the other end against the green of Mother's ferns, which, brought inside in October, filled the three octagonal windows, she would have given her attention to the large, tall glass comport which had been one of her favorite wedding presents. For this kind of occasion, it would have been filled with the golden-colored wine jelly, a dessert made with gelatin, Madeira or sherry, and lemon juice, and nobody had ever been known to refuse it. At a smaller table under the window to the south, the children would have had their own bowl of bright red fruit-gelatin.

The fourth in a family of daughters – there were to be no sons – we might wonder now, at so much celebration on the first birthday of yet another little daughter. Surely Mother and Father must have wished for a son. But, things being equal, babies are usually greeted with love, and since my three sisters were older by eight, ten, and twelve years, a plump, cuddly toddler of a year might be cause for a renewal of rejoicing.

By that time, I was no doubt struggling to form words and to catch on to what those about me happened to be called; those who were inclined to coo over my crib, to rock me to sleep, to bounce me on knees and to scrape a raw apple with a spoon as they fed me, spoonful by spoonful, from that delectable fruit. There were "Mother," and "Father," the oldest daughter, Mattie May, called "Sister," the next, Vivian, called "Sister Biddie," and Alice Bryan, named for Mother, but who, since she had been the youngest in the family for so long, was called "Baby Sister." What, I might have wondered, other than "Precious," which was Mother's form of address to me, and "Darling," from my sisters, and "Babe," from Father, who called each of us that all our lives, would my own designation be? The answer was not long in coming.

It was always going to be, I could tell, something with the word "Baby" in it. For as I grew, I was introduced by my sisters as just, *"Mama's Baby."* And Mother, as though I were an afterthought, would say, "and *this* is my *Baby.*" Even the domestics, at those times when I was in the kitchen where I would always love to be, listening to the rhythm of their speech and the recounting of what went on in their lives – in which they made even the dull into high drama – and when they were not doing that, were almost instinctively singing, would say, to whatever friend of theirs happened to be visiting, "Let me make you known to Miss Aal-ice's *Baby.*" For what it's worth, this was my ongoing distinction.

≈ ≈ ≈

In looking back to my early years over the struggle for assertion of the self, I can think of three ways in which, in a world of giants, of whom all I saw was their knees, the struggle was beginning to show. Even until I was five or six, I would have to be held for the dose of caster oil that was given for colds. I suppose the pouting habit was a second way of striking back. The third was what would have been termed a "fracas" with a chum over a new cap, resulting in my bitten thumb. To recall these things makes me very sympathetic with children.

Although I wasn't altogether a pouting child, the memory of a certain form of treatment for this childish trait as it was administered in my family, comes to me so clearly that I have a vague feeling that I used this form of resistance more than was entirely fitting.

I can recall situations when my sisters and I were all in the same room, where they were happily engaged in their own pursuits, embroidering, painting, reading, or writing letters, and I, having been denied some privilege that seemed important to me, as they would say, puffed up like a toad. Their remedy for this was that one of them would chant in a sing-song voice, from the eminence of her young lady-hood, without looking up from her work, "Smarty had a party, and nobody came." For some reason, the treatment was effective, and I would soon decide to rejoin the human race.

But my childhood progressed in the normal way, with dolls, and tea sets, and playmates: my two best-loved little chums, Velma and Margaret. At the time, little girls wore an undergarment of two parts. Both parts were made of white cotton; both were trimmed with narrow white lace. The bodice fit snugly, and at its waist it had a row of buttons. The other part of the garment consisted of short little panties made with buttonholes and edged with matching lace trimming.

In the afternoon of southern summer, a "grown lady" always took her rest. For this she would put on her long white nightgown. A small girl would be required to rest, too. But she had only to slip off her dress and take a nap in the undergarments described above, and spoken of as her "draws 'n body." A frequent half-pouting remark of hers might be, as though it were the beginning of a death sentence, which indeed it would be for an active child deprived of an hour of play, "and now I have to go and get in my draws 'n body."

After the nap, a girl-child would have a bath and with her mother's help or that of her nurse, would be dressed in a long-waisted short frock of white lawn with a wide pink or blue sash. For some unfathomable reason, a baby-cap would be the finishing touch for her afternoon attire. This creation resembled those close-fitting caps worn by the women and children of the French Revolution called "mobcaps." Our mothers, of course, made no such connection. Thus enhanced, a little girl was ready to put her doll-baby in its carriage, and take it out for a stroll.

For me, this meant joining my playmates, Velma and Margaret in one yard or another and taking the air jointly. But one afternoon I had on a *new* cap; one made of white handkerchief linen with the customary rosettes – mine were pink – on each side to match my sash, and a matching ribbon under the chin.

Why our mothers chose to put these caps on us in hot weather will always be a mystery. But they were handmade and, indeed, very beautiful.

Even at that early age, in that burgeoning pride that knows no pain, we were delighted, heat or no, on those occasions in which we had a new one to show off.

How wise Emerson was to take note of this feminine trait to the extent that he would leave this comment for posterity: "I have it on authority that the sense of being well-dressed for an occasion gives a woman a feeling of felicity which religion is powerless to bestow." But after all, Emerson was a very bright man.

On this particular afternoon that happened to be my good fortune. Margaret, too, had worn a cap. Velma usually did, but for some reason, that day she had refused to submit to her mother's effort at making her fashionable, and was now slowly coming to regret it. At the time, we were no more than four or five, which now makes the whole episode incredulous. Margaret's cap was not new, so the fact that she had one on and Velma did not, did not seem to unsettle Velma. I could soon tell, however, that mine was having that effect. And I was not surprised when she said to me, threateningly, as she shoved her doll carriage aside, "Take it off!"

"I will not," I said. Of course I was not going to, and so Velma bit my thumb. Margaret went flying for my nurse, screaming, "Koosa!" Koosa, who was sitting on the kitchen porch helping Julette shell butter beans, sprang into action. Arriving at the scene of my bleeding finger, Velma's scratched face, and a badly damaged cap that, although askew, was still riding high, she was able to prevent homicide by the promise of lemonade.

That Velma would grow up to have the world's nicest disposition, and that by choice we would be roommates in college, and that now, in our eighties, this long-standing three-way friendship among Velma, Margaret and me still flourishes, goes to show that, as everybody says, "You never can tell."

≈ ≈ ≈

As a young child, my concept of beauty was being formed by several things that were around me in my daily life. First, was our large wide hall and its fluted Doric columns and their pilasters. Against the four-foot-high dark, mahogany paneling, a feature that went up three floors, the white of the fluted columns and the pilasters in the downstairs hall I thought very beautiful. The stair landing to the second floor, lighted as it was by a palladian window with bevelled glass was beautiful in morning sunlight.

Just inside the entrance hall from the front door, on either side, were narrow coat closets; their doors held full length mirrors, and by some prismatic effect, when the afternoon sun streamed in between the large columns of the porch and into that area of the hall, for a short while, refracted light from the bevelled glass of the narrow windows on either side of the front door to the bevelled glass of the doors to the coat closets just inside produced all kinds of lovely coppery glints in a little girl's mouse-brown hair. That glorious light deepened the blue of her eyes as well. In such an aura of glamour, freckles were lost. No wonder I thought those mirrors the nicest things in our house.

The afternoon reflection encouraged me to believe what my – to me – beautiful sisters said when they sought to soothe me about my freckles. "Freckles fade," they would say. "By the time you're sixteen or eighteen, they will all be gone. And you know, you have Father's periwinkle eyes, the bluest in the family, and his black lashes. With your bronzy hair, it's unusual coloring." Comforted, I would go back to my dolls and my tea sets, my climbing and rope-jumping, taking what they said about my freckles on faith.

Going from the hall through the sliding doors into the library, Father's black, leatherbound *Book of Presidents* lay on the table. Its size was possibly sixteen inches by twenty-two. The soft sheen of its enormous gold seal – easily larger than a bread and butter plate – and its gilt-edged leaves that glowed when the book was closed, were further evidence to me of things beautiful. And although I wasn't quite sure that it was pretty, I did think the Tiffany lamp that hung over the dining room table handsome. It seemed too heavy for beauty, except that I loved the circle of light where it fell on the table at supper, a lovely circle that seemed made to measure for our family.

The parlor was the stiffest room in the house. It was there that in solitude, on the grand piano I pounded out my scales and practiced my pieces, which were often interrupted for me to compose a rendition of "the storm." With three sets of closed doors between the parlor and the sitting room, this creative impulse could hardly be detected from "Melody in F," "Gypsy Rondo," "To Spring," or "Moonlight Sonata." The escape into the storm gave me a wonderful sense of freedom; the lightening-like skip of the fingers over a few treble notes, and the swing to the heavy roll of the thunder far down in the bass, and then, around middle "C," the soft, slow, mellow return to the calm of sunshine. With this release, I could then run another scale.

The main thing wrong with the parlor was that except in summer, it was never really warm. Like many other rooms in the house, it had a grate built into the fireplace, and there was no way to get the piano and the grate close to each other. And since all the downstairs rooms had fourteen-foot ceilings, and music lessons went on in winter, I never remember having had warm fingers at the piano. I recognize this now as a handy alibi for my lack of dedication to the art. Yet I do love music.

That room was, however, saved by the most glamorous thing I had ever seen in the way of a picture, a large lateral painting that in its wide, heavy, gold-leaf frame, hung on the wall opposite the piano. It was a marvelously executed landscape featuring a castle on the Rhine. Every window in the castle, even those of the multiplicity of its turrets, shone with splendor. I seem to remember having been told that that great pearly iridescence came from the use of seashells. But how it had come into being held little interest for me. That somebody had produced this marvel for my enjoyment was enough.

The memory of it lingered with me far into life, and years after I'd been married, when young Tom was fifteen, Tom had to make a business trip to Germany. Father and son went, combining business with a five day trip on shipboard down the Rhine. They reported that the romantic river had now become industrialized to some degree, and I was glad that I had not been along, for my own earlier trip down the Rhine, as a young girl enjoying the romance of its castles, had only deepened the illusions created by the castle in our parlor.

Wanting to bring me some small present from Germany, my two men spent some time at a jeweler's, and had decided on a small gold pin, a shamrock, with chip diamonds at its center. Knowing that I would be pleased with something simple, they explained that they had looked at more impressive jewels, but that in light of my having no great desire for them, they had passed them up. Indeed, over the years, having lost several pieces of jewelry, I had come to see the care of it as just another responsibility. My conception of jewelry as a complication in life had begun with Father's having given me a small gold daisy-diamond ring when I was six, one that I promptly lost in a game of hide-and-seek. Wisely, it was not replaced.

I did love to wear my little gold cross on its chain, the one I had been given at confirmation. And now and then at Christmas, or on birthdays, I would be given a little gold bracelet, or something called a "signet ring," with my initials on it. Father liked to give his daughters a diamond solitaire when they became sixteen, but by the time I had reached that age, Father was dead. Even so, Mother saw that I had one. And after I was married, as times began to get better, Tom would surprise me with some little jewel on special wedding anniversaries. One of these was a diamond circle pin, which, woefully, I lost in Mexico. In Athens, for one of our anniversaries, he gave me a wide gold bracelet with a handsome gold disk, the head of Athena engraved on it, which I wore daily, and which, at Tom's death, along with my diamond bracelet, I gave to my grandson, Brad, for his future bride. All in all, I am not a jewelry person. I do, however, enjoy it on others.

It was not the castles on the Rhine, however, that drew me to Germany later. I was to see the Passion Play twice, thirty years apart. The first time, I went as a young girl with my mother and sisters, the second with Tom, and each time, was equally moved. Tom and I had combined that visit with a drive through Bavaria. It was early in October, the flower boxes in all the windows were still blazing with red geraniums, and every day our drives were full of charm.

A part of one day was given to visiting the palace of the mad Prince Ludwig. This small castle is one of the most beautiful I've ever seen. There is a great deal of the use of white inside: white marble floors, wide flights of marble stairs with white balustrades, white arches and white columns, with the added interest and contrast of beautiful paintings. This most picturesque of princes, as we learned in a little book we'd read in advance, would, under a winter moon, dressed in all white, in a white sleigh pulled by white horses, drive madly about the countryside. As I recall, his death came early; it was led up to by sorrowful years of being shut away because of his emotional instability. The castle is now preserved by the State.

We had made our plans to be in Munich for Oktoberfest, that celebration of the new wine. And what a celebration it is! We went at night, where, admitted by ticket to a large wide avenue lined with enormous one-story buildings similar to our American warehouses, we followed the crowds. Now and then we would go inside one of these, each of which represented a certain winery. There, at wooden tables for ten or twelve, seated on long benches, the revelers drank. Weaving in and out among the tables, the barmaids, in Bavarian costume, their arms held high, carried by the handles on each of their ten fingers, a beer stein holding a full liter of frothing beer, never spilling a drop.

Around the inside perimeter of these large halls there were a number of spits. That night each was roasting an ox; the aroma, strong and pleasant. As we wandered in and out of the buildings, more as onlookers than as participants, at intervals we would almost bump into one of a number of wheelbarrows, which, being wheeled by what we would call "bouncers," trundled along, carrying some inert figure to an approximation of an infirmary, a well-staffed place for overnight recovery. For this period of the celebration of the new wine, on which the livelihoods of the natives depend, the acceptance of human weakness that prevails is impressive.

But if there was, in the parlor, to engage my fancies for that scheduled half hour of piano practice, the distraction of the castle on the Rhine, there was, on the mantelpiece in the sitting room, the wonderful bronze clock, on one side of which, The Three Graces, in their long, soft, graceful garments, their hair bound in a circlet of some kind, were poetically twined and intertwined. The clock chimed the hours and the half hours, and I used to wonder if, when everybody had gone to sleep and the fire burned low, would not those three graceful figures have broken apart and done a little dance, then hurriedly gone back into place? To make them more beautiful, I was told that they represented Faith, Hope, and Charity. Less important than the fact that the clock told the time of day was the pleasant illusion that those ladies had a little life of their own.

In direct contrast to the Grecian maidens, however, was the earthiness of the two sets of companion prints that hung in our dining room. One wall held copies of two of Millet's popular paintings, the *Angelus*, and the *Gleaners*. Each was the scene of a field holding human figures. In one, the figures were bending over at their gleaning. In the other, in response to the Angelus, the figures were standing, their heads bowed in prayer. The prints were done in sepia, and to a child, neither the color nor the subjects were exciting.

On the other wall of the dining room, separated by the large bay windows, hung companion pictures of those two other subjects popular at the time, and spoken of simply as "The Fish and The Fowl." In one were two life-size, lifeless ducks hanging upside down; in the other, a large, lifeless fish, hanging with a string through its gills. Since these were more colorful than the Millets, and to a child suggested animation, they were my preference. But deep down, nothing could compare with the castle on the Rhine and the Grecian maidens.

In our own small part of the world, distanced as we were from classical art by at least a two-and-a-half hour's train ride to the nearest major city, there was not pervasive cultural exposure. Yet, scattered about in the rooms of the homes of the time, there might be a sprinkling of portraits done by not-very-talented family members, and as such, given places of honor. Mother's sister, Penelope, "Aunt Nellie" to us, was especially generous with her still lifes. Her years of the study of painting at Salem had left their mark. By my sisters' time, young daughters were being provided both painting lessons and those in china-painting from local teachers. Sister enjoyed china painting; Alice Bryan liked to do things in charcoal and oil.

From an earlier time when it was customary for itinerant painters to go through the South, there were a few unflattering portraits in which women were made to look particularly pious and sombre. Audubon had made his way in and out of the southern states leaving a trail of children's portraits in which the same body was used over and over, only the head personalized. On a higher level, there were a few portraits by Sully. Homes were likely to have at least one or two reprints of the old masters: Rembrandt's *Nightwatch*, Sir Joshua Reynold's *Age of Innocence*, Landseer's *Blacksmith Shop*, Gainsborough's *Blue Boy*, or Van Dyck's *Baby Stuart*.

Even if they did not intend to pursue painting, young daughters sent away to school studied the history of art, and by the time of my girlhood, were being sent to see, and sometimes to study, the art in Europe, where so much of it lies, particularly in the churches. For whether we are Protestant or Catholic or of any other faith, each of us must be grateful to the Roman Church for its preservation of art. In that the Old World, with its advantage of age, has provided us with so many majestic cathedrals, I like to think of what our beloved old Bishop Cheshire once said in a sermon. At some point he had made a journey to Europe; in that sermon he spoke of the beauty and the splendor of its cathedrals. In relating those to our own churches, however, many of them small and simple, as is the little St. John's where our family worshipped, which is one of the two to which I belong, and where the sermon was being given, he said, "In its own situation, the meadowsweet is as great as the lily." I was glad that Mother and Father had been married in that small church. I had always felt, that, when the time came, I would want to be married there as well.

≈ ≈ ≈

Contrary to what people think, country life is never dull. It would have been even less dull at the time when Father, Uncle Mark, Uncle Jim, and Uncle Tom, their youngest brother who was to die of yellow fever just before his graduation from the University of North Carolina, were leading their own brand of country life. It's possible that losing their younger brother made the other three feel closer ties. For as my first cousin, Mamie Braswell Battle, in her witty way, was to say of all of us throughout life, "Pinch one Braswell and we all holler."

As a child, as full as my life was of the interesting country things, there was pleasure of another kind when I went, often, the eight miles into town to spend the night or longer with my cousins on my father's side, Emily and Lillian, those nearest my age. At Aunt Zell's and Uncle Jim's, their houseman and driver was called Grimes, and Grimes had, what up to that time was the most unusual set of teeth I had ever seen. The rows across the front, up and down, were gold, and Grimes usually wore a wide friendly grin. As he waited on the table, the effect was dazzling.

At Aunt Mamie's and Uncle Mark's, their houseman, Gaston, though just as good-natured as Grimes, had some irregularity of pigmentation in his skin in that it was not evenly distributed, and gave him large white splotches on his otherwise dark skin. In no way did this seem to affect his health or his attitude toward life. It did, however, give Gaston an unusual appearance. I decided that Uncle Jim's and Uncle Mark's domestics were more interesting than ours. Life at both uncles' homes seemed more glamorous, because at both, there was the indulgence to growing girls when they had company, of having breakfast served in bed. The trays would be laden with silver, everything piping hot and delicious.

Ordinarily, however, each family was at the breakfast table by eight. At Aunt Zell's and Uncle Jim's, Uncle Jim would always start the day by reading from the Bible. Our own prayers at home came at the end of the day, and singly. It would have been unthinkable not to kneel by the bed and give thanks for the day's blessings. Even Alice Bryan tried to kneel by the bed to say hers. My own childhood prayers, like all children, ended with, "and please bless Mother, and Father, and Everybody." The exception to this pattern came at those times when Alice Bryan was in such deep pain that, without her knowing it, Father would gather us in a bedroom, and everybody kneeling, would read aloud appropriate prayers from the *Book of Common Prayer*. And then would ask God to take away Alice Bryan's pain and to heal her body.

Impressed by the style of living that went on at Uncle Mark's and Uncle Jim's, breakfast in bed, white-coated butlers serving at mealtime – of course, in a pinch, we could put white coats on Henry Slick, who took care of the fireplaces, or the combination yardman-chauffeur, Robert – in contrast, our own breakfast hour seemed very tame. We came down for it, company or no. And we came dressed. I liked it both ways, theirs and ours, for although the luxury of being served breakfast in bed was delightful as a novelty, it would never have become for me, an addiction. I would always have felt that I might be missing something that might be going on downstairs, and a lot went on at our house.

It and its premises were a self-sustaining unit which made things lively. There was always something going on, each one – in itself – interesting, and whether you were involved in them or not, you were aware of them. The same, of course, as already described, went on at Grandma Bryan's. And although my Braswell grandparents died before I was born, I'm sure their way of life would have been similar. Apparently Grandpa Thomas and his Emily, or "Emmy," were a happy couple, with Grandpa especially protective of his Emmy, even to the point of providing her the supervisory housekeeper, Miss Cornelia. Knowing that Grandpa had a pet monkey, and that Grandpa was often elected to the state legislature, leaving Grandma with four growing boys and a mischievous creature of the jungle who – until the cook shut up his tail in the kitchen door when he had come inside and mixed the salt and the sugar – was always underfoot, I can see that Grandma did, indeed, need special help. The feeling deepened when –for a calamitous week – a monkey entered my own life, a tale to come later.

My Grandfather Braswell's full name was Thomas Permenter. Genealogical sources say that the name Permenter was originally Parmentier, French for pepper. Whether or not Grandpa derived his zest for life from his name, I don't know, but it does seem – in modern lingo – that he never missed a trick, and that he enjoyed people. He especially loved the circus, and never missed one when it came to the community. The tale goes that so regular was he in attendance, that the ringmaster would always pause just as the performance was about to start, and with a roll of drums, would inquire from where he stood on a box in the center ring, "Is Squire Braswell in the tent?"

And when the genial figure with the snow-white beard that was Grandpa would stand, and with a sweep of his large black hat, make an all-encompassing bow, the show would begin.

≈ ≈ ≈

When I came along, among the children in the first grade there were several from very poor homes. Part of the learning process for each child was to stand up and read, or to try to. When those children, who had never had a book nor a written word of any kind in their homes, stood up to take their turns at reading, it was troubling. I felt pity and embarrassment for them, and to escape, my mind would wander. Daydreaming would take over. The thing that interested me most as the years went on was literature, mainly composition. While the other subjects received enough application to get me by, I knew early that I would never be a famous mathematician, nor a historian, nor a geographer.

Indeed, years later, when I came upon something Stanley Baldwin, when he was Prime Minister of England, said of himself, I felt that there were two of us. "What powers I have," he said, "I attribute to the fact that I did not overstrain them earlier." Finding this honest self-appraisal gave me the momentary pleasure of feeling myself in good company, but Chaucer brought me back to earth in relation to my dilly-dallying about my writing when I read in *Canterbury Tales*, "A busier man than he there n'as. Yet, he seemed busier than he was."

Shakespeare, too, could easily have had me in mind when he has a character say of himself, "I am a feather for each wind that blows." For I have recognized a weakness in myself for accepting invitations that have often pulled me away from my writing or something else purposeful that I was enjoying doing at home. For I have a double compulsion: I draw support from others, and this gives me a feeling that they just might draw something from me. For I believe that if we will take the time and the trouble to find out, every human being will, in one way or another, prove interesting. It is for these reasons that those interruptions bring into my life things that, for me, make it life itself.

≈ ≈ ≈

Perhaps in some families, illustrating certain truths by quoting maxims is more a way of life than in others. If there had been prizes given for the number and the variety used, our family would have made a good showing. To a young girl in such a family, they would be as familiar as the ABC's, and in the mind for life. But falling on small ears, some of them seemed to contradict each other: "A rolling stone gathers no moss," yet, "nothing ventured, nothing gained"; "look before you leap," yet, "he who hesitates is lost"; "still water runs deep," but how can still water run? These were the puzzlers. The one that never let up, and in that it had no contradiction, stood alone, and was painfully clear to an active and venturesome little girl was, "pretty is as pretty does."

Not only did my family speak in maxims in order to emphasize certain truths, they had other ways of getting across life's lessons as well. The laws of life seemed to have been thoroughly mastered by the older generation. When Grandma Bryan and I would be visiting in Oxford, making the rounds of seeing relatives in their homes, one of the more distant cousins, would, to my puzzlement, intersperse her conversations with the vague term, "and I know *whereof* I speak."

I'd never heard that expression, and it was a mystifying term. It did not serve to make me overly fond of Cousin Eula; I could only think of her as peculiar, perhaps even more so than another distant relative in Oxford, Cousin Ellen Bryan, who had gone to bed with a headache thirty years before, and was still there. When Grandma and I would call on Cousin Ellen, she would be propped up with pretty pillows wearing a frilly boudoir cap, herself, as bright as a cricket. I decided that there was no way to explain odd relatives, but that family was family, and that we must keep up our ties.

≈ ≈ ≈

Since grammar school I had loved words, and had once had the heady success of seeing something of mine in print under an assumed name. I had picked the name A. Julia Waters. Now I wonder why I chose such a business-like name. Certainly it was not a flowery one such as Rose would have been, or Lily, or Fern – perhaps I might have been thinking subconsciously that I wanted the name to represent strength of character. But then, I was only twelve, and had won a contest with an essay on the unlikely subject, "Why I Have Never Married." I wrote of having an invalid father for whom I felt responsible, all other family members being dead. My sweetheart was leaving to make his home in China, in tobacco. And heroically I sent him off. It oozed sob-stuff, and for a long time I kept the prize in the tray of my old doll trunk where I knew no grown person would find it.

My prize-winning essay was published in an inconsequential magazine called the *Progressive Farmer*, to which, along with the *Literary Digest*, and the newspapers, the *Raleigh News & Observer*, the *Richmond Times Dispatch*, the *Washington Post*, and the local *Evening Telegram*, Father subscribed. For diversion he read Bret Harte, O. Henry, Keats, Burns, Tennyson and Scott.

Looking back over Father's favorite poets, and his favorite novelist, Sir Walter Scott, I can see why Burns came first; he was a man of the earth. Although I doubt that father ever plowed a furrow, he may never even have held a hoe, he was very much a person of the land. And he had a deep feeling for those who tilled it. Genial, but not particularly voluble by nature, it was often said that when Father spoke, everybody listened. He loved laughter and enjoyed jokes, but in his innermost self, I now know that he was concerned with the deeper meanings of life.

While Father loved the brighter poems of Burns, he was especially drawn to those of his to which Thomas Gray, in his eulogy, referred to as "the short, but simple annals of the poor." A penciled check mark in a now very old volume of Burns' poems shows that of them all, the one Father loved best was "To a Mouse." And while perhaps one line from this poem is now as often quoted as any ever written, I daresay that the poem in its entirety is now rarely read. For that reason, I take time to explain how it came into being.

One day the Scottish Burns and his hired-man were plowing a field when the helper's plowshare destroyed the nest of a mouse. That night, tender-hearted man that Burns was, he could not sleep until he wrote the poem which he addressed to that small unfortunate creature who had lost its home. It is an apology. He begins by sympathizing with the poor cowering mouse over whom, in the scheme of things, man has dominion. He takes responsibility for having broken nature's social union, destroying the nest that the mouse has so long been building, and with the "bleak December's winds ensuin'...the fields laid bare and waste...and weary winter comin' fast," he will not be able to rebuild.

The poet goes on to say, "But Mousie, thou art not alone in proving that foresight may be in vain," for "the best-laid schemes o' mice and men gang awry and lea'e us nought but grief and pain for promised joy." And to comfort this small beast even more, the poet ends by saying,

> *Still thou art blest, compared wi' me!*
> *The present only toucheth thee:*
> *But, och! I backward cast my e'e*
> *on prospects drear!*
> *And forward, though I canna see,*
> *I guess and fear.*

It would be several years after Father's death that on a trip to the British Isles I saw the Burns home. In this, as he would have called it, "wee cot" where he was born, as I stood in the small, low-ceilinged room, I believe it was the kitchen, with its large fireplace, and in one corner, its heavily-carved oaken bed, I had a nice warm feeling that included thoughts of Father.

Mother read novels and poetry. At Salem Female Academy she had so consistently kept a diary that it now lies in the archives of Salem College and Academy, the record of a young girl who was full of life, of likes and dislikes for her teachers, who enjoyed flirting with the young men who made it their business to amble across the college square and sit on its benches, full of hope.

There were no bedrooms as such in the dormitories at Salem in those days. Space was petitioned by the use of white ducking into what was spoken of as alcoves, which two or three girls might share as roommates. Teachers had their own alcoves scattered among those of the students. Mother's diary tells of an exciting night, when one of the teachers, in cleaning her white kid gloves over a spirit lamp, started a small fire. But usually there was no more excitement than for the young girls to talk in whispers about plans to raid the school pantry. With Mother's enthusiasm for life, and her nature of taking chances, she probably was the instigator.

At any rate, in her diary, she confesses to having stolen a can of corn and one of pineapple, which were successfully, if laboriously opened with the hook of a shoe-buttoner. I assume that this began to weigh on Mother's conscience, for a few pages further along in the diary, she writes of a visit to the school's president, "Honestly, I am so sinful. After supper tonight, Mary Sue and I are going over to Dr. Rhondthaler's house to talk to him. He is the only one who I think can help me."

In spite of her youthful exuberance, Mother, as a young girl, saw the Moravians as the best people she'd ever known. The school had been founded by that religious sect. Even today there exists a friendly rivalry with Longwood College of Farmville, Virginia, for the distinction of which is the older of the two. Imbued with the spirit of the institution, Mother once wrote an appealing letter to Grandma, asking for permission to become a member of the Moravian Church. Permission was granted, and although there was no Moravian Church closer to where we lived than Winston-Salem, a distance of two hundred miles, always, at Christmas, Mother was sent one of the Church's small beeswax candles with a red ruff around it. For an hour or two, throughout the holidays, this candle would burn on the mantel of our sitting room throughout the holidays.

The last Easter of Father's life, Grandma Bryan and Cousin Anne Brown, the two who had gone to Salem in a stagecoach having now reached eighty, Mother decided it would be nice to take them back to Salem for the Easter services. Father was glad to help her with the undertaking. And I have a postcard that came back to my sisters and me at home on the Saturday before Easter Sunday. Properly addressed, as Mother would have, to: The Misses Braswells. This was her message:

> Saturday Night.
> Have spent a happy day. All feeling well and ready to retire and get up at 3:30 for the sunrise service in the graveyard. Went to the Love Feast this P.M. Enjoyed it very much. Guess we will be home Monday night.
>
> Hastily, Mother.

But Mother was essentially an Episcopalian, as were the rest of us. As I have already written, she and Father were married in St. John's in the village. The church was served by a visiting rector from the larger town, eight miles away. Since he always came by train, in a system of rotation, overnight hospitality was provided. This meant that the rector, Mr. Owens, went from the Marriott's to the Phillips's, to the Bunn's and to us.

These visits were ones of great pleasure to the host family. Best of all were the spring and fall visits of the Bishop. Bishop Cheshire, genial, round, and jolly, a little Santa Claus of a figure, even to the white beard, was one of the delights of my early life! I can picture him now at the lectern, his plump little hands extended from under the white ruffled cuffs of his surplice; I can see his Bishop's ring. His was a true Bishop's paunch, and on that paunch, as he sang and as he laughed, his heavy gold cross bounced up and down. At times of confirmation, when the confirmands knelt at the altar for the laying on of hands, the congregation, listening to his deep rich voice saying, "Oh, Lord, bless this child," felt that the petition had already been granted.

In or out of the pulpit, the Bishop could be playful. One day, when a handful of children were standing outside the church, waiting for the bell to ring to go in for the service, the Bishop stopped to ask a little girl her name. When she replied, "Swan Drake Wells," he said instantly, "What a *watery* name!"

With Bishop Cheshire's ecclesiastical duties behind him, he would become the world's most pleasing houseguest, and its best storyteller; however, as a teller of stories, Dr. Marriott ranked almost equally. When these two men were together at our house, having their toddies with Father, which, when Bishop Cheshire was there, were glorified into what was known as "Bishop Cheshire's Planter's Punch," our Sunday evenings were unforgettable.

The thing that made these Sundays especially lively, was the knowledge that Dr. Marriott's wife, Miss Emily – and it was the custom of the time to speak of your mother's friends as "Miss" – frowned upon the Doctor's indulgence in spirits. The Doctor had to keep his own in the stable, a handy place for them, especially on cold nights when he came in from a call in the countryside, which he had made with his horse and buggy.

On many weekday afternoons, as well, Dr. Marriott joined Father at our house for a toddy. Mother would sometimes have sherry. Often, it became my happy privilege to take the empty toddy glasses back to the kitchen. For I had found how delectable the moistened sugar at the bottom of the glasses was. The presence of alcohol was natural in our house. Father always kept a barrel of beer in the cellar. The fat, round, little brown empty bottles were useful to Velma and Margaret and me, when we went through the phase of playing "dairy." There was always a bag of lime in the toolshed, and with lime and water, it was easy to make "milk"! Parents would go crazy over such a danger now, but we were country children, allowed a great deal of freedom.

One of Dr. Marriott's tenets was that children should regularly have Scott's Emulsion Cod Liver Oil to avoid rickets (bowed legs). Every morning before I went to school, I had to swallow that awful dose: a tablespoonful. Mother would try in every way to make me get it down. She would start with lemon juice. She had lemon juice and hot water brought into her room for her own use every morning at seven. By putting some of the lemon juice in the bottom of a small glass and pouring in the cod liver oil, with lemon juice on top, she tried to get me to swallow the life-giving potion. But once having tried it, I refused, just as I did Mother's raw egg, which she offered under similar treatment. That was another of Dr. Marriott's suggestions, for use when anybody looked peaked.

There was never any success in getting me to take the raw egg, but as for the cod liver oil, when Mother substituted sherry for lemon juice, I cooperatively gulped the dose. I must have gone to school bright-eyed and bushy-tailed! That my growth was not stunted, and that throughout life I have required far less alcohol than the average is a testament to Dr. Marriott's skill.

Even Sunday was no exception to the Scott's Emulsion routine. Since the rector could not arrive until Sunday afternoon, our services were always those of evening prayer. I think few people would dispute the fact that this is the most beautiful of all services. And yet, I was always made sad by the hymns they sang: "Now the day is over, night is drawing nigh, shadows of the evening steal across the sky," or "Day is dying in the West," and so on. I think, now, that one of the reasons for the sadness connected with the evening services was, for me, the fact that Alice Bryan's crutches were, at those times, always lying under the pew, and that during the prayers she would be trying to kneel on one knee; the other would not bend.

During those times when Alice Bryan's osteomyelitis was in remission and she was able to use crutches instead of a wheelchair, we were happy and hopeful. We could even, as a family, takes trips to Washington and

New York, and in between those larger trips, Mother would take her daughters to Richmond to shop. Then, habitually, something would happen to change the whole tenor of family life.

In the middle of the night, we would be wakened by the eerie voice of the shivering owl, and although by day, the intermittent long tremors might have seemed musical, at night, they were ominous. Strangely, amid all the trees in our yard, the owl would have chosen the elm under Alice Bryan's bedroom window, and for some reason never to be explained, a few days after each visit, the symptoms of her osteomyelitis would begin to return. Understandably she had begun to associate these nocturnal visits with dread, and we shared her distress.

There were only two ways we could hope to drive the owl away: to turn on all the lights in the house, including those on the gate, and for Father to go out with a lantern, in later years, a flashlight, and throw pebbles up into the tree. For a time, this would bring silence; then another tremor would ring out into the night. We could only wait and hope, and as we did, try to divert Alice Bryan. Finally, Father would come inside, for he had heard a flapping of wings and had seen a shadow moving against the night sky toward the fields that led into the woods behind our house.

≈ ≈ ≈

For the village children of the time, Sunday School was something of a highlight. Our house was not too far away to hear the first bell. I knew that I had only to look out the south window of our sitting room to see the neatly dressed figure of Miss Emily Marriott walking fast up the hill; I knew that she would have her well-worn prayerbook in her hands. Miss Jesse Bunn, Margaret's Mother, would follow soon, as would Miss Mary Phillips, driving the horse that pulled her buggy. In the foot of the buggy she might have cookies and candy for the children of the Sunday School, for though, in the terminology of the time, Miss Mary was an "old maid," she was, in kinder terms, a happy-hearted spinster who loved and understood children. While Mother took no part in Sunday School, she always saw that her growing girls were there.

One or two of those three dedicated woman, on the day before, would have swept the church and dusted the pews, have changed the altar hangings if seasonally required, have selected the hymns for the service next day, and have put the numbers on the hymnboard. The next morning all three would be back again. Miss Emily would lead the prayers, Miss Jesse would play the organ, and the three of them would teach the lessons. Miss Emily had an entirely fitting, rather deep voice for opening the service, and when she stood in front of the first pew and said, "The Lord is in His holy temple," we settled down. And when she followed with, "Let all the earth be silent before Him," all the whispering and giggling stopped.

One of the most enriching experiences of my childhood was listening to the cadences of the prayers; I think that this may have given me a feeling for words. And any religion that I have now is attributable, in part, to the dedication of those three women. For me, they laid a foundation for the pleasurable experience of finding that the Anglican Communion is the same the world over. Time without number, this has given me a feeling of being at "home away from home."

Our St. John's, itself, with its paneled walls and slender Gothic windows, its tall steeple with the cross on top, could have been in any English churchyard, although there was no graveyard around it. The village graveyard was, and is, on the same hill, a field away, and is called "Cemetery Hill." With the church windows open on a summer day, the tombstones seem very near. In its shade, its moss-grown paths, and its ivy, there is indeed, an English flavor.

Often on a Sunday afternoon, Miss Ruth Hobgood would walk with a group of children up the hill to the cemetery. Walking among the squares, certain of the tombstones would suggest to Miss Ruth interesting stories of the ones buried there. Miss Ruth had a gift for dramatization, and those afternoons became fascinating. In spring and summer the little girls always carried flowers; we put the smallest and those with the shortest stems in small glass jars for the tiniest graves. In these ways, death was becoming, for us, a part of life.

≈ ≈ ≈

Mother had a delightful way of expressing things that would hang in the mind of her listeners. Mrs. George Strickland, one of her good and true and devoted friends, was to us, "Miss Mary Strickland." She and Mother had grown up together; they understood each other perfectly, but there was one point on which they could never quite agree.

I guess my own hit-the-high-spots method of going through life came to me from Mother. She was not one for details, and the matter of exchanging visits between friends with an I-go-to-see-you, you-come-to-see-me attitude was not her idea of friendship. But it was Miss Mary's. Often, when Miss Mary had made the most recent call, and Mother had not returned it promptly – or in a reasonable length of time – Miss Mary would, as Mother used to say, "Get in a huff."

They would meet at church, or at some social gathering soon after, and greetings over, in answer to Mother's, "How are you, Mary?" Miss Mary's answer would be, "Alice, I'm not coming to see you *another* time until you come to see *me*." On the way home from such an encounter, Mother's comment would be, "I declare, Mary Strickland is going to drive me to distraction with her bookkeeping."

Nevertheless, we would soon see Mother put on her hat, and put her foot in the path.

≈ ≈ ≈

Grandma Bryan had gone as a young girl of eleven, two hundred and fifty miles by stagecoach from Rainbow Plantation on the Roanoke in Eastern Carolina to attend Salem Female Academy. This had begun a family tradition: her daughters and their daughters, when the time came, would each attend that institution. From things from Mother's Salem diary, I can think fancifully, and with some pleasure, of a night in 1892 at Salem Female Academy when Miss Tientze had announced the end of Study Hall. It was my mother, the last of the young girls to stop writing in her diary, to whom Miss Tientze would speak in a loud, clear voice, "Alice, say goodnight with a flourish!" And it was this young Alice, full of zest for life, and, in a very normal way, full of mischief, who would later become my wonderful, brave, responsible mother, carrying with her, throughout life, her love of people, of trees, of the pen, and of books.

I can't imagine why Mother's diary was so long in coming to light. It was only after Vivian's death that I began to go through a trunk in her attic, one filled with old family papers. There were letters of all kinds, newspaper clippings, copies of business contracts, a few old college textbooks, our baby shoes, baptismal certificates, ledgers from the farms, some of Mother's and

Father's letters, written to each other before and throughout marriage, and a few of our grandparent's letters, as well, among other miscellany. Some of the books held pressed flowers. Obviously the books had sat unopened in Mother's attic during her lifetime, and from there, into one of several trunks that had gone, at Mother's death when Vivian came to live with me and my family, to sit in a large storage space adjacent to the servants' quarters over our garage, and then when Vivian built her house, had gone into her attic.

The night that I discovered Mother's diary, I sat up in my bedroom, reading it until one in the morning. I knew in a flash that it should be given to Salem to be placed in its library, and I set about doing that right away. The letter that came from Salem in response is given here:

Dear Mrs. Pearsall:

Several months ago you sent by Elizabeth Rose a diary kept by your mother while she was a student at Salem Female Academy. Alice Bryan's diary was faithfully delivered, and it has been safely incorporated into our archives in the Siewers Room of Gramley Library. I remember receiving the diary shortly before Christmas, and after reading the first few pages I knew that I had a real treasure in hand. I was determined to read the whole thing through, and not simply file it away for chance "discovery." I should have written to you at that point–for I had no idea how many weeks would pass before I could fulfill my resolution to read this marvelous account of student life at Salem. Yesterday and today I kept that promise to myself–and I can't thank you enough for enriching our collection of Salem's history with this gift.

Alice Bryan's account of her spring semester at Salem is an extraordinary document. The Diary itself is complete and remarkably legible–and anyone who has dealt with manuscripts knows the joy of that condition. The account provides fascinating insight into the daily activities, curricular and non-curricular, of the Academy students. But to tell the plain truth, the aspect I most enjoyed was the character of Alice Bryan. I couldn't help laughing when she stole a can of corn, punched it open with a shoe horn, and got caught cooking it in the stove. She crawled under fences, mailed unauthorized letters, giggled in church, and skipped classes. Despite her homesickness, Alice seems to have had a good time with her fellow students–and it's clear she admired many of the older people (Dr. Rondthaler, Dr. Clewell, Mr. Seaber, and Miss Ella) she met. Altogether I envision a very energetic, resourceful, brave, and loving young woman. It does not surprise me that, as you indicate, she achieved the heroism of managing a large farm and caring for an invalid child. She sounds exactly like the kind of woman Salem is so proud of helping to shape.

As you may know, we have a January term course called "Salem's Past" which will be taught during the next academic year. I have invited the professor, Dr. Inzer Byers, to read the Alice Bryan diary now so that it can be properly included in her course plans. Those of us who have dealt with the materials in the archives do not believe we have another diary as full, as interesting, and as delightful as your mother's. We deeply appreciate your thoughtfulness and generosity in making it available to Salem.

Sincerely,

Dr. Rose Simon,
Director of Libraries

When my own turn at Salem came, although I loved the school and the friendships I made there, after two years, I wanted to do what Father would have considered important – to have part of my education take place in the city of Washington. Although Father had endorsed the Salem idea, he felt that it would be broadening for his daughters to attend schools in our Capitol, as well. My sisters had gone from Salem Academy to two years at Ronald P. Macon Institute in Danville, Virginia, and then on to a school then called Gunston Hall, which had been started by that friend and neighbor of George Washington, George Mason, in Washington.

Those Washington schools for young girls, The Cathedral, Holton Arms, and Gunston were spoken of then as a finishing schools, but their obligation to education was not as shallow as the term implied. There was a certain amount of freedom in our choice of courses. It's true that we were taught manners and other of the social graces. We automatically sat at the French table for a month at a time, and speaking French there was compulsory. We had lessons in voice, piano, and dramatics. Art history and literature were required. Surprisingly, in a literature class, we spent three months on Dante's *Inferno*.

Mother and Father also subscribed to the theory that travel was broadening; that it "enlarged one's capacities," so travel became a part of our lives. All through those years I was busy writing chatty letters of many pages to long-suffering friends and relatives, and these, with a sporadic keeping of diaries and journals, seemed to take care of my predilection for the scrape of the pen.

In the South of my time, unless there happened to be economic necessity, young ladies were not brought up to be self-supporting. Piano lessons, voice lessons, painting, and elocution were the order of the day, with, of course, Latin, French, grammar and literature. Math, history, and geography were also included, but history was taught only as battles and the reigns of certain kings. Geography seemed a sing-song of the products of first one country and then another, so that all I remember from those two subjects is that Australia produces wool and that the Hundred Years War lasted that long.

Since I was the last child in the family, however, Mother had gone all out on me, musically speaking, starting early, even to violin lessons. But when I went to college, a few months of excruciating see-sawing in an orchestra mercifully soon put an end to that phase of my life. Where I really gave my all was in acting out Shakespeare at Gunston. For in a rotation of characters, we each learned virtually several whole plays, exchanging parts as we went along.

In between these pursuits and our recitals and exercising on our roof garden, we would walk down Connecticut Avenue for tea and cinnamon toast, as long as our expense money lasted – and making expense money last was important, for we had found out about marcels, that sophisticated way of making flat waves in straight hair. Although our parents might not have approved of this mutilation of our tresses, we went, now and then, to what became, for us, an adorable salon where we had the double excitement of conversing in French, and, at the same time, of making ourselves beautiful to go out with young men from Georgetown University on weekends.

On certain days of the year we were sent to the Capitol to observe our government in the process of governing, something Father would have endorsed whole-heartedly. On certain days we visited art galleries. Sometimes we substituted the trip to the Capitol for a sly trip by taxi to a movie, often painfully having to leave at the best part. Once a year we were received at the White House for tea, and Mrs. Coolidge, I might add, though not as dry-bones as the President, was not the kind of person you'd ask what color she put on her hair.

Although Father's motive in sending us to school in our national city was one of more importance, the experience brought with it certain of the spicier elements of human behavior which added considerably to our pleasure. Among the tales that were told was one of a former president. A great figure in his time and in history, in that he was being seen – with some degree of regularity – in the company of an attractive Washington lady who was not his wife, in some circles he came to have a humorous designation. The President would have been the last to know that, in that the lady was a Mrs. Peck, he was being spoken of around the city as "Peck's bad boy."

In that city of diversities of opinion, jealousies, and of striving to get ahead, gossip has always been rife. So much so, that the witty daughter of another president, the colorful "Teddy" or Theodore Roosevelt, Alice Roosevelt Longworth, crystallized that proclivity of our national city when she said to her dinner partner as she was being seated at the table, "Don't sit by me unless you know something bad about somebody."

And so it was, with the reality of a country upbringing for balance, that my education went along – not orthodox – but in my case, adequate for my building on throughout life. In a life that would include knowing a great many people, high and low alike, I was steadily being given a certain openness to experience. I was being provided as well, an interest in people as individuals. In that, down the years, I would come to know and to draw from so many, I would often, to a lesser degree – for her husband was Prime Minister of England – have something of the feeling expressed by Lady Cynthia Asquith, when she wrote, "I have often felt myself to be a bee in a herbaceous border." And here, in one of those characteristic plays of the mind, Lady Asquith and two other women come together in my thoughts. Although I did not have the pleasure of knowing Lady Asquith, she would surely not have pronounced the word "herb" in our American way, as "erb," or "herb," but in the English way, as "hub." I feel sure of this, because once when Tom and I were visiting in Oxford, our hostess, Jean MacClagan, whose husband, Michael, was head of Trinity College, said to me as Tom and I were ready to leave, "Oh, wait a minute. Elizabeth, come into the 'hub' garden with me."

We hurried out into her typically English garden, which looked as though the seeds might have been scattered by the wind, all varieties of flowers blooming companionably together, where Jean stooped to her patch of herbs, and pinching off a snippet for me, said, to delight my heart, "Rosemary, for remembrance."

Equally delightful, and undeniably as picturesque, is the pronunciation given the word "herb" by a wonderful African American woman who lives thirty miles away from me in the countryside of Eastern Carolina. Emma Dupree, a highly intelligent woman who spent many years taking care of a doctor's office in a small town, at the doctor's death, had gone back to live in the country near the small town of Bethel, where she was born and had grown up. From an insight into medicines which the kind-hearted old doctor had shared with her had come her own interest in nature's medicinal properties. She began roaming the woods to gather what she speaks of as her "yebs" for mixing with a variety of other ingredients to make health remedies. A sympathetic woman in the community, hearing of her interest, had given her a beautifully illustrated book of wildflowers which Emma would proudly say had cost fifteen dollars.

Emma's method of releasing the healing properties of the herbs is to select certain "yebs," and boil them in a large pot with a solution of water and rock candy, sometimes adding honey and lemon juice. The resulting liquid is then strained into large bottles which sit on Emma's dining room table where they are dispensed without charge. Her customers are legion. Some, who live in California, rely solely on her preparations for health, and keep her supplied with rock candy. Although Emma will never take any money for her remedies, it is acceptable to leave a bill or two inconspicuously on the table where the bottles of liquid sit.

I came to know Emma through Nannie, one of my two housekeepers, who always saves the empty bottles in my house for her friend, for Emma's bottles are supplied by her friends and patients. One of my pleasures is seeking out interesting individuals, and so it was, that when we had a large number of bottles saved for Emma, one pretty day when there was nothing on my calendar, I had the unique pleasure of driving with both Nannie and Laura and a trunkful of empty bottles the thirty miles to pay a visit to Emma.

Emma herself, is a marvelous example of preservation. Her enthusiasm for her "yebs" is contagious, and I have been several times. On every visit, in her great gratitude for so many bottles, she will urge one of her liquifications on me, but my ready response is, "Wait until I get sick, Emma. Let that go to somebody else." And although I write this in a spirit that is, in part, fun, my fun may just be due to ignorance, for on one occasion, five doctors from the Chapel Hill School of Medicine made the hundred-mile trip to see Emma. To prove it, she has their pictures, those taken with her and her bottles. So in a world in which the only thing we know –

relatively speaking – is that we don't know anything, "Who knows?"

Like Lady Asquith, I, too, have gleaned from so many, that as I have gone along, I have seen the truth of that homespun philosophy of Will Rogers which I saw lettered above the bookshelves of the library in his home once when Tom and I had taken our young sons on a trip to the West: "We're all ignorant," the lettering said, "it's just about different things."

And, not to put too fine a point on it, a combination of this philosophy and that of the founder of the Persian Empire, E. Publius Cyrus, that "everyone excels in something at which another fails," – to use that editorial "we" of the *New Yorker*, which has for so long delighted me – is to forge for "ourself" the most soothing of philosophies.

≈ ≈ ≈

Lawrence Durrell's beautifully written book, *Bitter Lemons*, begins with these thoughts on travel: "Journeys, like artists, are born, not made. A thousand differing circumstances contribute to them, few of them willed or determined by the will – whatever we may think. They flow spontaneously out of the demands of our natures – and the best of them lead us not only outward in space, but inward as well. Travel may be one of the most rewarding forms of introspection."

I suppose that, in this, that gifted writer refers to the fact that no matter how large the world, no matter how diverse its people and their customs, mingling and co-mingling among cultures evokes the feeling that in the basic ways, human beings are one. And that, loosely speaking, we are in one way or another linked.

The term "travel is broadening" had run all through my early life. Although as young men, Father and his brothers had gone to Europe, in our own part of the world, except for those involved in the tobacco trade, there had not, up to that time, generally, been much foreign travel. Father might have wished to take another voyage to Europe, for he loved Scotland, read and re-read Scott's novels, but by the time his family of its first three daughters were old enough to travel – I, the last of the four, had not been born – Alice Bryan had developed osteomyelitis. When her affliction came, the little girls were nine, eleven, and thirteen. By the time Alice Bryan had reached seventeen, her illness was occasionally in remission, and she and the other members of the family took a month's train trip to the West. In a party largely made up of North Carolinians and Virginians, Mother, Father, my three sisters, and Uncle Hugh Bryan made that trip.

Since I was only nine, I was left with Grandma Bryan. We spent most of the time visiting Grandma's son, my Uncle Charlie, who, with his wife and children, lived in Oxford. The seventy mile trip was made by train. Since it was summer, the train windows were open, there were no screens, telegraph poles, going in the wrong direction, whizzed by, and, using the corner of a handkerchief, passengers were always having to fish cinders out of each other's eyes.

In those days, little girls travelled in a dress made of a material called "pongee." It sometimes had a knee-length pongee coat to match, the length the same as that of the dress. The name seemed to denote its tan color, one useful for not showing smudges. And while Grandma travelled in her black bonnet with its long black veil down the back, its white ruching around the face, I rode in state in pongee and a wide-brimmed straw hat. The hat band was of inch-wide brown grosgrain ribbon, its streamers reached to the waist in the back.

Mother liked children to be dressed the way French children were: very short skirts for the little girls, very short pants for the little boys, and socks. If we had been travelling in winter, I would have worn my blue serge pleated skirt and my white midi-blouse with its blue sailor collar and its black silk sailor's tie done in a sailor's knot. There would have been the inevitable beret, always worn, in my case, low on the forehead, a simple solution to winter-chill that has remained in my life a veritable trademark. On average days in summer, little girls wore short gingham or lawn dresses, white socks and Mary Jane slippers. The one custom Mother couldn't have her little girls follow, was what we speak of now as wearing "long-johns." She said she'd never seen a child wearing them whose stockings were not wrinkled around the ankles.

Both the slippers we wore in summer, and the high-top shoes we wore in winter required a button hook, which meant that a lady's silver toilet articles on her dresser always held one of those important items for herself and her children. In winter we wore something called "Fay" stockings. These buttoned on to an undergarment at the waist and were worn with high-button shoes. My own "Sunday shoes" for winter had black patent leather bottoms, and for the upper half, white kid. With a small white fur cap and a matching muff, for Sunday School, this was quite an ensemble. But Sunday School over, I was torn between vanity and wanting to get out of my "Sunday clothes" and play.

Although, in Mother's conservative way, we had few clothes, they had to be of good material and well-made. If they were bought, quality was a first consideration. The second requirement after that was that their seams be French, which meant that there never should be a raw seam, and we were always taught to check inside a garment for that before trying it on.

Mother was not much of a seamstress, however. For real sewing she depended on Mrs. Joyner. Mrs. Joyner was the wonderful "revolving" sewing woman in our community. Her life was hard, and although her husband was a kind, good man, his health was such that he could not work. They had three children, the youngest, a boy just my age. Edgar was not only blind, he had to endure epileptic seizures, spoken of in those days as "fits." It was hard for Mrs. Joyner to get a neighbor to stay with Edgar when she went out to sew for the day, or for a week or so at a time as she often did, and so far as I know, Mother was the only one of her customers who would say, "Bring Edgar, too." Sadly, this boy once had had a seizure and had fallen into an open fire at home; after that, it was always Mrs. Joyner's great fear that that might happen again. And I suppose it was because of Alice Bryan that Mother was so sympathetic.

While Mother and Mrs. Joyner spread patterns on a large sewing table in what had earlier been our nursery and was now our sewing room on the first floor, I tried to help amuse Edgar in the adjoining sitting room. It was my daily job to clean our canary's cage to provide for his bath, and to replenish his water and seed. Edgar loved to sit on the floor and pat Gyp, our dog, and as he did, to listen to Dickie Bird, our canary, sing. Although I was too young to be a fluent reader, I remember trying to entertain him that way, telling him about the pictures. Edgar died young, and Mr. Joyner died soon after. In time, Mrs. Joyner was employed to do alterations for our best ladies shop. But during all those years of adversity and sorrow, she sang at her work. Mrs. Joyner was so accustomed to looking on the bright side of things, that when at around age forty-five, she lost all her teeth – and that was generally considered about the worst thing that could happen at so early an age – she continued to sing cheerfully, and to say often with a thankful heart, "Do you know I can still eat a raw apple?"

When I reflect on Mrs. Joyner's happy outlook, I think of Miss Bertha

Edwards, another woman blessed with the same. By the time I was married and our children were being born, Miss Bertha, who had long been a favorite nurse in the community, was getting on in years. She had been a part of Dr. Stewart McGuire's unit of nurses in France during World War I. This had been a high point in her life. At the time of the birth of our first child, young Tom, which had taken place at home, Miss Bertha stayed on in attendance for several weeks. She brought her scrapbook one day for me to enjoy. I kept it for several days. Somehow, looking at it when she wasn't there made me cry, for she loved babies, had taken care of so many, and would never have any of her own. I would be glad later when she came to nurse Aunt Zell, crippled with arthritis for several years before her death, and to stay on in Uncle Jim's home, looking after him until his death ten years later. His health was failing and he needed that kind of care.

Among Miss Bertha's fine qualities was a sense of humor, especially the ability to see herself as the butt of a joke. One day, when, after the birth of our second son, Mack, she was "on duty" with me, she shared one of her earlier experiences.

The war over by ten years, Dr. McGuire returned to his practice in Richmond, and decided to invite the nurses who had made up his wartime overseas unit to come to Richmond for a reunion. Excited at the prospect, Miss Bertha did something foreign to her nature, something extravagant.

It was winter, and she succumbed to the temptation of buying – for the celebration – a handsome, height-of-style, dark green, "worsted coat suit." So high was it in style, that it even had a hobbled skirt. Mrs. Crews, the town milliner, rose to the occasion by making a matching green turban, complete with a few small feathers on one side.

When the morning for the eventful departure came, Miss Bertha, in full regalia, stood at the head of the line of passengers standing by the tracks at the railway station waiting to board the train. But sadly, several attempts to get either foot up far enough to maneuver the steps failed. Modesty, of course, precluded lifting the skirt the necessary height. So that, Miss Bertha, thinking fast, gave up her place at the head of the line and said to the conductor who was standing by, helplessly, "Never mind! I'll take the *afternoon* train."

And a few hours later, she was back again; this time, relaxed and comfortable in her old, navy blue serge.

Was it Thoreau who said, "Beware of any journey that requires new clothes?"

As time went on, Miss Bertha was able to buy a nice large house in the country. She and her two sisters lived there, nurturing their vegetable garden, growing and canning all summer long, and more than generously sharing with anybody who came to see them. It was when she was in her nineties that, to the sorrow of the community, Miss Bertha fell and broke her hip. But nothing could get her down. If you went to see her in the hospital and said to her, "Oh, Miss Bertha, I'm so sorry," her answer would be characteristic: "Don't worry. The Lord has been looking after me for a long time. I'll trust him a little while longer." Until her death, Miss Bertha was like a member of the Braswell family. Mrs. Joyner and Miss Bertha are the kind of people we never forget.

But back, now, to my childhood. As children, we were clothed from Hutzler's in Baltimore, Wannamaker's in Philadelphia, and from either Franklin Simon, or Altman's, two department stores within a block from each other in New York. The latter two sent out catalogs. And when the store B. Altman closed a few years ago, I felt it was the demise of an old and trusted friend.

But I have strayed from the train trip to Oxford. Our dog, Gyp, black and graying around his mouth, was showing other signs of getting old. That summer when Grandma and I went to Oxford, our stay there was to be so long that I couldn't bear to leave Gyp at home, so we formed a conspiracy. We put him in a picnic basket with a top, and on the sly I fed him cold biscuits most of the way when I wasn't secretly rubbing the back of his neck. With an hour's layover in Weldon, between trains, I was able to give Gyp his exercise and his water. When we could hear our train coming down the tracks, blowing at every crossroad, I got Gyp back in hiding, and no conductor was ever the wiser.

Since our village and our town were on the mainline from New York to Florida, we had easy access to Richmond, Washington, Philadelphia, and New York. Richmond, as well as being where we went for medical attention, was gradually becoming our favorite shopping place, even though we were conveniently overnight from New York, and by boarding the train at ten at night in that city, would pull into Rocky Mount at nine the next morning.

My two older sisters, when they were in school in Washington, always came home on a night train spoken of as "85." In fact, at that time, all the trains were designated by numbers, not the glamorous terms in use today. When Sister and Vivian were coming home, since the through-train didn't stop in our village, Robert, the driver, and some members of the family would always arrange to be in Rocky Mount when the train arrived at 10:15. As was true of the larger town, the railroad track bisected the village with roads parallel to the rails on either side. Our house sat far back from the road among the tall old elms; some of us would stay at home in order to turn on all the lights in the house and those on the porches and on the gateway of the brick wall that surrounded the yard, so that, as the train sped by, our returning family travellers would recognize that brief, welcoming blaze of light. We knew that they would already have put on their coats, and for that instant, would be pressing their faces against the glass of the Pullman on that side of the car. The memory of those moments is one of the sweetest of my early life.

By the time the family car had come back bringing my sisters, we would have had the usual bedtime feast spread out on a table in the sitting-room in front of the fire, with Sister's hand-painted hot chocolate set on it, on a tray in readiness. For that set was one of the things that Sister had painted when she was studying china painting. The chocolate set was less impressive, however, than the beautiful punch bowl she had done, with its matching tray and twelve cups, each cup painted with pale purple grapes, and gold-rimmed to match the loveliest punch bowl I've ever seen. But the punch set was not half as often used as the chocolate. Underneath it is signed: *Mattie May Braswell, Randolph Macon, 1914.*

Possibly because we were a family of all girls, we had what I still consider the wonderful habit of what was called giving "last-go-trades." The rules were stringent. When you had heard something nice said about one of your sisters, in a strict system of barter, you would announce that you had up your sleeve *such* a compliment, but that under no conditions would it be divulged until it could be exchanged for something nice that had been said about *you.* The bartering could go on all day, because by some extrasensory perception, you could tell when your opponent was making things up. In that case, the compliment was not acceptable. One after another, they would be refused. I still think it's one of the best ways to instill self-confidence in growing children that I'd ever heard of, and it was so much ingrained in my nature that, for fun, sometimes on a winter's night, the children in bed, and Tom and I reading contentedly in front of the fire, in order to enliven things, I would suddenly say, "By the way, I have a last-go-trade for you."

He had lived with me long enough to know that this was a carry-over from the family habit, one that, for him, held little appeal. He considered it juvenile, and too girlish for the masculine psyche. He would not even lower the newspaper. But I was a bit of a fox; I *knew* that a smile was playing around his lips and that he wanted to know.

His first comment would be, pretending to be cross, "above" such things, "I'm not going to take part in any such foolishness. You're nothing but a fraud. I'm not going to play those games that you and your sisters played. Just keep it to yourself."

"All right, I will," I would answer, paying no attention to his "indifference." "But it was very *nice* and you'd be very much *interested* in knowing *who* said it." And finally he would say, "You're so foolish thinking that men sit around talking about things like that the way you and your sisters did. But if you have to have a trade, Mrs. John Jones thinks you're a very nice person."

"That won't do," I would answer. "It has to be something that somebody *said*. It's too easy to make things up." Then I would say, absently, "Let's just forget it."

After a while, maybe he would get up to put another log on the fire, and I would begin to relent a little. "If you just can't think of anything," I would suggest, helpfully, "I'll accept one from *you*."

And, coming round, he would offer, rather lamely, "Well, except for this fraudulent streak you have, I would say that you're a hundred percent." Then I would speak up.

Back again to train travel. On the Eastern Seaboard, the hours for daylight trains were more convenient than the night. All the daytime ones stopped in our village. The most inconsequential of these had just two passenger cars and one for baggage. A departure from the usual way of being designated by a number, this one was spoken of descriptively as "Shoofly." If you didn't mind giving the better part of the day to travelling a hundred-and-twenty-five miles, "Shoofly" would take you good-naturedly to Richmond, stopping at every pig path.

Number "89," going south, came at noon, bringing us the daily newspapers from Richmond and Washington. By boarding it in the village, in twenty minutes we would be in Rocky Mount. This would give us time to visit a department store, Daniels, and a shoe store, Cochran's, and something called "The Candy Kitchen." This last was the highlight. We could get store-bought ice cream, which we ate at small round tables while, overhead, ceiling fans ran a losing battle with flies, and we could take home assorted candies and crystallized fruits. This journey would also include a trip to the fruit stand, for we were a family with a great taste for Seckel pears, those small rust-colored pears which you would eat with the juice running down your fingers, still my favorite fruit, and a special reminder of Uncle Jim.

In reading an old tribute to my Uncle Jim, after his death, the writer spoke of how kind and genial he had been. He cited two examples, one, in which the writer had gone into a men's clothing store one day for some small article of apparel, and had overheard a conversation. A man he knew to be in reduced circumstances was trying on an overcoat, and had remarked to the salesman that it was beyond his price. Uncle Jim, a customer as well, then said quietly when the man had left the store, "Send that to John Jones's house and let me have the bill." The writer went on to say that it was always a pleasure to find Uncle Jim, at some hour of the day when he had walked from the bank of which he was president, across the railroad to the fruit stand, standing there eating a Seckel pear, and in the way of those in small towns, urging anyone who came by to join him in having one.

This was the same Uncle Jim of whom a nice little incident was told by one who had been one of his bank tellers. On this particular morning, Uncle Jim was seen going round in his quiet way, teller to teller, showing each of them a small piece of paper. He was trying to find out who had written a certain memorandum and placed it on his desk. He went from one to the other, courteously asking, "John, or Joe, or Robert, did you leave this note for me?"

The tellers, eager to please, and holding an affection for this father-figure, one by one, said, "No, Mr. Braswell, I didn't." Finally he came to the one who, tingling pleasantly to be sought out, acknowledged with some satisfaction, "Yes, sir. I did."

Then Uncle Jim said to the teller, "Well, next time you have a message, write it on a piece of scrap paper, not on the back of a printed check."

Still thinking of Uncle Jim: Frank Wilkinson and his family were lifelong close friends of our family, and so it was that when Frank had finished college and had come to start work in his family's insurance and real estate business, he came one day to ask Uncle Jim for advice. "Mr. Braswell, what do you think such and such piece of land (one Uncle Jim knew well) is worth?"

Frank always laughed at Uncle Jim's answer. It came in the form of a question, a short one: "Frank, are you buying or selling?"

Father and Mother had their glasses fitted in Baltimore, which meant that we had frequent trips there. I loved to see Mother, especially in cities, use her lorgnette, which she always kept in her pocketbook. In later years, she would use a pince-nez as well. This she wore attached to her blouse, but when necessary, pride would reassert itself, and she would rely on the less convenient lorgnette.

Father had a throat specialist in New York, for he was subject to sore throats, and he often took us there for several days or a week, combining these trips with business. Father's travelling bags were made of alligator, and there were three: the suitcase, the valise, and the grip. Even empty they were heavy, but there was always Henry, our yardman, or Robert, the driver, to carry them. Of the three bags, the one that, as a child, held my interest, was the grip. Not only because it sprang open in the middle in a very lively way, exposing all its contents, but because that's where Father always carried our presents, from New York, or Baltimore, or Richmond. The texture alone – the dark brown bumpy hide of the alligator – would have made those bags interesting in themselves, but the fact that the Jefferson Hotel in Richmond had a live alligator in the pool of its grand old lobby made it doubly so. Even to this day, that leathery smell of Father's bags comes to me, for that they were lined with heavy, saddle-colored leather added to their great weight.

In his earlier days in New York, Father had stayed in the Hotel Knickerbocker. With us, he stayed at the old Waldorf, sometimes the McAlpine; the two were at opposite ends of the same block. Sometimes we stayed in a small hotel called The Martinique, which was Uncle Mark's favorite. Father believed in making the most of your time in a city, and while we might be allowed breakfast in the room on one morning and were free to order things out of season such as strawberries and cream, for the rest of the time, we were supposed to be up early, and out. If we seemed

116

slow in getting up, he would come into our room and say, "Wake up and get up, Babes! It's too expensive to sleep in a city." It's an attitude I've never been able to overcome.

Except for those short stays away from home, Alice Bryan's repeated attacks of osteomyelitis and their subsequent operations, would, for the rest of Father's life, rule out more extensive family travel. However, a few years after his death, with Alice Bryan's osteomyelitis in remission, and with a Philadelphia doctor's recommendation that being on the water might benefit Alice Bryan, Mother began to make plans for the type of foreign travel that would include many days at sea.

For some reason, she chose the Canadian Pacific Steamship Line, and we liked their Empress ships. Since the first of the sea trips did seem to help Alice Bryan to stay well, we began to take more and more. There were cruises to the West Indies where I would fall in love with bamboo, and would say to myself that if I ever had a garden, I wanted to have some of it, and ultimately, did. When the time for that came, in a friendly effort to help me obtain this heart's desire, Burt Shaw, a close friend who had grown up in Littleton, a town thirty-five miles away, brought me a Jamaican bamboo root from her mother's garden. But, as beautiful as it was, the small narrow leaves quivering in the slightest breeze, my ecstasy practically uncontrollable, this plant would turn out to be a millstone around my neck. In our Carolina mixture of warmth and humidity, doing most of its growing during the month of May, it sometimes grew eight inches overnight, the shoots reaching the size of a broomstick handle. That the same thing was going on below ground among its roots, was a complication of which I was not aware. The time came when it was so frustrating to find a large sturdy shoot springing up in my prize-azaleas, or camellias, or cape jessamine, the fierce roots having tunnelled under twelve or fourteen feet to arrive at this strategic spot that Tom and I decided to have it all dug up. It would require three years to eradicate it, and I would not now touch a piece of bamboo with a ten-foot pole.

One of the longest of our voyages with the Canadian Steamship Line was a five months' cruise to South America and Africa on its *Empress of France*, in 1928. A country family, one with four marriageable daughters, I suppose, always has a certain romantic appeal. Unlike Mrs. Bennett, however, the mother so humorously treated in Jane Austen's *Pride and Prejudice*, Mother did not seem to worry about our finding husbands. Our family did, however, have a close friendship with another family of daughters in which the father jokingly voiced another opinion.

Miss Carrie Whitehead, Mother's childhood neighbor and friend in the village, for whom she had a life-long affection, was the daughter of old Dr. Whitehead, whose son Joe furnishes an anecdote later in this story. Miss ie – or Caroline – married Mr. Luther Huffines; much later, with their five daughters and two sons, one of whom died, the family moved from Rocky Mount out into the country to their farm, "Sunny Slope," the location now, of our large and flourishing Golden East Mall. Louise, the oldest of the Huffine sisters was a contemporary of my sisters; the life of their family was much like ours, and the families were often together. Both houses had swarms of young eligibles – and some not so young – eager to pay court to the older daughters, and, in between hayrides and watermelon parties there would be the exciting arrival, for the older sisters, of flowers and candy, floral boxes of long-stemmed red roses, of parma violets, and of lily-of-the-valley, to say nothing of five-pound boxes of Heyler's candy; things that had come by train from Richmond and Philadelphia. Seeing all this, the younger daughters in both families could hardly wait for their turn at this golden age.

Sometimes, when the suitors came to fill their evening engagements, Mother or Father would answer the ring of the doorbell and invite them into the sitting room for conversation until my sisters finished their primping upstairs. More often, the welcoming was delegated to me by a casual request from Mother where she sat reading, saying, "Precious, why don't you run to the door," – and I was always being asked by the family, why I didn't run and do something that needed doing – "and take the gentlemen into the parlor, and talk to them until the girls come down?"

Once I had the company in the parlor, my social grace consisted of rocking vigorously in one of the two red velvet-covered rockers that matched the settee, and of not very loyally, giving away secrets of the primping I knew to be going on on the floor above; the rouge on the cheeks, the mascara on the lashes, the last-minute look into the mirror, head tossed back so that the face in the mirror reflected slits for eyes that seemed to call for a little more mascara, and the deed was done. Further, I could even entertain them with an account of how, when Sister and Vivian were getting ready to go for a visit in Washington or Richmond, they would put on their new evening dresses for my benefit, even to the point of applying a beauty spot, and fluttering around with an ostrich fan.

But I don't know that these revelations from me did any harm, for at Christmastime – I must have been about seven – among the candy and the flowers and the silver card cases and mesh bags, there was a small jeweler's box, for me. It held a lovely little topaz ring from these nice young men who so often sang around the piano in our parlor. They knew that a year earlier I had lost Father's little daisy-diamond. It would not have occurred to me, that, in addition to their kindness, these young Galahads might be trying to curry favor with my sisters.

The routine of answering the doorbell when my sisters' beaux were expected and my sisters were still primping, ran through my early life. Because of his fun-loving nature, and his gift for telling tales, "Mr. Chambliss" became my favorite. In his tales, he usually made himself the butt of the joke. One of those had to do with a trip he had made a few months earlier to the city of Washington, one in which he combined business with calling on Sister at her finishing school. Dressed – as he said – in a new suit and a new overcoat, everything but a top hat and spats, at the appointed time, he rang the bell at the entrance to the school. With Mother's permission, and that of the Headmistress in his pocket, his self confidence was high. When the door opened, Norman – as he would be to me when I grew up – was prepared for the maid in her frilly apron and cap, but *not* for her silver card tray. But Norman was no slouch. In the wink of an eye, he had put a silver quarter on the polished tray. And it should be said, for the record, that Norman, who was born in Emporia, Virginia, and had come as a young man to work in Uncle Jim's bank, had a grandmother who was a friend of Robert E. Lee.

It was about this time, that one day, crossing the street on the way to his office, Mr. Huffines met a friend and they stopped to talk. The friend had just heard the news of the engagement of yet another Huffines daughter, and was commiserating with the father on his loss. Those of us who remember have laughed many times over Mr. Huffine's ready and altogether truthful answer: "Well, I didn't raise 'em to keep!"

The attitude of our mother and father toward marrying off their daughters appears, to me, now, easy-going, almost casual. I remember hearing that comment of Father's sometimes used in other situations, "Let nature take its course," and I suppose that was his philosophy about our getting married. In light of this, it was no surprise to find that when we started taking those long foreign trips on which we had a variety of beaux from other backgrounds that Mother's attitude remained the same. I really think she felt that if you were always a "lady," whatever course your life might take, things would turn out all right.

Yet the South of my girlhood was nothing if not romantic. It may have been that since, as a people, we seemed to find such significance in a sense of place, we tended to marry among ourselves, and that it came naturally to take that major step early in life. Which meant that every girl had proposals, not one, but several, or even many, in her home community. By the time of our major foreign travel, Sister was married, and each of the remaining three of us had our own romantic interests. Vivian was mildly in love with a man from Richmond, a tobacco buyer whom she had met when he'd been on the market in our home town. I had fallen in love with a young doctor in a metropolitan area. Alice Bryan, who, through having had an operation on her badly drawn knee, was, at that time, not confined to a wheelchair, but still limped and had to use crutches, had come to have the deep love of two fine men. One was William Decker, of Williamsport, Pennsylvania. Bill and Alice Bryan had met through his having been sent by his father to buy lumber in Eastern Carolina for their furniture factory in Williamsport. But the one who held her heart was Eugene Benedict, of Nashville, Tennessee, whom she had known first.

Gene's sister, Ruth, married a Rocky Mount man, Van Watson, a prominent farmer and developer of seed in the community. The Watsons had a large house in town, but for the summer months, they retreated to one of their farms. It was there, in a summer-in-the-country way, that Alice Bryan and Gene met, and for the last three years of her life, Alice Bryan had the happiness of being engaged to Gene. Always hoping to become well enough to feel that it would not be unfair to risk burdening him with her osteomeyelitis, she continued to fill her hope chest with lovely linen, and exchange daily letters with Gene. This period overlapped the year of my own engagement and the first year of my marriage, and the difference between what life had given *me* and was denying *Alice Bryan* continually weighed on my heart. But in Alice Bryan's there was no room for bitterness; that made it all the more poignant.

During our trip to South America and Africa, Mother, in her usual way, kept a diary. Pages are filled with her beautiful script, and never a smudge. She writes of our departure from New York:

120

Tuesday, January 24th, 1928
New York & later at sea

Weather, fair and cold. A beautiful day. We wakened at 7:30, dressed and hurried to breakfast, finished packing our bags, and left the Waldorf for Pier 59 at 10:00. Mrs. Decker, Bill's mother, his sister, Maxine, and Elizabeth and I, went in a taxi, and Alice Bryan, Vivian, and Bill, in another. The Deckers all went on board with us and looked it over. I had to leave them to reserve our deck chairs and our table sitting. Before I had finished, the boat's whistle blew for all to go ashore, except passengers, and I hurried on deck to wave to our friends on the pier. Before we were out of sight of New York, the bugle blew for lunch. After lunch, we unpacked, rested, took a bath, had dinner, and then the girls danced in the lounge, as Alice Bryan and I watched. By nine o'clock the boat was beginning to rock. By eleven, we were really getting into a storm, which lasted all night.

In her diary for the next day, Mother describes the severity of the storm, for we were opposite that "Graveyard of the Atlantic," Cape Hatteras:

The wind was blowing a hundred-and-twenty-five miles an hour. There was lightening every few moments. Rain, so thick it could have been a fog, the foghorns, blowing every minute – I timed it by the clock. Elizabeth and I watched it through a porthole for a long time. It was thrilling to see the huge waves. Vivian and Alice Bryan can't hold up their heads. Elizabeth has eaten three meals. I only had orange juice. After breakfast we went up on the top deck and talked to the pilot about the storm. The boat was rocking so that we had to hold to the rail. We lost four hours last night. Part of our ship's rigging blew away. Alice Bryan got up for dinner, but left the table at once. Vivian didn't get up. Few passengers out of bed today.

The diary treats shipboard life in detail. It records a masquerade ball where costumes have been provided by the ship's hostess and, with a mother's pride, Mother sets down that:

Elizabeth was beautiful as the Snow Queen, and won first prize. Vivian, with her coal black hair, was an enchanting gypsy.

On one of the long stretches at sea, almost a full page of the diary is given to describing a ball that had been held the night before. The imaginative ship's hostess had thought up what I still think is one of the most amusing things in the world. For that kind of occasion, the dancers drew numbers. A few of the numbers matched, but in the main, the numbers matched broomsticks. And if there's anything funnier than watching a dance floor of individuals moving in step as they keep time with a broomstick, I don't know what it is. Some of them took it so seriously, and they were the funniest. Others threw off inhibitions and clowned, even to flirting with their broomsticks with light conversation and beguiling laughter. Either way, it was side-splitting. Mother tells this:

> Elizabeth was one of those who drew a broomstick, but she was saved by the nice, tall, young red-headed man from San Francisco, who hurried across the room to say that he had her matching number.

If it was on the island of Trinidad that I had initially succumbed to the charm of bamboo, it would be in Barbados that I would come under the spell of its Planter's Punch. I was only eighteen, and except for homemade wine, sherry with cod liver oil and in desserts, and the sugar in the bottom of Father's toddy glass, I had never had any alcohol. But since Barbados was the home of that delectable iced drink made with rum, and called Planter's Punch, it seemed in order to investigate.

The day was what, on cruises was called, a "free day." We were in port, passengers left to their own devices. A New York bachelor, a Mr. Walsh, possibly in his late thirties, asked me to go for a drive with a native driver around the island and to have lunch. Mother's policy with her daughters was always to give them complete freedom, and I accepted the invitation. It was at lunch in a hotel by the sea that this Mr. Walsh felt that I should sample the island's favorite drink, and, with my consent, ordered one for each of us. Sitting on a cool porch, surrounded by tropical growth, and very hot from our drive, I took mine at a gulp, and since it seemed much like lemonade, without too much encouragement, I took a second.

By the time we returned to the ship, under delayed reaction, I had become enlightened about Planter's Punch. I could see why Bishop Cheshire, when he came around visiting in our parish, had always called this his favorite drink. It is endearing even now, to find in the back of Mother's old cookbook, with yellow smudges suggestive of cake batter, in her own handwriting,

Bishop Cheshire's Planter's Punch:

2 tablespoons sugar
Juice of 1/2 lemon
1 tablespoon rum
crushed ice

On shipboard, in the early part of the day, the Mr. Walsh of the Planter's Punch was pleasant to be around. But as the day wore on, he spent more and more time in the bar. Mother tells of an incident that came about one night:

Elizabeth is furious with Mr. Walsh. She was dancing tonight, when he came up to break in, and had hardly danced a step when he spoke angrily, "Aren't you ashamed of yourself, for dancing with that Jew?" Elizabeth answered, "Aren't you ashamed of yourself for saying that? He's a nice man and a good dancer." And with that, Mr. Walsh left her standing in the middle of the floor.

A few days later, Mother comments:

At tonight's dance, Mr. Walsh came up to where Alice Bryan and I were, and sat down by me. He said, "Why won't Elizabeth dance with me anymore?" He knows very well why she won't dance with him. But I said, "Until you apologize to her, she never will." Poor Mr. Walsh, so handsome and so well-groomed, but drinking so badly that people are beginning to shun him. I can't help but feel sorry for him.

Another excerpt:

Sunday, April 1
At sea in the Gulf of Aden

Hot, but a fine breeze. Elizabeth and I were the only ones to get up for breakfast. Alice Bryan not feeling well, and Vivian was up too late. Burrows, our dining room steward, reminded us that it was April Fool's Day by serving Elizabeth a plate with a silver cover over it – nothing underneath. After that, I had fun fooling people. Mrs. Ayres was the first one. I told her that her dress had a terrible tear in the back. She was distressed enough, until I told her "April Fool!" I also fooled Mr. Dermit the same way about a tear in the back of his jacket, and many others. The concert last night was very good. $1,130.00 was the amount given the musicians. They are paid to play, but have been so accommodating, we wanted to give them this in appreciation. I've been sneezing all day. Took some aspirin and lay down after lunch and slept an hour. Alice Bryan is better and on deck tonight. We entered the Gulf of Aden about nine this morning. Enjoyed seeing the mountains and the town of Aden from the deck. There is a fort there, English, of course.

On our longest period at sea, ten days, a man died of a heart attack. He and his wife had had the table next to ours in the dining room, and Mother records that with the message, she hurried to Mrs. Oliver's stateroom to offer her sympathy and her help. The purser took charge of the arrangements for the body to be received on our landing in Rio, where subsequent arrangements would be made. Mrs. Oliver, in her dignity, and her unselfishness toward the other passengers, was an example to be emulated. With her encouragement, shipboard dancing went on as usual each night.

It was perfectly natural that under the romance of life at sea, Vivian and I should have proposals of marriage. Her two main beaux both happened to be from the Americas, although far apart from each other. One was a South American, the other, a Canadian. My three were varied: California, England, and Hungary. The one from California, although he had inherited business interests, in that he had a beautiful, well-trained singing voice, did concerts, and was often called upon to give us concerts when we were at sea. He was tall, with wavy bronze hair, was thoughtful, had a nice personality, and was impressive when he stood by the piano and in his deep voice, sang from operatic scores. I can hear him now, starting out slowly in his deep bass tones, *"Oh I-sis, and O-si-ris,"* which seemed incongruous with the person with whom I danced, and swam, and usually, when we were having luncheon on shore, sat by, and with whom afterward, I shopped for souvenirs.

The one from England had some shipping interests, and being of the turn of mind that I am about England, I might have been swayed by his beautiful diction and his courtesy, but I had no intention of allowing myself to fall in love with anybody but an American, which I had already done, although I was not ready for commitment.

The third proposal, from the Hungarian, was a citizen of Budapest, and since his name was hard to pronounce, the other passengers spoke of him as "Buddha." To me, Buddha was the most attractive of the three. I suppose

I could almost have fallen in love with the way he said one certain word, "veat." His business interests in Hungary were in importing wheat, and the way he said, "I was in your country last year in Chicago, buying veat," was adorable, like some darling child. Buddha and I shared a passion for table tennis – or ping-pong – and at the end of the cruise, we both won prizes. We kept up our friendship until after Tom and I were married and deliriously happy with the birth of our firstborn. I had promised to cable him the news. His answering cable preceded the arrival of a silver spoon. The cable read: "Congratulations on the arrival of the Crown Prince."

With the revelation that Alice Bryan had been able to weather several sea voyages and that they had brought her pleasure, Mother began to talk of booking passage for a cruise around the world. In the back of her mind was the hope that when we had made the major part of the trip which would bring us to Europe, Alice Bryan might, in Vienna, see the world's foremost authority on orthopedics, a Dr. Lorenz. Now, for the first time, I find myself going back to put together the steps which may have led Mother to that decision.

And here I go into the digression to end all digressions.

Cousin Johnny Sherrod, son of Dr. John Sherrod, Grandma Bryan's brother, had always seemed to be Mother's favorite cousin. While Elizabeth Sherrod, or "Bettie" – to become Bryan – at marriage, had left Rainbow Banks in Martin County, at first for Granville County, and then for Edgecombe, her brother, John, the Civil War surgeon, had stayed on, on the Sherrod land. He and his wife, my great Aunt Lou, had only one child, a son, John, or to us, "Cousin Johnny."

Cousin Johnny was much indulged. So much so, that when he went to the University at Chapel Hill, he took with him his own body servant.

Cousin Johnny had a winning personality; something of a gay blade, with friends everywhere. But in his late twenties, he was stricken with total paralysis. Except for his speech, and barely enough life in one arm to hold a cigar in that hand and puff gently on it through the day, his life came to a standstill. His parents had died early, and since, after his illness, he was under the care of doctors in Richmond, it was there that he went to live. He had a large comfortable house in what was known as Ginter Park. The house was well-run by a competent staff, including a combination houseman and driver, who, with the help of one of his trained nurses, occasionally took him out for a drive.

One of these nurses was a Miss Beard, who had come highly recommended. All Cousin Johnny's relatives came to know her well, for this poor man loved having his relatives come for visits, and Miss Beard seemed to be something of a coordinator of the household. In that way, the whole of the two clans – the Bryans and the Sherrods – became fond of her. Yet, there was seemingly little levity in Miss Beard's nature. She was a large woman, tall and heavy, her face was full and ruddy, her mouth, tiny. Mother often said, not unkindly, but as a matter of fact, "Miss Beard presses out her words."

Her uniform and her nurse's cap were starched. Her long, stiff sleeves always had their gold cufflinks in place, her cap, with its little puff on top was never even slightly askew. But we could tell that she had become Cousin Johnny's security. We knew she was good and kind. Even so, it was a shock to have him marry her – Cousin Johnny, *of all people*!

He may not have been entirely selfish in doing this; it would, and did, ensure her future financially. With the marriage, off came the uniform, and at breakfast, Miss Beard – for we continued to call her that – would sit at the end of the table and pour coffee from the Sherrod service. So that, everything seemed to fall into place in the best way, that, under the circumstances, it could. Mother's only disparaging comment would be one made in private: "It's a pity for the best of the Sherrod silver to go out of the family, which it will. But then, Miss Beard takes good care of Johnny, and she deserves it."

All this is by way of saying, that when Cousin Johnny died – which came a year after we had taken the South African cruise during which Alice Bryan had managed to stay well – another travel-plan began to form in Mother's mind. Its high point would be the hope of having Alice Bryan see Dr. Lorenz in Vienna. And in that Miss Beard was now free, Mother could approach her with an invitation to join us, not in her capacity as nurse, but as friend and relative. For by now, Miss Beard had become a wealthy woman; she could easily afford the trip, and she readily accepted the invitation.

This meant days and weeks and months of shipboard intimacy on those long stretches at sea, of being seated together daily at our assigned table for five in the dining room, of being served by the same steward, and of our being together, generally. Would there be enough points of congeniality with a personality so unlike our own to invite so much prolonged intimacy?

For we had inherited a love of laughter and the play of the mind from both sides of the family, especially from the Irishness of the Bryans. But Miss Beard was intelligent, she read a lot, she had a very real admiration for Mother, she loved Alice Bryan, and she seemed to enjoy being with all of us. We decided that it would all work out, and it did. But for Miss Beard, I doubt that we would have undertaken the trip.

Miraculously, Alice Bryan did stay well, and that appointment of long standing which had been made by her Philadelphia doctors, was filled. This meant that toward the end of the trip we would leave the ship at Cherbourg and by pre-arrangement, would be met there by car and driver for the motor trip to Vienna, Florence, and Rome, leaving Miss Beard at Cherbourg to go back to America alone. As planned, we would have an audience with the Pope. In those days, this was widely done by tourists. Since women were not allowed to enter a Roman Catholic church bare-headed, black veils, or those little round white lace caps for borrowing were kept on hand by virgers at the door.

I remember very little about the ceremony and where it took place, except that it was in some part of the Vatican. For this august occasion, we were received by vergers in a large rectangular room with gilded straight chairs against the wall. Properly veiled, we sat waiting for what seemed a very long time. Then suddenly, at a signal from the vergers, we all knelt. The doors opened, and the Pope, followed by two Cardinals, entered. As we knelt, this high symbol of the church making his rounds among us, we each kissed his ring. In our own case, as Protestants, that our church had long ago broken with Rome made no difference. There was a feeling of awe at being in the presence of His Eminence.

Mother had worked out the mechanics of this experience herself, just as she had arranged, when we were in Paris, to use her letter of credit to increase our travelling funds. After that important visit to the bank, back in our hotel room, she divided bills of enormous size among us to be worn in those little aids to travel found in New York department stores called "bosom friends." These were two-inch square envelopes made of pale pink silk with a matching pink ribbon on either side to be attached to the straps of a lady's lingerie. There were no zippers then, but concealed fasteners made the bills secure. Mother was continually teaching us by example that where there's a will, there's a way. Thus individually equipped, I can remember with some humor, that after Mother's visit with her letter of credit to the bank in Paris, we sometimes travelled with as much as four thousand dollars riding safely on the collective family bosom. And by today's reckoning, I gather that would have been around twenty thousand dollars or more. Mother must have felt that we just might be stranded on an Alp as we went over this most beautiful of mountain ranges.

Naturally, our driver knew none of this. Luckily, he was an honorable man who spoke some English, and kindly put up with our fractured French as, with our guidebooks, we tried to get the most out of what we were seeing.

The cruise proper was to last six months, but adding another month's stay in Europe at the end in order for Alice Bryan to see Dr. Lorenz and probably have treatment, we rearranged our plans to be away for seven. We left for the long journey the first of December of 1929. Tom and I had become engaged that summer, the wedding planned for the following October. And although, in planning for the trip, I was torn by the thought of our long separation, I would not, for anything, have gone back on the plans Mother had made for giving Alice Bryan this final pleasure as a family, in a search of her health.

Mother was in the room in Vienna when the famous Dr. Lorenz examined Alice Bryan. She was to hear words that would break a mother's heart. "My child," said Dr. Lorenz, sadly, seeing her scars on her shoulders, her ribs, her arms and her legs, "You have suffered more than Christ."

Through some miracle Alice Bryan's face had been spared, which is not always true of osteomyelitis. She had seen the scars on the faces of other patients in hospitals who had the same disease, and always expected her own to be disfigured. It never was, and each bout with her affliction seemed, somehow, to add further radiance to her Madonna-like beauty, her brown hair parted in the middle, coiled low on her neck, and pinned in what was spoken of as a "Psyche." Dr. Lorenz confirmed the fact that nothing could be done for Alice Bryan to ward off further infections, which was, to us, no surprise, but we felt better for having made that final effort.

However, before filling this appointment with Dr. Lorenz in the spring, we would have the winter months on the far side of the world. As I had expected before leaving home, of these travel memories, China would take precedence; my brief stay in Tientsin has already been described. Then came Peking, and Shanghai, and Hong Kong. And although Singapore was then a crown colony, in that its population was mainly Chinese, I felt that it too, was a part of the mainland.

Our four lovely, cold days in Peking were each filled with exhilaration: that of walking on the Great Wall, of visiting the Summer Palace of the Emperor, and of climbing the innumerable steps to the Temple of Heaven. Coming into the warmth of a luxury hotel at the end of the day would have been enough, for the evening meal was superb. But after that there was another high moment for the female passengers of our cruise, when amiable Chinese tailors came, by appointment, to our hotel rooms. This was a period when travellers to China, without leaving their rooms, might make choices from bolts of beautiful silks to be made into garments, sometimes to be made overnight, complete with the embroidery of monograms. With our several days in Peking, a family of all girls, we made selections right and left. And true to her unselfish nature, Alice Bryan happily took part in the decisions connected with the collecting of my trousseau. The bulk of my lingerie was made there, and I bought a muted figured bronze and gold robe with matching slippers for Tom. My wedding veil, I would get later, in Florence.

But as joyous as I was with plans for my future, with the ever-present dancing with attractive men and the ship's officers that went on, both on shipboard, and when we were in port, there was always the shadow in my life that Alice Bryan could only watch from the sidelines.

...that favored spot! Where people have individuality and kindliness, and where oddities are tolerated, nay, greatly loved for the sake of the individual.

Mrs. Gaskell, *Cranford*

AT THE FALLS OF THE TAR

≈ ≈ ≈

W hen the well-known writer of historical novels of the coastal area of North Carolina, Inglis Fletcher, came to that area to write and to make it her home, in a sense, she was returning to her roots. In an interview a few years later, at the pinnacle of her profession, as always, gracious, she made this telling comment: "When I was considering coming, I realized, from having parked my car with its windows down on the main streets of a number of Eastern Carolina's town and villages, that it is an area where people laugh a lot."

Perhaps Mrs. Fletcher was right. A part of the tendency may come from a background of tale-telling, of recognizing the lighter side of life as an element in cohesiveness and, therefore, worthy of our time. We're inclined to make the most of a story, to spin it out, give it a little drama. Any chance meeting at the post office may become a visit to the village well, always with the come and go of laughter.

Incurably Tarheelian, two males, a world away from their native soil, might, on being introduced, fall easily and pleasurably and facetiously into the familiar country vernacular of, "See ya tomorrow if the creek don't rise." And no matter if the two should happen to be dining on nightingale's tongue in the most sophisticated of all the restaurants in South America, Europe, Asia, Africa, or Australia, from their incurably tarred heels, one might say to the other, "Where in the devil in this man's town can you get some grits?" With that word from holy writ, the friendship would be sealed in blood.

Should it be the rendezvous of old friends meeting somewhere in North Carolina, at football games, or in the halls of the State Capitol in Raleigh, and not having seen each other for some time, in greeting, as they shake hands, one might say to the other, "Hey, Sport! Wheah ya bin? Haven't seen you in a coon's age," the answer might then be, "I bin workin' on the back side of the fahm!" Tom was always answering that way, for although he was a lawyer with business interests, in that we had farms as well, he enjoyed that grassroots characterization that kept him feeling close to the land.

It may have been that in overhearing these jocular greetings Inglis Fletcher recognized a proclivity for laughter, something that has been bred into us, and that it is sustained by the healthful attitude of, "What better to laugh at than ourselves?" It's an attitude that often bubbles up, even in newspapers over the state.

But all this is not to say that North Carolinians don't have any gray matter to speak of. We just don't want it to show. We seem steeped in our state motto: Esse Quam Videri; to be, rather than to seem. We may tell you that we wouldn't like to have to live anywhere else, but it would not be done in a bragging way. We would leave our reasons for you to find out.

A few years ago, in a delightful story, one of the papers gave us the news that North Carolina would soon have a nudist colony east of Raleigh, not even in the metropolitan area of the Research Triangle, nor in the cosmopolitan scenic section of the mountains, but possibly sixty miles from our own Eastern Carolina town, near the Virginia line. The camp was making ready to open in the rural section of Vance County, near the town of Kittrell. We were told that several families had signed a petition opposing the vacation resort, but we gathered that the agitation was mild. Off-hand responses were generally that it was ridiculous. Others held that it was immoral; some didn't venture either yay or nay, they just shrugged and went on with whatever it was that they were doing.

Anne S. Milton, whose property was across the road from the proposed camp site, went into it a bit further. In an interview, she was quoted as having said, "We're not country hicks. We just don't believe in this sort of thing. We think it's degrading. How would you like this to move into your neighborhood? And with no way to stop it!"

The newspaper article continued, "Since they first heard of the resort a couple of weeks ago, local business leaders have been trying to find a way to talk about it without giggling. In the office of the Henderson/Vance County Chamber of Commerce, secretary Betty Smith doesn't just blush when someone says the word "nudist camp," she turns crimson. There used to be a settlement in the area, but with the coming of the railroad, most of the families moved to nearby Henderson and left Kittrell mostly to farmers like Mrs. Milton.

'Yeah, us and the sheepflies,' Mrs. Milton said after a day in the garden. Lifting the leg of her jeans, she exposed an ankle swollen and red with insect bites.

'I don't know what fun they're going to have over there with their clothes off,' she said of the camp across the road. 'I don't want to say it would serve them right... But we'll see what happens.' "

Morals aside, I'm aware that, to those of us who find it hard to understand that kind of commitment to the body beautiful, Mrs. Milton comes across as a pillar of common sense. I think the attitude of two of our neighboring states, Virginia and South Carolina, might be something of the same. For these are the two in which we feel most at home, and therefore, love best. Indeed, the four states of the Eastern Seaboard, Virginia, North Carolina, South Carolina, and Georgia, are all a lot alike. The speech in each, however, has variations. It's in a Virginian's pronunciation of "house" as "hoose," and "out" as "oot." In South Carolina, "dead" becomes "day'ed," and "late," "lay'et." Georgians in certain areas, say "ligh'at" for "light," or "nigh'at" for "night." And so on. Just what the distinguishing mark of North Carolina's speech is, I'm not quite sure, but apparently it's there. People spot it right away. Of one thing I'm completely certain, however. We will never, ourselves, make the word "Carolina" into something less than beautiful. For as my sister, Vivian, used to say, "The only "r" we roll is in Carolina." *Not* to roll it in that word is awful. For it was from Queen Caroline herself that our state took its lovely name. To pronounce it "Cal-lina" is beyond the pale. The twin sister states, North and South Carolina, sound totally unlike themselves in that version.

The state of Tennessee, another of North Carolina's neighbors, while just as southern as the Tidewater and Coastal states, seems far away from Eastern Carolina. South Carolina and Virginia have the same climate as ours, the same vegetation, and the same way of life. Most of us have friends and relatives in both South Carolina and Virginia. Until the 1930s, some of our relatives other than Cousin Johnny Sherrod lived in Richmond, and since the hospital and the specialists in Richmond were those nearest us, although I had schoolmates in South Carolina, and went there to house parties, I always felt closer to Virginia. So it was that I enjoyed the little story that came to me one day recently when a visiting Virginian and her local hostess came to tea.

This Virginia lady happened to live in the town of Portsmouth. At one point, her Bishop was in London for the Lambeth Conference, that convention of the Bishops that the Anglican communion, approximately every ten years, has at Lambeth Palace "to confer, but not to define doctrine, or to legislate on ecclesiastical matters." In a conversation between two Bishops, a certain English Bishop asked a certain American

Bishop where he was from.

The reply was, "From the Diocese of Southern Virginia."

The other man of the cloth disclosed that he was having trouble placing that diocese, and went on to say, "Can you *tell* me just where it *is?*"

Our American Bishop won the day when he answered that inquiry with another: "Well, my Good Sir, you've heard of *Yorktown*, haven't you?"

And the Good Sir agreed that he had.

But, if Mrs. Fletcher, when she was among us, heard the sound of laughter, another last summer's visitor gained a completely different impression. This young man was a farmer from Poland who had never heard southern speech. After being shown about in our community on the first day of his visit, he turned to his host and remarked, "These people, when they talk, it sounds like they're singing." However unique this observation, I find it delightful. It conjures up a picture of us as a flock of canaries, or as members of an ongoing opera. In either case, it's pleasant to think that he defines us lyrical.

≈ ≈ ≈

With the coming of the railroad shops several miles to the south of our town, in what we spoke of as "South Rocky Mount," five thousand people were gradually added to our population, and the town began to grow. For in the way that earlier towns had sprung up around rivers, towns later began to concentrate around railroads. In our case, the railroad followed the county line, placing us partly in Edgecombe, partly in Nash. Soon there would be two men's clubs, the Sagamore, and the Elks, and there would be a woman's exchange. Boarding houses near the railway station would be replaced by a large, and in our eyes, magnificent hotel, The Ricks. The smaller hotel, The Cambridge, would, for a few years, still exist.

Mrs. Nichols would teach China painting; Mrs. Lacey would give coaching in English. Miss Virginia Kyser, later Mrs. Carleton Noel, whose brother, Kay Kyser would attain radio fame with his "College of Musical Knowledge," would teach music appreciation. Virginia and Carleton Noel were to have no children, but after Virginia's death and Carlton's second marriage to my first cousin, Annie Lou Mayo Holt, Annie Lou's nieces and nephews, the children of her sister, Lucy, who, of course, was my first cousin as well, and of Lucy's husband, Boddie Bunn, became, in theory, the Noels' own children.

Now that I'm into this tangled subject, I will confuse the reader even more by including – for the record – that this Boddie Bunn would later become Bunn Boddie. Both he and his children, Nick, Mayo, and Lucy Ann, who was to marry Joe Brewer, were born at the family plantation, Rose Hill. To inherit the land, it was necessary for Boddie, then Boddie Bunn, to change his surname to Boddie.

This stipulation, that the property remain in the Boddie line, must have come to light in somebody's will. That far-sighted ancestor could not possibly have foreseen what this Rose Hill Plantation would come to mean to our community. Generous and public-spirited, the three inheritors of the plantation have continued to be one of our leading families. In an arrangement among themselves, Mayo Boddie came to own Rose Hill, and it has more than come into its own. Little was needed in the way of restoration, but with superlative taste, the house, its grounds, and the surrounding areas – still being farmed – have become in every way distinguished, a source of pride to our community, with which it is generously shared.

Since this name-changing in the Boddie Bunn or Bunn Boddie family went on when I was still a child, the proceedings are hazy, but it was often discussed in our family, and my impression is that the change required the consent of the legislature. I can remember hearing the grown-ups say that Boddie Bunn had changed his name in order to "heir" his land. For the word "heir," as both noun and verb, permeated conversation in those days. "Who heired what" was of great interest, as was whether or not the property inherited had been entailed. There was a prevailing feeling that keeping land in the blood line was important. The practice is still occasionally followed today.

This attitude toward the holding of land had often been the approach on both sides of my own family. Possibly even as early as when they had an acre and a few sheep in West Riding, England, they must have felt that we were meant to be people of the land. There were more lucrative ways of making money, but to invest in them heavily would, to us, have seemed short-sighted. A sprinkling of investments in commercial enterprises was a good idea for balance, but to have put all the eggs in one basket without the backing of land would have been considered unwise.

Land was something to be held onto as a hedge against a fluctuating economy. Perhaps it was in this philosophy that with the crash of 1929, when people were leaping to their deaths from windows in high buildings in cities, it hardly caused a ripple in our family's reserves. At that time, Father had been dead several years. Mother had been holding things together as best she could, and it was in that year that she took my sisters and me, comfortably, on what was to be a seven-months' voyage around the world. The year before, she had taken us on a five-months' voyage around South America and Africa, so that actually, out of twenty-four months, we spent twelve at sea, on luxury liners. That we had been able to do this at that economically uncertain time seemed to underscore the validity of the generation-to-generation family attitude toward the ownership of land. The attitude came to us from both sides.

And, although, in that both my grandfathers died before I was born, I knew them only through hearsay, Grandpa Braswell emerges as the most colorful of the two. Two remarks of his are still quoted.

I suppose that in early days, land sales must have taken place at county seats; the ones of which I was aware in my time all seemed to have gone on in Rocky Mount on what was spoken of as the "Planters Bank Corner." My impression is that they went on on Saturdays. Advance information having gone out, at noon a cluster of people would gather on that corner for the sale. In spite of the fact that Grandpa Braswell would say, sagaciously, to his sons, "Never buy land at a sale where there's a band," he would often come away from such occasions having just added to his store of acres more of what he spoke of as "God's fertile handiwork." Now and then, knowing what Grandpa's jolly reply would be, an affectionate bystander would ask, "Squire Braswell, why do you keep on buying land?"

"Well John," or Joe, or Dick, "I just don't want anybody to join me!"

But back to the story of our town. A railroad center, Rocky Mount, came early to have a YMCA. As time went on, the need for a YWCA was felt, as well, and funds were raised. Now, this many years later, we have a magnificent facility for women. Its work in the community is outstanding. Although the list of the many women who have brought this about would be a long one, much of the credit for its current and ongoing success is due Betsy Boddie, wife of the Nick Boddie of the Rose Hill story.

The Rocky Mount Cotton Mill is usually spoken of as the "Rocky Mount Mills." This plural term must have come about because at one time a long galvanized duct for blowing the cotton crossed the road from one building to another. The mill is probably the oldest structure in our town. Built in 1818, and at the time of the Civil War, making fabric for the uniforms of the soldiers of the Confederacy, it was burned by Union forces. But in two years it had been rebuilt, and has since been in continuous operation. From the beginning, the distinguished Battle family have been part owners, and have furnished seven of its presidents. Thomas B. Battle, my cousin, my Uncle Mark Braswell's grandson, is currently serving in that capacity.

At some point, there came to be a small secretarial school, and to add liveliness to the town's diversions, we had an opera house for assorted entertainment, almost everything except Grand Opera. By that time, there was a ball park as well.

I believe it was in some connection with The Woman's Exchange that Miss Nell Gupton Battle, the young widow of Judge Jacob Battle, and mother of two small daughters, Dorothy and Mary Long, started a small lending library. The outgrowth of this was the establishment of our public library, the Thomas Hackney Braswell, a memorial to Uncle Mark's twelve year old son. That sadness had caused Uncle Mark to give up the practice of medicine, for he had failed to suspect appendicitis when his young son developed a stomachache. By the time a raging fever had set in, and the deathly ill boy could be rushed by train to Richmond, peritonitis had developed and there was no hope. The sorrow would always be with Uncle Mark, one so deep that he covered it up with a certain crustiness. Among his relatives and his friends, his sharp remarks, quoted in affectionate amusement, would make the rounds.

The three Braswell brothers had all built Greek Revival homes; ours was in the village, the other two, in town. Uncle Mark's and Aunt Mamie's house sat two blocks from Main Street. Its backyard adjoined Uncle Jim's, whose house sat on Church Street. The homes were similar in size: each had large columns, wide porches, balconies, and porte-cocheres. Today these last would be spoken of as "carports."

In those days, porte-cocheres were decorative, their wide arches rising from brick pillars with elevated flower boxes between. On the opposite side of the arches, the high bottom step up to the side porch would be concrete. It would be both wide and deep for the convenience of alighting from carriages. Roads were still unpaved, and often muddy, so that vehicles had to have large wheels and sit high off the ground.

The Mrs. Sorsby/Uncle Mark episode came on a summer morning. Uncle Mark was out in his car, and, as was true of that period, those who had learned to drive in middle life never really mastered the art, nor would Mrs. Sorsby. Indeed, just the week before, Mrs. Sorsby had taken her car out alone for the first time, and once she had gotten going, had not been able to stop. And so she went round and round a downtown block until some sympathetic bystander jumped up onto the running board, which in those days would have been wide, reached over Mrs. Sorsby's plump form, and was able to reach under the steering wheel and thrust the spark all the way up. As the motor gradually died, he urged Mrs. Sorsby to put her foot on the brake – not on the clutch – and in this way, they managed to avert disaster. Since Uncle Mark and Mrs. Sorsby were neighbors, it was inevitable that they would at some time collide. When this happened, it took place on the most prominent corner in town, that of the Planter's Bank. People rushed to the rescue from all directions, but the collision was more frightening than serious, the two drivers hurriedly getting out to assess the damage.

Mrs. Sorsby began first, with apologies, "Oh, Dr. Braswell, I'm so sorry. It was all my fault."

"No, indeed," replied Uncle Mark. "The fault was entirely mine. I was sitting on my porch ten minutes ago, and saw you drive by. I should have known better than to come out!"

Even after cars had arrived, with the small salaries that ministers used to be paid, it would be a long time before they could afford such a luxury. And so it was, that Roddy Murchison, father of a family, and a devout Episcopalian, knowing that Mr. Diehl, the rector of the Church of The Good Shepherd, needed transportation on one Sunday of each month to the small town of Spring Hope, thirty miles away, in order to conduct Evening Prayer there, offered to drive the good man over.

When the two arrived at the church, and were getting out of the car, Mr. Diehl, picking up the small black bag that held his vestments, asked solicitously, "Roddy, have you cut off the gas and the oil?"

Uncle Mark, and Father, and Uncle Jim all loved baseball, and frequently took groups of their male friends with them to New York for the World Series. Their wives never went, but women had begun to enjoy the local ball games, and through the warm summer days, dressed in their cooling lawns, they would attend. And here I have to stop and look up the real meaning of the word "lawn," one so familiar to me, and yet so seldom used now. I find that it is a sheer linen or cotton fabric, sometimes printed. "Sprigged lawn" was another familiar term, for on a hot day, the delicacy of the design added to the impression of freshness.

Through Irene Castle, a famous New York dancer, bobbed hair had come in, but it would be slow to be taken up by mothers. Tortoise shell hairpins still held their chignons and their pompadours in place, and though in the twenties, a small inconsequential "beauty parlor" came to Main Street, older women stuck to the old ways, relying on the faithful "kid-curlers" for their soft waves. These so called kid-curlers were made of fine wire covered with gray kid-glove leather. For an hour or two before special occasions, two or three of these curlers might be placed about the face under what was called a "boudoir cap" to make waves, but only in the privacy of home.

And on the subject of women and their hair, only a modicum of travel to other parts of the world with visits to museums would be necessary to make any woman feel a bond with women over the ages, when she sees, in glass cases, the variety of tools which women throughout history have used in the effort to make their hair beautiful. Some of these would have been tortuous. They vary from museum to museum and country to country, but the worst I've ever come upon have been something from three to four inches long, apparently made of iron, but now crusted over and black, and resembling nothing so much as what we used to call a "ten-penny-nail." Could this have been in Tuscany? I believe so.

As far as *men* and vanity goes, I find it soothing to read, on the authority of a former Eton don in the "Lyttelton Hart-David Letters," six volumes that are now some of my favorite reading, that "Milton, like all Puritans, according to Macaulay, had invincible pride before man, and utter humility before God; that there is no evidence that he was proud of his poetry, but plenty that he was vain about his blindness not spoiling his looks; that Julius Caesar wasn't a bit proud of straddling the world like a colossus, but was vain of his looks, and liked the senate's permission to wear the laurel wreath on his bald head more than all his other honors." So there we are.

And so it was in our town, that in the era of our afternoon ball games, some of our ladies, delicately waved, lightly scented with toilet water, and, as they attended, sometimes using their palm-leaf fans, developed a real interest in the sport.

There were a few card clubs: Rook for the women, and Setback for the men. In spite of the fact that Tarboro was sixteen miles from my village of Battleboro, and Rocky Mount was only eight, in my early days, our family seemed to have had more contact with Tarboro than with Rocky Mount, and on certain nights, Father, and Mother's brother, Uncle Hugh, and some of the other plantation owners, would drive the sixteen miles there, at first by horse, then by car, to play Setback or Whist, perhaps a little poker. It's amusing to me today, to be aware that the small, quiet, old town of Tarboro not only has always had a poker club among men, but that one would also develop among women, in which mothers still pass their memberships down to their daughters, and meet for the game one night a week. I find this engaging, and at intervals will inquire of one of my cousins, "How's the Poker Club?" to be told, "Going strong!" And this in a small courthouse town in Eastern Carolina that will always carry a strong flavor of the old.

In Tarboro, there always has seemed to be a lot of "old money." Originally, incomes came from plantations. Gradually, landowners moved to town and continued to supervise their farming operations with the help of an overseer who lived on the land. This supervision required only half a day. With the custom of large midday meals, it was easy to follow them with a nap. The rest of the afternoon might be spent in the companionship of other men as they played Setback or Whist or Poker. These small gatherings inevitably needed a name. And the members began to call themselves, facetiously, The Sons of Leisure.

At one point, there developed a crisis in the Sons of Leisure. At the time, Ely Staton was president, and was suddenly threatened with impeachment from this high office. A called meeting was held: Rumour had it that Ely had been seen one night chopping wood for his mother. Ely was quick to deny the charge, explaining, in this way, to set the record straight, "I was doing nothing of the kind. I was only holding the lantern for my mother while *she* chopped the wood."

Miss Sally Staton, possibly a relative of Ely's, was another town character. Miss Sally, Tarboro's first Vassar graduate, never married. During the first years of our own marriage, Tom and I enjoyed going to Tarboro for Sunday afternoon visits. For not only did we both have relatives there, but we found pleasure in dropping in on Miss Sally, as well.

We knew, amusingly, but of course, never brought it up, that, independent and fiesty as Miss Sally was, until the day of her death, she would sign her important papers and her checks as, "Miss Sally Staton, by choice."

Another Tarboro native, who, with her marriage, went to live at some distance, said, of her reasons for looking forward to returning for frequent visits to the town: "Tarboro is, as it was in the beginning, is *now*, and ever *shall* be, world without end."

With the establishment of Rocky Mount's first country club, and the building of its clubhouse in 1922, came golf. The rolling site was given the name of the large farm which had formerly belonged to the Bunn family, "Benvenue," a name from Scott's *Lady of the Lake*, which, translated, means "small hill." Fortunately, the Bunn home, built when Benjamin Hickman Bunn was our representative in Congress, still stands, and though it has changed hands, is in perfect condition and filled with family life.

Strangers who visit in our community sometimes comment on the fact that though we are a small town, there is, here, an air of sophistication. That, I believe, is due to our so long having had a tobacco market. From around the turn of the century we had buyers come from other countries, the Far East, especially. Many of our local young men of the time would go there to live for a few years and return, still to be allied with the local tobacco industry.

An amusing little incident relative to tobacco is the one in which my father, having completed three years at the University of Virginia and one at a business school in Poughkeepsie, New York, decided to join his own father in becoming a planter. With this, he became aware that in Eastern Carolina we should not rely solely on cotton for our economy. And so, from some Virginia connection, he ordered what he thought was a suitable amount of tobacco seed. Entirely unfamiliar with the seed, he sent in an order for a small barrelful, which throughout his life was to give him many laughs, for, as he said, it turned out that a barrel would have planted something in the nature of five counties.

At any rate, Father planted a number of acres and shared the seed with other farmers. Then, with delving into the subject, he began to see a need for a tobacco market. Although he owned a diversity of real estate in town, and had partners in a variety of enterprises, he decided to start a tobacco market in Battleboro, for the village at that time was still more active than the town of Rocky Mount. It had a telephone exchange, and three churches.

The village had several stores, two newspapers, the *Battleboro Gazette*, and the *Battleboro Advance*, and two saloons. Gradually, however, with the impetus of the coming of the railroad shops to what we called "South Rocky Mount," the village's progress gave way to the faster growing town of Rocky Mount, which would, in time, have three hospitals: one of three stories, one of two, and a smaller one, spoken of as "The Clinic." For these benefits and others, the people of the village, the countryside, and the town were grateful. But Battleboro, proud of its age, would begin to speak of itself as the "Mother of Rocky Mount." It has been suggested that because no land owner in the Battleboro community was willing to part with any of his acreage, the shops were built in Rocky Mount.

As late as 1950 or 1960, old timers were still recalling the story of this area's first tobacco market. Josh Horne, then publisher and editor of our Rocky Mount *Evening Telegram*, revived the tale in his weekly column of local history and reminiscence in this way:

Stolen Leaf Market
By AN OLD REPORTER

Stolen Tobacco Market - Since the Worthy Grand Matron could not get to tonight's meeting I'll take you on Sam as to what you remember, and I'm wondering if you were around these parts when Rocky Mount stole the tobacco market from Battleboro. Yes the word is "stole" and Uncle Sam Davis, (the former post office employee who has the fetching goatee of gray hair and who marches in parades everywhere in his uniform of Uncle Sam), does and he was a resident here about the time. It is in the record (just where we don't know) but the warehouse and tobacco storage and prizery stood in Battleboro long after the theft was perpetrated. In fact, Uncle Sam Davis said he went to school in the old prizery building as a boy.

It's pieced together that the late T.P. Braswell sent his oldest son the late M.C. (Mack) Braswell to school at the University of Virginia and it was while he was up there, that he saw growing tobacco and became interested in a cursory sort of way. When he returned to Battleboro he told his father what he had seen and recited its possibility as an additional crop that might lend itself to cultivation in Eastern Carolina – that was in the late '70s or the early '80s of the last century. In fact, the University of Virginia student set in motion a use of some of the farm land of his father, and with parental

144

approval, set about to get some tobacco seed. He wrote a fellow student to "send him ten pounds" as he wanted to plant an acreage on his father's farm. The Virginia chum wrote him back that unless he was planting all of Eastern Carolina he could hardly use ten pounds and that instead he was sending him five ounces. It was from that effort that tobacco sales and auction was begun in Battleboro.

But it is of record that the sale lasted but for one day, and that wound up the season for there was a lack of experience by the auctioneer that was supposed to cry the bids, the ticket-markers lost track of the last bid, the bookkeepers that followed the sale couldn't figure the fractional bids to get them down on paper or to find themselves in agreement and there were no bills going to the cashier whereby the grower of the tobacco could get payment for his product. It was confusion compounded upon confusion, which was rampant, until in the afternoon the first day of sales efforts was halted. Everyone that had brought tobacco that day was identified and he returned home empty-handed, but with a satisfied promise that they would be paid later – but not to bring any more to market for a second day's sale. That second day hasn't happened and that's been more than seventy years ago.

And at this point a man named S.S. Berger had established himself in Rocky Mount and built a warehouse, designed for the reception and storage of cotton, and other farm crops. It was on the site of the present Fenners Warehouse No. 1. It was operated first by Mr. Berger and for years by Bucker Davis who had a young auctioneer W.E. Fenner, who in later years succeeded Mr. Bucker Davis as its owner.

But Mr. Berger was a wizard at figures and an organizer and he began receiving tobacco in a quantity that he knew that he could market daily. He enlisted a Mr. Chevasse, (a Canadian whose English accent caused him to be known as "Dutch" Chevasse,) but an organizer and wizard as a mathematician. It was around these men that the Rocky Mount Tobacco Market had its inception and quickly J. O. W. Gravely and Charlie Cooper built warehouses that carried their names. For they, too, were able to find men who could systematize the marketing of tobacco, knew of the last and highest bid, what tobacco of the many grades might well be started at for the buyers' bidding, and two men who could with lightning rapidity total the fractional pounds and the fractional price and have them agree so that a bill might be sent to the office and payment received in a brief time by the waiting grower.

But in that day and time a bell was rung from a steeple at the front of the warehouse when the sale started. Not a bad idea – we think. But did that go out when acreage control came in?

Father lived to be sixty-one. In February of that year, he had a long siege with flu. It left him with a daily elevation of temperature which was not to be explained. Malaria, that ever-present malady among the lower areas of the South, was suspected. After some weeks of treatment for this, with no improvement, he was sent to a hospital in Richmond. Mother went with him, and in the way of the times, was allowed a bed in his hospital room. Father's temperature gradually subsided, and after three weeks the two of them were to leave on the following day when, in the middle of the night, Uncle Mark and Uncle Jim came to waken my sisters and me at home in North Carolina with the shock that Father had died, of a heart attack. There had been no warning. He had suddenly sat up in bed to call out "Oh Alice, Alice...," and breathed no more.

Among the letters of sympathy that came after Father's death was one from a person who, in our family, had always been called "Miss Virginia." For several years she had been governess to my sisters, and had gone on to become Mrs. McCandless, wife of a Virginia lawyer and mother of several children. She was bringing up her family in Tidewater Virginia. She writes of her shock and the distress of hearing of Father's death in this way:

> Saluda, Virginia
> Sunday night

My Dear Mrs. Braswell;

> I had just read in a Richmond paper a notice of Mr. Braswell's death, and I so hoped there might be some mistake, when the telephone rang and your telegram came telling me the awful truth of the death of your husband. How I wish I could be with you and the dear girls! I can think of nothing else, and my first impulse was to go, tomorrow, to Battleboro, but on thinking it over, I'm afraid I can't get off right now.
>
> My heart goes out to you, my dear friend, in this, your hour of greatest sorrow, and I long to do something to bring comfort to your broken heart. It will take me a long time to realize that he has been taken from you. The sessions that I spent in your home were sufficient for me to know what a splendid man he was. It seemed to me he measured up in every way to the ideal man – a devoted and always considerate father, husband and son; always unselfish and ever ready to do a kindly act for anyone whom he felt needed such. I feel his death keenly, for I know I've lost a friend. I am glad to have known him, for I'm sure this world is a better place because of the place he has taken in it.
>
> As time goes on, you will find just how much he meant to many

others outside his immediate family, for his charitable acts were not known, save by those for whom they were meant. In other words, he was a real friend of humanity – he loved life and all that went with it, and whilst we *know* he has gone to reap his just reward, it is hard for his loved ones to *understand* right now.

Be patient, have faith, and never forget that underneath are the everlasting arms. My deep love for you and the girls. If you feel that I could be of any real comfort or help to you, I might run down for a few days a little later. But you know just how hard it is for a mother to leave home on short notice. I shall wait patiently to hear all the particulars; you know I am interested. Write me when you can and tell me all. If you need me, let me know, and I shall make every effort to go to my sweet friend. In these few hours, since I received the sad news, I have been busy making plans for you. I'm so thankful you have your mother and Mr. Hugh. I know just what a comfort they will be!

Love again in which Mr. Evans and the children join – may God give you strength to bear your burden bravely is the prayer of one who is thinking constantly of you and yours.

Devotedly,
"Miss Virginia"

Miss Virginia's daughter, whom our family always spoke of as "Little Virginia," was to grow up and marry Brigadier General Joseph Puller, who, at one time, was in command of Camp Lejeune, the marine base in North Carolina. He was honored by having the important highway which connects points in the Tidewater section of Virginia to the city of Richmond named the General Joseph Puller Highway.

After their son, Louis, had become a paraplegic from the Korean War, his life demanded a courage of another kind. While not to win as many decorations as his father, Louis continued to make his own contribution to the military by writing a book on the Korean War for which he won a Pulitzer prize. Recently – and very sadly – under increasing depression, this brave young man took his life.

Although I had not been in touch with his mother for several years, I was eager to reach her with my sympathy. After several phone calls, I was able to have a conversation with her daughter, who now, with her own family, lives in Alexandria, Virginia. And I was to find out that her mother is now the victim of Alzheimer's, where, living in a suspended state, she was not even told of that final great sorrow.

≈ ≈ ≈

No doubt, in the homes of other families rooted in our community, there will be today a scattering of copies of a small old faded book, which bears the simple title, Rocky Mount. Its subtitle, The Peer of Any City in the Good Ol' North State, and the Rapidity of its Growth and Development. Obviously the product of an emerging chamber of commerce for this town of eight thousand, the book came out when I was a small child. Its language is so flowery that we wonder, now, that the writers didn't run out of adjectives. Its hundred-or-so pages are given to photographs and to the individuals who were helping to build the "Good Town" that was to become ours. In Father's photograph, his dark hair is parted on the side, he has a moustache, and is wearing a winged collar. In his double-breasted dark suit which emphasizes his full chest and the squareness of his shoulders, he is very much a man of his time, and to me, is wonderfully handsome.

Worth noting is the fact that eighty-five years later, as recently as last week, a friend of mine, Meg Teagarden, who had lived among us for seventeen years and then, drawn away to live in a number of other parts of our country, was to say when she came back for good, "in no other place have I found the people so friendly and so genteel as here."

Since that book of information regarding early Rocky Mount includes my Braswell grandfather and the part he played in the community, bringing out the fact that he was able to transmit that sense of community obligation to his three sons, and since the idea of writing something about the Braswells to be placed in the Wesleyan College Library originated with the college, it seems fitting to reprint, at the very end of my story, an account of the life of Thomas Permenter Braswell and his three sons. As a gesture to women, I have to inject a thought here. In the way of the times, among all the lauditory things that were said about my grandfather, emphasizing, in particular, the fact that he had "raised" three fine sons to take their places in laying foundations for a good community, there was not a single mention of the mother of these sons, my grandmother, Emily Stallings Braswell. Thank goodness our world is becoming more realistic. Fairer.

*No man who has ever whole-heartedly
laughed can be irrevocably bad.*

Thomas Carlyle

≈ ≈ ≈

These early years of my life were the years when Bishop Cheshire, coming around for confirmation and often staying at our house, was entertaining us at night with so many amusing tales that he was giving us such a happy impression of the church that long-faced Christianity would always seem, to us, to miss the point. I don't mean to imply, of course, that we don't instinctively turn to our faith in times of trouble. I hardly see how we could get through sorrow without it. But to have had a jolly Bishop is a nice memory. And luckily, some of Bishop Cheshire's favorite tales still survive in his book, *Nonulla*, (About Nothing).

One of them recounts the story about Enos, a man who lived in the country. The story is paraphrased here. His neighbors said of him that, "he was kind and good," but that "Enos was not right in the *hay*-ed."

It was a Sunday afternoon in the country, and Enos had dressed himself up in his Sunday clothes to go to preachin'. Walking the several miles to the church, he was unusually excited, for he had some news to tell. When the first hymn had been sung, Enos could wait no longer, and he rose to his feet to tell the congregation that that morning when he was out slopping his pigs, he had heard the voice of the Lord, and the Lord had called him to preach.

The church members, sitting listening to this astounding information, could hardly believe their ears. Nobody could think of a way out of the dilemma, one that wouldn't hurt Enos's feelings. Then all at once, a quick-witted Sister among the flock stood up, the flowers in her small hat bouncing up and down, and spoke in a strong voice to Enos, "Enos, you ain't heard right! The Lawd ain't called *you*! You jus' overheard him callin' somebody else."

And poor Enos sat down and was quiet.

But from having listened to so many sermons, Enos felt that he had a fairly good knowledge of the Bible. Now and then, he would be troubled by some parts of it, and would have to go to the preacher to have the point cleared up.

Enos did his best thinking when he was at work, and one day when he was white-washing his barn, something came into his mind that unsettled him to such an extent that he laid down his brush and walked the several miles to the preacher's house to get an answer to the problem.

The holy man was at home and invited Enos in, but Enos preferred staying outside, hoping to get a quick answer and to go back to his work.

"Preacher," he began, "don't de Bible say dat de Lawd made everything in heab'n and on de earth, and all dat?"

"That's right, Enos."

"Well, don't de Bible say dat everything de Lawd made is good?"

"That's right, Enos."

"Well, den, how could de Bible say dat de Lawd made de Debil?" For Enos felt he *had* to know.

The preacher hesitated for a moment, before coming up with something that would ease Enos's troubled spirit. An answer that would send him home until another question rose in his mind, for the minister had spoken sagely, "Well, Enos, he's a very *good* devil, isn't he?"

And Enos, satisfied, went home to finish white-washing his barn.

≈ ≈ ≈

No doubt every small town has its share of characters, and here in Rocky Mount we've had ours. In current times, however, there seem to be few. Possibly because the town has grown, they tend not to stand out. Whether or no, our town is the richer for having had tales to tell, with affection and amusement, tales woven about those who have been among us who were different.

In memory, a few stand out. There were Mrs. "Wickie," and Mr. Spence Robbins, Mrs. Kyser, Mrs. Josie Bennett, and Claude Harris, among others. And, of course, "Dr. Joe" Whitehead, who had grown up in the village of Battleboro, and was, therefore, claimed by both the village and the town. His father had been the village doctor before Dr. Marriott came back from Jefferson Medical School to practice medicine. Much to the uneasiness of his wife, Dr. Whitehead had a great love for high-spirited horses, and she would often hold her breath, knowing that he was out in the buggy driving a horse that might as easily as not run away.

One day the doctor had the wildest of his horses hitched to the buggy, and Mrs. Whitehead and the cook stood apprehensively at the window, watching the buggy leave the yard with the doctor at the reins. Its wheels were already flying, the horse's tail, high in the air, his eye, the one on their side, rolled with what the two women thought was a fiendish light; his nostrils flared.

Mrs. Whitehead could hardly speak for worry, but the cook could still talk, and she spoke for all time when she said, "I declare Miss Mary! Mens is a strange nation, ain't they?" By that time, the buggy and the horse and the driver were disappearing from sight.

The younger Dr. Joe was my mother's first beau, his sister, Carrie, Mother's best friend. As an early sign of his favor, while he was doing his internship in Wilmington, the young Joe gave Mother, who was then Alice Susan Bryan, that popular article of the time, a tiny pearl-handled folding pocket-knife for her sewing basket, possibly for ripping seams. The young medical student had also given her the pin of his medical society. But even after these tender thoughts, Joe and Alice, having gone away to their separate schools, grew apart. Alice married and Joe went on to complete the study of medicine.

When the time came, Joe married a young lady from Winston-Salem, which might, at that time, have been our largest city. It had been settled by the hardy Germans – the first few covering the distance on foot – who had come down through what was known as the "Dutch Gap" from Pennsylvania, bringing with them some of their European ways. Naturally there was more sophistication than was to be found in our eastern section of the state, which had been settled by the less hurried temperament of those of the British Isles, who, as they gradually worked inland, were almost entirely given to agriculture. So that, at Miss Alta Cozort's engagement to this young man from "flat country," one of her cousins, being given the news, exclaimed in dismay, "Oh, Alta! You don't mean that you're going down there to live in the Piney Woods!" I must say, however, that it was to be the happiest of marriages.

Ironically, had the people in Eastern Carolina known how the people in the Piedmont felt about our area, they might have said, "Isn't it sad that those people in the Piedmont live so far from the ocean and lead such regimented lives that they don't have time to go fishing, and visit around among their relatives, and have all-day barbecues, watermelon parties, and at the same time, have access to everything on the Eastern Seaboard? We can get to New York in a reasonable length of time, either by rail or by water, and we are not the backwoods people they might think. From our point of view, we have everything the heart desires. We wouldn't live anywhere else if we could. It's true, our children have farther to go to college, but they're always in a hurry to get back home, and the schoolmates they bring with them will sometimes want to spend the summer." So might our thoughts have run as to our being satisfied with our sense of place.

But Miss Alta easily became one of us. Dr. Joe, however, always full of fun and, at times, wanting to appear a little rough around the edges, would sometimes place Miss Alta in a dilemma. These dilemmas usually involved the patient and the doctor.

Telephones had come in, and one night at their house, theirs rang. Miss Alta answered, and the woman launched into a tale of distress, anxious to consult the Doctor. When told that Dr. Joe was resting, the woman then said, "Mrs. Whitehead, please do me a favor? He has told my husband to stop drinking coffee, but he's begging for some. I wonder if I might give him just a little?"

Miss Alta went into the sitting room to lay the question before Dr. Joe. Without hesitation, his answer came, "Tell her to go to hell."

But he knew his wife, and he was not in the least surprised to overhear her say, when she was back at the telephone, in her customarily cultivated gentle voice, "The Doctor says for you to try giving him half a cup."

On another night there came another call, this time, from the worried mother of three small children. Mrs. George Wilkinson, a town character herself, was calling at three in the morning to say, excitedly, "Joe, this is Mary Wilkinson. Sarah is whining in her sleep, and is as hot as a fire-cracker. What must I do?"

"Lord, Mary," said the Doctor. "Go back to bed. Something's worrying the hell out of everybody."

Dr. Joe's succinct answer to Mrs. Wilkinson reminds me of the terse comment on life as quoted from an English maid to a titled English woman in whose service she had been so long that the two had formed the habit of a daily sharing of their troubles. Often, at the end of these unburdenings, the maid was wont to say, with resignation, "Well, it looks like the Lord didn't mean for anybody to be happy, so we might as well learn to be happy without it."

This Mary Wilkinson of the worried nighttime call to the doctor, formerly Mary Geiger, was an attractive, animated woman, with a deep interest in all that went on. Hers had been a northern background. With the coming of the railroad, as so often happened in our town, young northern men came south to work, and married southern girls. In an unparalleled example of the theory that opposites attract, George and Mary Geiger Wilkinson were blissfully happy. Mr. "Wickie," as we called him, loved the quiet things, especially wildflowers, and Mrs. "Wickie" liked to walk briskly all over town, finding out what was going on, and then impart it to whomever she met. Not only did she walk by day, but she walked, in the house, at night. Mr. Wickie good-naturedly complained that she was always waking him and the children up throughout the night to see if they were asleep.

A keen observer of the passing scene, Mrs. Wickie was frank in her appraisal of her fellow creatures. She saw through people like an x-ray, and would sometimes say of somebody who was inclined to show off, "I've never been able to see any difference between a snob and a damned fool."

Strangely, Mrs. Wickie got by with murder in the things she said, and would continue to hold everybody's affection. One reason, I suppose, was that she would say, unapologetically, "I'm just saying what everybody else thinks."

Something of this liveliness was inherited by her younger daughter, Charlotte. Sarah's death was to come in middle life. Charlotte and a brother, George, were to live on until recently. George went first. Indeed, Charlotte's death has just come. With her beauty and her love of life and people, and her artistic nature, her death has saddened the whole town. During the graveside rites she lay under a large spray of pink roses, the color she loved best and wore most. One of the prayers offered by the minister is so beautiful that it is being quoted here:

Prayer Of Thanksgiving For The Life Of
Charlotte Wilkinson Toler
July 25, 1911 - February 20, 1995

Loving God, creator of life, giver of our lives and the lives of all people, we give you special thanks for the life of a remarkable person, your servant Charlotte. We thank you for all she meant to so many and especially to her family and friends; for her love for your church, and especially your Presbyterian Church, and more especially your First Presbyterian Church, and for all she did to enrich its life. Thank you for her love of children, for the way they were drawn to her and found fulfillment in her interest in them. Thank you for her love of music, and art, and the dramatic; and for how she put those together in striking ways. Thank you for her eccentricities: her hats, her pinks, her insistence on living life her way, on her terms. We thank you that when she made her decision not to be seen, she stayed in touch with family and friends. Thank you for the glad reunion when that decision got changed, and that she died in the arms of those who loved her. Thank you that for her, pain is past, death is over, that life has just begun and your brighter day is enriched by her presence.

Through her life, we pray, teach us how to live lives true to ourselves and useful to you. Accept the offering of our grief and by your grace enable us to be better servants of our Lord Jesus Christ who taught us to pray saying "Our Father..."

Once again, a unique personality among us has left an imprint. Between customers, Mr. Spence Robbins, a merchant, was another. In warm weather, Mr. Robbins used to take a straight chair with a cane bottom outside his store onto the sidewalk and sit there until the customers came. In that way, he could pass the time of day with others who were opening their stores, going to their offices, and with the few early shoppers who were out. One morning, as he sat in this relaxed state, ready to speak to everybody, along came a tall young man whom he knew had just passed the Bar. Tom Avera, all spruced up for starting his career, was taking long strides, swinging his briefcase, looking neither to the right nor to the left. Expecting to be spoken to, Mr. Robbins withheld his own "Good Morning" until Tom had passed silently by, and then shouted, "Uh, Tom! When did the price of 'Howdy!' go up?" All heads turned, and Tom had learned his lesson.

Mr. Robbins' store was only one door away from Kyser's drugstore. Mr. and Mrs. Kyser were both pharmacists. Mrs. Kyser had been the first woman pharmacist to graduate from the University of North Carolina. She had been a member of the Royster family of that area, all of them very bright people. An outstanding member of this family in my generation was Vermont Royster, who was to become editor of *The Wall Street Journal*, and whom Tom and I saw often at Chapel Hill. With originality and patriotism, his parents had named all of their children for the states of the Union.

As the responsibilities of raising her children grew, Mrs. Kyser's professional life received less of her time. The Kysers lived opposite Uncle Mark and Aunt Mamie on Sunset Avenue. On summer mornings Mrs. Kyser was often on Aunt Mamie's porch, for in those days, no matter that they had domestics who could have taken care of these duties, many housewives, if they were domestically inclined, sat on each other's porches during the summer, visiting, and combining the pleasure of conversation with the usefulness of shelling peas and butter beans from their gardens. Mrs. Kyser talked fast, and always with spirit, and I remember overhearing her say one morning when I was a child and was visiting my cousins, Emily and Lillian, and we were playing jackrocks at the other end of Aunt Mamie's porch, "Why, Mamie, it doesn't matter that you don't want to go on that trip. You should go. Even a bad change is good for us."

Around the corner from Uncle Mark's and Aunt Mamie's house lived the Aleck Thorpe family. On the Pearsall side, through the Middletons of South Carolina and the Cape Fear area of North Carolina, Mrs. Thorpe was Tom's "Cousin Sudie." Much beloved and respected in the community, Cousin Sudie lived to be nearly a hundred. Her mind active until the end, one summer she suggested that we take our family, and that her daughter, Virginia, take hers, and we all go to Warsaw, a small North Carolina town near the seat of the North Carolina Pearsall and Middleton clans, to attend a Middleton family reunion. Although I daresay it is never mentioned except on these occasions, we came away reminded, by charts and records, that Arthur Middleton, the signer of the Declaration of Independence, was indeed a part of their heritage. Generous always, and charitable in her attitudes, Cousin Sudie's influence was wide. Even without the family relationship, her two older children, Aleck and Virginia, contemporaries of ours, would have been close friends of Tom's and mine.

A few of us know of the beauty of Cousin Sudie's will, at the end of which she said, "Now that I have taken care of the disposition of my material possessions, I feel that I can do no better than to close with what Patrick Henry said at the close of his own will, 'If I have left you these things and have not left you my faith, I have left you nothing.'"

A few years after Cousin Sudie's death – in conversation with Virginia – I asked if she'd ever considered writing anything about her Mother's singularly well-spent life. In her characteristically direct way, Virginia's answer was one to remember. "No," she answered, "I prefer to try to live it." Without the shadow of a doubt, she succeeds.

In memory, Mrs. Josie Bennett is a clear figure. For she was one of the most public-spirited women we were ever to have. In the depression of the 1930s, to give employment to some of the thousands of people without jobs, Roosevelt had initiated using Federal funds for regional projects, of which our City Lake would be one. Thus it was, that with wheelbarrows and shovels, at ten cents an hour, this small lake was dug. There were no funds for its beautification, and day in and day out, Mrs. Bennett worked tirelessly, taking a few laborers at a time into the woods to bring out and plant native trees and shrubs. She did, indeed, give the area lasting beauty.

Mrs. Bennett's mantle for doing good things for the town was to fall on the shoulders of another fine public-spirited citizen, Mrs. J.B.A. Daughtridge. Together and separately, these two, among others, furnished plants for the Elizabethan Gardens on Roanoke Island, and it was Mrs. Daughtridge who took tobacco plants from her own farm to start the patch of "Upper Wock," the Indian name for the "golden weed," that lies near the green house of the Elizabethan Gardens.

But that was only one area of Mrs. Bennett's unselfishness. Preoccupied with doing for others, there came a time, when, having been invited to a wedding and its reception, she would need her evening dress. But, to her consternation, she could not find it. The only thing she could remember was that she had lent it to somebody. Calling and asking around brought no results until, in desperation, she resorted to putting a notice in our *Evening Telegram.* While her plea ran on in the paper for several days, she still searched for the dress over the house, and just in time, it was discovered in what we used to call a "suit box," one which, at the bottom of several, had lain in a dark corner of the attic.

Mrs. Kornegay was French. As the wife of one of our most prominent doctors, she had come to live among us bringing with her a flavor of Grand Opera, but she quickly became one of us. For a while I had the pleasure of taking voice lessons from her. Her company was as culturally stimulating as it was pleasurable in a fun-loving way. One of the stories she sometimes told had to do with a trip that her native Eastern Carolina cook had once made to New York.

Mrs. Kornegay had built up such a glowing picture of the city of New York that Effie got it in her mind to go. She knew she wouldn't want to stay – all she wanted to do was to have a good look at it – and so she bought a round-trip ticket. She made the ten-hour train trip without incident, sitting up all night, and arrived early in the morning at Pennsylvania Station. There she spent the day. She could tell that it had a place for getting meals which she did not need to buy, for she had prepared for that contingency; she had brought her own food in a shoe-box. Not only was the station warm and comfortable, there were all the conveniences, and watching the people was, in itself, entertaining, and so Effie had a day of wondrous fulfillment.

Ten o'clock that night found Effie again on the train, headed back for Rocky Mount. She had spent eleven enlightening hours in Pennsylvania Station, considering it "New York." Then, her curiosity satisfied, she was southbound. She couldn't wait to see Mrs. Kornegay the next day to give her comments on the enormity of the city. Enchanted with the "dome as high as the sky," and the way the announcements ricocheted around the walls, and trying, with might and main, to describe the enormity of the city which now in her mind had a top over it, she declared, "I tell you, Mrs. Kornegay, ain't 'air" (Old English term for "nary a one"), "ain't 'air warehouse in Rocky Mount that big!"

Of these town characters, Dr. Joe and another man, Claude Harris, are the ones that most often come up in conversation, even today. Claude, amiable and attractive, always "good company," owned a stockyard. Spring was coming, and a farmer had come to buy a mule. And it was accepted as the preliminary to bargaining to – Mother's word – "prevaricate" a little. Claude gave directions to the stableman to bring a certain one out into the lot. This was done, and as Claude and the customer stood watching, the mule began to show a lot of life, which, of course, was to be desired, frisking about from one side of the lot to the other. But invariably he would lunge headlong into something. First it would be the barn, then the fence, then the wagon. After a few minutes of this, the farmer spoke, uneasily, "Look here, Claude. I don't believe that mule can see."

"Naw," said Claude, "he c'n see. He just don't give a damn."

Who would want to forget Dr. Looney, our eye, ear, nose and throat specialist, a husky man, and his annual fishing trip to Durant Island which he made in the company of a number of other men and a cook? Coming down to breakfast in the morning in their crude island house, in answer to James Salisbury's question – and James, himself was a town favorite – "What you having for breakfast, Doctor?" Dr. Looney's answer would be, "The same as yesterday and the day before, James. A slice of ham and nine eggs, fried on eighteen sides."

There are other tales, not so well-known perhaps, but which – in that they reflect the times in such a human way – continue to be dear to the hearts of those of us who recall them, and to wish there were more.

My father and my uncles belonged to the Elks Club. They also belonged to the Sagamore Club. With the coming of the Rotary Club, Tom became a member. One of the most popular after-dinner speakers in Eastern Carolina of the time happened to be a certain Edmund Harding, who came from the small town we still call "Little Washington." I believe he was, for many years, the organist in the Episcopal church there.

Whatever his occupation, Edward was, in a literal sense, that proverbial "barrel of fun." He could, as we used to say, "make a dog laugh." Time and again, he came to our town. His tales were made especially effective by the choice of names he gave the characters. Those names I've forgotten, but I do remember one of his tales.

It seems to have taken place at one of those large all-day church socials, spoken of then as the "Association." Associations were usually held at country churches. Buggies and surreys filled the churchyard, and all-day preaching went on, sermons delivered by a number of ministers. Naturally, there must be some reward for this horrendous day; it came in the form of food: fried chicken, deviled eggs, ham-and-biscuits, sweet-pickled peaches, watermelon-rind pickles, and layer cakes, as they would have said, "to beat the band."

One of the most long-winded of the preachers, and one of those whose appearance gave an air of being the best-fed, had come back to the food table a second time. By that hour, the fried chicken was getting a little low; the woman in charge thought that, unnoticed, she might sever the short-leg from the drumstick in order to have another piece left. But the preacher saw it out of the corner of a watchful eye, and spoke out in a commanding voice, "Stay thy hand, Sister Brown! Those whom God hath joined together, let not man put asunder!"

Another amusing story with a religious slant was one which Tom Avera – the same Tom who, in his younger days, had passed by Mr. Spence Robbins and failed to say, "Howdy!" – would, in later years, work up for his own pleasure, and the pleasure of his friends and local groups. By this time, Tom was a community leader, but not too busy to stop for a little fun.

The tale concerned a preacher who, although he had great respect for the Bible, and would often turn its pages, was unable to read. So strong was the spirit, that the good man somehow derived his sermons from a hazy impression of what he had been told lay in each of the books of the Bible. In those days, the Book of Psalms was often listed in the Bible as the

"Psalter," from the Greek word for a Greek instrument, and in some Bibles, was spelled *psaltre*. Apparently this word stirred the preacher's imagination. From it, he developed a marvelous sermon whose text he always announced as "The Story of the *Peezle Tree*." The heights to which he would carry his flock under this illumination, weaving in and out of the story incidents in the lives of those Biblical characters who by divine dispensation were allowed to sit under so remarkable a tree, were beyond compare!

By the time of the second World War, our town had its own Red Cross chapter with the appropriate offices. The head of the local chapter was a friend and contemporary of mine. Mary Robbins Oliver was a young widow helping to support her small daughter in that way. This very capable woman had, all through life, been called "Babe," and that continued. Babe was perfectly equipped for this work, which, day after day, dealt with human need and distress, family problems of all kinds; a veritable catch-all for the town's social needs. With not only a sympathetic heart, but with a wonderful way of seeing the humor in life, Babe would sometimes share with her friends some of the funny things that people had said. This one is too unforgettable not to pass along. For some years, Babe had had a steady client, coming regularly for financial assistance. Every year there was a new baby, but Cephronia did not have a husband, and seemed unconcerned about getting one.

One day when she had made her regular visit with the latest baby in her arms, Babe thought it might be a good idea to be practical. And so she said, "Cephronia, you say the same man is the father of all these children. Why don't you go on and marry him, and then he would *have* to help you support them?"

"Lawd, Miz Oliver," replied Cephronia, "he jes' don't *appeal* to me."

Another anecdote. In the spring and summer of the thirties, Mr. John Wells, the realtor who had developed the wooded residential area two miles west of the post office into what was to be known as "Westhaven," and where I've now spent fifty-nine years, used to enjoy driving slowly about among the curved streets, stopping now and then to talk to this and that person at work in the yard. At that hour of the morning, they were usually women, and they might be happily engaged in training a vine of Carolina jasmine to grow around a lamp post, or a gate post, or weeding or watering a flower bed that was visible from the road.

Ours was the sixth house to be built in the development, and on just such a morning, in the May of our first spring there, as I went up and down just inside our rock wall, encouraging ivy to cling, I looked up to see Mr. Wells coming through the garden gate. He had noticed me. When we had exchanged pleasantries, we moved on to the weather. Since it was unseasonably warm for May, I was dressed in the usual way for a summer morning at home in the Eastern Carolina of the time, in a sun-back sleeveless dress, feet and legs bare, and wearing sandals. Mr. Wells, a stout, bald-headed man of perhaps sixty, with a round, red, good-natured face, was, as usual, wearing a coat, a collar, and a tie.

"Mr. Wells," I said. "Let's go sit on the terrace for a few minutes – maybe drink something cooling. Aren't you burning up in that coat and tie?" For even the stiffly starched cuffs of his long-sleeved white shirt and their cufflinks were showing at his wrists.

"Yes, Ma'am," he began. "I *am* pretty hot. But, you know, I've been on the school board a long time, and at commencement we always have to sit on the stage. So I don't want to get used to being comfortable until after commencement."

At once I could see that school, and the podium, could hear the drone of its speaker, its recitations, its rousingly patriotic musical opening and closing, and in between, the lethargic motion of row after row of funeral-parlor, or drugstore fans, and I felt a great tenderness for Mr. Wells.

That I have dwelt on these personalities at some length is to say that I think these stories make us human, yet I would not like to leave the impression that we were not a serious-minded community, ready to take advantage of opportunities for our overall good. For, at the same time that we were doing the dear, cohesive, small-town things, we were moving purposefully in other ways, industrial, humanitarian, and cultural. And, among the nice things that have been said about our town by outsiders is that we are outstandingly generous. Our "drives" are invariably successful, often going over the top. Ours is, indeed, a good town.

To be happy at home is the ultimate result of all ambition,
the end to which every enterprise and labor tends.

Samuel Johnson
The Rambler, 1750

≈ ≈ ≈

Although the Civil War was nearly three-quarters of a century behind us when Tom and I were married, the South was still indirectly feeling its effects. She was undergoing, as well, one of our country's greatest depressions. In addition, the agricultural South was still dependent on the vagaries of agriculture. The transition to the introduction of industry, which, when it came, would slowly, to some degree, boost our economy, had not yet begun. The age of automation could not be foreseen. When that came, it again plunged us into economic instability. For with its coming, one segment of our population, that of unskilled labor, would be largely displaced.

For the first half of my life, there existed tenant-farmer methods of agriculture. In North Carolina, from Raleigh to the coast, there were no large cities. Wilmington was our largest town. There were innumerable small towns, these often linked by family relations. This gave the area an air of camaraderie which continues to set Eastern Carolina apart. It has made people from other sections of the state and other areas of the country seem to enjoy coming to visit us, since small town and country people are almost universally open and hospitable.

There was, at that time, little club life. Bridal parties took one of three forms: luncheons, afternoon teas, or bridge parties. As a bride, I was to have my share of each. But the one party I remember best is easy to recall because it is connected with something humorous.

In his neighborhood, Tom had been a favorite. In a block of large, comfortable old houses, that of the Pearsall's was at one end, at the other end lived a family spoken of as "the Harts." This block and dozens of similar ones were characteristic of our town, one in which its people lived largely on the same scale. With few exceptions, there was no great wealth, yet life went on pleasantly, and with a certain amount of grace. In those days, often relatives liked to live together. The Harts, a fine and gentle family, were no exception. There was "Miss Jesse," as we called her, though she had a perfectly good husband, and the same went for her sister, "Miss Alice." Mrs. Hart, their mother, also lived with them, and had the downstairs bedroom.

For the bridge party in my honor, the Harts had spared themselves no effort; they were determined to make it both pleasurable and beautiful. It was a lovely summer day when fifty-six of the community's young ladies, brightly clad, and wearing summer hats which we would keep on throughout the party, made our way up the front walk. Because it was a large party, so-called "progressive bridge" was played. At the tinkle of a silver bell, the winners moved to a "higher" table, this system enabled the hostess, at the end of the party, to present both a high-score prize and a sympathetic booby. According to custom, at a final signal from the hostess, card-playing would stop, and as scores were quickly added, beautiful Madeira cloths on the tables would replace the cards and scorepads on the tables.

Plates were served in the kitchen. Two cooks had prepared the world's best chicken salad, which was served with paper thin slices of the world's best country ham; each plate would have a "sweet-pickled-peach." Hot rolls so delicious they almost melted on the way to the mouth were passed, coffee was served from an old silver service, and the chatter was a continuous happy buzz. We wound up with chocolate cake, nibbling an after dinner mint from a silver bon-bon dish in the center of each table, then it was time to leave.

Thoroughly grateful for this beautiful party, as goodbyes were being said, I stood at the door with the hostesses. Plaudits had reached a crescendo when one grateful guest said, feelingly to the sisters, "It's so *wonderful* that you have this large house and can have fourteen tables at one time."

And Miss Jesse, the most vocal of the sisters, without the slightest wane of enthusiasm, replied "Oh, yes, and we *could* have had fifteen, if we'd taken down Mama's bed!"

And while we're on the subject of bridal parties, I can't resist sharing another anecdote. While the remark about to be quoted was not made in our town, it might easily have been. Indeed, I wish that we could have claimed this woman. I can just tell how much pleasure she might have given to the community. The story came through one of my dear friends, Eleanor Joyner, no longer alive, who as Eleanor Armfield, had grown up in the small town of Monroe, North Carolina. I've forgotten the name of the lady involved, but since she needs one for the tale, I shall call her Miss Flossie Blunt.

Miss Flossie was honoring, with a luncheon, one of Eleanor's older sisters, who was about to be married. As usual in small towns, just about everybody was invited. The house was large, there were flowers from Miss Flossie's garden everywhere, the dining room table was beautifully set for twelve, twelve more to be seated at card tables, two of these on the porch, under the ceiling fan.

In addition to being a gardener, Miss Flossie was a wonderful homemaker, as well, decidedly talented in the kitchen. Guests could count on her chicken salad to have been made with homemade dressing, in a double boiler. They knew that her rolls would be the lightest, and that the tall glasses of iced tea would have in them sprigs of her own mint. Miss Flossie and her cook had worked tirelessly for days, and the event was, indeed, a glorious affair.

When it was over, the departing guests poured out a Niagara of thanks. One of them, going all out, exclaimed, "Miss Flossie, it's the *nicest* party I've ever been to!"

Miss Flossie's ready reply was as heart-felt, "Well, I'm glad you enjoyed it, because it sure was a heap of trouble!"

≈ ≈ ≈

For the first two years Tom and I lived in an apartment. Ours happened to face on a street which ran by the side of Uncle Mark's and Aunt Mamie's large old house. Uncle Jim's and Aunt Zell's, while on the same block as Uncle Mark's, and just as large, faced on another street, so that I was in a stone's throw of these two wonderful and loving uncles and their families.

To get to Uncle Jim's I went through the vegetable garden and then the rose garden. I knew that every morning, before Uncle Jim started for the bank, he would go out and pick a rose for his lapel. In those days men in small southern towns often wore flowers; the men in my family did. It was a custom that Tom would follow all his life, as well. It could not always be a rosebud, but in our climate something is nearly always accommodatingly in bloom. Camellias start in September with our sasanquas, and in one variety or another, bloom the year round; a rose in December is not unheard of. This custom of wearing a flower was so much a part of Tom's life, that whenever his suits went to the drycleaners, before they left, I would remove a simple straight pin that was always kept under his lapel. And, as so often happens in my writing, the philosophical surfaces. Just the other day my son, Mack, remarked that he had read in a publication he subscribes to, called *American Demographics*, the following observation: "While the nineteen-eighties have been the age of conspicuous consumption, the nineties will be that of visible virtue." Should that be true, should we be, for happiness, swinging back to the simpler things of life, it would seem all to the good.

During these early years of our marriage, in addition to being prosecuting attorney for the city, Tom was, for seven years, superintendent of our Episcopal Sunday School. At one point, in need of a teacher for a class of twelve to fourteen-year-old boys, and a teacher being hard to find, I was pressed into service.

It was a horrendous experience, and I was soon replaced by a man. My enthusiasm for the church was not diminished, however, for I soon attended a series of lectures that went on for five nights in our parish hall.

A marvelously exuberant man and his equally exuberant wife, from somewhere out West, were lecturing on the subject, "Life Abundant." The secret of their youth and their exuberance was beet-tops. Not the vegetable itself, just the tops, boiled in water. The liquid, drunk in great quantities, would set you out on what was spoken of as the "elimination diet," and you would be on your way to life abundant.

Throughout his adult life, Tom had had migraine headaches. There was little known about the origin and the cure. Over time, several doctors would admit that the only thing they knew about these headaches was that they are inherited, usually from the mother's side. But that enlightenment would come to us later. And since these high-minded lectures at the church were going on night after night, the inspired couple harping on their miraculous cures with beet-tops, and offering their magic recipes in a cookbook that was for sale, it was natural that I should go home with a volume, entranced.

For five days, I boiled beet-tops, dropping in an occasional surprise for poor Tom, in the way of a potato, or a carrot, or an okra pod. So great was his devotion to his bride, that, day after day, he drank it. So earnest was my belief in this so-called "elimination diet" that I almost eliminated Tom. After that, he could no doubt have composed that verse of Landor's as he, himself, faced a lifetime of resignation in connection with my enthusiasms:

> *A woman is a foreign land,*
> *Though which he settle young*
> *A man will never understand*
> *Her mind, her politics, nor tongue.*

By the time our two sons were in grammar school, I was beginning to approach my church life with more common sense. From having become head of the Women of the Church for two years, in those days spoken of as the Women's Auxiliary, I would go on to become Chairman of the District for another two. This would automatically place me on diocesan committees. Since our diocese is a large one which takes in Charlotte, the largest city in the state, I was often on committees with many northern and western women. In our meetings, these women seemed so brisk, so sure of themselves, that there were times when I felt over my depth. Even in the meetings over which I presided in my own section, as District Chairman, I was often in a tangle of Parliamentary Law. My lifelong system of hitting the high spots and not worrying about details was suddenly being called into account. A few things saved me. Since the district meetings were always held in one of our Eastern Carolina churches, the clergy of the district came, by invitation. They usually sat in the pews farthest back, and were careful not to interfere. Somehow it was conveyed to me that they were "with me," that perhaps they felt, as I did, that some of the technicalities we argued over from the floor at such length might have been disposed of in half the time. In a hopeless barrage of, "Madam Chairman, may I suggest..." from here and there, gasping for air, I felt, "You certainly *may*," or "If you only *would*," I would lean down for a hurried conference with my secretary, Katherine Weeks, who had volunteered for the job. Katherine would be suitably engaged in taking notes at the cardtable which had been placed for us in the chancel, and although very bright, she had the same weakness that I had for seeing the funny side of things, and the two of us were continually lost in a shuffle of papers and in the mechanics of being in charge of "the Chair."

It helped a little, however, to remember that, although our bishop, Bishop Penick, was never there for these meetings, he and I saw church life from something of the same point of view. I had formed the habit of always writing to him in green ink, to symbolize the growth of the Church. He liked that. We shared the feeling that church life should be joyous and lighthearted, not necessarily solemn, with all its "i's" dotted, and its "t's" crossed. At the diocesan meetings, the Bishop always sat in the choir stalls with those of us who had to give our reports to the church full of delegates, and if my mouth was prone to dry a little before my time to speak came, I had only to look at the Bishop to be reassured. It also helped to recall that about that time, an article of mine had appeared in the publication of the National Episcopal Church. It had to do with what we speak of as the United Thanks Offering, and had caught the fancy of a dozen or so other women over the nation who were kind enough to write. Once a year, each woman in the church is given a small box, a duplication of the Mite-Boxes used by the children of the church, which, in their case, are brought to the church on Easter Sunday and laid upon the altar to be sent to foreign missions. Ours are turned in at what we call an "Ingathering," which takes place in October and March. Women are encouraged to form the habit of donating in this way for anything for which they are especially thankful. Among other things, our United Thanks Offering, at the time, was going specifically to the work of the church in Alaska, providing the airplane which enabled the Bishop, the Right Reverend William Gordon, whose roots, incidentally, were in our area of Eastern Carolina, to carry on his work, in covering those vast distances. My little story had brought a flurry of fan mail from others in the National church.

The other thing that I counted on to come to my rescue was that I had learned long, long ago, that valuable lesson, that if you have to make a speech, provided you have enthusiasm for your subject and know it well, almost with the opening of your mouth the butterflies will have flown. In regard to those impressive women of the North and West, who always seemed to know exactly where they were going all the time, I knew, inside, that it was their accents as much as their superb briskness that was making them seem so marvelously brilliant; that I was being intimidated by manner, and that we strove for the same things, each in our different ways, products of where life had placed us.

≈ ≈ ≈

In spite of the inability to collect legal fees during the depression, Tom was still excited about the practice of law. He was beginning to make speeches when the state Bar Association met; he never dreamed that with time he would give up the practice of law. But in a round-about way, fate intervened.

The day after Father's funeral service, the third day after his death, Uncle Mark and Uncle Jim came over together to talk to Mother. Mother had held up bravely through the shock of Father's death and through seeing the hundreds of people who came to offer their sympathy. That day, however, she had given in to grief, and they found her lying on the daybed in her sitting room, the daybed where Father had often dropped down for an early afternoon nap, the newspaper he'd started to read, rising and falling on his chest with his slow, rhythmic breathing.

Since it was October, and a chill in the air, there was a bright fire in the fireplace, but by that time, our old dog, Gyp, the one of my childhood, was gone, as was the canary, Dickie Bird. Babied and protected all my life, at Father's death, I felt my childhood slipping away. The feeling deepened as I heard Uncle Jim and Uncle Mark begin to bring the phrase "minor" into the conversation.

"Since Elizabeth is a minor, it makes the settling of the estate and the conducting of Mack's affairs more difficult," one of them said.

After a few moments of this kind of conversation, Uncle Mark came out with what, to Mother, was a startling statement, "Alice, we think Mack would like for you to qualify as administratrix of the estate." As a girl of barely fifteen, that large word was new to me, but I soon gathered, in a hazy way, what it meant. Father's brothers had so much confidence in Mother that they were suggesting that she assume overall responsibility for settling Father's estate and for managing the variety of his interests, including the farms, which, at that time, covered twenty-two thousand acres in Eastern Carolina, and smaller tracts in the states of Georgia and Texas, a diversity of which I would only gradually become aware, replacing the feeling that we just "had farms," in the way that a large number of people in our part of the world did.

I'm sure that Mother's mind would have leaped to the certainty that she could never be the father-figure to the tenants that Father had been. It was not to be expected that she spend hours in his office dealing with the cotton and peanut buyers and the day to day routine that had been Father's. That she could not hope to have that combination of business acumen and the appreciation of every tenant and his problems that came so easily to Father, the gentleness at the end of a weary day, when on the way through the store and out to go home he would be stopped by some timid tenant with a grievance which he felt neither the overseer of that particular farm nor the riding-boss of all the farms could understand. It was "Mista Mack" whom he wanted to see.

Father knew that the tenant might have been standing around the large stove that sat in the center of the store called a base-burner, humbly waiting for an interview. He felt for these people deeply. Mother did, as well, but she took care of their needs in other ways.

Father had inherited his own father's love of land. They had each enjoyed everything associated with making it produce, and had had some years of doing that in partnership. Grandpa Braswell had chosen to live on his main farm; there to bring up his four sons. But when Father grew up and began to accumulate a number of farms in his own name, he chose not to live on any of them, but in a village situated approximately in the center of his farming interests. The village would give him the country way of life he liked; at the same time, there would be the overall management of not only the farms, but their allied operations. The marketing of their products could be carried on there, providing him with the hum of activity which the other side of Father's nature required, and with an outlet for the application of those business principles in which he had been trained in Poughkeepsie. To Father, a breadth of interests was important.

There were the cotton gin and the cotton brokerage. There was the peanut brokerage, the oil mill, and a large mercantile business which included a branch store called "The Harness House." To my child's mind, the Harness House was associated with things that brought excitement; it sold the bright and shiny buggies, surreys and sulkies. Sulkies were those light, two-wheeled vehicles for one person, used mainly in harness races throughout the year, especially in summer. Some farmers used sulkies to ride over their fields. To me they were wonderfully picturesque. Once in awhile, I was allowed to go through the fields in the sulky with Father. I sat on a low stool in the foot. The fields would be green then, and Father

170

usually drove a beautiful young horse. In memory, they were chestnut or sorrel-colored. Trained to obey his master's slightest command, the horse would stand perfectly still, only shaking his head or swishing his tail against the flies, as Father, the reins held loosely in his hands, discussed the condition of the crops with one or two of the field-hands who would have come to stand at the end of the row for the consultation. That they always held their hats in their hands, I understood was a mark of respect, but somehow it touched me.

In a carry-over of relationships from an earlier era – the days of slavery – a few of the older hands would address Father as "Mahs' Mack." Yet, it was in an amiable, even affectionate way that had no air of subservience. If they happened to be at work in a watermelon or a cantelope patch, they would be all smiles in offering melons for us to take home. For in this system of sharecropping, there usually existed the trusting feeling of partnership between landlord and tenant.

There was, however, a term in use at the time, that with insight, now holds, for me, a degree of poignance. For whatever reason, some tenants would prove undesirable, and that kind were often spoken of as "shiftless." Though the men in the family, and the women, might be entirely able-bodied, and would have access to unlimited firewood, they would have been indifferent to going into the woods and getting it for themselves. They would have burned up the doorsteps or a panel in a broken fence. The cow they had been furnished would be allowed to go dry, leaving no milk for the children. Naturally these tenants were not rehired at the beginning of the next year. One of the saddest sights of my childhood was on a day early in January, seeing on the roads, a scattering of wagons, piled with the meager furnishings of a family of this kind; the father, the mother, and the children moving from one area to another. It was a foregone conclusion that the pattern of failure would be repeated. Yet I knew that the responsible tenants – the hard-working and thrifty ones – would continue to prosper, and would sometimes stay for as long as twenty-five years on the same farm, and that, in Father's case, if a certain tenant wanted to buy his own land, Father would gladly see that this was brought about.

Near the village there was a modest racetrack where harness racing was held. There were no seats for spectators; they stood at the rail. Between races, they returned to their vehicles for refreshment and drinks. The largest of the races was that to celebrate the Fourth of July. Both the spectators and those who had entered their horses for the feats came from far and near. Cousin Benjamin Mayo, a relative from Mother's side who lived farther down in the county, always had prize race horses, and was always there to see some of them perform.

Before and after the races we had open house, and there must have been several hundred guests on our porches, sipping the beverage of their preference. There would be large wooden bowls with peanuts grown on our farms and parched in our kitchen, one of the barrels of small, amber-colored bottles of beer packed in straw that Father always kept cooling in the cellar came up, and then another, and another. There was pitcherful after pitcherful of lemonade, of iced tea, and for those who wanted it, something stronger.

In memory, the day floats on a cloud of white. For the women were in white shirtwaists and skirts, and they wore white sailor hats with black or striped hat-bands. The men in their white linen suits wore white Panama hats. Everybody wore white shoes. There were always one or two "sportscars," as they were called, and even these would be white, two-seated, and would have their tops down.

Not only did the Harness House cater to the sophisticated things like sulkies and surreys, it offered wagons and other implements needed for farm cultivation: plows, discs, those horse or mule-drawn implements used after the breaking up of the land by the plow and the mule, and harrows, the rake-like implements which were next pulled over the fields for leveling and for breaking up clods and for rooting up weeds. After Christmas, the movement of any of these over the fields, the plow, the disc, or the harrow, in which even the horses and mules seemed to feel a new zest, were the harbingers of spring; they quickened the pulse.

There was, as well, a blacksmith shop. I suppose that out of all the farm-related activity, the blacksmith shop held, for me, the most fascination. I could ride up to it on my pony, or later, on my horse, and through its wide doors, opposite each other, and always open on either side, could see the leaping flame into which, with long iron tongs, the blacksmith would be working with his molten iron, shaping horseshoes or repairing axles for wagons or broken plows, or attending to the multiplicity of needs that always arise in an agricultural community. I especially loved the ring of the hammer on the anvil. From a distance, it was softly but clearly musical. At close range, it seemed miraculous that a horse or a mule would stand so quietly to be shod. Of course, now and then, one would be frightened, and would have to have blinders put on, but in the main, they were docile. As a child, I wondered why this hammering on their feet didn't hurt, and was told that their hooves are like our fingernails; they have no feeling.

Forty miles away from where we lived, a little to the west, and on "higher ground," there was Panacea Hotel, the management of which would have been a career in itself for Mother, had it not sat, unopened since World War I. For with those troubled years, the smaller resorts tended to lose their patronage, for better transportation, including air travel, was coming about. For a number of years it sat in this inoperational state, until its co-owners, Father and Mr. Johnson, made the decision to have the hotel dismantled, everything, including the land to be sold at public auction.

Yet, with the diversity of Father's other interests, Mother couldn't, that day, believe her ears when Uncle Jim and Uncle Mark suggested that she assume responsibility for their overall management. At first she said, "I'm not capable. Nobody knows better than you-all that I have been happy just being a wife and mother." (And I say here, parenthetically, that southerners never use "you-all" for just one person, in spite of all the jokes to the contrary. It's always used in the plural. Using it for two persons may be ungrammatical, but it's "us.")

But Father's brothers continued their persuasiveness. Apparently, they knew Mother better than she knew herself. They assured her of their help, and went on to say, "You have a good lawyer in Jim Bunn. Mack's affairs are in order, but we have a strong feeling that you should be the one to hold things together. You have your overseers on the farms; you have your riding managers who will report to you every afternoon. We know you can do it, Alice."

I can hardly imagine what Mother was feeling. While it's true that she and Father had sometimes discussed business affairs, and in a general way, had spoken of the farms, for Mother had a small one of her own that had been given her by her mother which she used to "run" – although Father did most of that for her – Mother was, by nature, a nurturer, always happy in taking care of her family. Except for Alice Bryan's affliction, she had been truly content as wife and mother. I wondered what her answer would be, and as I wondered, I saw resolution coming. For finally she said slowly, "If you think I should try to do it, I will."

"We'll go with you to Jim Bunn's office when you think you can," said one of the uncles.

And Mother, sitting up, answered slowly, "Will tomorrow be soon enough?"

≈ ≈ ≈

By the time Tom and I were married, Mother had been laboring under these responsibilities for seven years. It was beginning to show in her health. Insomnia was ever-present, but with the traditional fear of becoming a "dope fiend" – nobody ever thought of speaking of anybody as an "addict" in those days, I suppose, because they wanted to make the connotation as horrible as possible, and every community had its example of these – she would not take a sleeping pill more often than once a week. That meant six nights of lying almost completely awake. But once committed to something, Mother's resolve never swerved.

As time has a way of doing, however, it would provide an answer. As soon as Tom came into the family, he and Mr. Bunn together took over the legal part of everything. It was in this capacity, and in his exposure to Mother's trials and tribulations – to the enormity of her problems and the complexity of our holdings – that Tom was able, four years later, to give an affirmative answer to Mother's plea, "Tom, would you consider taking over for me? I hate to ask you to give up your law practice, but I don't know what else to do." That she felt she could appeal to Tom, and would do that, was very beautiful to me, and at the same time, very sad.

It required a great deal of soul-searching for Tom. I suppose he knew in his heart that in the end he would have to acquiesce. When he did, being Tom, he made her feel that he was not making a sacrifice. He knew that he would have to "learn" farming, for while it was true that his father had once had a farm, it had been sold, so that Tom could not relate to agriculture as closely as even I could. Yet it was his nature to be enthusiastic about whatever he undertook. He met challenge head on; he approached this new life with both humility and confidence, saying, "The only thing I know about farming is that I don't know anything. But I can learn."

And he set about having all our overseers, all our managers of departments, come together regularly so that they became a team. He sent the overseers to State College for courses during the winter when farm work was slack. He attended some of the courses himself and began to replace horses and mules with tractors.

From the beginning, the plight of the farm women and children had weighed on Tom, for he had an innately high regard for womanhood. He always said that it was the pioneer woman who had his sympathy – that they gave themselves, body and soul, to the men they followed, and in so doing, had to endure the drudgery of a life that was hum-drum, uneventful, and probably at times, even frightening for herself and her children, while the man had the thrill, even if it did carry major responsibilities for his family, of a day to day life in the wild.

This feeling was translated into our own environment. He hired a home demonstration agent to go from house to house, teaching the tenant wives hygiene and sewing and cooking. For summer use, he converted a large empty building in our village to a cannery, so that women would be encouraged to preserve their produce in order that their families be well-nourished during the winter. In Father's day, each tenant had always been given chickens and one or two pigs, corresponding to the size of the family, and a cow. But often the animals, especially the cows, as I've already mentioned, were not given proper care, and children went without milk. Many of them had rickets, but by some provision of nature, in their diet of pork, collard greens, sweet potatoes, and black-strap molasses, which they ate on cornbread and on biscuits, they were given reasonably healthy bodies. Dr. Marriott, Father's close friend, talked a great deal about pellagra, a disease which comes from a non-diversified diet, but I never heard of a case. And in a limited way, Mother had, ever since her marriage, tried to teach the farm woman not to have their families subsist mainly on fatback and cornbread, the way they were inclined to do.

Tom also hired a nurse to take the sick to Duke, and after the University of North Carolina Medical School came, to Chapel Hill. During those years, he was one of a committee of twelve whose dream had been that of starting a medical school at Chapel Hill, a dream that in a few years would become a reality. Concurrently, Tom left no stone unturned to better overall conditions for farm families in general, those over the state and especially our own, and in a few years would be awarded the Firestone Medal, "For Improvement in Landlord/Tenant Relations."

≈ ≈ ≈

I realized, as a bride, that I was going to have a busy life. Although I could not foresee in what direction life would take us, with an insight into Tom's capacity for leadership, and for hard work, I knew that inevitably these qualities would be recognized in other spheres. It was in this gradual recognition that he had begun to be appointed to this and that commission, especially those where there was controversy.

I told him, down the years, that he was something of a paradox, that with his unbounded energy – that energy which would prompt a Philadelphia doctor to say at one point when Tom was there for migraine headaches, "Mr. Pearsall, you have a dynamo personality" – he was yet able to get things done that required unlimited patience. His philosophy, "Things have to evolve," was always at work.

He had the patience to sit hour after hour in board meetings, waiting for this man and that man and the other to be led into making decisions which at first might have gone against the grain. Not only that, but he had the perseverance and the patience to stay on the telephone at night after these meetings, and to phone those persons whom he felt might have gone along had they had the feeling that their voices were being heard. In the application of this democratic, if slow, process, Tom would bring to bear the other part of his philosophy: that while the vision may be given to relatively few, it is only in the checks and balances of differing points of view at which sound thinking is arrived.

There was an effervescence about Tom that drew people to him. When it came to influencing men and women of high or low rank, he was a born psychologist. Not only that, but he had an understanding heart. People knew that, and they trusted him. They knew that there was never an ulterior motive where he was concerned.

With these gifts, it should not have been unexpected, but it was, that when the legislator from our city, Bill Fenner, died suddenly in office, Tom was chosen to fill out his term. Nor would it have been unexpected that at the end of the term, his interest in politics would have been generated, not as the perennial political animal, but on a deeper level. On both sides of my family, men had taken their turns in the legislature, and I now concurred in Tom's interest. For the next twelve years, much of our life would go on in Raleigh, the State Capitol. His political life would culminate with his becoming Speaker of the House.

It could almost go without saying, that having proven himself in many ways, he would be urged by the Democratic party to run for Governor. But neither of us wanted that. Tom's feeling was that he could continue to make contributions to his state in other ways. This decision was something that our friends at home and over the state, in general, never really understood, but it was a decision we never regretted. It gave us more time for our family, more time for each other, and more for travelling; and for the thing that would really round out our life: the twenty-three years to be spent, in part, in our second home, on Captiva Island. There we would be making additional friendships with people from all over the country, and from foreign shores as well. On that naturally beautiful island, in a simple, uncluttered way of life, in that we came and went, still pulling our oar at home, but at intervals, refilling the vessel at Captiva, we felt that we had the best of both worlds.

≈ ≈ ≈

The first and lasting sorrow that came into my own early life, and that of our immediate family, was Alice Bryan's long illness. From the stories I was told, I know that for the first eight years of her life, Alice Bryan had been a happy little girl, prettier and more sunny than the average. The story of her illness begins with the summer when the loving grandparents on Father's side took the first three little girls, Sister, twelve, Vivian, ten, and Alice Bryan, nine, to Wrightsville Beach for a stay of a month.

They made the four-hour trip by train to Wilmington, and the rest of the twelve miles by hack. The first two weeks were all joy, but there were mosquitos. Suddenly, as it was later explained, from having scratched a mosquito bite, Alice Bryan developed blood poisoning. With high fever, and terrible pain in one leg, she was rushed home by train. There was no hospital nearer than Richmond, 125 miles away, but with home care – that of Mother's around the clock – with nurses sent down from Richmond, and with Uncle Mark's daily visits – at that time, he was still practicing medicine – driving the eight miles in his buggy, and Dr. Marriott's almost constant attendance at the bedside of the beautiful little daughter of his best friend, she pulled through.

But at the end of six weeks, when she was well enough to get out of bed, it was found that her left knee was badly drawn. For the rest of her life, she would limp. Not only that, but she was left with the incurable disease, osteomyelitis, the dread infection which once in the marrow of the bone, never leaves. Even today, with all the miracle drugs, there is no cure. The intensity of the seizures may be lessened, but the danger of getting a bruise anywhere, especially by a fall, is always lurking. In Alice Bryan's case, over the remaining years of her life, she would undergo twenty-three operations. The first sign of the onset of trouble would be pain in whatever member of her body was under attack. The severity of the pain would increase, and six weeks would be required for the infection to localize. Only then could surgery be performed.

Surgery involved the scraping of the bone, and over time, nearly all the joints in her body and some of her ribs had needed that. As joint after joint stiffened from these operations, her life became one principally of wheelchairs and crutches. It began to seem that only the bones in her face would be spared, and by some miracle they were. That is not always true of osteomyelitis. As her body underwent all these ordeals, however, her face seemed to become even more beautiful. It shone with an inner light; the miracle of that is, in itself, unforgettable.

The fact that we lived daily with this affliction of Alice Bryan's may have encouraged us to be a laughing family, for laughter and tears can never be far apart. Further, Mother was Irish; she approached life with a bright outlook. Combined with her unfailing nurturing and fortitude lay the realization that humor makes the ordeals of life easier. We were always trying to make Alice Bryan laugh and it was her nature to be responsive.

Father died after he and Mother had had twenty-eight years together. As I have said, I was almost fifteen. When Tom and I had been married a year, Alice Bryan's death came, almost on our first anniversary, so that Mother's two greatest sorrows came – loosely speaking – ten years apart.

Knowing how she had met Father's death, I felt that she would bear up under Alice Bryan's. By that time, I had the immeasurable joy of feeling that I had given Mother the second of two sons she was not to have until late in life, and of having given Alice Bryan a second brother. Bob Gorham, Sister's husband, had been filling those roles for three years when Tom and I were married. In the few years that Mother was to live after Alice Bryan's death, she would have the joy of having two grandsons, as well. Sister's son came first, three years later, my firstborn. The pendulum in our family was now swinging from having been a generation of girls, to one of boys.

Mother's death came suddenly, when my son, young Tom, was two months old. She had had the pleasure, one day when I had gone to Raleigh, of "keeping" the baby in our new home, which we had been in for not quite a year. Taking turns with the nurse, and supervising the planting of the sugar-maple tree, which, with our appreciation, she was having brought in from the woods of one of our farms and planted near our driveway, she had had one of her usual happily useful days. For the next fifty years, every October, that tree, near the large old magnolia in the corner of our yard would become a blaze of gold, a beautiful link with Mother. Like nothing else, it would remind me of Mother's love of trees, of how she was always sending to the woods to have certain varieties brought out and planted about the tenant houses on our farms. The sugar-maple was her favorite. She wanted the tenants to have shade to sit in on Sunday afternoons, when, bathed and dressed for company, they sat in the yard on their straight-backed chairs brought out from the kitchen for the purpose. Often an older sister would be "wrapping" the hair of a younger one with tobacco twine. This was a slow process, but worth it, because it kept the hair neat throughout the week. They were happy scenes.

At some point in the long warm afternoon, the father would bring up a watermelon from where it had been cooling in the well. At the squeak of the chain, the children would begin to jump and clap their hands, and to make way for the father to put the watermelon on the floor at the edge of the porch. The mother would come from the kitchen with a long knife, and in less time than it takes to tell it, all ages would be at work on a slice of melon, spitting the seeds in all directions. There was no need to be circumspect about the disposition of the seed, because on the next Saturday, the yard would be swept with a brushbroom, those long stiff branches of the dogwood tree that, tied together for the purpose, were always kept on hand, lying under the house.

≈ ≈ ≈

Tom's years as a student at the University at Chapel Hill had been busy ones. He played freshman football, and soon became manager of the baseball team. To supplement his tuition he ran the fraternity dining room. Throughout his life, his fraternity brothers, who'd been there at that time, whenever they saw Tom, would start joking about the carloads of grits that they'd been served when he planned the meals. Not only did he like grits himself, but among southerners, they were, and are, a favorite "filler," and they cost little.

Johnson, spoken of and to as "Brother Johnson," the old retainer at the Deke house, could not pronounce the name "Pearsall," and since Tom's room was on the third floor, the whole house was awakened every morning at six o'clock with the sound of Johnson's voice, coming loudly from the foot of the stairs to get Tom up and on the job, "Mr. Peace, Oh, Mr. Peace!" It was in that way that Tom's nickname became "Peace." It was amusing to me through the years to read some of the letters that came to Tom from his fraternity brothers using that term in the salutation; especially amusing when the fraternity brother, Gordon Gray, had become President of the University of North Carolina, and later, when he had gone on to be United States Senator, to see that his letters to Tom continued to begin, "Dear Peace."

Having, as he said, always taken his athletics seriously, Tom did not drink. If he needed anything beyond his happy disposition and his joy of life to endear him to his fraternity brothers, the fact that he didn't take a drink would in itself have made him popular. The others could always count on him to drive them home after a dance.

One of his best-loved fraternity brothers was Norfleet Pruden from Edenton, near the coast. Prudy's father had been dead a long time. His mother, spoken of with affectionate amusement by the other members of the fraternity, and even by her son, as "Miss Penzy," was an Edenton town character. Although the Prudens lived in a fine old house with a lot of old silver, since their income had always come mainly from farms, they were often short of cash. There were times when he was at the University when Prudy, through various means and sundry, would have scraped the bottom of the barrel. At those times, he would wire his mother for funds.

Miss Penzy was never known to let him down, but mother-like, when she wired the money, she wired motherly advice, as well. One telegram Tom remembered as characteristically amusing was in dialect. This is what she wired: "Look here boy, cotton is five cents a pound and the mullet ain't runnin'. But here it is – divide with the po', and go to church Sunday."

This was a tale Tom always loved to tell, and one, now, that I like to recall. For, in a few years, that group of apparently languid young men would take their places in our state as hard-working businessmen and outstanding citizens and statesmen. That they would go on to blaze trails for the new things that were coming in, while at the same time, hold on to those of the old that had worth, would have been beyond credulity. But so it happened.

In addition to his other obligations while at Chapel Hill, Tom was given the responsibility for raising money to get the Deke Fraternity house out of debt, letters of appeal going out to all members of that chapter. One of these was an outstanding lawyer who was helping with the legal end of things, and who happened to be from Tom's own hometown of Rocky Mount. In this way, Mr. Joe Ramsey and Tom were often in contact. Apparently impressed with the younger man's enthusiasm and dependability, when Tom had graduated from Carolina and had gone on to study law and had passed the bar, Mr. Ramsey invited him to join him in his practice. But Tom was to have only one year of practice with this respected member of the bar. Mr. Ramsey died suddenly; Tom decided to go out on his own, and that was the situation three years later when we were married.

The first of Tom's volunteer public responsibilities after we were married, was that of being asked to take charge of something called "Bundles for Britain." Although now, the why's and wherefore's of this community effort have grown dim, it was probably that there was a depression in England at the time, perhaps even worse than our own, for the British Isles were hardly more than a decade away from the end of the first World War. I remember that every night Tom and I would go to a large old empty store to receive things like blankets, and warm woolen clothes, and, at intervals, would see that they were shipped out. It was reminiscent of our country's all-out effort during my childhood to provide food and clothes for the "starving Armenians," her willingness – even her habit – of sharing with other nations who were less-fortunate.

Somewhere along in this period, our town began a charity league. Not having the required population of fifty-thousand, we could not call ourselves a Junior League – we were possibly no more than thirty-thousand– so we became the "Junior Guild." Families in need were assigned to members, we gave our services to the baby clinic at the health department, and, in a general way, ferreted out community needs, giving them our support. These needs were an eye-opener to the more fortunate young women of our town. With our own children well-fed, properly clothed, and under a pediatrician's care – for one of those had now come among us –we began to see, firsthand, the unfairness of life.

During those years, Junior Guild members were assigned – in pairs – to certain families who were living on severely limited incomes. These troubled but deserving people stirred both our sympathy and our admiration, and we were often able to find ways to help them other than merely with funds. Mrs. William Wall, or Kay, formerly a nurse, was my partner, and she knew right away that since the mother of the family to which we'd been assigned was a chronic asthmatic, her own lot, and that of her children, some of them sickly as well, could not improve unless she, herself, had a chance at health. Fortunately, we were able to persuade a doctor to perform a tubal ligation. Almost overnight there was the joy – for us – of seeing the lot of the whole family change. The burdens of the hard-working father were lessened; the whole family would go on to lead fruitful lives.

It was in these years that the Children's Museum came into being. And here my mind goes back to our rector, Mr. Craighill, whose love of birds stimulated that of our family into subscribing to a small magazine called *The Chat*. For those who are not ornithologists, a chat is "any of several small Old World thrushes that have a chattering cry, especially the yellow-breasted chat." We began to pass our copies on to the William Joyners, Eleanor and Bill, in order that they might have their little daughter, Ellen, know and love birds. Already a naturalist, Bill was so inspired that he wound up giving lectures with slides that taught children in our town, and in others, about birds and their habits, and Bill gave lasting credit to *The Chat*.

Around that time, another naturalist, English by birth, and wife of a Universalist minister, came to live among us. Mrs. Mae Bell and Bill Joyner were members of the original board of our Children's Museum, Mrs. Bell becoming its very competent director. This woman of many talents is a published writer, as well. She has published books of poems, and at present writes book reviews that appear regularly in our local paper.

Somewhere along in those years, our Arts Center came into being. As I recall, a Mr. Harold Parry, employed in the music department of the city schools, was its instigator. His enthusiasm was shared by Bill Rawls, a native who had returned from a period of teaching design in the city of New York to go into business with his father. With a handful of those like-minded, a meeting was held, and plans laid for our prospective center for the arts. During that initial meeting, Bill telephoned Sunny – or Florence – Lea (Mrs. Bruce Lea), whose marriage had brought her from South Carolina to live among us, and who, in a short while, had shown herself to be generous to things for the public good. Sunny immediately subscribed. And I feel reasonably sure that that first exciting show of support amounted to five hundred dollars. With this, an old house near downtown was rented. Empty except for the immediate installation of a ballet bar and a much-used old table, a half-dozen mismatched straight chairs, and a crotchety furnace which consistently sent up smoke and layers of soot, the Arts Center was born. Soon, a variety of courses were being offered.

As early as possible, however, we gave up that house, for the city had given us its abandoned water tank. Its ground level floor became an art gallery, its second floor, our theater-in-the-round. The one-story, small brick building adjacent became the crafts center. Happily, we now have, on the same property, our impressive new playhouse, and its well-thought-out parking area. Charlotte Toler and Lula Carrington Shultz were early enthusiasts of the proposed Arts Center. And, down the years, Charlotte's attic has been a gold mine of assorted props and costumes on loan for the theater, everything from ostrich fans and feather boas, to lovely Chinese parasols, embroidered Spanish shawls and exotic necklaces.

This upsurge of interest in the arts followed what had, for some time, been the dream of some local preservationists that the stately old home, spoken of locally as the "Old Louis Place," more formerly as "Stonewall," be given to the city as a place of historical interest. When the Louis family, owners of Stonewall and stockholders in the Rocky Mount Mills, had all died out, the home and its surrounding acres were purchased by the Mills as a home for its superintendent and the superintendent's family. After some time, this use of the home changed. And, in a state of perfect preservation, the property was turned over to the Nash County Society for Historic Preservation.

The Tar ran between Stonewall and the Mills, and, loosely, at a halfway point between the two, near the river, a monument to the Confederacy was erected. After the building of Stonewall in the early 1800s, the Church of the Good Shepherd would possibly be our town's next landmark, for it came somewhere in the 1850s. Although, as I have said in this story many times, accuracy as to dates is not my longsuit, I might venture to say that next to the Good Shepherd and a few early storefronts on Main Street, there would be little of historical interest until the early 1900s when there was a spate of Greek Revival homes, our still handsome brick railway station, and a large brick home of simple elegance near the downtown area, that of the Hines family, who lived there for three generations.

With the inevitable changes that come about generation to generation, the home and its grounds became too much of a burden for Erwin Robbins Wilde, the only surviving member of the current generation of the Hines family, and the whole town wondered what would be the eventual fate of this lovely "Machaven" in which we had such pride. Then came the solution. It came out that, Henry Tharrington, a local young man of untiring energy and vision – to say nothing of taste – had for his dream, ownership of Machaven and its conversion to a city club.

Collective local breaths were held, but we need have had no fears, for architecturally, the house has remained the same. Even its draperies and some of its fine old wallpaper have been preserved. It has been brightened by the use of off-white woodwork, enhanced by dark floors. The few pieces of furniture which serve to make the rooms hospitable and gracious, are placed where they always were, their scarcity provides the necessary space for large receptions and other entertainment of that nature. All the space on the upper floor has been given to dining, with the good news that an elevator is to be installed during the coming year. Since my own family and the Hines family had a close friendship, this altogether perfect transition pleases *me* especially.

My new life had been slowly gaining momentum, as had Tom's. With the expectancy of our first child, we built what would be our one and only home. The choices of lots in Westhaven were many. We chose ours for three major reasons: the property faced a park, it was on a corner, and it had the poetic note of having a spring that, among ferns, trickled artistically down a ravine. Mesmerized by the gurgle of the spring, we were off on a romantic cloud about making that area into a garden. Tom had a great liking for dry stone walls – he could already see two sides of the garden so enclosed – so that the first step in our gardening life was to have this done. Even as the house was being built, I was planting ivy on that wall, and we were driving out together late in the afternoon to pour water on it and to sit and hear the trickle of the spring.

Time marched on, bringing us the double pleasure and excitement of moving into a new home and expecting our first child. By the first spring in our new home, we were working morning to night in the garden. When the wall around the garden had been built, there was a large pile of stones left in the corner for Tom to carry out his dream of building three dams over which the water would gently trickle and supposedly lull us to sleep, for our bedroom was on that side. Ferns and other wild things already grew along the banks of the stream; we even had a Jack-in-the-pulpit, and we were practically delirious about our garden. But when the dams were completed, there was one thing in the garden which I saw as an eye-sore: in one corner, a leftover pile of rocks, four or five feet high. Tom was reluctant to have them moved, for in that way of husbands, he insisted that "we might need them sometime." For months I was sympathetic with that point of view. Then I began to urge him to have them taken away. Always, I got the same – to his way of thinking – logical answer. So that one fine day, I shared a little plan with the yardman for the disposition of the rocks, and enlisted his help. Wheelbarrow by wheelbarrow, Joe moved the rocks to the vacant lot behind our yard, which belonged to us, as well, and one by one, buried them. The minor problem of what to do with the displaced earth was of no concern. We could bring that into the garden in a now empty wheelbarrow, and sprinkle it about under the shrubs where no one would know. By the end of the day, the job had been done. I kept the news to myself. One morning, a few days later, Tom, as usual, looking out over the garden as he buttoned his shirt, spoke. "Am I seeing things?" he asked. "Or are the rocks gone?"

"They are," was my reply. "Joe and I buried them in the arena," for that was the name we'd already given to that wooded area where we expected to have, later, a pony stable, a wigwam, and a long rope-swing from a very tall tree that would make wonderful swinging for our own children and those of the neighborhood.

Without turning away from the window, Tom said in disbelief, "Well, I'll be damned! All this talk about motherhood and tenderness and nurturing being a woman's stripe is dead wrong! The dominant trait in a woman is tenacity."

I just held my peace. The rocks were gone, and I was happy.

No doubt Tom was not the only husband to live to make that observation. Whether openly or deviously, if she wants something done, a woman will usually keep on until she brings it about. Not having been given the necessary brawn, we have learned to keep our wits nimble. But Tom wasn't really upset. For deep inside, I knew that he conceded to my point of view, although I did not press the point. And so it was, that the last unplanted corner of the garden could be made beautiful.

≈ ≈ ≈

With time and introspection, I have come to know something about myself that I believe must have been true – in the main – of my ancestors as well. I love homes to have beautiful names. Having come to the New World and plunged their roots into its soil, rewarded with her fruits, our ancestors came to give to their "homeplaces" names that were warm and lovely: "Rainbow Banks," and "Cotton Plains," and most evocative of all for a southern plantation, "Snowfields." Just to say them over is to brim my cup, for it gives me the feeling that my forebears and I have been irrevocably linked to the land.

Oddly, it was not until a year after our marriage that Tom and I discovered that our great-great-grandfathers and great-great-grandmothers had spent their lives as neighboring planters on the Roanoke. This was near the town of Hamilton, forty-two miles from our own. Once we'd made the discovery of our joint backgrounds, we drove to that area often.

The Prices of Hickory Hill and the Sherrods of Rainbow Banks must have met regularly on Sundays at St. Martins, the small Episcopal church in Hamilton, approximately a halfway point between the few miles by which their plantations were separated. No doubt, in shad season, the men would be out in their rowboats with a field-hand or two to help with the nets, excitedly seining for those large delectable fish. Certainly they would have been among the groups who gathered on the high banks of the Roanoke for the accustomed "rock muddles" that were a part of river life. To balance this, I have a mental picture of our great-great-grandmothers exchanging spend-the-day visits. I do not have to be told to know that as they did, they would have been sharing slips from their flower gardens, fresh vegetables from their gardens, and newly ripened fruits from their orchards. Nor to know that from their pantries, in a basket covered by a large white damask napkin would lie those true homemaker's delights, some of the things they had, themselves, "put up": jars of jams and jellies and pickles and preserves, especially that long-time favorite Eastern Carolina relish of red and green sweet peppers, a jar or two of "chow chow."

Fitting this discovery from that far back time into the fabric of our own happy life together, Tom and I began to feel that somehow, things for us must have been pre-ordained; in our beloved Julia Black's phrase, "As if they were meant."

≈ ≈ ≈

From the moment when we moved into our new home, Tom was moving more and more into political life, with all its obligations and social by-products. Luckily, I felt well during that, and my subsequent pregnancies, and all that season, Tom and I went to every football game that was played at Chapel Hill. We accepted a world of invitations in Chapel Hill, Raleigh, Greensboro, and Charlotte. And in a few months after moving into our home, our son was born.

In those days, babies were still being born at home. Out of our heads with happiness after young Tom's birth, the next morning at seven I phoned Mother; the friends and relatives that Tom didn't phone and invite to come and see the baby on the following Sunday afternoon, I did. For our joy had become a mild form of hysteria. The result of these widespread invitations was that by the end of the day of "the viewing," thirty-five people had come to share our joy. They filed enthusiastically through my bedroom to give me a hug where I lay, pillowed and primped, accepting all accolades.

Childbirth, and its way of keeping the new mother pampered and secluded in her bedroom for a month, had progressed from my grandmother's time to my mother's time, when two weeks and a few limited visitors were the norm. In my own time, this unique coddling had dwindled to ten days, yet lying-in was still an occasion to be made the most of. For what moment in life is greater than that of the miracle of birth? Realization and thanksgiving go hand in hand. On that joyous Sunday, the parade of well-wishers, moving through the bedroom and on into the nursery and out into the hall, might hope to find the proud father either upstairs or downstairs; he couldn't decide which was the better vantage point.

Unfortunately for young mothers in the 1930s, there was not that comforting presence, even if at a remove, of Dr. Spock. And there were, as yet, not many pediatricians. But the Federal Government had kindly printed a pamphlet of about forty pages in which they dispensed advice on getting the baby started. This became a young mother's bible. Its title was simply, "Infant Care." One of the rules it laid down was that after the first crucial month, in order that the infant stay dry during the night, it should be roused at intervals, taken to the bathroom, and with the appropriate mother-cooing by way of encouragement, urged to cooperate.

Nobody took this mandate more seriously than Dot Wilkinson and I. There was not a whit of difference in our intensity; there was only the slight variation in that her first-born was a girl, and mine, a boy. Our homes were not far apart, and everyday, we kept in close touch with regard to our nightly progress in the bathroom. But one night, there came an episode at Dot's house which ended the prescribed practice for each of us.

The application of this theory of infant care had gone on for several nights, much to the disparagement of the husbands, who deemed it silly to meddle with nature, especially in this way. Frank and Tom were close friends, and although I doubt that they had discussed this "home problem," they held the same point of view.

By the fourth night that Dot had been following the government mandate, Frank took action; Dot did as well. The book suggested that in order to enlist the cooperation of the child, who has been lovingly deposited on its own little throne, by way of inspiration a glassful of water be trickled slowly into the half-filled lavatory. Not only once, but repeatedly. And although Dot and I were considerate about closing doors and not disturbing our sleeping husbands, it would have been impossible for them, with all our billing and cooing, not to be aware of what was going on. And so, on that particular night, Frank – having had enough –jumped out of bed and strode purposefully toward the bathroom to file a complaint.

When he flung the bathroom door open, Dot, having just filled a glass with the required water, and knowing just what he was going to say, quickly changed course and threw the water into his face. Frank, his face and his pajamas dripping, bless him, had the grace to burst out laughing, and it was the end of the adherence to Federally prescribed principles of infant care according to the Pearsalls and the Wilkinsons.

In another two years, young Tom would have a little brother, and our family's joy would be doubled. Mack would be born in the hospital and named for my father. Once again, the relatives came from far and near to share the joy. My two Braswell uncles were especially glad for Father to have a namesake, wished that he could have known about it, and everyday that I was in the hospital, came for a visit. Having these two loving uncles never ceased to add beauty to my life, for though the Braswell clan has never been a large one, they are especially close knit. The fact that Father's and Uncle Mark's and Uncle Jim's youngest brother – named Tom, for their father – had succumbed to yellow fever in his last year at the University seemed to make the bonds between the remaining brothers even stronger.

The spring that Mack was born, Tommy developed a chronic case of malaria, and while I was trying to be in Raleigh with Tom, or in Chapel Hill as much as I could, I was busy writing letters to hospitals all over the country trying to find a cure for this disease which, with its intermittent bouts of chills, fever with fever-blisters, and aching all over, had, for a long time, been common to Eastern Carolina.

Malaria had always been the scourge of the lowlands. While for a long time, its source had been a mystery, there had come an increasingly strong feeling that it had something to do with our swamps, perhaps the vapors that rose from them and blew over the land. Yet, other than quinine, no treatment for the malady had been developed. The answers to my letters of inquiry were always the same: "The doctors in your malarial belt know more about the treatment than any other." And it was true that every family kept on hand a large blue pill-box stuffed with capsules of quinine. Many had been the time when Dr. Marriott had allowed some of the village children to watch him fill these capsules, I, among them.

That treatment had always consisted of large and consistent doses of quinine. There was also a belief in the possibility of effecting a cure by going to live at a higher elevation. Two good things were to come out of the Second World War, however. The discovery of a medicine called "atabrine," which was much more effective than quinine, and the discovery of DDT to control mosquitos. When young Tom had reached the age of fourteen, although ostensibly cured by atabrine, Tom and I decided to follow our local doctor's advice, which had always been, if possible, to go for a long stay in the mountains. In some mystifying way, the change from low country to high would bring on an attack of great severity. After that, in some cases, the attacks would never return. And so, young Tom spent the next five years at Asheville School for Boys, and after a prolonged and dreadful attack of malaria during his first year, it never returned. Finding it a top grade prep school, run along English lines, when Mack came to be fourteen, he would be entered there as well.

When Tommy was five and Mack was three, there would be a third little son for us whose life would last only four days. Our sorrow would be doubled by the shock of knowing then that there would be, for us, no more children. This beautiful little boy was given Tom's father's name, Leon Fillyaw. Happy in that knowledge, the next day, the old grandfather, accompanied by his nurse, came to the hospital. Walking feebly, with the aid of a cane, the dear man said, "My feet were never lighter than when I came down that hall."

This was the same man whose letter of an earlier time, with other things of sentimental value, Tom kept in a desk drawer throughout his life. At the time of the letter, Tom had just gone away to prep school for the first time, for his father believed in the discipline of military school; his older son had been sent to the Citadel, in Charleston.

In his letter to Tom, sent to him at Georgia Military Academy in Atlanta, his father was saying things which, with his reserved nature, he would have found it hard to say in person. He spoke of his pride in the traits that Tom had shown in high school: a medal for being the best athlete, and one for being the best all-round student. He went on to say that he expected him to attend the University of North Carolina, and that he hoped he would choose a profession. That, because of the aftermath of the Civil War, the men in his father's family had not had those opportunities. He was speaking of having grown up in Duplin county, where, at the time, there was a good academy, and the students had been schooled in the three "R's," reading, writing, and arithmetic, even a little Latin. Through able and dedicated teachers, those of his generation had been given an especial love of the classics, and of history, as well. But because of the economy, few were able to follow professions.

The letter closed by saying, "In these long stays away from home, you will be thrown with girls in a different way. There is nothing so elevating in the life of a young man as being in the company of a nice girl. But don't lose your head." He signed it in an affectionate way. Rereading it now, and remembering his father's reserve, I am reminded, once again, that still water runs deep.

In the hospital, the babies were kept in a nursery, brought in only at times of feeding. When the third afternoon came, and the baby was not brought to me, I wanted to know why. The nurse said they were trying out supplemental feedings, and that, I accepted. Nor was the baby brought to me at ten, and I was given the same explanation.

Awakening in the night, I asked the nurse what time it was, and she answered quietly, "It's three." Again I wanted to know why the baby hadn't been brought in at two. Always the same explanation. But at five, the door opened. As the brighter light came on, Tom entered the room. Startled and frightened at seeing him at that hour, I held my breath. He came to the side of the bed and put his hand on my arm. With him was our obstetrician and close friend, Adam Thorp. There was a third man, a stranger, and as he came to stand on the other side of the bed, I said, in panic, "You-all have come to tell me something!"

And then, with Tom holding my hand tight, tears rolling down his face, the visiting doctor began to explain, "Mrs. Pearsall, your little son has just given up life."

As though it would burst, my head began to throb with a thousand hammers. I could only cry out, "My head..." Adam gave a swift order to the nurse and I was given an injection. As my blood pressure lowered, and the pain began to subside, the Doctor quietly explained to me what had happened.

"Something new has come to science, Mrs. Pearsall, that when one parent's blood is RH positive, and the other, RH negative, there begins to be a form of warfare in the body of the mother. Nature does her best to overcome this. It has been proven that the mother's body can go through two pregnancies successfully. By the third, however, although at birth, things in the new little life might appear normal, it can only for a short while function outside its mother's body, and severe jaundice sets in. Doctors and nurses are trained to look for the first danger signals, red spots on the abdomen, and as soon as these appeared on your little son, your local doctor and your husband got in touch with Duke hospital and asked to have somebody sent down to administer the only known treatment for the condition. This treatment consists of giving emergency injections of Vitamin K every hour. These have gone on throughout the night, to no avail. Virtually no success has been had so far with this form of treatment, but we hope that research will steer us in the right direction."

Speaking so gently and with so much feeling, this kind man from Duke, who was trying to make it easier for me to accept the sorrow, went on, "With this condition, your little son would already have begun to suffer brain damage." And with that sentence, resignation began to come.

In a few years there would, indeed, come the miracle discovery that by completely transfusing all the infant's blood at a certain crucial moment after birth, as long as he is otherwise healthy, the infant will have a chance at survival.

There were streaks of dawn showing through the window, and I felt the need of the church as I had never before in my life. I knew that Tom did too, and I asked him to call Mr. Craighill, the rector who had married us and christened our children, as soon as he thought that good man might be awake.

On the following day, interment took place in my home village, with our relatives and our friends there to support Tom. The doctors had agreed that it would help me psychologically to go home as soon as possible to Tom and the children. It was thought that I needed to be among my loved ones. Once there, as any mother would have done, I hid my grief. Since I had bordered on uremia, I had to stay in bed for awhile. But I could be propped up there, and with a child and a pillow under each arm, could read aloud to them. Our little sons, themselves, were filled with disappointment, but they understood that it would take time for nature to reverse the preparation she had made for the new little life, and that, at that time, my breasts, excruciatingly painful and temporarily bound, the movements of the little boys needed to be especially careful. For them, this situation was a double early lesson in maturity.

I never loved my friends and relatives more than during that period of recovery when they came, so often, to visit me. Most of them were women, and it was moving to see that in nearly every case, as they approached the bed to kiss me, there were tears of sympathy in their eyes. They knew that Tom and I had hoped for a large family.

When I was able to get out of bed, with the nurse's help, I packed up the layette and had it sent as a gift to a woman who had had the room across the hall from me in the hospital. She was someone I didn't know, had never seen, but I felt that since she had given birth to twins while I was there, she might need more infant clothes. The only thing I kept was the family christening dress.

As has always been my habit in times of trouble and sorrow, I leaned on the prayer book. By then I had seen enough of life – that around me, and in the various parts of the world to which I had travelled – to understand the need for that supplication in the Book of Common Prayer, A Prayer for all Sorts and Conditions of Men:

"*Finally, we commend to thy Fatherly Goodness, all those who are in any ways afflicted or distressed, in mind, body, or estate, [especially those for whom our prayers are desired;]*" and if the prayer is being followed in a service, the priest will pause here for a full minute, "*that it may please thee to comfort and relieve them, according to their several necessities; giving them patience under their sufferings, and a happy issue out of all their afflictions."*

This sorrow came early in November, and for me it was to be a long, sad winter. I remember, that often, when I was alone, I would look through the window to the outside and think, *If only it were spring.* And, as it always does, spring did come.

≈ ≈ ≈

The shock and the way of Mother's death was beyond imagining. After Alice Bryan's death, she and Vivian had continued to live in the village, life going on in the same quiet ways of the country. No matter that the family had dwindled, in a general way the hum of activity had to be maintained, and Mother kept an eye out for its overall coordination. The poultry yard was still active, the garden, in its mixture of vegetables and flowers, was still planted, and tended, and regularly shared, but the stable was now empty. Although Vivian was then only thirty-nine, I had begun to feel that she would never marry, and was saddened. Yet she had had many opportunities and they would continue.

At the explosion of our gas house I must have been about six when Henry, the yardman, made the mistake of lighting his lantern when he was inside the fourteen-by-fourteen gashouse on his tour of inspection, and had luckily except for singed eyebrows and lashes, escaped without injury. Henry's head, completey bald before, did, somehow ever after, seem to appear slicker. After that, Father converted the house to electricity. This was generated by something called a Delco. Throughout the day, the merry little tat-tat-tat came and went, more up-to-date than Grandma's windmill, but the sound not half as poetic. In the same building, spoken of as the "engine house," the Delco also pumped our water from an artesian well. The carriage house had always been large, so that there was now plenty of room for our cars. These had begun to come into our lives when I was three, when we had moved into the newer and larger house.

One of the rules of the era for the upkeep of cars was that distilled water should be added to their batteries every two weeks. It was the yardman, Arthur's, responsibility, every fourteen days, to go through this ritual. Several gallon bottles of distilled water were always on hand for the purpose. Mother counted on this, coupled with the air-cooled motors of our snub-nosed Franklins, which we had two at a time, to give our cars life-everlasting.

It was another of Arthur's responsibilities to keep check on the boiler in the cellar that furnished our heat and hot water, and to keep check on the smokehouse. One of Mother's great prides had always been the way the hams from the farms were cured. She had learned to supervise the process for taking care of them from her own mother, who was a product of the Reconstruction. There was never a day during my early life when there wasn't a ham, cooked and sitting on a large blue and white platter in the pantry, ready to be sliced "as thin as paper," an art in which all southern husbands endeavored to excel, and in which Father certainly did.

In the South, a plantation mistress was judged by the quality of her hams. If they were not properly treated, somewhere along the line, they would spoil. Not in the usual sense, but through the invasion of a few "skippers," those small white worms, that boring into the tender meat, eventually turn into slender insects resembling silver, or paper moths. It was in the supervision of the steps in the protection of hams from these liabilities that a plantation mistress's reputation lay. Mother, herself, had coined the phrase which today would be out-moded, "A woman should always keep in her life a black lace dress, a string of pearls and a ham."

In our part of the world, the slaughter of pigs, called "hog-killing," could not be done until the weather was very cold. A sharp eye had to be kept out for its arrival, and here I have to inject a tale.

When air-conditioning had just come to the South, a farmer, walking to town one day in November, was offered a ride. It was one of those left-over days of early autumn when the sun shone so warmly that the thermometer was probably in the upper fifties. With the sun streaming in through the windows of the car, the driver quietly turned on the air-conditioning. Although they had not yet reached the town, the farmer suddenly asked to be let out. His hurried explanation to the driver, "I'm not going to town. It's cold enough for me to kill my hogs."

Now back to the ham-curing process. At the time of hog-killing, all farm hands turned to, to take care of the "meat." The half-dozen hogs were first shot in the forehead, then stabbed in the throat. None of this did we ever see, for that took place on the farms. They were then scalded, laid out on a board to scrape off the hair, and hung on large hooks for cutting open before butchering. This done, two or three of them were brought to us in the village, where far back from the house there followed the making of sausage, and the beginning of the curing of hams. One of the overseers was always there to supervise.

As the workers ground the meat into sausage, the overseer seasoned small batches, and when he thought he had put into it just the right amount of sage and salt and pepper, especially red pepper, would fry a patty or two in a pan over the red hot coals surrounding a large, cast-iron pot and send the samples "to the house" for Mother to give her decision. "A little more sage, a little less pepper," the message would go back, and by the end of the day there would be stuffed links to begin the day, and to share with the neighbors, a quantity of that in bulk.

The part that Mother oversaw was the treatment of the hams. With several people at work, the hams were first rubbed in salt and then laid on a wide shelf that ran around three sides inside the smokehouse. There they were to be left undisturbed for around three or four months, our coldest. In March, the hams would be washed and dried, then coated with a mixture of molasses, pepper, and saltpeter. The proper proportions of this, and the thoroughness with which it was applied told the story; whether the ham would be free of skippers or not.

In our part of the world, one of the gestures of hospitality had long been sending a houseguest home with a ham, and no self-respecting hostess would have dared do this unless she were sure of the quality of the ham. If she were, she could, with complete confidence send the yardman to the smokehouse to make a selection. The ham would be wrapped thoroughly by the cook, then placed in the car – in the earlier days, the buggy or the surrey – of the guest. That gesture of warmth carried over into my own life. Tom and I happened to be in New York at a time when, with World War II over, and the Marshall Plan for helping Europe with its recovery in operation, Churchill was in New York visiting his old friend, Bernard Baruch. As usual, when concerned about how their tax dollars are being spent, there were protesters. The newspapers, quick to seize the story, blew it up with large headlines. They carried pictures of the picketers; their placards shrieked, "Churchill go home! Keep your hands out of Uncle Sam's pockets!"

With our admiration for that great man, and what he had done to save the free world, I was indignant, covered with shame, as was Tom. Reading these ungrateful headlines in the newspaper, I said, "Tom, I'm going home and send Churchill a ham." Tom laughed, yet I think he knew I would. At the time, England was still in the grip of rationing. Butter was practically non-existent, meat allowances per person, infinitesimal, and we had been sending packages to our friends there. And so, a ham went to Ten Downing Street. Along with this product of Edgecombe County, went a letter of explanation as to its symbolism, and our personal apologies for our nation. A letter of appreciation from Ten Downing Street soon arrived, and I felt better.

We were never to know what went wrong the day of Mother's accident. It was after lunch on a warm day in March. Vivian had Uncle Dennis, the man who took care of the garden, planting flowers. For, of all of us, Vivian's love of flowers was greatest. Lucinda, the cook, was in the kitchen, Arthur was polishing the cars. As usual, Mother was taking her afternoon rest on the daybed in her sitting room, combining it with reading the morning paper, which, except for the headlines, she saved for that hour.

Perhaps the house felt chilly, and she decided to go to the cellar to check the pressure on the water tank that furnished our heat. For from a background of women who had filled the role of plantation mistress, it was almost instinctive for Mother to play that part. Though ours was not actually an antebellum sort of life, there was a discernable psychological carry-over.

The entrance to the cellar was at some distance from Mother's sitting room. She would have gone through the library into the wide front hall, past the sliding doors of the parlor, the side hall, and the sliding doors to the dining room, and through the breakfast room onto a porch from which stairs led down into the cellar. From the kitchen, Lucinda had glimpsed her as she crossed the back porch. In another two or three minutes there was an explosion. Unbelievably, the round, heavy cast-iron door, over a yard in circumference and held to the tank with enormous rivets, had blown off. It struck Mother's head, and she never spoke again.

With Arthur at the wheel, and Vivian and Lucinda in the backseat holding Mother, they reached the hospital in a matter of minutes, and the staff immediately went to work. Tom and Sister and her husband, Bob, and I, were there at once. When told that the skull would have to be lifted from the brain, and that it should be done by a brain surgeon, the decision to get Dr. Cole to come down from Richmond was immediately made.

Throughout the night, none of us left the hospital. With our baby two months old, I phoned the nurse every few hours. With sunrise, Mother was gone. Fifty-two years later, death would come to Tom at sunrise, as it had to Alice Bryan and to our little Leon. This has always made it easier for me. For with the coming of day – any day – comes duty. We gather our forces and go ahead.

≈ ≈ ≈

To have Mother's life end so abruptly at fifty-nine, when she was still so vibrant, and – as she had always been – responsive to the needs of others, such an example of meeting life with a calm and clear mind, a heart that was never judgmental, was unbelievable. But since Sister and I had both married in the time that lapsed after Father's death, now, in the shock of mother's death, we had both Tom and Bob to lean on. And Uncle Mark and Uncle Jim, who, after the loss of Father had kept faithful watch over

"Mack's family," or "Mack's children," as they spoke of us, were soon there.

This was where we had held Father's funeral and Alice Bryan's, for it was here, under a grove of lovely, old elms that Father and Mother had started their life together in what they spoke of as "Honeymoon Cottage," and which, in order to build a larger, more permanent home, had been moved to another site. The new home was called "The Elms," but since it was rarely spoken of in that way, a few years before Father's death, Vivian and I, the so-called "poetic" ones, suggested a more descriptive term, for we loved the way that with the softest of winds, the shadows of the long, sweeping branches of the elms slowly changed. And the name became "Shadowlawn."

For the last rites for Mother, the procession, would, again, move slowly past St. John's, as it had for Alice Bryan and Father, and would wind its way up the hill to the peaceful shade of the cemetery and the Braswell and Bryan mausoleum. Again, during the two days of waiting for that final hour, the house was hushed. Again, the venetian blinds in the parlor were lowered, their shutters, half-closed. Again, the light fell softly on the roses in the carpet, and gave to the floral tributes, most of them on easels, in their varying designs of crescents, hearts, crosses, and somehow, most meaningful of all, pillows, a mellowed beauty.

By the time of Father's death, however, Mother had developed a feeling of protectiveness toward the dead, had come to believe that they deserved the dignity and privacy of unopened caskets. And again, as had been done at both Alice Bryan's and Father's deaths, from the green world that Mother had so much loved, a point of view that became that of her daughters, we gathered a few magnolia boughs for sending to the florist to be made into a spray.

Yet, in early sorrow, no matter how many measures are taken to alleviate the pain of final separation, efforts to make death seem almost illusion, there must inevitably be the moment of reality. For my sisters and me, it came in the late afternoon of the day of the final service. Throughout the morning there had been little time to think, for the service was to begin at eleven. Early that morning, I had gone back to my own home to see that the baby was all right, to give him his bath, and then go back to Mother's. At ten-thirty, people had begun to arrive. According to Eastern Carolina custom, many of the friends and relatives would return with us from the cemetery to have a buffet lunch. A few stayed on through the afternoon, but by the hour of sunset, they had all gone. Tom and Bob had each gone for awhile "to the office."

The domestics, those current, and those who, although retired, for reasons of sentiment and affection had come back for the day, were now

196

congregated in the kitchen, and were, in their own inimitable ways, reliving the past. Vivian and Sister and I, standing in the hall, looking from the front door out into the western sky, knew that, in the come and go of conversation that was going on in the kitchen, there would be, "Do you recollect that time when Mr. Mack was in Baltimo', and one night a tramp cum lookin' in de winda and laked to sked Miss Alice and dat lady schoolteacha' from Virgina, and Lula and de three chillun to *deff*? And Miss Alice, she be in de family way, and all us sked that de new baby gonna be ill-defomed? And when dat baby cum, she be jes' as plump and pretty as dem udders was? And how 'bout all dem foeth of July bobby-kewes? And dat Foeth of July when evvybody be lookin' for Henry Slick, and he wuz down in de cella' drinkin' too much beer? And nobody don't know wheah he was? Won't dem de days doe?"

And so on.

It was March. Days, were lengthening, buds were swollen; some things were already in bloom. In the fields, that process that was bone of our bone – planting – had begun. But for us, one thought was paramount: the bedrock chapter of our lives was ending. We knew that the house would close.

≈ ≈ ≈

Although the house now belonged to Vivian, there was no longer any reason for her to live there. To have been, at thirty-nine, burdened with its upkeep, and subject to loneliness, would have been folly, and was never considered. Yet, I have to say here, parenthetically, that with her love of gardening and music, and of people and children, especially those around her, and with her pleasure in travel, it would have been hard to imagine Vivian as being bored or lonely.

In the South, one of the customs that was beginning to change, but that was still a pattern in Tom's family, and in mine, was that, at the death of her parents, a maiden sister would make her home with either a sister or a brother who was married. In Tom's family, it had been Aunt Molly; in Mother's, it had been Aunt Anne. In the plantation life of an earlier time – where the custom may have originated – in its preponderance of large houses, and an assortment of domestics, with the mistress of the plantation often overtaxed, the maiden sister would endeavor – and she usually succeeded in the effort – to make herself useful. These maiden sisters were usually seemingly bright and happy, but in that they played a secondary role, their resignation to this vicarious happiness had always had my sympathy.

By a dozen years or so, the youngest of the four daughters, I had early developed a sense of responsibility toward my sisters. Now there were only two of them. Sister was happily married; it was Vivian who lay on my heart. It was in this feeling, and Tom's all-loving nature, his "come one, come all" approach to life, that Vivian came to live with us.

She soon set about giving the old house for use either as a convalescent home for crippled children, or a home for the elderly. But because of the ever-present threat of fire to a wooden structure, both efforts failed. As these attempts at its disposition were being made, however, Vivian made plans for disposing of its contents. Alone, and with a strikingly positive attitude, she returned each week for several hours of applying herself to the monumental task of going through the rooms, one by one, item by item, even to the contents of cupboards and drawers, in the cellar, the rooms on the first floor, the second floor, and the all-encompassing attic, making lists as she did so, of what to offer to this or that institution, to this or that person, a detailed undertaking that only those who have closed the large, old house of a family who has lived rather well, and who believed in "keeping things" can appreciate.

At last it was all done, and except for the stair carpet, which was still held in place by handsome brass rods, the house sat empty. The sun streaked in through the now curtainless windows, Arthur continued to mow the grass. Now and then, the porch was swept. But flowers and vegetables no longer grew in the garden, and except for the birds, there was silence.

The doll house had long since been given away, but to stand now on the grass-grown spot where it had sat under the pear tree, was to hear, again, the plop of a large, heavy pear on the roof, and from the poultry yard, the cluck of a mother hen as she moved about, her brood instinctively following as she taught them to scratch for the all-important grit necessary for the craw, and to hear – again – the cackle of another hen, proudly announcing a new-laid egg.

Mother's roses that grew under the windows of the sitting room still bloomed, but as though half-hearted, sparingly. Indeed, to be there now, washed over by the way things had once been, was to be aware of the pulse of life only in the trees. For to see a tree, almost any tree, was to think of Mother. And now, to look up into the two pecan trees that grew near the kitchen porch, and to see nuts forming that with November would litter the ground, was to feel Mother's presence, and to remember, as we always would, that combination of the practical and the aesthetic that was her nature.

It was equally soothing to Vivian and me on our return visits, to sit for awhile on the steps to the front porch; to look up, again, into the old elms that always seemed to be dreaming away the hours; to find them, once again, nodding and swaying, impervious to time.

Yet, not everything about those visits into the past was somber. To recall the days of the dollhouse, my sisters so much older than I, that by the time I was ready for it, it was altogether mine, was to be taken back to that carefree happiness of early childhood, when, in my own case, some of the pleasures were mischief – inspired, there was a time when I enjoyed nettling my nurse by asking her the same question I'd asked many times, and that I knew the answer to as well as I knew my name.

Sometimes, in the lull of a summer afternoon, Koosa and I would be in the dollhouse. She would be shelling peas or butter-beans, or snapping snaps into a bowl on her lap, and I would be rocking and singing to my doll. Through the open doorway and the windows, we could hear Uncle Dennis, his whistling coming through the distance from where he was chopping his way down the long, straight rows of flowers and vegetables of the garden.

For the excitement of provoking Koosa to a fiery response, I might stop my rocking and singing, and puckering my lips in imitation of Uncle Dennis's performance, ask, lazily, "Koosa, why can't girls whistle?"

"Deah you go agin!" would sputter Koosa. "You jes' tryin' to vex me. You dun axed me a hunded times, and I done tole you a hunded. You jes doan never lissen, doan make you no neva mine. I'll tell you one mo' time. It's cawzen a whistlin' *gull* and a crowin' *hen* always cums to some bad *en'*!"

And having succeeded in producing this desirable explosion in Koosa, I would go back to my rocking and singing.

With time, robbers broke into the house and took the only things left: the bronze doorknobs, and the brass rods of the stair carpet. And, inevitably, the high school students in the community, seeking a thrill, put it out that the house was haunted. This set up regular weekend break-ins. Afterwards, the rooms would be littered with beer cans and cigarette stubs; this brought the question of fire. And rather than arrive one day to find the house in ashes, Vivian decided to have it torn down. In this way, all of us had the pleasure of knowing that young couples in the vicinity would be using its doors, its mantels, and its paneling in their own homes, and that the Corinthian columns would grace the porch of a church.

At the end of perhaps another forty years, the homes of all three of the Braswell brothers, which, in their preference for the Greek Revival style of architecture were so similar, would be torn down. Their materials would go on to serve the needs of others.

≈ ≈ ≈

There was no way for me to have foreseen that with time, turning the pages of our branch of the Braswell family, there would be for its oldest house something pleasant in store. That with the coming of 1994, the home and the farm of my grandfather Thomas Permenter Braswell, and my grandmother, formerly Emily Stallings, would pass from my Uncle Jim's descendants into the hands of the John High family of Rocky Mount, the younger John High family planning to live there.

This gives me the happiest of feelings, for this young couple is enthusiastic about restoring the house and grounds. Although it is now midwinter, and several months will be required before they take up residence, they have pansies blooming through the snow in what was once my grandmother's dooryard garden.

And although, by the time I was born, both those Braswell grandparents were no longer alive and the house was being occupied by an overseer and his family, all my life I loved driving down the avenue of its beautiful old elms, and began early to find it endearing that all the Braswells in our direct line would go on for four generations speaking of it as "The Homeplace."

≈ ≈ ≈

Ten months after Mother's death, with the approach of young Tom's first birthday, I went into one of my bursts of joy, those spells to which I've always been subject. This time it was to plan a party for a one-year-old who would have been just as happy having his zwieback all to himself. A dozen or so toddlers and their mothers were invited, and when the day came, great preparations were under way. The dining room table was moved out, the rug rolled up and taken away so that tops could be spun, tiny cars could be wound up for rolling across the room, and orange juice and crumbs could be spilled without harm.

The party was in full swing, mothers seated on the floor, children waddling about, and everybody happy, when the front door opened and Tom unexpectedly appeared in the hall. Making his way gingerly around toddlers, and a large rubber ball that was being rolled across the floor, he came into the dining room to where I sat on the floor at the other end, a toddler under each arm. Placing a small package in what was left of my lap, he said, quietly, "Something for you."

Inside the ribbon and the wrappings I found a small dark-blue velvet box. Inside the box, there was a ring; to me, the loveliest that could ever have been made. You would have to have known that, having been married five years earlier, during the depth of the Depression, there had been no money for an engagement ring, and that this was Tom's way of remembering, to have known, as any woman would, how I felt.

Before the day ended, I had my own surprise for Tom. I handed him a letter from two strangers in California. Unknown to us, a certain member of the widespread family of Pearsalls and his wife, a childless couple, had spent years researching the history of the Pearsall name. They had made frequent trips to England, and at the time the letter was written, had gathered enough data to publish three books. All three were to be had for the sum of twenty-five dollars. And without telling Tom, I gave an order for them.

When they came, the size of these three thoroughly authenticated books was startling. It has been a source of satisfaction to have them, even though, I must confess, they were to be used more to elevate small visiting children at mealtime than for research. Nevertheless, we liked knowing that the information was all there. For when this inspired and dedicated couple had gotten us back to William the Conqueror, they had barely started. One thing I do remember; the name "Pearsall" was "Peshale" in French, which these good people explained could have meant that they were either peers and lived in a hall, or were growers and pickers of peas. We could take our choice!

It would be many years before I came to know something of the original American Pearsall family. It came about through the discovery of the autobiography of a certain Logan Pearsall Smith. References to this writer in contemporary English and American literature had long piqued my interest, and when I finally was able to track down the writing for which he is most remembered, I found just what I wanted to know. Capsuled:

Three brothers came from England. One to settle in New York state as a clockmaker, one, in Pennsylvania to manufacture glass, and one, to Virginia to grow tobacco. The Philadelphia Pearsalls, coming under the influence of Benjamin Franklin, became Quakers, virtual leaders in that faith. Much of the family's time was spent in England at religious conferences, all the while, the mother of the family writing religious tracts. Growing up with the educational advantages of both worlds, their children, Logan and Mary became writers themselves. Mary was to marry Bernard Berenson, the world recognized connoisseur of art. After the age of twenty-seven, Logan lived quietly in Sussex, England. Logan never married, but his life was rich in friendships with the best literary minds of the time, and he, himself, became a "man of letters," his essays, brief, but exquisite. But for all his erudition, I felt particularly drawn to him for his witty observation that "youth is a kind of a delirium which takes years of painful treatment to cure."

A special friend of Edith Wharton's, it was on one of her cruises in the Adriatic, for which she chartered a large boat for her friends among the literati, that Logan withdrew to his stateroom one morning to begin his *Unforgotten Years*. Incidentally, that story tells of a family friendship with Walt Whitman, and the fact that they championed his *Leaves of Grass*. I especially like the section that includes the story in which the little Mary, knowing where the poet kept the key to his house, had the privilege of going in and out of a downstairs window, as well, in order to visit the great man as he sat upstairs in his study, composing his immortal lines.

Obviously, Tom's American ancestor was the one who came to Virginia to grow tobacco.

≈ ≈ ≈

There was never a day that I haven't appreciated my sons, more and more as they grow older and I see that they each have a social conscience. Early in their lives I began to recognize this quality. It was recognizable in young Tom at the age of four. Tom and I were out of town for the day; the cook and the nurse, in charge. It was summer, and in the late afternoon a storm had begun to "come up." The wind rose, and Julius, the elderly man who, although you could not call him a gardener, did the less strenuous things, such as weeding and watering, prepared to start home.

The nurse and the cook hurried about in the house, pulling down windows, and in the scurry, nobody missed Tommy until they suddenly saw him running out and down the front walk and through the gate, half dragging Tom's raincoat which he had hurriedly grabbed from our coat closet. In the splattering of the first raindrops he was scurrying across the road and a corner of the park to overtake Julius and give him the coat. Then he ran back home.

Greeted by Priscilla and Minnie in the front hall, Minnie asked, "Boy-ze, what were you doing out there?"

The open door to the coat closet in the hall helped to tell the story. Tommy's answer was succinct, "Julius was getting wet. He needed Daddy's raincoat."

Mack's social conscience showed up a little later, when he was in the first grade in school. A classmate came from a poor family, and he became Mack's almost best friend. At that time, there were no school cafeterias. Children whose homes were in walking distance went home for lunch that way.

Since our suburban area was too far to allow that, the children of our neighborhood were picked up by car pool. Two-thirds of the time, Mack brought Charlie home with him for that meal, and the family became our family's charge. Few things have given me more pleasure than having Charlie, the one in his family who was to finish high school, come by to see us on his way to the senior class prom. Dressed in his rented tuxedo, his appearance belied all the hardships that had gone before. After graduation, Charlie went to work in the midwest. He returned to Rocky Mount every few years, and we felt honored that we received a visit. Sadly he was to die young.

≈ ≈ ≈

At the point in my life when the children were not old enough to go to school, I developed a serious ear infection. Advised by our local specialist, I sought treatment at John's Hopkins in Baltimore. I was told there that I had a fragment of residual adenoidal tissue, which would respond to an infinitesimal amount of radium. For only one minute this would be administered through my nose on a small steel probe. Three treatments would be required, each one a month apart. This meant a five-hour train trip each way, which, in the way I had always enjoyed a train trip, I made the most of, with a book.

Each time, I had two overnight stays in Baltimore. The next morning I usually spent in a bookstore in which the salesgirl had come to recognize me. There being no other customers one morning, I felt free to ask her for a certain kind of help. I began this way: "I live in a small southern town, where a handful of us, as young mothers, are concerned that our minds are, at present, too much taken up with potty-training, and nose drops, and croup kettles, and although we're passionately devoted mothers, we feel that we should be doing something more with our minds. Can you recommend any book or books that we might study as a group?"

Without even answering, the young saleswoman reached under the counter, and pulled out a pamphlet. Handing it to me across the counter, she said, simply, "This is what you want."

I had never heard of "The Great Books," that list of time-proven, thought-provoking writings of some the world's greatest minds, compiled by Robert Hutchins – President of Western Reserve University of Chicago, I think – but I was fascinated. At home again, I called together five other women and we agreed to undertake this study.

But enrolling was not as easy as it sounded. In my first letter to Great Books Headquarters, I explained that we were not in a position to fall in line with the pre-requisite that our discussions be led by a paid instructor.

Not having a college in our community at that time, we had no such person. Could we not – since there would be enclosed with the book a paper spoken of as "The Gadfly" which would provide a list of questions to be answered among ourselves – do the study on our own? The purpose of the study, it had been explained, was to stimulate original thinking.

My letter upset them at headquarters. They did not see how the study could possibly be done without an instructor. That letter unsettled *me*, and I sent back one of pleading right away, pointing out what seemed to me to be entirely legitimate: "You know our eagerness to undertake this study. If the stumbling block is that we just can't find an instructor, and since you emphasize as the whole point and purpose of the study, the promotion of original thinking, why wouldn't our thoughts be as original as anybody else's?"

My pleading prevailed. Like any other of their groups, we were sent, piecemeal and in order, the books that, for the next twenty-five years would keep us engaged. By the time we had read and discussed all the assignments, our town had a college. We went on, having professors willing to give us their time for intermittent lectures on subjects in their fields. And now, forty-five years later, we are still meeting in homes as we always have, and still in pursuit of knowledge. Currently we are digesting the book, *Ourselves Among Others*, an anthology of short stories written by writers all over the world, stories that give insight into cultures other than our own.

≈ ≈ ≈

By the time our sons were four and six, war clouds were gathering over Europe and Asia. Although our country was doing its best to stay out of the conflict, in case that should prove impossible, it was quietly watching developments, and there was a change in the air.

Our town, less than a hundred miles from both the marine base at Camp Lejeune and Fort Bragg at Fayetteville, began to be aware of the comings and goings of servicemen, particularly on weekends. A U.S.O. canteen soon appeared at our local railway station. This was manned by volunteers, and – along with other townspeople – Tom and I took our turns. But the thing that gave us a real satisfaction was being able to go to the railway station on Sunday afternoons and pick up – at random – four or five marines and take them home with us for supper.

The fateful Sunday of December 7, 1941, was just such a day. Since it was cold and cloudy, by late afternoon, our family and five marines sat around the fire in our den. As we joked and popped corn with our long-handled popper that in winter rarely was out of sight, splitting our sides laughing at "Amos and Andy" coming in on the radio, the program was interrupted by a man's voice making the awful announcement, "The Japanese have just bombed Pearl Harbor! All men in uniform are to report for duty at once!"

Stunned, the soldiers would have left at once, but we persuaded them to first have a quick bite. And as Tom and I hurried to the kitchen to take chicken tetrazzini casseroles from the oven, and to stir the large wooden bowl of salad, the others gathered around the long, rectangular breakfast room table. Tom quickly poured coffee, while I dropped brownies into five separate bags. All I could think of, over and over, was, *And they seem so young!*

From that day on, our town opened its heart to soldiers, taking them into our homes for weekends, with or without their wives and their sweethearts.

It so happened that one of the town's most generous hostesses was Tom's sister, Louise, nicknamed, by a lisping two-year-old brother trying to say "sweet" at the baby's birth, as "Tete." At the outbreak of the war, Tete was a woman of forty-five, her husband, Ike Pettite, away in the Navy. Married late, they had no children. Blessed with the faithful Lula, a wonderful old-time cook, on weekends, their bedrooms were always filled with servicemen from either Camp Lejeune or Fort Bragg.

Lula shared Tete's patriotism, but was, herself, a curiosity to the visitors, for she was completely bald and refused to wear either a cap or a wig. She had lost her teeth as well, a fact that didn't keep her from laughing heartily at jokes as she served hot corn sticks, or from smiling broadly when asked for more of her apple strudel. Lula was a delight in her starched blue uniform and crisp white apron, handing things around the old Hepplewhite table that had come from the Jenkins side of Tete's family – a table that was always set with snowy hand-embroidered mats and large monogrammed dinner napkins which Lula would allow nobody else to launder. In this perfect blend of the old and the new way of doing things, the meals were unforgettable.

With one exception, Lula gave homey mothering to all the soldiers, and gracious service to their wives and sweethearts. For reasons of her own, however, one of those women did not meet Lula's approval. But until the morning after the weekend guests had left, the house returning to normal, she kept it to herself. It was then that Tete, hearing Lula coming downstairs muttering, went into the hall to ask, "What's the matter, Lula?"

"I was just saying to myself," said Lula crossly, "that it ain't laces and satins and fumeration that makes folks, but it be's some as don't never know it."

"Well, maybe we won't have any more of that kind," answered Tete.

"Yeb'm." And Lula moved on toward the kitchen, her irritation subsiding.

Besides, this was Monday, she thought. Friday would be there in no time. And that would mean another batch of company. Soon she must be deciding on her desserts. It didn't matter if some peoples didn't have no manners. *She* knew a thing or two, and *one* of 'em was that some people jes' ain't had no raisin'. The other was that won't *nobody* could do what *she* could with pastry!

"A sweater is something you wear when your mother is cold."

Source Unknown

≈ ≈ ≈

I knew that I wanted our sons to be as much like their father as possible. But, bringing up two small boys who were only two years apart, and who, if not any more obstreperous (that word that Mother used to apply to some children we knew) than other lively, normal boys, the process opened up a whole new world for me, one in a family of all girls. The first hint that we were going to be an accident-prone family came when Tommy was four, and Mack was two.

It was a rainy afternoon in summer. Minnie, the nurse, and the children and two of their playmates were playing on our side porch. Through the screen door, from the den where I sat, comfortably, reading, I was aware that Minnie had brought up the idea of having each of the children take turns making speeches, and I thought, with gratitude, of how inventive Minnie was. But the next page in the book was never turned. All of a sudden I heard Mack wailing. The children were screaming, and Minnie was yelling to Tommy, "Go get your Mama, quick!"

The small footstool upon which Mack was standing to address the group had flipped over, his face had hit the flagstone floor, and one of his front teeth had been knocked out.

With blood and tears everywhere – some of the tears, I confess, were my own, for I thought Mack might never grow any more teeth – I hurried to call our dentist for advice. With Dr. Hunt's assurance that he would be able to hold the space with a brace applied to the remaining teeth, and that Mack *would* have permanent teeth after all, things calmed down. The hitch, however, was that when the brace was applied, it had to be cemented, and Mack would have to be perfectly still for two whole minutes waiting for the cement to dry.

The brace was made, and when the day for the two minute ordeal arrived, Mack wanted Tommy to go along, so that, at the appointed time, our little party of Priscilla, the nurse, and Tommy and I all went too. With Tommy settled with a coloring book in the waiting room, the other three of us went *in*, for I had been warned that arms and legs would have to be held down for the important two minutes. As expected, as he was forced to a lying position and held, two-thirds of Dr. Hunt's hand in his mouth, Mack set up a howl. Tommy rushed to the rescue, pounding on the dentist's arm, and when that failed, bit him.

Somehow, everybody involved survived. The ordeal over, as we passed through the waiting room where, by then, several patients were waiting to be called, there sat Henry Gregory, an old friend who was quick to ask, "What in *world* is going on in there?"

My answer was cryptic. "Mack was the patient, but your godchild bit the dentist."

On another day, dressed for an afternoon of hospital-visiting to be done with a friend, Jo Vann, there was another disaster. Going from the back porch into the yard to tell the children and their chums goodbye, a visiting dog, lying on the top doorstep was uninclined to move, and I stepped over him just as he changed his mind. I was flipped over, to land on the brick edge at the bottom of the step, on my nose. Naturally, the nose broke. In ten minutes, bound for the hospital, I was in the back seat of my car, with the nurse and the children, and our dog, all of whom wanted to go, and with my head buried in a bloody bath towel, I was in no shape to argue, nor could I keep up with where John Henry was taking us. Many blocks later, the car stopped, and I asked in a muffled voice, "Are we there, John Henry?"

"Nome," he answered, "I made a mistake, we're at the ballpark."

Half an hour later, lying on the operating table, Tom on one side, and three doctors whom I knew well on the other, a bright white light in my face, they were discussing the relative merits of sewing my nose with catgut or with nylon – which of the two would leave less of a scar. Three days later I was again at home, and in time, the scar disappeared.

When the boys were ten and twelve, in the vacant lot we owned back of our property, they had a wigwam. It led to the disaster of a fire. How it happened I've forgotten. But I'll never forget the pandemonium that set in when they saw that the grass under the wigwam was burning. While Mack tried to stamp out the blaze, for luckily he had on shoes, Jimmy Crumpler, a playmate, ran to tell me to call the fire department. Lyle Crumpler, Jimmy's younger brother, ran with a twenty-five-foot hose when no spigot was nearer the tent than a hundred feet. Tommy saved the day by hurrying with a bucket of sand from the edge of the road past our house. That held the blaze until the firemen arrived. No real harm was done, except no more wigwams.

In a few years, Tom built his sons a tree house. The day after it was finished, there was a sudden commotion as both boys scuttled down the ladder, Tommy's face and head all bloody. He had been on the lower platform, while Mack, two limbs above, nailed something to the trunk of the tree. Tom suddenly needed the hammer, and said so. Mack let go, and it dropped on the top of Tommy's head. Sixteen stitches required.

Not to let the boys get ahead of me, I, myself, once set fire to *our* house. It was Christmas. As usual, I had gone all out to emphasize the spirit of the season. Among other things, I had made a lovely little snow scene on our dining room sideboard. At one end, there was a white church that played "Hark the Herald Angels Sing," as a dozen adorable choirboys marched, singing toward a night service. The two gilded wall brackets on either side of a large mirror that hung over the sideboard and that usually held "cache pots" of ivy, now each held a golden angel bearing a white candle. The candles, however, were lighted only when we were in the room. On this particular night, however, having blown them out after supper, I relighted them for the drop-in visit of two neighbors. As they were making motions about leaving, I asked them to wait a minute for me to cross the hall to go into the dining room to relight my candles in order that they might enjoy the Christmas scene, as well.

When I went back into the living room to *summon* them, I found the two ladies – in that slow way of leave-taking that men complain of – in no hurry to go. So that, unconsciously, there was a time lapse before we got around to crossing the hall altogether. In fact, we must have leaped across it. For, all at once, each of us smelled burning cotton. I had been guilty of using just surgical cotton; the asbestos kind had not yet come into being.

Tom's hands were so badly burned from trying to put out the blaze that they were bandaged for weeks. The sideboard had to have a new top and be done over. The room had to be redone; the dining room rug was lost, and *I* had learned a lesson.

Those were the years when even our dog seemed accident-prone. Run over in the street, he lost all of a back leg and an eye. Afterwards, understandably, he became fractious. But he lived for five years. I'm afraid we added to his misery by accidentally taking on another dog.

Sadly, one very cold night, the coldest of the winter, the dog, Nip, let out for his bedtime trip to the "bathroom," wandered off and was never seen again. We stayed awake all that night, and the next, and the next, bundling up to go out, whistling and calling, calling, calling..."Nip! Nip! Here, Nip!" Three weeks later his poor little body was found in a ditch in the park in front of our house. He had fallen in and had frozen.

When the boys were in college, the dog, Dink, who had come to us unawares, lived on for a number of years. As he grew older, he developed a habit of lying, in summer, on the cool of the concrete floor of the garage. One afternoon, late for an appointment, I forgot to look under my car before getting in, and I backed out to the horrible feeling that the lump I felt under the car was Dink. Crying and rushing, with the dog in the foot of the car in the front, I made it to the vet, but there was no life left. And as Tom and I came back in the house after having buried Dink in a corner of the yard, having run the gamut of pets by that time, and having our hearts, as a family, torn in two at their deaths, Tom, said sagely, one day, "*No more livestock!*" It was well, though, that he waited to say it until after we had had it in practically all its forms.

When Mama ain't happy, ain't nobody happy.

> – From a small boy on his way to being
> a sage

≈ ≈ ≈

But of all the episodes that went with having a family of pets, the week of the monkey is the most unforgettable.

Young Tom was seven, Mack was five. It was summer, and as was the custom in those days, men in small towns came home for lunch. Tom had done that, and following lunch and a short nap, had started out for an afternoon on the farms.

The children were playing in the backyard, and I was pulling a few weeds from the flower bed by the terrace, which was on the other side of the yard toward the front. I could not see the children nor could they see me. Tom had been gone only a few minutes when I heard the click of the front gate. I looked up to see that his car was back and that he himself was coming across the lawn toward me. Holding his finger to his lips, he wore a funny little secretive smile.

"Sit down a minute," he began, almost in a whisper, as he turned a wrought iron chair around for me, "and let me tell you something." Again his finger went to his lips.

"What is it?" I whispered back, dying of curiosity.

"I think I've had a sign," he began.

"A sign of what?" I asked, my voice already low with conspiracy.

We were used to the unexpected in each other's natures and were careful not to throw cold water until we felt it absolutely necessary. Tom often allowed, however, that I was impulsive and sometimes needed restraint, something that I would cheerfully acknowledge, but only after reminding him that he was also so flawed. And if it happened that something that seemed important to me was at stake and he was trying to cool me off, I was not above pointing out that some of the nicest things that had ever happened to us had been those in which I had acted on impulse. For over time it had seemed to me that too much looking before you leap is not always good. This time, however, I felt in my bones that it was Tom who was doing something impulsive. In light of my own proclivity for that, however, I could not afford – at the very outset – to be a killjoy. Anyway, I was dying to know what he had to tell me.

Endeavoring to relieve my curiosity quickly, and at the same time to build up a better case for what was to come, Tom went on to say, "You know, your father had a monkey when he and your Uncle Mark and your Uncle Jim were boys. You wrote all about it in your family history. And we had one at home when we were children; you've heard me tell our boys about Mary-Monk. Well, I've just since lunch picked up a man thumbing on the highway, who, of all things, is on his way to a monkey farm in Illinois to sell the cutest little monkey you've ever seen! I didn't know he had one until after he was in the car, and the little thing crept out from under his coat. He doesn't want much for him as monkeys go – just fifty dollars – and I've always wanted Tommy and Mack to have one. What do you think?"

I didn't know what I thought, but I stalled for time. My brain was whirling with thoughts which I was keeping to myself as Tom waited, and as I looked toward the gate, and the car, and at the man sitting in it, I felt the pressure of time. For the farm manager was waiting for Tom to pick him up. There came over me a feeling that this was the world's last monkey, or, at least, our last chance to get one. And now that the subject had come up in such a personal way, had not the Lord, perhaps, really sent us a sign? For after all, I told myself, our dog is old; he has only three legs and one eye. It *does* seem that the children should have a whole dog or a whole pet of some kind. Having applied this logic, it began to seem altogether practical to take advantage of so clear a sign. Of course, in a lapse of memory, I was forgetting the wide variety of pets they'd already had; some had not turned out well. Even the baby alligator that was brought by one of Tom's friends for the boys to take care of in the dammed-up stream in our garden had not survived the winter.

So I said to Tom, still speaking very low, however, for more than one reason, "All right."

Tom went around the house to tell the children. Two other little boys were playing with Tommy and Mack, and in less time than it takes to tell it, there was an eruption of shouts and shrieks of uncontrollable delight as the four came running around the corner. The monkey was paid for at the gate, and the man came into the yard with the little creature sitting cunningly (if that's the way you feel about monkeys) on his shoulder. The children were, by that time, jumping up and down; others in the neighborhood were gathering. Hardly able to make himself heard, the monkey-man suggested that we find some kind of bushel basket to tie to the monkey's collar so that we could keep up with him. With such a ball and chain, he couldn't run away.

In a wild hubbub, these matters were attended to. Then Tom and the monkey-man drove off, and I was left in charge. Tom was to drop the man off ten miles down the road where Tom would turn from the highway onto a country road to join Mr. Cobb, the overall farm manager of our several farms. As usual in the growing season, I would not see any more of Tom until dusk.

At the time, we had three domestics – a cook, a house-and-yard-man, and a combination laundress and housekeeper. All three of them gathered in consternation at this new turn in our lives – and theirs – and kept their counsel and their distance.

In a body we had all moved, by that time, into the backyard. Somehow, Priscilla, the cook, was able to hear the ring of the telephone in the kitchen and hurried in to answer. The call was for me. Barely able to leave the scene at this crucial point, I dashed into the breakfast room and answered with a breathless, "Hello."

Mary Hester Crumpler, a trained nurse, as we used to say before we knew the term "R.N.," wife of our pediatrician, and mother of two small sons who were tombstone buddies of Tommy's and Mack's, replied in a voice heavy with alarm, "Elizabeth, have you and Tom lost your minds? Don't you know that monkeys carry more diseases than any other creatures in the world?"

"Oh, Mary Hester, you don't mean it. What am I to do?" I cried.

"I don't know, but I wish my boys would come right home," she replied.

"Don't worry, Mary Hester. But, oh my, you've upset me to death. I'll have to think of something."

The only thing I could think of was to sanitize the monkey, and at the earliest possible moment.

Returning to the yard, I said to Henry, the yard man, who had been peacefully cutting the grass an hour ago, and now stood way off as though ready to take flight at the slightest provocation, "Henry, you go into the garage and get that large zinc washtub we sometimes use when canning," for preserving the produce which he brought home from the farms was one of Tom's passions, and it was before the days of freezing, "and get the hose and fill the tub with water. Minnie, you get the package of Super-Suds, and a brush, some rags, and a kettle of hot water to temper the water as Henry fills the tub."

The children squealed with even more delight at the prospect of bathing a beast of the jungle, and the monkey kept moving around the yard dragging his peach basket and sometimes carrying it under his arm – looking very much a man about town.

We finally got everything set up, and I delegated Henry to do the bathing. The tub was running over with the froth from the Super-Suds, and both Henry and the monkey had to have a lot of encouragement. At length, the monkey was in, but only barely, for he kept trying to clamber out, and Henry was getting more and more nervous, rolling his eyes to me in appeal. The chorus from the bystanders jumping up and down didn't help any, and naturally, the inevitable happened. The monkey bit Henry; Henry vamoosed. As the monkey leaped free, the children screamed and scattered. Priscilla ran into the house, and Minnie the maid, took refuge upstairs in her quarters over the garage.

I alone, was left to face the music with the frightened, insulted, soapy monkey. You don't have to read any further, however, to know who finally bathed him, for what are mothers for but to come into the breach in emergencies, and this was an all-time high. True to life, when these things happen, fathers are seldom at hand.

My emotions had to have an outlet, and I began to blame Tom, getting madder by the minute. Mary Hester had terrified me, and frustration and fear are a deadly combination! I had to make plans. In spite of himself, calmed a little by his bath, the monkey became more amiable. This made me feel that I could leave the scene long enough to go inside to call Mary Hester back and see if she could help me find a way out of the dilemma.

When I passed through the kitchen on my way into the breakfast room, Priscilla, late in getting her own lunch, had just served her plate with an assortment of summer vegetables –beans, corn, okra and tomatoes – and was sitting down to eat. As I picked up the receiver, I heard her scream, and ran to see. She had run through the house and had flown upstairs and was nowhere in sight, for the monkey had come into the kitchen toting his peach basket and had then taken both hands and flung everything on her plate all over the kitchen, even the ceiling.

That did it.

I couldn't wait for Tom to come home. My mind was made up; the monkey had to go. When Tom did finally come – smiling and whistling and eager to know what had gone on – I had an earful for him. He couldn't believe I really meant that the monkey couldn't stay, but I did.

"Well, don't be so hasty," he pleaded. "Just give me a little time to find out how to get rid of him. After all, I've got fifty dollars in him."

"I don't care," I said firmly. "I'll give you a week, no more, or I'll be at Dix Hill (the asylum for the insane in Raleigh). It's your choice."

Of course, it never rains, but it pours. The day of the monkey, our house also gave refuge to a wandering dog. He came up onto the side porch, and whined to get in. The children fed him, put a bath mat on the porch for him to nap on, and made him feel welcome in every way.

He had on a nice collar, and I knew that somebody had lost him and would be out looking for him. That was clearly explained to the children. For we had an old dog who was much loved, and they'd certainly have worried if he'd been lost. True, Nip wasn't all there physically; he had been run over, and had lost all of one leg, and one eye. But we loved him, and wouldn't have thought of upsetting him by getting another dog to share our affection.

215

Night came, and with the darkness, I heard a car driving slowly down the street in front of the house, and a woman's voice calling "Dink, Dink, here Dink."

I rushed out on the walk, cupped my hands and called out loudly into the night, "Have you lost a *dog?*"

"Yes, Elizabeth, a fox terrier. Have you seen him?" came the answer. I recognized the voice of my friend, Jamison Dowdy.

In a voice rising with graciousness, I replied, "He's right here on my porch, Jamison, hale and hearty and waiting for you."

With that, she parked and came in. The children led the way to the side porch, talking as they went. As she left with Dink under her arm, they patted him goodbye, and I breathed easy.

But the next day Jamison telephoned and said kindly, "Elizabeth, I've been thinking about your little boys. Their dog is so old and can't romp and play, and they were so sweet to Dink and all that. I want to give Dink to them."

My mind ran ahead, a hundred miles an hour as I answered sweetly, "Oh that's the nicest thing I ever heard of, Jamison, but I couldn't let you do that unless I gave you something in return. How about a monkey? Have you ever wanted one?"

Surprised, but amazingly interested, she said, "Well, truth to tell, I always have; but first I'd have to ask Daddy, (with whom she and her husband, Jessie lived), and Jessie. I'll let you know tomorrow."

For the first time in thirty hours I began to have hope.

I got busy. The monkey behaved. And knowing that Tom never broke his promises to me, I almost felt normal again the next day when Jamison appeared at the door with the news that her father and her husband had vetoed the idea of the monkey. They had pointed out that Falls Road, on which they lived, was a busy street and he might be run over. As she stepped into the hall, she had the dog, Dink, his basket, and his leash, mentioning casually as she turned to go and handed me a bottle, "This is for Dink's fleas." It was a drugstore bottle of a clear liquid which turned out to be a medicine for chronic eczema that the poor dog would continue to have under his arms for all the ten years we were to have him. That first summer, our vet bill was sixty-five dollars. What a thing to do to a friend! But then, I was guilty of having tried to do something evil to her.

The days passed. Tom's daily ad in the paper for the sale of "a gentle monkey" brought no takers. Finally, on the fifth day, I was afraid to ask him what he had in mind. On the sixth, however, he left home very early – wasn't gone long – and returned with a relaxed expression and a nod to me to follow him into the breakfast room.

Tom said, later, that he had had a serious talk with the boys. For this sober affair, he had chosen what we spoke of, for no discernable reason, as "the arena." That was the part of our property back of the garage behind our brick wall. It was enclosed by a split-rail fence, inside which, under tall pines and their dappled sunlight, there was a very long rope-swing hanging from the branch of a very tall poplar. In the hundred-and-fifty foot area, there was enough room to build forts and to play cowboy and Indians. At one side there was a path to our small dark green pony stable. Near the stable, all of them standing up, Tom explained the family dilemma. Leading carefully to the point, he let them know that there was a choice to be made. It had been found that the monkey and I could not co-exist. One of us would have to go!

Although their decision may have required a little time, I have no way of knowing how long their deliberations went on, nor by what slender *margin* it turned out that *I* won.

Now Tom was slightly unfettered. If only he could find a buyer for my adversary. Finally, the seventh day brought action. Tom was up early to slip out. At breakfast time he was back, motioning me into the breakfast room, out of earshot of the boys. His expression was relaxed, and he said seriously, "I've found a home for *him*." For by that time the word *him* was all that was needed.

"In the night I thought of Roland," he began.

Roland, who for many years had been the groundskeeper of the park onto which our house faced, had changed to a more leisurely job – that of caring for the horses in the riding stables not far away, and spoken of as a riding academy." Our children had had a few riding lessons, and Tom suddenly bethought himself of this: to ask Roland if he hadn't always wanted a monkey.

It continues to astonish me to this day how many people say they actually have. "I reckon I have," replied Roland slowly.

"Well," said Tom, swiftly and encouragingly, "you know, they're supposed to be good company for horses – makes them easier to handle and that kind of thing." Poor Roland didn't stand a chance. "How would you like one almost free," Tom urged, "and just let my boys trade it out in twenty-five dollars worth of riding lessons?"

A pleasant light was beginning to dawn for Roland, and he answered appreciatively, "It does sometimes get lonesome around hyeah." And the deal was made.

After due explanation to our children and those of the neighborhood, (who, by that stage of the monkey's visit, were beginning to regulate their lives by going to bed and getting up according to the monkey's schedule), the whole little company, including Minnie and Priscilla and Henry, formed an honor guard down the front walk, as Tom, with the monkey on his shoulder, and the monkey's peach basket under the other arm, made his way out the gate. I brought up a happy rear.

With both Tom and the monkey in the car, I could return to a personality of sweetness and light, could speed them off with a charitable last remark, "And Tom, be sure to stop by the store and get Roland a bunch of bananas."

≈ ≈ ≈

Whatever the generation, the custom of sending children to summer camp usually seems worthwhile to parents. This may not, to every child, hold appeal; parents may have to do a selling job. This successfully done, there is still the question mark in the minds of those parents involved in this first real separation from their young as to the matter of homesickness. With admirable self-control, they wait for the first letter to come, and the following small episodes are examples of what any parent may expect.

The Carey Whitaker family, younger friends of ours in another town, consists of the mother, the father, two sisters and the youngest child, a little brother. The little boy, no doubt understandably indulged, was told by his parents that they thought the time had come for him to have the pleasure of going away to camp. This unselfish move on the part of his parents was not greeted with joy. Carey's reason for this attitude was that he was afraid he would not be able to get all the peanut butter-and-jelly he wanted. With the most earnest of reassurances from his parents and his sisters, the little boy finally said he would go.

When he had been there a few days, a letter from Carey arrived, its contents, cryptic: "I'm getting along pretty good with my problum," he wrote, "and I'm the most behaved one in my cabin."

As did these, any parents who have ever sent children to camp for the first time will have saved some of these unique letters. For a long time, I kept one such letter that had come to us from young Tom on his first venture away from the family hearth. The camp, one in the North Carolina mountains, had kindly furnished the campers with a sheet of stationery and an envelope. To underscore to parents the lofty aspirations of the camp, in the left-hand margin of the sheet there was a column of small footprints, theoretically leading onward and upward. To young Tom, this suggested a way to "work" his parents. Thoroughly homesick, or seemingly so, his letter, like young Carey's, contained only one sentence and some arrows pointing to the left: "These are my little footprints trying to walk home," it said excruciatingly.

We never did decide whether Tommy was pulling our leg or not. Naturally, the uncertainty tore us to pieces. So although we laughed, the question in each of our minds was, "Shall we go and get him?" But common sense and a hastily dispatched box of cookies prevailed.

≈ ≈ ≈

World War II was over and the English children who had been evacuated to the United States were gradually returning. Sara and Aleck Thorpe, cousins of ours, as well as close friends, had for three years had the care of a little English girl, Valerie Goodwin. When plans for Val's return to her parents had been worked out, Sara and I went by train with her to New York, from where she would sail.

As those English children all seemed to do, Val had adapted well to the change; she had been a member of the Thorpe family from age eleven to fourteen, and had felt that Sara and Aleck's small sons were her own little brothers. So that at parting in Rocky Mount, there was a touch of sadness all-round. This was in some measure dispelled the next day in New York when Sara and I went shopping with Val and helped her select presents for her family. On the last day, we took her, now "half American," by taxi to Pier 29, an area familiar to Sara and me, for each of us had done some travelling, always, up to that time, by ship.

We were allowed on board the large liner to see Val's stateroom, and to find out if things were in order. As we said goodbye to this tall, softly feminine young girl, her large gray eyes filled with tears, Sara and I were openly weeping. For when the ship sounded that first note of throaty warning, "All ashore that's going ashore," there was that dismal feeling of finality. Last embraces were followed by a scurry of passengers toward the gangway; urged on in a brief interval by a second warning. With the third, the gangway was lifted.

By the time Sara and I had gone ashore to stand on the dock with the throng of other Americans who were there to say goodbye to their own war charges, we had recovered. We could wave and throw kisses and confetti with the best of them. Having watched Val's ship sail, to cheer ourselves up, Sara and I went back to the Biltmore, where we were staying, and had tea. We had tickets for a play for that night, so we decided to spend the rest of the afternoon getting our hair done in the hotel. We had made plans to have lunch the next day with an old schoolmate of Sara's from Converse college who now lived in New York. But I had an important mission to carry out the next morning between breakfast and joining the

219

other two at noon.

When asked before leaving home what they'd like for me to bring them, my small sons had been specific. Mack's need was for a new baseball glove. Tommy's was one more involved – homing pigeons. Somewhere he had read a story that had fired his imagination, and since New York is the "City of Everything," I was charged with what was to become a major responsibility.

Wakening early, dressing for a day that would include lunch in what I felt sure would be some nice place, I dressed with more care than I normally would have just for going on a search for saleable pigeons. I had spent some time the night before going through the yellow pages of the telephone book looking for a pet shop that would list, among dogs, cats, canaries, parakeets and hamsters, the words, "homing pigeons." I set out early after breakfast by taxi for a certain address in the Bowery. When the taxi driver and I had gone far enough for the meter to register five dollars (and in those days, that was a lot) the driver began to be curious as to why a lady so dressed should be making her way into that section of the city, and I explained. By the time the meter had gotten to six dollars, he was beginning to feel a sense of responsibility for me.

"Lady," he began, "You're going into a rough section. I would hesitate to take you there, except that I have children, and I know how you feel. But I would suggest this: If you ride up in a cab, they're going to up their prices. Why don't you let me put you out around the corner?"

I could see the wisdom of that. I divested myself of all my refined trappings, putting my gloves into my bag, my little navy-blue pill-box of shiny straw and my white scarf on the seat. And then I left the cab, hoping fervently that this stranger, who seemed to have become my friend, would do as I'd asked, "Please wait for me."

The pet shop was owned by an Italian who spoke limited English. His apron was as dirty as his shop was dirty and smelly. But he did have my birds. In a cage to themselves sat four white pigeons and they were the homing kind. The only words I could really understand from the shop's owner were "hooming peejons," and he would circle with his arms to demonstrate. We made the bargain, which was not excessive, and I was given a receipt.

Except that I felt I should have been fumigated, I was none the worse for the visit, and could get back to the hotel in time to freshen up and be ready to meet Sara and our hostess at that then favorite meeting place of young and old, "under the clock at the Biltmore." Many southerners stayed at the Biltmore. We liked the service, it was especially nice for ladies when they were alone, and the row of its handsome lanterns that hung from the

Madison Avenue side –and still do – were a beacon as they drew closer to those tired shoppers who had waited until the last minute before the rush hour to get a taxi, and failing that, had decided to walk back to the hotel.

Back home again in Carolina, the whole family awaited the delivery of the pigeons. Three weeks passed, and no pigeons. Then one day there came a telephone call. The person calling was a distant relative of Tom's who lived in a town near Wilmington called Rocky Point. The cousin's initials were T. F. (Pearsall), very similar to Thomas J. (Pearsall).

The conversation began, "Hello, Tom," and the man explained who he was. "Have you ordered any dirty white birds from anywhere? They've been delivered to me, and I don't know what in the world to do with them."

Both men enjoyed a laugh, and the next day the pigeons arrived. Tommy was in a state of ecstasy, could hardly bear a moment's separation from them, and gave them the hospitality of our pony stable. This was summer, and in order to hasten the attachment that he deemed necessary between himself and the birds, he slept at the end of the pony stable where the hay was kept, the area which the pigeons had immediately claimed as a roosting place.

Following information he'd gained from the library, the pigeons were kept for a month, and, for their release, taken to a point a few miles distant. "Old Town" was one of our farms, and the pigeon ceremony was to go on there on a Sunday afternoon. When the day came, Tom and the boys, with two other cars full of neighborhood children and two fathers, left for the exhibition. I stayed at home with instructions to sit in the garden and read a book so that there would be a familiar presence when the family birds flew back.

Hardly daring to read a page without looking up, I sat at my post. Time passed. No birds. Half-an-hour later, the pigeon-watchers, themselves, rounded the corner on two wheels in their hurry to join the pigeons on home ground. I could only say, "They haven't come."

They knew the answer. For as Tom said with resignation, "When we turned them loose, they circled over the field three times and headed north."

One more line: Two weeks later, Tommy developed viral pneumonia. He spent ten days in the hospital, and one of the first questions the doctor asked was, "Have you been around any pigeons?"

≈ ≈ ≈

On one of the summers when our sons were very small, Tom and I rented a cottage for a month at Wrightsville Beach. The house was built high above the sand, that lower area of all sand was enclosed by latticework, and for our children and those of our friends, it became the neighborhood sandbox, a spot to resort to when it rained. On the beach, in front of the vacant lot next to our rented cottage, to protect his family and our friends from the burning sun, Tom erected the top of an ordinary khaki tent of about twelve feet by twelve, and – in the Pearsall way – gave it a jolly name, "the shadyrella" (for "shade" and "umbrella"), which became the "shadyrilla," practically a household word. And no cabana at Newport or Bar Harbor could have given more pleasure.

"Who will go to the shadyrilla and tell everybody that lunch is ready?" would ask Fannie, the cook, coming out on the cottage porch where one or two mothers of the tent-children would be sitting in conversation. And soon we would all be busy, consuming fried chicken or crabmeat – in some form – or shrimp, along with summer vegetables with corn sticks and iced tea, all this to be followed by home-churned ice cream and layer cake.

To think of the shadyrilla now, is to be reminded of that general way of the Pearsalls for meeting life with enthusiasm, to remember, once again, the tales that Tom and his father and his brother, Harry used to tell of the Pocosin, that Indian name for the swamp, that half-scary area that, in Duplin County, bordered the land of the Pearsalls of earlier generations, and of their own experiences, during Tom's childhood, with something called the "Kitty Liza." For the Kitty Liza was the name given to a Civil War cannon that sat under the trees in the side yard of the Pearsall home in Rocky Mount. Only on the Fourth of July, however, did it ever come to life. It was then that, pulled by a dray-horse the distance of around two miles out of town to a wooded section, and followed to that point by the neighborhood fathers and sons, with the use of window weights, a number of patriotic rounds would be fired. With some refreshments between rounds, late in the afternoon it was pulled home again, to await another Fourth, and another celebration.

Those involved in the maneuver must have gone to a great deal of trouble to bring it off. I loved the way the Pearsalls and Tom's mother's people, the Jenkins, put so much into life, and, of course, got so much in return. There was not much money, but they had something better. Something that could never be taken away.

Sara and Aleck Thorpe, and Virginia and Henry Gregory had cottages near ours at the beach. Our husbands were there only for weekends. Mothers and children had been away for about two weeks, when, in his nightly telephone call, Tom gave us the news that since we had taken the two family dogs with us, he was doing battle with fleas. It so happened that the easy chair in our bedroom at home had long been the favorite of our old dog, Nip. Nip had gone to the beach; the fleas had stayed at home.

Another year, on another of our beach stays, in a nightly phone call, Tom said, "I suddenly have the funniest condition on the bottoms of my feet. They itch and burn and have something that looks like little tunnels under the skin. I think I'm going to have to go to the doctor."

I interrupted with my own tale of woe, to tell him that that morning I had taken our sons to the doctor over on the mainland for the same condition. I had been told that the children had tetter worms, that sometimes, cats, using the sand for a bathroom, deposit eggs, which, getting into a foot through a cut or an abrasion, will turn into worms that make those awful tunnels that become almost unbearable. I was glad to be able to tell Tom that there was an – even if painful – antidote. The tunnels had to be frozen by a strong spray which caused blisters, and refrozen at intervals, and that this treatment might take as long as two months. It did take that long – for both Tom and the boys.

All this, and the cat had not even been ours.

≈ ≈ ≈

It was about the time when the boys had reached the age of Cub Scouting – and I think Cub Scouting was new to our community – that I conscientiously became a Den Mother. The meetings were usually held, and always began, in our basement rumpus room. That room served in many ways: it held a large gun-case, always kept carefully locked, and a closet for Tom's hunting clothes. Almost one end of the room was given to a large fireplace, built from the same Nash County stone that had gone into making the rock wall enclosure for two sides of the garden.

I met the scouting challenge with enthusiasm: providing weeny roasts and marshmallow toasts, a few mild field trips where we identified by sight and call several birds and one or two wildflowers, excursions to places where the boys could pick up rocks for our collective museum, that small set of shelves that held our sea shells, seed pods, small and interesting rocks and arrowheads that the troop discovered when they were out with Tom on weekends on our farm, Old Town. For Old Town, which is situated at the bend of the River Tar, was once the homesite of a tribe of the Tuscaroras. As long as the boys saw me in this pleasant role, I was acceptable. It was with my adherence to the first rule of the Guidebook, however, which stated that meetings must be opened with the oath of allegiance to the flag, that my authority would break down.

As I stood before this group of ten little boys, their ruddy round faces under their little billed Cub Scout caps, their little yellow cotton ties looped loosely under their collars, all of us patriotically holding hand over heart, there would, at some point, be a loud snicker. Extra-sensory perception told me whence it was coming. I was an embarrassment to my young, and I could tell that they were covering it up with this form of mutiny. Inevitably this would set up a wave of sympathetic snickers, and though one or two held out bravely with me, I felt that my ship was foundering. And I was never so glad to have the time come when the little band reached the age of real scouting, with the role model of a man.

≈ ≈ ≈

During those years when I was trying to find the key to bringing up boys, the thrill they derived from danger – and seemingly, always would – their constant pranks, some of them done for the express purpose of scaring me to death, that just-below-the-surface "boyishness" which Goethe refers to in his statement that "the boy is always in the man," I would never have dreamed that certain favorable things would come to pass; that they would do anything sensible.

Many years later I was suddenly thrust back to that time by a request from the office of Jack Laughery, the president of the Hardee's chain of restaurants, a man of exceptional generosity to our community and our state. Mr. Laughery is a highly regarded citizen, both locally and nationally in the Republican party; at the time, he was frequently in conference with President Bush. I was notified that in two months, at the annual dinner for the Boys Scout's Distinguished Citizen Award, which was to be presented to Mack, Jack would be making the talk, one which would contain something of both the light and the serious. Mr. Laughery was to be out of town until near time for the meeting.

For the lighter part of the talk that he was to make, he was hoping that I might be able to furnish him with some amusing episodes that had gone along with Mack's growing up. I said that I would be glad to, and soon started making a list of things that might be used. But as the time drew near, and Jack had not returned, I began to foresee a last-minute rendezvous, for he had asked for an hour of my time, and for me to give these things to him in conversation would put me in a flurry; I might not at all say what I wanted to say. For that reason, I decided to put things in writing; to have it ready to hand to Jack so that he could take it home and read it.

True to his word, at the appointed time, this frightfully busy man and his secretary appeared at my door. For all I knew, he might just have flown in from the oval office.

As though I, myself, were the busiest person in the world, Jack started apologizing for taking up my time, and once we had been seated in the living room, he and his secretary each produced a long yellow legal tablet, and sat poised with their pens for whatever should fall from my lips.

Entirely overwhelmed with this deference, I felt I had to try to at least measure up. And so I said, "If you-all are going to write away like this – and I almost said, "carry on like this" – let's go into the dining room and gather around the table where you'll have a writing surface."

Turning up the dim lights from the chandelier to their very brightest, we sat down. The two visitors were on one side of the table, I was on the other. I excused myself for a minute to go back across the hall to get a hurriedly typed version of the thoughts I had to offer, a jumble of what, just an hour before, had lain – in handwriting – on my own legal pad. Rescued to cypherability by a public typist.

Returning with my document, I explained, as they sat with their ball-points raised, "Jack, I began to feel that you might just hop in at the last minute, and to make it easier for both of us, I've written down some little episodes that you may be able to make something of."

And so instead of their being engaged with writing, they put down their pens, and as I read, they listened to the letter I had written to give to Jack. It turned out that he would incorporate certain paragraphs in his speech the night of the dinner. In its entirety, the letter is included here:

> Dear Jack,
>
> Since Pauline called, I've had my thinking cap on about Mack, trying to dredge up things for you to consider on what I assume is to be part roast, part toast.
>
> There's not much, but for what it's worth, I'll jot something.
>
> In reply to your first question, "Were there any early signs of a bent for leadership?"
>
> Not really, that I can recall. He was a very average little boy, if you consider doing all right in school scholastically, but a "botheration" often to his teachers in other ways, often being brought before the principal (in this case a spinster) for playing rough or something on the school grounds and things like that. We had a car pool from Westhaven. There were only eight or ten houses there at the time, and one day, in the car of a neighbor of ours, Mack hit the neighbor's little girl. When word reached Mack's father, Mack was, of course, taken to task. When told that a boy never hits a girl, Mack's reply was that he'd never heard of such a crazy rule in his life! For the little girl had hit him first.
>
> Mack's favorite pastime, when he came to the age for a bicycle, was raiding the trash bins on Howard Street. He was always coming home with a lot of clean paper oddments. Not of much value, but he enjoyed the hunt. This may have foretold his attitude about waste. Always generous, he dislikes waste.

One outstanding thing about Mack, from early life, was self discipline. He loved playing football with the other boys on Fridays after school in our backyard, but even if the game had started, he wouldn't go out to play until he had sat down and hurried (or scurried might be a better word) through his homework. He couldn't stand to have it hanging over him, and this habit of concentration has followed him on all the boards he has sat on, where the comment has often been that, "almost more than anyone else, Mack does his homework."

An early bent toward social consciousness was evident. With no school cafeteria, our car pool brought its Westhaven children home for lunch. Often Mack would bring with him some child he didn't think had much to go home to. At Mack's instigation, our family discovered other families in similar disadvantaged plights, and he had us help them in small ways and seek help for them through local family services.

As for the "bad things" he did...

He and his brother, Tom Jr., nearly got our whole family put into jail one time when we were in New York.

It was this way:

The two boys were perhaps six and eight. We had taken them to the "Big Apple" for a week of sightseeing and various forms of entertainment. The last day, Tom had taken them to the Bronx Zoo, while I shopped. Dead tired, we all came back late in the afternoon to our hotel. (It was the Astor on Broadway and 43rd or something.)

We had tickets to one last show, so Tom and I told the boys to bathe and dress and give us a little while to put our feet up on pillows to rest, and to do the same. Then we'd have dinner in the hotel and see the play. All went well. They emerged from their rooms at the proper time looking neat and angelic.

When the show was over and we were going back to the hotel, Tom said, "Let's walk down to the Flat Iron building and see the news flash."

"You three go on," I said. "I'll go in and pack."

Dressed in navy blue with a small white hat, I felt I was dressed as a lady should be. But unknowingly, I was headed for rough treatment.

When I asked at the desk for my key, a grim-faced clerk asked in a gruff voice, "Are you Mrs. Pearsall?"

"Yes," I replied.

"Well, the hotel manager wants to see you and your husband right away. His office is that way," he said, pointing down the corridor.

I hurried to find out what terrible thing had happened at home. A death message?

The manager turned out to be about four-and-a-half feet tall. He sat, or slouched, behind a large, impressive desk. And he didn't get up when I came in. His manner was intimidating.

Hostile and furious, he hurled the information toward me that at seven p.m., seven enraged people had rushed off Broadway into the hotel to report that ink had been sprayed from the hotel windows on that side, and it had splattered all over them. One stout blonde lady had even pointed to her hair, others showed splattered dresses and suits. They were going to sue! The Pearsalls were being ordered to leave the hotel at that instant. My knees were knocking, but I knew in a flash what had happened. While out shopping that day, the boys had bought trick felt-daisies (the kind that squirt water). Having tired of water by the end of the day, they had gone on secretly to better things, namely, the squirting of ink. For – and this sounds like the dark ages – in those days there were ink stands in all hotel rooms. And by that time, I had learned a lot about boys.

The furious manager went on to say, "The security officer found the evidence on the window sill of one of your rooms. Both rooms are now padlocked, and you and your family will leave this hotel at once."

Without completely groveling, I had to confess that I thought I knew what had happened, and that I could certainly understand his anger. But that, no matter what, he was being discourteous to a guest, and I was going to have to demand that he allow me to go to my room to await the arrival of my husband. I remembered Mother's constant admonition, "Hold up your shoulders, look people in the eye, and always be a lady."

I held my breath and waited.

I knew the poor man was in a fix, and that he had a job to do. But I also knew, from being married to a lawyer, that you have to be careful what you say. And as I stood, and he sat, he phoned for the security officer.

A large burly person with a pistol in his belt (I think, I was too scared to look) came to escort me to the elevator, and together we reached the third floor; we walked down the hall, turned a corner, and came to a stop at a door which was, indeed, padlocked with a very large lock. I prayed that Tom would hurry. The officer allowed me in the room long enough to see the evidence. Sure enough, there, on the boy's window sill, were the now navy, sodden daisies; nearby was a dry ink well. After seeing this evidence of the crime, the officer and I went back into the hall to wait.

I asked if he had any sons, and felt my cause wasn't helped any when he told me his children were all girls – four in fact. I used that information, however, as best I could, by saying it had been that way in my own family, and that boys were something new in my life; that I'd already come to the conclusion that there's a streak in boys that women will never understand. They love both danger and daring. That as many of them get raised as do, is to me a constant miracle.

While not downright sociable, in the fifteen minute interval of this crossing of our paths, the officer and I were at least human.

227

I dreaded, more than anything I could think of, for Tom to have the news of what was happening. He'd worked so hard to show his sons everything he thought they should see, and we'd all had such a good time. I knew when I heard the elevator door open and close that the three men in my life, my very heart, were coming toward disaster. And when I heard Tom's characteristic little whistle, soft and thin like the highest notes on a violin, whistling his favorite tune, "The world is waiting for the sunrise, every rose is heavy with dew," I knew that he had the satisfied feeling of "mission accomplished."

As I listened, knowing how happy he was, I could have died. As the three rounded the corner, however, and saw me standing there with the security officer, I spoke in a matter of fact, steady voice, "Tom, this is the security officer. Our rooms have been padlocked. We have to leave the hotel tonight. The boys have sprayed ink on people under their window, and the manager is furious. He says we have to go right away." If I had been breaking the news that our train would be late the next morning, I couldn't have been more matter-of-fact.

The security officer opened the door and showed Tom the evidence on the window sill.

To the boys Tom said, "Stay in this room."

To me, "I'm going to talk to the manager."

I started packing.

Tom wasn't very long. I held my breath to learn the outcome of this visit to the manger.

And this is the sequence of events.

Being a lawyer, Tom could speak in a way that allayed the fears of the manager. A man of self-confidence to begin with, he had spoken in this way:

"I agree with you that it should not have happened. I hasten to say, however, that I am morally and financially responsible. Give me the names of those seven people. I'll get in touch with each of them. You have my promise that you will hear no more from them."

Tom was given the seven names. He showed the list to the boys. And when they wanted to know if we would have enough money to pay all those people, Tom's answer was, "I don't know. We may have to sell Belmont."

Belmont was Father's favorite farm, the one we all loved best. We rode its horses, petted its lambs, watched its crane where it waded at the lower end of the meadow, and roamed its woods. This was a language the boys could understand.

We were allowed to stay the night in the hotel, and as we went through Pennsylvania Station the next morning, unknown to the boys, I picked up several packages of chewing gum for their long, hard day ahead.

We had a compartment, and all day, the four of us sat opposite each other, our eight knees touching, but not in the usual light-hearted companionship. Now and then I brightened the lives of the culprits with a stick of gum. They had funny books, but those seemed to have lost their charm. And although I felt great sympathy for them, I had to stick by Tom when he had said to them the previous night, "Your mother and I have lived a long time without anything as humiliating as this."

I didn't see it that way exactly, but then I was in a different position. I wasn't a man. I felt in my bones that those unsettled people – under a nice letter – would cool off.

Tom had a *New York Times*, and all day he held the paper between himself and the boys; he spoke to them in monosyllables, and refused to fraternize. I felt compelled to talk to them.

Periodically, one of the boys would tap on the newspaper and say, "Daddy, will we have to sell Belmont?" "Have you decided what our punishment will be?"

Tom would lower the paper long enough to say, "I don't know. I haven't decided."

These questions continued all during the whole of the ten-hour journey, and for the next three months, at home. The answer was always the same.

For this, the most unforgettable misdemeanor of their young lives, suspense was their only punishment. It was enough.

A few other incidents stand out.

Marie Tyler Gardner lived across the park. Being an only child, she liked the activity that went on at our house, and was almost like a member of the family.

One day – and her parents were out of town to make it worse – she was playing in our yard. Mack had been given his first BB gun. He, young Tom, Marie, and other neighborhood children were out behind our house watching Mack's expertise, or lack of it, at shooting his BB gun. His targets were chosen for size, mainly an old oil drum which we used for trash. Marie was standing by Mack. He made a shot that not only found its mark, the oil drum, but turned around, ricocheted, and lodged in Marie's forehead. Pandemonium set in.

But the hospital assured us that the BB shot was gone. They did give Marie a tetanus injection, and life went along on its course. Her parents, Arthur and Elizabeth Tyler, were particularly noble about the whole thing. Marie, herself, wasn't concerned about the small scar on her forehead.

Although Mack was a daredevil – for that matter both our sons were, but they were daring in different ways – Mack was the one who couldn't stand crawly things. Young Tom liked having an awful looking salamander from the stream his father had dammed up in our garden, cling to his bare forearm while he admired it. But if he tried to put it on Mack, Mack ran. The same with garter snakes and centipedes.

Now, however, married to Janice, who must surely be the world's foremost environmentalist, I hear that Mack handles snakes with aplomb. That – and I daresay this is when Janice is along – when he sees an injured snake on the road, he will stop his car and administer first aid, something like dipping it in ice water and putting it under a lamp, I believe. Whatever the treatment, if the snake is only in shock, which often happens, I'm told that it will revive and slither off into the woods for a long and happy life. One which, I trust, does not include me.

At one time, many local children had lost fingers, and some even their eyesight, from shooting fireworks. When Tom was Speaker of the House, he sponsored a bill to do away with fireworks, and the tables were turned. Now it was our young sons' turn to be humiliated, for having their friends remind them of this stigma was hard to bear.

One dark night, Mack, young Tom – who had just gotten his driver's license – and their two cronies, the Crumpler brothers, had the use of the Pearsall family car, a big, dark-green station wagon.

Eleven o'clock came with no boys back at home, then eleven-thirty and midnight. As usual, in these circumstances, where worrying mothers sit up at windows watching for the lights of a car turning into the drive, fathers dreamlessly sleep. I've never understood the difference, it's just there and always will be.

Mary Hester Crumpler and I, in our separate homes, without communicating, for this would have disturbed our husbands, sat – gnawing our fingers and biting our nails.

Finally, at one-thirty my phone rang. A man's voice asked to speak to Mr. Pearsall. And this was the man's cryptic message:

"Mr. Pearsall, your two boys and the Crumpler boys are down here at the police station. They were caught shooting fireworks out near the concrete mixing plant...You'd better come down here and help us out."

The boys had driven across the Virginia line and bought as many fireworks as they had money for. They felt this was only right.

They then returned to Rocky Mount and went out near the concrete mixing plant and shot a few baby-wakers, and were at the peak of their excitement when the light on a police car was seen coming. They jumped back in the car, Tom at the wheel, gunning it for all it was worth. The car ran up on a pile of crossties. It could neither back off, nor go forward to get down, so passengers and driver all jumped out and ran for a ditch. It was not very deep, but they thought they were hidden. It was a cold night, however, and with their large searchlights, the police saw their breath smoking up from the ditch, and the lawbreakers heard the dread words, "Boys, come out."

From his early experience as prosecuting attorney for the city Tom never believed in indicting minors, nor did the city at this later date, so the whole episode passed quickly.

But what a moment it had been for their parents! One of the many traumas of getting boys to manhood.

We must have been a great trial to our neighbors. For example: One day, Tom, Sr. and I arrived home at the same time. We were surprised to find all the window sills in the kitchen filled with the handsomest and most exotic jonquils we'd ever laid our eyes on. Their colors were astonishing – purple, red and orange. Of course, we had to know something about them and where they had come from. The boys confessed to having pulled them from our neighbor's, Mrs. Clarence Griffin's, garden. They were her prize jonquils, properly called "Empress." But the boys had improved on nature. They had put them in bottles of vegetable coloring.

It was a bitter pill to be made to return them to Mrs. Griffin; to ring her doorbell and to say, hurriedly, "Mrs. Griffin, here are some of your flowers. We're sorry." But that's what they had to do.

Two more escapades:

Sister lived across the park, and this one came when she and her family were out of town. One hot July afternoon, her yardman, James, came running over to my house to tell me that our boys and Marie Tyler had taken oxblood shoe polish and written all over the side of Sister's and Bob's two-story limestone garage. Worse still, limestone is porous, and this side of the garage formed the background of one side of her lovely formal garden, the joy of her life.

I ran back with the worried James, as worried as he, but detoured enough to dash into Marie's mother's house with the news. I found her making sweet-pickled peaches and dripping with perspiration.

When the two of us saw what had been done, we called our husbands. They came in a hurry to stand with us and try to think of what to do, for written in letters at least three feet tall was the one word:

D E T H

And close by that misspelled word was a skull and crossbones – all in deep red.

The Gorhams would be arriving late that afternoon on the seven o'clock train. From three o'clock to six forty-five, Arthur, Elizabeth, Tom and I scrubbed first with with Bon Ami, then with steel wool, Skidoo, ammonia, and anything else we could think of.

At the last minute only a tinge of pink still showed. We scattered and ran home.

If the Gorhams ever noticed the pinkish tint on the side of their garage, family affection kept them from mentioning it.

During the years when our boys were away at prep school, for the Easter holiday the boys would come home, and we'd meet them at the local airport. On one such occasion, we were surprised to find Mack with almost shoulder length hair.

In the hub-bub of welcoming and hugging, no mention was made of Mack's hair until we got home. Once there, Tom said quietly, "Get that hair cut before we go to church tomorrow morning."

"Yes sir," Mack replied.

Being very late on Saturday afternoon, all the barbershops in town were closed, but during the years before the boys went off to prep school, when the four of us would be coming home at night after football games at Chapel Hill, near Momeyer, we always passed a microscopic, wooden barbershop, not more than ten-by-ten feet at the most, sitting off by itself near a crossroads. It always had a single light hanging from the ceiling, and the light was always on as we went by, even at ten o'clock at night.

Sure enough, when Mack came in at bedtime, he was shorn.

Asked where he'd gone to get his hair cut, he said, "Moe-my."

That's the way our community speaks of Momeyer. He had prevailed on an older friend to drive him to the little barbershop at the crossroads.

The next morning found us all sitting reverently in church, and on time.

Looking back, I conclude that the influence of a firm father, who undergirds his firmness with enduring affection is, I believe, the strongest influence in a son's life. It can be a battle of wills, but its rewards are not to be measured.

I've rambled on here at length, Jack. But once you start remembering, it's that way.

I hope there are one or two thoughts here that will serve your purpose, and I appreciate the time and thought you're giving to rounding out what will be an unforgettable experience for Mack. I know he does, too. For he values your friendship a great deal.

Sincerely,

Elizabeth Pearsall
February 11, 1991

≈ ≈ ≈

But those years when the children were growing up were not filled entirely with traumas. Tom had set in motion his program for the betterment of the farm families, and in a roundabout way, we would come to have a friendship with the writer, Archibald Rutledge. At that time, our town's local book clubs – and the members of these were entirely women – would come together for joint programs in our high school auditorium. Outstanding speakers would be brought in, and one of these happened to be the South Carolina poet, Archibald Rutledge.

Dr. Rutledge, or "Arch," as he was called, had taught at Mercersburg Academy in Pennsylvania for thirty years. At the time, he had retired and had gone back to live in his plantation home, "Hampton." While the house had long been in his family, it had gone down. It was badly in need of a new roof, and Archibald was endeavoring to get the necessary funds through his writing and his lectures. His most popular book had been *Home by the River*. There were smaller ones, *Beauty in the Heart*, and *Life's Extras*, among others, each one with its own charm.

For the visit to our town, he was our houseguest. His two-day stay happened to coincide with an annual gathering of our farm tenants at harvest time, for something spoken of as the "farm dinner." At that time, our tenants, including their children, numbered around a thousand. Some of the older ones were not able to read or write. For that reason, they were assigned to tables by swatches of colored cloth, and in the manner of southern barbecues, temporary tables for standing up to eat had been built among the trees. Temporary bleachers had also been built. In front of these was a high stage for the day's entertainment, such as cracker-and-whistling contests, clogging, and recitations. On the ground around the stage, tall, wooden crossbars had been erected, and there, the garments which the farm women had made and submitted for the contest for the best sewing were displayed. On the other side of the stage were displayed jars of their canned fruits, vegetables, jellies, and preserves, again, in competition for prizes.

Tom conducted the affairs of the day. At one point he had a cow brought in, the one judged to have had the best treatment throughout the year. The farm people were all neatly dressed, and there was a happy hum. Throughout the day, I never knew where our own two little boys would be, for they mingled happily with the children of their own age. Archibald Rutledge had said the night before that he would like to go with us, and throughout the next day, between my sister, Vivian, and me, he sat transfixed. Several times during the day he turned to me to say quietly, "There's so much love here."

I was to find later, that that night before he went to bed, he wrote a poem. Its title is "Signature," and this is the way it reads:

> *Before we were, who through this country came?*
> *Whose are these signs and signals in the night?*
> *Whose sign is on the darkness and the light?*
> *Whose symbol on the shadow and the flame?*
> *The constellations in their song proclaim*
> *Illustrious authorship. On depth and height*
> *His proud armorial bearings are in sight.*
> *Royal insignia reveal His name.*

All beauty bears His signet and His crest.
Upon the mountains and the sunrise shore
His sign is set, and on the wildrose west.
The evening star is His bright semaphore.
All glories to His glory must attest,
Acknowledging His sovereign signature.

Archibald Rutledge, Sept. 30, 1949
Written in the beautiful and gracious home of
Elizabeth and Thomas Pearsall, and of Vivian
Braswell

After that visit, Tom and I never went to Charleston that we didn't go the coastal route, by way of Georgetown, in order to stop and see our friend. In winter, we would find him at his typewriter which sat at one end of the dining room table, a fire would be going, and it seemed cozy. The first floor of the house, which was the only part we saw, was stark, meagerly furnished. Although there was no furniture in the ballroom, its beauty seemed to relieve the starkness of the house.

This loving man so much wanted to have something to give his friends when they came by, that he had one of his farm helpers pull up cypress knees from the swamp and place them on his wide front porch. On one trip, we had our young sons, then eight and ten, with us, and he allowed each one to chose the knee he wanted. This posed a problem. As they went among them, picking up this one and that one – boy-like, not being little saints – they went into fits of giggles, which Tom and I were hard-put to conceal from Archibald, our impoverished, but gallant friend.

For his lectures, Archibald carried out the flavor of the old in the way he dressed. If it were winter he wore puttees, laced to the knee, and riding pants, as well as a pinched-in coat. If it were summer, he was all in white. Although he was a little-known writer, those of my generation still re-read his books, and I find that my own sons and my daughter-in-law, Janice, find special meaning in two of his slender volumes, *Beauty in the Heart* and *Life's Extras*. In the second, he asks the question, "What if God had not put color in the sunset? That he did is one of life's extras." Those things make us think.

≈ ≈ ≈

As Tom's interest in politics deepened – and I shall try to speak objectively – that he was a man of stature was becoming recognized: one of ideas, and one willing to work for the common good. It was evident that he had that quality – a word much bandied about today, but not in use then:

234

charisma. In earlier times, that would have been spoken of as "magnetism." Undeniably he was, in that country phrase, "a man with an educated heart," at home in either high or low circles. Best of all, he was a man whose word was as good as his bond. Codman Hislop, a Captiva friend, once remarked that Tom was the kind of person who would make you feel secure were he around in an emergency. Paul Everett, another island friend, often pointed out, "Tom has a way of being able to 'galvanize' people together."

Excerpts from an interview with Tom in one of the newspapers of the Piedmont section of our state summarized Tom's interest in politics up to that time. The article starts out by explaining that Tom had been in political life since 1929. It goes on in this way:

> A year out of Carolina Law School, Pearsall became solicitor of the recorder's court in his home town. In 1940, seven years after he had left the first post, he was popped into the legislature by an accident of sorts, in the death of the elected member: "I nominated Kemp Battle for the place, and tried to get him elected. But the farmers of the county said they wanted a farmer, and they picked me."

Elsewhere in the interview, Tom goes on to say:

> "I'm not a real farmer, but I've studied hard. The only thing I can do is to hire good men who know their field. For example, the general farm manager, A. P. Cobb, is a State College graduate in agriculture and a former county agent."

Going over the article many years later, I'm struck with the accuracy of its tone – its informality and its down to earth conversation, because to me, it captures the person Tom was; not flowery, not pompous, yet there was a deep-down appreciation for things intellectual, and for the artistic.

Returning to the interview, Tom says of the overall of the family land, and the allied enterprises under his management:

> "I can't get involved in the details of any one operation, because if I did, I'd fall behind in the whole. I try to operate by a fixed set of principles. The most important, I suppose, is that the land is sort of like a bank account; you can't take out more than you put in, and we're blessed with diversity here, right on the fall line, near the extremes of many crop belts, and can grow them all. You can't miss with that kind of climate – and this year, for the first time since I started farming back in '35, we've hit the jackpot in everything: big tobacco crop, cotton, peanut and corn crops. All good."

The newspaper continues:

235

Pearsall oversees farms with six thousand acres, farmed by some nine-hundred people, and in Battleboro, the site of the Braswell enterprise, sixty to seventy people administer the more formally organized business end, [the cotton and peanut processing, a cotton and peanut brokerage, the sale of farm machinery, and the running of a general-store]...

... Pearsall looks to be in fine condition, perhaps because of his strenuous daily routine, perhaps because of the fifteen minutes of daily calisthenics, evidently taken between waking before dawn and his reaching for the morning newspaper on his porch at six a.m. He also rides occasionally...

...On his reading habit, he says: "I read the *Greensboro News*, the Raleigh and the Rocky Mount papers, and the *New York Times* on Sunday, a few magazines, mostly digests. My wife, Elizabeth does my heavy reading for me." I interrupt here to say that I wish Tom had included his love of history, of wars and battles, and of sailing stories.

By the time this reporter had spent an hour with Tom in his office, I think he would have drawn the conclusion from Tom, that few of us in Eastern Carolina would live anywhere else, that Tom believed in the future of our area, that he believed industry would expand here, and that with improved measures for our fine soil, there would be expansion in our agriculture. In his words:

"I feel that down here we live a little better than most folks, because we live close to the soil, and have time to enjoy other things. They say Eastern Carolinians are too busy living to make a living – but we manage to do both, I guess."

At the end of a long siege of questioning on his affairs, winding up with a visit to his newly operated highway restaurant near here, where he was hailed as "Governor," Pearsall said, "I'm not running for anything, but staying here and doing what I like. I don't want to seem presumptuous enough to shout that I'm not in the least interested in the idea of being Governor –I don't think a man has a right to feel so self-important. I made my decision long ago, and I'll stick to it. I won't say I'll never change, come what may. But I'm purely and simply content here. I don't want to leave. I'm busy, and happy."

The caption for the last paragraph in that comprehensive interview had read:

He's a contented man.

Although in the supporting role in our marriage, with the fulfillment of having our children, and knowing that I was playing a part in Tom's success, a nurturer by nature, I was to feel no lack of anything in my life. Indeed, I considered myself among the blessed. And in the thought expressed every now and then in a sermon by our beloved rector, Mr. Craighill, that "we can never earn our blessings," I felt that I could not be grateful enough for my own.

In time, Tom would receive three honorary degrees, one from the University of North Carolina, one from that branch of the University at Greensboro, (formerly the Women's College of the University) and one from North Carolina Wesleyan College.

In that Tom held women in such respect, and always wholeheartedly indulged any recognition of their merit, the citation included in this story is the one that accompanied the awarding of the honorary degree from the University of North Carolina at Greensboro, as conferred by its president:

> THOMAS JENKINS PEARSALL – lawyer, legislator, and dedicated public servant – has been a member, officer, director, trustee, and chairman of countless business, philanthropic, educational, religious, and cultural institutions, agencies, boards, and foundations, through which the lives of the people of North Carolina have been enriched.
>
> As a distinguished member of the bar, as an outstanding figure in the state's General Assembly, and as one of the most creative and forceful personalities of the University's Board of Trustees in its century and three-quarters of history, he has placed every citizen of North Carolina in his debt. Beloved and respected for his humanity, his wisdom and his wit, he takes rank with a select company of North Carolinians who have brought our state and our University to the favorable notice of countless thousands far beyond our borders.
>
> Mr. Pearsall, for your unstinting labors in behalf of the Commonwealth, and most especially for your inspired leadership as the chairman of the special committee of the University's Board of Trustees which was created to study the establishment of additional campuses of the University and to develop a rational plan for meeting North Carolina's future needs for higher learning, we salute you as the architect-in-chief of the plan that redefined and expanded the role of the former Women's College of the University and launched it upon wider seas as a co-educational institution of full university rank. And speaking for all those who would honor you in this hour, I now confer upon you the honorary degree of Doctor of Laws with all its rights and privileges.

Tom saw the University of our state and its allied institutions as vehicles for the state's collective advancement. It was beginning to be understood that its base must be broadened by the building of a medical school and hospital. Tom was active on the committee charged with this endeavor. I recall, clearly, one of several dinners for the committee, held in our home in Rocky Mount, where some of our local doctors were guests as well. These dinners came to be duplicated in other areas.

After a few years, the dream would, indeed, become a reality. Which meant that along with Duke Hospital, healthcare – on a large scale – was available for all our citizens. Even today, years later, a warm feeling surges over me when I overhear some person whose income would never have allowed medical treatment say, "I was treated at Chapel Hill and I'm well again." I'm continually thankful that our taxpayers' monies afford this.

During those years which Tom had spent in the legislature, he and I kept a suite in the Sir Walter Hotel in Raleigh. While I could not always be there, at those times when I was, it was pleasurable and exciting in that way that goes with politics. Tom, ostensibly the country boy from Nash, or so he described himself, harking back to the earlier years when he had, as he said, "taken his athletics seriously" to the extent that he neither smoked nor drank, had developed a reputation for serving a concoction in our suite which he had named "Nash Mash." It was a drink we had created at home for our own pleasure, one made of grapefruit and orange juice, crushed ice, and sugar – no alcohol. Among legislators the drink became a general favorite; they would end the day in our suite with the camaraderie of a "Nash-Mash," for it's surprising when you get right down to it, how easy it is for people to enjoy something simple. We would bring our blender to the suite, and off and on during those nocturnal political discussions, I could hear it from the bedroom in all its earsplitting whir. Its interference, however, instead of being a deterrent to the group, appeared to stimulate the flow of conversation.

With Tom's becoming Speaker of the House, we gave a dance for the General Assembly. It was held in the Sir Walter Hotel, where most of the legislature stayed for the session. Its large, lovely ballroom lent itself to those dance figures to which Tom and I had grown accustomed in Rocky Mount at the annual dance put on early in summer and spoken of as The June-German. The year before we were married, in that Tom was president of the Cotillion Club, we were given the honor of leading the Grand March of that annual affair, which at that time, had been going on for seventy-five years.

An old program, yellowed with age, which, for sentimental reasons I had saved, says,

FORTY-NINTH ANNUAL JUNE GERMAN
June Twenty-first, Nineteen Hundred Twenty-nine
Fenners Warehouse, Rocky Mount, N.C.
10:00 P.M. to 5:30 A.M.
– Music by –
Jack Crawford and His Victor Recording Orchestra

SPECIAL CLUB FIGURE 12:30

DIRECTOR
Mr. W.E. Fenner with Mrs. W.E. Fenner
LEADER
Mr. Thomas J. Pearsall with Miss Elizabeth Braswell
ASSISTANT LEADERS
Mr. W.G. Weeks, Jr. with Miss Susie Batts
Mr. R.H. Gregory with Miss Virginia Thorpe

INTERMISSIONS
FIRST – 1:00 A.M. to 1:30 A.M.
SECOND – 3:00 A.M. to 3:20 A.M.
THIRD – 4:30 A.M. to 4:40 A.M.

The "June-German" was, and still is, held in an empty tobacco warehouse, but a warehouse converted – for a night – to some large, beautiful, summer garden. The dance, according to custom, begins at ten, with intermission parties in homes at twelve, two, and four, breakfast at dawn. In the generations before ours, the ladies wore trains, they had plumes in their hair, and each carried on her arm a large spray of long-stemmed red roses shipped from Philadelphia, or, perhaps, Richmond.

Those attending would have come from all over the state, some from other southern states as far away as Louisiana, for it was a dance known, and to some degree, heralded, over the South. On the stroke of midnight, to the tune of a nationally known orchestra, we began the Grand March. In an archway made beautiful with smilax, which in the early days usually came from local gardens, or where it hung over some local porch, each lady would be introduced by megaphone, as was her escort, who, in white tie and tails, stood ready to receive her, so that on his arm, she might accompany him on the long, slow walk around the dance floor. This procedure would be followed until each young lady and her escort, the latter, those members of the cotillion club responsible for the dance, had been presented.

The first couple, having led this promenade around the inside of the gigantic rectangle, would return to the archway to be joined by other couples. There, facing the ballroom, perhaps two dozen couples abreast, they would – in this impressive formation – make the grand sweep down the length of the room, that final note done to ever heightening applause; a moment in a young girl's life that ranked close to that of being a bride.

Minus the introductions, but copying the figures, the dance in Raleigh followed that June-German pattern, even to its spectacular Grand March. Although the guests were a generation older, the response was as enthusiastic. Gowns were as elegant, the flowers the ladies carried, not so dramatic, but equally as beautiful, the only real difference was that instead of dancing to "Good Night Ladies" at five o'clock in the morning, the strains of that came at midnight.

In those political years, when I was consistently in and out of Raleigh, the Sir Walter Cabinet, an ongoing organization, played a large part in my social life. Tom and I already had a wide circle of friends in Raleigh, but in the general assembly, where each of the one hundred counties over the state is represented, I came to know many fine women who were there in the way that I was, in support of their husbands, or those women at large who were there to get legislative support for the causes which were their particular interests.

My friendship with Buffie Ives began there. Having come, each year, from Illinois, to spend time in her mother's winter home in Southern Pines, Buffie and Mrs. Hugh Cannon of the Cannon Towel family of the Piedmont, through their interest in historical preservation, had become close friends. Following that interest, the two ladies were often together in Raleigh at the Cabinet Meetings where they were busy laying the groundwork for the promotion of their joint cause.

That branch of the Cannon family had been fellow passengers with Mother and my sisters and me on the Red Star Liner, *The Belgianland*, when it made its 1929-30 six-month cruise around the world. And it was through Mrs. Charles Cannon – Ruth – that I came to know Buffie more intimately. That later friendship would ripen fast, for we had the twin interests of historic preservation and the fostering of democratic ideals. It was in the latter sphere that Tom and I had come to know Buffie's brother, Adlai Stevenson, as well, since Southern Pines and our hometown, Rocky Mount, are only a two hour drive apart.

Ernest and Buffie were frequently in our home and we were in theirs, as houseguests. Adlai was never our guest other than at Captiva, but we were with him in a variety of places: Southern Pines, Captiva, Chicago, Lake Forest, and in his own home in Libertyville. Later he would become

United States Representative to the United Nations. We were sometimes there with him in his New York apartment where Paula, the cook he had brought from home, would provide us a simple lunch.

Since Ernest had retired from the Diplomatic Service, the Ives' winters were spent, from November first to April, in Southern Pines. Along with the North Carolina delegation and with the Ives, Tom and I would attend the 1956 National Convention in Chicago when Kennedy was chosen as the Democratic Party's candidate for President. By pre-arrangement, we would stay at the same hotel as the Ives. Their home in Bloomington required for them, only a hundred-and-fifty-mile drive to Chicago, that city spoken of in earlier times as the "City of the Stockyards."

The convention hall was in the area of the stockyards, and while we were there, that earlier descriptive phrase kept coming into my mind. For to an easterner's nose, the air in that area was strongly infused with the odor of beef. Since for our pleasure and our convenience, the temporary restaurants that had sprung up around the convention hall to serve the delegates would offer their prize filet mignon, the aroma of these in preparation constantly seeping in to the hall was to add to the impression.

However, the city's elegance and sophistication is not to be disputed, a point that I would understand, when, later, Tom and I were visiting in the homes of friends around Lake Michigan, where, under the force of the winds that sweep across that large body of water, the ruffled waves could be those of a sea.

During that, my first visit to Chicago, I did not always stay at the convention hall for the evening sessions. And one night, I began to regret my choice, for there came the frightening experience of a fire in our hotel.

When I am in a hotel alone, to make it especially pleasant, I always remember what my friend Tillie Elliot used to say, "I love the anonymity of a hotel room, marooned as you are, against any and all demands." That night, I had had a leisurely bath, had gotten into bed, had phoned the family at home, and was happily at work on the list for a luncheon I had decided to give for the ladies in the North Carolina delegation who were there for the convention. Buffie was to be guest of honor.

When is a woman ever so pleasurably engaged as when she's planning a party? And since the luncheon was to be given in the hotel, with no responsibility for anything except the selection of the flowers and the menu, I was floating about on a cloud of anticipation when, suddenly, I heard fire trucks and loud voices under my window. I jumped up and ran to look out, and down. Sure enough, from the twelfth floor, I was looking down on a hundred or more firehats and firehoses, the hats scurrying like ants to carry the hoses into our building. I hurried to telephone the desk to ask, "Are we on fire?" and was told in a matter-of-fact tone, "Yes, Madam, but we think it's under control."

"Where is it?" I wanted to know.

"In the kitchen area," the desk clerk replied easily.

This was of no help. I didn't know what to do. To regain composure was beyond me, so, to the terrible thought, *I wonder if the elevators are working?* I flung on a few clothes, and was thankful, that, from the time I'd spent my first night in a hotel as a child, I'd been told at the moment of being shown into the room to look for an exit. And since it was a habit of Tom's as well, it was a safeguard we never overlooked. The only bright thought at that moment was that we had done that. Shakily dressing, I could see myself clattering down those twelve flights of metal stairs, clutching my pocketbook, and trying not to fall.

But the hallway was quiet. Not a soul in sight. *Are they all at the convention, or have they already suffocated?* went through my head. My hands shook as I pressed the button for the elevator, and it seemed an eternity before it decided to come. Finally it did.

In the lobby, there was hardly room to get out of the elevator, for the firemen and their alarmingly purposeful hats, their frightening picks and their large sturdy hoses, were all rushing by in the same direction. But they moved quietly, which was, in some dim way, reassuring.

There were no other hotel guests around. Pressing against the wall, and at the same time trying to reach the desk, where the clerk, in his usual position, stood – calm as a May day – I gasped, "What am I supposed to do?"

Again, his answer seemed peculiarly unconcerned, "Madam, there's only one thing for you to do. Take the elevator back to your room. Get in bed and read a book. This happens all the time. It's of little consequence."

I almost said, "Of little consequence to *you* because you're here on the first floor." But I held back. Instead, I decided to make an effort at being mature. After all, it was only my life that was at stake; I might as well be philosophical. Nevertheless, it was an eternity, for me, before two a.m., when, wide-eyed and propped up on three pillows, the light still on by my bed, I heard the welcome sound of Tom's key in the lock.

A few nights later, when the convention had nominated John Kennedy over Adlai Stevenson as its candidate, the eruption of excitement in the convention hall was deafening. But you could have heard a pin drop when Adlai made his concession. He referred to a quotation from a man of an earlier time who had suffered a political defeat. The man was Abraham Lincoln, who, quoting a little boy who had stubbed his toe in the dirt, said,

"It hurts too much to laugh, and I'm too old to cry."

The thousands of his admirers, listening, could have shed their own tears.

Soon after the defeat of his candidacy for the Presidency, Adlai came to Captiva to visit some of his Chicago friends. It was there, in that informal atmosphere, that we saw the person he was. He was not one to grieve over spilled milk. His sense of the joy of life and his spirit of fun had returned, and swimming with us in small groups – going by boat to another, uninhabited island to swim and picnic – he was his witty self. He enjoyed swimming, but he joked that his swims on that island were not as relaxed as they might have been because of the wheeling of the shorebirds over the surf and his uneasiness that they might mistake his rosy bald scalp for a large shrimp.

When he had become U.N. representative, Tom and I, seeing him often in New York, were inspired over and over again with what one writer describes as his having shown Americans that intelligence and idealism have their place in political life. This writer, Bill Severn, in his book, *Adlai Stevenson, Citizen of the World*, tells us that when the United States and Cuba were locked in confrontation over the presence of Russian missiles in Cuba, the Cuban representative to U.N. is supposed to have said of Stevenson, "Even when my enemy, he is a gentleman."

When, after five years at U.N., Adlai died suddenly on the streets of London, President Johnson paid him this impromptu tribute: "The flame which illumined the dreams and expectations of an entire world is now extinguished. Adlai Stevenson of Illinois is dead...for an entire generation of Americans he imparted a nobility to public life and a grandeur to American purpose which has already reshaped the life of the nation and which will endure for many generations."

From another tribute: "The disappointments were his in cruel measure, but the satisfactions were his as well. He died as he would have wished, engaged in his country's business and mankind's."

≈ ≈ ≈

During what I think of as the Raleigh years, among a wealth of pleasant social things, one in particular stands out. Mr. Josephus Daniels, editor of the Raleigh newspaper *The News and Observer*, which virtually blankets Eastern Carolina, and who, at one point, had been Secretary of the Navy under Woodrow Wilson, and who, subsequently, would become Ambassador to Mexico, was father to four sons: Worth, Josephus, Jonathan, and Frank. Frank and Tom had been fraternity brothers at

Chapel Hill, and later, had been in each other's weddings. In this way, Ruth, Frank's wife, formerly Ruth Aunsbaugh of Norfolk, and I, became close friends. Our marriages had come only a month apart, and when Mr. and Mrs. Daniels gave a large reception at Wakestone, home of the Daniels' family in Raleigh, for the bride and groom on their return from their wedding trip, Tom and I were invited to receive with the family of the bride and groom.

It was the first time I had heard Tom introduce me formally. Instead of introducing me as his "wife," in what would turn out to be his characteristic way throughout life, he would say to people coming down the receiving line, "Elizabeth and Tom Pearsall." With his Charlestonian pronunciation of the Pearsall name, as it had come up through the old North Carolina towns of Wilmington, Kenansville, Warsaw, and Fayetteville, it came out in a way I loved. It rhymed with "there," with a "y" thrown in after the "P"; "Pyeahs'll."

And here, still re-living that reception, my thoughts run to another digression, asking myself why it is that in formal circumstances the man always stands to the right of the lady. I recall the explanation of the custom, which came at the time when Sir Anthony Eden, at that time, Prime Minister of England, was being married. In the usual consternation of bridegrooms, at the time of the rehearsal, he asked, "On which side do I stand?" In answer, the time-worn couplet, was recited for him:

> *A gentleman's always on the lady's right*
> *leaving his sword-arm free to fight.*

I love the romance of that. I can see a white knight, with his left arm, snatching his lady-love up beside him on his horse, while, with his right arm, he wards off the competition with a sweep of the sword.

Another occasion at Wakestone that I remember well came years later, sometime after Mrs. Daniels' death. Mr. Daniels was giving a luncheon for their old friend, Mrs. Woodrow Wilson. This large, handsome, outstanding woman, as impressive in appearance as she was in manner, was driving through with her secretary on her way to Florida. As a stopover on her journey, she had accepted Mr. Daniels' invitation for lunch, where he would, as he had promised, see that she would be served something which, next to barbecue, is perhaps a North Carolinian's – certainly an Eastern Carolinian's – favorite food: turnip-salad, a cooked green new to Mrs. Wilson.

These small green leaves, so tender that they can be pinched off with the fingernails, are gathered with little regard to the developing turnip, which is diced and either put into the pot, or not used at all. The leaves require the usual several rinsings that go with the preparation of greens. Seasoning is simple. A small chunk of pork is allowed to boil for an hour or more in a large pot of water, then the tender leaves are added. At that time, a little sugar and a little salt go into the pot. The timing for boiling the greens varies with the tenderness of the leaves, which could be from thirty minutes to an hour. The last stage comes with the draining and chopping of the greens which are served in a vegetable dish. At our house, and in my own home throughout life, until knowledge of cholesterol came, this time-honored Tar Heel dish would be garnished with slices of hard-boiled egg, making the vegetable as attractive as it is tasty.

So that, on a bright winter's day, the little party often – all ladies, except for Mr. Daniels – gathered at Wakestone. Carrying out his promise to honor Mrs. Wilson, and at the same time, to glorify turnip-salad, Mr. Daniels had made plans to have the celebrated greens served as a first course. Of course, to Tar Heels, that was as wrong as wrong can be. A serving of this delicacy has to lie on the plate with something else, usually a meat and a starch. But for this luncheon, the service plates, from Mr. Daniels' days of having been Ambassador to Mexico, were silver, and to Sturgeon, the gray-haired butler, passing these homely greens from a large silver vegetable dish to lie in state on an otherwise empty china plate, with the silver one underneath, seemed so out of character that he appeared to be having as little to do with the process as possible.

Naturally, Mr. Daniels, at the head of the table, was having himself a high old time. Mrs. Wilson was a native of Staunton, Virginia, and that day, although the turnip salad was served in jest, it was an indirect reminder, perhaps even a little boast, that North Carolinians have always been down-to-earth. For no Tar Heel ever gets to be twenty-years-old without having heard what a long ago Tar Heel patriot said – and I daresay the words were spoken in our general assembly – that "North Carolina is a valley of humility between two mountains of conceit."

In those earlier years after our marriage, when Tom was making talks at Rotary Clubs and such, he would explain that in contrast to two of our Eastern Seaboard sister states, South Carolina and Virginia, we had had no deep ports; therefore, North Carolina did not have as many of the early elegances – the silver and the Chippendale – that those two had. And since, in the early days, the law of primogeniture still held (the oldest son inheriting the land), in many cases, the younger sons were sent across the borders to homestead in our state.

We know this without apology, and we think it worked to our good. For we remember that those earlier settlers who came to this country from the Old World were not all high-ranking Lord's proprietors, of which we, ourselves, had a respectable number. By and large, settlers were yeomen, some of them in this way, rescued from debtor's prison. For laws in the Old World were stern. To recall their severity in the British Isles, you have only to be shown one of those grassy mounds that, long ago, were thrown up at the end of a now well-kept walled and beautiful garden, and to be told, as Tom and I were once when we were visiting friends in Scotland, that those man-made mounds were for scaffolds, sometimes used for an offense as small as the stealing of a sheep.

I would not be able to agree with the "valley of humility" jest, however, for a degree of pride has its place. For balance, I recall two of the best biographies I've ever come across, those of Thomas Jefferson and Helen Keller. Each began with a telling paragraph. Thomas Jefferson, a frontiersman, had married into the so-called blue-blooded family of the Randolphs of Virginia. He retained many of his simple ways. When he had made his place in history, and was asked by some bright-eyed young interviewer, "Mr. Jefferson, now that you've become famous, are you not thinking of getting a coat of arms?" Mr. Jefferson's reply was a gem of wit and wisdom. Paraphrased, "I might sometime give a little thought to the matter," he said, "for I understand that by writing to London, one can be obtained as cheaply as any other coat."

The story of Helen Keller's life begins with the thought, again paraphrased, that it behooves none of us to be overproud of our ancestry, for a thorough knowledge of history, could there be such, would show that every slave is descended from a king, and every king from a slave.

It seems to me that North Carolinians have always been realists. Before we take action on major issues, we tend to think slowly and carefully. In that way we were the last of the thirteen colonies to distance ourselves from the Mother Country. Yet, when we felt that the time had come for us to take that bold step, in spite of our respect for authority, we were quick to form our Carolina Resolves. These papers were drawn up in two sections of the state, papers that pre-date the Declaration of Independence. It had become too galling to continue to submit to "taxation without representation."

As to the South in general, in connection with the Civil War, I was late in finding out that it was fought not so much over slavery as for the defense of state's rights. And although nobody would deny that the buying and selling of human beings as though they are cattle is wrong, our forebears had inherited a system. Somebody had to till the land, or it would have been non-productive.

In an old church graveyard I know, there is an example of how I like to think our forebears felt, generally, toward the treatment of slaves. In the shade of Old Trinity Church graveyard near the town of Scotland Neck, twenty-five miles from the area in which I've spent my life, there's a tombstone made in the shape of a large harp. One of its chords is broken, and this tells the story of a young woman who had fallen in love and was engaged to be married to a young man on a neighboring plantation. But he was cruel to his slaves, and the engagement was ended. This heartbroken young lady never married, and at her death, which came many years later, her family used this symbol to mark her grave.

In the same graveyard, there is a tomb that marks the death of another young daughter of the time. The lovely inscription is that used by Mark Twain on his own daughter's headstone:

> *Warm Southern breeze, blow softly, blow softly,*
> *Warm Southern sun, shine warmly, shine warmly,*
> *Warm Southern sod, lie light, lie light,*
> *Good night, dear heart, good night.*

Still on the subject of slavery, all women can now be proud that Harriet Beecher Stowe, a wife and mother with a house full of children and a multitude of duties, had the heart, and the talent, and somehow found the time to write, among other things, a book that would prove the impetus for the ultimate righting of the wrong of the owning of slaves. For, *Uncle Tom's Cabin* swept the country; its cry heard around the world. I have gone into these last subjects – ones so profound, that even the most informed minds still seek the answers – because it seems to me that any thinking southern woman, even at this remove from two turbulent periods in our country's history, is compelled to make the questions her own.

But now back to Mr. Daniels' luncheon for Mrs. Wilson. A tablespoonful of turnip-salad, alone on a china plate in front of a diner, is a flagrant mixture of metaphors. But there was so much merriment that day that it hardly mattered. With that course soon whisked away to avoid embarrassing the guest of honor, who could hardly have acquired a taste for it so quickly, the other courses, sumptuous and sophisticated, began.

Mr. Daniels had seated me next to Mrs. Wilson, and I found her charming. My sisters had been students at colleges in the city of Washington, when, after the death of the first Mrs. Wilson, she was in the White House. And though at the time, I was only a child, I had gained through them, and through Father and my uncles, a lasting respect for President Wilson. Hearing so much about the League of Nations, which had become his dream, and which, at the Geneva Conference would fail, I felt it a privilege to be in *her* presence.

I suppose that that feeling was something of what I had several years later when Tom and I were spending a weekend with Buffie and Ernest in their home in Southern Pines, when General Marshall was their luncheon guest as well. Tom and I had such a deep admiration for this great man, for the Marshall Plan for Lend-Lease after World War II had enabled Europe to reach economic recovery, that I, myself, felt tinged with greatness to be seated with him at a small table for five.

Still thinking of the White House: One of the millions who would come to appreciate that other humanitarian, Eleanor Roosevelt, I regret that I was never thrown with her informally, but I could, and did, have the satisfaction of apologizing to her for a small scathing book, written by one of our radio commentators, and addressed to her openly after one of her visits to our state. In frankness and sincerity, she had expressed to reporters her regret at finding, in our towns and our villages and along the roadsides, that there still existed shanties. Resentful of this critical observation, in a sarcastic vein, this North Carolina commentator had written a thin little book of denigration of Mrs. Roosevelt, and had given it the title, *Weep No More My Lady*. The book was on all the newsstands, and I felt a personal responsibilty for letting Eleanor Roosevelt, perhaps the greatest woman of our century, know that that was the voice of only one North Carolinian. I would have had to sit on my hands not to have written an apology for my state.

In order to preserve peace, we must always be working for it.

Eleanor Roosevelt (Paraphrased)

The only deadly thing in the world is cynicism.

James L. McCloy, Counsel at the
Nuremburg Trials, quoting his hero
Secretary of State, Henry L. Stimson

≈ ≈ ≈

As Tom moved into the busy years, in a small way, mine were being filled as well, but in less obvious ways. A nurturer at heart, a firelight kind of person, with a leaning toward supper by candlelight, I suppose it was gratitude for my own good fortune that forced me out into the larger spheres.

Now, looking back over my life, trying to see why I was taking such a deep interest in a movement for world peace – a new movement – then called "World Government Through World Federalists," I see that this came about through a combination of my background of travelling and my consistent involvement with the church. At the time, it was not a widely known movement, nor did its membership include any prominent names.

By that time, having given up teaching Sunday School, I had gone on to become leader of a small group of women of my parish, known as a "Church Circle." Later I became president of a much larger group of churchwomen, my title, District Chairman. In that way, I began to serve on diocesan committees, all the while being given more and more breadth of vision. With this added to the amount of travelling we had done as a family during my girlhood and young womanhood, my conviction that, basically, all human beings want the same things from life, grew.

My interest in world peace had begun at the age of eighteen, when visiting the battlefields of France. There was an indescribable sadness in the acres and acres of small white crosses in the green of those military cemeteries, and I had come to have the feeling that if there were ever any way that I could work for peace over the world, I would want to.

With the birth of our first child, the feeling of the futility of war became almost a part of my daily life. That nations continued to go to war against each other, appeared, to me, one of the imponderables. Yet there was a deep conviction that, with time, this tragic aspect of life might not prove insurmountable.

I had begun to study Woodrow Wilson's attempts, after the bloodshed of the first World War, at forming The League of Nations in Geneva. Around the time of my growing interest in peace, Wendell Wilke, an unsuccessful candidate for the Presidency of our country, gave us the phrase, "One World." It was a phrase to hold to the heart, and afterward, my own searched constantly for signs of hope toward that ideal.

In my church mail one day, I found a pamphlet telling of a certain Sam Levering, an apple-grower in the hills of my own state, who was committed to, and constantly working for world peace. Sam, a Quaker, through having taken part in the International Olympics in Germany as a young man, had come to believe in "One World" as well. Many areas of our country were

251

then isolationist, but there were scattered segments of those who were loosely banding together to form the organization called "World Government Through World Federalists." Sam Levering became one of its speakers, and it was in this capacity that I came to know him.

As head of "The Women of the Church," in my parish, it was my responsibility to provide outside speakers for our monthly meetings. The subject for our year's study in my home parish was "Racial Amity as a Pillar of Peace." I planned the program to start with Racial Amity at home, and to work outward. For one of our meetings, I had as a speaker a wonderful African American woman, Charlotte Hawkins Brown, president of Palmer Memorial Institute, a small North Carolina college of predominantly black students, not far from Greensboro. Born and brought up in the South, Dr. Brown had been befriended by a New England woman educator who recognized qualities in this young southern woman that made her want to help with her education. The fact that the older woman had held out her hand to this young girl of another race, and that it was bearing fruit was significant. The college was in the Piedmont section of our state, easily within driving distance of our town. To add interest to the program, I asked Dr. Brown to bring a quartet of her students for musical numbers. The meeting was held in the parish hall of our church and was well attended. From there, the base of our year's program was broadened to have people of other nationalities, by turns, come and talk to us.

We closed the year's study with a meeting on a subject that although it was not racial, was one that seemed important enough to be highlighted. For this meeting, a lovely young woman came from Greensboro to talk to us on this subject: *I Am An Alcoholic.* Our church, in some ways, had always been the village church, headquarters for Boy Scout troops, and, among other things, Alcoholics Anonymous. Later it would provide our community's first kindergarten for all races and creeds. Concurrently, it was providing its facilities as a shelter for the homeless, a step that soon become a communitywide beneficence sponsored by all our churches and our townspeople, the shelter having now grown to require a building of its own.

To help this world government movement, Sam Levering had given ten thousand dollars of the income from his own apple orchard near Mt. Airy in the foothills of our state. That generosity in itself was inspiring, and slowly, through this good man's efforts and those like-minded, the movement grew. At my invitation, Sam Levering returned to our town several times, always as our houseguest. To have him in our home was always a happy experience. His presence there at mealtime, at our family table, gave me the same feeling that I had once derived from having another houseguest for a week, when a certain Father Harrison from Holy Cross Monastery, an Episcopal retreat in New York, had come to conduct a mission in our parish.

The theme of the mission was "Love." Father Harrison was an elderly man, but one who had not lost touch with children and teenagers, and our meals were never more merry than when he was there. He sensibly confided to me on arrival that he had lost his teeth; that his dentures now left something to be desired, but that I was never to worry about what he did or did not consume, for he would always find enough.

This meant that at the last minute before meals, I would be in the kitchen with the cook, making sure that the spoon bread was right, or that the soufflé hadn't fallen. In a light way, the Bible story of two sisters would run through my mind; one, who chose to sit at Christ's feet and hear what he had to say, and the other, who, at the moment, was more concerned with what she was going to put before him to eat, and I would wonder, *Am I a Mary or a Martha?*, for I did not want to miss a minute of Father Harrison's company, but as a matter of being practical, I felt that it was more important for me, at that point, to be in the kitchen. Incidentally, this is a question that I have found pleasure in raising before small church groups of women throughout my adult life. It always brings out interesting discussion, for applied to herself, it makes a woman think, and whichever she feels that she is, she will wonder if she should not be the other; the kind of dilemma women are always facing.

On the wider horizon, my interest in World Peace was always there. True, there were not many members of that organization of World Federalists, sometimes spoken of as World Peace through World Government, but we were believers.

And here I bring in Mrs. Gaskell. Elizabeth Gaskell, the writer who lived in the time of the Brontë sisters, was a friend of Charlotte's; they kept up an avid correspondence. Both women were the daughters of clergymen, but Mrs. Gaskell had had a happier home life than the Brontë sisters and their unhappy brother. The happiness for Mrs. Gaskell would continue throughout her life. Her book, *Cranford*, is a delightful story of life in her village, where, bringing up her children, being a helpmeet to her husband, and trying to snatch a few moments of the day for her writing, she said, on the subject of optimism and belief, "A little credulity is a good thing; better than going around doubting things all the time." And, speaking further on the subject of life in general, Mrs. Gaskell writes, in her novel, *Mary Barton*, "The only solution offered is that, recognizing their common frailty, men should withhold judgment on each other." This is a person I would like to have known.

Members of World Federalists through World Peace wrote countless letters to their representatives in Washington. And finally, slowly, came what is today, United Nations, or simply, "U.N." Yet, there was still, in our country, a degree of pessimism as to how much that organization would be able to do. No matter. The small band of the faithful held on. The beloved President Emeritus of our University of North Carolina, and one of Tom's heroes, Frank Graham, became U.S. Delegate to United Nations, as later would Adlai Stevenson. Tom and I knew both of these men intimately, and now, in 1995, that the world has seen the real moral influence U.N. has and is willing to stand up for in protection of human rights brings global hope.

That the Berlin Wall has come down, that the Cold War with Russia has ended, with democracies now springing up over the face of the earth, when even Castro, our nearest Communist neighbor, seems to show signs of unbending from his rigid stance as dictator gives weight to that Oriental proverb: the wise bamboo bends with the wind.

≈ ≈ ≈

When I was a bride, I began to think of the overall kind of woman I'd like to be. For with my great happiness there came an urge toward more sense of direction for my life. And although I could never be thankful enough for having had Mother's wonderful example to measure life by, I knew that – to serve as further inspiration – I needed the example of a woman of a generation nearer my own. There were many women about me to admire, but I chose one as my ideal; the one person, whom, as an individual, I would most want to be like. That person was Maude Bunn Battle.

Some years older than I, I liked her lifestyle. It seemed to contain an admirable balance. She was a supportive wife, a beautiful homemaker, a fine mother, an untiring community servant and churchwoman. She was open-minded in race relations. She was a woman of education, as well, and she perennially saw the funny side of life.

Maude and her husband, Kemp, were as well-matched as any pair I've ever known. Tom and I considered them the ideal couple. As a young man, Kemp had had tuberculosis, and their wedding had to be delayed for him to spend some time in the dry air of the West for treatment. This highly intelligent man's family background was one that included outstanding lawyers and an early president of the University of North Carolina. A deeply respected lawyer himself, Kemp was a community leader, and a leader in the Episcopal church on both the local and the diocesan levels. He served on the board of the larger of our three hospitals. In spite of the difference in their ages, Kemp and Tom had a friendship in a dozen ways: the church, the legal profession, community loyalty, love of the University of North Carolina at Chapel Hill, their alma mater, their state, and their country.

With all of these bonds, we saw as much of Maude and Kemp as we did any of our younger friends, and I dare say that it was through Kemp that I was invited to become a member of the board of the hospital of which he was a member. I was the only woman member on that board, one on which I was to sit through the years until the institution became a county hospital.

Close friends and contemporaries of the Kemp Battles were Dr. and Mrs. Claiborne Smith, and I can recall nothing more pleasant than those times when, as couples, the Smiths and the Pearsalls would be invited out to the Battles' country home for supper. Their home was a copy of The Hermitage, President Andrew Jackson's residence, in Tennessee. On its wide front porch, the six of us would sit in rockers, sipping a mint julep or a glass of wine, and our laughter would ring through the large, old oaks of the grove.

Those visits were filled with the play of the mind. There was as much of nonsense among us as there was of the serious. If there happened to be a stranger among us, Kemp would ask him or her a favorite riddle. The riddle went this way, "There was an old man with a little *feebly* growing down on his chin. Tell me what a feebly is?"

The person being asked would screw up the face and think hard, and no matter how many degrees he or she had, at the end, would give up. Kemp would then repeat the riddle. He would say the same words, changing their emphasis. "There was an old man with a little feebly growing *down* on his chin." Then we would all burst into a laugh, considering nonsense a very sensible ingredient in human life.

As late afternoon gave way to dusk, the front door from the hall would open, and Susie, the housegirl, would step out onto the porch, crisp in her uniform and cap, to announce, not in the formal way of "Dinner is served," but in the soft southern way, "Suppa's ready, Miss Mawed." And the little party would make its way through the wide, gracious hall, past the opening of the double doors to the sitting room on the right, and those of the parlor to the left, and into the double doors of the dining room.

Maude and Kemp would take their customary places at opposite ends of the table, while Mary Lee, whom Maude had taught to be a skilled cook, would come from the kitchen to help Irene with the serving and to enjoy the round of compliments that would undoubtedly be hers. These preliminaries taken care of, Kemp, at his end of the table, would carve the roast, or the lamb, or serve the fried chicken, whatever the entree happened to be. And by the time the diners were giving attention to their food, Kemp would start telling a tale, something for which he had a great talent. He was one of those individuals who could tell a simple tale, but so pepper it with big words that it would make the tale doubly humorous. One night, as a particular tale unfolded, he set the stage for it with this opening. "It was a warm day in a southern town, and two men, meeting on the street, were engaged in *desultory* conversation."

My mouth dropped open, my fork fell, as I interrupted, "My goodness, Kemp! Is *that* the way you pronounce that word? I've only read it, and when I did, I always read it as de*zull*try, rather like that odd pronunciation that the British give to the word "laboratory": le*bor*itry."

We all had a good laugh at the British and ourselves, and of course, at me. But I didn't mind, because I could tell the others of having read somewhere in an autobiography, a confession from the writer, that until long after he left college, he read the word "misled" as "mistled." Yet, deep down, I must have liked Kemp's pronunciation of that special word – desultory – for ever since, whenever I have begun to say that two people were engaged in idle conversation, the word desultory comes to me first. I just don't have the nerve to use it.

Further, on the subject of words – one of which I never seem to tire – I have one jolly memory of something that happened once when Tom and I were on a cruise among the Caribbean Islands. I had had a hard time convincing Tom that we needed a cruise, one into the tropics. I had pointed out that the only time we'd ever been on an ocean liner together was the one that had come early in our marriage, which had taken us for a short stay with the Bar Association to Bermuda. My premise was that it seemed time to take another, this time to an area more tropical than Bermuda.

His reaction to the suggestion was that we would only be seeing different palms and different waters, and that nowhere could there be more delightful people than were to be found on the island of Captiva, that we would be exchanging this for days of lolling about on a liner that was, itself, lolling its way between shopping sprees. To Tom, the idea held little appeal. Yet, with a little gentle perseverance, and a reminder that our friends, the William Shaws, were booked for one a few months away, and had invited us to join them on the large and impressive *Rotterdam*, of the Dutch line, he gave in. As I knew he would, when the time came, he enjoyed every aspect of the interlude.

When we were ashore on any of the islands, Tom always sought out the marinas or those little stretches of coastline where the local fisherman beached their boats. It was on a day of this kind, that we reached St. Thomas and had gone ashore. Burt and William and I were having a happy day of wandering in and out of shops, buying things mainly to bring back to our family and friends: perfumes, watercolors, sweaters, linens, meerschaum pipes, and trinkets. In that British way of stopping for "elevenses," their version of our coffee break, we were seated at an outdoor cafe when something funny happened.

For that day, that area of the island was flooded with *Rotterdam* passengers, and we sat surrounded by them. In that genial way of fellow passengers, a man, sitting with his wife at the table next to ours, turned to our table, and although there had been no introduction, said to William, "Up to this point, I think this has been our best port-of-call."

Like a shot, William replied, with one of his favorite words, "Indubitably!"

And the stranger was so overjoyed at the sound of that word that he sprang to his feet and held out his hand, saying, "I'm John Rogers, and I've always hoped that some day I would meet someone who would use that word."

By that time, William was on his feet for the handshake, and for his own designation, "William Shaw." That little tableau is one of those nice ones that go with total recall.

≈ ≈ ≈

With the establishment of the medical school and its nursing school at Chapel Hill, I was asked to serve on that nursing board, and did for a number of years. While that experience was meaningful, it never brought me the satisfaction that being connected with my hometown hospital gave me. For one thing, I knew all the other members of the board intimately. As soon as I became a member of our local board, I began, for the first time, to feel the injustice of the hospital's having a cottage connected by corridor to the main building as the area for the black patients. At board meetings, this unfairness was often discussed with sympathy, but we hardly knew where to turn. Although it was only a drop in the bucket, I interested my sisters in joining me in a contribution to make that area of the hospital more attractive and more comfortable. Of course, now, in our beautiful new county hospital, those wrongs have been righted, and Kemp Battle was to spend the last years of his life leading the movement for its construction.

By that time, a committee on race relations had long been in existence in our town. At one point in those earlier years, a forward-looking

Episcopal minister in our area arranged for a three-night panel discussion, its subject: race relations. A panel of four from the University at Chapel Hill, two men and two women, conducted those meetings. They were held in the small Episcopal church, the Church of the Holy Hope, whose membership was all black. The name of the church has now become the Church of the Ephiphany. Together the Battles and Tom and I went for the first two meetings. The discussions were helpful. The meetings were not largely attended, probably forty in all, and other than the panel and the minister, we were the only whites. The third night, Kemp and Tom were unable to go. The regular vestry meeting of the Church of the Good Shepherd took precedence, so that Maude and I went alone.

Toward the end of our meeting, written questions were asked for. One of the questions was, "I am a schoolteacher. I'm married and have children, I pay my bills promptly. Why is it, that when I go to give my charge in the two leading department stores in town, the salesladies all say, when I have given my name as Mrs. John Jones, 'What's your first name?' and then they will make out the ticket as just *Mary Jones?*" For customarily in the South of the time, blacks were never given their titles, they were never addressed as "Mr." or "Mrs."

Another question came from a doctor: "Why is it," he asked, "that although I've had the same training as the white doctors, when I send a patient of mine to the hospital, I'm not allowed any part in his treatment thereafter? I can only see him as if I were an ordinary visitor."

Sitting quietly, Maude and I were filled with sorrow and shame. A laboring man in work clothes, who would probably have had a terrible time writing his questions, stood up and asked, "Mr. Spong," that was the name of the white minister who took care of Holy Hope Church and its Parish, "How is it, that when my peoples dug that City Lake," and Maude and I knew that it had been dug with wages of ten cents an hour, federally funded under Roosevelt's WPA, which translates to Works Progress Administration, "How come," he asked, "that when our peoples dug that City Lake, and my old mother-in-law laks to fish better 'n anything, she can't sit out there and hold a fishing pole?"

A woman with gray hair stood up to point out that, in the downtown area, the only drinking fountains and rest rooms that were available to blacks were at the railway station and the bus stop. Questions that seared the soul.

On these somber notes which were to lead to a prayer of dismissal, the meeting was about to close, when suddenly, a tall figure whom I recognized, a well-dressed man, speaking well and courteously, said, "Mr. Spong, I'd like to address a question to Mrs. Pearsall."

You can imagine what happened to Mrs. Pearsall. My heart began to race, but I knew the high standing of this individual. I felt that he would be sincere. Chauncy Stokes owned Stokes Funeral Home and was respected by both races. His question was this, "My wife and I travel extensively up and down the Eastern Seaboard. Why is it, that beginning with Chester, Virginia, and on through the South, we can go in no Howard Johnson Restaurant and be served?"

Chauncy Stokes was asking that question of me because at the time, Tom and I owned five Howard Johnson restaurants and motels. The question had come so suddenly that I was practically in outer space. Yet somehow words came to me that would turn out to have been the right ones. To begin with, somewhere from the depths of my being, I found myself, for the first time in my life, addressing a black man as "Mister." When I stood to say, "Mr. Stokes," it was as natural as breathing.

My response to his question ran like this, "Mr. Stokes, those injustices have long been on our hearts, my husband's and mine, and we are working toward change. But you must be aware of the fact that some of the husbands of the waitresses have declared that their wives cannot serve blacks. They will have them quit their jobs first. However, we are working on changing that attitude among restaurant personnel. In this, we have a strong ally in Mrs. Alma Brown, the head hostess, who lives out in the country, and for more years than you can count, has taught Bible Study to young adults in her Oakdale country church. She is not only working on the members of her Bible class, but on the young women under her tutelage in the restaurant. She thinks she sees a mellowing."

I thought I had seen it as well, for one day I happened to be at the Howard Johnson restaurant in our hometown when a bus load of soldiers came by. They must have been on their way to Vietnam. The passengers numbered half black, and half white. The blacks could not even come in to use the restaurant rest rooms. Their food had to be taken out to them in boxes. Watching this was almost more than I could bear. I was alone, and I began to move quietly around, asking each of the waitresses, one by one, how that made them feel. They admitted that they felt shamed.

But to go back to the meeting at Holy Hope. The meeting adjourned, Maude and I went to our homes, and I began to wonder if I had said what Tom would have wanted me to. So that, as wives will sometimes do in similar situations, when he came in, I was very busy. I was brushing my teeth. He called through the open door from the bedroom, "How did the meeting go?"

"Very well," I said, muffling it with the foam of toothpaste.

"Did they ask any questions?" he wanted to know.

"A few," I answered, still busy with the brush.

"What were some of them?" he asked.

And then I had to tell him, even including the surprise of my own part in it.

"What did you say to Chauncy's question?" he wanted to know. And when I told him, he answered sensibly, "Well, you can't beat the truth."

The next afternoon came another surprise. I answered the doorbell to find our own Rector, Tom Smythe, standing there. That lovable young, and enormously popular minister of ours was Irish. His sermons were profound, his laugh hearty, his prayers, spoken in his resonant voice, almost made you feel, when he intoned, "Oh, Gaud," that the omnipotent presence was there. It's hard to understand that a person with so many gifts would be given so few years in which to use them, for Tom Smythe died at an early age.

Knowing how busy his life of service was, I had told him, when he first came to our parish, not to put me on his list of those to be visited. "When I need you, I'll call for you," I said. "Give your time to those who need it more."

So that, that afternoon when I opened the door to say, "Do come in," I added, "What brings you?"

"I'll tell you in a minute," he said as he sat down in the living room. Then he went on, "This morning," he said, "I had a visit in my office from Chauncy Stokes. He said, 'Mr. Smythe, I want to tell you that last night, for the first time in my life, I felt that a white person has been completely honest with me – she was from your parish: Mrs. Tom Pearsall.' "

A month later, our five hotels were integrated. Only three waitresses left, and they were easily replaced. In two weeks' time, when Tom and I went there for a meal, the waitresses could hardly wait to tell us that the black customers were the most neatly dressed, that they were the most courteous, that they were the best tippers, and that their children were the best behaved. You could feel a difference in the very air, one of happy people, black and white.

In looking back now, I can see that it's possible that this, and a succession of other things in which Tom and I had tried to make ourselves felt toward the bettering of race relations, might have been leading up to Tom's having been chosen, when the mandate came down from the Supreme Court in 1964 for the integration of schools, to head a committee for devising a workable plan for our state. More on that later.

≈ ≈ ≈

By the time we had been married five years, the economic depression was lifting. We had gone from living in an apartment for two years, and in a rented bungalow for two, to having had a year-and-a-half in our own home. When young Tom was six months old, we would go with The Planter's Bank, which had been started by my grandfather and my Uncle Jim, on a week's cruise to Bermuda. For Uncle Jim had come to like Tom very much, to respect his enthusiasm for work, so that, as a very young man, Tom had become a director of that bank.

Other than that Bermuda trip, we did not leave the country until the children were up and out in the world. However, there had been for us, a variety of family trips around the country. The longest had come when the boys were ten and twelve, a month-long train trip to California with a group from Charlotte. Later, when they were in college, in that way of the times, the boys would separately retrace some of those steps, wherein four or five college boys would together invest two hundred dollars in some old jalopy and then head for summer work in the West, working their way as they went.

One of the funniest episodes of that period was when young Tom had taken a job as a cook's helper at Jackson Hole, Wyoming. He had been told by his predecessors of the summer before that the way to success in the kitchen of a temperamental chef was never to be without a cloth in the hand, in order to look busy. These instructions had been followed to the letter; however, even that demonstration of industry would, at one point, come to nothing, when obeying a gruff command from the chef to "clean up that counter," Tom saw a large pot of something half filled with what, to him, looked sodden and inedible, and dumped into the garbage can fifteen pounds of expensive wild rice that had been left to soak before cooking. When this appalling affront to the progress of the chef's gourmet meal was discovered, no time was lost in sending young Tom on his way.

But there were many tales of the kindnesses of strangers whose doorbells the boys rang, wanting to mow their grass. A little later on, when our sons had reached the age to go with college tours to Europe, the two sons took turns making those trips. It was only in the 1950s that Tom and I had come to feel free to do our own foreign travel. By that time, in a series of round-about ways, we had come to have foreign contacts that would develop into friendships, making our travels doubly interesting.

Through our local tobacco market, we had been continually meeting foreigners who had come over to buy tobacco for their firms. One of the most intimate of these contacts for us was to be with the Gore-Lloyds of

England. We had met Eileen and Ted through our local friends Aleck and Sara Thorpe. On one of the Gore-Lloyd's summer stays in Eastern Carolina, where there is a concentration of tobacco markets, their visit had extended into October, and they were then the guests of the Thorpes for a week of leisure. Since the football season was in full swing, the six of us attended a game together at Chapel Hill.

Because of Tom's long-standing membership on the executive committee of the University, we had a standing invitation for lunch at the Morehead Planetarium and seats for the game in the President's box. Greetings between old friends would begin in the circle for parking, an area which includes a large beautiful rose garden. Mr. John Motley Morehead, at that time, alive and well and into his nineties, after his own years at the University, had gone on to be outstandingly successful as one of the powers, if not *the* power, in Union Carbide. Though his adult life would be spent in New Jersey, he would always feel a strong allegiance to his alma mater.

By this time, his contributions had been many and varied. They had culminated in his having built the Morehead Planetarium, and having established what is known as the Morehead Scholarships. These scholarships were, and still are, awarded for the purpose of fostering leadership, irrespective of financial need. The selection of the recipients of these scholarships, which takes place once a year, begins in the local high schools over the state, from which students work their way up to the final selection. From the beginning Tom had served on our Morehead Scholarship district committee.

A particularly meaningful scene in connection with the annual awarding of the scholarships was to make a permanent imprint on my mind. It must have been the first year of the Morehead scholarships. On a Friday night before a certain football game, in the beautifully paneled oval room on the top floor of the planetarium, this distinguished-looking man of ninety, immaculate in his heavy, dark, well-tailored suit – and, perhaps this was an illusion, but I felt he had on a stiff collar – sat in a handsome Chippendale armchair, surrounded by those young students who had won the scholarships and were now seated on the floor. Mr. Morehead's voice was low, the words addressed to his recipients, warm and fatherly.

The next day, in this same room, in what I assume will be a never-ending pattern during each football season on those days when games are played on home ground, an elegant buffet luncheon was served. In a system of rotation, by the time the season is over, an impressive number of loyal North Carolina citizens will have been extended this courtesy.

Among jovial greetings, guests make their way around a beautifully appointed table, and then wander, plate in hand, to one of the now-glass-enclosed terraces on either side of the large room. Although a number of tables for four will have been arranged on the terraces, there will not be enough seating places to go around, but nobody minds; the parapet is chest-high and broad enough to hold a plate, and although the provender is superb, at that moment, fellowship transcends food. Looking over the treetops from there, it seems symbolic that the planetarium was built in the center of the campus, and looking down on roses that bloom through November, there is a feeling among Tar Heels that this is, indeed, God's Country.

But on these happily busy days, there is little time for that kind of reflection. Suddenly, between all the speaking and being spoken to, there will begin a general scurrying downstairs for a brisk walk through the campus in order not to miss that special moment, just before kick-off when "Hark the Sound" is sung. In the way that lumps come into throats when the flag passes by, there comes a choky feeling. For the melody is haunting, the words beautiful, the hearts, fervent. I always felt that in this fervor, Tom's was at the top of the list as the stadium filled with:

> *Hark the sound of Tarheel voices,*
> *Ringing clear and true*
> *Singing Carolina's praises*
> *Shouting NCU*
>
> *Hail to the brightest star of all*
> *Clear its radiance shine*
> *Carolina, priceless gem*
> *Receive our praises thine*
>
> *I'm a Tarheel born*
> *And a Tarheel bred*
> *And when I die*
> *I'll be a Tarheel dead*
>
> *So it's Rah, Rah, Carolina-lina*
> *Rah, Rah, Carolina-lina*
> *Rah, Rah, Carolina-lina*
> *Rah! Rah! Rah!*

As usual, after the game, socializing would continue in the fraternity houses. That day with the Gore-Lloyds, in order to visit both Tom's Deke fraternity house, and Aleck's Zeta Psi, our stops were brief. Then, in traffic that was still moving slowly, we headed east. Ted Gore-Lloyd liked "to shoot," as they say in England, and in Carolina, our dove season and

263

our football seasons overlap. As we drove along, on the way home, knowing that during the dove season, Tom always arranged and took part in intermittent dove hunts on one or another of our farms, Aleck asked, "Jefferson, how about inviting Ted to go on one of your dove hunts with you?"

Since Tom's first two initials were "T.J.," Aleck, an admirerer of Thomas Jefferson, from high school days, had facetiously addressed Tom as "Jefferson." Tom had another nickname, one more generally used. Although his mother died when he was seven, she had been given enough time to make a booksack for her little son, and to outline in red embroidery floss, the two letters, "T.P." What an albatross for a little boy! For within thirty seconds of his arrival on the schoolgrounds, the children fiendishly translated the two letters into "Teacher's Pet." Whether that was hard to live down or not, I'm not sure. But I do know that – to his contemporaries – with the exception of Aleck, throughout life, he was always "T.P."

"Gladly," was Tom's answer to Aleck's question about the hunt. "I could outfit you, Ted, we're about the same size. And I have a gun case in my basement. You can choose your own."

"I should be *delighted*," said Ted, crisply English.

These Saturday hunts always included going back after the hunt to our place in the country which was on another farm, a small rustic house spoken of as "the cabin," but since it was on our Belmont farm, I thought of it more poetically as "Belmont Lodge." For it sits in a wooded area on a rise above a lake. Tom kept his boyhood canoe there, and late in the afternoons of summer, he and I would often be there on the water, by turns, rowing and drifting around its edge.

Those dove hunts were all-day affairs. Each wound up with a supper, its main dish something called a dove-pie. This combination of birds and pastry was slowly cooked outside in a large cast-iron pot, the meal taken care of by several of the farm men, some of whom had been doing this kind of thing all their lives. Ted would say later, that he had never enjoyed anything so much, for during the interval of the cooking, the hunters sat around with their drinks, telling old tales of Eastern Carolina, nearly all of them humorous. And in just the way we – as anglophiles – drool over anything British, this seemed to Ted "vahstly" picturesque.

The day of that particular hunt, Eileen and Sara had come for lunch with me at home. After Eileen had been there awhile, she remarked, "Your houses here are very much like ours." And, in showing her around, she could see, from the kitchen windows, a new and rather large, round apparatus I had just bought, a collapsible clothesline made of what was then the new light-weight steel. In a very real way, the contraption struck Eileen's fancy, for her own home in England was in the country. The county was Berkshire, the nearest town, Newbury. I was to learn later, that to those in the village nearby, Eileen was the "Lady of the Manor." She taught the village women painting, and in summer took them to the seaside for a week with the brush. Eileen's background and mine, involved as we each were with country life and its people, were similar. This gave us an easy friendship.

When she saw my arrangement for drying clothes, she exclaimed, "Oh, we *cahn't* get things like that in England! I wish we could. I should be the envy of the village."

That remark went straight to my heart, for Tom and I seemed to have an inborn love of England. Tom, himself a member of the Bar, was always one to say loyally, "We get our system of jurisprudence from the Mother Country."

England had entered my own life at eighteen on a first trip to Europe. It would be a long time before I would return, but nurtured on her nursery rhymes, her fairy tales, and her other forms of literature, she was always, in some way, in a corner of my mind. Over the years, I was gradually coming to see, that England is, for me, the embodiment of most of the things that give life meaning. I admire the British as a people who withstood the Blitz with such courage that the advice of a certain headmistress to her parting graduates could be twofold: that they "function in disaster and finish with style." Yet, as a people, along with this steeliness lies a gentleness that reveals itself in many ways, small and large, so much so, that their leading newspapers feature – on the front page almost daily – small items of interest in the world of nature: the first bluebird, the news of the diversion of traffic around a certain road in spring in order that frogs might safely cross. An endearing experience that came to Tom and me was that of having, one spring, come upon a small handwritten note just inside the entrance of an old church in East Anglia. The note suggested, courteously, "Please do not close the door when you leave; a wren is nesting under the lectern."

Courtesy in England seems to be inborn. Their swift "thanks-very-much" permeates the very air, and although their restraint might be interpreted as coolness, I have found the way to an Englishman's heart. All you have to do is stand on a street corner with an open guidebook in your hand, and as you look up, trying to find your way, a passer-by will immediately come up, apologize for the intrusion, and ask, "I beg your pardon. Is it possible that I might be of help to you?" If necessary, he will devote the next half hour to leading you, block after block, until you have found your destination.

Nothing could appeal to me more than that tolerant attitude of theirs, laissez faire, which, in the dictionary, is defined as that "practice or doctrine of non-interference in the affairs of others, especially with reference to individual conduct or freedom of action," loosely translated, "Do as you will." In light of that, and with my own growing conviction that it is only through making our own choices that we grow, I am forever an admirer of those of the British Isles.

So that, when the Gore-Lloyds had gone, I impulsively decided on a course of action on Eileen's behalf. I would arrange to have one of those clotheslines sent to her from the New York store from which mine had come. In doing that, I had no idea what a complicated thing I was setting in motion. I said in my order, "By air," and immediately sent an airmail letter to Eileen, telling her to be on the lookout. But in answer to my order, the store wrote that because of its shape, the clotheslines could not go by air. It would have to go by sea. That was agreed upon, and another letter was dispatched to Eileen announcing the change, and the delay. But that letter – more's the pity – went astray, and everyday for weeks, the hopeful Eileen met the plane, a drive of thirty miles, arriving only to disappointment. It took three months for the wandering clothesline to make its way by sea.

Good-natured as always, Eileen wrote that the joy of having that spectacular convenience obliterated all foregoing complications. From then on, she and I kept up a happy correspondence, and whenever we were in England, Tom and I visited the Gore-Lloyds. The first time we were their houseguests, I did the inexcusable: I arrived with a sore throat, hoarseness, and the onset of a cold.

Eileen at once put me to bed "for the next twenty-four hours," and started sending up hot broth. My room and its bath were beautiful and fresh. There were flowers on the desk, there was a lovely view over the downs, two of the latest books lay on the night table. Under other circumstances, I would have lapped it all up, might have wished for a visit longer than the four days we'd planned, but not now. For my conscience was at work. I had known for some time, that Eileen had invited two special couples for dinner the day of our arrival, and that they had been hand-chosen for congeniality with Tom and me.

In one couple, the man was a farmer-businessman, the other, a banker-lawyer. One of the wives liked books and doing her own interior decorating; the other did some writing. Both couples were titled, and though not as impressionable as to titles as I once had been, my mortification at letting my hostess down was made slightly worse by the thought that around the table there would, indeed, be a sprinkling of these illustrious people. For I knew that I would have been given the place of honor on Ted's right. And here I was, not even able to make an appearance. There was nothing to do in my misery but to get up every now and then and gargle, and then go back to bed to wallow in sackcloth and ashes.

I "had been there" myself, often enough to know without being told, that just as Eileen had been building up to us the strangers we were about to meet, she would have been doing her best to embellish Tom and me to them. We had probably been made unbelievably colorful. And then – of all things – I had taken to my couch.

My feverish mind both wandered and wondered. How was it possible for those notoriously rugged Englishwomen to understand; walking all over the face of the earth as they do, and never gauging their miles like other people, always saying something casual like, "It's only a ten minute's walk," or "It's only a twenty minute's walk," an offhand remark that could send you off on a trek of five miles? How could they really be expected to relate? No wonder their cheeks are rosy, their complexions as famous as their gardens.

Yet at the same time that these thoughts were running through my head, I was giving thanks to providence, that until I could see what my malady was going to do, I was lucky enough to be snug, and most of all, warm. For I'm one of those, who, should a cold lead to complications, am at the disadvantage of not being able to take an antibiotic, and have been warned to be careful at the beginning of a cold. Fortunately, I seem fairly resistant to those kinds of viruses.

Collapsing on the doorstep of my hosts on arrival was a double blow to my pride. For nature, in many ways, seemed to have given me marvelous endurance. It has shown itself in my daily life, and often has been the envy of my travelling companions. If there is something of special interest to be seen, I can walk farther and climb higher than anybody. And although it may not be entirely true, my own observation has been that women often have more endurance than men.

Having picked up a small book called *London Walks* one spring on an earlier stay there, the next year Tom and I went to London, we decided to devote two weeks to "doing that City, the City of Sprawls," largely on foot. On those London walks, finding our way from one historical marker to another, there was the added delight of the names of the streets, so many of them evocative of a time when London was only a country town: Haymarket, Cheapside, Fishmonger's Row, Petticoat Lane, Threadneedle Street, Rottenrow, Bishop's Gate, Drury Lane, St. Martin-in-the-Fields, St. Andrew's Close; this last, one of those walled areas or enclosures, designated for the use of the church. When the various steeple bells rang out, it was almost too much for my already happy heart, for I knew that every London child grows up on the ditty:

"Oranges and lemons," say the bells of St. Clemmons,
"I owe you a farthing," say the bells of St. Martins.
"When will you pay me?" say the bells of Old Bailey,
"When I get rich!" say the bells of Shoreditch.

Even the street urchins of Old London would have this note of whimsy in their otherwise grim lives. Though our feet would grow weary, it was hard to go back to the hotel and save something for another day. But Tom, nearly always the better balanced of the two of us, would say at about three in the afternoon, "Don't you think we should call it a day? You remember, we'll have to have sandwiches in the hotel bar at five in order to make the theater at seven." For London plays start early, leaving time enough for a heavier meal later.

On those long-drawn-out walks, stopping to read house-markers and referring to our book for information, it was I, hail and hearty, who could have kept on going – on and on and on. But now at Eileen's, I was in a woeful state of indisposition, and with the maid's appearance in my room bearing a tray every few moments, making a succession of trips running abreast of the eight courses being served downstairs, for there was even a savory before dessert, my guilt increased. Between her trips, I was trying to lose myself in a novel. I knew that Tom could, and would, fill in for both of us, that since he liked people, people always liked him. Truly, he had "never met a stranger." The bedrock of his nature was self-confidence, all he had to do was to be natural, and he always was. Rounded and informed, he could take part comfortably on practically any level of conversation.

When the guests had gone, Tom came upstairs and I was given an account of things, something for which he had a knack. His main concern, however, was that at the end of my twenty-four hours in bed, I would be downstairs sitting about in those *"drahfts,"* which Englishmen so love.

"Two outside doors stayed open all the time," he told me. "By the time we'd finished dinner and had gone for coffee in the living room, I was all but frozen."

"Drawing room," I corrected. "English people speak of their living rooms that way."

"All right. By the time we were in front of the fireplace in the *drawing* room, my teeth were all but chattering." And this from Tom, the rugged. "No telling how many doors they'll be keeping open in the daytime," he concluded mournfully.

"How in the world do they happen to be so red-blooded?" I asked. "It must be something they eat, all those kidney pies and pork pies, and all that *ale*." But we gave up the matter, and as I went to sleep, I was thinking about our driver, Woodward, and that probably at that moment, he would be sitting in some pub enjoying his "pint," or the "*ayle*" to which he had looked forward all day.

By the second day, the trauma was lessening, and I was back on my feet. Even though Eileen's car had a heater, when the four of us set out for a day's drive around the countryside, lap-robes were part of our trappings. In that country area, Eileen and Ted knew everybody, and now and then, we would stop at a cottage to talk to the people who lived there, and were puttering outside. There was a drizzle, but in the hardiness of that race, those people kept on with their gardening and whatever else it was that happened to make up their daily rounds, which would surely have included a long-legged trek over a few country miles.

For lunch, Eileen and Ted had chosen an interesting old inn. For such a day, its heavy, old, oak beams, and its glowing fires were perfect. When we arrived out of the cold and the drip, nothing could have appeared so welcome as a glass of wine or a pot of tea. "Straightaway," as they say, we went into the dining room. When the waiter had come to our table for our order, I asked for tea. Eileen flew up in alarm. "Why Elizabeth, you *cahn't* have tea with your meal! It's gastronomically un*sound*." I knew she was thinking more of the assault against gastronomics than of my virus, but I longed for a steaming cup of tea.

By impressing it on the waiter that the tea must be weak, however, in order to mollify Eileen, and requesting a pitcher of hot water as well, the invitation to disaster was permitted. But all afternoon, Eileen would look at me questioningly and want to know, "Elizabeth, are you all right?" I knew what she was thinking.

Whether hot tea as my favorite drink is due to my love of England, or whether I like it for itself, I'm not sure. Of one thing I am sure, however. I do not like it so much as Dr. Johnson was said to have, as expressed in this limerick, which I quote from memory:

> *His hostess blenched*
> *to pour his*
> *twenty-seventh cup,*
> *knowing the doctor*
> *would*
> *drink it up.*

The remainder of our stay with the Gore-Lloyds was given to the homier pleasures. While Eileen and I sat by the fire, and "tired the sun with talking," Tom went with Ted over the farm to see his pheasants, which until the days of the shoot, were kept in large wooden enclosures. At first glance this seemed to me unsportsmanlike, irreconcilable with the British and their great love of animals, until I remembered that, in my own family, on land long family-owned, quail in great numbers are kept penned for the same purpose.

Then, I thought, *what could have appeared more callous to a stranger than what I was exposed to every day of my early life with its country ways, seeing the cook, Julette, and old Uncle Dennis, who looked after our vegetable garden and the chickens, go together to the poultry yard to wring off the necks of several chickens for our table?* But then, everything is, indeed, relative. Perhaps my initial reaction to shooting the pheasants was due to their beauty, and to their contrast with the hum-drum appearance of our dull-colored, thick-legged, Rhode Island reds, which Mother believed were the only breed of chickens worth bothering about.

The one concession the Gore-Lloyds made to the ever-present chill was that the fire in the drawing room was never allowed to go out. The four of us, moving after meals into that room, would always find Ted's old dog, Brewster, curled up in his master's chair. Ted would then ever so courteously lean over the sleeping figure and say, "Old chap, would you mind very much giving me my chair?" And the drowsy old dog would slowly relinquish his post. As this went on, I would have been cannily staking out my own territory on one end of the fireside bench, and with Eileen a few feet away pouring coffee, could began to feel that I might be able to make it through the cold.

Over the years, as our friendship grew, Tom and I were to feel that Ted and Eileen, in the main, represented many of those things we admired about the British. Though born to privilege –Eileen would say casually of Ted's family, "The title went the other way" – they themselves were thoroughly democratic. When they decided to pull up stakes and move to Portugal, leaving England in search of "suhvants and sun" (servants), and "to escape death duties" (inheritance tax), we visited them there, as well.

Tom and I decided to combine a scheduled trip to Spain with a visit to the Gore-Lloyds in Portugal. At the end of a lovely interval in Madrid, we flew to Seville. It was in one of those two cities – I've forgotten which – that we saw a bull fight, an experience that doesn't dim.

Behind my dark glasses, I could – unobserved – close my eyes to the goading of an animal to pure rage, then allowing it to lunge about in the ring, spears in its flesh, its blood dripping to the ground. Not wanting to present a "holier-than-thou" attitude to this ancient custom of a highly civilized country, I could remain outwardly calm. But, at the climax of the performance, the excited spectators tossing flowers to the matador, the animal, now dying, and by a rope around its neck, spears and all, being dragged from the arena, Tom and I quietly slipped out. I wondered, and still do, if certain of a country's customs always seem unfathomable to those of another.

But in travelling, the scenes change so quickly that usually another experience is at hand. And on the journey from Seville by car and driver, to find the remote village where the Gore-Lloyds now lived was, for us, unique. For most of a pleasant, sunny day, along dusty roads with a light sprinkling of those lovely, colorful, country carts of the Portuguese, past miles of slopes covered with the silvery green of almond trees, and stopping to ask the way, we covered the rather long distance. Those little adventures, arising out of not knowing how to get where we were going, were something we both enjoyed. Many times the driver would be as much at a loss as we were, but would become caught up in the spirit of stopping to ask this and that countryman for directions, which often turned out only to add to the confusion. But finally we were there.

The Gore-Lloyds had bought land in the Algarve, that section of Portugal to which, for its mild climate, Europeans often go on retirement. From their hilltop, the blue of the Atlantic three miles away was cleary visible.

The servants they'd looked forward to, however, were not entirely satisfactory. The cook did not take to uniforms. She liked to wear her accustomed all-black full-length cotton dress, and her never-to-be-removed head-covering arrangement which included a black cotton cloth tightly wrapped around her head, on which, riding high, sat her dull black, felt wide-brimmed hat. This made her a cross between a large crow and a Halloween witch. She spoke practically no English. Making her into a serving maid was laughable, but Bettina had a nice, friendly grin, and both Eileen and Ted, although they had been surrounded by a competent staff all their lives, now had the good nature and the good sense to adapt to a more casual style.

Bettina's only real success was with cabbage soup, and we consumed a lot of that. She was kept happy by the regular patronage that Eileen and Ted gave her husband, a fisherman. For he was one of the many Portuguese men of that poorer class who went out early every morning, alone in their small colorful boats, returning by noon to beach their boats and drag ashore bright red nets filled with their catch. Their sales were made right there, and for their purchases, Eileen and Ted always sought out Bettina's deeply tanned and weathered, jovial husband, Alonzo.

The Gore-Lloyd's house was of white stucco and was large, light and airy, and lovely. They had brought out their Chippendale and a few paintings in order to feel at home. The house sat on a hilltop overlooking the low-growing, silvery-leafed almond trees which ran down miles to the sea. Lunch was usually served around the pool, and their guests included some of the titled Portuguese. They all spoke English well, and although there were often three nationalities represented, there was that commonality that is nearly always present among people who have their families to talk about, their children, perhaps their grandchildren, and who, in a sense, live on comparable levels.

For dinner, we would drive thirty-five miles to the club of which the Gore-Lloyds were members. With this in mind, our swims came in the morning. When the luncheon guests had left, while Ted and Eileen read their mail, Tom and I would walk down a long flight of stone steps that led to a road where Portuguese laborers worked in the almond groves, and who, in great friendliness, would smile and wave, and call out greetings in their native tongue.

Thoughtful hostess that Eileen was, when I had gone to my room to dress for dinner, she would come knocking on my door to ask, "Elizabeth, are you wearing something light or something dark? I'll join you either way."

With drinks at the club, and meeting more of the Gore-Lloyd's friends, the evening would pass delightfully, and Tom and I early decided that the Gore-Lloyds had made a wise move in going to the Algarve. Yet, deep down, there was something poignant about the fact that Eileen had made up her mind – at the cost of any effort – to have an English garden in that far-off spot. For the purpose, a large area around the pool and down its vista toward a beautiful Moorish summerhouse had been left for flowers. Brick paths led through the rectangle, between hoped-for flowery borders, but sadly, Eileen's hollyhocks were puny, the foxgloves had not filled out, the Sweet William was stunted and pale, and in the corners, the rhododendrons were slowly giving up the ghost. Eileen had been used to the near-perfect gardening conditions that exist in England. Yet I felt that, with time, she would adapt her garden to the change. Our friends had exchanged one thing for another.

The sounds that went on in the summerhouse, however, made up for what the garden lacked; they were indescribably exotic. Rectangular and airy, its interior pavement was of small colored tiles laid in large, intricate patterns. Its walls and its arched openings were of interlacing fretwork that suggested lovely pale apricot alabaster. Against the blue of the sky it was very beautiful. But, for some unaccountable reason, flocks of swallows and swifts seemed to have chosen the summer house as their flyway. And dawn to dusk, incessantly whistling, they endlessly darted through. Wakening to the sound at sunrise was like coming to life in the *Tales of the Arabian Nights*.

As poetic as it all was, by the time Tom and I had been there a few days, we began to wonder about long-range happiness there for Ted and Eileen. For although they were making a joke of the structural inadequacies that were continually cropping up, we wondered how many more faulty things would appear as time went on. Still, I do treasure the memory of hearing Ted, the epitome of the English gentleman, telling us on our first night there something of how the next day would go. We'd already been told that construction with inept carpenters, and electricians, and plumbers had made the building process for them long and drawn out, and that although they'd had to undergo taking up much of their tile floor in order to find out why they couldn't get hot water, they hoped we liked cold showers.

Ted went on to say, "It's very likely that our houseman, Manuel, will be late tomorrow morning. In that case, I, myself, shall roll the tea trolley down the hall to your room, bringing you a kettle of hot water for your shave, Tom," with Eileen joining in to say, "And there will be another kettle on the trolley for morning tea for the two of you."

As sporting as Eileen and Ted were being about these things, and as much as I was enjoying the informality, for it always delights me to feel the bonds of reality among people, and Tom and I always leaned backward trying to adapt to things, because we realized that if you don't, you miss so many of life's pleasures, it did make us think that the Gore-Lloyds might not always stay in Portugal.

When our visit was over, and Eileen had driven us to the airport, for the first time in our many goodbyes, she had tears in her eyes. I felt it meant something, and was not too surprised, when, several years later, one of her letters brought the news that with Ted's need for eye surgery they were going to England, and that it might be for good. At home, in Carolina, reading the letter to Tom, I remarked, "As the poet said, 'There will always be an England.'"

And his answer – and I knew it came from the heart – was, "And always one to go back to. I sometimes wish that a ring could be drawn around England, and that like some wonderful museum she could be preserved; she has influenced so many nations and their people. Has shed her light so far."

≈ ≈ ≈

The first twenty-five years of our marriage were to be the busiest of my life; they were filled to the brim with bringing up the children, with Tom's management of the farms and their allied interests – the cotton, the peanut, and the corn brokerages –and with those twelve years of his given to politics and to University of North Carolina affairs. Through long membership on the university's executive committee, he became closely involved with three consecutive university presidents. First, there was Frank Graham, president from 1930 to 1949, who, according to Charles Kuralt, "performed the miracle of making a first rate institution out of the hard depression years," and greater still, "to make it an outpost of challenging inquiry in a region not always devoted to the same....." The origins of the University of North Carolina, Kuralt went on to point out, "reach back to the ideals of a new nation, sprung experimentally from liberal revolution and the Enlightenment values still blazoned in Latin on its seal: Lux/Libertas – Light and Freedom.

"Against considerable odds, UNC has remained uncommonly true to those ideals for two centuries."

As a student during Frank Graham's presidency, is it any wonder that this great man should become the hero of Tom's early manhood?

Through his friendship with Gordon Gray, who followed Frank Graham as president, Tom's involvement increased. With Bill Friday's assumption of the office of the presidency, Tom's interest in the University and the dedication of his time and his effort toward its effectiveness reached its peak. The close association between these two men would continue to the end of Tom's life.

As a young man emerging from law school, Tom had begun to be called upon by a succession of governors – Cherry, Broughton, Umstead, and Hodges – to serve on committees. Having served Governor Umstead on a committee for the bettering of race relations in the state, when the decree for integration of schools came down from the Supreme Court, Tom was appointed head of that state committee. At Governor Umstead's sudden death, he was succeeded by Lieutenant Governor Luther Hodges. Governor Hodges then asked Tom to continue with the school integration responsibility. Since, with assuming office, Governor Hodges would have to dispose of a Howard Johnson franchise he owned, he offered to sell the franchise to Tom. In that way, our family entered tourism, gradually adding Howard Johnson motels and restaurants of our own until there were five, all of them on Interstate 95.

By the second phase of our marriage, which was to last another twenty-five years, there would be a partial let-up of outside activity, and our sons would no longer be at home. The Korean War had ended, but the draft was still in existence. The options for young men were two: to enlist in either the Standing Army, or the National Guard. By joining the National Guard, unless our country should again become involved in war, the opportunities of going to college, and perhaps, of doing graduate work, were pretty well ensured. Basic Training was required by all. For our sons, this went on at Fort Jackson, South Carolina, supplemented by returning for duty a certain number of weeks and a certain number of weekends throughout the year – in this case, at Fort Bragg. This enabled each of them to finish college and to receive graduate degrees as well, Mack's in Law, Tom's in Interior Design. From then on they would be out in the larger world.

During the years between 1947 and 1954, with Tom not so active in politics, travel became important to us. If possible, we were on foreign soil for short stays each spring and fall, timing the stays always, not only with an eye to business obligations, but to those involving Tom's work for the state as well. With 1954, however, with responsibility for the implementation of the court's mandate concerning schools, there were several years when we were not travelling at all. When it was resumed, we often travelled – as private citizens – with the Hodges. For the four of us enjoyed a rare congeniality.

When Luther became National Secretary of Commerce, the pattern resumed; always we took care of our own expenses. Tom and Luther shared political philosophies, the four of us saw the funny side of things, and we all knew that the cornerstone of Luther's existence was that of being on time. Martha, herself, declared that in their long marriage she could truthfully say that she had never kept Luther waiting for one minute. What a record for a life's partner!

There might have been a few other things about Tom and me that enabled us to pass muster, as well. In addition to our respect for other people's time, we were not fussy about soft beds and fine foods. Our attitude had always been that the pleasure and enlargement of experience outweighed comforts and luxuries; that interesting things, as well as interesting individuals do not always come with impressive trappings. Often it's the reverse. Too, we had been around enough to understand that no matter on what level a person's life is lived, in that we all have our joys and our sorrows, we are alike underneath, and that ways of communicating can usually be found.

So that, when Luther and Martha invited Tom and me to go with them on a three weeks goodwill trip to South America, we accepted. For most of my life, having sporadically kept a diary or a journal of sorts, on this trip, in order to share it with my home community by way of our town newspaper, which I had been invited to do, I began to make notes on what we were seeing and doing. And since a friend of mine, Mrs. Thomas MacMillan (Vivian), was editor of the Woman's Page of our *Evening Telegram*, I wrote the account of the trip to her in the form of a letter. In that way it could be more casual – a pleasure, rather than a burden. Installments of that letter appeared daily for a week in our local paper.

Although Tom was, then, only on the fringe of politics, his interest in state affairs was such that he was always being called on to help with its problems. He continued to sit on committees, and his undying love for his alma mater would keep him closely involved with endorsing its philosophy of academic freedom. I can recall a minor crisis that took place at Chapel Hill during these years, called the "Speaker Ban Crisis." Pursuing the policy of academic freedom, an outstanding Russian communist had been invited to University of North Carolina at Chapel Hill to address the students. The meeting was to be held in a large hall, and when word of this came, daily demonstrations against it were staged.

The peaceful village filled with a wave of hostility. Tempers were inflamed to the point of fighting, and our newspapers followed the turmoil. Tom hurried to Chapel Hill in Bill Friday's support; the demonstrations were allowed, the meeting was held, and the school's academic freedom was not endangered. It was gratifying to begin to read in periodicals from around the country, that the University of North Carolina was consistently considered a bastion of intellectual freedom.

While all these things were taking place, when we could work it in, we continued to travel in spring and fall, and in some ways, we were as busy as we had been earlier. I doubt that we could have kept up the pace, had it not been for something that had never occurred to us – the possibility of having a second home, one out of the state, far away from what we had come to consider our across-the-board obligations. It was in this way, that we came to cast our lot with Captiva Island, which was to become the island of our hearts.

Oft I longed to speak of things that make life so sweet –
the wind, the clouds, the flight of birds.

The source of this quotation I can no longer recall. But, in its simplicity, I find it very beautiful. Memory suggests that it was the reflection of a woman who had grown up in a lighthouse. However that may be, once I had heard them, the words would forever echo in my heart.

Nowhere would this have been more true than during our years at Captiva. For it was not only in the island's beauty, in its sun and sea and its sky, but in the people it drew, many of whom, if they stayed long enough to think of it as "our island," must often have felt that tug of the heart that said, *There's something here that should be held.*

The language of birds is very ancient, and like other modes of ancient speech is very elliptical; little is said, but much is understood.

Gilbert White,
The Nature Conservancy

"Oh, it's very tantalizing driving down your island!" exclaimed the lady to whom Tom and I had just been introduced one afternoon at a cocktail party on a neighboring island.

"I love the combination of your green jungles, and your sea, and your wheeling shorebirds that almost seem to be the only form of life. But then there will be the glimpse of an occasional house through the jungle. But there's no one in sight. And it stirs the imagination."

BEYOND THE SEA GRAPES

≈ ≈ ≈

*E*arly one morning, one of those clear, crisp mornings of Carolina winter, Tom brought our bags down from the attic. They now sat on one side of the fireplace in our bedroom. I daresay not many homes of today or of that era have a fireplace in an upstairs bedroom, but when we built our house sixty years ago, we took the advice of those of an earlier generation as they urged us to build in that way. And, I will have to admit, that, during the first years that followed Pearl Harbor and its attendant fuel shortages, when most of our rooms were kept at a temperature of sixty degrees, that that fireplace in the large master bedroom became an early morning and evening family center worth its weight in gold. But far later that morning, after breakfast, when Tom had left for the office, I went back upstairs to begin to pack.

For several days, I had been getting out our summer clothes; some of them now lay on the twin beds of the guest room. I knew that I would leave Tom's packing to him, for as a bride, I had once made a fatal error, depending on which way you look at it. When he was suddenly called away on a business trip, and had phoned from the office asking me to pack his bag, I conscientiously, but hurriedly, did so, in order that the bag be ready when he came by to pick it up. Unwittingly, I failed to put in his razor. After that, he didn't trust me, and in a way, that was to prove convenient.

As usual, after Christmas, we began to plan a winter holiday. With our two sons now in college, going away for three weeks in the dead of winter had become a habit. Those trips took us to the resort area of the East Coast of Florida. Often we were joined there by hometown friends, making it doubly pleasant. Once having arrived, among our pleasure would be swims and long walks on the beach. On some days, there would be, for the men, deep sea fishing. On others, tennis or golf.

The wives would go to Palm Beach for shopping in branches of the New York stores in which we had charge accounts. We might venture to an art gallery, have lunch, go to a concert or to a matinee.

Best of all, as couples, we would meet for dinner, those happy, casual gatherings among old friends where we were ready to laugh at anything and everything. One of the wives might be wearing a purchase she'd made that day, and, to the accompaniment of a round of compliments there would be the sympathetically facetious groans of some supposedly long-suffering husband who knew that his own turn would come soon.

At times, we would patronize a well-known restaurant which had the distinction of having seven-inch meringue on its key-lime pie. When the waiter came to take the orders for dessert, the heavy decision would begin. Arthur Tyler, an immensely lovable man, and part owner of a number of chain stores, had a peculiar weakness for this pie, but being short and inclined to stoutness, indulging required persuasion. On one of those occasions when we had all succumbed to temptation, including Arthur, getting his minutes and his miles mixed, he came out with the dismal pronouncement: "I read the other day," he said, "that it takes a thirty-five mile walk to work off a slice of pie." And we were sunk. For at the end of a day of varied activity, much of it spent in the open, the prospect of taking a long walk could only bring on a long, collective moan. But it would have taken more than that to cast more than a momentary gloom over us.

Foreseeing all these pleasures that day in January, I could hardly wait for the time to come when we would begin the two day drive to Del Ray. Yet, as I looked out of an upstairs window over our yard, Carolina winter seemed almost too lovely to miss. At eight that morning, the thermometer stood at forty degrees, across the lawn there was the flutter of birds. Under sunlight, the giant old magnolia growing in the corner of our white picket fence was a thing of a thousand shimmering mirrors; the hollies, the myrtles, and the long, green needles of the pines cast their own sheen.

Leaving for the office, Tom had stopped for a minute or two on our front stoop to look up at the sky, to glance about the yard, and, then, standing still, to take several, long, deep, noisy breaths. Then to say, with satisfaction, "And *this* is what the Yankees at Southern Pines and Pinehurst leave home in winter for." We laughed together and he left.

After lunch, I went out for the afternoon, and when I came in at dusk, the mail lay on the hall table. Annabelle, our housekeeper, was thoughtful about things like that. At the top of the stack of letters, she had even placed one in a familiar handwriting. Its postmark, however, was a strange one. *Where can Buffie be now?* I wondered. And, in a well-lighted chair in the living room, I began to open the mail. Buffie's letter came first. I had no way of knowing that with the opening of that particular envelope, Tom and I would soon begin what I would forever after think of as the Captiva years; no way of knowing that from that point, the direction of our lives, and, to some extent, that of our family, would begin to change. For it seemed an average letter between friends. It ran this way:

Dear Elizabeth,
    You will wonder at my being in Florida, for as you know, the few times I've been in this state, it's always seemed to me too windy, too cool, or too hot, its weather altogether unpredictable. I much prefer the crisp, cool days of Carolina winter, but my cousin Lena Ewing, of Bloomington, who has had a house on this island off the West Coast has been after me for years to come and give it a chance. This time

Ernest and I decided to do that. We're not Cousin Lena's houseguests, however, because she's old and her white housekeeper is, too. Her house is on the bay and has the charming name, "Fiddler's Green." Nothing in the house has been changed in the last forty years – simple furnishings, wicker, grass rugs and iron beds – the perfect setting for Cousin Lena. But we didn't want to get her excited about houseguests, so we decided to stay at this rustic little inn. It's owned by an FFV who started the inn some years ago because her husband, a doctor, from Bristol, Virginia, and his medical friends liked coming to the island to fish, but had no place to stay. Now the people who come regularly for the winter book their small cottages a year ahead. The guests are all delightful, and terribly interesting. On one side of the island, there is the gentle lapping of the surf – bathing is wonderful. On the other side there's the quiet bay. In their small boats, men fish those waters – the catch of the day is prepared by the inn. This furnishes much dinner table conversation. The unspoiled beauty of the island, and the fact that the people who come seek an uncluttered way of life – absolutely without show – gives a sophisticated simplicity that is as charming as it is unique. You and Tom must try it sometime. Ernest and I will be here for two more weeks. After that, back to Southern Pines. Write me there. If you have time, send a letter here.

Affy,
Buffie

P.S. There is one tiny store of oddments and groceries. It's owned and run by a former New York producer of plays. The island stories that are told of this character, Parker Mills, are delightful. I will give you an example: One day, on the rare occasion when a crate of strawberries had been brought over on the mail boat, a customer found Parker seated near the cash register, comfortably absorbed in the reading of *War and Peace*. The crate of strawberries had been placed nearby. The customer was hesitant to interrupt, but after waiting a few minutes, did say, "Parker, how much are the strawberries?"

Without raising his eyes, the storekeeper said, absently, "I haven't any idea."

Don't you love that kind of atmosphere?

With or without househelp to take care of the aftermath, lingering at the table over the evening meal has always been one of my great pleasures. So it was, that afternoon, that as soon as I had read Buffie's letter, I placed it on the dining room table for sharing with Tom at supper. When I had read it aloud, I looked up to find his eyes like stars. He could hardly wait to ask, "Doesn't that sound like a wonderful spot? What would you think of trying it, instead of going back to the East Coast?" And as I was getting used to the surprise, he went on, "Truth to tell, I'm beginning to be a little tired of the East Coast. I enjoy the deep sea fishing, but only occasionally. Of course, I enjoy tennis, but it's hard to get into the right kind of game. And as you know, I've given up golf because it takes so much time. I know you and the girls love going to Palm Beach to shop and visit the galleries, have lunch, and go to matinees... and I hate to suggest a change. But for just this one time, what do you think?"

What, indeed, *did* I think? I could hardly have warmed to the idea as much as Tom on such short notice. But something told me that I must try to match his enthusiasm or I would be letting him down, and so I said, "I think that *would* be nice."

I knew that Tom would not have suggested this lightly, and trusting his judgment, as I nearly always did, I acquiesced. Ordinarily, this change would not have given me concern, but I'd been ill for several months. I'd had a digestive disorder, with stays in three hospitals. One, in Boston under the celebrated late Dr. Sarah Jordan. True, I was physically better, but I was hardly ready, psychologically, to go to an unknown island for three weeks, to be away from doctors, nurses, and drugstores, or even in the loose sense, any stores at all.

But I found that I could put up a good front for Tom's sake, when he said next, "I have to go back to the office to do some work tonight. How about telephoning Buffie to see if she can get reservations for us at that little inn for three weeks, starting February the fifth?" And he was gone. Out into the night.

In half an hour I was at the telephone asking a long-distance operator for a Florida island spelled C-A-P-T-I-V-A. I wasn't even sure of its pronunciation. By spelling it, the operator understood, but had no idea where it was. She asked for a little time, said she would call back. When she did, she had found that the island was thirty-five miles from the town of Fort Meyers, but that there were no telephones there. This was hard to believe. Since the operator seemed friendly, I began to explain to her in some detail that I had an important message for somebody on the island, and asked her what I must do. "Can you think of anything?" I pleaded.

Perhaps it was a dull night at the telephone exchange, for she became sympathetic, and soon came out with this: "Well, I don't know whether this will help you or not, but just this week, a man who lives on the island has put a ship to shore telephone in his car. It's possible that I could get him, and that he might deliver your message."

I thanked her in twenty languages. She told me to hang up, that she would call back.

In about ten minutes the phone rang. A man's deep voice was saying brusquely, "Hello, hello, hello. This is Captiva Island."

I chimed in with a syrupy little tone, "Oh, hello, are you the man with the telephone in his car?"

"Yes, I've got a telephone in my car, Lady, but what about it?" he asked.

"Oh," I said, in a pained voice. "I have such a *problem* on my hands." And then, I must confess to a little name-dropping. "I have an important message for someone who is on that island. She's Mrs. Ernest Ives, sister of Governor Adlai Stevenson. It's terribly important that I get in touch with her. Could you please get her to the phone?"

"Lord, Lady," he said, "I know that lady's on the island, but she's three miles down the road, it's dark as Egypt here, and everybody's gone to bed."

And this, at eight-thirty at night! However, that only whetted my appetite for adventure. "Oh, oh," I came back, "if you could just do me this favor, I would hope that I might be able to return it sometime."

Then, either because he was a nice man, or probably, since the "boy is always in the man," and he was glad of a chance to try out his new gadget, he came out with, "I'll see what I can do."

"Will you please tell Mrs. Ives that her friend in Rocky Mount, North Carolina, is trying to reach her?" I asked. He agreed to try.

After that I sat quietly, thinking and twirling my thumbs. Sure enough, in about fifteen minutes, the phone rang again. This time it was a lady's voice saying, excitedly, "Hello, hello, hello?"

My answer was, "Hello? Buffie, it's Elizabeth!"

"Elizabeth!" She exclaimed. "What on earth has happened?"

"Nothing, nothing," I hurried to allay her fears. "But your letter came today. It has set Tom on *fire*. We want to come to that island. Will you please see if you can make reservations for us at your little inn for three weeks, beginning February fifth?"

"Oh, my dear," Buffie answered. "I doubt very much that you can get in here. The same people occupy the same cottages year after year, booking a year in advance – but I'll see what I can do. After I find out, I'll drive down onto the other island to the ferry-landing where there's a telegraph office in the general store and will let you know."

I said, "I hope you don't have to go very far."

"Only about fifteen miles," she said, and I felt some sense of remorse, but not much, because by then my excitement was mounting.

Apologizing for waking her out of a deep sleep and having her come out into the night in her bathrobe and slippers to talk on the phone in a stranger's car, and thanking her ahead for the trouble that I was putting her to, we said goodbye.

The next afternoon, the wire came.

ABLE TO PIECE TOGETHER STAY OF THREE WEEKS ON THE
ISLAND **STOP** FIRST FIVE DAYS AT THE INN **STOP** AFTER
THAT GUESTHOUSE OF A FRIEND OF THE MANAGER **STOP**
GLAD OUR STAYS WILL OVERLAP **STOP** BUFFIE **STOP**

Allowing two days for the drive, on a bright, clear February day a week later, Tom and I set out. From looking at the map, we had decided that Walterboro, South Carolina, was about halfway. We spent the night there, and knowing that the last ferry of the day left the mainland for the island at five in the afternoon, we were up and out at sunrise. There was no sun that day, and secretly, the venture, for me, was beginning to lose some of its glamour. This was especially true when, at around four o'clock, we finally arrived at the town of Fort Meyers and turned west.

At first, this drive toward the ferry-landing was beautiful. We passed Thomas Edison's home, with his laboratory across the road, where – I would later learn – under his canvas cot, sat his overshoes. The great man did, literally, have an Achilles heel, for history tells us that as a young man, Mr. Edison had a severe attack of pleurisy. Afterward, he never left the house without putting on his overshoes, even in that divinely tropical area. Had I known that at this point, it would have made my own apprehensions about going away from doctors, nurses, and drugstores more respectable.

The Firestone home was next to Edison's. Each was surrounded by the lushness of tropical growth. Royal palms of great height lined the avenue that ran past their homes, and, having always had a weakness for palms, that day, in a rising wind, they seemed momentarily picturesque. For I do not agree with Mark Twain that all palms look like featherdusters that have been struck by lightning.

Soon this kind of beauty fell away. While the road was not too bad, it seemed desolate. On either side, as far as the eye could see there was sawgrass; it was dotted with palmettos, and pepper trees, with a scattering of cabbage palms, and now and then a century plant. The scenery hardly varied for twelve miles. Then we rounded a curve onto a point called "Puntarassa," and stopped at its inconsequential ferry-landing.

In the distance, making its way toward us across the choppy waters of San Carlos bay, was a tiny ferry; a toy bobbing among the white caps. As it drew nearer, I could see that its name was the *Islander*, and would find later that it had two sister-ferries: the *Rebel* and the *Best*. For years, the three faithful little vessels had plied those waters and made it possible for people to live on the two sister islands, Sanibel, the larger, served by ferry, and Captiva, at Sanibel's far end, the two connected by bridge.

The sky was turning more and more to gray, the wind becoming stronger, and my heart more fluttery. Far across the water, against the horizon, was a dark-green stretch of fringe, beyond which, my future – should there be any – lay. My apprehension about leaving the mainland for three weeks was deepening by the moment. It was strange for me to be this way. I'd always loved adventure, but, as our family doctor, Dr. Claiborne Smith, who was still actively practicing medicine told me, I had temporarily "lost my grip."

Once on the ferry for the four mile crossing, Tom got out of the car, stood in the wind and the spray like some happy Viking, and I redoubled my efforts to put on a good face. Later, however, when we had both come to love Captiva next to home, he said that he had been aware of my nervousness; that after leaving Fort Meyers I had chattered like a magpie.

Once we had landed on the island of Sanibel, there was a simple sign with an arrow pointing to the right. It bore only one word: "Captiva." For a mile or two, the road was tree-lined and lovely with tropical growth. Then it turned sharply to the left, and again we were driving through that type of pale, yellowy-green Florida stubble to which we were becoming accustomed, except that now there appeared yucca. There were more and more of the exotic century plants, the pepper trees were enormous. The sturdy, rounded sea grape trees were twice as tall as our car; their branches were so low, their leaves so large and round and thick that stretches of that kind of growth seemed impenetrable. Pepper trees were laden with red berries that had been left untouched, for the birds knew better than to eat them.

As we drove toward the northern end of Sanibel, we passed, perhaps, half a dozen scattered homes. There were roads leading toward the sea, which told us that there must be a few more homes nearer the shore.

Finally, we came to a short bridge. This spanned a narrow channel known as "Blind Pass." After that we were on Captiva. And we seemed to feel a difference. The road was bordered by a jungly growth into which narrow sandy lanes led and disappeared. At each lane was an inconspicuous house-marker, and these bore evocative names such as "White Shores," "Sanderling," and "Bay Barlin." In the half-light, as had been true of a part of Sanibel, the road, arched over by tall, graceful casuarinas or Australian pines, held a kind of fairy tale beauty. I did not know, then, that it was the composition of the island's soil, a mixture of sand and shell, that had made it easy for a few of them, long ago, to be transplanted from other tropical islands, and that, once there, they had sprung up all over our own island.

Suddenly, the road curved to the left, a turn which we would, for the next twenty-three years, speak of as the "S" curve. The road then paralleled the beach. Even at that hour of dusk, there was enough light to see the churning sea, its white caps rushing to shore on our left. Very soon, the inn, with its central dining room and its cottages, everything seemingly built of driftwood, appeared on our right. A small sign on a side door of the main building said, "Office," and when Tom came out of that, he was followed by a white-coated bellboy. Genial and hospitable, he led us to our cottage, explaining, as he took care of our bags, that dinner was already being served. There was hardly time to glance at the white-iron beds, to see that the bathtubs sat high up on legs, or that the closet had a flowered curtain instead of a door. One small rug lay on the floor between the beds.

We hurried across the yard through a scattering of palms and casuarinas into the dining room. As we entered, the other guests, already halfway through their meal, looked up, smiled and bowed. At tables for two or four, with snowy cloths and fresh flowers, they were being served by waitresses who'd come down from Virginia. They wore powder-blue stiffly starched cotton uniforms and long, crisply starched white aprons and white caps, which against their dark skin, added to the dignity of the scene. The women who were guests were simply and quietly dressed. The men wore coats and ties. The hum of conversation sounded friendly, but refined, and instantly, any fears, any misgivings that I might have had, were no more.

In as little as fourteen hours, Tom and I had completely succumbed to the enchantment of the island, and as luck would have it, as much as we regretted not being able to stay more than five days at the inn, the Russell Karrs, who were nice enough to allow us the use of their guesthouse, would turn out to become some of our closest friends. For the next two years we rented their guest house for the season, for having found Captiva, Tom and I knew that we would never want to stay away very long. We couldn't have known, at that point, however, that even in the heat of summer we would be drawn to return, and that those stays were to be some of our most unforgettable. For, there alone, and living within the rhythm of nature, we seemed to belong to the island, and in a peculiar way, she to us. The momentary pangs we might have felt on seeing the houses of those we loved, shuttered and empty, would soon pass, for we knew that with the coming of October, our friends would begin to return.

By the second winter, I was so happy there, that Tom could leave me for as long as a month at a time, and come and go. In the same way that I felt a part of my home community, I had become a part of the island. We'd quickly made wonderful friendships, and my self-confidence about my health

had returned. I had regained my zest for life.

By the third winter, we took the plunge, and, casting our lot with Captiva, bought a house. While the Karr's guesthouse was ideally situated (it faced the bay and the bird life over both land and water was a constant show), the little house had one drawback – studio beds. One night, after a long day on the water, as usual, we sat reading. Tom, sunburned, tired, and drowsy, said, as he glanced toward the studio beds and their multiple pillows, "Let's go out before we leave, and rent something for next year with real beds." I said I thought it would be a good idea.

By that time I was taking a few watercolor lessons, and one day, soon after the suggestion of renting something else, when Tom had gone out on the boat to fish, I took my easel and my brushes out on a nearby point. Almost on the tip of the point was a small charming white house. On its front door, a sign read,

FOR SALE

PRISCILLA MURPHY

SANIBEL ISLAND

By the time Tom came around the point, several hours later, I was fast building air castles. I stood up and waved, and as he came closer, he waved back. Cupping my hands, I called out, "Come ashore! I want to show you something." Good-natured about my whims, he found something to tie up to, and taking off his shoes and socks and rolling up his pants, waded ashore.

"What are you up to?" he asked.

I couldn't wait to tell him. "I've found a home for us," I said. "Look." And I led him around to the door where the sign was.

He did not seem to mind going to look, but failed to fall in with the degree of my enthusiasm. "You're just having one of your spells," he said. "You know we don't want any more houses to worry about. All those tenant houses on the farms that keep a carpenter going from one to the other all the time. Rotting screens, fallen doorsteps, sagging doors – it's better for us to rent."

"That may be true," I said, "but I believe in signs, and why would this nice little house that's almost next door to where we are, be empty, if it were not meant to be ours? Please, let's get Priscilla Murphy to take us inside to see it? We don't have to buy it."

He agreed to explore the possibility. But once inside, the house did not cast the spell over me that I expected. The walls were incongruously of dark paneling. It seemed to bear no relation to the happy, light-hearted spirit of the island, so that was that.

But the day came, just four before the one of our leaving for the season, when we drove up the island to see an older woman, perhaps sixty-five or seventy-years-old, with the engaging name, Phoebe Peabody (pronounced in New England, from where she came, "Peab'dy") who, in a quiet way, handled nearly all Captiva real estate. We found her at home.

Tom explained our need, that we wanted to rent a small place for the next winter. She was quick to say that that was impossible. The only two houses available for rent were large, old, two-story ones that sat far back in the jungle. These we knew about and felt them to be too ghost-like to be appealing, and indeed, they did usually remain empty.

Tom explained that these would not do; that most of the time I would be there alone. Then Phoebe said, "Well, there's one house that sounds exactly like what you want, but it's for sale, not for rent. It belongs to Dorothy Thompson, a spinster from St. Paul, who, in January, had a heart-attack. At the end of her convalescence she came to the decision to sell her Captiva property. The house is to go as is, completely furnished."

Then Tom, who could always seem to think of the practical thing to do, answered, "Well, Miss Thompson may not be able to sell it. In that case, she might change her mind about renting, and if you don't mind showing it to us, should that happen, you could let us know."

So we drove down the island, turned into a lane through the jungle, drove about three-hundred feet to a slight rise, and there sat a small, white, one-story house. Phoebe took us in through the kitchen. She led the way, and as she passed by one of the cupboards, stopped long enough to fling open its doors.

On its lower shelves sat blue and white china, on those above, chunky, cobalt-blue goblets. Something inside me flipped, and going through the door from the kitchen into the living room, I flipped even more, for there, in the glow of those walls made of Florida cypress, to which had been applied a thin coat of white paint, leaving the grain of the wood to show, was a lovely pearliness, a glow in harmony with the island's own loveliness: its sunlight, its sea, its sky, and its luminous clouds. There were Delft tiles around the fireplace. Triple windows faced the sea, and on either side were built-in bookshelves of the same pearly finish, not filled with books, however, but beautiful pieces of coral and an assortment of seashells.

The furnishings were simple and tropical, reminiscent of an island in the Caribbean. There was an unstudied look, one that suggested soft winds and the stir of palms. And from that moment on, I was never to be the same. Up to that point I had not really even thought seriously of living for a part of each year at Captiva. Seeing that appealing little house would be just something pleasant to remember, I mused. And in a business-like way we were shown the other rooms. Across the breezeway from the living room and kitchen were two small bedrooms and a bath. On the bay side of the property there was a small, one-room structure for Miss Thompson's maid, and we were shown that as well. Later, back in front of Phoebe's own house, ready to say good-bye, (Phoebe had been driving, Tom sat on the front seat, and I sat in the back) Tom gave Phoebe our name and Carolina telephone number in case the house should ever come up for rent.

Then, in some kind of daze, I suddenly had the sensation of being a spectator in a little tableau; without consciously willing it, I saw my hand reach over and touch Tom's shoulder, and heard my voice say, calmly, "Tom, don't you know that little house was made for us? Why don't we buy it?"

In a properly masculine way, Tom made no sign that he was having the same feeling. Later, it was to become one of his stock jokes, that I had pulled the rug right out from under him as to any possible negotiating that might have been done. Just the same, in a matter of minutes, he was saying to Phoebe, (and somehow, in that state of euphoria that was mine, this was no surprise), "Phoebe, is it in order for me to make you a firm offer?"

Completely rattled, Phoebe's tiny hands were shaking as she reached up to pat her hair and adjust her collar, but she found her voice enough to say, "I suppose you could."

And Tom, who had never been known to let any grass grow under his feet once he had decided something, said, "Then why don't we drive down to the Sanibel ferry-landing now, and let you talk to Miss Thompson?" For there was a telephone on Sanibel at the ferry-landing.

By this time, Phoebe's hands were trembling so that they could hardly find the ignition. Turning out of her driveway, we started on our *fourth* trip of the morning down the island. Before she had gone very far, she made a turn away from the road by the sea into an area of openness and scattered palms, beyond which, sat the home of Alice O'Brien. Though open to the sea and the bay, Alice's property was enclosed by jungles on either side. Phoebe asked to be excused for a moment, and hurried from the car into the house. In less than five minutes, she and Alice O'Brien hurried out together. Al, whom we knew only slightly from having attended small gatherings for drinks in homes up and down the island, had her arms opened wide in a welcoming gesture, saying, "Of course I would like to have these nice Pearsalls as next-door neighbors. I should be delighted."

Twenty minutes later, we had again covered the fifteen miles to the phone booth. Phoebe was explaining to Miss Thompson what had taken place.

As we stood outside the booth, Tom said to me, "I've been thinking.

I'm excited too. I can arrange my affairs at home to stay one more week so that we can start making some changes if this deal goes through. I would want to see water in both directions, wouldn't you?"

"Of course," I said. I knew that he was referring to clearing out the growth, both to the sea and the bay.

"We will have to get a bulldozer to remove the jungles, and we don't ever want to feel that we don't have room for the children and our friends. Don't you think we should go on and enlarge the guesthouse; get it all started, so that it will be ready by next fall?"

I could see the wisdom of all this. Over the years, I had found that if either of us had an idea that could be immediately supported by the other, we would be off at a gallop, the bit in our teeth, and that, in the main, those swift joint decisions would prove to have been right. I had come to trust things for which we felt equal enthusiasm.

Tom went on to say, "We might even ask Miss Thompson to allow us to spend this last week in the house before we leave for the season. How would you like that? I think that with the season coming to an end we can get the workman without any trouble."

Of course, I was all for that. With this, Tom tapped on the glass of the telephone booth to interrupt Phoebe so that she might ask Miss Thompson if we might be allowed to move in right away for a week.

By nightfall, our clothes were in the closets of this enchanting house. The jalousies of the breezeway were open, and although there was not as yet a vista to the sea, nor to the bay, there was the sound of the sea. The soft, night wind stirred the chimes on the breezeway to a delicate tinkle, and there was the papery rustle of the palms. I could have died of happiness. Sleep was blissful, and the next morning we could not get up early enough for the beginning of what we knew would be, in Virginia Woolf's words, "one blue day after another – smooth, round and flawless."

While we were sleeping the sleep of the just, however, in Minnesota, Dorothy Thompson was tossing on her pillow. In a telephone conversation with her lawyer, she had been reminded that since possession is nine tenths of the law, were we the wrong kind of people, she might be in trouble.

Early the next morning, she sent a nervous telegram to Phoebe in care of the store on Sanibel. In spite of its urgency, the delivery of the telegram would not begin its fifteen-mile journey to us until a Captiva resident, who needed something from the store had made his or her morning purchases and had gone back.

But by noon the telegram had reached Phoebe. Relaxing on her porch from so quick a sale, when the telegram arrived, this new slant on the situation threw her into a state of panic. She hurried down to us to find out what was to be done. I can't recall all the in's and out's, but in some way, Dorothy Thompson was reassured. We spent a happy week drawing plans for the guesthouse, watching the bulldozers clear out the tangle of growth so that when we had our meals on our breezeway, we would have lovely vistas in two opposite directions, one to the sea and one to the bay. Every hour of that week deepened the feeling that we had, indeed, found our Eden.

It was in this swift springing into action and other instances that Jim Gray, a fellow Captivan, would be led to say, down the years, "The Pearsalls are a catalyst. When they're here, things happen."

Jim was probably right. We were different from the other Captiva residents. Since most of them had retired, they spent the seven winter months on the island, and their lives developed a routine. Since Tom had not retired, and indeed, as time proved, he never would – in order to have time for Captiva and for travel, when he was at home in Carolina, except for weekends, he worked literally sixteen hours a day – for our *own* island stays we came and went, engaged all the while in a very active life in North Carolina. On the island we nearly always had guests, and a variety of them. For it was impossible not to want to share so much beauty and tranquility. Many times, we would have preferred just being there quietly alone, but what is paradise, unless you share it?

But I'm ahead of the story. I must speak of the various ways of travel from Carolina to Captiva that, over time, would be ours. No matter what mode of travel we had used, nor at what hour of the day we had arrived, the stir of our arrival would be intense. But, somehow, between all the little things to be done, by the time the long twilight had deepened, and had slowly disappeared, I would have prepared a light evening meal. And in our breezeway, in the glow of candlelight and to the tinkle of wind chimes a few feet away, we would linger on and on at the table, our contentment indescribable.

≈ ≈ ≈

From the very first of our having become islanders, we fell into the pattern of going on sand-picnics with other boat-lovers. After the simplest of lunches – each one consuming his or her own sandwich, although a jug of iced drinks might be shared – the little group, sitting on the beach of an uninhabited island, one without anything but bird life, would reminisce as to how each of us had happened to find our way to Captiva. This was long before there was any advertising, and each person's tale of discovery had elements of humor.

In the first place, even if you had heard of the island, unless you had entrée to the aristocratic Virginian, Mrs. Grace Price, who owned and ran Tween Waters Inn, and whom we called Grace, there would have been no place to stay. She had no need to lower her standards by advertising to fill her cottages, and she didn't. We always said that nothing less than a recommendation from St. Peter would get you in! A gross exaggeration, of course, but you did have to be spoken for.

Anita McCulloch's tale was, like Anita herself, one of the most colorful. With her husband's frequent long stays in South America as a geologist, one winter, Anita decided that she would leave their place in the North Carolina mountains and do a little exploring of her own. She wanted to find an island where she and Paul could be warm, as in a winter home in Florida, keeping their summer home in the mountains, with plans to live, by turns, in both areas, as simply as possible and yet be reasonably comfortable.

Although Anita had spent the night on the mainland, and could have come over to the island on the mailboat, which had a few benches for passengers on top and arrived every day at noon or thereabouts, she chose to come by hired car. Its driver was an old salt who lived on Captiva, and that day, was taking home with him a goat, which he hoped would help to clear his jungle. For travelling, Anita was wearing a large, straw hat, and all during the drive, she sat in the front seat, unaware that the goat was working on her hat. When they pulled up to the inn, she made the discovery that her hat had been chewed to shreds, but somehow the gods were in a favorable mood: Grace Price took her in, and eventually, Anita and Paul would have their own place on the island.

On our joint picnics, the largest boat would be that of the Bixbies of the "Bixby Compound." There were two such compounds on the island. Ours was the "O'Brien," that name derived from the fact that in the twenties, the Minneapolis spinster, Alice O'Brien, once she had discovered Captiva, had bought a tract of the unseen land and parcelled it out to her friends.

Harold and Debbie Bixby were parents and grandparents to a large clan; the clan gathered frequently on Captiva. Nobody would have known that Harold, a banker of influence in St. Louis, had been largely responsible for financing Lindburgh's flight to Paris. Harold and Debbie had lived in China for many years. Thoroughly global in his thinking, Harold was connected with the pioneering of Pan American Airlines, but their house on Captiva was perhaps the least impressive on the island; not large, there was a small adjacent guest house, equally rustic.

Debbie's hobby was the collection of shells; her collection finally grew to such proportions that Harold gave her an old barge and had it pulled up to the shore on their property. Debbie's shell collection was world-wide. I remember that one winter, when she and Harold went to the great barrier reef off the coast of Australia, Harold had the pleasure of giving Debbie, as an anniversary present, a shell that we knew had cost a thousand dollars. That shell lay in the weather-worn old barge along with the common Captiva varieties – fans, olives, and cockleshells – and with Debbie's junonias, which are the rarest shell found on either of the two sister islands. Debbie and Harold are both no longer alive, but I'm sure that Debbie's shell collection has been well placed.

On those picnics, a boatload of Bixbies of assorted ages could well have been a boatload of immigrants from the "old country." As was true of all Captivans, they cared less than nothing for what they wore on picnics. There would be straw hats, sunbonnets, baseball caps, yachting caps, head scarves. Even some freshly arrived houseguest, hoping against hope to preserve a hairdo, might wear a shower cap. That was the charm of Captiva.

What a contrast though, to visit the Bixbies in their place on Lake George, New York. That impressively large, beautiful, white home of theirs stood at the water's edge. The Bixby electric boat could easily have held thirty passengers, and sometimes there were that many of the clan under one roof. As times changed, the house was divided into apartments, but was still solely for the use of the Bixbies.

Sometimes there might be another boatload of Bixbies, the Ralph Bixbies. Ralph and Harold were brothers. They, too, had an active social life in St. Louis. On Captiva, however, Ralph expressed the fun-loving side of his nature. Their house was built out over the bay. At the time of its construction, Ralph whimsically had a trap door installed, through which, by raising it, he could easily fish. This was always a conversation piece when there were houseguests there for the first time. I doubt that it was ever used for any other purpose.

Ralph's wife, Lucy, was so good-natured that she went along with the fun, yet Lucy's love of the beautiful, and her taste, were both shown scattered about in this simple structure where she had placed some of her fine antiques. Lucy loved flowers. She'd been president of the combined garden clubs of St. Louis, at that time, a city of six hundred thousand people, and from the island soil she was able to grow things that almost seemed a miracle.

Lucy and Ralph usually drove north to Lake George in April. Sometimes they stopped over with us in Carolina. One particular spring, they happened to be here when the dogwood was at its peak, and they would never stop raving over the dogwood in our hometown. It was on this visit that Ralph had a cage on top of his station wagon. In the cage were his two pet coons. Two nights after the stopover with us they would draw up to the Plaza in New York, coons and all, for Ralph enjoyed nothing more than indulging in these little eccentricities.

As to picnic food, that on Captiva picnics was altogether different from that in Carolina, where preparation might go on for days. On the island, capricious winds and unpredictable seas precluded advance planning, so the picnic fare was always uncomplicated, and it was never overabundant. But, as we sat in the sand munching our sandwiches, using a tarpaulin for a tablecloth, the play of wit was always delightful.

Usually we had to drop anchor something like fifteen or twenty feet offshore and wade in. That in itself put us in a laughing mood, for going overboard holding a picnic basket and trying to keep its contents dry as you waded in at least waist-high water made for laughs. Once, since it was Tom's birthday, I had over-stepped the rules of simple fare by bringing a commercially baked and frozen cake. But it was only a *small* cake, and it had only *one* layer. Its icing was orange, Tom's favorite. Feeling some obligation as a host, in passing around the cake, which I had cut into small blocks, he said, "Do have some cake. Elizabeth thawed it herself!"

Bert and Janet Lynch of St. Louis, who were to prove our most constant boating companions, were always ready for a picnic. It was on that one that Bert, looking up at the numberless shore birds who were wheeling over the edge of the sea, said, "This is as near heaven as I want to be."

Instantly, Marietta Raymond of Buffalo, came in with, "I agree. I never really felt that I would fit in – in heaven, anyway."

Sitting by Marietta, our beloved Julia Black of Pittsburgh, Pennsylvania, and Port Hope, Canada, spoke up quickly, "Oh, but Marietta, you would! You're so musical!"

Tom and I were to find that on these picnics, new friendships quickly ripened to the pleasure and intimacy of joining in collective reminiscences of individual upbringings; the ups and downs of growing up, and those that inevitably go with the early years of marriage. These shared experiences brought us together in a delightfully homey way. For example: It was as hard to imagine Connie Stanton, as she lay curled up sleeping on the floor of our inboard/outboard on the way home after a day of swimming and shelling, in earlier days, dancing with the Prince of Wales, with plumes in her hair, her train on her arm as it was to imagine Ernie, her husband, now with his gray hair and a matching small moustache, and his beautiful manner of speech, as the little boy he said he once was. Ernie's family had lived on the ten mile long island of Gross Isle near the Canadian line, and since he had to walk two miles to school in the severity of northern winter, his Mother would put a very hot hard-boiled egg in each pocket.

In this friendly reminiscing, everybody had a tale of his own to tell. Tom's contribution was that when his older brother, Harry went into the army during the first World War, Tom, in a burst of pride, replaced his own knickers by commandeering Harry's long pants. But the war was soon over. Harry came home, and Tom had the humiliation of having to return to the wearing of knickers.

On sand-picnics we swam before lunch, and immediately after lunch, Tom wanted a nap. To that end, our boat always had under its bow an old army blanket. Stretched out on the beach, with a handkerchief or a towel over his face, he would fade from the scene. The rest of the party would usually pick up shells; the search, always rewarding. On the larger islands of Captiva and Sanibel, however, if you really were a serious conchologist, knowing that the storms always brought in shells, on the morning after a storm you would be out on the beach at four. Tom and I were never addicted to collecting the rare ones to that extent. To me, all shells are beautiful, but my favorites are the small luminous jingle shells that sparkle in the sand. I enjoyed putting them into small decorative jars to have ready to give to departing guests for their bathrooms. Since our house was entirely unpretentious, we gave it the name "Cockleshells." Our guest house became "Jingle Shells," the two shortened to "Cockles" and "Jingles." The names themselves, seemed, to us, buoyant, suggesting the light, lilting quality that was, and is, in the spirit of the island.

≈ ≈ ≈

The morning after our initial stay on Captiva, Buffie and Ernest at once began to include us in their plans. Almost the first thing Buffie said was, "Elizabeth, Cousin Lena is eager to have you as a guest at a small luncheon she is giving over on Sanibel the day after tomorrow. The luncheon is being given at The Nutmeg House. Now, Tom, I know you and Ernest will want to fish, so you'll be deprived, briefly, of our company. I want Elizabeth to meet Cousin Lena's interesting friends. With you always so busy and involved in Carolina, she might come to the island alone sometime."

Tom, already enamored of the island, answered, "I don't know about that, Buffie. I think I'm going to want to come here as often as I can. This is the kind of place I've been longing for. The bright lights and bumper to bumper traffic of the East Coast are all right for those who want it, but this is my kind of place. Elizabeth says she already feels the same. We can't thank you enough for finding it for us."

At Cousin Lena's luncheon, the second person to whom I was introduced was Virginia Van Vleck, called "Gigi." Right away, I thought, *You're either the tackiest person I've ever seen, or the most sophisticated.* Her cinnamon-colored corduroy skirt had seen better days, her long, droopy overblouse was of coarse natural-colored cotton, her cotton stockings were black and ribbed, her shoes, saddle colored, while of good leather, were worn. She had an attractive, slightly husky voice, and she interspersed French phrases in conversation in a completely natural way. We happened to sit next to each other, and it was the beginning of a deep friendship that would last until her death eighteen years later.

She and her husband, Joe, were to visit us in North Carolina several times; we went for stays with them in their home in the Poconos, in Pennsylvania. The homestead of the original Dutch Van Vleck family had been a farm which was to become the center of Montclair, New Jersey. At this time, Joe's mother was living in the large home on that property, at the edge of which, Joe and Gigi – since this was a second marriage for both, and there would be no children for them – lived in a small, stone house that had been the original home of the Van Vlecks when the Dutch were settling the states of New York and New Jersey.

Joe and Gigi spent most of their time travelling. Joe was on the international board of Planned Parenthood, and wherever they went, Gigi always wanted to couple it with some time in France where she had grown up. Gigi's family were Americans transplanted to France. Her parents, however, had seen to it that Gigi and her sister, Dorothy, had some years of education in their own country.

It was Gigi who gave me, one morning, when she had come by to have a cup of tea, which she often did, what she considered essential advice for all women. She and I were both fifty-two at the time. I had said half jokingly, that we were getting old! This set Gigi off. "Oh, my dear!" she exclaimed. "Never let me hear you say that again. The French woman never mentions her age. She goes on the premise that if she keeps her mind alive, she's more attractive at eighty than she was at eighteen."

I promised never to forget. Sifting it, I think it's a sound philosophy, and I offer it to all women as a hedge against the inevitable.

Two other women at the luncheon immediately became my friends. The two were sisters-in-law, Marie Clark and Julia Black. Marie, of Orange, Virginia, daughter of a professor at the University of Virginia, was widely travelled, and had recently lost her husband, Julia's brother. Julia had been a widow since the age of thirty. The daughter in a wealthy Pittsburgh family, she had brought up her son and daughter between

Pittsburgh and Port Hope, Canada. At that time, several wealthy Pittsburgh families had second homes in Port Hope. When I met this lovely person, twenty years my senior, I would never have imagined what a close friendship would develop between Julia and Tom and me, her daughter, Mary, and her son-in-law, "Bookie" Book.

Marie would die a few years after we came to Captiva. With the same delightful approach to life which she had shown through the years of battling emphysema, since she had always wanted to go to Sicily, she went. Before leaving, she made plans for cremation, should death come over there, burial to take place at Port Hope. And that was the way it all happened.

When our friendship with Julia had deepened to the point that we visited her in Canada, we visited Marie's grave, then returned to Julia's beautiful home which overlooked her garden twenty-two steps below, one made distinctive by being planted in the colors and design of the Union Jack. Of all the homes I've ever been a guest in, this was the most elegant, the most beautifully appointed, and the most beautifully run. Julia's domestics were English and white-haired. They cared for her with devotion, and could never understand her going for six months of the year to a tiny island where she would live in a cottage not more than fourteen by twenty feet, part of this space given to a bath and a narrow screened porch, while they, themselves, remained in her comfortable and spacious and richly furnished house.

Through Julia, we came to know an older man whom everybody called Uncle Carroll. This handsome, attractive, old widower lived the life of an English Lord. He, too, was from Pittsburgh. His summer home, also in Port Hope, was "East House" on Lake Ontario, next door to Katherine Cornell's house, separated by beautiful gardens and hedges, and known as "West House."

One winter, however, Uncle Carroll decided to see what there was at Captiva that his old friend Julia found so attractive. With an attendant, he came for a stay at the rustic inn which had aroused his curiosity. Uncle Carroll was in and out of our house a great deal. In spite of the difference in age, he and Tom liked each other right away, and before he left, Uncle Carroll insisted that Tom and I come for a summer visit, half of it to be spent at Julia's and half of it to be spent at his house.

Uncle Carroll liked to play bridge, and on the island, while he was there, we had a short game every night. The game went on in our living room, the French doors open into the breezeway where Tom would sit, reading the newspapers that had come from home by mail, especially those from our hometown and from Raleigh, and going over charts for the daily boating expeditions that he and Bert had in mind.

When Uncle Carroll said that we must come to see him, Tom demurred, saying, "But Uncle Carroll, what would I do while you and the ladies play bridge and drink tea?"

"I've already figured that out," said Uncle Carroll. "I have an Irish friend who reminds me very much of you, Tom. He's an outdoorsman, and I will arrange that you and he have several days of fishing in Ottawa."

So before the summer ended we found ourselves in Port Hope. It was a marvelous experience. Julia was indeed the Grande Dame of the town. It was she who had entertained the Queen on her visit to that part of Canada. Uncle Carroll's hundred-and-twenty-five foot yacht, which he no longer owned, had taken him all over the world. He and Andrew Carnegie had been close friends.

For our stay, Tom and I were given Uncle Carroll's wife's bedroom. Her silver toilet articles still lay on the dressing table. Her chaise longue was there with its lovely throw; *The Book of Common Prayer* lay open on her prayer-desk. She had been dead many years, but her presence was still felt in this room. At night, lying in bed, the foghorns blowing on the lake, I could almost feel that we were characters in some Gothic novel. Yet, by day our surroundings were so beautiful, with sun-lit gardens and the wide porch overlooking expanses of well-kept lawn and fine old trees, that every moment was one of pure delight.

Immaculate and rosy, Uncle Carroll chuckled as he said that at his age, he was living on milk and whiskey, which was virtually true. He gave beautiful dinners for us with as many as fourteen or sixteen guests. At the head of the table, entirely serene, and the life of the party, he sipped his milk and whiskey. That was all.

One of the things Uncle Carroll enjoyed most was reading aloud. One night after dinner, when we had collected in the drawing room, the fire at one end and a bridge table at the other, he read some delightfully humorous story, the title of which I've forgotten. It had to do with an American's visit in one of the great houses of England, and of his not knowing what to do when he fell into the hands of a polished manservant. Uncle Carroll was a wonderful reader, and as he read, it was so funny that we had to wipe our eyes.

Bob and Irene Murison were the Irish couple of whom Uncle Carroll was so fond. The Murisons spent about eight months of the year in Canada where Bob had a chair factory. They chose to live in Port Hope where Irene could carry on her riding, for she had been brought up to cover as much as sixty miles in the saddle in a day of hunting. In that little golden thread of friendships which now seems, experience after experience, to have been handed to us by fate from the beginning of our life together, Tom and

I would soon be in the habit of visiting the Murisons in Ireland, but only in the warmer months. They would come to us, both on Captiva and in Carolina, depending on where we were at the time.

From the instant that Irene and I met at Uncle Carroll's (her name pronounced, "Ireny," the Irish way), we were as two bugs in a rug, for all my Irish ancestry surfaced. We both loved books; fantasy was second nature. Each of us had grown up with horses and dogs; however, horses had played a much larger part in her life than in mine. As a young girl she had often been excused for those days of the hunt from the French school she attended. In my own life, while our horses were nice enough, and usually five-gaited – the ones Father enjoyed most were the Tennessee Walkers, mainly for riding over the farms. As a child, still riding my large pony, Belle, I used to long for the day when my legs would be long enough to ride the larger, sleeker, horses; old enough to inherit Sister's black and white checked riding habit and her fine black boots, her black velvet cap and her white ascot.

Belle had a peculiar disposition. She seemed to consider being hitched to the pony cart an insult, an opinion which she kept to herself as she was being backed into the shafts and her girth being fastened; even until we were riding along on the road she would seem happy, enthusiastic about the outing. Then suddenly, when we had gone, perhaps, half a mile, she would balk. Stopping firmly in her tracks, she was immovable. No amount of wheedling, coaxing, shouting, or flapping of the reins on her flanks, could induce her to change her mind. Then suddenly with a jerk, she would be off, the occupants of the pony cart in a scramble, and nothing you could do or say would slow her down. Still, we never considered getting rid of Belle for a more amiable pony. For as anybody who has lived around animals knows, you learn to adapt to their ways.

Irene could recite Irish poetry by the yard, and through the green of the Irish countryside, as we drove in their fourteen-year-old Mercedes which still ran like a top, she would obligingly entertain us with some of her favorites. Our long-suffering husbands usually matched their moods to ours, and we knew how lucky we were to have mature, manly men who were not embarrassed by or frightened of having the poetic side of their natures show. A couplet I remember, that Ireny recited with marvelous dramatic effect, went like this:

> Time, you old gypsy man, will you not stay,
> rest not your caravan just for one day?

Another poem was given in the mood of the romantic, Ireny's voice, gentle and wistful:

> *I was married young to a decent man*
> *As many would call a prudent choice,*
> *But he never could hear how the river ran,*
> *Singin' a song in a changin' voice;*
> *Nor sought to see on the bay's blue water,*
> *A ship with yellow sails unfurled,*
> *Bearin' away a king's young daughter,*
> *Over the brim of the hearin' world.*

Both Irene and I wanted to visit the Isle of Innisfree, where Yeats had written his beautiful poem, "The Isle of Innisfree." It was one I knew and liked.

> *I will arise and go now, and go to Innisfree,*
> *and a small cabin build there, of clay and wattles made:*
> *Nine bean-rows will I have there, a hive for the honeybee,*
> *and live alone in the bee-loud glade.*
>
> *And I shall have some peace there, for peace comes dropping slow,*
> *Dropping from the veils of the morning to where the cricket sings;*
> *There midnight's all a glimmer, and noon a purple glow,*
> *And evening full of the linnet's wings,*
>
> *I will arise and go now, for always night and day,*
> *I hear lake water lapping with low sounds by the shore;*
> *While I stand on the roadway, or on the pavements gray,*
> *I hear it in the deep heart's core.*

Innisfree sat in a quiet bay, but we did not, that day, take time to find a boat and somebody to row us over to this almost insignificantly small island. Still, we had seen it across a narrow strip of water, and since – except where there are examples of poverty and its continuing strife – nearly every part of Ireland has some aspect of beauty, we drove on.

Irene's father had been a bank president, spoken of as a "bank manager" over there. His bank was in Dublin, but they chose to live twelve miles away, in the small town of Greystones. The name of their home was "Rochfort." It is there that Bob and Irene still live, their three sons scattered about over the English-speaking world. Bob had been an RAF pilot during World War II. Irene had been a WREN and it was in those war spheres that they had met. When I asked her what she did during the war, she said, in her jocular Irish way, that she had put the pins on the maps in the military offices. But Bob said, in reality, she was a highly respected secretary.

On the first night of our original visit to Rochfort, going up to bed, Irene called from the lower hall, "Elizabeth, there's one thing I didn't tell you. You'll be wakened at dawn by the mistle thrush in the magnolia outside your room. I hope it won't disturb you too much."

Disturb me too much? I thought it was the loveliest thing I'd ever heard of, awakening to matins in bird song. *What beautiful, poetic nature had thought of so fitting a name for a bird,* I wondered? For my mind had leaped to an incorrect spelling of the word, "mistle"; it had fallen on my ears as "missal," the term for a book of prayers or devotions. And since all birds waken at dawn, what an honor, it seemed, to be the one chosen to open the day with prayers? And this would be going on right outside my own window. I could hardly sleep for its anticipation, and every morning, when the four of us were not on a motoring trip, there was this wakening to the poetic.

In my euphoria, I was swept back to another lovely experience that was centered around another member of the thrush family. Once, a long time earlier, I had been on my way to Greece for the first time, when an English friend, preparing me, said, "Whatever you do, don't miss the nightingale at Delphi." She was right. For to hear that golden voice coming from the bough of an olive tree, and to see the bird's tiny throat quivering as it sang its heart out, was to have a lasting memory. And, as if these two outstanding thrushes were not enough, I had memorized three lines that appeared in the *Christian Science Monitor*, lines written by the poet, Ruth Lambert Jones, that seemed to say it all:

> *Sun down, a thrush.*
> *One liquid note, a catch in*
> *the throat.*

Since it would never have occurred to me, however, that the word "missal" in this context would be spelled in any way other than the way it had fallen on my ears, I did not discuss it with anybody, and there was nobody to set me straight. Knowing, as we all do, that the song of the thrush is, in sweetness, next to that of the nightingale, that indeed, they are of the same family, it seemed entirely logical that *one* should open the day – and if you're inclined to extend the fantasy, that it should do so with a prayer – and that *another* kind of bird should sing the day to sleep. And for a dozen or so years, I lived with that lovely illusion.

Then one day, back at home in Carolina, a certain unfamiliar warbler in a bayberry bush in our yard sent me to the bird book. Its pages fell open, oddly, at "The Thrush," and for the first time it occurred to me to stop and learn more about those members of the species that had so enchanted me under my window at Rochfort. It was almost more than I could *bear*, certainly more than I wanted to *believe*, to find that there is no such bird as the "Missal Thrush." The feathery creature in the magnolia who had so caught and held my fancy was given its name for the prosaic reason that it eats the berries of the mistletoe. Perhaps other kinds of birds don't. No matter; I had had a nice long time to enjoy my illusion.

On one of our visits to the British Isles, the Murisons joined us in London in their same old Mercedes and we drove about for ten days visiting their English relatives. One of our stops was to visit a friend Irene had known when they were both WRENs. Reaching that small, isolated house, its name "Mere Cottage," "Mere," of course, being the English word for meadow, required miles and miles of driving on roads tightly enclosed by hedgerows. At times we felt we were riding in a long, narrow, green trough, only occasionally glimpsing the countryside. When these glimpses came, however, the rolling green, accented now and then by a lone copper beach, was thrilling. It was dusk when we made it to a point where, in the distance, there appeared a light. Expected for dinner by Katherine and Roland, with apologies for arriving late, we drove up to the cottage door. The delightful stop included being offered homemade dandelion wine, freshly grown peas from the garden cooked with mint leaves, a rack of lamb, and the inevitable Yorkshire pudding. It was midnight before we could bear to say goodbye. So concerned were our hosts that we might lose our way back into town and on to our bed-and-breakfast that they led us, in their own car, the long, lonely distance of fifteen miles.

Visiting so many people in such a short time, we could sometimes stop only for tea or lunch with those friends or relatives of the Murisons. These stops were carefully planned, and were met with sincerest hospitality. One of Irene's sisters was married to a retired University professor. This couple lived in York. At retirement, the Professor had assumed responsibility for raising the millions required to restore Yorkminster. Being shown over that ancient cathedral by a person so informed was wonderful, yet equally wonderful was the suggestion that we leave those dank, chilly walls to return to their home for tea by the fireside.

As we drove along, day-to-day, with the Murisons, sharing tales from our separate backgrounds, one day, Bob gave us the story of their tinkerman. It seems that this type of repairman, the Irish tinkerman, still goes around the countryside with his covered wagon, mending pots and pans and umbrellas; whatever needs to be attended to. One day, when the tinkerman was working at their house, Bob came through the mud room where the old man was at work, and, in his jovial way, said that he hoped the good man had had enough lunch. The tinkerman's answer was simple and philosophical, "I may not have had me 'nough, but I've had me share," he said, and went on with his work.

Motoring on another day, Bob and Irene thought we should have the experience of eating pork pies for lunch. Having bought them in some village, we stopped outside under a tree to consume them. For those who have never seen a pork pie, I will say that it is, to my way of thinking, utterly unappealing in appearance. It could be a very large, tall, heavy biscuit of three layers of anemic-looking pastry, and three layers of pale pork, all of it stone-cold and white. Washed down with ale in pubs, it may make a proper lunch, but I prefer our hamburgers and hot dogs.

My Braswell ancestors are supposed to have come from West Riding in Yorkshire, and I kept thinking of them while on that visit. The tale goes that they were either weavers, or that they lived by a stream, since "Brace" means water, and indeed, the name was spelled "Bracewell" until three generations ago. So that, in that part of the world, my imagination could run wild. I could see them with their rough garments, their shepherd's horns and staffs, wandering over the moors with their flocks. Fantasies that cost nothing, didn't call for any proof, and that, as usual, brought me pleasure.

LIFE WITHIN THE COMPOUND

≈ ≈ ≈

Although our autumns in Carolina are beautiful, I knew that with the coming of October I could expect Tom's thoughts to return to the island, and that, one morning, standing at the window as he buttoned his shirt and looked over the garden, he would say, enthusiastically, "The robins are here! You know where they're going. And I can't let a robin be smarter than I am."

My answer would be the habitual one, "Well, it won't be long now." For the first of our winter stays on Captiva always fell in December.

During those first years, we went down by train. By pre-arrangement, on a certain night at eleven-thirty, a taxi would appear in our driveway in Carolina. The accommodating driver would come into the front hall and help carry out our bags, as well as a gigantic picnic basket, in which we would often have a country ham and several dozen one-pound bags of shelled and roasted peanuts, those grown on our farms and roasted in our kitchen, for the northerners had gone wild over our "goobers." We had taught them to speak of them that way, and if, at times, we arrived without a fresh supply, they pretended not to be glad to see us.

The train trip required all night and all the next day. By five-thirty the next afternoon, the by then bobtailed little train, that of one passenger car and one baggage car, which had been switched from the more important train at Lakeland, would begin to back along slowly, blowing constantly, into the railroad station at Fort Meyers. Arrival would be too late for the ferry, which meant that we would spend that night in Brown's Hotel in Fort Meyers, a dependable little place that, year in and year out, upheld its reputation for good food and was the winter home of the Pittsburgh Pirates.

The next morning, our caretaker, driving the fourteen-year-old little white Chevy that had come with our house when we bought it, would pick us up. Invariably, we would have to go by the marina to get something for one of Tom's boats. With this stop, and another to load up with groceries, it would be noon before we would drive up to our little house. We would have spent thirty-six hours en route.

In later years, we could make the last part of the journey by seaplane. By hurrying in a taxi from the railway station to the airport, we could be flown over by a man with the unlikely name of Buddy Bops, to land, before dark, in the bay behind our house. This was always exciting, because daylight would be fading, and Buddy Bops would have to fly back as soon as he had put us out.

The whir of the seaplane would announce our approaching arrival, and five or six of our friends would be on Al O'Brien's dock to greet us. The jokes about our goobers would begin, and everybody would volunteer to carry the picnic basket. In this happy reunion, the little party of friends, laughing and talking, would make their way, diagonally, through a scattering of palms and gumbo-limbos the three-hundred-and-fifty feet from Al's boat-slip to our cottage. Later on, we would come to have our own boat-slip and its dock.

The island soil, in its mixture of bleached shell and sand, is powdery and almost white. This meant that we never wore good shoes, but it was in this white powdery feature that the island reflected both sunshine and moonlight in a way that made it impossible for me ever to decide under which of the two lights the island lay the more beautiful. The unanswered question brings to mind another one that Tom and I, often, in idle conversation brought up, "Why do we love the island so? Is it its beauty, or the people?" In our hearts, we knew it was both. For to have that combination of natural beauty and delightful, interesting, and responsive friends, was to live under a shower of blessings.

Changing from city clothes quickly, Tom would hurry back to the boatslip to check on his small fleet: the nineteen-foot inboard/outboard which was the *Carolina*, the sailboat, one so small that he could handle it himself, spoken of as the *Spoonbill*, and the *Skiff*. If there were enough daylight left, he would then rush to the water tower to get our house-marker. The water tower stood at the side of our property, halfway between the bay and the house. The marker was one Tom, himself, had made by burning into a shingle the word, "Pearsall." He would hang this from a bracket on an Australian pine of ours, four-hundred-and-fifty feet in the other direction, where the road ran parallel to the sea.

As he was doing these things, I would be opening windows, and for such a small house there were many. The house itself was of that board and batten tropical construction which in times of storms enables it to breathe; its windows and doors were placed for cross-currents. Before changing into island clothes, I would have begun to unpack. I would have gone to see if there were messages in the weather-worn basket that hung by our door on the side toward the sea. There always were. These welcoming notes were only one of the joys to return to. The breeziest of these notes usually came from Ruth Lowry. One that I kept, reads:

> Dear Elizabeth and Tom,
> I hear that you impend. We have houseguests from Vermont that we're eager to have you meet. Weather permitting, can you join us on a picnic to Treasure Island on Friday, the fourth? If your boat is not feeling well, we'll have plenty of room for you in ours. The

Hudsons will be with us for a week. We will be wanting you to come
over for drinks one afternoon soon. For your special pleasure,
Elizabeth, Ed has brought down the sweater of the Henry James
portrait by Sargent, which he told you about. He says that if it is a
cool afternoon, he will wear it for you. So glad you're here.

Love, Ruth

Ed Lowry's father and the writer, Henry James were friends. At the
writer's death, Mr. Lowry was given the sweater of the Sargent portrait. But
this delightful information had come out only after we had been friends
of the Lowrys for years. That was the Captiva way; this modesty was typical
of Ed and Ruth, and indeed, of all Captivans.

Many people who spent the winter on the island were those of
distinction. It almost seemed that the greater the distinction, the smaller
the house they lived in. There were retired ambassadors, editors of large,
well-known newspapers, writers, painters, and ornithologists. Somewhere
along the line, Tom and I would find ourselves entertaining at cocktails
for Thornton Wilder and his sister, Isabel. There would be the experience
of having lunch on the beach with Marianne Moore, and while Anne
Lindburgh did not return to the island during our years, we barely missed
being there as she was writing her beautiful book, *Gifts from the Sea*. The
house in which she stayed was near ours. She had come to Captiva
because her mother and Buffie's Cousin Lena had been classmates at
Smith. Since Cousin Lena was to become something of a Godmother to
me, I always felt that I knew Anne.

Down the road from us there was Madam "Alex*ahn*dra" Tolstoy.
Through a prominent Philadelphia family, a member of which came every
winter to an incredibly small and simple house tucked into the palms,
Madam Tolstoy had discovered the island. For this family had been
instrumental in starting an asylum for White Russians near the city of
Philadelphia, where Madam Tolstoy had gone to live after she fled Russia.
What she lived on, I don't know. The Captiva tale was that she had brought
the family jewels over in a walking stick. But I believe this was a familiar
way of describing the flight of White Russians. It may, in her case, be true.

Madam Tolstoy was what, in a small town, would be called a character.
In her careless attitude toward dress, she could have been a peasant in a
Russian field, and she was not inclined to social life. She spent her days
fishing, and was a continual worry to Ted Levering, from whom she rented
her nondescript little house, because when she dressed her fish, which she
always did on a shelf on the outside, she left her fish heads lying about for
any wildlife that might happen to come by in the day or the night. This

practice of hers led to horrendous fights among the coons on their nightly prowls. Yet Ted was fond of her, and when she yelled out all through the day, as though it were something calamitous, "Tad! Tad!" he would come running.

Every day on Captiva was one to be played by ear. Perhaps life on an island is governed by the weather more than on the mainland. Ours had become a do-it-yourself little place. We often said that we did everything for ourselves except fill our own teeth. Although I never did lose a filling on the island, should it have happened, I'm sure that I would have resorted to the use of chewing-gum the way I had once done when Tom and I were motoring around the provinces of France. We had enjoyed stopping in small towns and country inns for lunch. Our driver, "Gastonh" (Gaston), allowed to make the choice as long as it was a country inn, always chose one where, on the premises, there was a large glass tank in which swam the several live, wriggly eels which his own palate called for. Ours did not, but other seafoods would be available. I would have been much better off, on a certain day, however, had I chosen an eel for my lunch and nothing else, for, while eating one of those very good, but also very hard, French rolls to go along with my chicken, I lost a filling. We were soon in a village, and Gaston found a dentist's office where I was expecting to find help. But the door was locked, and even in my rusty French, I could read the notice: "Will be back on Thursday." This was Monday. Tom suggested that I buy chewing-gum and keep a lob of it over the hollow. It worked so successfully that I held on to that remedy for the remaining ten days of our stay.

In that spirit of making do when we were on Captiva, instead of driving the thirty-five miles to town, Tom's workshop in the water tower, for any and all repair work – other than dental – came into its own. Everybody knew that Tom was a willing and zealous jack-of-all-trades, his services, of course, always free. Since our house was in the center of the compound and since Tom, when he wasn't on the water or tinkering with his boats, was usually to be found happily puttering in his workshop on the ground floor of the tower, by a drop-in morning visit there, the members of the compound could find out just what, for that day, would be going on at each house. You could find out if somebody had found it imperative to go to town. In a system of reciprocity, you could ask of him or her to have your own errands taken care of, for it was considered a great deprivation to have to leave the island for anything.

The exception to this was when some imaginative member of the female of the species would decide that it was time to go to Naples to have lunch in one of the swish places and to enjoy the elegance of the shops. As exciting as these excursions were, in that delightfully feminine way of which nothing else takes the place, when they came, they would make us more than ever content that we had chosen a simpler way of life.

Often these excursions would originate with Janet Lynch. And from the beginning to the end of our Captiva years, this couple, Bert and Janet Lynch of St. Louis, were our constant companions. Tom and Bert were deep-dyed boaters; they were never happier than when they were in one boat or the other, exploring channels, bayous, making trips to marinas, or, best of all, each in his own boat and perhaps a third man in his – a happy little flotilla – taking family and friends to an uninhabited island for a sand-picnic on the beach.

By the time we started going to Captiva, lights and water had come, but the water towers in the compound remained. These had always been painted white to match the cottages. With their four-sided roofs rising to a point, more than anything else in structure, they resembled Dutch windmills without the windmills. Scattered among the palms, the view of these from the waters of the bay made the area of the compound fantastically picturesque. In a way they suggested Bermuda, yet the tropical growth, especially the palms, could have been those of the South Pacific. It was a rare combination.

Some of the families of the compound converted the upper story of their towers to a small area for guests, and that was the disposition we made of ours, but only when Chuck Rogers, a young Pole, showed up on our island wanting work. At that point, in need of a caretaker, we hired him and gave him the use of our tower. But that is a long story, one to be covered later, full of sorrow and strife for one who had been a drifter. Fortunately it has a happy ending.

The use of the water tower had evolved in this way: In earlier years, the water tank filled the second floor, then water was finally piped over from Pine Island. The tank was taken out, that relatively small area then usually used for storage, mainly for luggage. This was the use to which we put ours, except that we placed a rollaway up there, and installed a half bath, complete with shower, as Tom said, "Just in case." Tom's workshop and our bicycles were on the ground floor.

Usually our guests came for only a week, with the exception of the Murisons from Ireland, and Julia Black's daughter, Mary, and her husband, Bookie, who stayed longer on account of Bookie's terminal illness.

Knowing that Bookie's health was giving way, in our invitation, we urged them to come for a long stay. This once strong, husky man, who all his life had loved sailing, was now reduced to sitting on the dock at our boatslip in conversation with Tom, as Tom worked on one of his boats. It was a new friendship, but a meaningful one, especially since Bookie would soon die. It was in that sweetness in Tom's nature, that he could make Bookie feel that he was still a man. As I've written in so many ways in this story, Tom had that sixth sense of knowing exactly how to help people.

Often, when we couldn't go to Captiva ourselves, we offered our house, or the guesthouse to other friends or to relatives. In one of those instances, Mary and Frank Lowe, from our hometown, went down for three weeks. The story of Mary's illness and death is one so beautiful that is should be told.

Mary had grown up in the way of an average small-town southern girl: a happy girlhood, followed by college, marriage, and family. She had always had a turn for writing, and being a mother and homemaker at heart, as she stayed at home to be there for her children, she began to write articles for church magazines. For awhile, she acted as society editor of our local paper. But when the youngest of her sons was, perhaps, eight or nine, she developed cancer.

Treatment was sought in a number of places, including Duke. All to no avail. Then Mary, who was Roman Catholic, began to long to go to the shrine of healing at Lourdes, so that for three years, she and Frank went, annually, to France in search of her being restored. Nothing could be done, but by the last visit, Mary had become a different person. She had gained inner peace and strength. This made her want to share what she had found, and she wrote what was accepted and published after her death in the *Reader's Digest*, an article called, "The Miracle at Lourdes." She knew that it would be published.

Mary describes her first days at Lourdes giving full credit for thinking of going there and going with her, to what she speaks of as "my good Episcopalian husband." Toward the end of the article, she says:

> In the blue twilight, I've walked a short distance to the bank of the Gave de Pau. As my gaze drifted over the water, I felt a light touch on my arm. It was the young Irish girl I'd seen earlier at the baths, a young woman who was there for treatment.
>
> "Please forgive me for intruding," she said, "but I had to come." She hesitated, and then the words tumbled out: "The look on your face back at the Grotto – would you tell me, did you have a miracle?"
>
> My first impulse was to say, "No," but something held me back. A still, small voice seemed to ask, "Didn't you?"
>
> And then I knew. I *had* had a miracle. No healing of the body, no cure for my disease; but, far more important, a healing of doubts and fears. I wasn't afraid anymore. I knew God's love would sustain me, would give me the quiet strength to face whatever the morrow held – pain, or even death.

There was one more thing that Mary wanted to do. She had heard of Captiva, and wanted to go there for its natural beauty and tranquility. As soon as we were aware of this, Tom and I went to see Mary and Frank, and urged them to take our house for as long as they wanted it. We couldn't be there at that time. They chose the guesthouse, and everyday, Frank would carry Mary in his arms to the beach where she would sit under a palm-thatched umbrella and against a quiet sea, would watch the sandpipers, listening, as she did, to the never changing high pitch of their whistling. I think I can guess what her thoughts might have been. That these outward and visible signs of the order of the universe were – as was her own life – but symbols of a larger design, a design that would later unfold. And, that, with the faith she'd been given at Lourdes, her heart would remain at peace.

The Lowes were able to stay for three weeks. When they had returned home, Mary would have only three more weeks of life. This was in November, and when Tom and I went down in January, there was the sadness of finding the medicine bottles that were the mute evidence of her suffering.

≈ ≈ ≈

During our first visit to Captiva, having quickly overcome my fear of going away from doctors, nurses, hospitals, and drugstores, by our second visit, a year later, in the simply built guest house of the Carrs, I began to come to terms with my lifelong fear of crawly things.

As anyone who's ever spent time in the tropics knows, there is a running battle with insects. With the average, or perhaps more than average, aversion to crawly things, it was hard for me to get used to having a pale green lizard flirt his tale and stick out his tongue as he ran around the edge of a room, as lizards sometimes do.

Still, I was not quite the kind to jump up on a chair at the sight of a mouse; when a lizard appeared, by trial and error, and what I considered commendable courage, I learned to prop open an outside door, one on the sunny side of the house, if possible, and by closing off all the other inside doors, and never taking my eyes off the lizard, I could, after a while, see him go back into the outer world.

Spiders were different. Although I had been told years before, when the boys were in early childhood, and Tommy's chronic malaria had sent us to Florida for the winter months, that there are such things as housekeeping spiders, I was not enlightened enough on the subject to know when a spider was that kind; nor could I recognize the red spider which can lurk in the toe of your shoe and cause you to have injections for three months, nor was I sure what a tarantula really looked like.

As for the lizard, my mind went back to my early travels, where in India and Ceylon and Java I had been told by other travellers, half jokingly, that unless my hotel room had a lizard clucking as he nestled in the chandelier, a sound I would be able to hear throughout the night, I must order one from downstairs to keep away the mosquitos. In no other way would I be able to sleep.

I never saw any such lizards in my own hotel room, but I had a sneaking feeling that they were lurking somewhere. With youth, however, and with someone else in the room as well, I was not too much concerned. Yet alone – Tom was back in Carolina – and shut up at night in my room on Captiva with a large spider who came and went from the pocket of a sliding door, and who would stand three feet from my bed in the same position for about an hour, I was not that indifferent. He was black and heavy-set, and about the size of a small teacup. How could he not be a tarantula?

The first time he appeared, I sat propped up on three pillows throughout the night. The light was on, and except for blinking now and then, my eyes did not close. By morning the spider had disappeared, and when I talked to Susan Carr about it after breakfast, she suggested that I think of it as a friend. But that was too much. And before the day had gone very far, I made a trip to the island store and came back with a can of insect spray. Friend or no, I had to have some sleep.

For several sleepless nights he continued to come out to take up his usual position. With the can of spray on my bed, almost without having to move a muscle, I could set up an instant attack. This became my nocturnal arrangement, and sure enough, for the next three nights, when he came for his visits, I was ready with my barrage. Each time, he would retreat into the pocket of the sliding door which separated the living room from the bedroom. The fourth night told the story. I think he either gave up or needed some sleep himself, and by that time, half dead myself for lack of it, I could say to myself with a measure of resignation, "What is to be, will be." And I slept.

In addition to lizards and spiders, in the tropics, enormous beetles are around. A shiny one of an inch-and-a-quarter, running across the floor, cannot be anybody's idea of delight; worse, still, if you're inclined to go barefooted. We were told that Captiva has no snakes, but one day a black one crawled out from under my car. In India, some years before, watching a snake charmer and his mongoose had not been for me. Standing in the group, I would, in the same way I did when I saw a snake on a movie screen

318

or on TV, close my eyes; otherwise, I would dream about snakes at night. On the bleached soil of the island, this snake looked very black, but he went on his way, and I was not frightened. I was now on rung two of learning to be an islander. Scorpions were something else. When we'd been going to Captiva for several years, one day, I went into the jungle to find a dried coconut shell. As I picked one up from where it had fallen on the ground, a two-and-a-half or three inch scorpion lay underneath, and he bit me. It hurt very badly, and I hurried to find Tom at the boat slip. Having been brought up in Eastern Carolina where scorpions are considered poisonous, we were terrified. No doctors, no drugstore – what to do? We immediately thought of Dr. Malone, retired from somewhere, possibly Michigan. He had a house on Captiva, and luckily, he was at home. He said that the swelling would go down, the pain would stop, and that Captiva scorpions are not poisonous.

To have had a country upbringing, and to have spent so much time in the woods, you wouldn't think I would have this aversion to things that crawl. Yet, without rhyme or reason, some people do. Even now, an octogenarian, I have no love for something as harmless as a cricket. To have one come out and sit and stare at me, frozen, is almost worse than when he's in motion, because I get the feeling that he is brooding over when and where to pounce, mainly in my direction. This can be a major disturbance to an otherwise peaceful evening. If a cricket wants to sing, let him find somebody else's hearth. I refuse to share mine with him. I don't bear these supposedly endearing little creatures ill will; I just don't want to dwell with them.

Luckily, I did not pass these quirks onto my children, who consider me, in this area – and probably if the truth were known, in other areas, as well – slightly demented. The only insect that ever seemed to bother Tom was the mosquito. One of them whining around his head in his bedroom at night was his undoing. His swift and sudden method of dealing with the situation was often amusing. The ceiling light would be popped on in half a second, which meant that the mosquito would soon have lighted on the ceiling, and all Tom would have to do would be to take his pillow and pitch it broad-side against the ceiling. No more mosquito. By the simple procedure of changing the pillowcase, sleep could be restored.

But seeing Tom go through this with such a grim face against such a tiny enemy always made me laugh, for he was the kind of man who could enjoy a rendezvous with a rattler on one of his walks through a large timber tract we owned. The description of a rattlesnake given by a tenant farmer of ours who was sometimes with him on these inspections of the timber pleased his fancy. For the countryman, Charlie Strickland, always spoke of rattlers as "sewing machine snakes." Of course, Charlie had arrived at his description of rattlers from the old peddle-type Singer sewing machine that did, indeed, make an intensely rapid clicking sound. Although Tom and I must have taken thousands of walks through woods in our other farms on Saturdays and Sundays, I have never yet seen a rattler. But Tom always walked in the woods with a walking stick in case, and always walked ahead of me, blazing the trail.

Nor did I ever see one in my earlier life when at girls' camp. Camp *As You Like It* in Little Switzerland, North Carolina, was owned and run by a bird-like spinster from Charleston, a Miss Ravenal, whom we were allowed to call "Bunny." We slept in floored tents with all the flaps up at night, and one morning, my two "tentmates" and I found that we had the company of some kind of snake. Naturally, we went crazy with fright, but it happened on a day when a group of a dozen campers were going for the first time with a counselor to the top of a mountain to sleep out, and in our joy and excitement, the snake was forgotten. The spot we chose was in a daisy field, and if you haven't slept in moonlight on the top of a mountain in a daisy field, you've missed one of life's most beautiful experiences.

At the other end of North Carolina, three-hundred-and-fifty miles east, in Eastern Carolina, we have the daisies, but we don't have the mountain-tops. In our flat country, in my time, girls did not sleep out, and somehow I missed knowing that there are such things as flying squirrels. I had known that bats sometimes get inside houses. We had had those to contend with occasionally during my childhood, and one had come into the home we built and moved into four years after we were married.

It was in a wooded area. Tom was out of town, and a friend of mine, Sara Thorpe, and her two children, were spending the night with me, and ours, when we discovered a bat upstairs in a bedroom. Terrified, we did what we'd always seen done: we tied our heads up in towels, opened all the windows in the room the bat was in, closed the doors, and peeped until we saw him go back out into the night.

A few years earlier, when we were expecting our first child, one night I went to bed early in the downstairs bedroom. It was before air-conditioning, so that all the windows over the house were open. Only the hall light was on; it shone dimly into my room, and I was awakened suddenly by the knowledge that some creature was flying back and forth over my bed. Tom was in his workshop that sat across the backyard adjacent to the garage, and I screamed. He came running, and by shutting himself up in the room – which I had hastily vacated – armed with a bath towel in which to catch the wiley, biting animal who could give you rabies, for it turned out to be a flying squirrel, was able to capture him and take him outside.

Thirty years later, in another run-in with a flying squirrel, I came to realize that I was not quite as squeamish as I had once been. Tom and I had had the first winter stay of our regular November winter stays of three weeks at Captiva. Hometown friends, the William Shaws, had spent the time with us, and now, two weeks before Christmas, the four of us had driven home in the Shaws' car. Plans for our return had been made to arrive in Carolina on a certain date, the one on which Tom was due in Fayetteville, North Carolina, a town ninety miles south of Rocky Mount, to attend a meeting of the North Carolina Gas Commission.

The two day drive had gone along without incident, except for one thing – William Shaw liked to drive, and bank president that he was, he ran a trip with precision. In such a long-time friendship, we didn't have to make polite conversation. William and Burt were in the front seat; Tom and I, in the back. It was almost like being in a limousine with a glass partition so far as communication was concerned, for it was that first of cars that had come out with built-in high neck supports. They, in themselves, gave a feeling of separation, and added to that, we had bought so many oranges on the way, that those boxes and the odds and ends that we travelled with when we went by car, almost made the car into two compartments.

Cruising along with the sun on my side, I became drowsy and went to sleep. Tom did, as well. Apparently, William, doing what he always did, suddenly announced, in a matter of fact tone, as we slept, "We'll stop here at Stuckey's for lunch." He had driven up to that building, and without ceremony, had parked, none of which was I aware. When I knew anything, I was in the car alone. Through the wide front window of the store, which the car faced, I could see what the other three passengers were doing. To my dismay, and a terribly deflated ego, what should they be doing, but standing up around one of those little stand-up tables, munching their sandwiches. I was locked in the car. Scoundrels! What on earth? Such treatment from my old, old friends, and my husband of forty years!

I set to work to get out, but the car doors were controlled by the lock in the front, by the driver's seat. I was too far away to reach that, and was separated from it by boxes of oranges, of seashells and pepper berries being taken home to use indoors – almost everything you could think of. By no stretch of the imagination could I reach that important little knob. All but insulted at not even having been missed, it did seem, to me, funny. A large fat lady with piled up blond hair was arranging oranges and grapefruit in the wide front window of the restaurant, and laughing my head off, I waved to her and pointed desperately toward the knob of the door to the car on my side, which, of course, confused the lady. Assuming that I was the village idiot, she waved back and kindly smiled, and this exchange went on, back and forth, for four or five minutes.

Finally, a maintenance man, trundling a wheelbarrow came along close enough to hear my beating on the glass, and I said, "Come *help* me!"

By shouting and pointing to my friends inside the restaurant, I was able to make him understand something of what the situation was. He hurried in, and Tom hurried out.

"What on earth did you-all think had happened to me?" I wanted to know. And I tried to be sharp, but was too tickled.

"We thought you were still in the rest room," Tom said matter-of-factly, and went on, "William is such a one for not wasting time, that I was hurrying to give our order. I knew you'd want a hamburger and a glass of iced tea. I didn't want to hold William up."

Everybody has his store of these kinds of funny little family incidents. I considered myself admirably mature, however, not to hold a grudge against the other three, not to sulk for the rest of the journey.

According to schedule, on the second day, we dropped Tom off in Fayetteville for his meeting, which was to begin that night. And so it was, that on a winter's night, ninety miles farther north, William stopped the car in our driveway in order to put me out. He brought all my things inside and then said, "Do you want me to go over all the house and look under all the beds?"

"Heavens, no, William," I declared. "You and Burt go on, and thank you for everything."

The first thing I did was to call my sister, who lived across the park, to tell her that I had arrived safely, and to ask about any news. As I sat in the den, with my feet propped up on an ottoman, comfortably talking, a flying squirrel jumped from the curtain pole over one window to that of another, and my heart leaped into my mouth. I didn't want to alarm Sister, to have her think that I was frightened to death, because hers was a nervous temperament. And I was pleasantly surprised that I could say, cheerfully, "Sister, I can't talk any longer. I'm starved to death, I'm going and boil myself an egg. I'll call you back." And then I flew out of the room and banged the door.

I could have left the squirrel in there all night, but I knew that he must have come down the chimney through an unclosed damper and would be sooty, and that I would have to have the ceiling painted and probably have chairs recovered if I left him there to fly about. There was nothing to do but figure something out. So putting on a shower cap, I scooted in and hurriedly opened wide a door that led outside onto the porch. I popped on the light on the porch and flew back through the room. And, by watching the lighted porch from a window of another downstairs room, I finally saw him hop out. After that, we put chicken wire over our chimneys, and had no more visits from what country people call "varmints."

≈ ≈ ≈

Among our first and deepest friendships at Captiva was the one with Sid and Kitty O'Donohue. This couple had been friends of Buffie's and Ernest's in their earlier years spent in the Diplomatic Corps. One of Sid's posts had been Rumania, and there, they had become close friends of King Carol. During our Captiva years, King Carol and "the woman he loved," Madam Lupesco, had been exiled and had gone to live in South America, but by correspondence and by telephone, the friendship between the King and the O'Donohues continued, and one of my pleasures was to have Kitty, at bridge, wear for me the enormous topaz ring which had been given her by the King whom she spoke of as "Carol."

Dropping by to see Kitty one morning, I found her hurrying off for the mainland to answer an SOS from "Carol." Lupesco, as she was called, was critically ill. She was in need of a certain antibiotic that could not be obtained in South America. Kitty was on her way to take care of the situation. So many things like that were always happening at Captiva that I began to feel that everything either began or ended, or went through that small island.

At that time there were still no telephones. Who would have thought that when telephones did come, ours would be the first on the island? Or that, this being so, the first phone call on the island would be one piped into our simple cottage, and that it would be from the White House? But so it was.

It was a morning when Tom and Luther Hodges and I had gone out early in the boat to fish. Martha, Luther's wife, was reading on the screened porch of the guesthouse. By nine o'clock, I was settled on the patio to do what I often did, culling the best of those from our yellow plastic bucket of shells which we had scooped up the day before when we went for our swims. The residue of the assortment would be poured about the foundation of our cottage in order to keep insects such as large, shiny beetles from straying inside, for, in its simple board and batten construction, some of the knotholes were not quite bugproof.

Protected from the sun by an enormous floppy straw hat, and wearing Bermuda shorts and an old short-sleeved shirt, a long, flowered kitchen apron tied around me, my hands were gritty with sand when our telephone gave its first startling ring. Since the patio led into the back door of the breezeway, and since we had had the phone installed on the breezeway, with the jalousies open, the ring came to me loudly, and imperiously. Needless to say, I ran into our breezeway to be told over the wire by a crisp feminine voice, "This is the *White House* calling!"

Feeling a few palpitations, but not as many as might have been expected, I answered back, airly, "Oh, you must want to get in touch with Secretary Hodges." For Luther had just been appointed Secretary of Commerce by the President.

"I do, indeed," the voice said.

I explained that the Secretary was out on the water for a day of fishing, and that, in case of emergency, I *could* reach him by going down the island two miles to Andy's dock and asking Andy, who knew the fishing waters, to go out in his putt-putt and find Tom and Luther. But with the assurance of knowing exactly where this Head of State was, and with knowing just how he could be reached, she seemed satisfied. With that I could go back to my bucket of shells.

≈ ≈ ≈

The first summer we had our house on Captiva, in spite of knowing that the heat and the insects would be a drawback, Tom and I couldn't stay away, and we went for two weeks in July. To be there at that season, in those days before the use of the insect repellent DDT, was almost a test of endurance. Certainly it was a test of love for the island, and ours never wavered. The island store and post office were still open. Other than that, it was as if there were no other life on the island, except that of its wildlife. We knew, by that time, however, that a very old couple, Allen and Larry Weeks, had spent most of their marriage in their secluded home on the island, and that they were still there; that although they were not quite anti-social, they purposely saw few people.

Allen, who had grown up on the coast of New England, was currently engaged in something to do with the Geodetic Survey, which, as I look it up for the first time, sounds intensely interesting and demanding. That this small, mild-mannered man was engaged in "the branch of applied mathematics that deals with the measurement of the shape and area of large tracts of country, the exact position of geographical points, and the curvature, shape, and dimensions of the earth" now seems impressive. But I rather suspect that the responsibility was not much of a tax on him, for I suppose there are degrees of involvement. In any event Allen did always seem to be vaguely busy.

"Larry," for Laura, had been born and brought up in the city of New York. She had been secretary to Harold Ross, when, in 1925, he created the *New Yorker*. Knowing that piqued my interest, for since the first year of my marriage, sixty-four years ago, my subscription to that magazine has never lapsed.

We knew of this island couple, but that was all. On that summer stay, however, one of those on which I had ridden my bicycle down the island to the post office, carrying my "swisher" in my basket, for to stand still for a moment at that season was to be peppered with those tiny mosquitos with strangely large, black wings, creatures which had to be swished off as rapidly as possible, for they tended to cling, Larry happened to have gone for her mail at the same time. Her short gray hair hung just below her wide flowered cloth hat, she was tanned to bronze, and her arms and legs, from her short flowered shift, were leathery. From earlier descriptions, I knew exactly who she was, and I said, "Good Morning."

She answered, "This heat must be very hard for you."

I wondered how she knew that much about *me*. I didn't know I was doing it, but she said later that I won her heart when I replied, as I swished mosquitos right and left, arms, legs and torso, "Oh, this isn't so bad if you come from Eastern Carolina."

Allen and Larry had a cabin boat that can best be described as spartan. It was painted pale gray, trimmed in black, had two folding chairs on the stern; its name, taken from those black-and-white birds that waded in the bay in front of their house, was the *Stilt*.

The afternoon of the day after Larry and I chanced to meet at the post office found Tom working on our inboard/outboard, the *Carolina*, which, at that time, sat grandly in the large yacht basin which our neighbor, Alice O'Brien, had kindly urged us to use, whether or not she happened to be there with her *Wanagan*, until we could build our own boatslip. She had made the same offer to her old friends, the Weeks, who had never had a boatslip for their boat, the *Stilt*, and when Allen came down the bay in the *Stilt*, as he often did on a summer afternoon, and slowly brought the craft into Al's basin alongside our own boat, in that friendliness among mariners, Tom hurried to catch the bow line from this stranger, and to help with the mooring.

The two men introduced themselves, and after exchanging a few pleasantries, Allen explained that he and Larry would like for us to come up the next afternoon for a drink. We were to come to know that a spontaneous gesture such as this, coming from the Weeks, was rare. They guarded their privacy with a vengeance, but Larry had loosened up enough to send me word that she was especially eager for me to see her royal poinciana tree in bloom.

And so, the next afternoon we went, by car. First, we entered the road that led into their lane, which, around curve after curve, led through their jungle. Finally we came into a clearing, and there sat their house. Without question, it was the smallest and the simplest year-round residence of sophisticated people that I've ever seen. Wooden, and with a screened porch, like the *Stilt*, it was painted gray inside and out; its floors were black. The windows were the casement kind, with large panes, and except in storms, were always open. The starkness of the little house was softened by bright yellow straight curtains of a coarse see-through material. Most of the time drawn back and far apart, they framed the wide expanse through which they could enjoy their poinciana. The other walls were lined with books, and as much as anything, books have their own warmth, so that the house did not seem austere. In that, the living room, were two easy chairs, a desk, a table, and a long window seat. There was a small bedroom, a bath, and a tiny kitchen. Yet these two individuals lived a life of perfect contentment, and they were unusually interesting. The glory of the whole set-up – the house and its large property – was their royal poinciana. The size and shape of a middle-sized oak, it was perfectly rounded, and in summer, through the hours of daylight when they were not watching the shore birds over the bay, Allen and Larry were on their terrace, in the other direction, drinking in the splendor of their magnificent tree as it blazed with flame-colored blooms.

Now and then, we had heard the Captivans who had been coming to the island longer than we had, laugh affectionately at the perennial expedition Allen and Larry made early in January when they left Captiva for three months on Cabbage Key, saying they must get away for the Captiva season, as though our island's simple way of life were that of Saratoga, Palm Beach, or Newport. Knowing that there would be more people on our island through January, February, and March, they felt threatened. On that even smaller one, which had once belonged to the writer, Mary Roberts Rinehart, the cottage they always rented was hardly more than a doll house. Their meals and those of the occupants of the other four or five smaller cottages were provided in the unpretentious home of the current owner of the key. With April the Weeks would return to Captiva.

From that summer afternoon when we had gravitated to each other, the Weeks and we were close friends. Knowing their habits, we felt free to drop in on them, summer or winter. We knew that they would always be glad to see us, and sometimes I would go alone to sit with Larry, in lazy conversation, as we enjoyed her poinciana and her several cats. So far as I know, except in emergencies, neither Allen nor Larry ever left the island after they found it. Not many people are so self-sufficient. To these two, our own lifestyle, Tom's and mine, must have seemed that of a pair of whirligigs. But we and they had found common ground.

≈ ≈ ≈

Fortunately, a few years after we discovered Captiva, through the massive spray of the powerful repellent DDT which had come into being, mosquitos came under control. But in the years before that, during our summer stays, we often joked about the way the mosquitos escorted us to the beach, and waited patiently for us as we swam, ready, after that, to escort us on the return trip to the house, or so it seemed.

Finally – although for fear of where it might lead, our island abhorred the idea of any kind of organization – something called the Captiva Civic Association was formed. Its first accomplishments were important ones: zoning, and mosquito control. A third was an all-out effort to stem the tide of the movement by the county commissioners of Lee County to replace ferries from the mainland to Sanibel with a four mile causeway and bridge. The two sister islands went together and hired lawyers to fight it, but the County foresaw a way to fill its coffers from a toll bridge, and we were doomed.

After several years, their dream – and our nightmare – became a reality. As often happens, however, it didn't take long for us to consider the bridge a blessing. We could reach a hospital at any hour of the twenty-four, we could meet plane schedules, and could go into the town of Fort Meyers for its very good seasonal theater. The winter residents, who stayed for six months and one day, as nearly all of them did since this gave them a tax benefit, could fill regular appointments to doctors and dentists. In many ways it made life easier. Naturally, it brought the tourists. Usually, however, on Captiva, with nothing for tourists to do or to buy, their visits would consist of only a drive up its five miles and back down the same road, where, once again, they would cross the short bridge that connected us with the island of Sanibel, and in forty minutes, they could be back in Fort Meyers.

The coming of the bridge made it easier for us to consider having telephones. Yet those two milestones, as important to us as they were to become, were not to be compared to the change for the better that mosquito control would bring, especially for Tom and me. For not a summer went by that we didn't go down for two stays of two weeks each.

327

With the coming of mosquito control, the Civic Association bought a truck. It was a truck we never saw, however, nor its driver, because the fogging went on at night. It seemed entirely incongruous to have drifted off to sleep in the silvery light of the moon, and the serenity of the pervasive quiescence, to be suddenly wakened at two or three in the morning by the awful racket of what must have been the world's oldest truck, first weaving its way in and out of the palms in the four-hundred-and-fifty foot span of ours to the sea, and then in the four-hundred-and-fifty foot span to the bay in the other direction. In five or six minutes, however, the noise would be gone, the fog would soon settle, and the night beauty would return. And with it, several more hours of sleep.

≈ ≈ ≈

While there were no lawns as such on the island, just to keep the jungle at bay required some care. For in the tropics, plants never seem to sleep. Help for this work was hard to come by. For our first years at Captiva we were lucky enough to have the help of Willy, an ebony-skinned, cheerful and willing worker, who divided his time among a handful of other winter residents. Willy lived in the smallest house I've ever seen, perhaps ten feet square. Wooden, and almost hidden by palms, sea grapes, buttonwoods, and gumbo-limbos, the house sat at the end of a path of white sand; it was painted red, but Willy had trimmed it with white. Orange-colored bougainvillea tumbled over its roof.

Whenever we wanted to find Willy, we would wait until late in the day when we knew he would be at home. Invariably, at that hour, he would be standing outside his house, his shirtless black skin in contrast to his trousers of some bright color, and giving himself a shave. For this purpose he had built a small shelf and had hung over it a small mirror. When he turned to greet us with his characteristic bright smile, his face covered with lather, it would create as picturesque a little scene as any I've ever come upon. I've wished many times since that I had tried to paint it, and always had planned to, but never did. As soon as we arrived, Tom would begin to tease Willy about getting ready to go courting, and Willy would be more than pleased, and smiling.

"I know what you're getting ready to do, Willy," Tom would say. "You're gettin' ready to go a'courtin', that's what you're going to do!"

But Willy would deny it. "Naw, suh. I ain't studdin' no coatin'." But his smile would turn into an all-out grin.

When Willy came to work, he always had in his bicycle basket two paper sacks. One held his lunch, the other, a Big Ben alarm clock.

Everybody was fond of Willy, and we were sorry when he decided to leave to live on the mainland. It was then that Al O'Brien kindly offered to share her own caretaker, Bud Petersen, with us.

≈ ≈ ≈

The name O'Brien on Captiva means many things. The observatory in the wildlife refuge bears the name "Alice O'Brien," for Alice O'Brien was a great benefactress. Her father had owned extensive timberlands, some of them in Florida, so that when the houses in the compound were being built – by people who were already friends – all of them at about the same time, they were built of Florida cypress, ours included, although at that time the house belonged to Dorothy Thompson. When Tom and I, through our decision to buy property, landed in the compound, although we knew the compound families, our closest friendships were not, at that time, among them. But we became a part of the compound family immediately. That first winter of having our house, when Tom was going back and forth to Carolina and leaving me there for three weeks at a time, Alice O'Brien felt responsible for me. She had not yet learned that southern women can stand on their own feet.

When the first storm came, Al was so sure that I would be frightened that she had Bud rig up a cowbell from my bedroom window to her maid's. According to the forecast, the wind rose, the storm raged, and the cowbell tinkled merrily all night. The next morning the cowbell came down and I said, "Don't worry about me at night, Al. I will tell Bud that every morning when he sees a blue sweater hanging on the doorknob outside, he's to know that I'm alive and well. Unless it's not there, there's no need for concern." Because Bud roamed the compound all day long with his tools in his little electric cart, that seemed to take care of the situation.

Bud, a Norwegian, had been captain on Al's yachts, the *Wanagans I, II,* and *III.* Now that Al no longer had her yachts, for she said she grew tired of entertaining all the time, she lived quietly with her two white maids. She continued to wear her yachting attire, white pants, and a navy blazer and yachting cap. Seemingly masculine, Al was very gentle. When she decided to give up her boating life, Bud became her caretaker, both in Marine on St. Croix in Minnesota in the summer, and at Captiva, where she spent the winter. Al gave Bud and his wife, Helen, a small house down the bay. There was to come an incident involving a chronic circulatory problem of Helen's in which I played a small part.

Once when Tom and I were on the island, when a flare-up from this condition came, following doctor's orders, Bud was struggling to keep warm moist towels on Helen's leg. Inquiring of Bud one morning as to how he was managing, he confessed to not knowing how to cope with wet dressings. If there was anything I had been brought up on, it was – because of my sister, Alice Bryan's, illness with osteomyelitis – the application of warm moist dressings. For at times the trained nurses, in today's language, "registered nurses," who were so much a part of our family's life, were out of place. In those days, for that particular affliction, poultices of hot flax seed in cheesecloth were in use. Thirty-five years later, in an entirely different situation, I was asking Bud if he'd like for me to go with him to see Helen and try and work something out which would make the compressing easier for him and for Helen. Bud readily accepted.

While large pieces of plastic were not available then, and we had no pieces of oilcloth, I showed Bud the simple procedure of using a raincoat to wrap the whole leg, encased as it was, in warm, wet, turkish towels. In that way the warmth would last for several hours. Bud and Helen were so grateful for my help, that every day until Helen's leg had recovered, I went down, at intervals, to change the hot towels. And I could soon feel that in my Captiva friends and neighbors there was dawning a new conception of the pampered southern woman.

I felt that I had climbed another rung of the ladder in their estimation, when later, at one point, in order to save Tom's having to leave the island for one day of his approaching stay of two weeks, I decided that I would surprise him by going to the marina and bringing back his boat, the *Carolina*, which had been in for minor repairs; it would save him from spending a whole day away from heaven. We had had a trailer hitch put on our ancient little Chevy, but when it was in use, Tom always drove the car. The maneuver of driving onto the small ferry with a boat attached, I faced with some apprehension, but that day, the weather was fine, and I set out.

The distance I would have to cover would be thirty-five miles, four of those over water. Going toward the marina with the trailer empty was not very difficult, except that it felt a little funny to be dragging something, especially around corners. Yet, by three in the afternoon, the car, the trailer, the boat and I, could leave the marina for the return trip. First, I had to get through the town of Fort Meyers, and if my Captiva friends had seen me there, they would have fallen in a faint. By coasting up to stoplights, and by maintaining a careful distance between myself and any vehicle that might lie ahead, constantly keeping my eyes on the rear-view mirror and my appendage, finally – slowed then to a snail's pace – I arrived at the ferry landing. I had a terrible feeling that once on the ferry, my car and its heavy boat might, at any moment, pitch into the water. As I sat waiting, watching the approach of the same small ferry that I had watched with such uneasiness on the day of our first visit to Captiva, I thought, with pride, how far I had come in the eradication of fear. Having conquered the one of going away into the unknown, away from a doctor, a nurse, and a hospital, this feeling was secondary. All the same, I had never quite trusted those chains on ferries, or those small blocks that are all that keep a car from plunging into the water. And this brings on another of my digressions; this one includes Mother.

When Williamsburg was beginning to be restored by the Rockefellers, being made beautiful and historically interesting, Mother, my sister, Vivian, and I decided to go and see for ourselves.

As I've mentioned already in writing of my girlhood, Mother thought the only car worth buying was a Franklin. For some reason, the salesman's talking point – that it had an air-cooled motor – had found its mark. Thereafter, we had nothing but Franklins, two at a time. They had less power than an old horse, but I assume that because Mother was conservative, she believed in buying what she considered the best, taking care of it, and using it the rest of your life, if necessary.

But Franklins had a snubbed nose, and on a highway, were easily recognized. I always had the feeling that people sailing by in a more high-powered car smiled a little, for they generally waved. But on that day, when we had started out for Williamsburg, where we would spend a day or two, roads were not as well-marked as they are today. There was little traffic, and we were lost several times. There were a number of ways to cross the James. We decided on the nearest. The dirt road led through the pines for a mile or so near Dinwiddie Courthouse, and at a very homemade-looking ferry landing sitting up on a few pilings, we sat, waiting.

After a quarter of an hour, another car drove up behind us. Seeing this, Mother sat for a few minutes in thought, and then to our embarrassment, got out and went to the window of the other car and speaking in her well-bred voice, said, "I beg your pardon, but may I ask a favor of you? When the ferry comes, do you mind getting on first?" And then went on to explain, companionably, "Because *our* car jumps."

Everybody laughed, and this accommodating man went first.

That day at Punta Rassa, with earnest concentration, I managed to get both my vehicles on the ferry. I got out of the car, and stood, as Tom often did, for the four mile crossing, facing the breeze and the spray. But I was showing off. What I was really doing was keeping my eye on the man who was taking care of the blocks and the chain. By the time I drove off the ferry at Sanibel, I was entirely self-confident, and could breeze along the remaining twelve miles to Captiva, even humming a little tune.

To get the full pleasure from the moment, I decided to stop at Elizabeth Beal's, a friend whose house sat near the short bridge over Blind Pass that connects Sanibel and Captiva. Elizabeth was from Buffalo. Her perennial winter houseguest was Marrieta Raymond, also from Buffalo. These two were much older than I. They had been kind to me from the beginning, and I suppose that, more than everybody else on the island, they felt that southern women were entirely helpless. When I blew the horn that day, they ran out, throwing up their hands, and ran back for the camera. In some of the pictures they took I posed outside the car, leaning nonchalantly against the fender; in others, I waved gaily from under the steering wheel.

While the arrangement with Bud as our caretaker on Captiva was, in part, the answer for us, with Bud's age a factor, there were times when we needed to have heavier work done. By riding in and out through the compound in his golf cart, Bud could manage to do the small things, but during the first few days of each of our stays, Tom would, himself, climb the ladder and chop off dead palm fronds; things that made me worry, and in that he was not used to that kind of exercise, made his arms and shoulders sore and stiff. Yet, that working-like-a-Trojan continued to be the pattern.

Then one day, he came up from the boatslip for lunch and said, "A young man wanting work rode his bicycle back to the bay this morning. He wanted work so badly that I've had him helping me. He knows nothing about boats; in fact, he's clumsy about everything, but he's very thin. I know he needs work. He has nothing except what he has on his back and in his duffle bag which he carries on his bicycle. What would you think of allowing him to stay in our tower? He seems educated. His mother and father are both Polish, but he was born in this country. He says he's ridden a bicycle all over Europe. At one time, he worked for an airline and was able to get some free trips that way. There's something about him that gets my sympathy."

And so Chuck, or Charles Rogers, came to live in our water tower. This arrangement was to go on for some years. For Tom had endless patience when it came to helping people, or to teaching them how to help themselves, and in no time, he became Chuck's idol. Throughout the eight years of our association, Chuck was to say to me many times with tears in his eyes, "Mr. 'P' is the first person in the world to make me feel a sense of worth." I, myself, came into the overflow of Chuck's affections.

Now and then we invited Chuck to join us for a sandwich on our patio at lunchtime. The first time he came without a shirt, just wearing his cut-offs. I was still inside, when through the window, I heard Tom say, "Chuck, Mrs. Pearsall is having lunch with us. You must go back and put on a shirt."

Chuck had many delightful European ways. He loved flowers with all his heart, and made the area around our water tower the loveliest of small gardens. He would even clean the house for us before our arrival. The beds would be beautifully made, the corners turned back for our convenience. There would be flowers in each room, the refrigerator stocked – all the things to make life easy for us, for he had the year-round use of our car. Chuck was musical, and after a while he bought an expensive accordion which he would play upstairs in the tower in the darkness of evening.

With this going on, Tom and I would be sitting reading on our breezeway. The music was very beautiful, but it made me sad. Tom didn't feel that way, or if he did, he didn't encourage my thinking of the lonely life that Chuck led, for as he said, "Chuck says he's happier than he's ever been in his life." Then he would add, "You can't make the *world* happy," a sentence not as callous as it sounds when I write it. Tom was only being practical.

But, and here comes the sad part, we did not know that Chuck was growing marijuana in our jungle. After a few years, however, his letters to us in Carolina were becoming fanciful. In one of them, he enclosed a clipping of a letter he had written to the newspaper in Fort Meyers, which, in good faith, the Fort Meyer's *News Press* printed. In that letter he explained what his dreams for Captiva were. He developed his thoughts into three beautiful paragraphs – that gradually the island would become a park: Park Pearsall. He said that he was working very hard toward that end.

Eventually, the sheriff found out about the marijuana, and Chuck landed in jail. This came right at the end of our Captiva years. He was released, and on our recommendation, was reinstated as keeper of our grounds, employed by the people who bought our property. This was done around the time of the onset of Tom's terminal illness. When I wrote to explain that sadness to Chuck, he began making a scrapbook, drawing and painting the tropical flowers that grew on Captiva, writing poems that were interspersed among the paintings. But I had to stop reading Chuck's letters aloud to Tom after he became terribly ill. It would have broken my heart, for they were full of tenderness. The sentence that killed me was at the very end of his last letter. It said, simply, "Good Sailing, Sir." For among so many other things, Tom had taught Chuck to sail.

Chuck and a partner now own a nursery and landscape business in the town of Fort Meyers. He's doing well in every way. One of the things he does between seasons is drive the cars of certain winter residents to their northern homes in order that they may fly. Usually, he travels on Interstate

95, which takes him through my town. When he does, he always phones me a few days ahead, in order that I be available for an hour of conversation. He brings me the island news. Sometimes he brings me one of his paintings, and for that hour I feel a deep sense of communion.

And here I have to stop and think, as I continually do, of Tom's philosophy, often expressed in this simple sentence, "Things have to evolve." For after so many years of trial-and-error, it was discovered that Chuck is manic-depressive. Having been put on lithium, by keeping up with the necessary checks on the condition of his blood which he undergoes at intervals in a hospital, life has smoothed out for him.

≈ ≈ ≈

A casual attitude toward merchandising had always been the Captiva way. An amusing tale comes from an earlier time than ours, when an enviably laid-back islander ran an approximation of a snack bar at the end of the pier in the dock house. From time to time, his meager supplies would be brought over by the mail boat.

One day, one of the winter residents, getting ready to go out in his boat for several hours of fishing, inquired of the storekeeper, as he sat in a canvas chair near the cash-register, as to the absence of a certain favorite candy bar, "You never seem to have Mounds anymore, John. Why is that?"

The answer that came back kept us chuckling down the years. "I decided not to stock them anymore," was the pleasantly matter-of-fact answer, "because they sell out as soon as they come in."

≈ ≈ ≈

"There goes the real Philadelphia," Cousin Lena was saying one morning as she and I were leaving the island store and a woman – apparently of some years – dressed in the clothes of winter, with a small grey winter hat, was walking toward the beach. The simple white wooden building of the store had a small announcement hanging from an inconspicuous wrought-iron arm on a wooden post standing near the entrance. The sign said, almost apologetically, in small black letters on a white board, "The Island Store of Groceries and Oddments." It was in this picturesque little store that meal and flour and grits often sat until they were buggy, while its interestingly eccentric owner, Parker Mills, read the classics – some of them plays – for at one time, Parker had been a successful New York director. Still, the other items, the canned goods and the straw hats and the writing materials, including ballpoints, helped to make life easy for us. And on the wall behind the cash register, on a tacked-up nondescript piece of paper on which the figures changed from day to day, the temperature of the surf was posted.

On our first visit to Captiva, when Buffie and Ernest had left the island to return to the sandhills of North Carolina for the rest of the winter, Cousin Lena took me under her wing. It was a nice wing to be under. She not only had been coming to Captiva for so long that she knew everything about it and knew everybody who came, but she now considered me her particular charge. This had come about in a number of ways. In her relationship with Buffie, I assume that on leaving, Buffie must have said, "Take care of Elizabeth." It was to be a happy connection for both of us.

At seventy-five, Cousin Lena was soon to give up her island property and its responsibilities to live down the bay in a wing of the commodious home of her friends, the Russell Karrs, who happened to be the owners of the guest house in which Tom and I had been placed for the latter part of our first stay at Captiva. A wing of the Karrs' house was made ready for Cousin Lena. There she was to live comfortably under the affectionate eye of the Karrs who were considerably younger. I was younger still.

At that time, however, Cousin Lena was still well enough to shepherd a flock of Midwestern home demonstration agents to a summer conference in Amsterdam. This gave her great joy, for she and Lady "Something-Or-Other" in England had long ago recognized the need among rural women for an organization of this kind, and had joined hands in getting the movement off the ground. The Amsterdam sortie over, back on the island, Cousin Lena took *me* on.

Strangely, when people make up their minds that you're "delicate," that old-time phrase that somehow, is always slightly amusing – so Victorian – and that you're helpless, as well, its easy to be associated, in their minds, with the vapors. That I am fair-skinned and slender seems consistently to create that image. At any rate, since Buffie had mentioned that I had been wrestling with something of a digestive disorder, the short, plump Cousin Lena got busy.

At that time, there was a simple eating place down the island near where Cousin Lena's house had been, and it was aptly named "Gulf View Inn," for with time and erosion the simple structure almost stood in the waves. Through the open windows, the sound of their slow splashing, their slow receding and their returning to splash again, combined with the evening sunset, made the hour of the evening meal incredibly beautiful. In that I knew that with a few more storms, the building would either have to be moved back, or that it would go out to sea, those late afternoon hours were made doubly beautiful.

To my embarrassment, Cousin Lena had taken it upon herself to discuss my bland diet with the owner of the inn and with the "chef," a glorified term for the cook in this small rustic place of a few tables. For Tom had insisted that I go there for the evening meal so that I wouldn't be lonely. With this chain of individuals interested in my well-being, I was receiving the care of a soft-boiled egg. But like a general who has given his orders and retreated, Cousin Lena would stay at home for her own evening meal of cereal and a glass of milk.

The lonely part for me came during the two mile drive down the shoreline back to the Karrs' guesthouse. In the dying sunset, especially if it were a cold night, I did have a momentary feeling of emptiness, but I fended it off. I had books to read and letters to write, the first one would always be, of course, to Tom. Following a habit that had begun with our marriage, whenever he and I were separated we wrote to each other every day. It was not until decades later, when I came upon boxes containing letters of Mother's and Father's that I realized that throughout their marriage, they had done the same.

I have saved a dozen or so of those letters; they tell me much about Mother and Father that I would never have known in any other way. Mother was twelve years younger than Father, and I can sense the protective feeling he had for her. As did Uncle Mark and Uncle Jim, Father always sent his little family, Mother and his three daughters – at that time I was not yet born – to escape the summer heat and humidity of Eastern Carolina, for at least a month, to Roaring Gap, a resort in the mountains of North Carolina. It's tender to find how much Mother and Father depended on each other for happiness. One of Mother's letters is both tender and amusing. For two days, none from Father had arrived, and Mother wrote to complain. Father's puzzled reply, when it came, was, "Alice, I don't understand, I write *everyday*." Her answer to that, a few days later, was, "But sometimes your letters are *short*."

Wherever he was on business, in Richmond, Baltimore, or New York, or when he was at the World Series with some of his male friends, Father never failed to end the day with a letter to Mother. The last line of the earlier ones was always, "Kiss Baby for me."

If Mother were the one absent, perhaps visiting her brother, our Uncle Charlie Bryan, and his family in Oxford, although the trip was only eighty miles, including a train connection in the town of Weldon, forty miles from where we lived, the trip required all day. In those times, a trip on the train was spoken of as a "trip on the cars," and in Father's letters, looking forward to his family's return, he would write to Mother, "I will meet you in Weldon by the cars," which meant that, by the end of that day, together they would all board "the cars" for the rest of the journey home.

After I had finished my nightly letter to Tom, I would read for a while, and then turn out my light – and except for my three-night ordeal with the spider – the nights would pass peacefully, and I would be up early for a pre-breakfast walk on the beach. With a morning and an afternoon swim and more beach walks – the day would fly.

Although I did not feel the need of friends, for I was finding that being alone can have its rewards, I was gradually getting to know people. Each one was interesting, each one seemed genuinely glad that Tom and I had come into their midst. I was not, at that point, aware of the expression used by Captivans concerning newcomers. In a quiet way, newcomers would soon be assessed by islanders as either "Captiva material" or not. In some mystical way, Tom and I apparently passed muster.

I was soon to learn further, as our roots plunged deeper and deeper into the sand, that the island has always had a built-in screening process. If you don't like its quiet way of life, you don't stay. As for us, who from the very first, thought that not to love the island would be impossible, we always worried that our own stays couldn't be longer.

But back to the "Real Philadelphian" Cousin Lena had spoken of. She was a figure quietly, even soberly dressed; a tall slender lady of dignity. On cold days she usually wore a very long gray coat and a dull gray turban. By speaking of her as "the real Philadelphia," Cousin Lena meant that she was an aristocrat. She lived in a simple house among the palms, near the equally simple one of Madam Alexahndra Tolstoy, and their natures could hardly have been more different. In this mixture of personalities, that the stolid, slow-walking figure – the "Real Philadelphian" – should have the spring-like name of May Peas, seemed, to my agricultural heart, entirely out of character. As unlikely as the fact that Madam Alexandra should be the daughter of one of the world's most renowned writers. Of such paradoxes is Captiva made. To us, the island would have been heavenly had it offered nothing but its natural beauty; to have all that, and to have as well, its interesting personalities, and the gradual but steady accumulation of enduring friendships was to have heaven twice over.

≈ ≈ ≈

Among the other types of Philadelphians who – year after year – returned to Captiva for the winter, there was Mary Mason. As a young woman, this Alabama native had gone to Philadelphia to study art. There she met and married a much sought after young Philadelphia lawyer, Will Mason.

Will died young; Mary continued with her painting, and whatever her staid in-laws may have thought of it, Mary bought and lived in a large old barn. Her ability as a painter was recognized. She was often on art juries; her free spirit never changed, even as a grandmother. When Tom and I began to go to Captiva, Mary had been coming for fourteen years. For all those years she had rented one of the tiny cottages that belonged to "Tween Waters Inn."

Mary had heavy and exceptionally long hair. This, she parted in the middle; it hung below her waist in two long braids. A devout churchwoman, every Sunday morning, she could be seen striding down the beach on her way to The Chapel By the Sea. She never wore anything but tennis shoes. Her churchgoing dress was a soft yellow, linen, button-down-the-front style. It had its matching yellow, close-fitting Dobbs hat with its small brim, a yellow feather tucked jauntily in its band. For fourteen years, this ensemble, reserved purely for church, hung in the curtained-off closet of her tiny cottage at the inn, and it hung there the year round, even when she was back in Philadelphia.

As nobody else, Mary could capture on canvas the yellowy-green of Captiva palms as they filter the sunlight. One winter, at her suggestion, ten of us on the island, all women, were being given the first of ten water-color lessons by a very old former art teacher from Vermont who had long wintered on the island. The class had been hurriedly formed in order that Daisy Pitcher – whom we called "Molly" for the Revolutionary character – might pay her bill at the inn, for it was to be her last winter on the island.

One day, as the class met under the palms at the home of one of its members, without my knowing it, Mary was sketching and painting me. Although she did not give it a title, "The Beginner" would have been appropriate, for as I sit at my easel, you can tell I am in deep earnest. To remind me of all these happy things that comprised our Captiva life, this painting now hangs in my living room in Carolina.

The Captiva lifestyle, surrounded by sunlight inside our house and out, among simple furnishings, soon began to be reflected in the interior of our home in Eastern Carolina. My family and my oldest and dearest friends almost had what we used to speak of as "nervous prostration" when they realized that, in my living room, I was having my green grass cloth, which had been put on by a celebrated decorator some years earlier, pulled off. That I was taking down the draperies in my living room and dining room, and going largely to scatter rugs was hard for them to understand.

Agitated phone call after phone call came in the hope of rescuing me from the grass-cloth-mistake before it was too late. My two sisters, who believed in hiring professionals for home decorating, with the emphasis always on quality, were in a frenzy, reminding me that grass cloth grows more beautiful with age, something I very well knew, but I knew as well, that it was absorbing light.

One terribly candid friend asked over the phone, "Do you know what you're doing, Elizabeth? Have you forgotten how expensive grass-cloth is?"

"No, Katherine," I answered. "I haven't forgotten. Wait until you see what I have in mind. Don't be nervous."

I overheard one of my sisters say to the other, "Elizabeth always was an extremist. She's so impulsive."

I pretended not to hear. The only endorsement I needed was Tom's, and I had that. I can see now, that this was a forerunner of the pervasive feeling about indoor light that exists today; nearly everybody now likes light and more light, and while I still find pleasure in dark, richly furnished rooms that belong to other people, I, myself, am happier living with light. At the moment, my home has become a combination of Captiva and Carolina, a few good old pieces giving it that sense of continuity which my nature calls for.

Although I did this about-face for purely personal reasons, it came as a surprise to me, a year ago, however, to have a friend, Skipper Parker, herself a grandmother, and currently program chairman of our local chapter of the Colonial Dames of America, ask if I would allow the members and their husbands to come for a cocktail hour to end our social season.

My response was, "Skipper, you can't be serious. With all those beautiful homes among younger members, to choose mine is ridiculous! It's true that my walls are reasonably fresh, but nothing matches. My books and my tiles and my bowls of fruit are everywhere, and I really don't want to start worrying about whether or not my lampshades are time-worn and need replacing and things like that."

"I don't care," said Skipper. "I want those younger women to see something like this, and I want it just the way it is. Promise me you won't change a thing."

"But why?" I wanted to know.

She had trouble giving her reasons. I had more understanding them, for they were flattering. And this from a person who had been born and brought up in, and still keeps her ties with beautiful Charleston.

In the rosiness of being chosen, however, my answer to Skipper was, "Yes."

≈ ≈ ≈

When Tom was no longer in politics, there were often pleasant little experiences that would come to us in Raleigh-Durham airport where we would be waiting for our flight, either to Captiva, or to Europe. Now and then, a younger man, recognizing Tom from newspaper pictures, would come over and introduce himself, and have nice things to say about the contributions Tom had made to the State. Always genial, and of course, duly appreciative, I knew that at the same time, Tom believed that Adlai Stevenson had hit the nail on the head when he said, "Flattery is all right if you don't inhale it."

On one of these occasions, the younger man said, smiling, knowing that we were going to Europe, "Mr. Pearsall, what's the State going to do with you not here to take care of it?"

And Tom replied in the same spirit of banter, "Oh, I think they'll manage." And then, quoting Kemp Battle's often used jolly expression, "They'll just have to bear it with fortitude," and soon boarded the plane.

As often happened, some of these young men had made trips down from Chapel Hill to Tom's office to interview him concerning the so-called "Pearsall Plan" for integration of schools. Recognizing those indefinable qualities that constitute sincere dedication to public service, they would say, "Mr. Pearsall, why don't you get back into public life?" That too, was something that Tom could turn off with a smile and a light touch. "No, John (or Joe, or Harry), I'm not running for anything now, but the Kingdom of God." And on that light note, the subject would close.

≈ ≈ ≈

For the first three years of our having our own home on Captiva, the Ross house, next door, continued to be rented by the season. The oldest daughter, Sissy, had died. Hie and Jay Ross had not yet retired, and as was their custom, they came down for the Christmas holiday. But Tom and I were always in Carolina at Christmas, so we did not, as yet, know them.

We did, however, get to know, very well, the people who had taken their house for the season, Joe and Marilyn Bowler from Briarcliff Manor, New York. At that time, Joe was illustrator for stories in *McCall's*, *Ladies Home Journal*, *Cosmopolitan*, *Redbook*, and *Woman's Home Companion*. The women in his illustrations were intriguingly beautiful, each one almost a portrait, and indeed, Joe was beginning to go into portrait painting. At that time, one of the rooms with a northern light at the Ross house had become his studio. Anne Lindbergh's book, *Dearly Beloved*, was about to appear in serial form in *McCall's*, and Joe Bowler was the illustrator she had chosen for that story's wedding scene.

The Art Editor of the magazine had suggested two illustrations for the story: one, a large close-up of a hand-clasp of the bride and the groom – nothing else, the other, an illustration of the wedding ceremony, painted at an oblique angle. One day Joe came over to tell us that he had already sketched in the bride and the groom and the minister, but that he needed two figures of more maturity to represent the parents of the bride. He also needed a triple window, for it was to be a home wedding. The result was that he asked if Tom and I would stand-in for those parental figures at an improvised "altar" in front of our triple windows. So that, the sketching done, day to day, in Joe's studio, we gradually came to life as the parents of the bride, and in proper wedding attire. Naturally, we felt covered with glory, and I could hardly wait to mail notes to my scattered friends, telling them to be sure to see the June issue of *McCall's*.

What a letdown to have a phone call from Joe in May, when we were back in Carolina, and he and Marilyn were back in Briarcliff, to be told that the *McCall's* Art Editor had decided that the story would be more effective with one simple illustration – the clasped hands. And so we lay, ungloriously, on the cutting room floor.

But Joe gave us the original. In that, we are very handsome. Tom, with his graying hair and fine profile, looks like a Roman senator. I have been given blonde hair; it's short, as was mine, and my tiny hat sets me off. My shoulders are made fetching, with a V-neck down the back in some soft, sheer, pastel material. The best thing about it – indeed, the only reality – is that it shows Tom's sturdy build and height in relation to mine, the more slender, and not so tall.

Joe and Marilyn had had a tragedy early in their marriage. When their two little girls were about four and six, they had all flown to Europe for Joe to study. On the flight back, Joe developed a terrific headache. By the time they reached LaGuardia airport where they would be met by an ambulance, paralysis had set in. It was polio. After months in the hospital, in which Joe was trying to regain the use of his right side – and he painted with his right hand – seeing Joe losing his spirit, Marilyn asked the doctor if she might take a course in therapy in order that Joe might be taken home and the therapy carried on there. That was done. In addition, every day she rolled his wheelchair into his studio, pulled out his paintings and showed them to him, one by one.

Gradually, the use of his right hand and arm returned; the full use of his left leg never would. He began to paint again, using the dark-haired Marilyn as his model. She is very beautiful, and the first Christmas that

Joe had regained enough strength and skill to recover his appealingly impressionistic style, Marilyn was the Madonna on their Christmas card. I never saw a Madonna more beautiful. Joe continues to have a decided limp and must wear a heavy, built-up shoe. He has given up illustration and has gone entirely to portraits. His portraits of children are enchanting, and his success has been astronomical. After their Captiva years, the Bowlers started going to Hilton Head, finally making it their residence. Now they live in the nearby town of Bluffton, Joe's studio, in the home.

Joe's limp kept him from playing tennis and golf, but he loved to row, and sometimes, on a windless night with a full moon over Captiva, Tom and I would go out with Joe and Marilyn in their boat. I have few memories more picturesque than those of our moving slowly and quietly in that silvery world where, now and then, Joe and Tom would rest their oars, and as we drifted in that dreamland, Marilyn, in her clear, now muted, lovely soprano, would sing. I love things written in minor keys, and on those nights, Marilyn would sing for me that most hauntingly beautiful of folk melodies, "Greensleeves."

Over the years, in driving north or south, the Bowlers always stayed overnight with us in Carolina, and once we visited them in Briarcliff Manor. They gave a party for us, and we were happy to meet their friends, the many who had supported them through the years of Joe's illness.

After the Bowlers stopped going to Captiva, the next occupants of the Ross house were Buffie and Ernest, and, as next-door-neighbors, the four of us had many happy times. The Ross house was always rented with the proviso that it be left vacant for their own Captiva Christmas holiday. But, since Tom and I were never there at that time, it would be several years before I met them. During that time, however, Tom had once gone to the island between Christmas and New Year's in order to have some work done on our boatslip. Because of complications at home, I didn't go until we went together at the end of January. When Tom returned to Carolina, having met Hie and Jay, he made the understatement of the century when he said to me, "You're going to like those women next door."

But several more years would pass before Hie and Jay's retirement, at which point, they would come into my own life.

After our friendship had begun, and had so quickly developed into intimacy, I would sometimes, in fancy, think of some hypothetical night in earlier years, when, leaving Washington on a southbound train for Florida for their brief Christmas stay, their train would have stopped for a few minutes at one or two in the morning at the brightly lighted platform of the railway station of a middle-sized town in Eastern Carolina. Raising the shade to look out, they might have seen, at the end of the platform, the words, "Rocky Mount." Sixteen blocks away, in a wooded suburban area, had we had the bedroom windows open, we might have heard that train blow as we did often at night in those days when everybody slept with fresh air. Looking back, it pleased my fancy, and still does, to think that, on that night, our lives almost touched. For it was all but incredible that the friendship between the four of us, when it came, should instantly have become so deep.

≈ ≈ ≈

With the Rosses having become our permanent winter neighbors, we never knew what illustrious individual might be coming for a stay with them. One of these was Katherine Cleary. On one of her visits, Katherine arrived straight from Japan, where, as the first woman to be an executive on the board of a world-wide business enterprise, she had attended a meeting of General Motors. Katherine might have been expected to be masculine, or coolly self-confident, even a little brittle. She was none of those things. She went into old clothes promptly and easily, she loved our sand-picnics, and to see her with a broom in her hand, sweeping the crumbs from the kitchen floor through the door to the outside, was to dispel any idea that she was not a homemaker.

In this combination of a career – well managed – but one to which the other side of her nature had not been sacrificed, there was much to be admired. True, since Katherine was not married, the complexities of her life were less than those of the woman who must do the juggling act of being supportive wife, mother of a growing family, and at the same time, be trying to follow a career of her own. A situation which, in some cases, fills a woman's life with a mixture of responsibilities that make for constant frustration and an overall sense of defeat. Yet, I'm glad that there is not, now – in the struggle for fairness to women – the stridence and abrasiveness that characterized those first early movements, and that, in some cases, widened the rift between the sexes. Whatever we do, as women, even though there are still some injustices, let us not forget that we are feminine, and that whether the involvement is with co-worker, friend, brother, or husband, let us remember that we and they are created for complementary relationships. For, to quote Hie, "Manners and friendliness oil the machinery for all of us."

There was, at a time, a perceptive French novelist, one of the most widely read of her time, and one of many female writers who knew that her work would not be considered for publication unless it were submitted under a masculine pen name. This Aurore Lucie Dupin became George Sand.

To the consternation and envy of her older friend, Flaubert, in spite of the exhausting combination of her roles as country housewife, mother, and homemaker, she managed a routine of sitting up half the night to write the thirty pages to which she had committed herself. From this remarkable woman, come these beautiful thoughts, here paraphrased: *In a world of brutality and harshness, it will always fall to women to offer the softening influence of pity, comfort, and abiding love. When this is no longer true, the world will be the loser.* This is something to write in our hearts.

≈ ≈ ≈

"Where are you going?" asked Tom, as he looked up from his workbench in the tower and through the open doorway where I stood in the brilliance of morning sunlight.

"Into the jungle to gather cathedral bells," I answered. For on the island, those lovely air plants grow everywhere. Brought into the house, in their pale-green and ruby loveliness, they live without water for weeks at a time.

"Well, would you take these scraps to the gulls for me? I stopped here to work on our bicycles and on the oars to the skiff, and it has taken me longer than I thought."

I took the paper bag of scraps, and knowing that the gulls would see me coming and begin to circle over the water, made my way back to the bay. Hie usually fed the gulls, but she was leaving that morning for New York for one of the meetings of the Fields Foundation. She was being driven over to the mainland and on to the airport by our mutual friend, Sarita Van Vleck, Gigi's step-daughter.

As Tom and Jay and I later stood by Sarita's car saying goodbye to Hie, I put a plastic sandwich bag filled with small shells into her hands. They were for Dr. Jean Luke, also a psychoanalyst, with whom Hie would be spending her stay in New York. Through Hie, Tom and I had come to know Jean. We had once had the pleasure, and the inspiration, of having dinner with her in her apartment. This remarkably happy woman, who, from poliomyelitis, had been in a wheelchair since the age of twelve, was living a busy, useful life. Had I not been drawn to Jean for any other reason, I would have felt an immediate attachment to her for an off-hand comment she made after dinner. Searching the top of her desk for something she very much wanted to show to us, a clipping of some kind, she said, "Life with a Mrs. Tiggy-Winkle can be difficult." Her eyes twinkled as she said it, and Beatrix Potter fan that I am, I immediately felt close to Jean. For under Beatrix Potter's deft hand, the hedgehog, Mrs. Tiggy-Winkle, tidiest of all the animals in the forest, has become a favorite of mine. Laundress to all the small animals, Mrs. Tiggy-Winkle takes pride in her work, as she speaks of herself as a "clear-starcher." The drawings of her in her little ruffled cap and apron as she dips tiny garments up and down in a teacup, and the drawing of her as she fills her small laundry basket with those in preparation for her deliveries around in the forest, never lose their charm for me.

Jean longed to visit Captiva, but always felt that the trip would be too much for her, and in her note to me, after that visit of Hie's when I sent her the shells, she gave me a charming thought to remember, "I have those lovely shells in a small bowl on my desk," she wrote. "They bring me a special kind of company."

≈ ≈ ≈

After Captiva had been in our life for some years, once, when we returned for one of our winter stays, we found that the house that had been Al O'Brien's and that had belonged to her nieces and nephews, was occupied by some of their friends from Minneapolis. This nice young couple, Bruce and Sarah – and their last name escapes me – were often with us; in our house, out on the boat, or in Tom's workshop in the tower, and we quickly became friends.

The morning Sarah and Bruce left to go back to their three young children, and to the hum of life that goes with growing families, and with careers, and with the complexities in general that go with these middle years in which – in spite of the joys and the excitement they bring – can be trying, Sarah and Bruce had come to say goodbye. They found me in the patio, writing; Tom was out in the boat. Dressed in their city clothes and hurrying, they seemed, already, no longer a part of the island.

"Do, please, say goodbye to Tom for us, won't you?" began Bruce.

And Sarah went on, "You know, Elizabeth, before we came to Captiva, we were beginning to wonder, 'Is this all there *is?*'. Our two weeks here with you and Tom and the other delightful people on this island have changed all that. It's been inspiring, and we hope that a year will never go by for us without a renewal of the Captiva experience."

≈ ≈ ≈

That morning, one of the things that Sarah said she envied me was my pleasure in books. "I find that I have neither the interest nor the time," she added.

"Don't worry. You'll have both later on," I answered. "But try to read something other than a newspaper, or a magazine everyday, and you will soon come to make the time for rounding out life this way. Don't worry about taste, that will come later. You have such an aesthetic nature, Sarah. I can recommend a lovely book of only a few pages to be ordered from The Metropolitan. The story is told in poetry, and its illustrations are beautiful. Read it, and see what you think."

"I'll certainly send for it," answered Sarah.

"We'll read it together," said Bruce.

The story takes place in the twelfth century in Japan. A young lady of high birth – so much so that she is accustomed to having cherries brought to her in a silver bowl – is suddenly abducted. For years her father sends out search parties, all to no avail. Finally she is discovered where she has been forced to live as the wife of the rough, tough, unwashed chief of the bandits, with whom, she has a son, now twelve years old. When her father's men finally arrive with a large ransom the chief is willing to bargain for her freedom, but only on the condition that she leave their son to grow up with him and to live with his nomadic tribe.

The night before she is to give her decision, to the music of the flute, the young mother sits all night singing her sad thoughts. And that is where the poem gets its title, "Eighteen Songs from the Nomad's Flute." We're not told how the story ends. At times, over the years, I've retold the story and have asked my listeners to figure out its ending for themselves. Inevitably, if they're women, they say, "She stayed with her son." The men are not so sure.

≈ ≈ ≈

I was late in discovering the writings of the Goncourts: the two brothers, who, I was to find, for forty years held their place as art and literary critics in their native France.

Not only did they depict the Parisian life of the period, but their travels over Europe furnished the material for their frequent essays and short stories. One of their stories tells of an incident in the life of the Russian writer, Ivan Turgenev, an incident that was to have far-reaching implications.

Born into a family of means and vast estates, Turgenev's father died young; the upbringing of the young boy and his brother was left to a tyrannical mother. The only thing good about this horrible woman was that she saw that her sons had a broad education, not only in Russia, but in Berlin.

Early in life, the young Ivan began to feel a sympathy for the plight of the serfs in his country. Yet, he felt no sense of injustice when, under the prevailing custom of the times, on visiting the family estates for hunting, he regularly availed himself of the favors of the wife of one of the vassals. This had been going on some time, when, one day, as he prepared to go back to the city, it occurred to Turgenev to ask this countrywoman, who had for so long had no choice but to submit to this indignity, if there were something in the city that he might bring to her on his next visit.

Her answer came swiftly, "Oh, Sir, there is! I should so much like to have a little of that fine soap with which the ladies of gentility wash their hands."

Startled into reality and humility, Turgenev fell to his knees and wept.

Searching out more about Turgenev and his life, I find that in his *A Sportman's Sketches* of 1852, along with his beautiful descriptions of country settings, he attacked the institution of serfdom, works which would later influence Alexander II to emancipate the serfs. With that emancipation, Turgenev was one of the first landlords to free his own. The sadness of that story has remained with me. I feel sympathy for both Turgenev and the peasant's wife. But the real beauty of the story, to me, is that two individuals, trapped by time and circumstance, each found a way to a triumph of the spirit.

≈ ≈ ≈

I suppose that the "funny papers" that came with the Sunday newspaper all through my early life, must have given me a taste for cartoons. For the antics of *Mutt and Jeff, Happy Hooligan,* and *The Katzenjammer Kids* kept me laughing from one Sunday to the next.

For many years I subscribed to the no-longer-published English magazine, *Punch,* enjoying equally its cartoons and the humorous articles. Certain paragraphs from some of those are with me still.

The pleasure of having copies of *Punch* arrive regularly from England, and the cartoons in the weekly *Saturday Evening Post* made the birth of the *New Yorker,* for me, another delight. And who would have thought that many years later, one of my closest friends on Captiva Island would turn out to be Larry Weeks, a woman who had early in the life of the magazine, been secretary to Harold Ross, founder of the *New Yorker?* It still amazes me that this so-called "tough" editor, who did not himself have the gift of writing, but knew good writing when he found it, had the wit to put across to his writers the sophistication he had set out to accomplish, by saying to them, "This magazine is not to be for the little woman in Dubuque." One of his writers who, in time, would become my favorite was E.B. White. So much so that I once offered him a plot for a children's book,

347

one to teach them, effortlessly, I thought, the identification, the songs, and the habits of birds. It was to be called *The Wedding of Benny and Jenny Wren*.

At the time when this marvelous aide to children's knowledge of birds presented itself to me, I was not only very busy, but I also wanted it to be done with the magic which E.B. White had brought to *Charlotte's Web* and *Stuart Little*. Mr. White answered my letter, which had offered him the plot, the characterizations, and the situations – all free – but his reply revealed that he had many plots of his own that he couldn't get around to, and wound up by admonishing me to, "Stop being lazy. Write that tale yourself."

I may do it yet.

≈ ≈ ≈

With the discovery of Captiva, we found that one of the things we enjoyed most, in summer or winter, was going far across the bay for clams. For these sorties, we always went in the *Carolina*, the inboard/outboard, and when we came to the clear shallow waters, Tom would gradually reduce our speed and let the motor idle. At that point, in order not to go aground, I would have to sit far up on the bow while Tom stood up behind the wheel, steering with one hand, as he had a passion for doing when we were on the water in that boat, for seeing the coloration of the water from that angle was an aid to gauging its depth. And my hundred-and-sixteen pounds on the bow seemed just right for lifting the stern and the propeller enough for us to move slowly and carefully through the long grasses.

In the shallows, it was beautiful to look down into those grasses, fascinating to watch the sea life as Tom, his left hand on the steering wheel, would use his right to dip the net for clams. By our second trip of this kind, I had bought a little book on clams. We could hardly believe the startling enlightenment that each clam has thirty-two blue eyes. Interestingly enough, they do. Each eye is the size of a pin head, a beautiful shade of sky blue. The eyes, as though they are a mouth, sit like a row of tiny blue teeth, that curving toward the back, follow the shape of its shell. And it always gave us a queer feeling to have a bucketful of those tiny accusing eyes staring up at us.

Nevertheless, we did enjoy the clams, and we enjoyed going out to get oysters as well. For that, we had to take our sharpest pruning shears, for the oysters were always clustered on a mangrove root, and it required cutting off the whole root and bringing the oysters home that way. After one of these excursions the whole compound would come, by grapevine invitation, to our tower for the feast. Tom had built a rough shelf on the outside of the tower for that purpose, and although I've never liked oysters, I enjoy seeing others enjoy them. As usual among oyster lovers, those busy at their consuming would count with some pride the number of those they'd already downed. Everybody seemed bent on reaching a peck. Meanwhile, Tom and Jimi Gray were busily opening shells.

My mind would run back to the days when every banquet worthy of the name, even in our unsophisticated Eastern Carolina, would begin with oysters on the half shell. Bluepoints, brought by train from Norfolk, formed the first course. Invariably, I seemed to sit next to the host, and as we talked brightly, I would keep my oyster fork busy, but not in the usual way. Round the plate it would go, concealing oyster by oyster under the lettuce or the ice, until all six were out of sight, my unobserving host assuming, that like everybody else, I was replete. But our oyster feasts on Captiva were a far cry from such formality. They were more like those open-air oyster roasts given at home by Father in our backyard. It would be on a cold night in midwinter when the all-male guests, Father's friends and relatives, would gather to consume the barrel of Blue Points that had been ordered from Norfolk. With Henry Slick and Robert, Father's driver, and two or three of our overseers from the farms to open the shells fast enough to keep the guests supplied, and with the barrel of beer that was always brought up from our cellar, there was little chance that such a hearty masculine nocturnal feast could fail.

Some of the Captiva winter residents went in for fishing. While Tom fished at times, it was not his favorite pursuit. He just liked being on the water. He had built a small shelf at the boatslip and had water piped there, so that at the water's edge he might dress his catch. The fish heads he would save for fertilizing the palms, and it was, indeed, nice to have him come in in the late afternoon with a trout or two, and in a burst of pride, cook them himself. His recipe: broil seven minutes on each side with mayonnaise. Serve with lemon wedges.

Among my Captiva memories associated with the catching of fish, there is one that brings on a tale. From time to time, we would visit Luther and Martha Hodges in their second home in the North Carolina mountains near Linville, or in Chapel Hill; they would visit us at Captiva. This went on with some regularity, but when the Hodges were on Captiva with us, Martha, who was not much of a camp-fire girl, only wanted to play bridge, so that, for one stay, Luther came alone.

This was only a few years before Martha would lose her life by suffocation in the fire which burned their home in Chapel Hill. Martha's bedroom was on the first floor. In the panic of getting outside, she became entangled in heavy draperies and perished. Luther, who had recently had a cataract operation, was sleeping in the room above. In those days, after the removal of cataracts, patients were supposed to be completely inactive. True, science had progressed from the stage when the patient would have to stay in bed and have the head made immobile by sandbags, yet a jar to the head was still considered dangerous. I suppose it made medical history when Luther jumped from that upstairs window, since it had no effect on the success of the operation, although he did suffer broken legs.

I knew what Luther liked for breakfast, and always had those things in the guest house when he arrived. On the first of these visits when he came alone, I explained to him the house rules: "Luther, your breakfast things are there in your quarters. We will have our lunch together, either on the water, or on the patio, and we'll go out for dinner."

His face fell. "Oh, my dear," he said, "Let's not go out for dinner. *I'll* catch the fish and *I'll* cook them. I always enjoy doing that."

"All right," I answered, making an effort to sound pleased, but, knowing men, I did not trust that. However, I could only agree to the plan. Luther was an attractive man, handsome, genial, witty, and we were to have many happy times that week. On one of the days, however, when he and Tom were far out from land, fishing from the inboard/outboard, in nautical language, they sheared a pin. This was a pretty poor predicament to be in. They could only hope that another boat would soon come by. Finally, one did. It was a crude little craft, but the putt-putt of its motor in the distance was heavenly to the two men. When the owner had come near enough to hear, Tom shouted, "Will you tow us to Captiva?"

"Nope," answered this seaworn-looking little man, his small boat sitting low in the water.

"Well, then will you tow us to Pine Island?" For they had assumed that that was where he was going.

"Yep," he answered.

And so, they hooked up their lines and started for Pine Island. But that was far from what Tom had wanted. It was true that he could have telephoned me from there – and by that time we had phones on Captiva – but it would have required a twenty-five mile drive for me over to get them, and twenty-five miles back. So, Tom kept thinking.

After a while, as they skimmed along over the water, Tom cupped his hands and shouted again, "Have you changed your mind about taking us to Captiva?"

"Nope," came back again.

Then from Tom, "Would twenty bucks do it?"

There was no answer. But the boat swerved, it made a full circle, and then headed straight in the direction of Captiva. The day ended happily.

Every afternoon of Luther's visit, however, wondering if he would bring in anything of a catch, I would be afraid to rely on it, which meant that from four o'clock on, I would be doing intensive cooking. Sometimes the catch of the day was only whitings, which were not considered edible, and my foresight would prove to have been prudent.

When the catch was good, however, I would have all the side dishes ready, as well as the salad and the dessert. I knew that Luther would soon emerge from the guesthouse, showered and rosy and handsome, his starched white shirt open at the neck, and his cuffs attractively turned back. I would put Tom's oyster-opening apron on him, and he would become a prima donna, floating about in the kitchen, adding glamour to his catch.

He had asked me the night before to get some cornmeal so that we could glorify this last catch with cornmeal muffins. That night I had the cornmeal, and as he called for other things, could produce the needed bowl, the sifter, and the right spoon for stirring. Then he said, in a commanding tone, "Now the baking powder!"

I had *never* had any baking powder in all my years on the island, and I was in a tizzy. Thinking fast, I said, "You do things with your fish, while I run to see if I can borrow some."

Hurriedly turning over in my mind all the houses in the compound wherein I might possibly find baking powder, it stood out that if *anybody* would have it, it would have to be Betty Gray, of Betty Crocker and her GM radio program fame. And I went leaping down the path through the jungle, back of the Ross's house to the Gray's.

Betty and Jim were having two couples in for drinks. They were sitting in the serenity of watching the sunset from their screened porch when I came bounding around the corner of the house to say, breathlessly, "Excuse me, Betty. Do you have any baking powder? There's a crisis at our house. Luther is in the midst of making cornmeal muffins and has to have some."

"I very much doubt that mine has any life in it, Elizabeth," Betty said in her clipped Minnesota accent, "but I do have an old can." And excusing herself from her guests, she rummaged in her kitchen cupboard and brought out a can so rusty that it could have been lying out in the rain. For even this creator of the mythical "Betty Crocker" of an earlier part of her life, now retired and on our carefree island, had gone the way of all flesh; to light housekeeping and limited cooking. I arrived back with the magic ingredient in the nick of time; the muffins were a success.

As usual for that week, however, Luther said to Tom as soon as dinner was over, "Tom, let's walk to the beach and look at the phosphorous."

And off they went. I felt like Little Orphan Annie. I had a mountain of used dishes; countertops were piled high with pots and pans. To make it worse, Tom had always been one of those thoughtful husbands who, after the last meal of the day, couldn't settle down with any comfort to reading until I was free of the kitchen. Now I felt abandoned. For always at the end of the evening meal on Captiva, where we had no dishwasher, Tom would suddenly say at some point, as he pushed back his chair, "Let's get up and knock out these dishes."

The statement was absolutely true, because he declared that with me in the dish pan, and him in charge of drying, it took too long. He preferred a reversal of the procedure. Not wanting to break his spirit, or have him give up his attitude of helpfulness, even knowing that it might mean handleless cups and chipped glasses, and forks that might, by the light of day, have to be gone over, I would obediently take up my post with the towel.

But naturally, there were times when Tom had to be a proper host, so that for the duration of Luther's stay, I had begun to feel a little put-upon. That last night of his visit, when the two men returned from communing with the stars, the three of us settled for conversation in the breezeway. Although aggrieved, I didn't let it show. What woman does?

After half-an-hour of this and that, Luther turned to my chair, and putting his hand on my arm, said, "Honey, you've been so sweet and kind, you've made this visit so wonderfully happy for me. I know that you and Tom are going to England in a few weeks. Is there anything I can do for you?"

The question took me by surprise. But as often happens, our best thoughts come to us quickly. "Oh, yes there is!" I answered. "I've always wanted to meet Lady Astor. I remember that you and she were both born in Danville. I was sorry we couldn't accept your invitation, and Martha's, to spend the weekend with you when Lady Astor was your guest at the mansion. Do you think I might be able to meet her?"

"Of course," Luther answered, "I'll see to that as soon as I get back." And in no time, things were set in motion.

I had long been intrigued by the fact that that young Virginia woman had had the spirit to go into politics in England, the perseverance to subject herself to the raucous kind of heckling – even sometimes the throwing of tomatoes – that goes with political life there, and to withstand it for twenty-five years. To my way of thinking, she was the most interesting woman in the England of her time. A newspaper clipping that I have saved through the years describes certain aspects of her character that I admired:

> [Lady Astor and her husband, Waldorf] were both exceptionally public-spirited, and were ready not only to donate funds but to work themselves really hard. But her most valuable work was to make it possible, often behind the scenes, for able and worthy people, welfare

workers and social reformers, to get a hearing and a chance to act. She was among the impresarios of the Welfare State.

As for her unique personality, Nancy frequently brought Queen Elizabeth I to my mind. She, too, had the heart and courage of a man, had a tongue like a whip, was unpredictable and wilful, yet had great funds of feeling, which often showed in almost childlike tenderness. They would both behave like men, with great shrewdness and determination, but, when it suited them, fall back on their femininity without scruple. They would rant or sob to get their way, and watch you out of the corner of an eye all the time. You never knew quite where you were with either of them, but they knew where they were with you.

Wealth and power, though she had them and used them, did not mean much to Nancy except in terms of people. She loved company, the more varied the better, and she could exchange compliments or insults on equal terms with dukes or dockers. She was larger than life. She had values, personal as well as social, and the fire and drive to project them. People like Nancy Astor, quite apart from their good works, are atmospheric. They make things hum. One does not see many people of her calibre in public life today, which is a pity.

We soon had a letter from Lady Astor's secretary inviting us for lunch at her apartment at Eaton Square in London, on the day after our arrival. There was to be one other guest, Lady Ogilvey, who had been Lady in Waiting to Queen Mary. I could not have imagined Lady Astor without her flattering turban, and that day, as usual, she wore it. Lady Ogilvey also wore a hat, as did I, for those were the days before women had discarded hats.

Lady Astor was as friendly and as folksy as could have been wished. Sherry was served, but Christian Scientist that she was, Lady Astor didn't have any. For lunch, the four of us were seated at a small table in the dining room where we were served by her faithful butler, whose name escapes me, but who could have easily have doubled for Mr. Henderson of the *Upstairs Downstairs* TV series. Lady Astor was eager to know what was going on in her beloved South, and when the chops were served said, genially, "Now, Mr. Pearsall, you're a large man. You need two chops. I'll admit, there's nothing in England quite as good as our fried chicken at home, but this will get you by."

By the time we left, Lady Astor had decided that she wanted to do something else for us. She wanted to have her driver take us to Clivedon, the Astor country estate. Excusing herself for a few minutes to telephone her daughter-in-law, wife of her son, William, she came back to say that she had arranged for us to have coffee with her daughter-in-law the next morning.

And so, on the following day, one beautiful with sunshine and warmth, we made the trip. Her daughter-in-law was a tall, attractive young Welsh woman, with abundant, shoulder-length red hair. Thoroughly cordial, she showed us the whole first floor of this beautiful home, pointing out the fact that the heavy, gilt, ornate woodwork in the dining room had been that of Madam Pompadour. I loved the "Englishness" of the entrance hall, which, to one side had highly polished hunting boots, ready and waiting. After that, we walked about the lawn to where the Astor baby sat in its pram with its nurse. Then she said, "I want you to see Bill's azalea garden. He's especially fond of it."

This took us on another long walk, which led past a swimming pool and its bathhouses to a pond, one encircled with the bloom of azaleas and of rhododendron. There seemed to be flowers everywhere, most of them in bloom. On the lawn near the house, where the baby was in its pram, we were served coffee, the whole of it a lovely, very natural, and homey experience.

≈ ≈ ≈

For Tom and me, these were indeed the years of travel. Sometimes we went alone, sometimes we went with the Hodges. Often, we travelled with Hie and Jay. But those travels with the Rosses will be gone into later.

When Luther had left the island after the stay that had led to our visit with Lady Astor, one afternoon Tom and I went for drinks with friends on Sanibel. As usual – a failing of ours –we arrived late. Tom could never resign himself to leaving the water at sunset, that most beautiful time of day. I had often suggested a compromise. "Why not accept invitations for cocktails only on weekends?" I asked.

"No," Tom would answer. "That would be to deprive you."

I knew he was not speaking of the cocktails, themselves, for one of the medical rules in my own life and the lives of others who had ulcers or minor digestive disorders, was no alcohol. That had been no great sacrifice for me. I had learned to say, "Just something soft, please." Tom, having always taken his athletics seriously, from boyhood on, had gone through life only occasionally enjoying wine, and that with meals, as I sometimes did. But wherever we were, our house always had alcohol for our friends. And we loved being with our friends in their homes for drinks.

That was the afternoon referred to earlier in this story, when Tom and I were introduced to the visitor who had found the drive down our own island tantalizing. She was tall and tanned, her short gray hair was well cut. When we were introduced as "the Pearsalls, Tom and Elizabeth, from

Captiva," the visitor exclaimed with real feeling, "Oh, it's very tantalizing driving down your island!" It came out that she had recently bought a house on Sanibel.

We knew what she meant by that comment about our island. It's everybody's reaction on their first visit to Captiva. But for occasional glimpses of houses, the impression is that the island is all jungle, and you think, *But where on earth are the people?* with the next thought, *And what on earth do they do?* For no homes are visible for perhaps two miles. And although the single road follows the shoreline, and you can hear the sea, it is not, at that point, visible. After perhaps a mile, a dozen or so houses, whose owners have cleared away their jungles, appear.

One of the most interesting of these houses was one of Spanish style and was occupied by Clara Gallagher, a widow, from the Midwest. She had lost her only child, a son, in the Korean War, and ever after that, her life was saddened. As time went on, one of the things Clara wanted most to do was to visit her son's grave in the Philippines. Arrangements were made, which meant that for that winter, she would not be in her home on the island. When she told Tom and me of her voyage, which was to be one around the world, we realized that the ship she was to take would be the one on which my first cousin, Mamie Braswell Battle, and her husband, Hyman, would be passengers, on the same trip for the entire voyage, so I asked Clara if she would like for me to put them together. She was glad to have this done, and I was to find that the companionship of my relatives meant a great deal to her, for Clara's husband was dead, she was travelling alone, and for visiting her son's grave, she had their support.

Soon after that, Clara's house was sold to Mattie and Betty Matthiessen, a couple from the Eastern shore of Maryland. The four of us became close friends. Often we went in their boat or ours for a part of the day to what was known as Treasure Island, a very small key with a few windswept trees, and nothing else but shells and water birds. We knew that the Matthiessen's son, Peter, was a great naturalist, one of promise. Incidentally, it has been interesting since those years to follow Peter's career, to be aware of the important books he's written, and this past year, to have had the pleasure of watching him in a documentary on TV.

The Matthiessens were one of the few families who lived formally on Captiva. They had a white couple who took care of them, their meals beautifully served, their parties, delightful. Mattie had been a well-known New York architect, his wit was a joy. Next door to them on the island was a simple house – simple in the way of the old Captiva – but these neighbors had decided to enhance their natural surroundings with a tiny, shallow, almost minute pond for two or three lily pads. This prized focal point of theirs even spouted a little water, and Mattie, overcome with grudging admiration, said one day jestingly, to a group of us, "We think we'll have to move. It's like living next to Versailles."

Betty was to die suddenly. It was a shock to the whole island, for she was a favorite. But happiness was again in store for Mattie. In the course of time, the attractive lady we'd met that afternoon on Sanibel and Mattie Matthiessen married. They came to live on the island which she had earlier found so tantalizing; in every way Captiva material, she became a part of the island.

≈ ≈ ≈

During the first half dozen years of our having our Captiva house, before Hie and Jay had retired, in addition to having Buffie and Ernest as neighbors next-door – since they had rented the house for the season – in succession, there were other couples with whom friendships would be equally lasting. These were the Bowlers, Joe and Marilyn, of Briarcliff Manor, New York, of whom I've already spoken. And then the Donnellys, Stan and Marne, of St. Paul, Minnesota: Stan's business, which in some way was involved with plastics, was in the twin city to St. Paul, Minneapolis. Later, Tom and I would accept invitations to visit all these friends and neighbors in their northern homes; they would come to us in Carolina. In Minneapolis, to my surprise, we were shown the tiny trickle of water, that, on its way south, gradually becomes the mighty Mississippi.

Al O'Brien died suddenly on her way to Captiva. At her death, her nieces and nephews became owners of her island property, and since the property adjoined ours on one side, this gave us a close friendship with the younger members of Al's family. It was they whom we visited in Minneapolis, for it is one of life's beneficences, that in friendship, age is not a factor. It had been flattering to have Stan and Marne insist that Tom and I fly out to St. Paul for their twentieth wedding anniversary and its celebration. We found the Donnellys in their permanent home, a large, lovely one on White Bear Lake, the same warm, happy, kind and witty family we'd so quickly come to love on the island.

Among the O'Brien clan was "Grand John," a marvelous character we had known on Captiva, as well. Grand John gave a lavish dinner in our honor. Xandra Kalman gave a small luncheon for us in her beautiful home, high on a bluff overlooking the city of St. Paul. Judy, one of the younger of the O'Briens drove us about the countryside, one of our destinations, Marine on St. Croix, where Al had had her home. There, it was my special delight to have pointed out to me the nearby hill on which several of Al's aunts had lived, a spot spoken of in her jolly Irishness, as "The Ant Hill." It was our impression that many people in the twin cities are of Irish extraction. Indeed, the O'Briens and the Donnellys are not far-removed from the Emerald Isle. Perhaps it was my own Irish ancestry – the Bryans, formerly the O'Briens – and Tom's Welsh "Hail-fellow, well met!" philosophy that made all of us congenial.

Stan and Marne did everything they could think of for our pleasure. Stan spent two days away from the office, driving Tom to see the process of Minnesota farming, and to attend an impressive Minnesota farm fair. As this went on, Marne and I were doing the "girl-things" with Marne's friends.

On top of all these pleasures, Tom and I went for lunch with Mike and Tillie Elliot, beloved neighbors of the compound at Captiva. Their attractive home stood at the edge of the campus of the University of Minnesota where a psychology building that was to be given Mike's name was under construction. Tillie prepared our meal, and as she did so, the two of us indulged in one of our old-time conversations. We had been simpatico from the word go, especially as to books. One day on Captiva, in idle conversation, I asked the question, "Tillie, why do you think we enjoy reading published letters so much?"

Tillie's answer was instant, as in her beautiful diction, she gave to our predilection for letters a quite honest appraisal of which I had not even thought. "Oh Elizabeth," she said, "It's such an *ell*-e-gant form of peeping."

With time, and a deep love for Captiva, the Donnellys wanted to buy property there, and build. But nothing was available, and they built on Boca Grande. This took them, as measured by water, fifteen miles north. Their going there for parts of the winter brought another pattern to us and their other Captiva friends: frequent exchanges of luncheon visits between the two islands.

As is true of our own island, Boca Grande is small. Its lifestyle, however, is much more sophisticated – more given to organization. Settled by the DuPonts in the days before automobiles and planes, it was not easily accessible. So that, in order to be able to go there for the tarpon fishing and the club life, the DuPonts built a causeway and a railroad. I remember that my father and my uncles used to go there by private car with their local friend, Mr. Newell, president of the Atlantic Coastline Railroad, and the picturesque tales they told of catching tarpon by moonlight.

There is a good golf course on Boca Grande, and a fine old inn, with the pleasant flavor of pillow shams and white wicker furniture, and quality service. There is, as well, a beautiful –if small – public library, where classical music is piped into the garden for afternoon concerts. Homes are impressive, and when Marne and Stan built theirs next to one of the DuPonts, it gave rise to constant joking among their Captiva friends, something the Donnellys could never hope to live down. Their own home is a reflection of their great store of common sense and their love of family life, and since Marne is a person of taste and style, it is a marvel of simplicity. This made no difference in the affectionate joshing from Captiva. And when it came Captiva's turn to invite the Donnellys over for lunch – perhaps a picnic – we would suggest that it might be a novelty for them to go "slumming."

We knew in our hearts, that no amount of luxury could ever replace, in theirs, the simple joy of things such as our Captiva Hoot'nannies, held on a warm night, either on the Donnelly's screened porch, or ours. For these sing-alongs, there would usually be their houseguests and ours, enough to make a goodly chorus, as, to the strumming of two guitars, we sang into the moonlight.

Some of those nights especially stand out in my memory. In one, our long time Carolina friends, the Shaws, Burt and William, of our hometown, and the Adamses, Bill and Waddy, of Greensboro were there. William Shaw, president of a chain of banks, was musical, and although he did not have his violin with him, he sang along and kept us on key. Bill Adams and Stan would strum their guitars, and to get the rest of us going in song, Bill, who was marvelously tall and very thin, wearing his gold-rimmed glasses, was as earnest in his performance as though he were earning his living that way, which was comical. That same Bill, the respected attorney and scholar of Greensboro, formerly of Sanford, who would, now and then, in daily conversation, paralyze us with the use of such words as "rapprochement" and other jawbreakers, would be chanting over and over, in deep seriousness, verse after verse: "On the sand, sifting sand, Marianne." It was so amusing that I could hardly add my own reedy contribution to the chorus when it was time for us all to come in.

Nor, I knew, would the Donnellys probably ever, on Boca Grande, indulge in the kind of camaraderie where Stan would announce, early one morning, to Tom or to me – whichever of us he saw first – that he would be favoring us at the evening meal with his culinary masterpiece: a batch of his hot popovers. It was accepted that at a certain hour, he would come dashing over, bearing his offering. I was expected to have the table set, the butter melted and in a proper receptacle on the table, Tom and I to be suitably arranged in our chairs there, our eyes alight with anticipation of the feast.

To see this entirely lovable man, the fine father that Stan is, the gentle, thoughtful, husband to Marne, who is handicapped with a limp, a man who is – withal – highly successful in business in the city of Minneapolis, has been a joy.

It was amusing to us that in making plans to go to and from St. Paul to Captiva by piloting his own airplane, he would announce to his family that any who were faint-hearted would not have to go. And nobody ever stayed.

Even now, twelve years since we've been together, the Donnellys and I keep in touch. They are dear in writing long letters, telling me the news of their children and their grandchildren. Like all our Captiva friends, they have asked me to visit them in Florida. But I know when a chapter is closed. Anything less than what Tom and I had there together would be warmed over. It would take away something forever beautiful.

One thing that always brought the Donnellys back to Captiva was what we spoke of, with tongue in cheek, as "The Regatta." The day began at our boat slip. For some days, Tom would have been building a low stage among our palms that grew near the water. Other than a well-preserved old porch rocker, the stage would hold no furnishings. That illustrious chair was known as the "Roosevelt Rocker," for it was in it that President "Teddy" had sat – between his fishing excursions – to take his ease. The day's exercises – that old time word, rarely heard used in this context now – would be entirely those related to fun.

Through the winter season, there was so much conversation among the small boaters as to who had, and who had not recently gone aground, that I decided that the worthiest of those seamen should have a trophy. For this mixture of small boats had come to be spoken of facetiously as the "Captiva Fleet." I found what seemed to be the perfect trophy: a comical little sea captain, exactly like Popeye.

For the award, Popeye would have to assume importance, so Tom mounted him for me on a small block, which he then stained. On a trip to the mainland, we took Popeye, and a jeweler added a small brass plate to be engraved later with the name of the boater who had that season, gone aground on sandbars the fewest number of times. To further the element of the comical, we needed a booby prize. For this, I went to the jungle and found an empty coconut husk which still had its fibrous hair, and with the help of Waddy Adams, my life-long friend who, along with her husband, Bill, was visiting us, the two of us made the husk and its hair into a wig to be awarded through acclamation, and worn throughout the Regatta. By shaping this scratchy, grotesque, coconut arrangement, and molding it, bent double with laughter, Waddy and I kept trying it on until we decided it was large enough for a man's head.

In a juxtaposition of the usual order, Bert Lynch, the most skilled of our seamen, for he had been in the Navy in the second World War and had spent more man hours on Captiva waters than all the others put together, and because he was jolly and good-natured, was awarded the booby prize. The trophy, Popeye, went to Lloyd Bowers from Chicago, who, though used to the deep waters of Lake Michigan, usually had a hard time making his peace with the shallows and the sandbars in the bay.

For these affairs, Tom was always dressed as Neptune. I made him a paper crown to which I had attached long sea-egg-sacks for curls. At the proper time, with his large conch shell, he blew the mermaids up from the deep (actually they appeared from our jungle) and from there, the script, which had come to life under my hand, went on from bad to worse. There was a mock trial as to the offenses of one or two boating-offenders. Neptune gave out their sentences, the crowd, sitting about near the stage in non descript folding chairs which they had brought, joined in to endorse each sentence with, "It is meet and right so to do." Those who wanted a brush with fame were invited to come up and sit in the Roosevelt Rocker.

After an hour or so of these chuckles, the flotilla would get under way for its picnic to Upper Captiva, that small uninhabited island that had come into being with the 1924 storm which had cut it off, making the inlet which, from then on, would be spoken of as "Red Fish Pass." There was no way that such a day, in its mixture of frolic and nonsense and love of our island could fail. I'm told now that in a different way, the day of the flotilla, a tradition which began under Al O'Brien, and that was recharged under Burt and Tom's enthusiasm for boats, and for being on the water, and for picnics, still survives.

≈ ≈ ≈

As for friendships between couples, our own most lasting Captiva friendship in that category was to be the one with the Lynches. Bert and Janet still go to their Captiva home. By letter and by telephone, they keep me posted on our mutual friends, and on island affairs. I know that Captiva now has a yacht club, a simple one, and that it has not basically changed the island. And that although a few condominiums have come, they have been built in accordance with zoning laws. Since there is no more vacant property, and since, what is already owned is in "firm hands," for the present, the flavor of this unique island is assured. Erosion, that world-wide imponderable, is now its major problem.

Among the colorful winter residents during our Captiva years was Mary Spalding, wife of the violinist, Albert Spalding, of the tennis racket family. By the time we knew her, Albert had died. Mary was like a bright, ageless, cheerful bird. Her simple house was made beautiful inside with large tropical plants; her dining room table, at which she entertained formally, had come from Florence, for Mary lived, becomingly, with the flavor of the Old World. After all, she and Albert had crossed the Atlantic by ocean liner sixty-four times. But at heart, she was simple. It was she who gave me the answer to my cocktail dilemma: what to ask for when for medical reasons, you do not get along well with alcohol. I was already in the habit of watering my wine, a habit, I might add, to which Montaigne, Thomas Jefferson, and the Pope, to name a few, have all confessed.

"Just ask for Quinine water," she said. "It will make your host happier than if you ask for ice water, or a coca cola, or ginger ale. The twist of lemon or lime will please his eye, and soothe his worries as to your having a good time. Besides, it's entirely refreshing." As indeed, it is, and has my firm endorsement.

Mary's description of Captiva was equally succinct: "A wild, semi-tropical island, inhabited by civilized people." I can think of no more apt description.

≈ ≈ ≈

At Captiva, since everybody had come to the island for reasons that had nothing to do with money, the amount of your own worldly goods was of no consequence; therefore, there was no display. In fact, it was just the opposite. If you had more than two pennies in the bank, it was something carefully hidden. Looking back on it now, I smile, affectionately, at this amusing little game we played. One incident, in particular, comes to mind. Since, at that time, the Lynches and we were a few years younger than the average Captivans, and now that Al O'Brien had sold her yacht, in a much diminished way, we were the island's four most active boaters. And we had a fine, firm, and jolly friendship. That they came from St. Louis, a city, at that time, of four-hundred thousand and our town was only about forty thousand seemed to add to the friendship.

The Lynches owned a box factory, which they carefully played down as making the smallest of boxes for the smallest of pills. They came and went from Captiva in a small aircraft which they said was put together with scotch-tape and picture wire. Nevertheless, that private mode of air travel singled them out for teasing.

The joking had gone on for a long time, especially between Tom and Bert, at Bert's expense, when, one season, the tables were briefly turned. Earlier, at home in Carolina, as the day for starting out on our usual complicated two-day trek of getting to Captiva by train drew near, my nephew, Bob Gorham, called to say that he was sending his Lear jet down to Florida on the scheduled day of our departure and insisted that we make use of it. It was true that Bob had sent Vivian and me to New York a time or two that way, but Tom and I had never reached the island with any such ease. And we were delighted.

With the windfall of this magic carpet, however, it occurred to us that here was a wonderful opportunity to take along a person to help with reclaiming our grounds from the rampant growth of summer. We had an office factotum, a general handyman between home and the office, who could work with Tom and Willie, the island's rotating yardman, as they did the heavy pruning and the hacking off of the lower palm fronds. That part of the work required a ladder and was a job that always fell to Tom because heights gave Willie "a swimmin' in the head."

That morning, with our usual assortment of nondescript luggage, and our customary mammoth picnic basket filled with one pound paper bags of parched peanuts, we were driven out to our local airport. James Sherrod was pleased to have his first trip to Florida, and in such style. As planned, he joined us at our local airport at nine o'clock on the morning of the important day. When he was driven up, however, we had to laugh, for, as to attire, Tom and I might have been setting out for one of the island's sand-picnics, while James had gone all out. He had on his Sunday clothes, a well-cut business suit, his felt hat sat at the proper angle, and he was wearing his dark glasses. Under his arm was a folded copy of the *Wall Street Journal*.

The overall plan was to turn out very well. James enjoyed the sunshine and the warmth, and Tom's companionship as they worked together on the growth and did various things to the boats. After two days at intensive labor, however, Tom suggested that they "knock off," and taking their lunch, go out in the inboard, possibly to do some fishing. But the prospect of being in a boat *on the water* was unsettling for James, for he said he didn't know how to swim. No amount of reassurance could reduce his fear, and Tom didn't insist.

In a week's time, according to plan, we sent James back to Carolina by bus. Two weeks later, when Tom and I had returned by train, James was to provide us another laugh. Our two housekeepers, Laura and Nannie, were interested in knowing, from us, how James had gotten along in Florida. In telling them, Tom made an amusing little story of James's refusal to get in the boat and gave his reason. When the tale ended, Laura then broke us up with one of the most sensible comments we'd ever heard: "Well, that's funny," she said, "he can't fly neither, can he?"

But the irony of our trip down by Lear jet was, that the day we were set down at the Fort Meyers airport, Bert and Janet had just flown back from Key West, where they had gone for lunch, which we sometimes did with them. And here we were, all on the same runway. Tom and I were guilty of treason; we, they said, had arrived like Barbara Hutton. Bert would not have taken a million dollars for the eyewitness opportunity to razz us, especially Tom, and to hurry back to the island with the tale.

≈ ≈ ≈

But travel for us was not always so pleasant. Indeed, one night in midwinter, when the Florida tourist season was at its peak and we needed to get back to Carolina on short notice, there being no other available transportation other than by bus, we had a unique ride for a part of the way on something called "The Gladiola Special."

It was a little journey I would not have missed. For around midnight, we boarded the caboose of this merry little train of two baggage cars filled with gladiolus which had been picked that day and were on their way to northern florists. Although we didn't see any of these, we felt the sense of urgency involved, and it was mildly exciting.

The flagman was so pleased to have passengers that he outdid himself with hospitality. He brought out snowy "pullman towels" for headrests, and offered us soft drinks and iced tea. Although at best the lights were dim, as we slowed for crossroads – of which there were many –each requiring repeated long blows of warning, the lights all but went out and had to build up again, and the train rattled and creaked, the three of us managed to make companionable conversation. After, perhaps, thirty minutes on this friendly chariot, it stopped in the middle of nowhere to put us off at a tiny railway shelter that consisted of a park bench and a bit of roof with a single light. Surrounded by darkness, we could have been the only two human beings in the world, with only the night insects for company.

With no luggage to speak of, we were prepared, when the moment should come, for sprinting to whichever car of the long line of the twenty-four that we knew to be the usual number of those speedy East and West Coast Florida specials should open for us. But the train never seemed to come. Finally, however, there was the faraway approach of a headlight, and although we were aware of the impressive speed of those trains, even then, this one seemed to crawl. Then, suddenly, out of the silence, with a hissing roar, it lunged halfway its length past us and with precision, stopped only the length of a car and a half away. By the time the porter and his block were down, we were in place for the leap up the steps, and in the wink of an eye, the train began to move.

Variety in modes of travel was becoming, for us, a way of life.

≈ ≈ ≈

It must have been in the sixties that I began to read the writings of Virginia Woolf. That interest led me to read Lytton Strachey, another of the so-called "Bloomsbury Group," for Mr. Strachey is said to have revolutionized biography with the informal style of his *Eminent Victorians*. A generation later, Leon Edel's book, *House of Lions* gave us an insight into the unorthodox lives of that fascinating group of Britons who chose to live together in a large house in London. In every way they flouted convention, but their respective talents flowered. Sadly, the life of Virginia Woolf, who was to become the Bloomsbury Group's most illustrious member, ended tragically in a pre-meditated suicidal-drowning in a lake near her home, where, after her marriage to the writer, Leonard Woolf, she spent her most productive years.

As subject to depression as Virginia was, however, the women she wrote about seemed, to me, to be by nature light-hearted. They are full of charm, and as I read them, I was drawn to each. In a self-characterization, one of these, a Mrs. Dalloway, in a novel of that name, expresses a philosophy that I feel might apply to most of us as we grow older, and, we hope, wiser. Walking down Bond Street in London, waiting at stoplights, and crossing streets, Mrs. Dalloway reflects that she "would not now say of anyone that he or she was this or that. She would not now say of *herself* that she was this or that."

She then adds a thought that could easily be my own about myself, "How she had got this far on the few twigs of her knowledge she could not know."

≈ ≈ ≈

The history of Captiva had never been recorded until 1984, several years after Tom and I had disposed of our property there, when an informal history of the island was published by the Captiva Civic Association. Its title is *Voices from the Past (True Tales of Old Captiva)*, which is truly a book of essences. Nineteen individuals were interviewed for the book, their contributions to the story of the island preserved by tape recorder. Two Captiva friends sent me copies. Reading from these voices brought to mind what Tillie had once said in one of our philosophical conversations as we took a long walk on the beach, "Yes, there is an essence here."

Thoroughly folksy, the book's casual style holds much of the island's charm. From one person to another the story is passed along, a story of the gradual narrowing of the island by as much as a hundred and sixty feet, the result of storms and tidal waves, the story is told of how salt water ruined a large grove of grapefruit and limes and drove those owners to the mainland; of fishermen's camps, and of how the small cemetery came into being when a perfectly well little girl, walking over a part of the island one day, said to her mother, "It's so beautiful right here. When I die, this is where I want to be buried." In a few years, that would happen; it was the beginning of the cemetery.

With time, the story goes, the Methodist Church, feeling that the homesteaders on Captiva needed a place to worship, built a small chapel, which is still being used. Later on, the chapel was closed. It sat empty for many years, until Susan Karr started a movement to get permission from the Methodist Church to have the islanders take over the church building, to make it interdenominational, requiring no support from the Methodists. With this accomplished, it became the "Chapel by the Sea."

Those interviewed for the oral history, spoke of "Ding Darling," the cartoonist, retired from his work with the *St. Louis Dispatch*, who came to own a large Captiva property. Ding was a born naturalist; he made a study of everything that grew on the island, and came up with the fact that no native tree there grows taller than fourteen feet. It was Ding Darling's extensive property, a jungle, and a large clearing on the bay side of the road that was, all of it, later bought by the Van Vlecks. For their guests, they used what was spoken of as the "Fish House," a complete and attractively furnished small house that sat on pilings high above the water, and was reached by a five foot wide drawbridge, and had been Mr. Darling's studio.

Some of those individuals sharing their memories orally with the two winter residents who were doing the interviews for the book, spoke of the time when the Lindberghs came regularly to the island. Nobody seemed to be quite sure how Lindbergh had discovered Captiva. It's assumed that, as a young man carrying the mail from St. Louis to Chicago, he shared the news of his find with the Bixby family in St. Louis, where, one of four outstanding businessmen, Harold Bixby would soon help to finance the young aviator's flight to Paris.

After Lindbergh and Anne Morrow Lindbergh were married, they came often to the island together. Anne's mother had been a classmate of Mrs. Ewing's at Smith, our island "Cousin Lena." Private by nature, the Lindberghs were made even more so by the tragedy which English speaking people over the civilized world shared as they waited for news from kidnappers of their little son of eighteen months. Beginning with the pictures of the ladder that leaned against the upper story window of their home in New Jersey, the newspapers followed, daily, the pleas of the distraught young parents for the return of their fair and curly-haired firstborn. All to no avail.

Anne Lindbergh became a model of heroism for other young women. Surely this sorrow helped to deepen her insight into the pathos of life. For I can think of no other woman of my time of which the news of publication of another one of her books is greeted by such a widely admiring public.

Speculation was that, while at Captiva, the Lindberghs sought no social life other than to see the Ewings informally from time to time. One of the island old timers, speaking of the years after Lindbergh became famous, said that when the Lindberghs came to the island, Mr. Lindbergh was so afraid that their stays might be spoiled by being recognized that he expressed his concern in advance to the Ewings, making it clear that he and Anne preferred not to mingle.

By grapevine the word made the rounds. At the end of their stay, Lindbergh asked his two island friends, the Ewings, "What on earth did you tell those people?" For whenever he or Anne met another person on the beach, the other one would not only fail to speak, but would quickly look away, would busy himself, or herself, with bending over, looking intently for shells. So much for Captiva manners. I doubt that anybody even peeped.

These collected reminiscences go on to tell of the school for young boys that, at one time, went on on the island in winter. Kent Curtis, the headmaster, and Alice O'Brien had met in Paris in the 1920s. They became friends, and in that way, Alice's interest in Captiva was aroused. Almost on sight, she bought a very large property for a home, and after that, every October, she came down the Mississippi in one of her three consecutively owned *Wanagans I, II,* or *III* to spend the winter, always bringing with her a party of eight. Her property, in the center of the island, was soon parcelled out to five other families to build their own homes there, in what would later always be spoken of as the "O'Brien Compound." From the beginning, Al would be the island's chief benefactress.

I could go on and on with these personalities, for in the epilogue of *True Tales,* it lists notables who, down the years, were to come. Bringing the story up to date, it says, "Amateur Captiva artists are too numerous to mention, but Captiva is home to Rauschenberg, who is at the top of his profession. All islanders are grateful to him, for buying up, in the name of preservation, many of the old properties, thereby rescuing them from the axes of the developers."

At the death of Allen and Larry Weeks, their property became that of Rauschenberg. It seems especially fitting, for what artist's eye could fail to respond to the bloom of Larry's royal poinciana tree? And this large property provides him with the seclusion which, no doubt, he needs for his work.

The book goes on to say, "Another well-known artist who has a home and haven here is Roy Lichtenstein," and continues, "but it is authors and writers who have felt the attraction of Captiva the most: Robert Frost, John Dos Passos, Anne Morrow Lindbergh, Rex Stout, Alexandra Tolstoy, Joe Brewer, and Allen Drury have all spent time here. However, it is to the permanent, long residents of Captiva, friends to us all, that we owe the most gratitude. There aren't too many of you left, but thank you all."

Knowing as I now do, all these steps in Captiva's history, and the names and stories of the people, there is still one person, who, in my mind stands out. In our years there, Tom's and mine, she was spoken of by one and all, as though we had all known her in person, as "Grandma Dickey," for she was a personality to engage and to hold the attention. All of us knew the debt we owed this Mrs. Julia Hoffman Dickey for the beauty of the casuarinas or Australian pines that grow on either side of the island's road, some of them now so near the beach, that from the sea they appear as a line of sentinels, holding fast against the onslaught of the waves that threaten the shoreline. Grandma Dickey's story was told me, at my request, by her granddaughter, Marie Dickey Kalman.

Everybody on the island loved Marie; she seems, somehow, to embody the spirit of her grandmother and the island. Marie and her childhood friend, Dottie Wakefield, whose mother for many years owned and ran Tween Waters Inn, as young girls, were always in their canoe exploring when they were not swimming, or gathering shells to be studied. They must have been a charming pair; Dottie, fair and blonde, Marie, the opposite. When we knew Dottie and Marie, they were both married and mothers. They brought their children to Captiva for their winters, and went back north for their summers. Dottie returned to Bristol, Virginia, where her mother spent the warm months, Marie, to Darien, Connecticut.

The Captiva community finally decided to take one small step in the direction of organized life by constructing a community house, a simple building, one end of which would house our library. The library that emerged was small, but well-stocked with current material. Since reading was an important part of island life, the library held many more volumes than you would have expected, for islanders were always buying them and giving them for the benefit of others. With this, the "book-boat" ceased to come on its weekly visits from Boca Grande.

Once the community house had been completed, we celebrated the opening with a semblance of a masquerade ball. Our "make-do" costumes were screamingly funny. Even Parker Mills, the owner of the store, left off reading *War and Peace* at the cash register long enough to deck himself out as a Greek youth, even to the laurel wreath on his graying hair. We could hardly believe the change in personality wrought by this role, for Parker was the life and the fun of the party until Marie came.

Nobody could compete with Marie, however. Once there, she stole the show from Parker, for she came as a Javanese Girl, her tall slimness draped in batik, her black hair wet and clinging to her shoulders. The Indonesian look became complete with the side-splitting affect of two of her front teeth blackened, seemingly with the use of the customary Javanese beetle-nut. No other woman I know would have had the courage and enough of the love of fun to make herself look so horrid. Marie smiled her awful smile right and left as she danced, all the while, engaged in animated conversation with her partner, and speaking to her friends between numbers she made such a ludicrous exhibition of herself that the rest of us were in stitches.

At some point in our years on the island, on one of our picnics, I expressed my interest in her grandmother. The things I had heard of Grandma Dickey seemed unique. I felt that if I should ever write anything about Captiva, she would often be in my subconscious mind. And so, one day I said, "Marie, sometime this summer, when you have time, would you be good enough to mail me a few facts about your grandmother?" She said she'd be glad to, and in June it was sent to me in Carolina. Marie wrote:

"Julia Hoffman Dickey was born in Milwaukee in 1865. Her father was a Lutheran minister, and she played the organ in his church at the age of nine. In her teens, she returned to Germany, which had been her father's birthplace, to study with VonBulow and progressed so well that VonBulow asked Franz Liszt to hear her play his "Hungarian Rhapsody." At the age of eighty, she was still indignant as she told that Liszt's first words were, 'I would never have believed that so tiny a girl could move so great a piano.' It took a while before she could be convinced that he wasn't being insulting.

"Her intention was to come back to the United States to teach. She had a job, but a cholera epidemic forced her ship to be quarantined for so long that it made her too late. So she did concerts, and because of that, was asked to teach at Virginia Intermont College in Bristol, Virginia. Dr. John R. Dickey was one of the founders of the school, and he married the new teacher."

Characteristically, at this point in her letter, Marie had drawn a round pumpkin of a face with a broad smile. The pumpkin-smile and the beetle-nut teeth go well together in characterization of Marie: the gift she has of seeing the lighter side of life. This Dr. John Dickey was one of two sons, one a doctor, one a pharmacist, from Bristol Virginia, who, in the early nineteen hundreds, went one year to fish on Sanibel Island. The next year, Dr. John, the pharmacist, lost his voice, and decided to take his family, his wife and three children, a cook and a yard man to spend the winter on Sanibel in the hope of recovering his voice, which turned out to be the case. They rented a house, but Sanibel is a wide island, and the house was not situated conveniently for the Doctor to do the fishing he loved to do on the bay, and at the same time, for his wife to collect the shells she loved, on the beach. To get to the bay, he would have to go in his horse and buggy.

"And so one day, having heard about Captiva, he went up by boat. He spent the whole day walking over the island. At that time, there were only five homesteaders there. By the end of the day, he knew what he wanted. He wanted to own a half mile of the island at its narrowest point. At that time the island was not nearly so narrow as it now is. He built far back from the beach. Since that time, a hundred-and-sixty feet have been lost to the Gulf.

"The next year he made the purchase. Before he left for the summer, he drew a plan for a simple two-story house, and left it with a carpenter to build, to be in readiness when he should bring his family down from Virginia in November, bringing a tutor with them. So that, in the fall of 1905, Grandma Dickey settled into her island home."

Equally as deeply embedded as her love of music was her love of all things beautiful. Finding that the beautiful casuarina trees had such shallow roots that pulling them up from the sand was easy, she decided that she would make the half-mile of road of the Dickey property more beautiful than it already was by planting on each side of it those fast-growing trees. The spread of their graceful branches would eventually arch over the island road. With their great height, which far exceeds fourteen feet – and nobody knows from where the first casuarinas on the island came – their long plumes make the road a lovely, feathery, green tunnel. Gradually, more trees were added until, by the 1930s, they lined the island's single road all the way from Blind Pass to Redfish Pass, and are now responsible for one aspect of the island's great beauty.

Dr. Dickey had had nine children by his first wife, so that in all, Grandma Dickey brought up a family of twelve. She brought her piano to the island, and somehow, kept up her music. Many years later, one of her neighbors told the story of how one afternoon she saw a "little old lady" chopping wood for the stove. Later, she heard a piano being played, and peeked in the window. The little old lady who had been chopping the wood was playing beautifully.

To return to Marie's letter, "My greatest memory of her is at sunset, when she was to play beautiful sounds in a beautiful place. One sad note: In the late years, one night the music stopped, and we went to see if she was all right. She was lying over the keyboard, crying. She said, 'My eyes don't work, and my fingers don't remember.' But believe me, she still kept busy!"

Marie's letter ended, "Hope this helps, and that it is what you asked for." It was, and indeed, it did.

Marie is not the only member of the Dickey clan who still goes back to Captiva. Her aunt, Dorothy Dickey, from Bristol, Virginia, who spent her honeymoon on the island, is still there for her winters – hale and hearty – making her own contribution to island life. For the relatively recently taped interviews which were to go into *True Tales of Old Captiva*, Dorothy's memories cover many interesting pages.

≈ ≈ ≈

In my own accumulation of island memories, I was to discover yet another source of island lore. It came at the home of Andy, the former dockmaster, who is now incapacitated. For some years, a heart condition had confined Andy to the house. Tom and I knew how hard this change in his way of life must have been for him, and Tom often dropped by to pass the time of day. At those times when we were planning a trip to the mainland, Tom would always ride his bicycle the mile down the road to Andy's house to find out if he had any needs in town. When Andy had given Tom his list, he would invariably say, at the last, "Be sure to bring me some girly magazines." Tom always did.

One afternoon I went with him to see Andy, and we found another old sailor there. These two graying men – Andy and his visitor – who had spent their lives on the sea, were busy with their memories. Andy's house was small; it sat under the palms not too far from that area on the bay where he had been dockmaster.

Andy's wife had been Dessa, an island character. Dessa did not care much for housekeeping. She preferred sitting inside the dock-building where the breezes blew through the windows and doors, talking to this and that boater in nautical language. She was very fat. She wore a low-cut sun-back dress, was always ready to philosophize, improving the time with beer. In the glow of the drink, she became quotable. The last thing Dessa happened to have said that made for good conversation would make its way up and down the island until replaced by another.

But Dessa died, and after Dessa's death, Andy managed to keep his house as best he could. The afternoon of my first visit to him at home, Tom

370

and I drew the two old sailors out, and it was when we were getting ready to leave that the visitor spoke in a way that made my heart sing. "Well, you know," he began, speaking to Tom and me, "in the early days, that area of the island where you live was a fishing camp. There was nothing else there, and that part of the island was so pretty under moonlight that the fishermen named their camp, 'Moonover'."

Oh, I thought, *the poetry of that name! How endearing that those rough men of the sea felt the night beauty to such an extent that they gave their camp so beautiful a name.* I knew in my heart, that although our area was always spoken of, up and down the island, as "The Compound," or "The O'Brien Compound," it would always be, to me, just "Moonover." And it always has been. Wherever he is, I wish that old man – and he's probably no longer alive – could know the pleasure he has given me in adding that to my life. And although it's unlikely that the old sailor and his fellow fisherman had ever heard those lovely, lilting lines of the essayist-poet Joseph Addison's, which so enchantingly depict the arrival of moonlight, had they known them, there would surely have been response to the charm of this:

Soon as the evening shades prevail
the moon takes up the wondrous tale
and nightly, to a listening earth
repeats the story of her birth
While the stars around her burn
and all the planets in their turn
affirm the tidings as they roll
and spread the truth from pole to pole

To recall Captiva in this and similar ways, to close my eyes and to imagine our days, our weeks, our months and our years there is to bring back a sense of Utopia.

≈ ≈ ≈

In my life now, almost always within reach, lies a certain book. To open it, is to find on its flyleaf, in my own handwriting, this notation:

This was Tom's favorite book, and mine. He kept it near his bed in North Carolina to transport him back to the island when he couldn't be there, for to both of us, the writing is as beautiful as its contents. To re-read this book now is to feel that we are, once again, reading it together. This notation is being written five years after Tom's death.

The book is Rachel Carson's *The Edge of the Sea.*

≈ ≈ ≈

With our discovery of Captiva, Miss Carson's sea books were rarely out of sight. For, not only did this dedicated marine biologist teach us much to look for on the shore, but she gave us an understanding of the beauty she found in her broad studies of the whole of marine life. Her writings have something of the fluidity of the sea itself; to read one of her paragraphs is to become deeply conscious of being, ourselves, a part of the natural order of things, to see that we are linked to every other form of life. An especially beautiful paragraph of hers reads this way:

> The shore is an ancient world, for as long as there has been an earth and sea there has been this place of the meeting of land and water. Yet it is a world that keeps alive the sense of continuing creation and of the relentless drive of life. Each time that I enter it, I gain some new awareness of its beauty and its deeper meanings, sensing that intricate fabric of life by which one creature is linked with another, and each with its surroundings.
> ...The shore at night is a different world, in which the very darkness that hides the distractions of daylight brings into sharper focus the elemental realities. Once, exploring the night beach, I surprised a small ghost crab in the searching beam of my torch. He was lying in a pit he had dug just above the surf, as though watching the sea and waiting. The blackness of the night possessed water, air and beach. It was the darkness of an older world, before Man. There was no sound but the all-enveloping primeval sounds of wind blowing over water and sand, and of waves crashing on the beach. The little crab alone with the sea became a symbol that stood for life itself – for the delicate, destructible, yet incredibly vital force that somehow holds it place amid the harsh realities of the inorganic world.

Many times Tom and I were to have similar experiences on the night beach, for perhaps the only thing more beautiful than the island as she lies under the brilliance of daylight is the island as she lies under moonlight. With the coming of the moon and the stars, she lies quiescent. Gone are the sounds of the day, when, from the edge of the bay, coming into the stillness and against the lovely soft coo of the dove, there would have been the nasal twang of the fish crow and the reverberating toneless cackle of the laughing gull, and from the beach, that constant, thin orchestration, the pipes and cheeps of the shorebirds. By the hour of dusk, there would be only two sounds: the papery rustle in the palms, and the long, slow swish of the sea.

Often this night beauty would rob us of sleep. Sometimes, I would waken and sit for perhaps an hour on our breezeway. For a while I would look toward the sea, where, in the pale half-light of a sapphire sky, the long plumes of the casuarinas that grow along the shoreline would be at their never-ending slow dusting of the sky. In the other direction, through another scattering of palms, moonlight would glisten on the bay, the two vistas equally beautiful. Sometimes Tom would be the one to waken to the night beauty. For him, this would mean a walk to the beach or back to the boat slip. Roused from sleep by the click of the door as he started out, I would call to him, "Wait for me. I want to go, too."

Once on the beach, if it were a night of stars there might be the play of phosphorus on the water. If the moon were full, she would have laid a silvery path across to the horizon. True to Miss Carson, a ghost crab or two would scuttle at our feet. We would speak little. In a combination of that hope and yearning that comes at such times as this, there was the feeling beautifully expressed in a sentence from Isak Dinesen's *Out of Africa*, that, "at any moment the universe might give up its secret." For, to be in the beauty of night on a solitary beach is to compress time as we know it; to have the deep feeling of belonging to all that has gone before, and that of being linked to all that is to come. In some vague way, it increases the belief in immortality, the belief that the order of the universe is too marked not to have some ultimate purpose toward which human life is moving.

Finally Tom would say, "Well we'd better get some sleep." And we would start slowly back to the house. Even so, when we reached the cottage we wouldn't go in. Drawn back to the bay, we would sit quietly on Tom's white gearbox, a large plain one he had made and painted himself. Looking far down the bay, we could, in imagination, place each of the channel markers, for we knew them by heart. Now and then the noiseless leap of a mullet from the water would make a silver streak of a few feet, then the waters would again be still. Leaving it all would require almost superhuman effort. But, as Virginia Woolf has the character Mrs. Dalloway say, tomorrow would be "another blue day, smooth, round, and flawless."

On our summer visits to the island, windows and doors open throughout the day and the night, there would be added to that warm loveliness the tinkle of our wind chimes. Somehow the delicate sound always suggested to me the China Sea. Ours, suspended from an arm inside our breezeway, added the final note of romance and beauty to island night. With summer visits, our evening meal always came later than in winter. For, in addition to our three swims a day, there would usually have been a sail and perhaps a short trip in the motorboat. We soon learned how to plan, in partnership, with the weather of island summer. We could count on the coming of a small quick shower at noon. During the shower the sun would sometimes not even go in. The raindrops would be the size of marbles and the prismatic effect would turn them into a shower of small round rainbows. The air, then cleansed and briefly cooled, would be filled with birdsong that, coming through moisture and sunbeams sounded more lyrical than ever. In midafternoon there would always be a squall. Invariably we would be out in one of the boats, but we knew certain coves in which to take cover, and we always had our rain gear along.

Often, on the summer island stays, the nighttime reading we both always enjoyed at home in Carolina had to be sacrificed. For one reason, from so much outdoor activity, we were tired. The other was the "no-see-ums." These tiny insects came through the screens and they either stung or bit, we never knew which. On those nights when we were able to keep the lights on without attracting them, as we sat on the breezeway reading, we would have a visit from a group of five coons. With the island virtually empty of people, and no garbage, they would come to our patio, and sitting up on their hind legs with their forepaws moving, their bodies weaving from side to side, would mutely beg for a hand-out. At such close range, they seemed so companionable as to be almost human.

And, although I would not say that coons are my favorite animals, in that little stage production these were appealing. Tom could never resist going to the refrigerator and taking out bread to toss on our patio for them. When he first started this practice, I half-jestingly said, "You're going to make them dependent, like those gulls who followed the shrimp boats on the other coast so long that they lost the capacity for finding their own food, and when the shrimp boats moved, they starved."

His answer was, "But we're not here for that long a time."

And I didn't say any more, for in the bay behind our house we had, several times, come upon the sadness of seeing a coon, who in an effort to get an oyster from its shell had drowned. Clusters of oysters attach themselves to the spidery roots of the mangroves that lie below the surface of the water, and mangroves grow thickly up and down the shallow edge of the bay. The coon, timing his feeding to that point between high and low tide, at which the mouth of the oyster would be open and feeding, would reach his little black paw into the shell. The oyster would clamp down, and in the rising tide the coon would drown. One of the many lessons the island was giving us in survival.

≈ ≈ ≈

As I have written, Hie and Jay, equally remarkable in their separate fields, were to have a great influence on my later life, then and now. Jay is five years older than I; Hie was thirteen. When our friendship had existed for about fifteen years, one day, while Hie and I sat on the beach waiting to be joined for our swims by Tom, Jay, and the other members of the compound, Hie spoke quietly and simply, "Elizabeth, you should write."

This took me by surprise. Our two sons had long been grown and were now out in the larger world, one of them married. I was mentally prepared to coast, and as Tom was no longer in politics, we were looking forward to spending more and more time together. Yet, so highly regarded was this beautiful little lady of seventy-five, that no one ever doubted anything she said. In this instance, however, I did; I was uncertain as to my having the real qualifications for the craft. Could a love for the scrape of the pen be enough to be regarded as talent? Even so, with all the other things to make life full: family, friends, books, and some consistent attempt at being aware of the needs of others, every single day a joy, would I have the necessary self-discipline? For a long time the question remained unanswered. And nothing happened.

Nobody on the island would ever have had the effrontery or the bad manners to solicit professional advice from Hie in her retirement. Her suggestion that I write had come about informally. All I could do that day on the beach was to try to analyze the analyst herself, to get inside Hie's mind. My thoughts ran like this: *Darling Hie! In her fondness for Tom and for me she thinks that when we're on the island I need something to do. She believes that I build my life too much around Tom's needs, not that she loves him any less than she does me. But she doesn't know how busy Tom is at home, how hard-working and how unselfish he is with his time for the benefit of others. That in a small town where your roots go deep, you're called upon for everything that needs doing. That, in addition, you feel an obligation to attend every wedding, christening, and funeral. That, as someone who loves his state and his Alma Mater in the way that Tom does, he's never going to turn down an opportunity to put his shoulder to the wheel for either. With all these things, I want to make our island stays all his, for relaxation. To be ready to swim, to sail, or to drive, on short notice and in a hurry, the thirty-five miles to a marina on the mainland, although it often involves a wait for the ferry and then a half hour's ride across a sometimes choppy bay. And all this for just a nut, or a bolt, or a pin – any of those tiny things on which so much of the well-being of the boater depends. Filling these needs is my joy.*

Hie knows, of course, that I don't need to spend much time keeping house.

Ours is so small and simply furnished – two things I wouldn't change, for I know from experience, the encumbrance of possessions. She knows that I write long letters, that I almost devour books and that I play a little bridge, but she thinks I need some real interest of my own to occupy me while Tom putters among his three boats. She's used to women who fully develop their powers and do something satisfying with them.

However, all I said was, "I think you're being nice, Hie." Yet there was a note of conviction in her voice that was pleasing.

"No," she answered. "You observe closely, you have a fresh way of saying things, and you enjoy telling a tale."

"But, Hie, I don't have anything to say," I countered.

"Start writing, and something will come," she suggested.

We heard the others coming down the path between the swaying sea oats on the sandbank, and as usual, we gave a little "Yoo hoo!" That was hardly necessary, for sitting in the sand under the palm-thatched umbrella, we were already in sight.

Nevertheless, Hie had planted a seed. As life went on, however, only at intervals would the seed receive any water. There were long dry spells between. Yet, Hie understood me more than I knew. Vague as it was, I did have the feeling of wanting to find out who I was.

≈ ≈ ≈

A few days after the suggestion of Hie's, I did manage to take a small step in that direction. That morning, those of us in the compound who enjoyed the surf, and in addition, three houseguests of the Rosses, sat on the beach before our morning swim. Our short-legged beach chairs formed a half circle; our feet and legs, stretched out as they were on the sand, could have been the spokes of a wheel. Contentment reigned supreme; conversation was idle.

The sea and the sky were blue; the clouds, slow-sailing and tufted. There was, as usual, the enchantment of watching the tripping sandpipers who were playing tag with the surf, chasing a fleeing wave as far as they could, and as they did, were snapping up from the wet sand the coquina and any other sea urchins that might have been offered up, then running quickly back just out of reach of another incoming wave, their timing perfect. Behind us, on the sandbank, where the sea oats were always in motion, the beach rose, and in that distinguishing feature of our island, the tall graceful casuarinas grew there along that elevation of the shoreline. It was in recognizing that dark fringe against the sky from the sea that one sailor might say to another, "And there's Captiva."

For he would see it as one of the strand of islands which begins with Boca Grande and goes through Marco. All but one of the strand have Spanish names. Going south, there is Boca Grande, for wide mouth, Usseppi, for Josephine, next, Cabbage Key, a small island which once belonged to a well-known writer of another time, Mary Roberts Rinehart, who spent her winters there. Then comes Upper Captiva, an island perhaps a mile in length, which, as has already been said in this story, became separated from Captiva proper by storm in 1924, the breakthrough forming the inlet now known as "Red Fish Pass." This is a favorite spot for Captiva fisherman to anchor their small boats, even if there are no fish, for there is the pleasure of watching the pelicans happily bobbing all day on an incoming or outgoing tide. After Captiva, there is Sanibel, for beautiful saint. The largest of the islands, and one of its most beautiful, Sanibel is well-known to conchologists over the world, for it is one of – I seem to remember – two beaches which face due south. The other is the Great Barrier Reef of Australia. Finally, there is Estero, for channel, and then Marco, for Marco Polo, I assume.

Because of their proximity to the sea, there is some peculiar air current over the shoreline casuarinas at Captiva that enables a few pelicans at a time, in V-formations of three to five, on a single wing-beat, to coast above them downshore. Seeing this patrol from either the surf or from our house for the thousandth time since Captiva had come in our life, and knowing that someday the beauty of it all would hardly be believable, I longed to write something that would hold it for us, and perhaps for those others of us who had a deep feeling that we were having the island at its best.

With hardly more sense of direction than that, that morning of Hie's suggestion to me about writing, in the circle of friends on the beach, all of us tightly bound in affection, I found myself saying, vaguely – if surprisingly – in the lull of conversation, "You know, I've decided to write."

Strangely, the sky did not fall, the horizon stayed in place, and so far as I could tell, the fish still swam in the sea. Even more, my announcement had been greeted with delight. The first remark was Jay's. Although I had not known her during her teaching years, I had been told by some of her former students that whenever she came into the classroom of young girls, the usual hubbub of conversation in full swing, at the flute-like sound of her voice at the end of the room, saying, "Young Ladies, we must have order here," the girls would fall in line and turn in their desks in happy anticipation of another charmed hour.

Jay's reaction to my announcement came in that same lovely, lilting voice. "Oh, Elizabeth, I'm so glad!"

Then Hie, "Very good, Elizabeth."

Jim Gray's comment came next, and Jim was, himself, a writer – a novelist – and former *Saturday Review* drama critic. "Splendid, Elizabeth," he said. "Of what shall you write?"

"I don't know, Jim. About life, I suppose. Life as I've known it."

"Well," Jim went on, "if it's to be autobiographical, may I come over soon and give you some pointers?"

"Oh, please do," I answered gratefully, terribly startled by being taken seriously so soon.

Betty Gray, Jim's wife, the wittiest person in the compound, a writer herself, and formerly in charge of Pillsbury's radio hour, herself the originator of Betty Crocker and *The Betty Crocker Cookbook*, was, as usual, practical. "Don't let it become a burden, Elizabeth," she cautioned.

I wondered what Tillie's reaction would be. Tillie had grown up in France, her real name, Mathilde, was pronounced the French way, "*Mateelde*." Her married life had been spent in the academic world in this country, however, and her husband, Richard, or "Mike" to us, had, for a long time, held the Chair of Psychology at the University of Minnesota. Some years older than Tillie, he now spent his time at Captiva editing books and becoming a quiet student of astrology. Mike had a wonderful telescope. On certain starry nights, in a space that was open to the sky, "the compound" would gather around Mike as he gave us simplified information on the galaxies, patiently supervising our turns at the telescope.

In the daytime, Tillie and I sometimes rode our bicycles together the two miles to the post office. Ours was the kind of friendship in which you philosophize a lot. One day, Mike, sitting high up on the screened porch of their small house, looking down on us as we stood by our bicycles in earnest conversation, called out laughingly, "What in the world can you two be talking about?"

Tillie answered cheerily, "Life and death and the afterlife!"

"Oh my Lord," said Mike, and went back to his bird-watching and reading.

Not only did I enjoy conversation with Tillie, I adored the way she talked. Her diction was flawless. After Mike's death, Tillie wrote to me in a sad letter, "Now Mike is all right, but what shall I do with *me*?" Her wonderful manner of speaking ultimately led her to volunteer to record for the blind at the University of Minnesota. Her reading selections were those of her own choosing.

But that morning on the beach, Tillie spoke casually, "I hope this doesn't mean that there won't be time for us to figure things out and set the world to rights."

378

"You know me better than that, Tillie," I answered, laughing, "Don't worry."

The three guests were the last to be heard from. All three had been colleagues of Jay's when she was teaching at Vassar. Pamela Askew is an art historian, taking her students regularly for one of the winter months to Europe. Although my own days of the study of art history were far behind me, I had read, with interest, one of Pam's published articles which she'd brought down with her. It was scholarly, as you would expect. Having no dictionary on the island, I was stumped by a word that appeared in the first paragraph. When I returned the article the next morning after having read it overnight, I could be sincere in my praise, but I also had to be honest.

"Pammy," I asked, "What in the world is a paradigm?"

She laughed and said, "Oh, Elizabeth, don't worry about that. I wrote that paper a long time ago when I was very young. I was just showing off."

That did a lot for my morale, and when Pammy said, in answer to my announcement, "You're going to enjoy writing, Elizabeth," I knew that she meant it.

Mary McLaughlin, the other of the three Ross houseguests, taught at Vassar as well, her field, medieval history. She was on leave to do a study of Abelard which would lead to publication. At this time her work on this French scholastic philosopher, teacher, and theologian had been going on for several years. Abelard's love for Heloise, and that of her for him, is one of the most famous romances in history. I knew that the introduction to this work of Mary's was one of five hundred pages; naturally my head was in the dust, and one year, when Mary and Pammy and Earl returned to the island for their annual visit, I felt I must – indeed I *wanted* to –inquire about her work. In an affectionate and laughing way, Mary had taught me some years earlier what the proper way to inquire about a book-in-progress is. I had said glibly and graciously, as though I were inquiring of a member of the family, "Have you finished your book, Mary?"

Her blue eyes twinkled with merriment, as she exclaimed, "Oh, Elizabeth! You *never* ask a writer that. Some books are twenty years in the doing."

"But then, Mary, what is the polite thing to say?" I wanted to know.

"Just ask, 'How is your book progressing?' " she answered. And I was happy to be thus enlightened.

Earl's opinion was the last. This six-foot-three, husky man, to whom the reader has been introduced earlier as head of the Music Department at Vassar, was encouraging, as well.

"Not a bad idea, Elizabeth. We never know where something will lead, once we get interested."

Tom, who had been listening and sifting sand through his fingers, and of course, ultimately feeling that something from him was called for, said jokingly and good-naturedly, "I hope you're not taking the veil – shutting yourself away and all that – on a whim."

But the others drowned him out, and in the usual camaraderie of the compound, we got up to go into the surf for our swims. The swims over, we separated, Tom, lugging our beach chairs. He and I walked back down the undulations of our driveway to our house.

This distance was three-hundred-and-fifty feet, and around halfway, Tom spoke, protectively, "My love," he began, and always when he began that way I knew he was getting ready to advise me about something, "I hate to hear you say you're going to try to write. You're down here among all these writing people and you've just caught writing fever. But they all have a *field. You* don't. I would hate to see you shut yourself away. You enjoy people too much for that, and in the end I think you might be disappointed."

In the same way that I respected Hie's judgment, I respected Tom's. We had gone through too many things together for me not to. I knew, as well, that I was impulsive, but, however little I had to back it up, I did not think that this was just an impulse. So I slowly agreed, "Well, maybe so."

Yet after lunch, before the glow of the morning's conversation had worn off, I rode my bicycle down to the island store for some kind of tablet or notebook and a few ballpoints. The next morning, with breakfast over, Tom, back at the boatslip at work on something, I put up the cardtable in our breezeway.

I'd just finished doing that when I heard the sound of footsteps, which was easy to do, for a wide strip about our house was strewn with small shells to keep down the tropical grasses, and footsteps had the sound of those on crusted snow. These were Jim Gray's. In his bright, cheerful way, Jim had come to give me those pointers on autobiographical writing which he had mentioned.

There was very little of the concrete to offer, except, "In autobiographical writing, do not be afraid to put in the sadness, Elizabeth, for every life has some of that. It's something that people can relate to."

But Jim had another suggestion to make. "You must not try to write here, in this spot, Elizabeth. It's too public. You won't take yourself seriously."

I had thought it was divine – the swish of the sea in the distance toward the west and the bird cries from over the bay to the east, palms swaying gently in both directions – but it was true that since the breezeway was in the center of the house, people came and went there from both directions.

"All right, Jim," I said. "I'll move the cardtable into the living room."

When he had gone, I did that. But, although I don't type, I had some loose pages of typewriter paper that were not weighted down. And with the windows and doors all open, while I was in the kitchen getting lunch, the pages blew up and scattered over the living room.

Tom, coming up from the boatslip for lunch, seeing the cardtable in the living room, wanted to know, "Are you having a bridge game?"

"No," I said. "This is where I'm going to write."

By that time, we were both gathering up the scattered sheets of paper from all over the floor.

"Do you mean to say," asked Tom, "that you're going to take the only decent room we have for the clutter of your writing?"

"Not really," I said. I was already thinking of moving to my bedroom.

He agreed that that was wise, and we had our happy little lunch on the patio. By three o'clock I had changed the location of the cardtable. Finding a spot for it had been a puzzle, for the room was crowded as it was. Still, there were double windows in the back toward the bay between the two single beds, which made writing from there a pleasant prospect. It seemed plausible that the muse might just find me there, and I sat down to wait.

Through the long lovely vista through the palms, light shimmered on the bay. I had not, at that time, come upon Edith Wharton's suggestion to writers, that "It's better to write facing a warehouse." In the lull of afternoon, except for the coo of the dove coming through the jungle, and now and then, the voice of a gull or fishcrow against the everpresent pipes and cheeps from the beach – the songbirds taking their usual siesta – the island was quiet. Nor had I come to the information that when Henry James was stumped for the right word, it was his habit to stand in front of the mantelpiece of his study until the word came, and that a depression in the floor proves it. Nor had I chanced to read the dismal statement of a professional who said, "Writing is easy. All you do is sit down and open a vein."

In this uninformed euphoria, I sat dreamily for a few minutes, unwilling to break the spell. Then, in less time than it takes to tell it, there came a little "*Yoohoo*ing!" from the kitchen, and on through the living room, and across the breezeway to the bedroom side of the house. Without getting up, I answered with my own "Yoohoo!" followed by, "Here I am in my bedroom. Come and see something," for I knew it was Jay. We always entered each other's houses through the kitchen, and wandered about until we found each other. In the doorway, she took it all in at a glance, and being the schoolteacher she was, took charge.

"Oh my goodness, Elizabeth," she began. "You can't write here, it's too crowded. Why don't you get Tom and Earl to move one of these twin beds into that little storage spot on the other side of your guesthouse?"

Right away I could see the wisdom of that, because we had plenty of room for the children in the guesthouse, and Tom and I, having developed different sleeping habits, each had a small room of our own in our cottage. The extra single beds in each room were there only in case of an overflow.

As the afternoon waned, happily expectant and poised for writing, Tom still at work on his boats, I suddenly decided to go over to the Ross's to see if Earl might be there. He was on the porch working on his tackle box, and my greeting was, "Earl, how strong does your back feel?"

"Strong enough," he replied, looking up. "What do you want moved?"

And I told him the sequence of events. I wound up by saying, "Now, Earl, Tom is not going to want to do this. He thinks we should have as many beds as possible for our friends, and our children, and their friends. But I think that if I can spring it on him when you're there, and you can back me up with an offer to help with the moving, he will go along."

Earl understood, and by prearrangement, came over after supper.

Tom and I had finished our own and were still sitting at the table in the candlelight in the breezeway when Earl joined us for a cup of coffee, and said, casually, "Did you want me to help move something, Elizabeth?" And then I told all. In half and hour I had a new room. I could hardly wait for morning to be up and at my spindle.

That night, after his visit and his help, Earl went back to the Ross's to convey the news. It brought Jay over in a hurry. "Well now this is an improvement," she agreed, as she surveyed the cardtable, now comfortably situated under the double window.

"But it's the *smallest* cardtable I've ever seen. Far too small for writing. Maybe Tom can build you something." I saw nothing wrong with the cardtable, however, and went to bed happy.

When morning came, I had not wakened as early as I'd expected. Every morning of my married life I had been roused to the sound of Tom's starting off his exercises in the middle of the room with long, slow, deep breathing, which would lead to twenty minutes of calisthenics, allowing me that much extra time to snooze. When we were on the island, I could always hear this preliminary dramatic inhaling and exhaling coming from our breezeway. I knew that for the next interval, there would be all kinds of gyrations, including lying on the floor for leg exercises, leading to the grand finale of standing up and jumping, arms flung.

But that morning there was silence. I hurried out of bed to see what had happened. Tom's bed was empty. In the breezeway in the middle of the floor lay a legal pad, and on the pad he had written, "I've gone to Fort

Meyers to buy a door and some turned legs to build a writing table for you like Jay's. Back by lunchtime, I hope." And my heart sang like a bird's.

By Tom's return, by grapevine, the news that I had a desk-in-progress had travelled around the compound, and one by one, everybody sauntered over to our tower to supervise the project. By three-thirty Tom had the legs in place, the table sat upright. When the neighbors came by to check his progress on the way to their afternoon swims, they all landed there at once. I had been sitting happily on a barstool as things went on. Having us all there together, Tom said, "You're going to want to paint it, aren't you, Elizabeth?"

"Yes," I answered.

"What color?" some of the ladies wanted to know, altogether.

"I don't know," I said, "it depends on whatever Bailey's has in stock." That was the general store twelve miles away on our sister island. "I'll have to go and see."

Bailey's did not have much to offer, but from the color chart I selected two shades. One "Avocado," the other, "Coral." Hurrying back with a paintbrush and a can of each, but uncertain as to which color to use, Tom solved the dilemma by turning the table upside down and painting one half of it coral, the other half avocado, which meant that one half was a soft green, the other, a pleasant, corally-pink. The swimmers on their way back stopped at the tower again, and in the spirit of doing everything together that always went on among us, and thinking in terms of quorums, Tom said, "Which color shall I make it? Let's take a vote."

They all chorused, "Avocado!"

In my room, with its white walls, its white furniture, and its straw rugs on a light gray floor, either color would have been a nice accent. But the choice was mine, and suddenly it came to me, as I sat perched on my barstool, that things had gotten out of hand. After all, whose table was it? And so I spoke in a loud, firm voice, "Coral!" And coral it became.

I had bought quick-drying paint, which meant that by nine that night, the table was ready to be moved. With Earl and Tom shifting the furniture and placing the writing table, the night was becoming a lark for all concerned. But just how much of a lark, I would never have suspected, when, half an hour later, while Tom and I sat reading in the breezeway, we heard the sound of voices. Coming across our patio, which, from the back, led into our breezeway, were the members of the compound.

Laughing and joking, they had come in a body, to see the new table. In some way, we all managed to scrounge into my bedroom at one time. It was then that Earl produced a bottle of champagne and enough paper cups to go around. I felt like a bride, and when they raised their glasses "to the coral door!" I could envision a space that was being held for my works in the Library of Congress.

≈ ≈ ≈

For as long as I can remember, it has interested me to see what somebody has written: on tablets in old churches, inscriptions on public monuments, on gravestones, on the flyleaves of old books, diaries, journals, and published letters. When I travel, almost more than anything else, I seem to search out the written word, always slow to leave an empty old church that has tombs and memorial tablets in it. And, in England, as in St. John's of my home village, the church doors are never locked. That makes them particularly conducive to sitting quietly for meditation. Tom enjoyed that, too. The writer, Ronald Blythe, in his book, *Akenfield*, quotes a passage from T.S. Eliot's *Little Gidding* to describe the gentle peacefulness that empty churches offer: "If you come this way, taking any route, starting from anywhere, at any time or at any season, it would always be the same; you would have to put off sense and notion. You are not here to verify, instruct yourself, or inform curiosity or carry report. You are here to kneel where prayer has been valid."

Always, after those experiences, and, indeed, after every lovely experience that has come to me, I have felt a longing to hold it, and perhaps to communicate something of it to others. That may have stemmed, in part, from my trying to bring everything back to Alice Bryan, the habit that began when I was a year old. With that bent, I suppose it was natural that I should develop an interest in writing, and beyond that, an interest in papyrus. So that, as Tom and I continued to travel, I sought the history of papyrus in a number of museums.

The first growing papyrus I ever saw was in Sicily, in the city of Syracuse, or "Siracusa," as they say, where there was a fountain in which it grew. The notation in our guidebooks said, "This paper, made from the papyrus, is manufactured only at Siracusa, and it is identical to the Egyptian papyrus used by pharaohs. It is the best-known feature to foreigners because it is the rarest and most esteemed relic of ancient civilization."

The dictionary tells us that papyrus is a tall, aquatic plant, native to the Nile Valley, a material on which to write prepared from thin strips of the pith of this plant laid together, soaked, pressed, and dried, and used by the ancient Egyptians, Greeks, and Romans for that purpose.

With the purchase of our Captiva property, my interest in papyrus came full circle, for I soon discovered that in the assortment of tropical growth under the double windows of my bedroom were several sturdy green stalks of that significant plant.

On the morning of the first day of my having the splendid writing table which had come to life in our tower under Tom's now more than sympathetic hand, it was irresistible, if you were of playful mind, not to let it flit over the symbolism of having a small bed of papyrus, alive and well, in so appropriate a spot. It was undeniably elevating.

Spending a while in this euphoria, trying out different colors of ink, selecting various shades of blue, green, purple – never red or black – I then moved on to the subject of a title, one that would allow for free-wheeling, a mish-mash of subject matter, and an informal style of presentation. It did no good to remember that a title is the last thing that happens in the writing of a book. And although, in the recesses of my mind, I could hear the professionals emphasizing that point, in a matter of minutes, I had the perfect title. It had fallen into my lap: *Papyrus Grows Under my Window.* And as it fell, my pen began to move across the page.

Light, disjointed, entirely without direction, my thoughts flowed. Then, gradually, they began to form into some semblance of a conversation, one between what I was beginning to think of as my writing self and the more familiar self of being a busy and happy wife, mother, sister, aunt, cousin, community and church member and reader of books.

From the bookish side of my nature I was approaching my writing with high-flown notions. And for the sake of argument, the conversation was taking place between the "writing self" and what, for lack of a better term, I was designating as the "reading self." The writing self spoke first, "I can see that there's more to getting a book started than I had thought. Declaring yourself a writer, and being accepted in that light by those around you was all well and good, but now what? How do I begin my memoirs?"

The reading self had a suggestion, "Why not," it began, "do something in the way of Proust, who, by introducing that tiny cake, one so associated with his childhood, that, all those years later, the taste of one of the kind would call up such a flood of memories as eventually to fill seven volumes?"

"It's worth considering," said the writing self. "But I don't really care about writing more than *one* book. Yet, I suppose I might build a tale around something as delectable as the taste of an East Carolina sweet-pickled-peach. For, truth to tell, I'm not as averse to pillaging from another writer as I once was. I'm now more enlightened on the subject. Indeed, I have read that a writer of prominence, advising amateurs on the matter, says, 'Not only is it acceptable for you to borrow, go ahead and *steal!*' "

Nevertheless, my two selves came to the conclusion that, since my Proustian imitation might be easily detected, my potential reputation as a writer might flounder early. It was not a risk I could afford to take. But my reading self had an alternate suggestion, "Why not," it said, "follow that example of Montaigne's first essay? If his essays are being read after four-hundred years, you could hardly do better. His style is casual and folksy, really endearing when he apologizes to the reader at the outset for using himself as subject matter. 'I want to be seen here,' he writes, 'in simple, natural, ordinary fashion, without artifice, for it is myself that I mean to portray.' As if the great man couldn't foresee that, in his humanness, by the end of his writing life, his essays would have portrayed every man."

But, at this point, rescued by a small store of common sense, which showed that the morning had all but gone, with nothing to show for it, I decided to exchange the view to the bay through the double windows of my bedroom for the same view through the windows of my kitchen, and to begin the preparations for lunch. As I stood in the kitchen in front of the open door of the refrigerator, waiting for my mind to catch up with me, from some corner of it, something came back. It was a line that had once appeared in a commentary on the life and work of a writer whose name was regrettably lost to memory – and I was never to read any of her works – but whose characterization, I felt, might have been mine as well, when she said of herself, "She never considered herself an intellectual. Relieved of that onerous responsibility, she absorbed essences." There it all was, in a nutshell.

I had been rescued by a fellow spirit in the nick of time. For all the while it had been just essences that I hoped to capture.

≈ ≈ ≈

For the rest of that island stay, I hardly left my writing table. It brought me such joy that I couldn't foresee that anything would ever have me put it aside.

Yet that happened. Life back in Carolina was so busy that the enthusiasm for writing that had been mine on the island waned. After all, what did I have to *say*? Once more, however, before we left Captiva after what I felt had been one of our most significant stays, I had a chance to declare myself to *another* group of friends, a small incident that – although it was amusing – was a small step in the progress of my decision to write.

The day had dawned as one perfect for a picnic, and by grapevine, one had been worked up. It would include our boat and two others. The other boaters were those of some of our dearest friends, Ruth and Ed Lowry, Janet and Bert Lynch, Lloyd and Faffy and Louise Clow.

At eleven o'clock I was busy in the kitchen making ham and cheese sandwiches and filling the ice chest, putting soft drinks in a styrofoam container, providing the usual things we took on these impromptu affairs, when Hie came into our kitchen. She had come to return something borrowed from our larder.

"Sit down and talk to me, Hie," I said, and I explained what I was doing.

When I had finished, she said quietly, "You don't *have* to go on that picnic, Elizabeth."

It stopped me in my tracks and I turned to answer, "No, I don't, do I, Hie?"

She left, and I finished filling the basket and hurried with it back to the boat slip. By that time, the three other boats had arrived and were circling in the water. The tide was out, Tom was standing down below the dock in our boat, ready to cast off. Taking the picnic basket and holding out his hand to help me, he said, "Jump in."

"I'm not going today," I said.

He did not seem surprised. "You're going to write?" he asked.

"Yes," I said.

And he answered, "We'll miss you." I knew that he meant it. Ours was a marriage where, if you were doing something pleasant and the other one wasn't there, half the joy was gone.

Still, I cupped my hands and shouted across the water to the other boats, "I'm not going today!"

"You're not?" they cried in astonishment.

Janet called out immediately, "What are you dying *of?*"

"Nothing," I called back. "I've decided to stay here today, and write."

"About what?" called Faffy.

Again through cupped hands I shouted back, "About all of *you.*"

"Oh Lord," they groaned.

And Bert, pulling a long face, called out a small plea, "Then treat us kindly!" he begged. But he knew the admonition was unnecessary.

With that, the third step in the evolution of my writing career – such as it was – had been taken.

≈ ≈ ≈

Yet, the very thing that – when we were at Captiva – made me *want* to write, made it difficult for me, as well. For what Tom had said was true – I enjoyed every moment and everything and everybody too much to sacrifice any of it. I was too busy living to write. A further description of life on the island will point this up.

Perhaps, on an island, mail assumes more importance than on the mainland. Certainly the arrival of island mail was a highlight, especially in the years when it was brought over by the mailboat. You could hear the little boat's throaty whistle as it approached, and by waiting half an hour to go to the post office, you could gauge the time just right for the letters to be "put up" in the individual mailboxes that this tiny building now boasted. Before the coming of the mailboxes, it would have required a wait by the window while the postmaster sifted through a pile of letters, looking for those addressed to you.

Since the daily life between our house and that of the Ross's was especially intimate, our joint outgoing and incoming mail usually came and went in one large basket. Sometimes Tom bicycled to the post office for the mail, more often, I went, either by bicycle or in our little old Chevy. By the time the day was over, news of what the incoming letters had brought to the Rosses and the Pearsalls had been shared.

One day, in her characteristic way, Jay came into our kitchen, calling me, and saying, "Elizabeth, I have something to tell you."

She had an opened typewritten letter in her hand, the contents of which she went on to explain, "A movement has been started in England to make amends for a conspicuous oversight in the literary world. Because of the irregularity of her lifestyle, there isn't anything in the way of a commemorative tablet to George Eliot in the Poets' Corner of Westminster Abbey. Funds for it are now being widely solicited. I shall certainly send them ten dollars, and I felt you would want to, too."

Indeed, I did want to. George Eliot did deserve to join what some literary wag of another time spoke of as "the best literary club in England." What a commentary this was, and is, on the susceptibility of customs to change. Apparently, once the movement began, response was immediate. And in that fine book, *Parallel Lives*, by Phyllis Rose, the author tells us this regarding George Eliot:

> A hundred years after her death, a memorial stone was installed in Poet's Corner of Westminster Abbey. It bears the name she was born with, Mary Ann Evans, and the name she lives by in our memory, George Eliot....Inscribed around the four sides, from "Janet's Repentance": "The first condition of human goodness is something to love: the second is something to revere."

On another morning, as I went over next door with my mail basket with my own letters already in it, those of the Ross's to be added, at the top of the neat stack being handed to me was a postcard which Jay explained, "This postcard is for Eric Severied." At the time, this aristocratic TV commentator with the scholar's face ranked next to Walter Cronkite as a TV commentator of popular appeal.

Jay went on, "It annoys me inordinately that he pronounces the word, 'affluent' incorrectly."

"Well, what is the right way, Jay?" I inquired.

"The emphasis goes on the first syllable, as in 'apple.' The word is '*af*fluent.' "

And I hurried down the road on my bicycle with this urgent message for the famous man. High time, as we now say, for him to get it right!

On the same subject, in Carolina some years later, when my life alone had begun, I had a nice folksy visit from the Bishop of our diocese, Bishop Estill. Somehow the conversation turned on the aptitude of all of us for making errors in speech. The Bishop countered my Eric Severied story with a tale of his own, an incident that had taken place early in his ministry. It, too, had to do with the mispronunciation of a word.

As a young seminarian, he was sent to the eastern shore of Virginia for the summer. We can imagine how many hours had gone into the preparation of his first sermon. When the time came, he gave it his all. At one point, bringing to bear his descriptive powers, he reached the heights by imparting to his flock that something had been "heartrendering." The service over, the young minister, in the accustomed way, stood at the entrance of the church, speaking and being spoken to. It must have been a lovely picture; the sun shining on the youthful face above the white surplice, a face now aglow with the praise being so generously poured out by a supportive congregation.

The young man's cup literally ran over when an elderly lady, shaking hands, slipped a small piece of paper into his. When he could get a chance to read it, it held one word: "heartrending." That this kind woman should have been so impressed with his ecclesiastical powers that she had found the sad story he had told heartbreaking, was heady. For the next few days, the young cleric – who was later in life to wear the bishop's cope and miter – trod on air. Before the end of the week, however, there was some social gathering in the community, and recognizing the lady who had gone all out in appreciation of his sermon, the young seminarian couldn't wait to thank her for her kindness.

"Oh, I'm so glad you took it in that spirit," she began. "Afterward, I worried that I might have offended you. But you know, as we get older, we feel an obligation to younger people to help them with their pronunciations." Poor young man. But it was a timely lesson.

It gives me pleasure to relate these incidents in this simple story of my life. For, should it fall into the hands of some who are just beginning to try their wings in any field that requires public speaking, they will know that if they make mistakes they are in good company. And they will always remember that nobody is born all-wise. Knowledge has to accrue, often painfully.

≈ ≈ ≈

It was one of those times in summer, when, although we had been away from the island only three months, we began to long to be back, and that time we drove. As usual, I had a large basket of books, not only for island reading, but for the trip down and back. The selection of books was varied, some for me, some for Tom. When we had gone possibly fifty miles, Tom taking his turn at the wheel, I asked, "Shall I begin to read?"

He acquiesced. Then I said, opening a paperback, "When I went over to say goodbye to the Grays before we left in March, I said, "Jim, can you suggest some summer reading for me?" and he said, "Why, yes. The seven novels of Proust. It may be slow going at first, but plow on, and you will find it rewarding."

As I began to read that day in the car, I said to Tom, "I haven't really had time to get into it. Overall, the seven novels are called *Remembrance of Things Past.* I've read only about fifty pages, but already I'm hooked. Would you like to be exposed to it?"

He nodded, and I began. When we had gone, perhaps, twenty-five miles, as I was turning a page, Tom spoke up to ask, "You don't find that *tedious?*"

I burst into a laugh. My answer was, "I wouldn't dare tell you that the introduction is thirty pages long, and that another writer has said, "If it takes a man thirty pages to turn over in bed, I'm not interested," and it does, indeed, open with Proust, the young asthmatic, lying in bed in a cork-lined room, beginning a study of life as he has known it among the almost upper-crust class of his native France. As I was to find, he had developed the ability to back away from life, and in a convoluted and involuted way of long sentences and endless paragraphs, to record it in all its nuances; the kind of ruminative reading I enjoy.

Tom's point of view was understandable, however, and I scrounged through the basket for Barbara Tuckman's *Guns in August.* For this woman's analysis of the conditions that had led to World War II and each of her books which were to follow, supplied Tom with some of his favorite reading. Possibly it was through his father, who had been a student of history that Tom developed his own love of the subject.

≈ ≈ ≈

On one of my stays alone on Captiva, when Tom had gone back to Carolina for two weeks, I had a novel experience involving a white pelican. These large beautiful birds, unlike our brown pelicans, kept to themselves on a distant, uninhabited island. To see them at all meant going by boat to a certain spit or sandbar where they could be seen through binoculars from a far away approach as they sat quietly in the contentment of dozing, or thinking, or resting from winging out to fish for their food. At the first faint noise of the approach of a boat, one neck could be seen to go up slowly, inch by inch, to its three or four foot length, very much like a periscope. In an instant, all necks would have gone up to a length of three or four feet, until, as the boat drew near, a kind of nervous cackling would have begun. The large beautiful white wings would begin to flap in alarm. Unless we changed course and drew away, pandemonium would set in. At first, only a few birds would take to the air; gradually the whole flock would be circling, refusing to come down until we had gone. We loved the beauty of all that; we always took our houseguests for the spectacular display. But we couldn't help feeling a little cruel for having disturbed the pelicans on that spit which they considered their own.

It salved our conscience to go regularly, however, to Kyuna Key, a small island used by all the shorebirds as a nesting ground, to bring them nesting material. The birds there were always desperate for that, for every type of vegetation had long been stripped, and they depended on the few twigs that would float up on all sides of the key. It was fascinating to see a brown pelican fly out and swoop down to pick up a stick or a twig from the surface of the water, and on his way back to whatever limb had become his territory, to have another pelican intercept him and steal the material for his own nest-building.

In the pity of all this, Tom came into our house one day when he'd been pruning the growth in our yard, to say, "I have an idea. I have a tarpaulin full of twigs. Let's take them to Kyuna Key this afternoon. We can let the motor idle, and as we slowly circle, can throw the cuttings out on the water. The birds can come out and get them." We did that, and the grateful birds nearly went mad with delight at this sudden beneficence. It was thrilling.

These trips became a habit of ours, made with regularity. In spite of the fact that Kyuna Key was made of nothing but a growth of stripped trees, in addition to the brown pelicans, there were so many birds of white plumage, herons, egrets, terns, and gulls, interspersed that there was a certain kind of beauty. Yet, in that pattern of nature where the enemy is always at hand, high above the island there was ever the menacing circling of the frigate or man 'o war birds, as they are sometimes called. Large and black, with their long forked tails, they seem the personification of evil, for with their keen eyesight, without the slightest warning, they would swoop down to a nest and rob it while the parents were out searching for food.

One day in a spirit of adventure, Tom and I anchored in the shallows and waded ashore. As much as anything I've ever done, this brought me a feeling of the primeval. We knew that the ground would be covered with droppings, so we wore our oldest and roughest shoes. I had on a bathing cap; Tom, one of his time-worn grocery store yachting caps. As we moved about slowly among the trunks of the low-growing trees, the birds seemed not to mind our presence. They continued to sit quietly on their perches a few feet above. Their cries, however, could have been those of the dawn of creation, and they were constant, far louder to us than when we were circling the key in our boat. Yet, we could see that our own presence was, to them, less to be feared than that of the black, fork-tailed men 'o war birds, which, when one appeared above, even at that characteristic great height, it set up cries of pandemonium and a great flapping of wings. For in that provision of nature, these birds knew instinctively their natural enemies. As thrilling as this experience was, for us, however, it was not one to be drawn out. For the odor of the droppings soon drove us away. Yet that brief interval was something we would not have missed.

With that strong ammonia-like odor I was swept immediately back into my childhood. For in the days before commercial fertilizers, North Carolina planters depended on shipments of "Guano," that mixture which, in its combination of bird droppings and fish scrap, came from islands off the coast of Peru. Long before spring planting in Eastern Carolina, carloads of this guano would began arriving by rail. In our village, we knew by its odor when the shipment had arrived. Its arrival would be followed by a constant flow of wagons that, having been loaded, would take the large, tightly packed burlap bags of this vital product to be spread over the fields. Fertilizer has always been important to the growth of crops in Eastern Carolina, for the area was once covered by the sea, and our soil is made up mostly of sand. This condition, however, is more than offset by its temperate climate and the abundance of its rainfall.

But back to my unusual experience that involved the disposition of a single white pelican who had wandered away from the flock and died. It was a day when Gigi had come by our house for her morning cup of coffee and our swim. She was full of excitement. A dead white pelican had been found that morning on Captiva's beach, nearer her end of the island than ours. Sarita, Gigi's step-daughter, going to the island store for something, had heard about this, and immediately decided that it would be a wonderful opportunity to draw the structure of the enormous white bird's wings for the book she was writing on birds which was to be called *Growing Wings*, a book later reviewed in *Time* magazine, the last line of the review saying, "and the book includes more sex than *Peyton Place*," for Sarita's book was to be a serious study of bird's habits.

After being told about the pelican, some of the island men went with Sarita to the beach and helped her to get the large dead bird into her station wagon. They then followed her to her home to lift it out onto the grass. It had lain there under a gumbo-limbo tree all day while Sarita spread its wings and drew their structure in detail.

That afternoon, after our swim, Gigi and I decided that when Sarita had finished her drawing, we must help her with the disposition of the enormous bird. I was to meet Gigi and Sarita at the inn at six-thirty for dinner as we sometimes did, and we would work something out. It was in the middle of winter and darkness came early. We met at the inn, and the whole dining room soon wanted to know all about the pelican.

As we were leaving, Sarita suddenly had a thought. "Elizabeth," she said, "I don't want to leave the pelican there overnight. The coons will tear it to pieces. How about following us in your car to our house and helping us take him somewhere far down the island to leave in the jungle?"

I was more than willing. It sounded adventurous. As it turned out, this adventure was to be a vivid learning experience. Nothing could have made me realize more the enormous size of those shorebirds. Stretched out on the ground, this one had a wingspan of more than seven feet, and from the tip of its beak to its toes, equally as much, if not more.

After a brief discussion as to how to get it into the Van Vleck station wagon, it was decided that since Sarita was not very strong – she had developed mononucleosis in her senior year at Vassar, and had managed to graduate, but had been told to be careful about lifting and to live in a warm climate – and since Gigi had a mild heart condition, the heavy part of the bird would be mine to carry.

I found this beautiful white body soft and spongy, a feeling that was a little eerie. Getting the bird and all its parts into the station wagon, assembly fashion, was relatively easy. Then the three of us and the bird started up the island.

We wanted to leave him somewhere in the jungle, far from any houses, and as we drove along, we tried to decide on a spot. But then I suddenly had a thought, "Wait a minute," I said. "Don't you think it would be kinder to try to get him into the sea? There will be an opening into the jungle somewhere. We can angle the car across the road so that its light will shine to point our way, and it's not far at this point through the jungle to the beach."

This appealed to our collective aesthetic sense, and we soon found such an opening. Again, we took up the carrying of our separate parts, but this time, there were obstacles. Two fallen trees lay directly across our path. They had been there a long time, and were that beautiful color of driftwood which, lying on white sand, seems always to call for an artist's brush.

Carrying the head, Sarita clambered over the first trees without any trouble, but in the language of childhood, in this assembly-line maneuver, my "tickle box turned over." Perhaps people from other regions would express it as a "fit of giggles." Convulsed, I was practically helpless as Sarita, having maneuvered the first tree with the long white neck, now stood perfectly still, waiting for me to recover, and Gigi stood patiently waiting in the rear with the bird's feet. Somehow, I managed to pull myself together.

By the time we had crawled over the second tree, we were worried that the battery in our car might be weak and our lights go out, which would have been the last straw. So that, nearing the beach we gained speed, and as we arrived, lined up parallel to the surf. Quickly counting "One, two, three!" we heaved the bird into an incoming wave. Then we dashed back to wait and see what had happened. Nothing.

After waiting for several more waves, we could see the futility of our efforts. We consoled ourselves, however, by saying that there was an incoming tide. And that by morning the beautiful white creature would have had an appropriate burial at sea.

≈ ≈ ≈

Herman and Elizabeth Wiel had long been North Carolina friends of ours. Their home and ours in the eastern part of the state were only forty miles apart. Down the years we had been thrown together at social gatherings connected with public service committee meetings and in social functions over the state. Many times we were together at Chapel Hill, and when we had had our house at Captiva for six or eight years, the Wiels, as they sometimes did, came one winter for a month on Sanibel Island. The inn in which they stayed was run in the manner of our "Tween Waters Inn" on Captiva. Residents spent their stays in a cluster of cottages; their meals were served in a central dining room.

At that particular time, the playwright, Thornton Wilder, and his sister, Isabel, were staying at that Sanibel inn for a month. They had become friends of the Wiels and on one of our island stays, the Wiels invited Tom and me over to have dinner. The other two guests were to be the Wilders.

We were charmed by Thornton's ebullient personality, sometimes described by the press as "bombastic." He spoke rapidly; obviously he was full of the joy of life, and it was hard for me to reconcile all this vivacity with that dream-like, heart-achingly beautiful and unforgettable play of his, *Our Town*.

In the light conversation that ran around the table, I said to Mr. Wilder, speaking of the play, "Oh, but you made it so sad."

Smiling broadly, he answered, "That's what they all say." As though he didn't find it that way. But, of course, the play showed, in every line, that he understood deeply the pathos that can, and often does, lie underneath everyday life – those things spoken of by E.B. White and so often portrayed in his own flawlessly clear writing as "the near things, the dear things of this living." How can anybody who's seen the play ever forget that somber scene when the young daughter who has been taken by death, revisits earth and in her mother's kitchen, tries to thank her unknowing mother for all those dresses she had ironed, and all the other loving things that her mother had done for her.

Mr. Wilder expressed some interest in Captiva and we told him a few things about our island. Tom asked him if he'd like to go out fishing in our boat. He said he was sorry, but that he was having trouble with an ear and had to stay out of the wind. Then we asked if he and Isabel would like to come over some afternoon for drinks to meet a few of our friends. They liked the idea, and in about ten days, we gathered at our house.

I suppose there were about twenty-five of us. Captivans were used to celebrities. Unless they gave evidence that they wanted to "mingle," the famous were left to their own devices. To have intruded on their privacy would not have been considered honorable. To ask for an autograph would have been beyond the pale. So it had been with Anne Lindbergh when she was there writing her *Gifts from the Sea*. And would be later, when the well-known artist, Rauschenberg had come to Captiva to live. Even though his picture appeared on the cover of *Time* magazine, unless he made the first move to speak as he came and went to and from the post office, he could ostensibly go unrecognized. But he was to show a oneness with the spirit of the two islands when he gave two of his works to hang in the newly and jointly-subscribed conservation building which was built on Sanibel.

So that afternoon, although we had that famous literary figure and his sister in the intimacy that went with our small and certainly not impressive cottage, it went on as any other of our get-togethers would have.

After the party, however, Tom and I laughed together, remembering how two of our dearest island friends had happened, either by accident or by design, to be sitting on either side of the guest of honor. Strangers to Mr. Wilder, the two were, themselves, old friends. Both were women, and women of spirit and sophistication. So flanked, Mr. Wilder seemed happy enough in the ensuing light conversation which Tom and I had to interrupt now and then as we brought up other guests to be introduced. Because of his age and his health, Mr. Wilder did not rise for these courtesies.

The person who sat on Mr. Wilder's right that afternoon was Buffie Ives. Statuesque and articulate, she easily held Mr. Wilder's interest. Thornton had, as well, at times shared podiums with Buffie's brother, Adlai Stevenson. But Gigi Van Vleck, of whom I was equally as fond as I was of Buffie, although she had no particular reason for filling the chosen seat to the left of Mr. Wilder, and was in no way a caterer to famous people, for some reason sat through the party as though she, too, were unable to rise. Had the tone of the party needed to be elevated, however, Gigi's occasional lapses into her French phrases in her attractive, husky voice, would have sufficed.

True to habit, however, Gigi had brought with her to the party, her French poodle, Smokey. Understandably, Smokey became jealous of Mr. Wilder and stood, planted, in front of him and growled. Usually when we entertained, Tom was the most responsible of hosts; it might even be said that he sometimes kept our parties rolling more conscientiously than I. It was a just accusation to have him point out to me jokingly after one of our parties that I had a perennial way of greeting the guests upon arrival and of then turning into one myself. So that, although I was unaware of it that afternoon, Tom was spending much of his time luring Smokey into the kitchen with cheese and anchovies.

After the party I couldn't wait to ask him, "Where in the world *were* you?" For somebody has said, a description of a good marriage is the feeling that there's always an eye to catch, and that afternoon I certainly could not have caught his.

When he answered, "I was busy feeding Smokey," I had to excuse him, and it gave us a wonderful laugh.

The next winter, Mr. Wilder and Isabel were scheduled to come to us again, but one day we had a hurried note from him, saying that his ear was giving him trouble, and that they were leaving immediately for home.

I suppose that among all the famous people we were to meet on Captiva over the years, because of our admiration for Thornton Wilder's writing, he was the one I remember most. After knowing him, I would never feel that I could judge the personality of the writer through his writings. At those times when Mr. Wilder came south for several weeks of work, this bouncy side of his personality surfaced only in the late afternoon. The dining room at the inn had standing instructions to deliver his breakfast tray at seven in the morning; his luncheon, at one. He neither spoke, nor was spoken to throughout those hours. That was the man who wrote.

≈ ≈ ≈

By the time I had become a grandmother, the dream, in our hometown, of having a college had come true. All generations rejoiced, and a small group of mothers of young children were quick to supplement their own college degrees by enrolling for audited college courses. In one such group, the course was poetry. At the end of their winter's study, Jack Teagarden, the professor, assigned to the class the writing of a poem of no more than ten lines, the subject to be "masks."

These collected, Jack Teagarden found one so good, that, as a member of our Church of the Good Shepherd – the mother church of the three Episcopal churches in our town, and the one in which Jack was often a lay reader – he arrived early one Sunday, and copied the poem on the blackboard in the hall of the parish house. He explained to Tom and to me after the morning service, as we went from the church into the parish house for coffee, that he had found Annie Gray Thorpe's poem "electrifying." We were impressed, as well, and later I asked Annie Gray, a favorite of mine, for a copy. Now, twenty years later, I include the poem here:

The Mask

I hope that others can not see –
what surely has become of me.
For if they knew what I had known
and what to others, I have shown
I hope a mask is all they see –
For could they face –
what's really me?

When I recently sought permission to include the poem from the composer, Annie Gray's answer was, "Oh, I was so young then. Now I find it depressing, don't you?"

I answered that I did not find it depressing. For I am struck with the insight of a young woman, who, at the time under thirty, had the maturity to understand that each of us does, indeed, wear a mask, that masks are nature's protective coloration, a unifying characteristic of the human race. For, as one of the sages has said, *Life would be unendurable without illusion.* And in deluding others, we delude ourselves.

BACK HOME FOR AN EVENING
AT BELLEMONTE

≈ ≈ ≈

W̲hen you've lived all your life in the same community, and people know that you like books, and that, from time to time you have written a little harmless poetry, more than likely, some of the people will consider you an intellectual. As applied to me, nothing could be further from the truth.

Having by this time, however, come to know a great many creative people – on the island, at Chapel Hill, and in other areas – and finding them thoroughly human, I had begun to take the great and the near-great in stride, and I was not as startled as I might once have been to receive an invitation to join – in a microscopic way – the ranks of the illustrious. After all, to have a little light layer of glamour of my own might not be a bad idea, especially if it's done in the interest of a cause.

But this kind of surprise was one of which I would never have dreamed. It came like a bolt out of the blue when, for five years, I had been a Grandmother, and although I was not sitting in the corner knitting, neither was I planning to go out and conquer any new worlds.

We were on Captiva Island when a telephone call came from Carolina. The aforementioned, Jack Teagarden, English professor at North Carolina Wesleyan College, was calling to lay before me an improbable situation. Although Jack phrased his request more flatteringly, the substance of the call was to tell me that he was in a jam. In order to qualify for a North Carolina poetry grant, he must have a local amateur poet appear on a program with three Carolina professional poets. The appeal was to ask me to serve in that key capacity. When I had gotten over the shock, I promised Jack that I would call back the next day with my answer. Since the date proposed was to coincide with a stay of ours in Carolina, Tom's advice was, "Go ahead. Help Jack out. But be sure that he doesn't misrepresent you. Tell him that you must be described as a person who enjoys poetry rather than as a poet, and that you would like to stimulate the interest in others."

With telephoning Jack that I would be there to take part, the strangeness of it all began to increase. For Bellemonte – with time and usage to become Belmont – had been Father's favorite farm. Although two hundred of its original acres had now become the groves of academe, certain of its earlier scenes would always be vivid to me. I can still see the crane that in the warmth of spring and summer spent the hours in the stream in the meadow, and the loveliness of two figures against a winter sunset: a woman – with her arms wrapped in her apron against the cold – is on her way to the woodpile, as over a distant hill there comes a man holding a gun

401

over his shoulder. From his other hand dangles a dead rabbit, held by its ears.

With the recurrence of those scenes, I knew that for the hour of the joint poetry reading, whatever my own poems might lack, there would, for me, be the compensation of feeling that, in a general sense, I would be speaking for things in which my family believed. It seemed, in some way, right.

When Tom and I arrived home two weeks later, we found that the local newspaper's announcement of the coming event had stirred the interest of the town, and there was a hub-bub of anticipation. This write-up followed the day after the program:

NC Wesleyan Poetry Evening Draws Over Capacity Crowd
By Patty Lambert

Three professional poets and Mrs. Elizabeth Pearsall of Rocky Mount sparked a literary renaissance in the community with their program at Wesleyan College last week.

Overwhelming attendance at 8:00 p.m., Thursday, February 11, took Wesleyan officials by surprise. More chairs were carried into the faculty lounge, Wesleyan students began to sit on the floor, benches and tables were shifted, and latecomers were packed in the corridor. A Rocky Mount banker was just offering a lady his lap, when Dr. Jack Teagarden announced that the audience would move to the more spacious Wesleyan cafeteria.

The large crowd of townspeople was in part attributed to the sudden discovery that a long-time friend and neighbor, Mrs. Elizabeth Pearsall, was a published poet.

The revelation apparently struck a secret chord in the community. Mrs. Pearsall herself, in remarks prefacing her reading, said that the newspaper announcement of her share in the Wesleyan program had uncovered dozens of poets among her acquaintances. People had approached her at the supermarket confiding, "I've been writing too, but never dared tell anybody."

As he introduced the four poets, Dr. Teagarden said that the program was made possible through funds from the North Carolina Council of the Arts. Wesleyan College was one of the few colleges in the state to receive this grant, though many had applied. The grant was specified "to foster dissemination of the arts throughout the state." Terms included "three professional poets and one local poet in an informal setting."

First on the program was Professor Ronald Bayes, writer-in-residence at St. Andrew's College in Laurinburg. Some of his readings were taken from his latest volume, *The History of the Turtle*. His poems reflected his experiences on the West Coast and in

402

the Orient.

Bayes communicated to his listeners his acute shock at the realization of conflicting values in the East and West.

Next to read was Hal Seiber of Greensboro, who works as coordinator of the Chamber of Commerce in Greensboro. He commented on the attitude of the business world toward poetry. He said he dared not read his poems in Greensboro, for fear of undermining his image as a tough practical businessman.

He amused the audience by saying that if Professor Bayes thinks we are as different from Orientals as cats from dogs, then he must be a dog who has married a cat – Seiber's wife is Oriental.

Another remark which nailed listeners' attention was Seiber's suggestion that Shakespeare's Dark Lady of the Sonnets was black indeed. The later Sonnets abound with clues supporting his theory.

Last of the professional poets was Dr. Tom Walters, assistant professor of English at N.C. State in Raleigh. Walter's contribution to the evening was a series of vignettes based on his boyhood employment at a moving picture theater in Tarboro.

His poems showed how the larger-than-life images built up by the old Hollywood star system have produced a new mythology. He ended his series with a penetrating portrait of Ava Gardner.

Intermission-and-coffee-break was the scene of confession and exchange of confidences in an audience composed of young and old, black and white, schoolteachers, students, faculty, administration, senior citizens, housewives, nurses, clerks, soda fountain employees, and many more.

At this time James Van Laan invited all present to inspect and buy copies of ASPECTS, the Wesleyan literary magazine. Van Laan is president of the college literary club and editor of the magazine.

For the friends and neighbors of Mrs. Elizabeth Pearsall, the last section of the program was the highlight of the evening. She read from her book *Kernels from the Compound* and other works. Her mood was a sweep from gaiety to sadness. Her topics ranged from love of nature to social consciousness. Settings reflected life on a Florida island, earlier days in Rocky Mount, and vivid experiences in bygone Peking.

Amid the triumph of applause, Mack Pearsall brought her a sheaf of roses and a poem from her grandson which began, "Roses are red, violets are blue..."

During the discussion the poets were asked at what age they began to write and what caused them to write. The answers were all different. Mrs. Pearsall, formerly Elizabeth Braswell of Battleboro, said that her childhood shyness prompted her first verses. Too shy to ask her father for something special, like a pony, she would put her wish in a poem and leave it in his room. The results encouraged her to continue writing.

Other points discussed were working methods, habits of revision, publication versus privacy, and sources of inspiration.

The departing audience was invited by Wesleyan student James Van Laan to submit creative work to the editorial panel of ASPECTS. Many from the Rocky Mount community expressed a desire for another Wesleyan poetry reading with more local participation. Townspeople interested in attending such a gathering should contact Jack Teagarden at Wesleyan, 442-7121.

Since my Captiva friends had expressed real interest in my public appearance, with shameless immodesty, I sent them copies of the poems I had read, including the ways in which I had woven them together. The poems I chose were mainly those relating to the island, but there were two that were the result of a growing social consciousness on my part. The one with the title *Annie* is self-explanatory. The *Rickshaw Boy* was written years later when I came across the information that because of their exposure in the bitter weather that swept down over the steppes over China, thousands of rickshaw bearers died young from tuberculosis.

A Salute to Gasparilla for the Discovery of our Island
and for Providing it with a Name

Sharp-eyed pirate
of Mexican waters
Capturing sisters,
Wives, and daughters
Leaving them under
The Banyan tree
To mend your nets
As you roamed
More free.
You never knew
The breath of romance
You gave to us
As a thing of chance
For we took
The name of
Your Spanish Maids
And almost came to
Bless your raids
For the name was
One born to beguile
No other would
So suit
Our Isle –
Captiva –

A Walk on the Beach Following the Sanderlings

Keeping time, and
Companionably gay
You move downshore
In your water
Ballet.
You weave in and out
Of the surf's sea lace
I saunter behind
At an accepted pace
We move to music
Adajio
Bound in the rhythm
Of
Ebb
And
Flow

Stopping for a word of explanation before the next poem, I said to my listeners, "One of the nicest customs on the two sister islands is that, often, two or three are gathered together in late afternoon to watch the sunset. It is usually done to the accompaniment of drinks. The hour is always filled with the excitement of hoping that on that particular afternoon there will be, once again, what is known as *The Green Flash*, that moment when, as the fiery ball drops below the horizon, there appears a long, lateral, flash of green.

"But with twelve years of watching for this phenomenon and no luck, I had almost given up hope, when, one afternoon at a neighbor's house my patience was rewarded, and I dashed home to write the poem which I sent to the island paper where it duly appeared."

Once Upon a Flash

Hadst thought me
That that celebrated
Flash of green
(Just by the
Quick-of-eye
And then, seldom seen)
A thing of myth.

Hadst begun me
To associate

This sometime
Phenomenon
In some dim way
But firmly
with "the fifth"

When lo,
Upon an afternoon
Behold,
Mine hostess
Coaxed for me
This boon,
From Paleolith

So now,
No longer skeptical,
It waxes me
Poetical
To find me
That the legend doth
Have pith.

In the thoughtful life there is always an element of looking back, of trying to weave the past into the fabric of the whole, as we know it, and to give it meaning.

Two unforgettable incidents in my own life, far back in time, and widely separated geographically, illustrate a delayed perception on my part.

We Are the Products of Our Times

The corporate guilt
Of blinded man
Becomes a part of
His being.
In looking back
With the sight
Of seeing
May we not be more
Free?

Ten Thousand Miles Apart

There was Annie—
Annie was a maid
Not the one of romance
But a domestic, who never

In any way displayed
Displeasure with her
Meager wage

She had two children
The children had no father
And from the protection
Of my own sheltered life
And its lack of insight
I thought of Annie's morals
As a Pharisee

Later
I tried to find
Annie
To make some small
Retribution
But she had
Left.
And I?–
Bereft.

From the other side of the world I also have a clinking chain.

The Rickshaw Boy

For often
On a winter's night
You wouldn't
Know
Where my thoughts
Go.

The eye of the mind
Travels fast;
Like light
It speeds a distance
Vast.
Mine comes to rest
In old Peking.

I see a party
Of tourists
On holiday
Being drawn about
By human horses

in rickshaws, painted
Gay.

Night where bitter
Winds swept down
From China's old great wall.

Our errands were only
Those of pleasure
To the rickshaw boy
Our pennies,
Treasure.

The riskshaw boy waited outside
To furnish my returning ride

Between the shaves
In the animal-sleep
Of a stall-less, strawless bed
He wouldn't have dreamed
Of tomorrow's meat
But of some small share
Of rice, or bread.

I emerged
From a rich-hung
Room
To bid him
Pant into
The gloom
As my
Bearer

And stirring the
Night
The sound was
Light
Of his padded
Feet
On the old
Cold stone
Of the narrowing
Street
Bringing my hotel
Nearer.

But his wracking cough

and the smoking
Breath
Floating back
To me
On my smooth
Ride
To his too-young
Death
Will be
As lasting
As
The
Sea.

These two fragments of life,
A world apart
Strike small fears
Within my heart;
Of man's
Continuing
Inhumanity.

Yet in the very fear
May lie
A kind of
Pilgrim's Progress.

One package of poems to Captiva friends went to Ruth and Ed Lowry of Peterborough, Vermont, another to Jim and Betty Gray in their summer home in Stanford, Connecticut. This was particularly bold on my part, because, as I've mentioned, Jim had been a literary critic and had written seven novels. From the Lowrys:

> Elizabeth dear,
> Thanks for your poems folder. How I should like to have been there! Keep on expressing in your clear melodious directness what so many people muffle in irrelevant hurry and scurry –those verities which, as they live the years along, people who are not sentient, fail to perceive. Have a glorious summer!
> Affectionately always,
> Ruth

There's nothing like being seen through the eyes of supportive friends. From Jim Gray:

> Thank you for letting us see these lines. You have a gift of gaiety

that enables you to turn phrases gracefully and to play with words, ideas, and attitudes in something of the way of Emily Dickinson. (Did you ever?) She might be a good model for you. For another one, Dorothy Parker, but you have none of Dorothy Parker's harshness or bitterness. (Thank goodness!) Of the things which I had seen before, I liked the one about Molly best. Of the overview, I especially enjoyed the one about the green flash and the one called "Richshaw Boy." Betty joins me in congratulations and affection.

Jim Gray

A true sample of affection and understanding encouragement.

But a few days after that moment of glamour, we were back on the island, and except for a flurry of fan mail, life was the same.

≈ ≈ ≈

Everybody on Captiva and on Sanibel knew that among the natural beauty by which both islands were surrounded, there were alligators in the canals and in the bayous of Sanibel. These canals were fed by our own island waters as well. Sometimes, by looking over the sawgrass into the canals that ran along the road on Sanibel you could see one of those scary creatures. In the wildlife preserve they were always on the prowl, and driving slowly on the sandy roads that wove through the waters, we sometimes witnessed that pitiable violence of nature, as an alligator slithered up and grabbed a lovely wading bird in the grip of its jaws. The struggle would be brief; after a few seconds, the bird would lie limp. Gradually, feathers and all would disappear.

Fortunately for us, and I daresay it was the pattern, there was rarely what would have been the doubly sad sight of an alligator seizing one of the roseate spoonbills. For in the softness of their color, and the gentle flapping of their wings as they came into the preserve late in the afternoon to feed in the shallows, their beauty was poetic. The most stately flamingo, in all its flamboyance – and we had no flamingos on this strand of islands – could not have upstaged them. It would have been the other way around.

These threats to our wading birds went on at a distance of four or five miles from Captiva. It was not generally believed that alligators ever came into our own waters. All the same, one day in summer, Tom and I had a frightening experience with one in a bayou very close behind our house. There had been a storm that afternoon, so that we had not gone out in either of the boats. But by sunset the air was clearing again, and we decided to go out for a short row in the skiff.

We loved going into the quietness of the bayous, especially at that hour, for many of the birds would have settled in the mangroves for the night. With the tide out, however, one or two might be still wading in the shallows, standing – on one stalk of a leg – transfixed, ready to pounce on any kind of food that came by. The tide happened to be out that day. This always changed the beauty of the mangroves to the grotesque, for it exposed in their entirety their eery three or four foot deep, spreading, dark, spidery roots. Instead of their then being the lovely masses of thick, deep green roots that they appeared when showing through the clear water, they now became sinister. And since mangroves grow quickly and very thick, a seed always fighting somewhere for a foothold in a grain of sand, they were everywhere up and down the bay. But for a small opening, they enclosed every bayou.

Always, at low tide, when I saw those exposed roots in a bayou, I would think, *What a perfect setting for a Charles Adams cartoon.* For the evil-looking figures of that cartoonist, with their chalk-white faces and their long black hair, seemingly always plotting malevolence, were, themselves, the personification of evil. I could see them cast-off in one of the bayous, trying desperately to gain a foothold in the tangle of roots. The pain would have been unbearable.

That afternoon, after a five minutes' row, we turned into the narrow opening of the bayou nearest our house, a small one, and were quietly drifting when we saw that we had the company of an alligator. There was no wading bird in sight to attract his attention. Tom and I were wearing shorts and short sleeves, and it crossed my mind that the alligator might consider an arm or a leg a convenient supper. My heart was in my mouth. I spoke in a low voice, "I'm scared to death!"

Tom's voice, too, was low. But he answered, "We'll be all right. Just sit perfectly still." And we drifted quietly for what seemed an eternity.

Straining the water through his teeth, the alligator slowly explored the side of the bayou opposite ours. Then, to complete the circle of his exploration, he slowly turned toward our side. "Don't make him mad," I whispered, in a frozen state as he eased toward the skiff.

"No," answered Tom. And as we held our breath and watched, at a distance of three feet, the alligator appeared to hesitate for an instant in indecision; whether to have his meal there, or whether his taste buds really called for the more familiar flavor of feathers.

To our relief, the decision was made in favor of feathers, and as though in no hurry to leave, he quietly glided out of the narrow opening of the bayou into the bay. And we began to breathe, for those powerful jaws had been very near, and the skiff sat very low in the water. We could easily understand, after that, why the bay waters of this strand of islands were never used for swimming.

≈ ≈ ≈

Of all the water birds on our strand of islands, the cormorant must surely be the one of least popular appeal. Black all over, not quite as large as a pelican, its small head on its long neck gives it a snake-like appearance. We never saw them in numbers, but there was always one, wet and sleek, perched high – and in bold relief – sitting alone at the top of one of the many channel markers. Engaged in its solitary fishing, it would wing out silently to dive and to gulp, and then return to the perch. There, its jet-black wings spread to dry, it was a forbidding creature from another world, one sleek-winged, but reptilian, mysterious and sinister. Choosing a channel marker for its lookout meant that when a boat passed – necessarily within a few feet of the marker itself – the cormorant would fly up and wheel out, and as soon as the boat had passed, would again settle on his perch. They never seemed to utter a sound.

Admittedly a legitimate part of the natural world, to me they were a blot on the landscape. Yet, I hardly ever watched their little routine without thinking, with some sympathy, of those cormorants in Japan, which are sometimes used in a way that seems a little cruel, where, by tying a string to the foot of a cormorant, as soon as the bird has swallowed its catch, a native can quickly snatch the bird from the water. Quickly bringing it into his boat, he can force the cormorant to disgorge the fish for his own benefit, and then repeat the process.

≈ ≈ ≈

In all of our coming and going to and from Carolina and Captiva, as any person, especially a woman, living in two homes does, I was always carrying along things from one place to the other. The largest item I ever travelled with by air was one of those long ago discarded battery jars, used in some way in connection with the generation of electricity by Delco. In the years of my growing up, the Delco engine that generated the lights for our house throbbed off and on through the day. We had gone from gas to electricity after Henry Sessoms had forgotten not to enter the gas house with a lighted lantern, and the gas house had blown up. Henry was not seriously hurt, but his eyebrows and lashes were singed, and the balding that had started was finished off. After that, the members of his family, because of his shiny head, called him Henry Slick. Henry took this with his usual good nature.

Naturally, Henry took kindly to the change in the way of lighting our house, and one of the things that he enjoyed was washing the empty glass battery jars and lining them up on a shelf where their thick aquamarine color gave them beauty. Year in and year out, the battery jars sat there, of no use to anybody. Then suddenly, there was a fad for using them in homes, where, filled with tall flowers, they are effective. Seeing that I had brought one down for our island cottage, Janet Lynch began to long for one of her own for her Captiva house. And that was the reason, that on one of our flights down from Carolina, one of these jars flew down with me.

But usually it was the other way. I would be bringing things home with me from the island. Some of these were the large, lovely green ceramic salad plates that Susan Karr had begun to make from the pattern of a real sea grape leaf. I have them still, a dozen, another small tangible link with Captiva.

Among Susan's many talents was this one, discovered only after she had become a grandmother. At one time, her five-year-old grandson was spending some time with her on Captiva, when one day he showed her a kit of modeling clay he'd been given. The little boy didn't know what to do with it, and grandmother-like, Susan took the time to sit down and help him. As she shaped the clay, not knowing in which direction it would take her, the head of the Statue of Liberty began to come through.

The next day, Ding Darling, the well-known cartoonist of the *St. Louis Post Dispatch*, came by to see Colonel Karr and Susan, and seeing the clay head, wanted to know who had done it. With the explanation, he went back down the island to his own home, to return soon with a bucket filled with ten pounds of modeling clay, saying to Susan, "I will come back in a week to see what you've done with it."

The days went by, Susan was busy. But the last night of the seven, not wanting to face her friend without attempting anything, she started with a larger ball of clay than before. Her mind went like this: *St. Francis of Assisi is my favorite saint, but I've never seen a statue of him that really pleased me. He's always portrayed as a well-fed, plump little monk. And for the life of me, I cannot picture that man of God, who had given all his worldly possessions away, never thereafter, to have any thought for his own well-being, as anything but ascetic.*

And as she thought, a figure more of the spirit than of the flesh began to emerge. His cheeks were hollow, his body thin almost to emaciation, the cord of his robe hung loosely. And of course, his feet were bare. When Mr. Darling saw this product of Susan's artistic nature, his judgement was sustained. With his encouragement, Susan went into ceramics. Her trade name became "Sea-ramics by Susan." As time went on, she would have a small shop. Firing her kiln gave the Colonel an interest to replace his years in the army, and by word of mouth, Susan became relatively famous.

During those first three years of ours, when I spent so many weeks alone in Susan's guest house, it was fascinating for me to watch her work. And, as was the case with so many of our Captiva friends, she and the Colonel would make a visit to us in North Carolina. In reflection, I see that Susan's influence was another of the components that was to make the Captiva community what it was and to make a contribution to my own life.

≈ ≈ ≈

For a long while, the community meetings on the island were held in the chapel, which was very small. Gradually, it came to be felt that it would be more democratic to construct a larger building and to urge more islanders to attend community meetings. This change was approached with fear and trembling. Captivans were always afraid that the simple life we loved might be slowly and unknowingly sacrificed. But when it began to be discussed that we might include a library in the building, the idea took hold. And once it did, there was enthusiasm for the project.

In time the community house would become a place to hold our combination rummage and bake sales, the money going toward the fire department and the rescue squad. It was fun to go down and buy each other's clothes. In a way, it was an exchange of personalities. Our Irish friends, Bob and Irene Murison, were so filled with the delight of buying quality things from L.L. Bean and other good brands which were so well suited to their life on the Irish sea, that when they came each year to visit us, they brought along empty suitcases.

I remember, with special pleasure, how handsome Bob was, with his wavy red hair and his good physique, his handsomeness multiplied when he wore a natural-colored linen jacket for which he had paid fifty cents. Irene was just as proud and just as distinctive with her soft, short black hair and her green eyes, when, in cool weather, she would be wearing a pair of well-cut gray pants, or "trousers," as they speak of them in Europe, with one of her own good Irish sweaters. Irene's concession to evening was to replace the trousers with a pleated plaid skirt, and add to the sweater a short string of real pearls. I liked it immensely that Bob and Irene could be so marvelously self-possessed in their openly-acknowledged second-hand fifty-cent attire, Irene adding the grace-note of real pearls.

At these jumble sales, so-called in the British Isles, we even bought each other's cooking utensils, and cocktail glasses and oddments. It was jolly to have these show up on tables and coffee tables other than our own, so easy to recognize each other's, and to laugh among ourselves over the swaps. This, instead of running off to Naples, a thirty-five mile drive, to shop in its swish stores, although undeniably, those "sometimes" trips did rejoice the hearts of Captiva ladies, as, in that sophisticated environment, our credit cards came out of hiding, and for a few hours, we lapped up the feeling of being, again, in the mainstream.

≈ ≈ ≈

The chapel at Captiva was small. In our time, from tropical storms and simultaneous erosion, it sat no more than a hundred or more yards from the sea. It is a wooden building with a steeple and a cross. Painted white, inside it is pale blue. Its gothic windows hold no stained glass, but since they were usually open, worship went on to the sound of the sea. In a system of rotation, interdenominational retired ministers came for two years at a time; often they stayed longer. For the minister and his wife, a small house near the chapel was furnished, and in a loose sense, the couple carried on a form of parish life. Ministers were chosen by a small committee.

Tom and I were always there on Sunday mornings, for church on Sunday mornings had been, for each of us, a way of life. Sometimes, at the height of the winter season, when there were a lot of houseguests on the island, we and others and our guests and theirs would have to sit outside on folding chairs. It was inspiringly lovely. Purposely, neither Tom nor I took on church responsibilities on the island, however, that went on at home in Carolina.

But at one point, when our close friend, Ed Lowry, who had been chairman of the church committee, gave an especially comprehensive annual report of the chapel at a morning service, I asked him afterward if I might have a copy. In the deep-down feeling that someday I would want to write about Captiva as I had known it, I wanted Ed's statement for my story. He agreed to send me one, and after some months, when he and Ruth had almost ended their usual trip north through the inland waterway on their boat, the *Sundog,* Ed answered my request.

Ed's letter to me, accompanying the church report, was typically Ed:

Aboard the "Sundog"
April 29, 1975

Dear Elizabeth,
    Here's the report I promised you. My typing is vestigial at best, and on a slightly rocking boat, it is a disaster – but here it is.
    We've arrived at the Eastern shore after a good trip, even though

the wind did blow out of the North for two solid weeks. Ruth is in Washington for her meeting and I'm doing ship's chores.

We set off for Peterborough next week.

We've been almost a month now without mail and I'm eager to get caught up on events when we get home – especially what happened in the erosion vote. There's a certain peaceful quality about the living vacuum on a boat – but after a while you need to plug in again. My best to you and Tom,

Yours, Ed

President's Statement
1975 Annual Meeting
Chapel by the Sea

For those of you who are not familiar with the operational side of Chapel by the Sea, let me briefly describe the set-up.

Chapel by the Sea is not a parish. It has no members and no parish roll. It is, quite simply, a strong and active fellowship with a unique capacity to weld together a changing and fluid group. The Chapel season begins the third Sunday in November and this year ends with the service on April 13th. The fiscal year is from April 30th to May first.

Its modest business affairs are run by a board of fifteen Associates elected for three year terms with the term of five ending each year. No Associate may serve more than two consecutive terms. Under that salutary rule the current president (myself) and the current treasurer (Susan Karr) go off the board next month.

Your officers for next year will be:

Bud Hemphill, President
Jim Scholefield, Vice President
Kay Schultz, Treasurer
Milt Prince, Recording Secretary
Dorothy Dickey, Corresponding Secretary

The Chapel has had a happy year. It has again demonstrated an almost magical capacity to evoke help and support in its affairs; and it has, I believe, been a warm and effective force in the community.

On a more mundane level it is in good working order. Its buildings are in good condition. The livability of the rectory has been improved by a good deal of interior rehabilitation and further interior painting has been contracted for and will be done when Bill and Virginia leave for the summer. A washer and dryer and a new television set and serial have also been installed.

Encouraged by the success of last year's do-it-yourself project (the painting of the outside of the rectory, garage and study) we carried out this year a chair painting project with a large number of willing volunteer helpers. I spoke a moment ago about the Chapel's capacity

416

to evoke support. Let me give you an example. Among those who worked hard all three mornings were a couple staying at a Sanibel motel who, I believe, had never been here before and who were down here on a ten day vacation.

The Chapel has at the moment no serious problems and sees none immediately ahead. As the treasurer has reported, operating expenses for the year to date have run about two thousand above operating income. In that calculation the board treats as income only plate collections, individuals gifts, and interest received on capital funds. It does not treat gifts to the Tribute Fund as current income but regards such gifts as capital contributions, even though their use is not restricted. If the experience of prior years is repeated this year, as I hope it will be, remaining plate collections and end of season gifts will close that two thousand dollar gap and put us in the black for the fiscal year ending May first.

Next year you will have a new president and a new treasurer. They have both already demonstrated their total commitment to this Chapel and their ability to translate that commitment into effective action. I thank them both for all the help and support they have given me, and I'll be rooting for them from the sidelines next year.

You will also have next year three new board members:

Mrs. Charles Fenton
Charles Stevens
P. Corbin Kohn

On behalf of the entire fellowship of the Chapel I welcome them to the board.

I've saved the best news for the last. Bill and Virginia Little will be with us again next year. This Chapel has been fortunate in its ministers but never more fortunate than this last year. We have all been stirred by the incisive quality of Bill's mind, by its brilliance and by the scholarship and experience upon which that mind draws. And when with all that, come two warm and delightful friends, how lucky can a congregation get?

That's your president's report. It ends with his warmest thanks to everyone of you who HAVE GIVEN of yourselves to make this little Chapel what it is.

≈ ≈ ≈

The Captiva way of meeting death was natural and impressively realistic. Since most of the winter residents had their permanent homes in northern climates, making interment in winter difficult, the usual way was cremation, interment deferred until spring. With the death of an islander, a handwritten notice, posted under the palms on the billboard outside the tiny post office, would announce the hour of a memorial service, to be held the next morning at the Chapel by the Sea.

At one of those services, Bill Little, the minister, quoted a beautiful poem. It spoke of death as only a door in a garden wall. The connotation was one of quiet, and rest. But in the memorial service of a later time, another of these interdenominational ministers spoke of death in another way, as the extinguishing of a lamp; for the light of morning has come. Of the two interpretations, I prefer the latter. It suggests continuity, work still to be done, perhaps even a progression from world to world in the honing of our souls.

After these memorial services, island life would go on in the usual way. The day of the memorial service, the family of the deceased might even have its lunch pleasantly on the beach. And under those circumstances, this oneness with nature seemed particularly fitting. To be exposed to that healthful attitude toward death was to have it relieved of much of its sting.

≈ ≈ ≈

For the first half dozen or so years of our Captiva life, Vivian was still making her home with us, but with more and more single women beginning to have their own homes or apartments, Vivian began to plan for a home of her own. Yet, in her nature there was a certain cautiousness; possibly it was this vein of weighing things carefully that, over time, had kept her from marrying. She certainly had plenty of opportunities.

A mild form of thrift had always been a part of Vivian's nature. This was, in a sense, a nice balance. She was the kind who, in late life, would darn a worn place in an old sweater, and on the same day, write a large check for some person's favorite charity. She never let it be known just how much good she did, such as the paying of hospital bills for others. One of the needs close to her heart was, in medical vernacular, to "put-on" a trained nurse for those who'd had surgery and who could not afford that kind of care. Furnishing that service incognito became one of her pleasures. She helped finance college educations, she gave trips to Europe among young members on Mother's side of the family, and she lent her time and effort to community and church service.

In retrospect, my sisters and I were all different. Sister, the oldest, or the "eldest," which I love to say and don't, was the painter, her continuing artistic inclination revealed in the beautiful Mediterranean house and the formal Italian garden which she and her husband Bob built; Vivian's forté was music, for although each of us played and sang, she and Mother were always the ones who played for the family to sing around the piano. And like Mother, she could play for hours for her own pleasure. All her life, Vivian attended concerts in Raleigh and Richmond, and travelled widely. Alice Bryan was the domestic one, often in the kitchen in her wheelchair, where she and the cook made delicious layer cakes, petite fours, and fancy candies. Alice Bryan also painted landscapes in oil and made charcoal drawings. I, the youngest, except for a predilection for the written word, was neither fish nor fowl.

Since Tom and I had each had a happy family background, it carried over into our homelife. We believed in making the evening meal the high point of the day. With everybody glad to be together, conversation would be sprinkled with laughter. Even when Tom's business and political life required his being away during the week, the supper hour was such a happy one, that as often as he could, he would call home around that time, speaking to each one in turn, often asking us what we were having for supper – all of the small heart-warming things that make for human happiness. And he would let us know how much he wanted to be there. On weekends he would try to make up for these times of separation.

In my own early life, at bed-time in winter, the family, as likely as not, would be gathered around the hearth in the sitting room, eating such unlikely things as sour pickles and crackers and sardines sprinkled with lemon juice and – something at which current generations would shiver – a jellied substance made of pig's feet and well-seasoned with vinegar and red pepper and called "souse." Small blocks of it were kept in the pantry in a large stone crock, and on a cold night, from a cold pantry, to have a block of this on a small plate with sardines and crackers in front of a bright fire made it delectable. At times, apples would be substituted for sardines, and the eleventh commandment in our family was "Don't throw the apple core into the fire!" You did not waste something that a lower form of life might need. No matter how cold the night, you had to get up and go out on the side porch and toss the core over the banister, leaving the door open to a chorus inside of, "Hurry up, we're freezing!"

But these nighttime feasts in my own little family, when the time came, would become corn popped in the fireplace, and the cracking and eating of nuts. For our generation was scaling down its menus. All this family happiness had its part in making Vivian, as she lived with us, continue to postpone the building of the home that she had begun to speak of as her "dream house." Against that time, however, she would, now and then, on her travels, buy some good piece of antique furniture and a few objects of art. These were stored upstairs in our garage in the rooms that had earlier been servants' quarters. When her friends, having known for a long time that she owned a beautiful lot in our own suburban area would ask, "Vivian, when are you going to build your dream-house?" her answer would be, "I'm not sure that I could face eating all my meals alone."

Many times through the years, knowing as we did that she wanted her own home, Tom would make the understanding, affectionate comment to me, privately, "Vivian is a fine woman; she's just in the grip of fear. It's understandable."

Time and two things made it less threatening for her to take the bold step. With the discovery of Captiva, Tom and I were spending more and more time away. Vivian seldom went with us. She didn't like staying overnight on an island that had to be reached by ferries that ran only in the day. In that our sons were no longer at home, Vivian was, in effect, for long intervals, living alone. The reality of that gradually dawned on her, and she began to manage her own life. Once plans were set in motion for building her home, the apparent indecisiveness in her nature became altogether the reverse. Vivian knew what she wanted, and she set out to get it.

Television had recently arrived, and whether or not we complain about its violence, the preponderance of its bedroom scenes, and the lack of taste in its commercials, and although we freely acknowledge the fact that, except for the educational programs, its lure has indirectly reduced the quality of education in our country, we have to admit, that, as no other one thing could have done, it has made us one world. And we have to admit further, that for those people living alone, especially the elderly and the sick, it has been a blessing. Probably the prospect of having some of her meals on a tray with TV for company, as half the population now does, made Vivian's decision easier. So it was, that at sixty, after having been a part of our family's daily life for twenty-seven years, she suddenly announced, "I've decided to build my house. I've already been to see Harry Haarles, I've told him what I want, and he's drawing the plans."

Sharing her excitement, all of us wanted to know what style it would be. Cape Cod? Colonial? What? For we had assumed that it would be something small and cozy. But her answer was indicative of the practical in her nature. "No," she replied, "It will be Georgian. I've noticed that a Georgian home has a better resale value than any other style."

From then on, things fell into place in a way that was all-round joy. Williamsburg and other fine colonial homes had given Eastern Carolinians a deep love of beautiful interiors, so that I suggested, "I hope you'll have the most beautiful woodwork in the world."

While her house would not have so bold a distinction as that, it did, and does include beautiful paneling, a winding stair, heavy cornices ornamented with dental work, and over-door treatments of broken pediments. I would not have dreamed that someday it would become my own home, that with the ending of that sad, sad year following Tom's death, which I spent in the home he and I built and had lived in for nearly fifty years, a year in which Vivian's health was failing, at her death, I would come to live in hers, the more compact of the two homes, the one with the smaller grounds.

In a veiled way, Vivian had suggested that she hoped that was the way things would turn out, and since the last, and possibly the happiest twenty-one years of her life had been spent there, my going to live in her home gave me the feeling that there was something I could still do for her.

From our local paper:

In Our Opinion
Invaluable Citizen

She had a habit of contributing generously to the annual community support program for North Carolina Wesleyan College and it came as no surprise to those who knew this great lady to find that the same amount had been provided in her name again this year, even after Vivian Braswell's death.

No wonder the recent death of Miss Braswell, a member of one of the most distinguished families in the area, caused a representative of one of the institutions she had generously assisted in a financial way, to comment that "she was a real good friend."

And it takes only a casual examination of her role as a citizen interested in all phases of the community to realize how very much she meant to so many individuals and institutions.

Perhaps Miss Braswell's assistance was most evident in her role as benefactor of Wesleyan College. First there was the Braswell contribution, in which she played an important role, of the site for the college.

Not content with helping to provide the land, Miss Braswell then concentrated upon other phases of the college. For example, there was the substantial gift made in her name to the library.

Then, there were gifts in the capital gains program of the college starting with a $25,000 gift in 1970 and another large contribution five years later.

Not only that, but her annual support to the college was significant, including the large amount contributed in her name that came about even after her death.

Thus, Miss Braswell's contributions have been immense to the college, but other community activities also were remembered. There was the $50,000 contribution made by Miss Braswell and her sisters to the YMCA building fund when that institution undertook an expansion program several years ago.

Miss Braswell's physical presence no longer is possible, but her lifetime of assistance to her community will be remembered.

≈ ≈ ≈

Now more of the Captiva story.

In our stays on the island, we would occasionally decide to go by boat across Pine Island Sound, a distance of perhaps, five miles, to one of the fish houses. This one sat several miles from the shore. Our purpose would be to buy a mackeral or a few blues or a trout. It might be that even a pompano would have come up in the commercial fisherman's net that morning.

We would tie up at the base of an unpainted one-story structure sitting high above the water near Pine Island, and climb the ladder up its side, sometimes to the disappointment of being told by the young man in charge that there were none of those fish that day, for, as he would express it, "Mullets are sellin' high, and we're goin' after them now."

After we had admired the tubs of the day's catch, we would back down the ladder into the *Carolina*, and cast off for Captiva. One day, headed home, and halfway across this open stretch, we saw a small motor-boat going in the direction from which we'd come. Thinking the owner of the boat might be a commercial fisherman, we steered toward him, and when we were in calling distance, Tom yoohoo'd, "Do you have any mackerel or any pompanos?"

"No Pompanos, one mackerel, and one small blue," came back across the water.

"Will you sell those two to us?" Tom wanted to know.

"No, I'll give 'em to you."

By this time our boats were drawing close to each other. From his nets in the bottom of his boat and their contents of squirming, silvery mullets, now glimmering in the sunlight, he handed Tom the two fish. Tom insisted on paying, saying, "You'll never make a living that way."

"I won't make a living out of them two fish, neither," the old man said philosophically, a pleasant smile on his weathered and wrinkled face.

Headed toward home and into a rising wind, we increased speed, it was hard to make conversation, and I fell to thinking: *Is life spent under the open sky and on the open sea conducive to thinking larger thoughts than in other areas; to applying values that are not commercial to a situation?* I decided it was. For I have noticed the same generous trait in people who live close to the soil, people who, under large open skies, in a similar relationship with natural forces, draw their living from the fruits of the earth.

≈ ≈ ≈

A great many retired U.S. Ambassadors, and those who had formerly been connected with the State Department and had held foreign posts had houses on Captiva. One of these was Randy Harrison, from Charlottesville, Virginia. As a young man, Randy had been injured in an automobile accident, and afterwards, was confined to a wheelchair. He had to have an attendant always with him, and had been lucky in finding a younger man who had started out to study medicine, but had given it up to take care of Randy's needs. This young man was a Seventh Day Adventist, a sect which, from once having had a hospital experience in Tacoma Park, in the city of Washington in one of their health institutions similar to Battle Creek, I've always respected.

Almost as much as Randy, Leslie, whose Polish surname I can neither remember nor spell, was an island favorite. At his death, Leslie was given Randy's house, and even now, a great many years later, if I want to reach Leslie by mail, all I need is to write on the envelope the word "Leslie," and, Captiva Island, Florida 33924.

Among island favorites, there was Paul Everett, a year-round resident who had, at one time, taught French in a New England prep school, but had received injuries to his kidneys in the Korean War that made it necessary for him to live in a warm climate. Since Paul's eyesight was, to a degree, failing, to make a living, he took care of people's yards. He spoke almost "Oxford English," and he lived in a tiny house – perhaps twenty by twenty-five feet, that, painted blue, was called "The Robin's Nest." From there, very often, he would emerge the gentleman that he is, in late afternoon, to be a guest at one of the few formal dinners that went on on the island. And there, among a small group of remarkably distinguished persons, he would make his own contribution to the success of the evening. That was one of the charms of Captiva.

≈ ≈ ≈

One day, knowing that Tom and Bert were going out on the water and that Tillie's husband, Mike, would be busy with the editing of psychology textbooks, I invited Tillie over for lunch. Coming in with her lively step she found me in the kitchen preparing our salad.

"May I help you?" she wanted to know.

"No. I want you to do something else for me, though. I want you to record something."

"All right," she answered. "But what would you like?" We went into the living room together to select something, and from a stack of second-hand books I'd bought the day before from the book sale at the library, I picked out two. One was that slender volume of Thomas Wolfe's poetry, *A Stone, A Leaf, A Door.*

"How about reading these lines written after his brother Ben's death?" I asked. For I had found them very beautiful, and wanted to hear them spoken in Tillie's lovely diction. She was glad to comply:

Artemidorus, Farewell!

We can believe in the nothingness of life,
We can believe in the nothingness of death
And of life after death –
But who can believe in the nothingness of Ben?

In Tillie's voice it was as moving as it was beautiful. For who among us, in the early despair of having given up a loved one to death, has not had those thoughts? To have something in Tillie's voice in a lighter vein, however, I had her read one from the same volume, entitled, "Magic."

And who shall say –
Whatever disenchantment follows –
That we ever forgot magic,
Or that we can ever betray,
On this leaden earth,
The apple-tree, the singing,
And the gold?

The other one was from a collection of Victoria Sackville-West's *Country Notes* that appeared in a newspaper column in London. It referred to a flock of sheep, which, transported to another meadow, became melancholy. We were told that: "They stood still and scraped the days away." With this we learned that even sheep can be homesick, making homesickness a part of the natural order of things.

But then I said, "Now Tillie, you must record something for me in which you use the word *matinee.*"

We laughed together at this because I thought it delightful the way she sharpened her "T" in that word. Indeed, all her "T's" were sharp. To the same degree, she found my Eastern Carolina pronunciation of that word amusing. For one day, when we had gone together on errands to the town of Fort Meyers, one of those main errands being to reserve tickets to an afternoon performance of *Fiddler on the Roof,* she declared that at the box office I had asked, as though I were inclined toward horses who were a little off their rockers, for, "Two tickets for the *mad 'neigh* please,"

Her jocular recording, which she composed spontaneously on a loose sheet of paper as she sat in the kitchen, went something like this:

> *My friend Elizabeth has an idea*
> *Somewhat peculiar, not quite clear,*
> *That "matinee," when said by me*
> *Is not the same when said by she.*
> *And so to please her – who would not! –*
> *I'll gladly do no matter what*
>
> *The nuns with "matins" start their day*
> *But never see a matinee.*
> *Their sainted heads at ten recline*
> *After the office of Compline –*
> *But once in Paradise I hope each day*
> *Front seats are theirs for a matinee.*

What a happy friendship Tillie and I had, our conversations swinging easily between the ridiculous and the sublime.

≈ ≈ ≈

At one point, when, for about ten years, Captiva had been a second home for Tom and me, soon after the new year came in, we went down for one of our winter stays of three weeks. As usual, the first two days were given to getting settled. Now it was the third, and we sat on our patio, having lunch. But for the calendar, you would not have believed it was midwinter. There would be two more visits to Captiva for us during that winter season, but April would find us in Carolina, for who would ever want to miss Carolina spring? And since our income came largely from the land, for this and other reasons, we both liked to be at home for the growing season. We were not often lured away in summer, although, sometimes homesick for the island, we would pull ourselves away for a two weeks' visit there.

Always, by the third day on the island of one of our winter stays, which this was, we would have forgotten the long journey of nine hundred miles, one which, at that time, still required for us three modes of travel: car, plane, ferry, and again by car. On that third January day, Tom had spent the morning back at the boatslip working on our sailboat. After helping him for a while, I'd gone back to the house. Around noon, he came up to say that he was going on his bicycle for the mail. This would give me time – allowing his three-quarter-mile ride and a chance conversation of his with some friend at the post office – to prepare our lunch. This which was always simple. And we now sat at the table on the patio as we consumed our sandwiches and our salad, opening letters, occasionally reading aloud to each other from their contents.

When we'd been at Captiva for our fall visit that year, which had extended into December, we'd had a steady stream of houseguests and had made plans for more. For not only did we enjoy having our friends and relatives with us when we were there, but we felt that Captiva was so perfect that to have looked out toward our guesthouse with it sitting empty, even for a few days at a time, our hearts would have smote us. With the growing popularity of winter vacations, and friends and relatives travelling around Florida in their cars, there had come a perennial joke among Captivans, "If you're considering a house in the tropics, you'd better build it guest-proof." But it was said with tongue-in-cheek.

The visitors we were looking forward to with peculiar pleasure that day were our family: our two sons, our daughter-in-law, and our three-year-old grandson, Brad. Although their arrival was two weeks away, we'd already ferreted out from the bottom floor of the tower, the bucket and spade, and a kite to be flown on the beach. I had my shell-book-for-children within arm's reach, and everyday Tom was busy getting his fishing gear in order. It was almost like starting over again for us. And with this anticipation, the present was, for us, a lovely little interlude.

One of the flies in the ointment of living in a tropical paradise, however, is that when you have houseguests, you feel responsible for the weather. Those days when island weather was off-center, rainy, chilly, or blustery, were the only kind that made it easier for us to leave it for a few daylight hours.

On those kinds of days, if we had guests, we might entertain them by taking them to the mainland, combining lunch with a visit to the Edison Laboratory. This one-story, unimpressive building sat across the road from a typically comfortable southern home, one of porches, with emphasis on windows and doors. The Edison home and the Firestone home next door, were similar. The houses sat back from the road in the shade of their grounds, each of which held a variety of palms and an assortment of other tropical growth.

On one of our early trips to Mr. Edison's laboratory, our guide gave us a comforting thought to remember and to apply to our own lives, when he recounted a little incident that had to do with the invention of the light bulb. Experiment after experiment had taken place without success. With the failure of so many, the great man's colleague asked, one day, "Mr. Edison, we've now done 999 experiments. Each one has failed. Aren't you

426

discouraged?"

"No, indeed," replied the great man, "we now know 999 things that won't work."

On those bad-weather excursions in which we were trying to entertain our houseguests, with time on our hands, we would choose a nice restaurant in Fort Meyers for a leisurely lunch. A particular conversation, during one of these lunches, I remember very clearly. Having just left the Edison home, naturally, the first part of the meal was given to conversation about the inventor. And then, since we were in such awe of his genius and his accomplishments, for the fun of it, I tossed a related question into the hopper. For a few days earlier, I had come across a short newspaper clipping that, yellowed with age, had to do with Leonardo da Vinci. At the close, the writer made the intriguing statement that his was one of the three great minds over time. He did not list the others. My question to these two visiting cousins of mine from Atlanta, and to Tom, was, "Who were the other two?"

One after another of the great minds was suggested, only to be talked down by a conflicting opinion. There was nobody to confirm or deny our answers, but I think there was more agreement on a triumvirate (and since we were concerned on such a high level, I like running in that word): of Leonardo da Vinci, Charles Darwin, and Albert Einstein. Could we have been right?

≈ ≈ ≈

In another pattern of island weather, one of those rare spells of severe cold, something unusual and interesting happened. The temperature had fallen to thirty-five degrees; we were aware that all over central Florida the citrus grove owners were in a frenzy of keeping their smudge-pots going against the freeze. Where we were, much farther south, although the sun shone, even those sun-pockets we loved were not warm enough to lure us outside. When these spells came, for four or five days, we would stay off the water and do our indoor jobs. At those times, we might drop in on each other to talk, mainly about the weather. Our fireplaces would be going, and the change of lifestyle was not unpleasant. Indeed, coping in our own little icy home was rather exciting. On one of those afternoons, I had driven over to Sanibel for groceries. On my way back, I overtook three young girls who were walking. While warmly enough dressed, in something like hiking clothes, I wondered if, in such cold weather, they could possibly be camping. When they had accepted my offer of a ride, I asked them a few questions, and discovered that their accents were northern. It seemed that they were indeed camping at the far end of Sanibel. Along with them were three other college students – male. It was spring break, and they had come down from the University of Rochester, in New York state.

The winds were rising, not those lovely warm winds we were accustomed to, but strong and icy, and the wheels in my head began to turn. Keeping my thoughts to myself, they ran this way: *Our guesthouse is empty for this week. Why not offer it to these girls?* When I did, they could hardly believe their good fortune. Only then, however, did I realize that, once again, I had done something impulsive, a perennial pitfall which all my life I had been warned against by my two older sisters. After I was married, Tom sometimes good-naturedly did the same, but in a more understanding, not-so-blunt way. After all, a spouse has to use a certain amount of diplomacy.

It was clear to me immediately, that I might have approached the situation with a little more restraint. Nevertheless, I was now into it, head over heels. Cruising along in our ancient little Chevy, I was trying to carry on polite conversation, and at the same time, to devise a little plan. The plan required a little dinky. And so, I said, "Come with me first, while I go home and take something to my husband. He's waiting for it to work on his boat. Then we'll go back and get your clothes." For I was counting on Tom's good judgment to help me out.

When we had driven the twelve miles, and had turned into our driveway, I stopped the car and excused myself to go to the tower where I was sure to find Tom busy and happy and carefree in his workshop.

I explained what I had done; as always, he was sympathetic with my plight, and with the plight of human need in general, and understood the need of the girls for a roof over their heads. But he was characteristically practical.

"Tell the girls," he answered, "that we cannot offer hospitality to the boys, and that we would prefer having the boys stay out at their campsite entirely, rather than run the risk of disturbing our compound with six youthfully exuberant college students."

I knew that Tom was right; he nearly always was. He understood that to have given the boys an inch might have meant that they would have taken a mile, and not knowing what kind of boys they were, we could not do that, either to ourselves, or to the compound. He followed me to the car to meet the girls, and in his genial way, laid down the rules. By late afternoon, the girls were settled in the guesthouse, they were showering and washing their hair like mad, and we invited them over for supper, explaining that thereafter they would be on their own, and that the island store was in walking distance. After supper, the girls went back to their quarters and Tom and I settled down to read.

As we did so, it suddenly occurred to me that I must go next door and explain to the Rosses that we had guests – who they were, and how it had all happened.

With the news of our unusual houseguests, Jay went into shock. "Elizabeth," she said, "Do you mean that you have picked up a bunch of hippies; that we now have hippies in the compound? How do you know that they're not on dope? I can't imagine what got into you!" It was my sisters all over again, reminding me of my impulsiveness.

My answer could only be one of speculation. "Jay, I believe they're nice girls. I don't think they're on dope, and I don't think I could sleep in my bed tonight if I were thinking of their being out in a tent on a windy beach at thirty-five degrees." In some measure, Jay was mollified.

The girls did appear grateful; they had told the boys about our house rule, and for those three days and nights, they seemed thoroughly happy to be there with Tom and me. If the weather had been right, I knew that Tom would have been taking the whole little house party – girls and boys together – out in the boat, giving them the pleasures we tried to give our other guests: picnicking, and swimming and shelling on other islands, seeing the white pelicans en route.

Every day for exercise, the girls walked down the beach to "the island store," and one day they brought back the makings for cookies. When the cookies were baked, they brought me a plateful, and we sat down together for tea. It was really very nice; we enjoyed each other. On the fourth day, the whole group, boys and girls alike, had to leave in order to get back to Rochester in time for classes, and we said fond goodbyes. When a week had gone by, I began to look for a bread-and-butter note of some kind. Another week went by. Tom knew that I was expecting something like that, and after the second week, he said sympathetically, "Your girls have let you down."

"No," I answered, "They're doing something handmade for me, some lovely little token." And I went on laughingly, "They're hem-stitching handkerchiefs."

It became a joke between us. Tom would ask, when I came in with the mail basket, "Have your handkerchiefs come yet?"

"No," I would say, "They've decided to monogram them, too, and those things take time."

Nothing ever came.

It left Tom's mind, and rarely came into my own. When it did, I tried to rationalize the oversight: *It cannot only be that they're northern, and that I'm southern. It cannot be our different stations in life, for underneath, people are the same all over.* Yet, looking back, I saw that it was indeed, as it was declared, the decade of the "me generation." In their minds, the cookies had been enough. The custom of the written word as a follow-up, was, to my regret, fast going by the board. But as William of Wycherley said over three centuries ago, "Manners maketh man." Not only that, but in the language of today, Hie's frequent observation was that manners oil the machinery for all of us.

During this period of waiting for some kind of communication from the girls, the island of Ithaca began to spring up jokingly in conversation between Tom and me. For in the spring of that past year, we had taken a cruise through the Greek Islands, during which, our ship had put in at that island in the Ionian Sea. Tom jestingly likened the situation with our recent houseguests to that of Penelope, wife of Ulysses.

His wry comment was, "Those girls must be doing what Penelope did when she knit on that scarf all day and unraveled it every night."

For, reading up on our Homer during that cruise, we had been reminded of the famous story which our generation had had read aloud to us by the teachers in our classroom. Of course, both Penelope's dedicated knitting and unraveling were being done to high purpose. With her husband away in the wars for thirty years, her life was filled with a wealth of determined suitors. She is much to be admired for having thought up a wonderfully effective way of keeping them at bay, assuring each that he would be seriously considered when she had finished knitting her scarf. Indeed, thirty years were not to be enough for its completion.

The island of Ithaca had not been a scheduled stop on our cruise, but stormy weather had made us change course, and in order not to make it a lost day, our ship suddenly made Ithaca a port of call. At the end of the island where we were anchored, a few of us went ashore in lifeboats, but there was nothing to see. When told that, only a few ship's passengers accepted the opportunity. Tom and I were among those who consumed two hours sitting on a sea wall, allowing the realization of where we were to sink in.

Walking along a desolate shore, in a short while, we came to a small building about the size of an automobile. It proved to be a shop, if you could call it that. Its owner had hurried over from her small white-washed stucco house, its flat roof made picturesque by a handful of potted plants that under the constantly bright sun were heavy with bloom. The woman's hair was as black as her dress, parted in the middle and pinned into a neat bun at the back. She swiftly let down the front shutter on the side of her tiny store where it faced the sea, and inside a space so small that it seemed more filled with her plump form than with her trinkets, began to chatter to us in Greek.

This typically Greek, dark-skinned, dark-haired woman smiled happily.

She spoke no English, and the sales were conducted more in sign language and smiles than anything else. There was no item in her meager stock for more than a dollar. The only thing that appealed to me was a round pendant on a leather thong, a marine-blue ceramic disk with one widely opened eye painted on it, the rim of the eye bright yellow, the eye of Cyclops. This simple pendant has been one of the daily joys of my life. As women will do, when it has been admired and questioned, I have not been above boasting, offhandedly, "I got it on the island of Ithaca for fifty cents."

Hearing me say that one time, Tom amused the gathering when he came out with a droll remark, "Well, it cost a little something to go and get it."

This inexpensive reminder of that rare experience has a parallel. Not being given to a great deal of shopping on our travels – for I had gone through that phase earlier in life – no matter where we were, I did usually make a hurried survey on our stops in order to bring home small mementos and a few gifts. In this way I've come to have a collection of letter-openers – something of which I never seem to have enough. But on the island of Corfu, near that of Corsica, Napoleon's home, which we would visit two days later, as we left a monastery, a nun was standing outside the door with a tray of crudely made necklaces. The price lay on the tray with the necklaces: one dollar each. One of these, made of narrow strips of braided leather into which small ocher-colored beads have been woven, is very often the single adornment I reach for when I dress casually for the morning.

Tom's comments as to the inexpensiveness of these items from my casket of jewels reminds me of how witty he was. Yet at times he could be poetic – in a homespun way. Once on a gray Saturday in Carolina, when unpredicted snow had suddenly begun to fall, he called me excitedly to come and look, and as we stood at the window, he said, reflectively, "The first snow makes a child of everybody." He would never have considered himself literary, but imbedded in his ever-so-practical nature was the soul of a poet. Indeed, I have a conviction that the urge to creativity and to the poetic lies in each human being. I agree thoroughly with something I once came across in E. M. Forster's *Passage to India*, in which it is said, "All men, whether they acknowledge it or not, love poetry," (in this sense, to me, poetry and beauty are synonymous) "they desire that joy be restrained, that sorrow be august, and that infinity have form."

Who would argue, that things being equal, human beings begin life with a love of the beautiful, even if, in many cases, it becomes warped and twisted? I believe as well, that the average person admires a certain restraint in joy, and wishes that sorrow be ennobling. Certainly I would dare to claim there's not a person alive who does not wish that infinity have form.

≈ ≈ ≈

During those years when we were intermittently visiting our Captiva friends in their permanent homes, and they were visiting in ours, Joe and Gigi Van Vleck came several times to us. They were the nicest kind of houseguests. Resourceful, they played Gin Rummy in our sun room, they took long walks, either with or without us, and they liked to read. And I'm sure I'm not the first hostess to feel that there is, indeed, an art in visiting. In my opinion, the art extends even to the occasional feigned need of a nap. Certainly the art includes that restraint of not forcing help on an unwilling hostess, for, as Hie used to say, "The hardest people in the world to take are those determined to give you help when you don't want it."

Joe was unlike anybody we'd ever known. To begin with, his father, a wealthy New Jersey man, as a parent had been severe, and although Mr. Van Vleck had had a large yacht, the Dutch note of thrift in his character was firmly established. Joe had inherited this habit of thrift to the extent that each of his six children – there had been a former marriage – was required, from the teenage years, to keep an account of every penny he or she spent. I recall an incident when, with all his children on the island at the same time, Mary, the youngest, a college student, couldn't join the boating and swimming and other family pleasures for the first two days of their stay because she couldn't get her bookkeeping straightened out. To the Van Vleck friends, this seemed harsh treatment. It may have worked out all right in the end, for the younger Van Vlecks all seem happy and well-adjusted now that they, themselves, are parents. When we came to know the Van Vlecks, Joe was dedicating his life to working for Planned Parenthood. He had been appointed to the international board, and regularly attended their meetings in New Delhi, Cairo, Tel Aviv, wherever and whenever the conferences were being held. In this way, he was ahead of his time. His enthusiasm for the movement to stem the tide of overpopulation had become a crusade. So much so, that it came into his conversation on social occasions. And once when Gigi and Joe were with us in Carolina, this propensity of Joe's was almost the undoing of my oldest sister, who was present when we had invited a few friends to meet our houseguests.

That night, some of the party guests had gathered in the sun room around Gigi, others were in the living room around Joe. It so happened that Sister, walking through the hall toward the living room, overheard Joe, who was seated on the sofa, surrounded by people whom he had hardly met, expounding on his favorite subject. I was coming from the dining room, and Sister and I almost collided in the hall, for she was so excited that she was hardly looking where she was going. Pulling me by the arm farther back into the hall, her breath coming in gasps, she whispered, "Do you know what Joe Van Vleck is talking about in the living room?"

I didn't know, but I could guess. Trying to convey what she had overheard, Sister went on, "I've never in all my life heard anything like it. He was talking about birth control, even – I think – about *devices*, something about a loop in India that is having some success. What in the world would Mama think?"

Although, like Sister, I did not consider Joe's topic of conversation parlor talk, I couldn't be as hard on him as Sister was being. The twelve years between her age and mine had made a difference, and I was beginning to understand that overpopulation was at the root of much of the world's misery. Earlier in life, by the time World War II had ended, the organization Foster Parents Plan had come into being. It was a pleasure for me to adopt a child in some foreign country, a policy I followed until three years ago, when informed that the mother of the family I was helping to support had just had her seventh child. It struck me as wrong, and I withdrew my support. For Planned Parenthood and abortion have long been interests of mine.

It seems unfair, to me, to bring children into the world who are neither wanted, nor will they have an opportunity of a reasonably good life. It seems unfair, as well, to deny a woman the basic right as to what concerns her own body. In a perfect world, the question of abortion would not arise, but our world is imperfect; we cannot live by illusion. We must face reality.

Working toward that end, perhaps, far in the future, when universal woman, through having been given her own choice concerning abortion, will have grown to the point of making her decisions responsibly, I believe that abortion should remain legal. Although I am aware that there will continue to be abuses in the system – for a while they might even increase – I have enough faith in human nature to believe that in the long run, women everywhere, will, in this complete freedom, fill their roles, as "mothers of the human race," with honor.

But there was no time to go into this with Sister. I could only offer a palliative, "I think the party will be breaking up soon, Sister. Come with me back into the living room. I'll bring up a new topic of conversation."

When we, in turn, visited the Van Vlecks, they were at their home in the Poconos at Forest Lake Club. This was a very old club; its members all seemed to have Dutch names. The clubhouse was simple, well-run, the food, without question, the best I think I've ever had, and the families lived, daily, in close touch with nature.

After the evening meal, people would go back to their cottages, change their clothes, and go canoeing on the lake. It was from a canoe that Tom and I saw the first beaver we'd ever seen at work building his dam. So thoroughly engrossed with his task that our presence a few feet away did not for a moment distract him, he was an engaging creature, and I can still hear that loud, rhythmic flap of his tail as he packed the mud he was using to construct his residence.

Not long after our last visit to the Van Vlecks, Gigi developed leukemia. For the year-and-a-half leading to her death, she discovered lump after lump over her body, those ominous signs of the progression of the disease. She and I often talked by telephone, and I felt that she was being heroic. Frank about her condition, one night she said, sadly, "I've just come upstairs and I've discovered another lump. I shan't even tell Joe."

In a few weeks, she was gone. Her death came when Tom and I were at Captiva, and the family soon came down, bringing her ashes. When they had all arrived, her friends were told that on a certain night – from the so-called fish house that sat on pilings behind the Van Vleck property and served as their guest house, her ashes would be spread on the waters of the bay. It was a moonlit night, and there was a soft wind. I did not close my eyes. Far into the night I sat on our breezeway, looking toward the silvery light on the bay, listening to the sound of the sea. I felt I could almost hear Gigi's voice – certain things she had said and the way she had said them. A much stronger character than an initial impression might have suggested, I mourned the loss.

From as far back as the time after Alice Bryan's death, and three years later, Mother's, I had found that, after the death of loved ones, that to sit for a while at a window, looking out into the moonlight, brought me comfort. This pattern of searching for answers in the moonlight would follow through the death of our little son, and many years later, the death of my brother-in-law, Bob Gorham, Sister's husband, who died suddenly on his boat off the coast of Carolina, with Tom and two other men along. It would be with me through Sister's death fifteen years later, when she had succumbed to a long, drawn-out illness, and through the death of my beautiful and much beloved first cousin, the unforgettable Mamie Braswell Battle.

For Mamie had had all the gifts. In addition to beauty and charm, hers was a keen wit. She was a devoted wife and mother, as well, and possibly the nearest thing our town has ever had to a Grande Dame. As one of her contemporaries said at her death, "Mamie's death affects us all, for we thought of her as indestructible."

In Carolina some years later, when death came to Tom, in almost a sense of desperation, I again spent hours searching for answers in the moonlight.

Yet, I felt that a moonlit night on Captiva would have broken my heart, and I would never undergo the test.

≈ ≈ ≈

With his love of history and his interest in world conditions, Tom proved a natural for travel. That, I might have expected. But I was surprised at how quickly he developed a very real interest in art. For when he and I were growing up, our town was just beginning to develop in cultural appreciation. As for music, almost all families had a phonograph, either a Victrola or an Edison. Our own music box was an Edison. We had the recordings of the Australian opera singer, Melba – and the current generation probably doesn't know that it was because of this singer's popularity that the dessert, *Peach Melba*, came into being, and that, in her taste for thin, hard, cold toast, *Melba* toast was given her name, as well. We had the tenor, Caruso's, records, the Polish Paderewski's piano numbers, and the Austrian Kreisler's violin recordings. Father's favorite was Kreisler's "Humoresque." His other favorite record was the blended voices from the opera, *Cavelleria Rusticana*. Our Edison sat in our parlor, but with the sliding doors open to the hall, and across the hall, sliding doors open to the library, and down the connecting side hall through still another set into the dining room, our house was literally filled with music. So that, even to homes in the country, that form of culture had arrived.

Our town had an opera house, and although Tom and I did not know it at the time, as children, we were often there for the same concerts, plays, and operettas. Down the years, we chuckled over how much we'd each enjoyed the comedy, *Mutt and Jeff*. The first operetta we ever saw, called *Flora Bella*, with its singing and dancing, its high kicks, and the romance of those moments when the hero and the heroine, in their duets, gracefully moved from side to side of the stage, the lady's slender waist held tenderly in the crook of the hero's arm, in retrospect, had almost carried each of us into delirium. Even today, every note in one of its melodies lives on for me, as do its first lines in the song, "Give Me All Your Love Dear." The words so truly express the longing of the human heart to come first with another:

> *Give me all your heart dear, or else give me none,*
> *Give me every kiss dear, or not one...*
> *Give me every thought dear,*
> *No matter how small...*
> *Give me all your love dear,*
> *Or give me none.*

The rest is lost in oblivion, but these lines were enough to last a lifetime.

Visiting artists of renown would now and then come to our opera house. While our family never missed anything that went on there, the variety of its delights usually took place in winter. My early life is filled with memories of cold nights when we rode in an open car, with lap-robes and steamer rugs – and there was a difference in these – the lap-robes were made of dark, heavy velvet, the steamer rugs were the kind made of woolen plaid and fringe. Our steamer rug was the one Father had bought on shipboard when, as a young man, he had gone to Europe. And that thought reminds me, again, of how in our family, we always bought with quality in mind. Therefore, nothing ever wore out. And you never stopped using it.

For the interval of the entertainment, Robert, our driver, would have gone to spend the evening in either Uncle Mark's or Uncle Jim's carriage house above the garage where the domestics lived. For the drive home, under the spell of romance, the theme song running through our heads, we sang all the way. Even Robert would join in with a hum. Once at home, we would indulge in one of our bedtime feasts. Surely, we thought, we had the best of both worlds, content, for the time being, only to *dream* of romance.

After Tom and I were married, following our custom of going to New York the last week in October for our wedding anniversary, in addition to seeing plays and musical comedies, we always went to an opera. Again, Tom surprised me with the pleasure he derived from this form of music, and twenty years later, when we had begun to go to foreign shores, it was interesting that as he registered in the hotels of major cities, he would turn to me and say, "Shall I speak to the concierge about getting tickets for an opera?" *Norma*, Maria Callas taking the part of the Druid priestess, was to be the most unforgettable of these. But *Madam Butterfly* would never cease to be our favorite. We heard it over and over.

In our travels, I found it endearing to see Tom approach art museums and the art in churches with the same enthusiasm he brought to everything else that came before him. Especially when, upon entering one or another of the many churches in Venice, where so much early art is found, to have him say, responsively, in something approaching a whisper, "I think these are mainly Tintorettos," or "Would they be Murrillos?" even pronouncing that name the Italian way, "Murie-oze."

This, his swiftly acquired knowledge of painters, had, to a degree, come through the habit of joining Jay on her regular visits to Venice and other European cities for her research in Medieval and Renaissance history. Jay had gradually settled on the Venetian libraries because, since that city had never been invaded, she considered them the best preserved in Europe. She would spend the first five hours of the day in the cold, dank rooms of these old buildings, where admittance was only to members of the learned societies of the world, bearing their credentials. It was comical to have Jay say to Tom and me, as though we were young students, on those days when, by pre-arrangement, we joined her outside the library on St. Mark's Square when her research for the day had ended, "Come along kids, we're going to pick up a few churches." After all, she was one of those who had pioneered the custom of taking groups of college students to study art history in the churches and museums of Europe for which they would receive credits.

But for us, this travelling with Jay, and some earlier done on our own, this exposure to the world's great art, came mainly after Tom's political years, when he had more time for it. At a point in his twelve years in the legislature he was appointed Chairman of the Advisory Budget Commission. During the convening of the legislature, that commission travelled over the state, endeavoring to devise and present a budget that would be as fair as possible to all the state's needs.

In the way of the times, members of the commission were all men. On several of their tours of investigation, in order that the women's facilities of various institutions might be evaluated in all their intimacy, the wives of the members of the commission would be requested to accompany their husbands and make independent investigations. In this way, I gained an insight into the workings of The School for the Deaf, The School for the Blind, and the State Insane Asylum in Raleigh. Certain pictures of that last institution are, for me, indelible.

After that, when our phone rang on weekends, and it would turn out to be some distraught father, mother, son, daughter, brother, or sister, appealing to Tom to find a way to have a family member admitted to the asylum, I was more than sympathetic. For there immediately arose in my mind a scene wherein a female patient, through a small window from the corridor, could be seen; the window through which she might be intermittently watched by an attendant. She would be entirely without clothes and sitting on the floor with her back against a padded wall, her head drooped in abject misery. In a similarly padded cell, another woman, absolutely nude, might be pacing the floor, clutching at her hair. To make it worse, I was aware that it is almost always true of our state, and perhaps others as well, that there is never enough room for individuals so afflicted. And how could a family possibly cope with such a situation at home?

Having gained this insight, at a later period, I knew what I must say when a handful of art lovers in Chapel Hill and Raleigh developed the dream of a state-supported art museum. At that time, Tom was Speaker of the House, and possibly in a combination of courtesy and acumen, the head of this committee, Mrs. Louis Sutton, whom I knew well, asked me to serve as a charter member. Without hesitation I gave my answer.

Although underneath, I had an inborn love of the arts, I knew that I must support Tom in his point of view toward priorities. It was a point of view which was gradually becoming mine. Although in a thousand years Tom would never have pressured me not to accept the invitation, I had once overheard him, say, in a little huddle with two other legislators in the next room, who were asking him what he thought of the proposition of a state-supported art museum, "I agree that we should have an art museum, but I think the money should be raised by private subscription." And then, going on in the roughly homespun, yet direct way in which we know that men communicate in the "smoke room" on state affairs, "So far as the State's budget is concerned, let's first get drawers on everybody before we begin to put lace on them. The museum will come in time."

Actually, in a few years the museum did come, and by that time it had been worked out with state support. When it came, Tom and I were both proud that our state could do this; we made it a point to visit the museum whenever, on a trip to Raleigh, we had time. It had been true that in our area, since we were not situated near any of the major metropolitan centers, North Carolinians had not generally acquired a taste for art, especially our men. When it was made accessible, they were quick to take advantage of this opportunity for rounding out life. In that we were, and are, largely agricultural, this might have been especially true of the eastern section of the state.

But, looking back, I should not have been surprised at Tom's interest in art, for he had an inquiring mind, and gave his best to whatever was at hand. In that strange way of life, this facet of his nature would for some years, lead to our joining forces with the Rosses, Hie and Jay, to plan and carry out many rewarding trips to European shores.

We felt that it must have been fate, itself, that had landed the four of us on a small island as next-door neighbors. Although we had liked each other from the start, our backgrounds and our lifestyles had, at first, appeared so different, that, at most, we expected only a pattern of being together intermittently at Captiva. That was far from the case; our friendship moved into the area of seeking all kinds of ways to be together, especially in travel. Friendship having survived that acid test, we arranged to have that pleasure more and more. Over time, we would make trips to England and Ireland, France, Italy, Sicily, Greece, Turkey, Syria, and the Greek Islands.

≈ ≈ ≈

On one of our trips alone to the British Isles, Tom and I had the experience of visiting in a Scottish home. It was a lovely place, not far from Loch Lomond, and the weather was as misty and cold as you might expect. The Flemmings, Margaret and Ian, had come into our lives through our Captiva friends, Oneita and Paul McCulloch. Margaret and Oenita, cousins, had both grown up in Kentucky. But Margaret had married a Scot and had spent her married life in her husband's country. She and Ian had a large old house and a large family to fill it.

They had a beautiful old walled garden, half given to vegetables, half to flowers. At the very back of the garden was a grassy mound on which, as our host explained, in earlier times, a scaffold for hanging had been mounted; it had been used for offenses as minor as the stealing of a sheep. In another area of the grounds, the family played cricket in the afternoons, and then came in for tea.

Tea was served in the dining room. Around a very long banquet-size table the family gathered, even to the youngest member, who sat in his high-chair. From her silver service, Margaret poured; talk was lively, and for crumpets and scones and cucumber sandwiches, and slices of currant cake, appetites were hearty. The baby seemed to enjoy it as much as anybody, and in this delightful mixture of the casual and the elegant, I wouldn't have been surprised if he had been given one of those small dainty cucumber sandwiches, for the atmosphere was entirely that of the carefree.

As was then true of Americans visiting in many very old houses in the Europe of the time, the bath hour was approached with apprehension. In this one, there was not a smidgen of heat in the bathrooms. You were saved from complete annihilation by one of those customary large, heavy, electrically-heated brass towel racks, holding bath-sheets in readiness for your shivers.

Back in our home town in Eastern Carolina, we still laugh at the way one of our local young men, on his first trip to Europe, described the ordeal of taking a bath. For some reason, John Daniel was spending time in the area near Edinburgh. He was lodged in a small hotel, and although a private bath went with the room, the bath was an inside one, without a window. Not only did the bath not have heat of any kind, but the fan was over the tub, and the fan and the bathroom light were on the same circuit; they came on simultaneously. So that, John, his teeth chattering with cold, had to take his baths with his hat on.

I'm sure that the bathrooms over the British Isles are not so frigid now as they used to be. But as much as our people and theirs are alike in other ways, I have a deep conviction that the inhabitants of the British Isles and we will always have a different approach to body heat.

≈ ≈ ≈

One winter, while we were at Captiva, through Jay's interest in visiting Sicily to see the Greek ruins there, Tom and I decided to join her in Naples for that extension of her usual working trip to Venice. Sarita Van Vleck, the ornithologist, regularly going to this and that part of the world to study birds, decided that she would like to join us as well, giving us a few days ahead in Palermo and Siracusa. For some reason, Tom and Jay and I decided to take the *night* boat over to Palermo, for Sicily, of course, is relatively near the toe of the Italian "boot."

The weather was nice, and after a leisurely dinner, the three of us went by taxi to the pier. As we drove up to it, as are all boats at night with their lights on, this one was beautiful. It was not large, but its crew, in their spic-and-span whites, jabbering to each other in what we assumed was nautical Italian lingo, were impressive. Our cabins – in those days spoken of as "staterooms" – while not palatial, were adequate.

We sailed at midnight, and from the sea, the city of Naples and its bay lived up to its reputation of beauty. We were to dock at Palermo at nine in the morning. But in the middle of the night, Tom and I had a fright. The lighter sleeper of the two of us, he had wakened to a sense that there was something wrong in our cabin, and had discovered that we had two or three inches of water on the floor. Our bedroom slippers were practically floating. Our suitcases were wet, and the water was rising. But the bell for the stewardess was working, and she came hurrying to answer.

I was more frightened than Tom; I had a feeling that the whole Mediterranean might be coming in. Tom expected to find a leaking pipe, which there was. For, as on so many passenger ships that are not luxury liners, the lavoratory, which sat between our two bunks, with the top let down, became a dressing table.

Without undue commotion, we were moved to another cabin. But for the first time, I understood the reason for the encumbrance of those characteristically elevated thresholds on ships, and the highly polished brass on them to act as a reminder to step up and over them. And, I suppose, one part of the pleasure of travel by sea is that you can expect everything to be, literally, ship-shape, the chief example the everpresent gleaming of the ship's brass.

Morning seemed to come very early. We were soon on that island, which, to me, has the most beautiful of all island names – Sicily.

In what must be one of the world's loveliest spots is the resort spoken of as "Taormino." We were lucky enough to have accommodations at an inn that hung on the side of a small mountain. Its lounge and its dining room overlooked an almost perfectly preserved Greek amphitheater. Service was superb, and we could have wished to have had more than our five days' stay.

At night we walked down a winding road into the village to lovely shops and dining places patronized by upper crust Sicilians. The lights in the square were bright, and strolling musicians wandered about. It was from there that the trip up to Mt. Etna could be made, an opportunity of which Tom and Sarita took advantage. Jay and I bore up under the disappointment of having developed colds and of being warned about how frigid it would be getting up to Mt. Etna – an elevation of about eleven thousand feet – partly by cable car. The two hardier ones, while they found the experience thrilling, returned numb with cold.

Jay's cold was worse than mine. She could hardly speak and had fever, but I was well enough to take a long walk. In our drives about the countryside, we had often seen old women out with their donkeys, dressed in the ubiquitous black, their heads bound in black scarves. They would be going through the woods picking up sticks and broken branches which were strapped on either side of their donkey. Usually they would smile and wave, but the impression was that their lives must be hard. Now and then, on a slope with the small-growing prickly pear trees, one of these old women would be there filling her saddle bags with the briary fruit. Surely it must have hurt their hands. That morning, just outside the hotel grounds, there was one of those women, hoping to sell her fruit. My impulse was to give her money and to try to make her understand in English and in pantomime that I was travelling and wouldn't be able to use the pears, but it was only an impulse, for I sensed that she was a woman of pride and would not have liked a dole. I bought as many as I could carry back to the hotel, which was only a middle-sized bag and gave them to the maid.

As I climbed back up the hill, my mind was filling with the never-to-be-solved problem of the poor. I had seen it in so many countries; figuratively, it sat and continues to sit on my own doorstep at home, and I'm aware of how much there is, on a larger scale, in cities. The beggar in New York, offering pencils or any little gadget he can lay his hands on, often gets to me, and did especially to Tom. We were aware of the cynical angle – newspapers often carried long articles attesting to the fact that people at this level sometimes led a double life, which might include fine cars and things of that nature – but Tom would often say, "Even though there might be ten who don't need it, we can't run the risk of passing by one who does."

Sifting these thoughts at this point in my life, I can understand our family's fidelity to the Democratic party, and although I would never deny the value of the checks and balances of the two-party system, I could not, politically, be other than as I am.

It was on that trip to Sicily, of which I've already spoken in relation to papyrus, that the four of us had an unfortunate experience of collective and sudden illness. We were staying in a beautiful hotel, one literally of marble halls, in which our fellow passenger on the elevator was often Audrey Hepburn, whom we found friendly and folksy – every bit as attractive in real life as on the screen, her eyes bright, and with what, in another era would have been spoken of as a "swan-like neck" – when calamity struck.

Everyday we went out sightseeing, and on the fourth, we'd had an unusual and delightful experience. We were having lunch in a very nice seafood place. At a glance, you could tell that its clientele was continental. As is often true of the best, it was a small place. Tables were necessarily close to each other. Indeed, there was only, perhaps, a foot between our table – a table for three, because Sarita had not yet arrived – and another table, even smaller, at which sat an immaculately dressed middle-aged man. There was gray in his hair, and in his small moustache. His eyes were dark-brown, and alive. There had been no communication between the tables until suddenly, Jay, in her good Italian, was giving her order to the waiter and had ordered scampi (pronounced *scahmpi*), which she had suggested Tom and I have as well.

The Frenchman at his table – at our elbow – immediately rose from his chair, and bowed in our direction to say, smilingly, "Bon Appétit."

It seemed that his pleasure in finding us, obviously Americans, ordering something so sophisticated, was uncontrollable.

According to schedule, Sarita had come to join us for a week's motor trip around the island, where we were to see some of the best preserved of Greek temples. The night of her arrival we had dinner in our hotel, and in the mood of "when in Rome, do as the Romans," we each ate squid. My sole comment might have been, at the time, that it was as tough as whit leather, those pieces of leather too small to use. Since we were to set out on our trip early the next morning, we went to our rooms right after dinner.

At one o'clock I wakened to stomach pains and violent nausea. At two, Tom did the same. We spent a miserable night longing for seven in the morning when we felt we could decently call Jay and ask her to get the house doctor for us. To our surprise, her own voice was weak, and not only did she have her own tale of woe to relate, but that of Sarita's, which was the same. Like us, she had been waiting for seven, to call the doctor.

It was obvious, when this symbol of mercy came into the room, that he spoke no English, and we began to pour out our miseries, mostly in pantomime. My own demonstration included the alternate rubbing of my stomach and waving my arms in the air, like the tentacles of an octopus. Although his English was, indeed, limited, he quickly put two and two together, exclaiming – possibly in the only two words he knew in our language – "Polluted waters!" And we gathered that he would send us the antidote for our malady.

In a day's time, the four of us we were able to start on our tour. Needless to say, as long as we were in the area, we avoided consuming things from the sea. It had later been explained to us that the Sicilians are conditioned to the bacteria that invades the marine life on which much of their economy has always depended. Possibly, some of those canned sardines that my early family long ago ate around the fireplace at bedtime in winter had come from this island, for it had always been one of their chief exports.

But even without the things from the sea, we found the food good. Particularly fond of the flavor of lemon, it pleased me to have nearly everything they served using the juice from this fruit. The two things I enjoyed most were their very thin steaks swimming in a delicious lemon sauce. Every home, no matter how small, had its citrus trees. The other thing I found delectable was the constant use of French artichokes; there seemed to be miles of them, pale and yellowy-green in their long, endless rows.

So that, to obliterate the memory of the squid, I took away from Sicily the pleasant memories of the papyrus that I had seen growing, and the temples, which were, indeed, well-preserved, the friendliness of the people, and the memory of lemon steak and artichokes.

≈ ≈ ≈

On one of our motoring trips in France – and this time Jay was with us, and, as always, she would lead us to worthwhile places – we visited the Cave of Lascaux. I'm told that, because human breath was proving harmful to the seventeen-thousand-year-old paintings on its walls, a delightful representation of bison, horses, and other animals done by Stone Age artists, soon after we saw it, the cave was closed to the public. But there are books on the subject, and speculation as to the use made of the cave itself. My own, and that of many of the historians is, that, before the hunt – and life, of course, almost depended wholly on the success of that – the hunter climbed the hill to the cave, and inside, offered prayers to his gods.

≈ ≈ ≈

It was on a cruise on the Adriatic, that Tom, and Hie, and Jay and I would be fellow passengers with the Right Reverend Robert Runcie, Bishop of Lincoln Cathedral, who, in a few years, would become The Primate, Archbishop of Canterbury. At that time, Bishop and Mrs. Runcie were making the tour to historic Greek sites as the guests of Swan's Hellenic Tours, on which the Bishop would serve as the ship's chaplain. So that, when I say that we had the pleasure of swimming in the Adriatic with the Archbishop of Canterbury, I'm not far afield.

The British are a hardy race. They have not lived on the North Sea all these centuries for nothing. No matter how cold the weather, if the calendar says it's spring or fall, they will never fail to carry their swimsuits with them if they think they're going to be near water. Day after day, on that so-called Hellenic Cruise, in going to and from historical ruins or temples, our bus would stop at some out of the way spot on the sea, to allow the passengers time for a swim. An enclosure for dressing and undressing was not considered necessary, for each passenger would have brought from the ship, his or her bath-sheet, and in some adept way, a few feet apart, and in complete modesty, those of both genders would manage to robe and disrobe inside their respective oversized Turkish towels.

Tom, who was, himself, half fish, took to the system like a duck to water. And Jay, for whom a day without a swim was almost a day lost, and as Hie often said, "Jay never feels the cold," splashed with the best of them. The lure of cold water so early in the season, however, was something that both Hie and I could resist. The warm waters of Captiva were more to our liking. But at these beach stops, bathers and non-bathers alike joined in the fun. With the word that it was time to buckle up and go, we would clamber back into our bus, and in the way of happy children, all chattering at once, seat ourselves in hodgepodge fashion.

I remember, with particular pleasure, having one day happened to share a seat with a British Dame, her name, I don't recall. But the title implies her having made a singular accomplishment in some field. It was the first Dame I'd even known. She was an older woman, her long gray hair, I had earlier observed, was usually falling away from its pins. As friendly as could be, and jolly too, the Dame and I had a wonderful time getting to know each other. I was reluctant to ask how she had become a Dame; I resorted to subterfuge, for I think the magnificent title, Dame of the British Empire, was bestowed for something she had done in math, a subject it seemed better for me to avert. Such is life, however, that the Dame seemed to find me as interesting as I found her, and I must confess, shamefully, that it had been gratifying for me, all through the cruise, to see that her stockings were always wrinkled. I adored the lighthearted way in which she divulged that her cabin was so small that it was almost impossible to find a place to hang her "smallies" when she laundered them, introducing me to that descriptive term.

On that same bus ride, the bus clipping along, Jay's seat companion was a fellow historian with whom she was chatting on a high level; Tom was in glib conversation with an Oxford don who liked to sail as much as he did to teach, and I thought, *What a nice way to take a cruise; such interesting people!* For when I wasn't talking on my right to my Dame, I was talking to the person across the aisle on my left, the attractive Mrs. Courage, of the famous Courage Ale, that word on enormous billboards all over England: "Drink Courage," or just, "Courage." And when I asked her how her hair always stayed in place so well in the wind, she answered, "Oh, my dear, twenty years before the 'mahst' have taught me always to have a wig handy." That was her secret. She and her husband had a sailboat which they kept at Falmouth.

Taking that particular cruise in that particular year – being at the right place at the right time – was, for Tom and me, to lead to the making of rewarding new friendships, one, in particular. Michael MacClagan, an eminent scholar, historian, and former Lord Mayor of Oxford, whose father had, at one time, been Director of the Victoria and Albert Museum in London, was the head lecturer on the cruise; as were the others, he was an Oxford don. The lecturers' wives made the cruise as well. One day, when passengers were having lunch ashore, Tom and I were thrown with Michael and Jean, and from that time on, the four of us spent a great deal of time together, especially when we were ashore.

Because of Hie's age, she and Jay did not always do the more rugged sightseeing. This was a sacrifice Jay gladly made, for the relationship and devotion between these two sisters had, from early life, been an approximation of that of mother and child. In Hie's words, "I was thirteen when J.B. was born," for unlike the rest of us, she used Jay's initials. "Our family had little money, and our father, who had been a journalist, because of failing eyesight, had to give up that work. He went intermittently to the West to prospect for gold. Our parents, both people of education, did their best to see that we had that opportunity. In a system of helping each other, the oldest child, assuming the responsibility after graduation from college, for the education of the one next in age, each of us wound up with

University degrees. When I was seventeen, and J.B. was four, I recognized the scholar in her, and I made up my mind to see that it was developed."

I well knew the rest of the story. Concurrent with her own continuing advances in post-graduate work, and with carrying the double burden of her own expenses, including her years of study in Vienna, Hie was seeing that Jay had her own years of graduate study abroad. For a time, these studies of Jay's went on in France; by that time, she had become an instructor in Medieval History. Ultimately, her research would lead to Venice. Her studies there went on in summer, and in that beautiful city of canals, there were times when Jay, and one, or sometimes two of her colleagues, would rent a certain apartment on the top floor of a villa, which meant that they had to climb ninety-nine marble steps to their quarters.

Sometimes Hie, having made her annual visit to Anna Freud in London, would spend some time in Venice with Jay. Several times Tom and I would be there when she was, and I liked to watch Hie's lovely, gentle face as she sat about in one of the squares. There is no other place in the city for children to play, and as she sat there, on some old stone bench where you could hardly hear your ears for the squeals of children, there was, on her face, a soft, happy smile. She laughingly told us that in getting about the city, she had surprising luck with the verbs she invented. Her simple rule: end everything in "O."

But I think Hie would have gotten along with verb inventions anywhere; there was something so gentle about her presence. I've seen people in airports not only stop and hold doors for her, but smile as they did so. This always affected me in the same way that I've choked up when, in the scurry of life, people of different nationalities become suddenly and spontaneously united in something that shows feeling: standing back for a person in a wheelchair to board a plane, or people in collective concern over a lost child. Strange how, as time goes on, these things move us to tears more than funerals, which, in early life, nearly choke us to death. With maturity, of course, there is the realization that life can be sadder than death.

The devotion between the Ross sisters would be especially apparent after their retirement, when they were able to live together again. This went on between their home in Washington, the one on Captiva, and their cabin on Footprint Island in Michigan. Being the younger, Jay was especially tender toward Hie, and endeavored always to make travelling easy for her. If, on a trip, Hie had to miss some part of sight-seeing, Jay would manage to convey the impression that she, herself, had work to do on her papers, and made it believable. For indeed, the translation of the notes which she had taken and was continuing to take in Latin in the Venetian libraries, were with her wherever she was; almost a part of her daily life.

When, on that Swan tour, it came out in conversation with Michael that the MacClagans would be coming to the United States for six months where he would be teaching at the University of South Carolina, Tom and I invited Michael and Jean to come to us for a visit in North Carolina. They readily accepted, and one weekend in May, when the school term had ended, they arrived. For some time, telephone calls had gone on between us, working out plans. One of the last of our calls to Michael and Jean had been to ask if they would like to meet a few of our friends, or if they preferred a quiet visit. They chose the first, not knowing – nor did we at that point – that we would wind up giving a barbecue at our country place for a hundred-and-fifty.

We liked Michael and Jean so much that until the eleventh hour the guest list continued to grow; for Eastern Carolinians feel the tie with the Mother Country to such an extent that we could hardly bear not sharing the MacClagans with as many as possible. When the day came, the sun shone bright, the weather was warm, and with everybody out in summer clothes, the hundred-and-fifty were scattered about among the trees around our "cabin," gathered for that ambrosial feast: Eastern Carolina barbecue.

Done in the traditional way, a large tender pig is roasted all night over a pit, and as it roasts, is basted throughout the hours with a mop made of a long dogwood stick, its end wrapped in a soft white cloth. All night, the "mop" is dipped into a bowl containing a mixture of vinegar and fiercely hot red pepper, then applied to the browning pig. After twenty-four hours, the pig, now done, is chopped, and with the addition of more of this strong seasoning, it becomes "barbecue."

Served with this tastiest of all delectables – or so we think – there is chopped raw cabbage, well-seasoned as well, something we call, simply, "slaw." Indeed, barbecue-an'-slaw could almost be one word. Not content with these, there must be, as well, at this meal, Brunswick Stew, for these southern barbecues originated in late summer, when the crops had matured, and butter beans, corn, and tomatoes were still at their peak, and were cooked together with the ever-present chicken, which forms the base of the stew. The consistency of soup, Brunswick Stew must be eaten with a spoon. In addition to "stew," it would be impossible to serve barbecue without corn meal in some fashion, made into bread. In Eastern Carolina, we like corn sticks. Until a few generations ago, we had never heard of hush-puppies, with their flavor of onion, sometimes even a little taste of sugar. I believe these came to us from Georgia. And to me, they've never seemed authentic.

Against these highly seasoned edibles, there must be, of course, gallons of iced tea. It would not be expected that dessert would be a popular item after such a meal, but what person in his right senses can resist a tray of tarts, half of them lemon, and half of them pecan, that will, at the appropriate time, be temptingly passed around?

Standing up to eat barbecue is par for the course, yet a few chairs are usually brought out, in deference to age. On that special day, in honor of the MacClagan's visit, before the meal began, we sang "God Save the Queen." In the fulsome of things, I nearly burst, and I will venture to say, mine were not the only goose pimples. Somewhere toward the end of the meal, Michael made a little talk about our mutual ties, those of his country and ours. And I don't think anybody wanted the day to end.

In six weeks Tom and I would be winding up a three weeks' visit to England with four days as the guests of Michael and Jean, in Oxford. We had extended our stay from its original plan in order to be present at Garter Day, that day in June when the service of the investiture of the new knights takes place at St. George Chapel, Windsor Castle. The chapel is home to the Order of the Garter, Britain's most prestigious order of chivalry, founded in 1348 by King Edward III. In that Michael was, and is, one of the thirteen of the Queen's Heralds – those responsible for the research and the presenting of those to be knighted – he was able to extend an invitation to us to attend this service.

I knew in my bones exactly how the English ladies attending would be dressed. They would wear calf-length fitted coats and small flowered hats, neither of which were part of my travelling wardrobe. There were lady's shops in Oxford that I might have patronized, or I might have taken the train to London. I did neither. It was easier and more natural for me to go just as an American. I had with me, a well-tailored, slightly feminine-looking suit, the kind spoken of in other times as a dressmaker's suit. It was woolen, which was necessary, for June, near the North Sea, is not hot. Its color was between bone and gray, and I had my perennial small, silk, handmade hat that happened to match, and "went" with anything. Soft and crushable, the hat had travelled many miles in the pocket of my tote bag. My alligator pumps were good enough, should the Queen look at my feet. These were the days when we were still wearing the skins of reptiles without compunction. And I never wore alligator shoes or carried an alligator pocketbook that I didn't think of Father's three alligator travelling bags and remember the childhood delight of being allowed to open the grip to find the presents that he always brought to each of us from his trips to the North. The only really necessary amendments to my Garter Day ensemble were two: a smaller pocketbook than the one I travelled with, and matching gloves, both of good leather. These articles, in a suitably conservative saddle-color, I found in a good store in Oxford.

On Garter Day, according to custom, the thirteen Heralds and their wives met at noon near Runnymede, the site of the signing of Magna Carta. Then came that phase of what, in American football language, would be called "tailgating." Only theirs was more touched with glamour. As we do in the States, a card table was put up at what the British speak of as, "the boot," and spread with a cloth; however, those Fortnum and Mason picnic baskets of theirs, than which there is nothing "whicher," opened up to lovely china and silver, the elegance of the traditional amenities. Ours incline more to paper plates and plastic knives and forks. They also carry in the "boot," folding chairs. Here we prefer to stand, to be able, at a moment's notice, to mingle and co-mingle with other tailgaters.

But this higher level tailgating at Runnymede was delightful. In American terms, there was good plain fun and fellowship. Although in their red costumes, their knee britches, their buckled shoes, and their black-plumed-hats, the Heralds suggested Baronial Halls and roast joints and the swigging of mead, these Heralds were happily munching away on watercress sandwiches, and tongue, and fruit and cheese.

Soon however, some time-keeper in the group reminded us that we should make our way to Windsor. From then on, things were executed so smoothly that I hardly remember being shown to our seats in the Chapel. The seats faced the aisle, and we did not have long to wait before we could hear the sound of trumpets coming downhill from the castle. We knew that the Queen and her entourage were slowly following the winding road, and we stood, breathless with anticipation and respect. We knew that she would be wearing her black plumed hat, that her robe would be long and heavy and heavily embroidered. By the time the trumpeters had reached the entrance to the chapel and were standing at the back announcing Her Majesty's presence with their fanfare, I was practically a basket-case.

As the Queen entered, and the procession started toward the altar, like wheat before the wind, there was a wave of curtsying. Tom, in that way of husbands, would later make a great tale of my having gone down so far that he had to pick me up, an insult to which I paid not the slightest attention, because, once the service was over, as we filed out, I could see that his own eyes were brimming with tears, as were mine.

The ceremony itself was a combination of beauty, and reality, and fantasy. Each of us had been given a leaflet. Its cover read:

THE
MOST NOBLE
ORDER OF THE
GARTER.

In the middle of the page was what I assumed was the Crown Seal. Under that:

THE PROCESSION
17TH JUNE 1974.

Inside, there was the order of the service:

On the arrival of THE SOVEREIGN at the West Door a fanfare of trumpets will be sounded.

The combined Procession will then move up the Nave, while a voluntary is played by the Organist and Master of the Choristers, Dr. Sidney Campbell.

On arriving in the Choir the Minor Canons and others of the College of St. George, the Constable and Governor of Windsor Castle, and the Military Knights of Windsor, will go to their appointed places; the Canons, the Register and the Prelate will proceed to the Sanctuary.

The Officers of Arms will go to their appointed places.

The Knights Companions to be Installed will be conducted to their places in the midst of the Choir where they will stand facing inwards; and the other Knights Companions will proceed to their Stalls.

Her Majesty Queen Elizabeth The Queen Mother and His Royal Highness The Prince of Wales will be conducted to their Stalls.

The Secretary, Black Rod and Garter will go to their customary places, and the Chancellor will proceed to his station.

His Royal Highness The Prince Philip, Duke of Edinburgh, will be conducted to his Stall.
THE SOVEREIGN

having entered the Choir, the Service will begin.

For that blissful hour I had the feeling that the British Isles and the rest of the civilized world, including our own country – especially its southern area, more specifically, Eastern Carolina, and Captiva Island – were all joined in something mystical, something far larger than ourselves. And it came to me anew, that the reason that Tom and I loved England so much and felt so at home there, was because of its philosophy of laissez faire, "do as you will," and that one of the reasons why we liked being a part of the

Anglican Communion is that it places so few doctrinal restrictions on its members.

Still in this euphoria, following the service, on some magic carpet of which I have no memory, we arrived at a fine old home, where, in its garden, we were served drinks and canapés. The group here was larger than that of the thirteen Heralds and their guests. It may have been that many of those who had attended the service were present. The Royals, of course, had gone back to Windsor Castle. The only person I clearly recall having met was the sister of the writer, Graham Greene. Fortunately, I had read her brother's books, and communication was not difficult; in that way of adoring sisters, all I had to do was turn her on.

The next afternoon, back at the MacClagan's, when Michael was in his study, writing, for he had published several books and was busy on another, and Jean was in the drawing room by the fire, reading, Tom and I decided to go for a walk. When we came back, the four of us drew together in the dining room for tea. That over, Jean suggested a game of "carpet bowls," something of which we'd never heard. It was played in the drawing room, as its name implies, on the carpet. I recall, vaguely, that it is something of a cross between croquet and those controlled strokes that, in golf, take place on a putting green. In order to clear an area of the room for the game, chairs were pushed slightly back, and in the doing, I was delighted to find the homey touch of a long cylindrical bean bag effectively keeping out a draft from a door into the garden.

The day before we were to leave to go back to London, soon to fly home, it was rainy and cool, but we had a cozy lunch with Michael and Jean; there were lots of laughs. Michael furnished us the best when he told a funny story about a tourist on her first visit to Oxford. It may have been good manners on Michael's part to say that the lady was Australian rather than American. At any rate, the town of Oxford, having grown in the way it has, now has the dilemma of traffic jams. Caught in one of these, the lady in the story is said to have declared to the other passengers in the car, "You would think that they would have had better judgement than to locate a University here, wouldn't you?" We did not know that within a few weeks, Michael was to become head of Trinity College, the largest of any of the colleges that comprise either of the two universities, Oxford or Cambridge.

That joke lodged in a corner of my mind, along with a certain cartoon which I had once seen in the *New Yorker*. A lady and her husband are seated on a plane. Obviously, they've been to Europe, and they are laden with shopping bags. The lady is seated next to the window, the plane has taken off, and they are now high in the air when she turns to her husband, and says, brightly, "I do hope we fly over Venice. I would love to include it in a talk to my book club." It's always healthful to laugh at ourselves in these kinds of exaggerations.

After lunch, bundled in what the British speak of as mackintoshes – their term for raincoats – Tom and I walked to the center of town. We wanted to go back to Blackwell's, which, at that time, was the world's largest book store, one enormous floor of it underground. After browsing there for an hour, we pulled ourselves away, in search of a tobacco shop. For our hometown friend, Frank Winslow, an elderly lawyer, then retired and a semi-invalid, smoked a pipe. An avid anglophile, we wanted to take Frank some tobacco for his pipe, and on a note of whimsy, we bought a box of snuff for him so that he might have the experience of elegant sniffing from a small elaborately decorated snuffbox, the kind that in earlier periods would have gone with lace cuffs. Good sport that he was, on those occasions when we would later go by for visits with Frank at his home, he would jovially sniff and sneeze.

So dear a man was he, and such a devoted husband, that now that they were both invalids – for Miss Nimi, as we spoke of her when we were younger, had developed Alzheimer's – late in the afternoon at their house there would be a little ceremony. This was the hour when, with Tom's having left the office, he and I would sometimes drop by the Winslow's together. Frank and Miss Nimi would have had their afternoon rest. Now, with the help of their respective attendants, they would put on their best robes, and, in wheelchairs, be brought into the sunroom to sit by the fire. That room faced west, and with the glow of the fire, and the deepening of the sunset, it became for that hour, a lovely spot. Frank's male attendant would wheel him in first, would then leave the room to return with a tray on which there would be a decanter of sherry and four glasses.

As we sat there, the men talking of things that two lawyers would, and of politics, and touching on world affairs, I sat listening with one ear, more inclined to muse into the firelight than to take part in the conversation. I had long thought there was something of a physical resemblance between Hie and Nimi. About the same age, they were both small, their voices were soft, there was an unmistakable air of refinement about each. Nimi had been the mother of four and had once said something very beautiful about motherhood, which had been told me by one of her daughters. When her children had grown up and had themselves become parents, Margaret, one of the Winslow daughters, in conversation with her mother, one day asked, in surprise, "Mother, do you mean that in your generation, pregnant women had absolutely no pre-natal care?"

"I do, indeed," said Miss Nimi. "During each of my own pregnancies –

and fortunately there was no trouble – I needed only the happiness of knowing that there was a baby growing under my heart."

Hie, possibly since she was one of the older Ross children, and was therefore feeling the responsibility of helping to educate her younger brothers and sisters, never married. But throughout her life, she had had the joy of helping children who needed the kind of help that she, by disposition and training, and by sound judgment and common sense, was in every way qualified to give. Those were the things that gave distinction to the practice of her profession.

That afternoon, no matter how many minutes would have passed before Miss Nimi's nurse came in, wheeling her charge, not a drop of sherry would have been poured until this beautiful little lady was there on the other side of the fireplace, opposite her husband. Frank's devotion and respect made you want to cry. For Miss Nimi never spoke, she only smiled.

≈ ≈ ≈

Anybody who has had the experience of travelling in a foreign country with a driver knows that after a few days of being together, the relationship between driver and passenger usually becomes one of friendship. From having had a number of drivers over the years, each of whom we liked, perhaps, for Tom and me, Woodward most clearly stands out.

Woodward was a young man of about thirty-five. By any standards, he would have been considered homely. His hair was bright red, curly, and grew far back from his forehead. His features were irregular, his complexion – as Mother would have said – was florid. For that was one of Dr. Marriott's ways to describe a red face. To be of a florid complexion was entirely different from having a "hectic flush," however, for that – a large red spot on each cheek – was a sign of consumption, even the galloping kind. And, since Dr. Marriott, having a toddy with Father nearly every afternoon, gave vivid accounts of his rounds, our family had something of a medical vocabulary.

But florid complexions and hectic flushes were the extreme opposite of having a "pallor." Pale ears meant that you needed iron, and since Sister and I were fair, we were continually being put on doses of something called nuxated iron. As a matter of course, all four sisters received a daily dose of Scott's Emulsion Cod Liver Oil, which was taken in a wine glass, a horrible combination of a layer of sherry at the bottom, a layer of cod liver oil in the middle, and a layer of sherry on top, a formula of which I have already spoken. In the way of the French children being given watered wine, this had Dr. Marriott's approval. So far as I knew, neither their growth nor ours was ever stunted. Nor did any of the four of us grow up to be alcoholics. Alice Bryan and Vivian, however, having pink ears, usually escaped the iron prescribed for Sister and me.

On the first morning of what would be our three weeks' drive over the British Isles, making our way out of London, I reined in my thoughts about Woodward's florid complexion and its ramifications, and began to consider that in his chauffeur's livery, seated at the wheel of his agency's shiny black car, he was not unimpressive. And with Tom at the helm, me in the back seat with that comprehensive traveller's "blue book" on my lap, we set out.

For that length of time, the blue book would become my bible. I had long ago learned that no matter how well a trip may have been planned in the hands of the most reliable of travel agencies, it is in searching out the byways on your own that the benefits of travel are doubled. With such a detailed book, you will avoid the disappointment of finding later that, at some points, you had been within a stone's throw of something that, had you known, you might have very much wanted to see. In travelling over the British Isles, it's almost a case of keeping your finger in such a book as you move about.

Only a few blocks from our London hotel that first morning, Tom said in his democratic way, "Woodward, may we call you Bill?"

Woodward's face and neck flushed; though respectful, his reply was swift. "Oh, sir, if you don't mind, I should very much prefer to be called Woodward." This was, to us, a reminder of the Britisher's predilection for addressing people in their employ by their surnames as opposed to their given. To the good old American heart, however, it would have seemed more friendly the other way.

A mile or two further along, Tom tried again, "Now, Woodward," he said, "If you don't want to wear that heavy cap, it would not matter at all to Mrs. Pearsall and me to have you put it on the seat beside you." This was a strange remark, for a chauffeur with a cap was, for us at home, so much a part of life that it went unnoticed.

Again there was polite resistance. "Oh, Sir, I hardly know it's there. I always wear it."

With these two instances, it did not take us long to conclude that in foreign cities, car-hire agencies instill a certain pride in their drivers. Every morning, drivers are out early polishing their cars, making ready for the day, and those who happen to have passengers in the same inns intersperse the polishing with conversation. They like to brag about their passengers. Car drivers, we discovered, have inter-agency friendships. They recognize each other in cities, keep up with each other's schedules, and at the end of a day, will go together to find a pub. So that in a sense, a chauffeur's cap becomes a status symbol.

After these wonderful three weeks, Tom and I flew to Paris for a week. The morning on which we were to take the plane for Paris, Woodward was at our hotel door with the car rather early. I asked for ten minutes before our start to go around the corner to a book shop to buy a copy of the British *Gazetteer*, for I had found that almost every name in the English speaking world is listed there. Information includes the seat of the clan, the current population of the hamlet or village or town of the seat, and brief information as to whether or not it can be reached by rail or highway.

Allowed time for that, when I came back around the corner with my treasure, both Tom and Woodward were standing outside the car; Woodward was holding a sheath of three-foot-long stemmed red roses, properly wrapped for my flight.

I was already laden, and ready to board the plane with my usual effects. As always, Tom would dutifully help with my conglomeration of an oversized pocketbook, a carry-on bag, a shoe-tote, a topcoat and raincoat, added to which was the most vital accessory of all, a commodious shopping bag, the veteran of many travels, made of a sturdy printed persian cotton, large enough to hold my writing materials, a book or two, and an occasional tile I'd bought, those things for which I've always had a passion.

Although Tom was indulgent to me in just about every way, he could never understand why I had to buy something as heavy as a native tile, and carry it home by hand. I didn't know, either, except that when I saw something I liked, I liked it very much – and, there being so many slips twixt cup and lip – I preferred keeping it with me until we were back at home. Having anything so close to my heart sent by water took too long, and I suppose it never occurred to me to sent them by air. Eventually I learned to conceal some of these tile acquisitions in my shopping bag until we were back at home. In transit, when Tom – the good husband – would ask to be allowed to carry that bag, I would hurriedly exclaim, "Oh, it's as light as a feather!" when all the while, I would be listing hard to port.

Whether he knew or not, I wasn't sure. It was just a trait in me he had to put up with. I hardly have to explain that once we were home and I was using the tile as a reminder of a pleasant trip, he was as glad as anybody. On top of all these appendages, however, to arrive at a Parisian hotel of some standing with this wonderfully impressive floral spray of Woodward's on top of everything else, was, like things that happen in so many areas of my life, a combination of the sublime and the ridiculous.

Tom and I had found Woodward so pleasant and trustworthy, that once back at home, the glow of our drive with him through Devon and Cornwall still fresh in our minds, I decided that since my sister, Vivian, who was not entirely well, needed a trip, that if Woodward were available the next spring, I would take her with me to England and do some of the things that had given Tom and me such pleasure.

As it turned out, Woodward was engaged, but we found a suitable substitute in Baker. For *that* trip, Vivian and I asked a friend of hers, and mine, to go along, so that early in May, Vivian, Katherine Weeks and I flew from Friendship Airport in Baltimore to London, where Baker was waiting for us at Heathrow.

Once in Baker's car, I asked, as we drove into the city on the way to our hotel, "How did you so quickly know me, Baker?"

"Oh! Indeed, Ma'am. I should certainly have known you, in any airport."

That was not as flattering as it sounded. Aware that, because every foreign airport has drivers or tour guides walking about holding up the names of those whom they have come to meet, the conversation turned on that system. It was then that Baker made an illuminating observation I would not forget. "I never have trouble recognizing the American women I've come to meet," he said, "even though they're strangers."

"How in the world can you do that, Baker?" I wanted to know.

"Well, Ma'am, I think perhaps it's because in America you drive your own cars that American women seem so self-assured. I can pick them out every time."

"Goodness, Baker!" I exclaimed. "I'm not sure that that makes us sound very nice. It suggests that we may appear hard-boiled, not very feminine."

"Oh, no, Ma'am. That's not what I mean. I like American women, but there's a difference." And we drove on, joining in the congestion of traffic in which those short, black, and intensely shiny taxis move courteously, where the bright red double-decker buses make their stops, and, illusion or not, they, and all the other transports on that unique island always seem to me less hurried, almost leisurely; I felt myself being distanced from the usual American purposeful tempo.

In a different way, that second trip would be almost as perfect as the first. John Gore-Lloyd and his travel agency had done just what I asked, including booking us almost entirely in small, old "musty inns." If there happened to be no bath on the floor of our rooms, that was a small price to pay for creaky, old, oak floors, for narrow winding stairs, and for a small fireplace in the bedroom, the last hospitable note, a decanter of sherry sitting on a table by the fire.

From an earlier trip to England, when soon after arrival, Tom and I had first stepped into the Milbank Travel Agency, we knew that we were in the right hands. For although the service of the larger and better known agencies could not be improved upon, this smaller one, less well-known, with its slightly Pickwickian air, was just what we wanted. Milbank had a very good address, but its pace was unhurried, and to my utter delight, its filing system was, in part, one of shoeboxes. The personnel, however, were on their toes.

To make this trip – which was being done mainly for Vivian's pleasure – more interesting, I had hatched up a little quest connected with our forebears, a notion that had sprung up on the trip the year before as Tom and I were driving with Woodward through the Cotswolds. Having by that time, spent three years delving into my Braswell genealogy at home, which had culminated in being shown the 1608 records of our original American ancestor's matriculation at Oxford, housed as it was, and is, upstairs in the rare books corner of the Bodleian Library where it sits next to a volume given by Henry VIII to Cardinal Wolsey, it had occurred to me to try sometime to find the seat of the Braswell – orginally Bracewell – clan. The information about this Robert Bracewell was meager, for it said only,

> *Robert Bracewell, Gentleman of London*
> *Son of Richard B., Gentleman,*
> *Matric. Hart Hall 20,*
> *Feb. 1608, Aged 15.*

Scant as the information was, it gave me a feeling of awe. Tom and I had been allowed there because we were with our host, Michael MacClagan, who, as I mentioned earlier, is Head of Trinity, one of the twenty-three colleges of Oxford University. As Michael copied the information for us, he and we spoke in whispers. I could hardly wait to get outside to ask Michael what the term "gentleman," used there, would have meant.

"Not very much," was his reply. "Only that he could pay his tuition." And my heart settled to its usual beat.

Knowing that the young man, Robert Bracewell, had "gone out" as the British say, to help to bring the Anglican faith to the New World, a nice little picture formed in my mind. I could see a day when the Bishop came to Oxford in search of candidates for this kind of ministry. I could picture a young hand going up, but then I wasn't sure what kind of personality the hand of the applicant would indicate: would it have been the hand of one who possessed my Grandfather Braswell's genial manner and love of people, and circuses, and adventure? Would it have been a person of my father's temperament: direct, reserved, gentle, but a man of decision; one whose favorite poet was Robert Burns, and who often read to us the poem,

"Wee Mousy" in which the poet, having witnessed the inadvertent destruction of the nest of a mouse, the plow in the hands of his hired man, so endearingly makes an apology to the mouse?

Not being able to go any further with fantasy, I had to be content with the reality of knowing that Robert Bracewell, "whose death came when he was serving as minister to Lawn's Creek Parish and St. Luke's Church, a few miles away near Smithfield, Virginia, had been a well-read man who had left a library valued at four-hundred pounds of tobacco." The ruins of Lawn's Creek Church are still there; St. Luke's, beautifully preserved, still has services on certain days. A brass plate on the back of one of its pews is a tribute to Robert Bracewell's memory. Robert, at one time, was elected to the House of Burgesses in Williamsburg. But, amusingly enough, he sat in that body for only one day before the small band of earnest founding fathers came to realize, with a shock, that in doing this, they had failed to separate Church and State.

With this smattering of information as to the Braswell clan and my search for its origin, jumping in feet first – for I have never been bothered about rushing in where angels fear to tread – I began with a small, stream-lined survey. On that earlier trip with Tom, every night, I took the telephone directory of whatever city or town or village we were in, and looked up the name Bracewell. For that is the way it was spelled until three generations ago. I would then call, at random, one or two of those of that name, and would explain that I was an American over there looking for roots; that I didn't have much time, but if he, or she, had any information as to the seat of the clan, I would ever so much appreciate having access to it.

Although it began to look as though I would never get any definite information this way, the conversations were always delightful. The strangers might chuckle at such strange behavior, but not one of them would fail to be courteous and kind.

After two weeks of this, it was beginning, indeed, to seem a fruitless quest. But among others, the search had included an interesting interchange with a Sister Monica, who had interspersed her response with a musical little upscale laugh, saying, "Oh I'm so veddy sorry I *cahn't* help you. But how veddy like you Ameddicans to be doing this!"

Then I thought, *I will give myself one more night, one more phone call tomorrow night, wherever we are, and that will be it*.

That admonition from the first grade, "If at first you don't succeed," was never more proven than what that final phone call brought. On our way back to London to end our trip, Tom and I, with Woodward, were somewhere in Essex when I made that last and rewarding call. Ronald E.

Bracewell of Green Village Hollow, Essex, a jolly dentist, at once became my hero. By the time I was halfway through my spiel, he was interrupting me to say, "Yes, yes, yes. I know exactly what you want. The seat of the clan is in Northern England, West Riding, near the town of Barnoldswick."

With the mention of West Riding, my heart began to beat fast with visions of moors and gorse, and heather and sheep-in-the-fold or roaming-over-the-wold. I was beside myself with delight.

"There is a village there called Bracewell Parish," Ronald went on, "It has a post office, and a very old church with a Norman tower. Bracewells are buried in the church graveyard. One of the earliest graves is that of a Canon William Bracewell."

I could have hugged him. "There is an historical booklet called "St. Michaels, Bracewell Parish," he continued. "If you will let me have your address, I shall be glad to send you one of those."

"Oh how nice of you!" I cried. "Am I in driving distance of that place now?"

"You are, but I'm sure it would take you two days to find it," he said.

My reply to that was that I'd have to leave the search for another time. And then I asked, "You say that you're only a hundred-and-fifty miles from there. You've been there, of course?"

"Oh, no," he said, laughing. "It's only you Ameddicans who do those things."

But I was determined to have the last word. "Shame on you," I declared. "If you people over here didn't have so many roots, and such old ones, you'd be doing this very thing."

On this exchange of banter, we concluded the conversation. Tom, sitting in the corner reading the *Times*, or trying to while this was going on, then remarked, "You seem to have made a friend."

"I think I have. It's a pity you men miss so much of this kind of fun. Every last one of you is so contained. You just won't do things like that." But he was back in the newspaper. And my sympathy was wasted.

The ensuing year passed quickly. Through the mail, with John Gore-Lloyd's help, my plans to take Vivian were laid, and the next spring found Vivian, Katherine, Baker and me in the car on our way to Barnoldswick. The two-day drive through Devon and Cornwall and on was so lovely that it became automatic to expect something beautiful around each curve; a thatched village, a country scene over the downs, or a gateway leading into the grounds of an estate which the British speak of as the "Park."

Finally, on the afternoon of the second day, we reached the village we sought. Although repairs were being made to its church, regular services were being held, and had been since 1153. We walked about in its graveyard reading the tombstones, went back into the church proper, and, as is the custom when visiting old churches, signed our names and left our addresses in the book that was lying in the vestibule. It was a significant moment for Vivian and me. Naturally we left a contribution in the alms basin.

We took pictures of the microscopic post office with the word "Bracewell" over its stone arch. The postmistress had obligingly come outside to appear in one of the pictures. From the vestibule we each had picked up one of the booklets that had on its cover, *The History of the Church of St. Michael Bracewell, 1153-1953*, the later date referring to its restoration. And as I closed the door, I had a deeply satisfying feeling.

During this little quest, Baker had been as interested as if he were a member of our family. According to plan, our little party then headed for the Shakespeare country, for it was Katherine's first trip to England, and Vivian and I wanted her to have the pleasure of seeing Stratford. On the day when we had almost reached Stratford, however, and had stopped for lunch, Vivian nearly fainted, and we were frightened. With lunch, she felt better, and we continued to the town of Broadway, and to our inn, the Ligun Arms.

Vivian did not feel well enough to go to the play that night, which meant a drive of twenty-five miles each way, and I did not feel free to leave her until I had had a doctor come for a visit. A very nice young man came. He saw her in her room, in bed, his diagnosis was simple and was to prove correct.

"You should reduce your blood pressure pills," he advised. "Take only one a day until you get back to your own doctor." I was never so happy to be reassured. And all this for the modest fee of three dollars. This knowledgeable man had driven twenty-five miles, and would have twenty-five more back, but then, this was socialized medicine. With overnight rest, Vivian would be restored, her only deprivation, that of not having been able to see *Othello* the night before.

For that play, Baker had driven Katherine and me to Stratford and back, as Vivian rested. Afterwards, according to the custom of after-theatre-supper, Katherine and I went into the hotel dining room for ours. We had hardly begun to order when the maitre'd came up to say that our driver would like to come in and speak to me. When Baker came in, he was as excited as a child.

It so happened that our car had parked on hotel grounds next to another London car-hire car, and in that friendly way in which drivers engage in conversation about their current passengers, Baker told the driver of the other car, who happened to be Woodward, that his present passengers were from North Carolina; their names, Pearsall. Woodward was now eager to come in and speak to me. When that happened, naturally, the dining room became old home week, and the evening ended on a light, happy, note all-round. Vivian was going to be all right, and I felt doubly lucky, because I was reminded that, on future trips, if Woodward were not available, Baker would prove as satisfactory.

≈ ≈ ≈

In a few years, Vivian's sight began to fail rapidly. It was only a matter of months before she said, "I can't read a word." Soon, she couldn't see to dial telephone numbers. It was poignant to find that with bright red nail polish, my own phone number had been highlighted. After that, she could no longer enjoy television. Yet her spirit never flagged.

Loved by so many for her generosity, her good disposition, and her wit, she had many visitors coming to keep her company. Her nephew, Bob Gorham, and our sons were especially devoted and attentive, always bringing gifts that might help her to cope in an almost sightless world. One of these devices was a small talking clock, brought to her by Bob. A light sleeper, it would be company for her to be able to know the nocturnal hours as they passed. And so, on the first night after the gift came, Vivian settled down at midnight in the high, wide, old, four-poster bed with the clock on the other pillow. She awakened in a dark room at one o'clock to the sound of a deep masculine voice, saying solemnly from the other pillow, "It's one o'clock in the morning."

Always a good sport, and by nature and by training, refined, she was, however, perennially witty, and she enjoyed telling this tale, the punch line of which was always, "And I thought I was in bed with a man!"

≈ ≈ ≈

Since my travels have been more to England than to any other country, I have in memory a few of the hotels in which I've stayed. They begin with the Thackary, when as a girl of eighteen, with a group of college students, I first saw London. This hotel was opposite the British Museum, which made it convenient for the two college teachers who were in charge of us to open our eyes to some of the wonders of the world. After that, the London hotels I was in varied from the small to the large, from the quiet ones on narrow streets, to those larger and more opulent. On the trips that Tom and I made to England, our hotels would become two: Brown's, which was old and had an air of gentle aristocracy, and the larger and better-known Savoy.

It was on one of these stays in the Savoy that I had an amusing experience with two English ladies. Tom and I had been in London for a week, and were leaving that morning to go into the country. Our bags had come down, the car and driver were waiting outside, and Tom was at the desk checking out. The lobby is not especially large, and a part of it is given to the delightful feature of having a flower stall just inside the entrance. And if there's anything lovelier on a spring morning than seeing a young girl with that English peaches-and-cream complexion, dressed in a rose-colored smock, filling her stall with the freshest of flowers, I don't know what it can be. The cool morning air was coming in through the open doors; the girl could, herself, have been a flower, and I sat a few feet away, mesmerized.

Drawing my attention away, however, were two English ladies of some years, quietly and perfectly dressed, tip to toe, one in navy, one in gray. Even their umbrellas matched their attire. And they were talking to each other in low tones. The fact that each small hat had a flower or two on it, suggested that they might be attending the Queen's Garden Party that afternoon, for the papers had spoken of one. I began to long to talk to them, but I didn't want to appear boorish. I know how reticent the English are – Tom kept reminding me – and I tried to talk myself out of starting up a conversation. I finally made a bargain with myself in this way: *If Tom doesn't come in another five minutes, I will have to move over to where they are.*

I doubt that I waited five minutes. It was simple enough to beg their pardon and to ask if I might come over and talk to them, to explain, which I'm sure was entirely unnecessary, that I was an American, always filled with this great yearning to communicate with people in the mother country. The ladies, I discovered, were sisters, and at my overture, melted like butter in the sun. By the time Tom came, we had practically promised never to be separated. We had covered so much territory that I felt free to say, "I suppose you think it's odd for me to be travelling in these comfortable old walking shoes, and hatless."

One of them, in a burst of honesty, but not unkindly, replied, "Oh, but you *know* you *should* wear a hat. Women of our age need the dignity of a hat."

In spite of the fact that I had asked for it, that got my dander up a little, and I suppose that, subconsciously, I was thinking of Tom's so often quoted football maxim, "the best offense is a good defense," that I found myself, for the first time in my life, pronouncing a certain word in that Churchillian way I loved, "Oh, but you *see*," I declared, raising my voice an octave, "in *America*, we like to be mo*bile*," emphasizing the last syllable and giving it a long "i."

The ladies were taken aback. To my pure delight, one sister turned to the other and said, feelingly, "Oh, Bessie, we just may be a couple of *squares*."

In a ladylike way, I was now wreathed in smiles, and if, while he was checking out, Tom had been aware of the little tableau, apparently, he tried not to notice.

One of our stops on that motoring trip into the countryside was a hotel in what was spoken of as "The New Forest," and in the British way, it bears that name because it was replanted in 1200. Ours was a nice hotel, fine food, and after dinner that night, over coffee in the lounge, people were settling down to read. Waiters moved so noiselessly, you could have heard a pin drop. For some reason, when a group of people are in the same room in a relaxed setting, and are completely without communication, unless it's a library, it seems to me an unnatural state; yet I was trying to be restrained.

The atmosphere was so refined that the people seemed even to be reading small books, those with fine print; you had the feeling they were the classics, and all first editions. This was very hard on me, for no change was in sight. Tom, habitually the American, was reading a newspaper. I seemed to be the only observer in the room, and to attract someone's attention, I began to use mental telepathy. Sure enough, the lady nearest me soon picked up her coffee cup, laid her book on the table, and looking in my direction, smiled. It was a ray of sunshine. In response I practically mimed, "May I bring my coffee over?"

And she mimed back, "Please do."

We spoke quietly, but were off at a gallop. There were questions she very much wanted answered about Kennedy's candidacy for the Presidency. I could help her a little, certainly not as much as Tom, and so, at that point, I turned to him, and in a friendly way, explained that this nice English lady wanted some political information that he might be able to give. By that time I knew her name and introductions could be made.

She then turned to her husband and said, genially, "These are some nice Americans." After the customary standing up among the men to shake hands, there was a little shuffling and settling down again in the congeniality of a four-way conversation.

The other husband, a "Mr.-Chips"-of-a-man, whom we now knew as Matthew Humphries, suddenly looking over his spectacles, excused himself and disappeared. The three of us left were so busy talking that we hardly noticed, for quickly he was back, explaining his absence, "I was sorry to leave so abruptly, but I wanted to go to my room to get my hearing aid."

I was sure that Mrs. Humphries and I were having carefully concealed identical thoughts; once again, women had been the ice-breakers.

≈ ≈ ≈

One of the later trips for Tom and Jay and me, was a cruise into the Baltic Sea. Hie had chosen to spend that time in London with Anna Freud. We sailed from Le Havre with a French line, and had two delightful weeks in those chilly waters. Since there were three of us, we were placed at a table with three others, and it turned out to be an all-round happy choice. Never would it have occurred to me that I would be having three meals a day with Harriet Adams, the author of the Nancy Drew books for girls. But there she was, at my elbow, a slender, lovable spinster – probably then in her late seventies – who had brought along her prettiest clothes. Every night she arrived at our table for six wearing a different dress. Her hair was short and softly curled; it had probably always been red, and with each trip to the ship's beauty salon it became redder. But she was more down-to-earth than I make her sound. Tom and Jay and I liked her very much, as we did the two men who held responsible jobs in her publishing house. An only child, Harriet had followed her father in writing the Nancy Drew books, and even then was continuing in that work.

Yet as much time as we spent with Harriet Adams, when I think of that cruise, I think more often of another woman who was a fellow passenger. This was due to the fact that this unfortunate person's baggage had failed to be put on board, and good sport that she was, she wore the same dark-brown pants-suit for two weeks, giving it a different look by the silk scarves she could buy from the ship's shop. So far as we could tell, she lost no sleep crying over spilt milk. And at the end of the cruise, at the grand finale of the farewell banquet, this sensible woman received a large prize from the Captain, and a standing ovation from the passengers.

Our table for six had been a frolicsome one. When we said goodbye at the end of the trip, we each made a solemn promise to visit, back and forth. Tom and I were given more definite follow-up invitations by Harriet. Somehow, although it was not far away, for she lived in New Jersey, we didn't get to go. Through Christmas cards and occasional letters we kept in touch. And in a few years, word came of Harriet's death.

≈ ≈ ≈

Twenty years earlier, when it had been finally understood by the outer world that Hitler, that madman, the house painter, was bent on the extermination of the Jews in his country and the satellite countries which he was taking over, there developed a group of thinking people in other countries for ransoming members of that faith, especially those who were making notable contributions in their respected fields. It was in that way that Dr. Sigmund Freud, the neurologist, whose studies had brought about the breakthrough into the subconscious, had been ransomed and brought to England. There, with the help of his daughter, he would carry on his work. Whether the Freud School for Disturbed Children of the Blitz had begun during his lifetime or not, I'm not sure. I assume it had. At any rate, at his death, the father's mantle would fall on his daughter, Anna.

This school for emotionally disturbed children had become known all over the world. Troubled parents, bringing their children, would come from every point of the compass. Since, from the beginning, the school had been largely supported by the Marshall Fields Foundation of Chicago, of whose board Hie was a member, it became necessary for Hie to spend some time in London each spring. When she was there on these missions, she was always the guest of Anna Freud in her home in that area of London known as Hampstead. Not far from Miss Freud's home, in a small square around which children play, is a bronze statue of the great man who was her father. Memory tells me that he is seated, his attitude, one of thoughtfulness and kindliness.

Hie and Anna were about the same age, but Anna's life was to last several years longer than Hie's. Through Hie, we knew that from the very beginning of her work, Miss Freud allowed no time for things social. We knew that, for diversion, on weekends, she usually drove to her small country place in East Anglia, where she enjoyed riding. These weekends and occasional stays in her cottage in Ireland with the company of a colleague were her only escapes from the demands of her work.

Yet Anna's household staff apparently felt remiss that there were no invitations to some of Hie's closest American friends when their visits to London coincided with hers while she was a guest in Miss Freud's home. By this time, Paula, Anna's housekeeper, knew of the close-knit friendship between the Rosses and the Pearsalls, and in this scramble of friendships and connections, an amusing little incident took place.

At the time, another friend of the Rosses, Earl Groves, a part-time Captivan, was in London as well. Earl, who had been a colleague of Jay's at Vassar, and after Jay's retirement, was continuing as Head of the Music Department there, for that summer had been offered the use of an English musician's house while its owner was away in South America. This was an especially attractive guesthouse; it sat far back in the garden of a larger house, and Earl, with whom Tom and I had, earlier on that trip, travelled through East Anglia, had now invited Hie and Tom and me there for dinner. Dinner was to be prepared by Earl and was to be served early, in order that the four of us might attend the ballet at Covent Garden.

Tom and I were the first to arrive at Earl's, and when Hie came, she came in smiling. She was bearing a silver bread tray, loosely covered with an embroidered cloth. As she placed the tray on the table, which was already set for the meal, she explained, "This is from Paula."

Each of us knew Paula's role in Anna's household, and Hie went on lightly, "Paula is afraid that Miss Ross's American friends, the "Peeles" and "Meester Grove," will not think she is visiting in a "gude" house. For in that endearing way of family retainers, Paula's pride was involved.

Through Hie, Anna had found that Tom and I would, the following day, be leaving for Dublin, where we would be met at the airport by our Irish friends, the Murisons of County Wicklow, and driven the twelve miles to their home, Roquefort, in the village of Greystones for a week's visit. Hie and Anna and a much younger colleague of Anna's –the name escapes me – would soon be spending one of their intermittent weeks in Anna's Irish retreat, a modest cottage in County Mayo. Anna, knowing of our plans and Hie's, to fly back together from Shannon Airport to New York, had earlier sent a note to our hotel in London, asking us to have tea with her in Ireland on the afternoon when we would be making our way by car to Shannon for the night flight, and things were in place for that.

And that is how it happened, that on a dark and drippy day, our Irish driver, Danny McSweeney, finally found, on a hillside, the narrow and very old two-story house we sought. The wisp of smoke rising from its chimney against the gray, we knew must be coming from a peat fire inside; the peat had possibly been dug from somewhere on Miss Freud's property. It was understandable that such a busy and esteemed person as Miss Freud might often need such a remote retreat, a place where she might be virtually incognito.

The dooryard was enclosed by a low stone wall, outside which, who should be standing out in the mist, wearing her heavy Irish boots, and her father's full length, dark green, heavy coat – one of those from Vienna, spoken of as a "Loden" coat – but Anna, herself. Her head was bound in a silk scarf of dark colors. She had been engaged in some way with a short-handled spade, probably clearing the earth from the stepping stones that led to the door. Her manner was cordial and gentle, her dark eyes warm with welcome.

Once inside, there was the stir of removing our coats and hanging them on a series of pegs at the back of this so-called "front room" where, gathered around a simple table, Anna poured tea. The tea cakes were of her own making, the aroma of stewing chicken came through the door from the kitchen, and I sat, enthralled, yet perfectly at home, and joining in conversation.

I watched this dedicated woman open like a flower to Tom's warmth and the friendliness of the everyday that his presence always brought. In a combination of respect, whimsy, and the understanding of human nature, he did not hesitate to cut through formalities. "Dr. Anna," he began, and I'm sure she'd never before been addressed that way, "how did you go about finding this retreat of yours?"

And when she had explained, Tom went on, "What do your neighbors here in this part of Ireland do with their land?" For he was always, first and foremost, the economist. "I see a great many sheep, and I know of Ireland's production of wool, but what else?"

"There's a great deal more wool exported than you would imagine," Anna answered, her English spoken with an accent.

"What about industry?" Tom wanted to know. "Has much of it has reached this area?"

"There are pockets," she replied.

"And I suppose these country people get to the factories by bus?"

"Yes, there's bus service," she answered. "Sometimes getting to the main road for the bus will require a long walk, but then, you know, these people are rugged. Life has never been easy for them."

The conversation then turned on what we'd been doing during the week we'd spent with the Murisons, and how long it would be before Tom and I would return to our home on Captiva. Anna thanked me for the many letters and packages that over the years I had mailed to her from Hie when we were on Captiva, for being the youngest member of the compound, mine was often the happy role of fetch-and-carry-person. I loved seeing Hie do needlework, a bargello case for Anna's glasses which would be sent to her one Christmas, a pillow of crewelwork at another. Now and then Hie made these pillows as gifts for members of her family and a circle of close friends, each pillow, a work of art. Mine, of white silk, done in soft pastel shades, and signed in silk floss, "H.R., 1971" is one of my most prized possessions.

As Hie was making these gifts for Anna, I was aware, through Hie, that Anna might be knitting a sweater or a scarf for Hie. For even with their failing eyesight, these two old friends "gave" of themselves to each other. It seemed to me, very beautiful.

When our time allowed for the tea stop was growing short, Tom, being Tom, said, "Dr. Anna, you're not only due many laurels for many great things, but you're a talented maker of tea cakes. Or are these Paula's?" For we remembered, through Hie, that Paula was also Viennese. When the

Freud family was ransomed from Austria by their British admirers, Paula had accompanied them to London, and had continued to take care of the family domestic matters.

Anna's face crinkled into smiles, and she accepted the compliment, almost shyly.

Half an hour later, seeing her three departing guests off as she and her colleague stood by the car, Anna gave a few helpful suggestions to our driver, and the six of us embraced. And the use of that word, "embrace," makes me think of the way Hie always ended her letters, a habit that came from having spent so much time in Europe. She used the lovely, evocative phrase, "I Embrace You." Her letters to us always began with, "Dear Elizabeth and Tom," they ended with, "I Embrace You Both." As we drove along in the Irish mist to the airport, those thoughts were mine.

But it had not occurred to me to ask Miss Freud something that would later have significance for me. The question had to do with what had seemed, to me, an unusual coincidence. Once at home, I found, in unpacking my bag, something I'd written on the plane on our flight over; I had finished it on the return flight. The night of our departure for London, a few hours out of New York, on a 747, the three of us flying east, Tom and Hie and I were settling down for the night. Lights had dimmed, those who preferred a movie to trying to sleep had their earphones in place. The movie had started, the plane was quiet, and Tom and Hie had fallen asleep. I sat between them. As I looked at Hie's small sleeping figure, the character lines showing on her face, I wanted to write something about her. And in the tiny circle of light that was mine, I began.

I knew that on that same night, Anna Freud would be in the skies on a plane bound for New York. She would be on her way to Philadelphia where she would be giving a series of lectures. But in a week she would be back in England, where Hie would become her houseguest. There seemed to lie, in this coincidence of the skies, a little story, and that is the way my writing went. It included the backgrounds of these two women, the length of Anna's and Hie's friendship, and their dual accomplishments: two women of different continents, of different faiths, who singly and together, were making major contributions in their field.

When I came upon it that day at home, unpacking, I decided to write Miss Freud, to tell her what I had done, and to ask her permission to include the little story in what, at that time, I had given no name, speaking of it simply as "my writing." In answer, there came a long understanding letter, bringing an apology for not being able to grant permission. Anna explained how she cherished her privacy, especially those intermittent visits to her Irish cottage, and that, regrettably, she could not risk doing anything that might, in the smallest way, threaten that. I understood. And I respected her wishes. Now that she is gone, for her death came several years ago, I feel that I have the freedom to describe our visit.

≈ ≈ ≈

Hie was to visit us in North Carolina only once. The two sisters came together for that June visit a few years before Hie's death; since then, Jay has returned many times. For now that we two are alone, we feel the need to keep in close touch, at least – now and then – to be together.

When Hie and Jay came for their stay of three days, Tom and I, knowing that they would not want things social, that meeting a lot of strangers would perhaps be fatiguing for Hie, made a simple plan. On the first day we would all go to my sister Vivian's home for lunch. I regretted that my two other sisters, Sister, and Alice Bryan, were no longer alive to meet those two who now, to Tom and me, seemed almost sisters as well, and I was glad that they and Vivian could meet. They liked each other from the first, as we had known they would, each of them a realist. The Rosses admired Vivian's combination of common sense, good nature, and her "spunk" for having gone out at sixty to build a home and make a life of her own.

On the second day, which would be Sunday, we would go at noon for drinks to the home of my first cousin, Mamie Braswell Battle, mentioned before, and of her husband, Hyman, two of the world's most hospitable individuals. Although Tom and I rarely missed going to church on Sundays, we knew that we would on that day, for although the Ross family based their lives on Christian precepts, they spoke of themselves as "free-thinkers," and were not members of any organized religion. Indeed, certain members of their family had long belonged to something called The Ethical Society, an organization which for generations has held that life can be lived satisfactorily if carried on by a code of ethics rather than by adhering to doctrine.

In the early life of Hie and Jay, when the Ross family was living in Independence, Missouri, their father, a journalist, gradually lost his eyesight; he had to give up journalism. At a loss as to how to support his family, he went for a short while to the West to prospect for gold. There, with so much of life in the open, and among a wide variety of individuals, he would be exposed to new ideas that would come to have a strong influence on his life and that of his family. The family, however, were not Atheists; they knew the Bible well.

Mrs. Ross returned to teaching; Mr. Ross accepted the job of Marshall of the town of Independence, the city furnishing its marshall with a large brick house next to the jail. Hie liked to tell the next part of the story, which she did, merrily. Mrs. Ross had a sister who lived in Independence, as well, and on something of a grand scale. The sister, calling often in her carriage with her driver, began to deplore the fact that five little girls and a boy were being brought up next to the jail. But Mrs. Ross – well-adjusted person that she was – always ready with a smile, could give the delightful answer, "Living next to the jail is the safest place in town."

Incidentally, the Ross home was near that of Harry Truman's. In this way began the friendship between the young boys, Charlie Ross, and Harry Truman, that would last through life. The friendship was such that when he became President, Truman chose Charlie as his Press Correspondent. Hie happened to be visiting Charlie in Washington on the night of her brother's sudden death. The two were attending that now-famous Margaret Truman concert. Hie was in Charlie's apartment, dressing; Charlie appeared to have been held up at the White House for some reason when the telephone brought the message that he had died of a massive heart-attack. In telling me the little story, Hie said, and I agree, that the President's lambasting of the press over their unfavorable reviews of his daughter's concert was understandable. Hie ended with this simple statement, "But if Charlie had lived a few hours longer, he would never have allowed his life-long friend to blow off in such a rough way." Yet, I believe the very humanness of it may have endeared the President to the people, possibly even the press. Strange that, in the way of politics, the man unknown to many at the time, and who had earlier been publicized as "the little haberdasher from Independence," should come to be regarded in history in such a different light, and, as time goes on, is so often quoted.

When the President and "Bess" were in the White House, Bess, having her bridge club come up from Independence, southerners felt that the occupants of 1600 Pennsylvania Avenue could have been their own neighbors, next door. And had I not liked President Truman for anything else, he would have won me by what, at the end of his term of office, he was supposed to have said to a young news reporter. The interview was being held soon after the return of the Trumans to Independence.

"Mr. President," began the young man, his ballpoint deferentially poised above his notebook, "What was the first thing you did when you retired?"

The answer was simple: "I took the grips to the attic," replied the President.

Our cousins, Hyman and Mamie, both in failing health, and no longer going to church, loved to have their friends drop by on Sunday morning after the eleven o'clock service. That day, knowing how close our friendship with Hie and Jay was, our cousins pulled out all the stops just for the four of us. The visitors were impressed with the success of rallying a staff on Sunday, and with the bountiful variety of hot hor d'oeuvres, which almost made it into a brunch.

For the third and last day, Tom and I decided on the one local person we wanted to invite for lunch to meet our beloved guests: our close friend, Patty Lambert. Offhand, this might have seemed a strange choice, for Patty, a woman in her early forties, a hunchback, was pitiably deformed. How she had been able to get her education in that condition, to follow it with a degree in Library Science, and to hold a job as assistant librarian in our public library was cause for wonder. But Patty had a world of things to offset her deformity. She was cheerful, she was witty, she had a bent for things scholarly, and she knew not an ounce of self-pity. It was amusing to hear Patty describe those first years of hers in our town when she was renting a room from a lady so genteel that to have the rental fee pass between them would have been unseemly. To avoid so crass a situation, there developed between the two a better routine.

When it was time to leave the monthly check in the downstairs hall, Patty would call up, in a flute-like voice, "Oh, Mrs. Sawyer! (fictitious name) There's something down here *for* you!" and from upstairs, in the same elevated tone, the answer would drift down, "Oh thank you so much, Patty. I'll be down soon." But before that happened, Patty, in her discreet way, would have left for the library. Inviting Patty that day was to prove the happiest of choices. Hie and Jay, in the literal sense, were charmed. Knowing how the sisters loved a well-told tale, especially one that cut through the froth to the real things of life, after lunch, in the living room over coffee, we called on Patty for the story of the mattress.

This was a tale involving three characters. While Mrs. Lambert's name is her own, the names of the other two are fictitious. The rigmarole began with the fact that Mrs. Lambert, Patty's mother, who was a widow with three young children and almost no money – for although her husband had owned a sawmill, he died young – had pieced out her college education enough to teach. One year, with Christmas on the way, she decided to buy a new mattress. The family lived in a village just over the Virginia line from North Carolina, and I never heard Patty pronounce its name, Broadnax, that I didn't halfway smile, thinking it might have been derived from the words "broad ax," the present version having come with usage. For all the tales of Broadnax seemed to place it in an earlier time, when a broad ax would have been a tool of everyday life. Everybody in Broadnax kept up with what everybody else was doing, and the news that

471

Mrs. Lambert had given an order for a new mattress made the rounds.

The bargain with the salesman included his agreeing, at the appointed time, to take the old mattress, allowing a few dollars for the trade-in. Hearing of Mrs. Lambert's bold step, a neighbor came hurrying over to ask Mrs. Lambert if she would do her a favor. In Mrs. Hedgepath's mind, a little plan was forming. Since, on a certain day, a week later, the salesman was to pick up the old mattress from Mrs. Lambert's back porch, assuming that Mrs. Lambert's present mattress was in better condition than her own, the neighbor wondered if, secretly, before the return of the salesman, a little exchange could not be made, and asked permission to place her own mattress on Mrs. Lambert's back porch to be in readiness for the salesman, having by then appropriated Mrs. Lambert's old mattress unto herself. That this would be trickery was beside the point.

In doing this, nobody could have foreseen that for the next few days, there would be a merry-go-round of mattresses in the neighborhood, wherein five Broadnax homes would each, in turn, have the betterment of a newer mattress, the quality of the ones being discarded steadily going downhill.

When the day of the salesman's return came, the neighborhood housewives found themselves innocently, but busily engaged in baking their Christmas cakes, making their holiday pies, putting holly on the mantelpieces and over their doorways and pictures, humming as they went. Mrs. Lambert's own house was pristine, and appropriately decorated with berries and greens, and she must have been humming a little tune of her own as she kept an eye out for Mr. Pettigrew.

It was not long before his truck stood in the backyard, and hurrying to greet the salesman on the porch with a cheerful "Merry Christmas!" and deflecting his attention from the latest mattress that had been brought to her porch, the canny lady handed him one of her mincemeat pies, on which she had thoughtfully placed a sprig of holly. And, although when he saw the mattress, some kind of question must have arisen in Mr. Pettigrew's mind, in the spirit of Christmas, no questions were asked, and with a great many "Merry Christmases!" from both sides, the salesman, bearing the mattress, and the pie, went on his way.

One of the neighbors involved in the exchange, and the one who happened to live nearest the creek and the bridge, had been on the lookout all day for the saleman's truck, and with her eyes, now followed its movement. Having observed the successful conclusion of the conspiracy, the lady could hardly wait to throw a shawl over her head and rush over to Mrs. Lambert's to give her report: She had just seen Mr. Pettigrew stop his truck on the bridge, from which, with his pitchfork, he had consigned the mattress to the creek.

By the time Patty had finished the tale, her listeners were convulsed. I could go on and on about Broadnax, as seen through Patty's eyes. I can only regret that she didn't live long enough to get around to writing the stories of her village for publication. It is my joy to record this one and to recall Patty's expression for when you wanted to share some beautiful thought or phrase and wanted to share it with someone like-minded, *"deep calling unto deep."*

As usual, in those days when our house was so often filled with houseguests, in getting ready for that visit of the Rosses, I had given some thought to just what books to place on bedside tables. I knew that for reading matter, Jay's inclination would be toward the scholarly, those high-level things discussed among the learned societies of the world, but except for the books which she had written in her historical studies, and those of a dozen or so of ours, our shelves were not, in that way, well stocked. For her diversion, I chose something that would take her away from the scholarly, in memory back to some of the places we had visited together on our foreign travels, things such as the contents of the Hermitage in Leningrad.

By some happy fate, I placed only one book on Hie's night table. I made that choice, because of Hie's interest in children. *The Tale of Beatrix Potter* may have a frivolous sound, but it is a fine and moving biography of a wonderful human being. I had become such an admirer of this artist/writer, that on one of the trips Tom and I made to England, I had gone to see the originals of her illustrations in the British Museum. After that, we drove to her home in Sawry, somewhere in the North of England. Hie was so taken with the story of this woman's life, that during the three days in our home, she would now and then excuse herself to go to her room for reading. I urged her to take the book home with her, but she didn't want it that way. She wanted to finish it before she left.

That the selection I'd made had been the right one, would in itself, have been enough pleasure for me, but not, in a thousand years, could I have envisioned a time when Hie, standing before a group of psychoanalysts at the University of Pittsburgh, to which, after retirement she went spring and fall for several weeks of lectures, would be delivering a lecture built around the book, *The Tale of Beatrix Potter.* Her premise would be that deprivation in early life can, and often does, lead to a fruition that might not otherwise have come about.

She had woven into her lectures the story of how, in a large and comfortable and well-run house in an impressive section of London, a little girl was born to insensitive parents and was relegated to living on the fourth floor of that home, seeing hardly anybody other than her governess. She saw her parents for only a few moments before the evening meal, and then was returned to her own solitary supper of a chop and a pudding.

The only thing good about this arrangement was that the little girl was allowed to have small pets in her room. A mouse was one of her favorites. One of the rules in this child's regimented life was that in the afternoon, she and the governess must take a walk. In some way, these walks began to take the two of them to the British Museum, and there, as soon as she was old enough to lean over the glass cases and study the flora and the fauna of the British Isles, the little girl began to draw.

Providence was to send her a little brother, born when she was five. Another benevolence was that, for six weeks in spring, the Potter family and their servants went to their home in the North of England where the two children were surprisingly given complete freedom.

But strangely, even in this more free and open environment, Mr. and Mrs. Potter were to show the same lack of concern for their children that was true of their life in London. This did mean, however, that the two children could roam the fields and woods at will, could pick up small dead animals, and could bring them to their barn for Beatrix to draw. Sometimes, in order that she might study their anatomy, the children boiled these animals, and in time, coupled with what we now know was an inborn sense of humor, this basic knowledge of life among earth's smaller creatures, and the flora and fauna of that region, would lead to the writing and to the illustrating of the Beatrix Potter shelf of books, which, in my opinion, are the most charming animal stories that have ever been produced.

It was not until the following October when we were all coming together again on Captiva, that Hie told me of having used Beatrix Potter as a subject for one of her lectures. When she did, a humorous picture sprang to mind: A room full of serious-minded scientists have just been told that the subject of the day's lecture will be based on the author of *The Tale of Peter Rabbit*. That picture, and what must have been the consternation on the faces of her listeners kept me laughing all day. It was comforting, however, to feel that perhaps the hunch, or the intuition – whatever you may call it – that had sent me to select that particular book which would soon find its way into a scientific community, would confirm the fact that things only vaguely perceived may sometimes provide a valid sense of direction. And they don't have to be the large things.

≈ ≈ ≈

The recent re-reading of Lawrence Durrell's book, *Bitter Lemons*, a copy I had bought long ago in Cypress, where for a time Durrell went to live and to write, reminds me of his having said, at the beginning of the book, that the best of travels lead us inward as well as outward. How true this is.

Tom and Jay and I had, once again, made happy plans to travel together. The fountain of Jay's knowledge, her warm personality, and her adaptability to any and all situations makes her a delightful companion, especially in travel. Since she knows so much in her field, and by comparison, we knew so little, we enjoyed the roles that might have been reserved for a brother and sister, albeit, a brother and sister who were given to doing spontaneous things. We no doubt were thought slightly peculiar; something that, apparently, was not to be held against us. Strange, how different we four were, to be so congenial.

This time, only three of us were embarking on a cruise to the Mediterranean. Hie was not along. Although we had booked passage through an American agency, the ship was to be Turkish. It turned out that the crew spoke no English, but that was not a problem. Nor would the small staterooms and the lack of luxurious lounges be important, for emphasis was to be on the quality of the lecturers who would be on board to prepare us for the historical ruins and other sites that lay ahead.

We were to sail from Piraeus, a port near the city of Athens. That morning, we were up early and waiting on the dock with the other passengers. As usual, there was some time before we were allowed on board ship. Finally however, toward noon, we were being shown to our staterooms and were meeting our stewards and stewardess, communicating in gestures and smiles. As we expected, our cabin was small. There was no rug on the floor. The cot-like beds were without headboards, were made of iron, and were painted white. Between the two beds was a lavatory over which hung a small mirror. Closet space was negligible. The shower was unpredictable, the other bathroom fixture was so far out of date that it was operated by a ball and chain.

These things, however, were not enough of a drawback to dampen our enthusiasm for the trip. Although the current expression, "everything is a trade-off," was not being used, it was a philosophy to which Tom and I subscribed. Nearly always, no matter what ship on which we were sailing, we wanted to be on deck to watch the cast-off. But that day, I chose to stay below in order to concentrate on making the nest that would keep us going without too much of a scramble for the next three weeks, for our bags had arrived. As he hurried out of the cabin for the upper deck, Tom turned to say, "It will soon be lunchtime. When the gong sounds, shall we meet at the foot of the staircase to the promenade deck?"

I scuttled down the narrow companionway, turning out for passengers as I went, all of whom seemed to be in a high state of disorganization. I wanted to tell Jay to meet us at the suggested place.

I was the first to arrive at the broad stairway. The hustle and bustle was still going on: people going up, and coming down the stairway in two's and three's, some of them concerned over not having yet had their luggage delivered to their cabins, the usual excitement that is a part of sailing. As I stood at the bottom of the stair, I could glimpse on the landing, a large, impressive, highly polished brass plaque, too far away to read. Where there was an opening in the line of passengers, I climbed to the landing and could hardly have been more surprised at the information given on the plaque:

S.S.S. Ankara
Built and Commissioned at Newport News, Virginia
Formerly a U.S. Naval Hospital Ship

The information it carried explained the ship's absence of luxury, its possible association with war, and the pity of war's wounded. The name "Newport News," however, was familiar to us; in a large way, it had run all through my own early life. Only a two-hours' train ride from Norfolk and its environs, the younger males among the farm families often left our community for work there in the shipyards.

I could remember so clearly one day when I was a child, when old Uncle Allen Battle, one of our best farm tenants, was having a discussion with Father about spring planting. We were in what was probably our first car, the Overland; our driver, Robert, at the wheel. I sat in the back.

Uncle Allen, whose manners were as nice as his character, was saying, "Mahs' Mack, I don't have as many head to help me dis spring like I been had. My oldest plowboy, Isaiah, dun got it in his mind to go to New-Pote-News and wuck in de shipyards. I tell him he ain't usin' no jedgemint, leaving hyeah where he c'n have cut ham from de smokehouse any time he want it, and milk from de cow, and colluds, and sweet 'tatoes, and poke whenever we kill hogs, and through de winter, he can eat roasted peanuts left from de thrashin' in de fields. He goin' off where he ain't liable to get no good t'eat, and liable to come back in a box from consumption. I don't think nothin' of it."

But Father consoled Uncle Allen by saying that Mr. Tanner, who was our riding boss, when the time came, would see that he had extra help with his crop from another farm, and followed with: "You know, Allen, we have to let our children experiment with life. Isaiah may be bettering himself

476

more then you realize. And Newport News is not far away."

At once Uncle Allen brightened. "Yes Suh," he answered cheerfully, "I'se got a bunch o' smart wimmins too." For most of his children were girls.

I couldn't wait to tell Tom the origin of the ship. Discussing it with Jay over lunch, she wanted to know, "Did Isaiah ever come back in a box?"

"No," Tom and I answered together. As had been true of our family, Tom had grown to have an affection for our farm families. He finished the little story by saying, "He prospered over there in the Norfolk area, married, and raised a large family." But he died young, and according to his wishes, he was brought back for burial in the graveyard on Old Town, for that was one of Father's farms on which he'd always lived.

By the time we reached dessert, the portholes told us that we were fast leaving the sight of land. Gliding slowly and smoothly, our ship would soon give those two final, courteous, short blows of "Thank you!" to the sturdy little tug, which, turning back, would respond with its own brief "All's well!" and my cup would be at the brim. I knew that we would soon begin to pick up speed, and that cutting her way through the waves, to be followed by the never-ending beauty of her wake, the ship would soon begin to creak, to roll gently from side to side, and that – the lady she always turned out to be – she would be constantly bowing and dipping, stem to stern. Small wonder, the fascination of the sea.

It had been as far back as on my first trip on an ocean liner that I came to understand the title of the song, "Rocked in the Cradle of the Deep." It was a song that, on Sunday nights, when I was a child, Father and a few of his friends used to love to sing around the piano as Mother played. There were several bass voices in the number, and they kept going down deeper and deeper with their

Dee

Eee

Eee

EEP's

until, as a child, listening in wonder, I couldn't see how their rumbly voices could possibly go any deeper, and yet, they did! At the end it was hardly music at all. But I felt it meant something lovely. From the very beginning of my sea travels I understood how instinctive it is to love your ship, how natural to have confidence in her seaworthiness and her crew, so that even in times of storm, when she's rhythmically creaking, and pitching, and straining, and you feel that every rivet is being tested, you can lie in your berth, quietly thrilled at being rocked in the cradle of the deep.

≈ ≈ ≈

The last winter that we were to have on Captiva, brought into our lives and that of the compound, the great sadness of Hie's illness. Her trouble had not as yet been diagnosed, but Jay and others of us who knew her intimately, felt that her lack of strength and her loss of appetite must mean something dire. As plucky as ever, she would try to take part in things. It was saddening to see her make the effort. During that winter, several of our other island friends had developed illnesses. I was more aware than Tom of how many times the rescue squad had hurried toward the mainland; I could glimpse it through the palms as it sped along against the sea, and could hear its siren as well.

One day, when this had happened several times in a relatively short period, I began to think. When Tom came up from the boatslip for lunch, he was aghast at my suggestion, which surprised even myself: that the time might have come for us to consider giving up our Captiva house. I pointed out the fact that we were nearly nine-hundred miles from home, that we could not expect to be immune to heart attacks and strokes, and that since we had acquired a hotel at Nags Head on the Carolina coast, we might find spending more time there in our apartment pleasant. Our boat, the *Carolina*, and the sailboat, The *Spoonbill*, could easily be taken care of there in the quiet waters of the sound. And I asked what he thought of the idea.

At first he couldn't think I was serious, but in twenty-four hours he reopened the subject by saying, "I've been giving the matter thought. There's no use hiding our heads in the sand. It just may be that we've had Captiva at its best. With our friends falling away, it will be different. I believe you have something." As usual, wives and mothers having given more time to the sifting of family matters, I had acted on intuition.

It was at our usual pre-Christmas stay that I had made that statement. By February, our house had been placed on the market. When we told Hie and Jay of our decision, the four of us had to wipe our eyes. One thing we knew, and we assured them of it, was that we could not, and would not, ever sell the property to anybody who wouldn't be congenial neighbors for them. To some extent, that slowed the process of the sale, not that Hie and Jay interfered, but we acted on the basis of affection. However, by the last of March, acceptable buyers had been found.

The morning in April when the Lynches came to say goodbye there was a further very real tug of the heartstrings. While, over the years, Janet and I had not spent the hours together that Tom and Bert had – for so many of theirs were spent on the water in one of the two boats – ours was, indeed, a close friendship. As usual, when the four of us were together, conversation was more banter than anything else, but bonds were deep.

Since the Lynches had their own small plane, the four of us often went up in it for the pleasure of looking down on the strand of islands to which ours belonged. Once in a while, we would go to Key West. A few hours in that exotic atmosphere with Hemingway's home in the heart of a triangle of a few sophisticated restaurants and a handful of shops in which the art of printmaking – silkscreening and other things – went on, was a lovely change for us. The Lynches and the Pearsalls had come to know many of each other's close "back-home" friends, and were always helping each other to make their visits to our island pleasant. There could hardly have been a more congenial friendship.

That morning of the goodbyes, to hide our overall sadness, conversation followed the usual light-hearted pattern. But when Tom and Bert shook hands, Janet and I had to look away.

Hie and Jay were to stay until later in the season. When we told them good-bye, we were all in tears. As Jay said, "Things can never be the same again," it was something we all knew.

But as I kissed Hie, I said, "Hie, I will be back in two weeks to take care of the things from our house that I will want sent to North Carolina. I will stay here and see you and Jay off, and we'll have a nice, quiet time together."

I did make that return trip. Hie was weakening every day, but she had said privately to me, in her unselfish way, "I long to be at home. But Jay enjoys the surf in the spring so much that I wanted to stay on for two more weeks."

Everyday I went over to the Rosses with a tray of something I hoped would tempt Hie's appetite. Bravely, she would try to consume at least a part of what I had brought, and the last night that the two were there, they came over to our house for the evening meal with me. At long last I had come to feel some self-confidence in cooking, and I had the things Hie had always enjoyed most. Jay had taught me how to use a rotisserie. Hie was fond of roast chicken, yet, as usual, she wanted only the wing – just one – for she was very small, and moderation had been the keystone of her life.

I had her favorite ice cream for dessert. For a few last moments, there in the twilight, with just enough light to still be able to see the sea in one direction, and the bay in the other, and in the softness of candlelight on the table, the three of us were together for the last time. Jay and I helped to get Hie to their house again, and at the door, Hie turned to kiss me again, and to say, "Elizabeth, we love you very much."

I had seen, several years earlier, the serenity with which Hie had met death in one of the ones she loved. Dr. Marion Putnam, or "Molly" to us, with whom, in a friendship of fifty years, Hie had had the bond of being in the psychoanalytical profession, had spent all her vacations with the Rosses, wherever they were, which meant that Tom and I had developed a great fondness for Molly as well. Molly had a heart condition which she knew might take her away at any time, but she did not restrict her movements on its account. She swam, she gardened, and like Hie, she wrote. The last of her writings was the publication of a book; her father's biography. For Dr. Putnam, her father, had been an outstanding neurologist in Boston. It was at his invitation that Dr. Sigmund Freud had made his first visit to this country.

Molly's death had come several years before Hie's, on a Thanksgiving night when all the members of the Compound had come to our house for the festive meal. As usual, each member had brought some item of food. A family of some of our oldest North Carolina friends were visiting us; John and Josephine, or "Jo," Vann, with one of their adult daughters, Molly. In a burst of Carolina pride, Jo and I had cooked the turkey and made a sublimely delectable and beautiful dessert, a mousse encircled with Lady Fingers, topped with whipped cream, and properly called "Lemon Float." We had prepared as well, two large casseroles of scalloped oysters, using real cream and cracker crumbs. By putting odd tables end to end, we managed to seat thirteen. Everything was, as we used to say at home when I was growing up, "as merry as a marriage bell."

At ten o'clock the guests went home. Jo and I attacked the kitchen, and at eleven, she had gone to the guest house to sleep and I was in my bed. I had hardly fallen asleep before the ceiling light in my room suddenly came on and Tom was saying, "Molly Putnam is terribly sick. The rescue squad is on the way. I'm going over."

He had to use the term Molly "Putnam," instead of his usual "Dr. Molly," because for the duration of the Vann's visit, we had come to speak jauntily of their daughter as Molly "O," the other, as Molly "P." In our overflow, our son, young Tom, was using the guest room at the Ross house. It was he who had phoned the rescue squad and had come to waken us. It was he who, with Jay in the car, would follow the ambulance to the mainland and to the hospital. But death would come enroute; resuscitation would prove futile. As Molly was being taken out on the stretcher from the Ross house and across its screened porch, all of us standing in our robes in a circle on the porch, Tom impulsively took the two steps necessary to touch her shoulder, and Molly said quietly, "Thank you, Tom." She never spoke again.

When young Tom phoned from the hospital that Molly had gone, Hie quietly went to her desk. She took out her address book, and as Tom and I sat there with her in her bedroom, we heard her say, without a quiver in her voice, over the phone to Molly's niece in New England, "This is Hie. Molly is dead. She wanted cremation. Will you make the proper plans, and let me know?"

This made me feel that when the time should come, Hie would have specified cremation, her ashes to be spread on Footprint Island, that beloved tiny island that so often came into conversation among the Rosses. Footprint Island lies in Lake Michigamme, Michigan, several miles across the water from where, for many years, Hie and their older sister, "Sis," had their girls' summer camp. Gradually, it was to become a family retreat. Sis died in her middle years, but the camp continued. As Hie's reputation as an analyst grew, the camp became possibly one of the best known in the Midwest, many of its campers, however, those who would attend eastern colleges. At one point in what was to be Hie's last years at Captiva, a group of her former girl campers wrote to ask permission to have a reunion of Hie's former campers of all ages in celebration of her seventy-fifth birthday. Gracefully, but swiftly, Hie declined. She felt that she had had honors enough. Possibly the crowning one for her had been the establishment by the University of Chicago in 1976, of the Helen Ross Professorship in Social Welfare Policy.

Hie's last letter to me, referring to her illness, contained these moving lines, "Let it (this news) not cloud our communication. I have had a good life – remember."

Those sentences, "Let it not cloud our communication. I have had a good life – remember," was the way Hie was to sign each of her farewell letters to her loved ones, including her close friends.

I had seen so many snapshots of Hie and Jay taken on Footprint, as they sat with four or five guests, enjoying a picnic lunch on a large rock at the water's edge where they often went, that to have Jay tell me over the phone when Hie had gone, that it was from that rock that Hie's ashes were to be given to the blue waters of the lake seemed especially beautifully fitting, the final beautiful note in a life well spent.

Tom's death was to come a year later. When I called Jay to tell her what had happened, both of us were in tears. The letter which she wrote right away, expresses the depth of the affection in which the four of us had been bound.

> Dear Elizabeth:
> I am reading *Ecclesiastes* for comfort, especially Chapter three, which was read at Hie's grave in Footprint,
> To everything there is a season and a time for every purpose

under the Heaven,

A time to be born, and a time to die, a time to plant, and a time to pluck up that which is planted.

Verse 12: I know that in these things of God, the good is *for a man to rejoice, and to be good in his life*, and that was Tom's way of life, *to rejoice* and *to do good in his life*.

And I shall think of him in his *rejoicing*, in his *good works*, for I have shared them both and observed them for many years.

I feel as if I had lost more than a friend, rather a brother, but I know he is, and will be, living in my thoughts and feelings as long as I live.

Dear Elizabeth, my tears are shed for you more than for him, you who knew and loved him best without reservation or doubt.

> With infinite love and compassion,
> Devotedly,
> Jay

In a few weeks she came to see me in Carolina.

With both Hie and Tom gone, we clung to each other, always knowing that we would keep in touch. For several years after Hie's death, Jay continued to go to Captiva. Then suddenly, as usually happens, she was aware that the time had come to dispose of her property. Having done that, she returned to the city of Washington. She has access there to the Library of Congress, to which she still goes, once a week, for her research. Last year, she sold her condominium there to enter that Episcopal retirement center, Collington, which is not far from the city of Washington, on the Maryland side.

Recently, I visited her there. I found her the same warm, loving friend, and in her new environment, the commanding small figure she's always been. All about the walkways of this well-run establishment, she is addressed deferentially, as "Miss Ross." I can tell that she is a favorite, and since this facility has the unique feature of having, on either side of the fireplace in its main lounge, built-in bookshelves for books which have been written by its residents, Jay is represented there in several volumes. I find that very pleasing.

For my visit, we talked over old times, we laughed a lot. She takes her evening meal in the main dining room, breakfast and lunch in her apartment. The first morning at breakfast, for which she was using her best china, her prettiest teapot, and the Earl Grey tea which she knows I like, as we sat cozily in her small kitchen, I said, laughingly, emphasizing the last syllable of the word, "Oh, Jay, I feel like a little princess."

Her comeback was swift and smiling, and freighted with a sincerity I did not question, as she raised her cup and said, "Only the best."

≈ ≈ ≈

There is now, no more available land on Captiva, but in order that more people may be accommodated, several condominiums have come. Relatively small, they are allowed to have only two stories, and they are required to conform to the island's taste for simplicity.

At the tip of the island, on a beautiful point, there is the old South Seas Plantation. Now enlarged, it has a small golf course, and tennis courts, which winter homeowners on the island may use. There is a yacht basin, even a sailing school. That inn, however, from the beginning, has been patronized more by short term occupants than that of the rustic Tween Waters Inn, midway down the island. "South Seas" had once been a citrus grove. A great many of its guests come now by seaplane, and unless they happen to have friends among the property owners of the island, their stays tend to go on entirely at that end.

During our time, South Seas added a gate house. When this sophisticated change came, the residents of the island were momentarily unsettled; it seemed an affront. Larry Weeks, who had always, from far back, had the habit of making that beautiful point a part of her daily walk, was one day turned away. You can imagine what that did to the rest of us. I must add that apologies were swiftly forthcoming, but it was never the same for Larry.

For a change, winter residents might, once in a while, take their guests to South Seas for dinner. It was interesting to be among such a concentration of youthful energy, bodies lean and lithe, minds intent on packing every experience the island offered into their short stays. There was, as well, the novelty of being served by Puerto Rican waiters who spoke almost no English. The feeling was that of being out of the country.

Although Captivans joked among ourselves that the only thing wrong with our island was that there were too many delightful people, our constant fear was that with more people coming – however delightful they might prove to be – things would change. Yet common sense told us that change was inevitable, and we tried to accept it with grace when a booklet came out called *The Story of the Island*, one that had been put together by a realtor. It was nicely done. Indeed, we liked having that condensed information about the island, information as to the tides, the descriptions of our twenty-eight varieties of native shells, and the illustrations and "Hints on Cleaning Shells," for the booklet not only informs, but pleads in this way:

Live shells which are cast up by storms usually do not live to propagate, but shells found at low tide in normal weather, are the ones we should gather, but sparingly. So, in your aim to collect beautiful shells, remember to leave sufficient so that the island may continue to be a "SHELLER'S PARADISE."

There are as many as 188 kinds of island birds listed, as well. In that paradise, Captivans were often aware that though we were at heart, conservationists, we might be considered selfish in hoping that more people wouldn't come to the island. Yet at the same time, we knew that when lovely quiet places come to be discovered, generally, they tend to lose their loveliness. Although I can't think that Captiva won't always be beautiful, I doubt that it can ever again provide that blissful feeling that we each had, that of having found something unique. And although it may have appeared at first that for each of us, our being there had come about by chance, there was a deeper meaning. We had been directed there by our common approach to life. It was the final note in an overall felicity.

≈ ≈ ≈

Sundays at Captiva were both traditional and non-traditional. Tom and I usually attended morning service at the Chapel By the Sea; once in a while, we changed the pattern and went to St. Michael's, the Episcopal church on Sanibel. Father Madden was the warm, happy, loving rector of the lovely little wooden church painted gray, and trimmed with red. Sitting back among the palms, it was aesthetically appealing. In a small building that matched the church, the women of the flock collected second-hand clothing, for Sanibel had a segment of people who were usually in need of help.

It was at St. Michael's that Tom and I met Emmy Lou Louis. Emmy Lou's husband, editor of a Minneapolis paper, was no longer alive. Their house, separated by tropical growth, sat as close to the wide, lovely Sanibel beach as possible. It was on a clear sunny day that Tom and I went by invitation to have lunch with Emmy Lou on her sun deck. As simple as the house was, there were a great many books. The magnet that books are, for me, as we had our drinks, and she and Tom talked, I was drawn to see what was on the shelves. The title of one immediately struck my fancy. Its author was Monsieur Guillaume Godeket, husband of the writer Colette. Emmy Lou, seeing that I was absorbed in the book, suggested that I take it home. It was not a large book, but I found one sentence in it that I would never forget. Monsieur Godeket, paying tribute to the love that exists between two individuals when it has stood the test of time, expresses it in this beautiful way:

After thirty years together, we loved that trustful silence between us,
a quietness based on affection that had no need to proclaim itself.

Each of us who has had a long and happy marriage knows the feeling. Those of us who are now alone find warmth and comfort in remembering. In that first pain of the grief of separation that is almost despair, when we are trying to hold up for those around us, we will have been supported by our loved ones, by our friends, by letters of sympathy, which, since they can be read and reread in private, will have brought us the release of tears. In the deepest sense, to give us hope, we will have felt underneath us the arms of the church. And although we may cling desperately to our memories, some sense of balance will make us know that they can be only a part of our groping toward light. Yet, they will be a vital part.

THE HOMING INSTINCT

≈ ≈ ≈

The alarm concerning Tom's health had first come in May. From then on, there would be a "stone in my heart." We had been back from Captiva and all its outdoor activity for a month when he began mentioning a feeling of constant fatigue. It was not enough to have to give in to, and he continued going to the office. The night before he was to receive an honorary degree from our local North Carolina Wesleyan College, however, he became very ill; his temperature went to 103, and I could hardly wait for morning to call our doctor. By four in the morning, Tom had said, "I just can't go out to the college."

My answer was, "Don't worry. I'll go and receive the honor for you." This seemed to bring him comfort. For most of that day Tom would be having tests. Although this was the third of the honorary degrees to be given him, one from the University of North Carolina at Chapel Hill and one from the branch of the University at Greensboro, this one was, for him, equally significant. He had been a founder of our North Carolina Wesleyan College, my own family had given the land for the college, and Tom had worked very hard for the college's growth.

The tests revealed a kidney infection. With medication, he began to feel slightly better, and in June, we drove to Nags Head for a few days. For five years – the last public service he was to render – Tom had been Chairman of the Roanoke Island Historical Association. The meetings were always held on Roanoke Island. In this capacity, he had succeeded Mrs. Fred Morrison of the cities of Washington and Nags Head. North Carolinians by birth, education, and deep allegiance, Fred and Emma Neal Morrison had, from the beginning, contributed generously of their time and their means toward the continuation of Paul Green's open-air symphonic drama, *The Lost Colony*, the first of its kind in our nation.

At that time, *The Lost Colony* had been going for some thirty summers, with nightly performances from June to September. Paul was almost ten years older than Tom, and except as loyal alumni of the University of North Carolina, the two had not known each other. Late in life, for what would be the last five-and-a-half years for each, they were thrown together intimately. They were to die two days apart.

The home of Paul and Elizabeth Green was in the open country near Chapel Hill. Sunny – and in its simplicity, charming – it reflected the natures of these two remarkable persons. Parents of four children, several months after Paul's death, in a talk given by Janet Green Catlin, one of their daughters, her parent's taste for simplicity was to be underscored. The talk was given at the National Honor Society for American Junior and

Community Colleges at the State University in Purchase, New York. Among others of their friends, I was happy to receive a copy of this tribute to her father, and it gives me pleasure now to share these insights into the life of this native son of North Carolina, who was to write eighteen symphonic dramas, any number of plays, and who was voted by the North Carolina legislature of 1979 as North Carolina's Dramatist Laureate. The note from Elizabeth Green that came with her daughter's paper was this:

> Dear folks,
> Today would be Paul's eighty-eighth birthday. We thought on this occasion you might like to receive a copy of our daughter Janet's paper about him.
>
> > With love and best wishes–
> > Elizabeth

From the paper I learned that Paul overcame poverty in such a way as to, at twenty-two, become a teacher at the University of his state. Janet speaks of her father in this way:

> Paul Green, for much of his career, was not in the mainstream of the American Theater. He avoided gratuitous violence, loveless sex, miserable introspection, ironic ambiguity, sophisticated banter, and fearful despair as subjects for the stage. He opposed the death of the dignified and hopeful behavior in drama, and he believed in heroes and heroines. At the height of his powers, he moved away from Broadway, once his habitat, and devoted at least half of his life's energy to what he called The People's Theater, free of the commercialism and concentrated clichés of Broadway...In the beginning, he was a regionalist. As the first white playwright to write about blacks, dripping in dialect, the parts were often taken by white actors in black-face.

Apparently this was disappointing to the playwright, and he moved away from that sphere. Mr. Green's daughter goes on to say:

> If you asked about any native of N.C. – we call them Tar Heels – "Who is the most famous North Carolina writer?" the reply would be inevitably, "Paul Green."...
> ...So he was writing, writing, writing all the time. He did it by hand or by dictation or on an ancient beloved typewriter. He always had a simple two-story cabin to work in, one that he built himself: no phone, book-lined shelves, full of paper, pencils, old drafts, boxes of notes –always mysterious places, rather dusty, silent, full of hope.

The photograph of Paul attached to his daughter's paper shows him in his late years. His hair is gray, his kindly face wears a smile, he has on a business suit and a shirt and tie. As he leans on his writing table on his right elbow, that hand, held up against the cheek, holds a pencil. A blank sheet of paper lies before him on the table, and in the foreground of the picture, anchored to the edge of the table, is a pencil sharpener.

I had long known that Paul Green considered himself a humanist. His daughter recounts an amusing incident wherein her father, on entering a hospital for treatment, was asked about his faith. He replied to the nurse taking down the information that he was a humanist, to which the nurse answered, "The computer is not going to recognize that answer. Can't you give me something else?"

Today for the first time I have sought the dictionary for the full meaning of the word "humanist." From several parts of the definition, in relation to Paul Green, I chose the one which I think he would have liked applied to himself: a person having a strong interest in, or concern for, human welfare, values, and dignity.

Tom and Paul were both products of Eastern Carolina, both were devoted to their state and saw the University of North Carolina as one of its strongest forces for good. With these things in common, that these two men should be – in their last years – joined in an effort to perpetuate the state's history, seems fitting.

When Tom became Chairman of the Roanoke Island Historical Association, Emma Neal Morrison was the producer of the pageant, "The Lost Colony." She always spent the entire summer at her Nags Head beach cottage, giving the play and its cast her constant attention and support. With a successful law practice in Washington, her husband, Fred, drove down to the beach for weekends in summer. Since Fred's death, Emma Neal has continued the pattern of her life, both in Washington and at Nags Head, her interest in preserving in drama, the story of the first settlers on our shores would still be - and remains - for her, a consuming interest. She continues to occupy possibly the oldest cottage on the beach, one of its smallest, perhaps its most modest. Innately hospitable, however, the Morrisons have long owned a more roomy cottage next door. I have especially happy memories of the time when Ida and Bill Friday, and Tom and I, were there together as houseguests. For much of the time, it is this from which the Morrison's daughter, Myra, and her husband and children come and go.

One of the pleasant by-products of Tom's involvement with the Roanoke Island Historical Association was, that for a few hours, I was to have an experience that would make me feel as though I were almost hobnobbing with the Queen!

For several years, North Carolinians had been making plans for the celebration of the four-hundredth anniversary of the landing of what had become "The Lost Colony." Now the time had come. Tom had gone down to Manteo a week ahead of the official ceremony. I was to arrive the day before the celebration. Knowing this, Bill Friday thoughtfully called me to say that he would be flying down with Lord Lothian, the Queen's emissary to the celebration, as his guest – his wife, Ida, had gone ahead – and that he would pick me up in Rocky Mount and bring me back. In that way, I had the pleasure of informal conversation with Lord Lothian. I recall that he was inclined to be casual, that he was enjoying the experience of being in our country at this special time, and that he was deeply impressed with our ongoing affection for the Mother Country. The *Coastland Times*, dated Thursday, June 17, 1976, ran this account of Lord Lothian's visit:

> A British Peer, Lord Lothian of Great Britain, a descendant of Sir Walter Raleigh, visited Roanoke Island and the Dare Beaches last Saturday. Three of the photographs made of him and his party, which included Mr. and Mrs. Tom Pearsall of Rocky Mount, William Friday, President of the Greater University of North Carolina, John Kerr of Durham, and a Mrs. John Kerr of Warrenton, are shown. In the Elizabethan Gardens he is shown as Louis Midgett pointed towards the water over which the first English colonists probably sailed during the sixteenth century. Pearsall, Chairman of the Roanoke Island Historical Association, is the third person in this picture. Another photo shows Lord Lothian as he was shown a patch of "Uppowoc," which was the Indian name for tobacco that was discovered growing on the island. New York photographer George Thames shot the photo of the group as they read the inscription on the tombstone-like marker which had been erected in the 1890s by The Roanoke Colony Association. Later the party was given a guided tour of Waterside Theatre. (Photos by Aycock Brown and George Thames.)

At the end of the five years during which Tom had joined Emma Neal and other committee members from Nags Head and over the state in this ongoing endeavor, he felt that his position on the committee might well be taken by a younger man, and was able to persuade John Kennedy, a committtee member, then Secretary to Bill Friday, the President of UNC, and formerly a successful lawyer in Charlotte, to assume that responsibility. Emma Neal would continue as producer.

These were the years when Tom and I were seeing a lot of John and Barbara Kennedy. We were often guests in their lovely old home in Hillsborough. With our love of England, that Barbara was English made our stays a double pleasure. They had chosen to live in Hillsborough, they said, because it was the nearest thing to an English village they could find in our part of the country. Barbara and John had met when he was a Rhodes Scholar. Barbara's mother, Lady Whitby, came over from England every summer to see her daughter. Tom and I were often being thrown with the Kennedys and Barbara's mother, either in Hillsborough, in our home town, or at Nags Head. We were continually delighted with the adaptability of this lovely English lady, who, in her eighties, flew the Atlantic alone as a matter-of-course.

The Kennedys had a summer cottage on the Carolina Coast, not far from Nags Head. That area of the shore was spoken of as "Stumpy Point." And my pleasure in the incongruous was continually surfacing in regard to the meshing of unlikely things. For I knew that Barbara's father had been physician to King George V, and that after the King's death and later, that of the doctor's, Barbara's mother had been given, by the crown – for life – one of those grace-and-favor apartments at Hampton Court. Barbara's mother did needlework, as does Barbara. And one afternoon, when the Kennedys and Lady Whitby had stopped at our house in Rocky Mount for tea on their way to the beach, I was surprised at Lady Whitby's interest in a small square of needlepoint that lay on the table in our living room. She picked it up, examined it carefully, and asked me about it. Her interest deepened when told just what it was.

I began by saying that for a long time, Tom and I had had a simple house on a small island off the southwest coast of Florida. That it was a place that I felt she might have liked; that there, in a setting of natural beauty, life went on in a completely natural way, the emphasis on simplicity. I explained that next door to us there was the house of two unusually interesting sisters, and that since theirs was a large house, and since they knew a great many people, it was usually filled with interesting houseguests, those who came season after season for either long or short stays.

One of their regular houseguests was a woman of, perhaps, forty-five. Her name, incidentally, was Helen Hayes, no connection with the actress. "Haysey," as we called her, loved the out-of-doors, fishing and swimming and sailing, and was also creative and handy with the needle. And that small square of needlework – a gray background centered with a cobalt blue emblem of some kind, something Helen brought out of her mind – had been worked in threads which she had dyed from native berries. It is, indeed, a charming little thing. But as Lady Whitby held it in her hand, the symbolic charm of it for me, was, that that microscopic bit of needlework, for a moment, became a connector between Captiva, Chapel Hill, Hillsborough, Hampton Court, and, of all things, Stumpy Point!

The fact that Lady Whitby had expressed interest in Haysey's bit of

needlework brought her into that intimate circle of connectors that even included Haysey's brother, whose given name, I think, was Ralph. At that time, Ralph was curator of the Gardner Museum in Boston. He and his wife came often to visit the Rosses. In the usual camaraderie between the Ross house and ours, the couple loved going out with us on our boat, and found pleasure in our sand picnics on other islands. Wanting to repay us in some way, at the end of one of their visits, they urged us to visit them in Boston in their penthouse above the Gardner Museum. On the last of their visits to the island, we were urged to "come soon," for Ralph was nearing retirement.

It was a tempting prospect, but somehow Tom and I never did get to go. Nevertheless, reliving that afternoon's pleasure, I had that companionable feeling that had so often occurred in my life, that of being, for a moment, very near to the heart of things. I knew that Mrs. Gardner had employed Bernard Berensen, mentioned earlier, as an outstanding authority on art to make the selections for her museum in Boston, and that Mr. Berensen and his wife, Mary Pearsall Smith Berensen had gone on to establish for Harvard the scholarly European retreat, I. Tatti, near the city of Florence. Knowing as I did, that among others, Jay, as a member of the Learned Societies of the World, was often invited to study there, brought it all very close to home, for, by prearrangement, Tom and I had once had a stay in Rome as we waited for Jay to complete her visit to I. Tatti, after which, the three of us would tour Rome and its vicinity together. All of it centered around that unassuming piece of needlework, created from the natural growth of our island.

≈ ≈ ≈

Our Captiva property disposed of, we spent more time on our North Carolina coast, at Nags Head, where we owned a hotel which included a spacious apartment for our own use. Although walks on the beach, swims, and sailing seemed to give Tom a certain temporary strength, he had to rest after any form of activity. When he came in from what was to be the last sail of his life, for we were to leave the next morning, he was more tired than I had ever seen him. That afternoon the two of us had had a beautiful sail on Currituck Sound. The waters were quiet, and I had not noticed that Tom seemed more tired than usual. I now know that he had been putting up a front. It was not until we were back in our apartment in the hotel a few miles away that he said, "When we get home I'm going to see John Chambliss." This meant our local doctor.

"Of course," I acquiesced, wishing that we were already at home.

Still, when Tom had showered and dressed for dinner, so crisp and healthy-and-young-looking in his white pants, his blue shirt and a figured ascot, his coat hanging on the back of a chair ready to put on for going down to dinner, momentarily, I regained a sense of balance. But then he said, and my worry returned, "Give me a few minutes to rest." This was wholly unlike Tom, and I began to feel a premonition.

As he stretched out on the long, brightly colored sofa of our living room, I sat down quietly at the glass-top table at the other end of the room to try to read. There was never any absence of books in my life, and as usual, the table held a stock of them. Whenever or wherever I was, as I've commented earlier, whether it was in the car, in a hotel room or its lobby, I always had something of an assortment of a travelling library. I never left home without a bag or a basket of some kind with reading material, a legal pad and a few ball-points, my provisions against the delays that often came into Tom's life, and in that way, indirectly, into mine. Tom came jokingly to call these hedges against boredom and loneliness my sidearms. That afternoon, on the coffee table lay several books on sailing and Barbara Tuckman's latest book, his current reading.

We had already decided to leave on the next morning. When it came, with our bags in the car, Tom said, "I think I'll ask you to drive if you don't mind."

Each of these small things gave me a terrible sense of change. The feeling increased as he kept his head on the back of the seat, his eyes closed most of the way of the three hour drive. We spoke little. Knowing the road well, Tom would sometimes ask where we were.

Once he said quietly, "You know, we never talk about death and separation. It's as though we felt it would come to everybody but us."

This, too, was different. From long years of protecting each other, now, as though we were having a conversation about ordinary things, we exchanged a few thoughts on the mystery of the afterlife. Finally, we could remind ourselves of what Hie always said, "the sooner you realize there are no certainties, the better off you are."

And Tom answered, "Yes, when all is said and done, it requires that leap in faith."

But I had one more thought. "Do you know, I read the other day something beautiful. It asks the question, *How to believe? Love. How to love? Believe.* Don't you think that's true?"

And he answered quietly, "Yes."

My heart felt that it could take no more. I added, trying to speak lightly, "Well, we've almost come to Tarboro. There's not much traffic today; I'm glad we made an early start." All those inconsequentials we use to tide us over the rough spots when thinking is unbearable. And we moved along as though the sun were not beginning to drain from our lives.

Two weeks later, when tests at our local hospital had shown an alarming blood deficiency and a shadow in the chest area, we were sent by our doctor to Duke. Our two sons were with us, and when Tom had been admitted to the area in which he would see a specialist, the other three of us sat in the waiting room. One of our sons said, quietly, "Mother, do you know what building we're in?"

I couldn't answer, but I bowed my head, and he understood.

Our other son, trying to help, came in quietly with what we already knew, "But the doctors at Duke are wonderful. People come here from all over the world."

A nurse who had been sitting behind her desk in the waiting room, came over with a handful of pamphlets. On the outside of each was that dread word – cancer. And my life began to crumble.

Tom became a patient in Duke North that day. Several days were devoted to making tests before the biopsy. We liked Dr. Silberman. He did not mince words. The night before the biopsy he told us the seriousness of going into the chest wall, but that it had to be done. As all this was explained, he stood on one side of Tom's bed; I stood on the other. Then Tom lifted his right hand toward Dr. Silberman and said, "Well, Doctor, we both believe in the same God," and these two men of different faiths were, for a moment, joined in hope.

As they clasped hands, I nearly choked. Yet by some gift of God, I could hold a tight rein on my emotions. I had already learned to turn quickly away so that Tom would never see my tears. Not to, would have made it harder for him. My voice I could control, but not my tears. He had done his best to protect me for fifty years, and I could tell that now he worried as much about how his illness would affect me as he did about his own well-being. He had seen me go through the loss of other members of my family, and he'd often said, "You love too much. Life will hurt you so much." But underneath, he was the same way.

And so, we played that little game that loved ones play for each other, taking the blows, one by one, as they came. After the biopsy, Tom was terribly sick. Dr. Silberman came to his room to say, "Mr. Pearsall, you have a thirty percent chance. We'll start the treatment right away." And I knew that I, myself, was beginning to die those deaths that are a part of watching a loved one's life ebb away.

This was three days before Christmas. Tom told our sons that he wanted them to send out a typed letter to our relatives and close friends, bringing them up to date on his illness, approaching the subject with a positive attitude. The letter would say that since somebody had sent him a Santa Claus cap, he would be wearing it in bed on the meaningful day. He had given Tom and Mack instructions to have a home-made cake made for the nurses on the hall, and to bring two dozen small bags of roasted peanuts for those members of the hospital personnel with whom he was in daily contact.

The letter ended by saying, "Our father says he's ordering pizza for lunch – the first time we've ever heard of his having any! In this season of hope, he sends all of you his love and appreciation for your concern and your prayers."

Christmas day came. The hospital had all but closed down. Physically, it was a terrible day for Tom, but the whole family came, including our fifteen-year-old grandson, Brad, whom Tom spoke of as "my boy," and Tom tried to be bright. By late afternoon they had gone, and as the sun was setting, there came a knock at the door. It was Terry Sanford, formerly Governor Sanford, at that time, President of Duke University. When he came in, he said, "I couldn't let Christmas day pass without coming to see my old friend." He could see how sick Tom was, and it was not a long visit. As he left, Terry and I walked down the long hall to the elevator together, our arms around each other, each of us too moved to speak.

Bill Friday, at that time still president of UNC, a few miles away in Chapel Hill, had been in constant touch, and came over many times during that, and our subsequent hospital stays. Our Bishop came several times, as did Heywood Holderness, Nancy's son, a cousin on my side of the family, a Presbyterian minister in Durham. One afternoon, Bill Friday and another close friend of Tom's and often a fellow committee member, Paul Johnson of Chapel Hill, came together. I heard Tom say to them that he sometimes worried that in the attempt to integrate our schools, the blacks might have felt that by the "escape valve" of pupil assignment by request, he might have dealt unfairly with their race. The two men assured him that that could never have been the case. Yet it disturbed me that Tom had that feeling, and I wrote to our Governor Hunt, explaining the situation, and asking a favor: "Was there an outstanding black person in the environs who might possibly be sent to see Tom for reassurance on that score?"

In a few days my request was answered. Benjamin Ruffin, an executive with Reynolds Tobacco Company, drove from Winston-Salem for a quiet visit with Tom. I was sorry not to have been there to meet this kind, understanding man. But the fact that he came, and his reassurance that the members of his race, as well, understood that with the coming of something as new as the integration of schools, time for acceptance must be given, meant a great deal to Tom, and to me. Gratitude that I could later express to Mr. Ruffin by telephone.

Although Tom had three registered nurses, I was always there. I left only to go to my meals, and to go back to the inn at night. The last minibus from the inn that served the hospital left at nine-thirty; the first in the morning from the inn, at six-thirty. That became my routine. I felt I had to be there when the doctors came round, which they sometimes did as early as seven o'clock.

The only thing Tom ever said by way of preparing me for the worst was the morning after the biopsy when he said, "You know, I may or may not get well."

But I would not have it that way. I knew that he wanted reassurance from me, and that would be my way to the very end. He wanted me to feel that he was going to be all right. One day, he opened his eyes to say, "I always worried how it would affect you if I were ever very sick, but you're so calm."

"That's because I can stay right here with you and help to get you well," I answered.

Then as he slowly closed his eyes, he said, "I'm just drifting – every word is an effort."

For the thousandth time I gave prayerful thanks for sedatives. My response would be, "I know. We don't need to talk. Just rest." And the hours passed.

Months later he would say to me – but only once – when the orderlies came with their stretcher to take him for more tests, "Why do they continue to make these tests? They don't contribute anything."

As I followed him to the door with my hand on his arm I could make myself say such hollow things as: "In a teaching hospital, breakthroughs come every day. This might be that day." For us, these statements held no hope, but I could never not hold out hope to Tom.

Sometimes he would urge me to take a walk, which I would do. Once he said, "Why don't you go home for a day or two?"

I could treat that suggestion with disdain. "Wild horses couldn't drag me away, and you know it."

With that he gave a weak little smile, remembering – I knew – my lifelong habit of making a point with exaggeration. And I sat remembering sadly, his never-failing affection and acceptance of that part of my nature. In a way, I think he liked it. And it now helped both of us momentarily for me to pretend to be my old self.

As he closed his eyes again, I said, "I'm right here where I want to be." He knew that, and he answered, "You're my only joy."

Of Tom's nurses, the oldest was one named Eva. Stout and motherly, I could tell that she brought him comfort. When I left her at his bedside at night, her presence eased my heart. One morning outside Tom's room, she told me that he had said quietly during the night, "Eva, when people with my trouble go, how do they go?"

"Well, Mr. Pearsall," she had replied. "You've been sleeping a lot. The sedatives will keep down the pain. I think you'll just go in your sleep."

"Thank you," he said. When Eva repeated this to me the next morning, I thought it would kill me.

All the nurses in the hospital – there, and in our local hospital – had commented, and would continue to, on the fact that Tom was the only patient they'd ever seen who thanked them even for the medications they brought. He was like that. He took nothing for granted. His was an understanding nature that reached people right away. For as long as I'd known him, small boys were addressed as "Partner," those a little older, as "Chief." Boys beyond that age, even into their middle years, if he knew them well, others were greeted as "Sport." Small girls were addressed as "Little Lady." Teachers, in a half-jesting way were addressed as "Professor," and all women who waited on tables in restaurants, no matter what their size, were courteously addressed as "Little Lady." The sincerity of an overall goodwill was conveyed through the light touch.

As Tom's pain grew, my prayer became that simple one I had finally used in the terminal illnesses of others of my loves ones: *Please God, give him peace, and give me strength.*

Now and then, over the years, in speaking of someone he admired, Tom would use the word "steadfast." Certainly during his illness we could have applied that word to our sons. Not a stone was left unturned for their father's comfort and the constant assurance that his business affairs were being taken care of. They had inherited Tom's nurturing nature, perhaps a little of mine, which at times, I confess, I carry too far. It comforted me to see our sons when they were with him, week after week, and month after month, doing those small thoughtful things that go with family illnesses, a capacity usually given only to women. It did not need to be voiced that their father was never far from their minds.

For eight months there would be repeated stays at Duke and at our local hospital, with intermittent stays at home. The nurses were kind enough to come home with us each time. During our stays at Duke we were in close touch with our home doctors, Dr. John Chambliss and Dr. Dan Crocker. Through the whole of the ordeal, those two skilled and compassionate men bore us up.

On one of his last stays at Duke, one of our local doctors, Kenneth

Weeks, spoken of as "K.D.," and his wife, Mildred, came to see Tom. Mildred, standing at the foot of his bed said, "Tom, I've had cancer for twenty years. You're going to be all right."

When they had gone, knowing that K.D. went to Duke one day a week to teach, and that Mildred went back and forth for treatment, Tom said to me, "Wasn't that thoughtful of K.D. and Mildred to come by to wish me well? K.D. so busy and Mildred so frail." Two years later, Mildred would lose her own fight with cancer. But of all the letters that were to come to me at Tom's death, I think hers expressed it best, for she said simply, "Everybody loved Tom."

A MOONLESS SEA

The Gift of Vital Strength

Some people are born with the gift of conveying to others a lifting sense of life. They say that when Bishop Phillips Brooks walked down the streets the sun shone brighter on everyone.

Blessed is the man who raises the level of life wherever he goes. He raises it by the way he walks, the smile of greeting, the word spoken, the whole atmosphere of exuberance which marks everything he does.

In the words of Isaiah, "Let thy light break forth as the morning and let thine health spring forth speedily."

God has made a world in which glory is catching, and the most contagious thing is a soul at peace with himself.

From a sermon delivered on October 16, 1949, by the Reverend Alexander Winston of the First Parish Church in Portland, and sent to me at Tom's death by Dr. Claiborne Smith

≈ ≈ ≈

Long ago, when I was but a young girl of fourteen, during what was to become Father's fatal illness, Dr. Smith, as a consultant, entered the life of our family. From then on, we would have two family doctors, but with Dr. Marriott's death, we relied solely on Dr. Smith and his recognized skill as a diagnostician and his unfailing interest and kindness. By the time of Tom's illness those many years later, Dr. Smith had retired, but still remained a close friend, and with Tom's death, was to administer to me in another way.

In the letter of sympathy that contained the sermon, Dr. Smith wrote, "There was another man with Tom's illness. This young doctor, Tom Dooley, of Cambodia, aware that he was about to die, said, 'To achieve happiness, one has to strive for the happiness of others.' By this yardstick, we can say that Tom achieved happiness."

There were many other letters to reach my heart. Bill Friday wrote, "Whatever I am, I owe to Tom."

Grace Johnson of Chapel Hill, expressing her sympathy, and that of her husband, Paul, sent another beautiful letter. Paul, as a young lawyer, had become a protégé of our Governor Hodges when he was in office, and under his guidance, had gone on to become an immensely successful businessman in New York. Grace and Paul then lived between there and Chapel Hill. Paul and Tom had served on many state committees together, and in Grace's letter to me, she had written, "Paul considered Tom the perfect man."

In this outpouring of sympathy, many messages came from our Captiva friends. In one, Grace Severinghaus, of Seattle and Captiva, who had lost her husband a few months earlier, wrote, "You and Tom would not have known it, but of all the wonderful men at Captiva, Elmer admired and loved Tom most. He felt that he and Tom shared a life-commitment to the betterment of human life." Dr. Severinghaus had been distinguished in his profession. His field was international health care, specifically nutrition, and this took him all over the world. At the time of our friendship, Elmer was making an extensive study of the newly discovered effects of cholesterol. One of his findings was puzzling. Often, in the poorer countries, shepherds, who existed almost solely on mutton-fat, when tested, had low cholesterol. It was assumed that their rugged lives took care of the excessive fat.

A letter that had come from Jane Gordon Thompson of Pittsburgh was typical of the other letters of sympathy from Captiva:

Dear Elizabeth,

We will all miss Tom so much. He was "Mr. Captiva" as far as the Thompsons are concerned. He was always so generous with his boat rides and made the difference in the children's having a super-special vacation many times. I wish he could have been around to give us a few pointers on Gordon's new boat. Tom will indeed be missed and remembered on Captiva with great happiness.

I hope someday you will come back to the island. We have a little guest house to offer now that we have added to our high-in-the-sky house.

Much love to you, and our sympathy,

Jane and Gordon

July 1981

From Codman Hislop, a warm, gentle man, and a widely recognized historian, then retired to Dorset, Vermont, and Captiva, comes this:

Dear Elizabeth,

Mail, even as the seasons, moves slowly and erratically in these parts. My mail, if it goes first to Captiva and then up to Dorset, "rusticates en route."

Delayed or not, I was thankful to you for your thoughtfulness in sending those fine newspaper tributes to Tom. I suspect that Tom, himself, might have read them in some astonishment, for he seemed to me first among modest men. But you knew, and the people of Rocky Mount and of North Carolina knew, that he measured up to all that was said of him. Tom was the kind of man I would always want around me in an emergency. I wish I had known him when he and I were young men.

Little but rain here since my return about ten days ago. I've never seen the "Green Mountain State" greener, nor my weeds more numerous and vigorous. If I win a half-victory against them, I'll think the summer well-spent.

If I drive South this fall, Rocky Mount will be a stage-stop. If I weaken and fly instead, then I will see you on Captiva. You have too many devoted friends there to turn us down.

Much love,

Coddy

Codman, driving north the last of May, did stop over. That night we had dinner together. Codman understood my sorrow because he had lost his wife some years before.

From Dorothy Horne Hinson, Tom's early secretary and a life-long friend:

507

Havng known Tom all my life, I realized at an early age, that he possessed those qualities which would cause him to stand out above the ordinary man. I share in your sadness at his death. His vital and worthwhile life will long be remembered.

My love and my sympathy to you and the boys.

Devotedly,
Dorothy

I was never able to read to Tom a certain letter that, among the many, came to him during his illness. For strangely, it moved me more than any other; it had been written by a wandering soul whose life, in a peculiarly meaningful way, Tom had touched; that of our Captiva caretaker, Chuck:

Saturday, 27 December 1980

Dear Mr. P.,

I have not written earlier not because I had nothing to write or did not want to write, but rather because I did not know how to write the many things I want to say.

It saddens me greatly that you are in the hospital and why you are in the hospital.

It has been my hope that when exit time came, as it must for us all, yours would be in your hundredth year with a nice "flashy" bolt of lightning while sailing your boat. If I could have any wish I've ever had, that would be the one I would choose.

If I could have a second wish, it would be for you to have received all the letters I have written to you in my mind over the past four years. Some of them were really great.

I will not wax sentimental and say all the things I want to say but only say that when I wrote that presumptuous story "Adam and the Pig," I chose the name "Adam" because of its Hebraic meaning: the first man, mankind, and dust of the earth. If nothing else in the story was correct or appropriate, the name was.

I have so much for which to thank you, the greatest being the three happiest years of my life. Mr. P., I admire and respect you more than any man I've ever known and I am grateful that our paths have crossed.

I truly have no idea what comes after this phase of existence, but if there be anything else, I hope our paths will cross again.

I'm sorry for the concern I must have caused you last summer – if there was a way to erase it, I certainly would.

I think I'm all right now. The only real damage I did was to myself. I can't change what has already happened, but I am trying to reestablish myself here on Captiva. It's difficult because I alienated many people with my strange behavior last summer. Fortunately, I've been able to find work. I have not been able to find a place to live which is distressing because I feel like I am in "limbo," but perhaps that will change.

I take care of the Carter place which I like very much. The Carters are from North Carolina also and are very nice people. I've done the best job I've ever done on their place and I'm really proud of how nice it looks.

The place I love the most is your place here. Unfortunately, I can't have that again.

The remodeling the Burrs are doing is going to make your place the grandest looking place on the whole island. In my thoughts, it will be "Park Pearsall."

The Burrs are really fine people and I think very dearly of them. Probably the worst thing I did during my sickness was to alienate them. But, anyway, I am glad they were the ones that bought your place because they are doing so many nice things with it.

When they are finished with the remodeling, I'll ask them if I can take some pictures and send them to you.

I was invited to J.B.'s for Christmas dinner. It was a very nice occasion.

I'll close now. Mr. P., I hope your life brought the things you wanted and I thank you for that part of it you shared with me.

Good sailing Sir – I love you.

Chuck

It was the "Good sailing Sir" that broke my heart.

≈ ≈ ≈

When the end had come, according to Eastern Carolina custom, all the relatives from both sides of the family assembled at our house for the service. Bishop Fraser was there to assist our own minister, Charlie Penick. For the prayers offered at home, to begin the service of graveside rights, Bishop Fraser stood in the hall at my side. He was perceptive enough to quietly hold my hand, for with the sound of his voice in the opening prayer, I began to tremble as though I might fall, yet outwardly I held my composure.

The only thing that our sons and I wanted over the pall was a spray of green, a combination of magnolia boughs from the giant old tree in the corner of our yard, and pine boughs from a timber tract long held by Tom's family, a tract which, long ago, when the widely scattered heirs to the land decided to sell it, Tom, in his capacity as overall manager of Father's farms, realizing its future value, suggested to Mother and our family lawyer that it would be a good investment for Father's estate. Had Tom had the money himself, he would have liked nothing more than to have bought it in his own right.

Tom's vision had proven correct. Ever afterward, with the judicious marketing of the timber, for we had hired a forester for the purpose – the nature of farming, itself, unpredictable – this would be our family's most dependable source of income. When we began to think of travelling, we would sometimes say among ourselves, lightly, "Well, let's just cut a few trees and go."

Of all the land we owned, Tom loved this wooded area most. It held a hunt club, and although I do not believe Tom enjoyed killing anything, nothing gave him more pleasure than being in that kind of country atmosphere, among people who till their own land, and have the earthy wisdom that goes with that kind of life, and who are usually, as well, good tellers of tales. This ten thousand acre tract had originally belonged to Tom's Uncle Dick and Aunt Penelope Price Gatling, a couple who had died childless. Incidentally, his Uncle Dick had had the distinction of having invented the Gatling gun.

Following Carolina custom, the relatives returned with us from the cemetery to our home for an informal luncheon. Once there, there was laughter. That was the way Tom would have wanted it. I realized then, that I had become two persons: Inside, I could be with Tom. But I felt it a strong obligation not to burden any of those around me – nor, indeed, anybody – with my sorrow. I must smile, I must laugh, I must take part in things, for I have long believed, knowing that every life has trouble or sorrow of one kind of another, that we owe each other bright faces. I was determined to wear mine. Grasping at straws, I made a quick little pledge to myself: I would find some joy in each day and would provide some for another. It was such a simple rule that it was in the realm of the possible, and with its practice, healing slowly began.

Yet, in my anguish, I found myself superimposing Tom on God, or the reverse, asking each equally for help. In my despair, the irrational thought was constantly in my mind, *Where is he? How can he still not need me the way I need him?* When sorrow is fresh, sleep is virtually impossible. I kept a basket of letters of sympathy by me on the bed, reluctant to turn out the light, for saddest of all was awakening to the slow tears of realization. On one of these nights, I wrote a few lines of poetry that seemed somehow to help:

> *Weep heart, in the silence of night*
> *Listen heart, for the voice far away*
> *Peace heart, in the songs of the morn*
> *For death could not make that heart afraid*
> *and mine is now but a heart overstayed*

And with the first soft, scattered bird calls of morning, I slept.

In a few days something beautiful happened. It was afternoon, and knowing that somebody would be coming soon, I sat alone on our terrace. For the first time, the sounds of summer hurt me, for Tom had so loved nature. Although we were a week into June, my heart was so filled with grief that my thoughts could have been those expressed in a poem which I later came across, its title, *Surrender*. A little-known poet, Carrie Benson, had written:

> *I hid away from April*
> *because my heart was sore*
> *I feared her sudden loveliness,*
> *for I could bear no more.*
> *and old griefs have a sharper sting*
> *when April's at the door*
>
> *But I could not flee her lilacs,*
> *her drifting silver rain,*
> *her dagger-thrusts of daffodils,*
> *her rapture and her pain –*
> *I flung my heart to April*
> *and let it break again!*

For me, the heartaches were, in part, the sights and sounds of early summer: its birdsong, the voices of children at play, the flutter of birds across the lawn, the flit of a butterfly, a bee moving from flower to flower.

Enveloped in this sadness, my thoughts were interrupted by the slam of a car door, and around the corner of the house came my sons. Everyday I was finding how many of their father's fine qualities they had inherited. Now, as never before, they realized that they had lost the one who had given them a blueprint for life. And while their interests were not to be the same – Mack has his father's enthusiasm for business and politics; Tom's nature is more mine, a leaning toward the arts – my sons have always respected each other's interests and are wholly congenial. In this family sorrow, there was an even greater strengthening of those bonds, and a constant mutual effort to shield me from heartache.

That afternoon, the two were bringing me a book. It had no cover, its size was average, its binding, dark blue. Handing it to me, one of them said, "Mother, we've been going through Daddy's desk." And at home, they always used this affectionate term.

"Did you know that at one time, he kept a diary?" the other asked. "It was the year of your engagement and it ended on your wedding day."

They had put a marker at that place. I opened it, and there it was:

511

October 28, 1930. Under the printed date, in Tom's handwriting, was one word: *Married.* And on the next line, *My life begins today.*

If anything could have brought my tears, it would have been that. But they were sweet tears. For Tom and I had always known that life did indeed, for each of us, begin that day, and this, I felt, was somehow a last beautiful message from him.

≈ ≈ ≈

Of the tributes written over the state at the time of Tom's death, the one from the *News and Observer* reads:

The Complete Tom Pearsall

Thomas J. Pearsall wore the mantle of political and civic leadership naturally. His long and varied career of public service never bore the taint of narrow self-interest. Many North Carolinians, unfortunately, had a one dimensional view of Pearsall as the chief author of a 1956 plan that shaped the state's approach to school desegregation. That view is too limited to embrace his gifts to the state.

Secure in identity and ability, Pearsall reflected a greater desire to serve than to be served by his state. He became Speaker of the House in 1947 and found fullfillment thereafter in public and private accomplishments short of statewide elective office. He chose that route even though the governorship probably could have been his had he chosen to pursue it.

Pearsall's aid and counsel, especially in higher education and the public schools, were solicited by a number of governors. As a member of the Carlyle Commission and other study groups, the Rocky Mount attorney-farmer-businessman helped lead the way in establishing a community college system and reorganizing the Consolidated University of North Carolina. Much of his work is still around paying dividends to the people of the state.

Pearsall's stature and his willingness to tackle tough issues prompted Governors Umstead and Hodges to seek his help after the U.S. Supreme Court's school desegregation decision in 1954. Today, depending on one's interpretation of history or indulgence in hindsight, the so-called Pearsall Plan is regarded as a reasoned path of accommodation, a clever way to avoid desegregation of the schools or something in between. Pearsall himself saw the plan as a safety valve that cooled emotions and avoided closed schools.

At a time when leaders in most other Southern states preached defiance and advocated resistance, the Pearsall committee rejected the advice – including that from a hotbed of segregationists in the state Attorney General's Office – that North Carolina take the same course. Instead, the committee persuaded the Legislature and the public to vote for a plan that 1) transferred pupil enrollment, assignment and transportation from the state to 167 school boards, 2) offered tuition grants for private education to students who wanted to leave desegregated schools and 3) gave local people the option of closing one or more schools if conditions became "intolerable." It was a decade before a federal court found portions of the plan unconstitutional.

The Pearsall Plan's assurance of "gradualism" instead of desegregation "forthwith" of all schools deflected the emotionalism of the white majority and reduced the influence of race-baiting politicians. No schools were closed, no tuition grants were given and little violence attended early desegregation. Given the temper of the times, it qualified as a moderate approach. But the plan's effects lingered long after the device had served its intended purpose. It ultimately let state leadership off the hook in pushing for school desegregation. It also contributed to local administrative delays and "freedom of choice" dodges until well after the Civil Rights Act of 1964. To the extent that black students and their parents suffered prolonged denials of justice and constitutional rights, the Pearsall Plan proved a mixed blessing.

But no one who knew of Tom Pearsall's labors on behalf of the education and training of both blacks and whites, and his prescience in helping shape the policies of a state rapidly changing from agricultural-rural to industrial-urban, ever felt he acted contrary to what he believed best for all North Carolinians. He never wanted one school door closed, one tuition grant given, one black child hurt. And Pearsall's death leaves poorer the state that he labored to make rich in every resource and human relationship.

The title of another editorial was *A Patrician in the Trenches*. And from another newspaper, a description of Tom, which, except for its reference to physical appearance, a phrase so favorable that, knowing Tom, I'm sure he would have turned off as a joke, is a tribute by which he would have felt deeply humbled. For it said:

> *Impressive in appearance, gentle,*
> *frugal, humble, articulate, moderate*
> *in all things, a disciplined man.*
> *Tom Pearsall was a complete citizen in the Jeffersonian sense.*

There is now a very large, handsome book called *Making a Difference in North Carolina* devoted to individuals who have more recently made an impact on the lives of North Carolinians. It was published in 1988 by Hugh M. Morton and Edward L. Rankin, Jr., "...a joint venture between two well-known North Carolinians whose careers, experiences and friendship have spanned a half-century. Their first-hand and intimate knowledge of North Carolina and its leaders would be difficult to match.

"Hugh Morton, a talented photographer often cited as the father of photojournalism in North Carolina, has recently produced a number of wildlife films that have received national and international awards. He owns and operates Grandfather Mountain in Western North Carolina, and was the developer of Grandfather Country Club.

"Edward Rankin is a seasoned political advisor, communicator/writer, and former corporate executive who has held senior appointive positions with three governors, a U.S. senator, and two major textile companies in North Carolina. His career in business, corporate communications, politics, government, and journalism spans more than forty-five years in the state."

The book is full of photographs selected from Hugh Morton's collection since the age of thirteen. Some of the portraits are almost life-size, Tom's, a close-up in profile. It shows that it was taken late in life, the hair is gray, and there are lines. But I like the photograph. To me, it reveals some of the strength that was Tom's in whatever lay before him. The three pages devoted to Tom's contributions to the state following the Supreme Court's 1954 decree for integration of public schools are defined under the title *Courage in the Midst of Tumult*. I particularly like the way the tribute ends:

"Tom Pearsall, in a 1960 interview, said, 'If anybody is ever going to record the history of this effort in North Carolina...the golden thread that ought to run all the way through it is the fact that we have had in this state leadership that was realistic and was determined to preserve the public schools in this state, and would not use the situation to their political advantage or selfish personal advantage.' "

≈ ≈ ≈

Among the people who had come for the funeral service from Chapel Hill was a cousin by marriage, Bill Perry, husband of my cousin, Emily Braswell. Emily had been dead a few years. Their two sons were now fathers themselves, and Bill continued to live alone in the distinctively attractive home which he and Emily had built on a wooded hilltop at the edge of Chapel Hill. The house, though built of brick, was Mt. Vernon-style. From an opening in the woods, on a clear day, from their front porch, there was a view seventeen miles away to the city of Raleigh.

Bill was continuing to teach education at UNC-Chapel Hill, and was a keen student of psychology, and I suppose it was from that and his own warm, gentle nature, that he called me a few days after having come for the service, to say that he wanted Dot Wilkinson, who had been a life-long friend of Emily's and mine and who had lost her husband, Frank, only a few months before Tom's death – and the two of them had been some of our closest friends – to come together and spend a quiet weekend with him on his hilltop. The anticipation of a stay at Chapel Hill without Tom was almost unbearable, but knowing that sooner or later, it had to come, with Dot to help me through it, we made the visit.

≈ ≈ ≈

I was beginning to realize that one of the hardest things after Tom's death when, after fifty years, it had become almost second nature to use the plural of the pronoun "I," was to absorb the shock of no longer being able to say "we." No longer able to say, "Come to see *us*." "*We'll* let you know," or "*Our* children."

Almost consumed with that searing grief of the finality of separation, my mind whirled endlessly over the question, *How did we happen to have such a beautiful marriage?* For from the very beginning, long ago, we had felt that those beautiful lines of Emily Brontë's, where she says, *No other sun would ever shine for me, no other stars light up my sky*, might have been ours.

As always happens in sorrow, friends and relatives brought me books. None of them were very long, for those who have had sorrow understand that in grief, the span of concentration is so reduced that at times it is hardly there at all. One of these books contained the writings of the Perisan poet Tagore, and in there I found a thought that, in part, gave me the answer to what seems to me our near-perfect marriage: "Let my love like sunshine surround you, and yet give you illumined freedom."

Aware from the beginning of my having to face life alone, that my sons were secretly trying to figure out a way for me not to be alone at night, even in the depth of sorrow, I knew that I must begin to stand on my own feet. I explained this to them, and after the second night, I was, indeed, alone, alone in our large old house, every corner filled with memories. *Alone now, adrift on a moonless sea.* But I would remind myself of how many millions of women had gone through this kind of final separation. I knew that, throughout time, women had found it necessary to draw on an inner strength, that each woman had had to find her own North Star and that somehow I would find mine.

Already my sons and I had decided that we wanted to do something in the way of a memorial to Tom at Chapel Hill. An interview at Chapel Hill was arranged, and after spending some time there with the proper people, the decision was made to endow the chair of Political Science which we felt might have been what Tom would have wanted. For a family whose holdings are mainly in land, as are ours, working this out would require time. As soon as he had heard of Tom's death, Albert Coats, head of the Institute of Government at the University there, telephoned me to say, "Elizabeth, we're going to want Tom's papers. When you feel that you can, I'd like to come down and talk to you about it."

Several weeks later Albert came. Since John Chambliss and Dan Crocker, our local doctors through Tom's illness, are alumni of the University and keep their ties, I invited these two wonderful doctors for lunch with Albert. As busy as they were, they came. My mind went back to the days before the University of North Carolina had its medical school, when Tom had been one of those instrumental in bringing that about. In the first stages of its planning, twelve outstanding North Carolina men, a mixture of doctors and those influential in state government, had sat gathered around our own table for dinner.

THE NORTH STAR

≈ ≈ ≈

With that visit from Albert Coats, I now saw how much of my life would be filled with those kinds of memories, and I knew that I would always feel an obligation to take part in some way, large or small, in the things in which Tom believed. Brought up with the philosophy that duty is the answer to sorrow, there were things of my own that I wanted to take care of. One of these was the placing, for historic preservation, of a house I owned, a very old small plantation home, "Old Town," its name derived from the tribe of Tuscarora Indians who had settled there on the banks of the River Tar. It had stood there, undamaged since 1742. Our father had bought that portion of the plantation in 1908, and was careful about the preservation of the house, as was my mother when the farms came under her management. My sisters and I had continued, and now that I was the last to survive, ensuring the future of this small house, which, according to the archives, is the earliest inland house in North Carolina, became important to me.

Under Father's ownership, for many years the fifteen-hundred acres had been given to cotton. During that early period, the house had been the home of the overseer of the farm, but when the price of cotton had fallen to five cents a pound, the land began to be given to other crops. With that, a more modern home was built for the overseer, but the original homestead, sitting empty, was carefully preserved.

With North Carolina's belated interest in historical preservation, I had begun to try to find a way to be sure of Old Town's future. This gave me an interest, and after acknowledging the expressions of sympathy – and there had been such an outpouring that I had to have the help of two secretaries – I began to seek the channels through which this transference might be made. In that, I had the help of Dot Wilkinson, to whose ancestors Old Town had early belonged. The remaining part of the Old Town tract still belongs to Dot and to her family. It is of such significance to her that she has gladly given a number of acres of her own part of the Old Town tract to the Historical Association in order to have a comfortable feeling about the house's future.

Removal of the house, two miles down the road near the sight of her family's earliest burial ground, was brought about and supervised by Chris Wilson, an artist and teacher of art in a nearby college. Chris is sought daily on questions on historical architecture, and he immediately began making this interesting house his own home, where, at the end of a long and impressively beautiful avenue of cedars, it now sits. For me, the wondering and the searching, month after month, seemed to have come together in an especially fitting way. But in my first sadness, that there would be preoccupation with things of this kind to take me out of myself, was not to be foreseen.

I was coming to understand that there is now a more pervasively healthful approach to death than that of earlier generations, when wearing mourning clothes and the other visible signs of sorrow seemed important. With the arrival of Mother's Day a week after Tom's death, as hard as it was to do, I joined the family in going to the country club for lunch. I knew that I would see and be spoken to by one and all. That I dreaded. My defense was to say to the first person who came up to greet me – it was Dick Oettinger, coming up with a warm hug – "Don't say anything sweet." I knew he'd understand. And everybody else did.

≈ ≈ ≈

In one of those strange ways of a beneficent providence, in addition to the support of old friends that was so generously offered, there had come, during Tom's last stay at Duke, a new friendship. Marion Martin lives in Farmville, Virginia. Our chance meeting came about at the end of one of those sad days at the hospital, when, at 9:15 at night, those who had been at the bedside of a loved one all day were gathering inside the hospital entrance to wait for the shuttle bus to take us back to the inn. We were all women. Among us, there was an unmistakable air of weariness, mainly of the spirit. Conversation consisted of, "How did your day go?"

That night, when I came to take my place among the group, I happened to sit near someone who had not been there before. Her hair was gray, she was well-groomed, she did not seem to droop as did the rest of us, and she was reading. She wore a pale gray suit, and she was well shod. You had the feeling that her own patient was there only temporarily.

As I sat down, she looked up and smiled, and I said, "You're scanning poetry."

With that, a conversation began; in almost no time, the bus arrived. Boarding that, we sat together, and in the exchange of information about ourselves, I found that her husband, Tony, had come to Duke for a scheduled hip replacement which the doctor had decided to postpone; they would be leaving the next morning to go back to Farmville. We said goodnight at the elevator, never expecting to see each other again.

When I came down the next morning, however, and was turning in my key at the desk, the clerk handed me a letter. It was from this stranger. She had left early as planned, but not before having been given my address by the clerk. Having discovered our mutual love of books, she

wondered, in the note which she had left in my box, if she might send me
one or two of her own favorites.

As dependable in this, I was to discover, as in all the other ways, the
books began to arrive. And when, a week later, in a thank-you-note for
her thoughtfulness, I told her that I was in bed there in the inn with flu,
she re-doubled her efforts to help me through this difficult time when I could
not spend those precious hours with Tom. A "care-package" soon came.
It held memo pads, ballpoints, a silver book-mark with my initials on it,
a wide assortment of small things to divert me. With that, our bonds were
forged.

A month after Tom's death Marion began urging me by phone to come
to Farmville for a few days with her and her husband. She promised
quietness and music, for she is an accomplished pianist, and with the
thought always before me that I must reach out, I accepted the invitation.
With the help of a North Carolina road map, and one of Virginia, I set out
for the four-hour drive to find this small, historic, college town that lies
at the beginning of the foothills of the Blue Ridge. I chose the country
roads, for it was June, and I needed the sense of the renewal of life.

On that visit to the Martins' home, Marion and Tony were so perceptive
that they gave me the feeling of being old friends. I could understand the
happiness that this second marriage has brought them. Tony's first wife,
in another happy marriage, had had a long illness. Before the onset of that,
the Martins had been in the habit of going, in February, for a month's stay
at a seaside club, Ponte Vedro, near Jacksonville, Florida. It was at that
club that the Martins of Farmville had become friends of Pete and Marion
Kilgore from Florence, Alabama, with whose winter vacations theirs
usually coincided.

Around the time of the death of Tony's wife, Pete Kilgore's business
plane went down without survivors. This left Marion to finish bringing
up their five children alone. Continuing to live in Farmville, Tony had
his sons and their families for solace. For the next three years there was
no return of either Tony or Marion to Ponte Vedro. Then, call it fate if
you like, without having had any contact all this time, one February, both
Tony and Marion landed back at the club at Ponte Vedro for a short stay.

After dinner on the night of their arrival, completely unaware of
each other's presence, Marion went into the lounge, and since the room
was empty, began to play the piano. After several numbers, from a dimly
lighted corner came unexpected quiet applause, and there sat Tony Martin.
He and his first wife had loved music, and he had been drawn to that little
private concert. From then on, there was to be for the two, a chance at
a second happiness. When Marion came into my life, she and Tony had

been married only a year. Transplanted to Farmville, a smaller town than Florence, Alabama, the one in which she had grown up, married, and had continued to live, there were, for Marion, adjustments to be made.

When it came out early that we both liked to write letters, we started our correspondence with the suggestion from me, with which she agreed, "Let's not edit." Undergirded by this attitude, over the years since then, we've kept the postman busy. For both of us subscribe wholeheartedly to the theory that "Life will never be dull so long as there's mail." In some of her earliest letters to me, she would often enclose small poems, which she had written during that fresh grief after the loss of Pete. In one of the letters, she told me that their life together had followed a pattern similar in some ways to mine and Tom's: life with an unusually active husband, and one who liked to spend time on the water. They had had a house on the Tennessee River, and from there they would take their family in their boat to Chattanooga. Marion, in her wise and witty way, would advise the group at the outset of these trips, "Unless we are as polite to each other as the Japanese, there may be some murders on board."

In one of her letters to me, she had flatteringly confided that she had had a friend in Alabama whom she had lost through death, one whom, because they liked to exchange letters she had thought of as her "literary friend," and that now I had come to answer that need. In the parallel of our lives, and in the pleasure of writing letters, ours has been a sustaining friendship.

After that visit, young Tom was eager for me to come to New York for a few days with him, and once there I was coddled in every possible way. He chose a few plays that he knew I would enjoy. When asked about an opera or a concert, I asked him not to urge that upon me. They would have been my undoing. I was so afraid that he might get seats for *Madam Butterfly*, that favorite opera of Tom's and mine, the music of which, after stereos came in, more than any other, filled our house. Museums and art galleries were a wise substitute.

The coming of August would find me visiting an old friend in her summer home, which was only fifty miles away from me, on Lake Gaston. Both of them now gone, but who live in my memory, Mebane and John Burgwynne lived a country life in an area of Eastern Carolina called "Occoneechee Neck," which is an area of fertile fields at a bend in the Roanoke River. Their two homes were perhaps twenty-five miles apart, and all summer they came and went between them. John, a dedicated farmer of various crops, and a high-ranking member of national committees which serve to promote the interests of farmers, oversaw with particular pleasure, the management of his five-hundred acres of cotton, which means that in summer, he rarely had time to spend at the Lake. So it was that sometimes Mebane began to go without him, taking with her a friend or two, or their children or grandchildren. Always thoughtful, Mebane was quick to recognize ways to help me through those first sad months, and sympathetically asked me to spend a few quiet days with her at the Lake, and a few with her at home, where every morning she brought breakfast to me in bed using her loveliest china, her nicest linen, and a rose she'd just picked from her garden.

As Mebane's children came to their high school years, she became a guidance counselor. It was from those qualifications that she was chosen as the only woman to serve on the executive committee of the University of North Carolina when the time had come for the University to consider the possibility of expanding into what would ultimately become fourteen community colleges throughout the state. Mebane went with this committee to various parts of our country, making a study of these types of educational institutions. It was on this committee that Tom had grown to admire Mebane, and in that way, she and I were to become friends. The inclination we shared toward writing made the friendship ripen fast.

With her usual spunk and courage, Mebane was to face years of illness. First, from collagen disease, one of the connective tissue, and later, a malignancy.

A writer herself – a professional – Mebane had published seven books, six of them for children. The seventh is built around the life of a young girl who has returned from her first year of college. In part, the story is autobiographical. The book reveals the emotions of the young girl as she tries to adjust to the loneliness and simplicity of life in the deep country. She has found it difficult, until one night, sitting on their front porch, she is aware that the flowers of the vine that grows at the end of the porch have opened to the moon. Their beauty transforms the young girl's thinking. It's possible that this was the beginning of the introspection that led Mebane, who was, indeed, that young girl, to write, for one of Mebane's early books bears the title *Moonflower*. And it was that book that Mebane had put on my bedside table when I visited with her at the Lake.

With the coming of that last spring of her life, nine years after my first visit to Mebane and John, I drove, with another of Mebane's old friends, Katherine Nicholson, to Occoneechee Farm for an afternoon's visit with Mebane. As we were preparing to leave, I went into her lovely country kitchen to thank Susie, the daily helper from the farm, for the tea she had served, and I noticed something unusual hanging by the fireplace. It was a sampler explaining the various kinds of woods that might contribute to life around the family hearth. In that my life, until I went to college, consisted solely of open fires, this old rhyme struck a note of response. When I asked Mebane if I might copy it, she hurried to say, "Of course. But not now. I'll have my son, Steve, make a copy of it for you and put it in the mail." And she kept her promise. The source of the poem is unknown, but it means more to me if I give it the title, *Firelight*. It begins this way:

Your own experience – and experiments – will be your most reliable guide in choosing wood, but you might like to remember this old English rhyme that sums up the firewood story:

Beech wood fires are bright and clear
if the logs are kept a year.
Chestnut's only good they say,
if for long it's laid away.
Birch and fir logs burn too fast,
blaze up bright and do not last.
It is by the Irish said,
hawthorne bakes the sweetest bread.
Elm wood burns like a church yard mould;
e'en the very flames are cold.
Poplar gives a bitter smoke,
fills your eyes and makes you choke.
Apple wood will scent your room
with an incense-like perfume.
Oaken logs, if dry and old,
keep away the winter cold.
But ash wood wet and ash wood dry,
a king shall warm his slippers by.

My visit to Mebane was followed by one of several days in the home of Marie Oldham and her husband in Ahoskie, North Carolina. Although I had not met Burr, for several years, I had been frequently thrown with Marie through the Roanoke Island Historical Association, where she had been, and still is President of the Elizabethan Gardens Association. Marie timed her invitation for early December in order to be able to take me the relatively short distance to Edenton to see the historical homes with their Christmas decorations. Back at her home, we walked about in her garden. She identified the perennials that, although inactive at that season, would begin to come to life with early spring. Burr loves historical reading, and the latest biography on Robert E. Lee, *Lee: The Last Years* had just come out. I took a copy for him with me, and while Marie was preparing delicious meals, Burr and I sat by the fire in the den enjoying the discussion of books.

Marie continued to be so thoughtful of me that often when she was going to attend a meeting of the Board of the North Carolina Museum of Art, she would call me ahead, and ask me to let her pick me up so that we might have lunch together in Raleigh.

Among the first two who had come to me in my sorrow, was my childhood friend, Velma Coburn, whose home is in Williamston, fifty miles east, and Mary McCarroll, from Warrenton, fifty miles west. Mary had grown up in the small town of Warrenton. One of her uncles had been very successful in tobacco. He and his family lived in the city of New York. Visiting them, Mary met and married a Kentuckian, Shipp McCarroll. Among the many interests they shared was a love of horses, and when their daughter, Lina, was a young girl in boarding school, Shipp retired, and they chose to live in the country, near Warrenton, North Carolina, where they could have their own stable. Friendships from Mary's earlier life were picked up, and Shipp and Mary were often in our home and we were in theirs.

All that we knew about Shipp at first, was the glamorous note that had come out in the write-up of their wedding in New York papers, which, in the way of the times, going into detail, wrote that the bridegroom, Shipp, had given his groomsmen gold-headed canes. With that, we rather expected Shipp to be the ultimate in sophistication, and while he was, indeed, a man of polish, it was a pleasure to see him adapt to the life of a sleepy little courthouse town in Eastern Carolina.

A few years after Shipp's death, Mary went to live in a retirement center in Charlottesville, Virginia, for her daughter and her husband had retired there. Mary and I continued to keep in close touch. Now and then I would go to Charlottesville, to see Mary, always the guest of Mary's daughter and her son-in-law at that beautiful and aristocratic old Farmington Club, Mary coming over to have lunch or tea. She too died two years ago.

Nearer Rocky Mount, my first cousin, Nancy Holderness, in a deepening relationship that has become almost that of sisters, was repeatedly urging me to come for stays. There, with not only her own great thoughtfulness, but that of her husband, Dail, who came into this story as having Alzheimer's, I felt that quiet affection and sympathy that, offered by a happily married couple to one who has just lost the love of her life, seems so generous that it brings a kind of healing.

Yet, side by side, was the discovery that from that time on, in such situations, there would always be, for me, that subconscious feeling of slightly intruding on the happiness of a couple, a strange new attitude for me, but one in which I knew I was not alone. I was reluctant to accept all of Dail's and Nancy's invitations. I knew that I must not always be seeking a harbor, that I must build a life of my own.

≈ ≈ ≈

The first Christmas without Tom having come and gone, I knew that the time had come for me to face Captiva. That if I didn't, all my life I would feel that I had been a coward. Although our property there had been sold the last year of Tom's having his health, I had many invitations to come back, none of which I accepted. I knew myself well enough to know that I must consider Captiva a closed chapter, yet I knew that I had to go, if only once. I did not have to stay; I preferred not to. I did not feel that I could have borne a moonlit night on the island.

I found a way to go. I knew that I couldn't go alone, and providence came to my rescue. Elizabeth Rose, generally known as "Lib," and I had been friends forever. The two of us had a mutual friend, Lee Kiel, who had gone to live in a retirement center in Bradenton, Florida. I knew that Lee was always eager for her Rocky Mount friends to come for a visit, and I asked Lib if she would like to drive down with me to Bradenton for a day and night with Lee. The two of them could then go with me to Fort Meyers where we would spend two nights. That would give us a day to go over to the island. They agreed to go, and that is the way I chose.

Jay was there in her house. Even *she* could not prevail on my staying longer than several of the daylight hours. She had told our closest friends that I was coming, and that is how, on a beautiful day of the brilliance of Captiva sunlight, I sat on her porch for the early afternoon, while friend after friend came by. Each one stayed until we had a circle of a dozen or so. And although Tom was not mentioned, he was there.

After lunch, Jay had walked back with me to our boat slip, now in other hands. I looked down the bay, touched the large white gearbox that Tom had made; then we walked slowly back to Jay's house. Then she left me in her bedroom to rest for half an hour of sad remembering. Why I felt I had to hurt myself by making this pilgrimage, I'll never know. Lib and Lee had thoughtfully gone to explore the island and to walk on the beach. As planned, they came for me at four and we started back for Fort Meyers.

I had known for some time, that Bill and Bumpy Stevenson – Bumpy, formerly "Miss Bumpstead," was Cousin Lena's niece – two close friends of ours, had given their Captiva property to their two daughters, one of whom was married to the then Governor of New Jersey, and that Bumpy and Bill had gone to live on the mainland in Shell Harbor, a retirement center not many miles from our island. I knew, too, that Bumpy was confined to the health-care unit there, and that every day Bill came to sit by her bed. Bill had, at one time, been President of Oberlin College, later, Ambassador to the Phillipines. During the Korean War he had been in charge of the American Red Cross, while Bumpy made her own contribution to the war effort by serving in the Red Cross on foreign shores. Later she compiled her experiences in a book, *I Knew Your Soldier.*

In making my plans for what I had come to think of as my "Captiva Pilgrimage," I left the visit to the Stevensons until the very last, a stop to be made, when, for the last time, I would have crossed San Carlos Bay on my way back to Fort Meyers. I counted on the thought of that, something that I could do for others, to lessen the sadness of saying goodbye to what, for twenty-three years, had been our Utopia.

Bumpy and Bill were surprised to see me. They wanted to know about Tom's illness, and as I told them, we mingled our tears. Then I began to ask Bumpy if her shell-hut on the edge of her island property was still intact. This was a simple one-room Polynesian structure, built in their side-yard and as close to the beach as it was to their house, filled throughout the years with shells, mainly from the South Pacific. Since their property was still in the family, she assured me that the shells had not been disturbed; that through her own interest in shell collecting, their grandchildren were starting a collection of their own on Captiva. This visit over, my friends and I drove back to the hotel in Fort Meyers. I had done what I had to do.

With each of those visits to the homes of understanding friends, I was coming nearer to finding my way, and by the time Marion Martin came for her first stay in my home, I knew that, although without Tom, I could never return to being the person I was, I was gradually discovering – and it was vital that I should – another self, one of those many of which Proust speaks when he says "We are many selfs, but there is a core of the original always." I was beginning to glimpse that "core of the original."

Luckily, from my country background, I knew early what Anais Nin confessed to have taken a long time to learn, that "happiness is in the quiet things."

I knew, as well, that for me, the most important of the quiet things would prove to be books and words, "that lifelong intoxication, that subtle joy not chilled with age."

THE QUIET EYE, THE QUIET THINGS

When is human nature ever so weak as in a bookstore?
Henry Ward Beecher

"What shall I do with all my books?" asks the question in Sir Winston Churchill's *"Churchill on Books."* His answer is this: *"Read them, but if you can't read them at any rate, handle them and, as it were, fondle them, peer into them. Let them fall open where they will. Read on from the first sentence that arrests the eye. Then turn to another. Make a voyage of discovery, taking time to make another voyage of discovery, taking soundings of uncharted seas. Arrange them in your own plan, so that if you do not know what is there, you at least know where they are. If they cannot be your friends, let them at any rate be your acquaintances. If they cannot enter the circle of your life, do not deny them at least a note of recognition.*

Thoughts and Adventure
Winston Churchill

≈ ≈ ≈

Having had Claiborne Smith in my life to lean on, medically, since the age of fourteen, and even beyond that, as a family friend, that "older-person" who can mean so much in the life of a younger one and in the life of a young couple and their growing family, I now found myself turning to him emotionally in the hour of my life's greatest sadness. And since he had retired, and his sight was beginning to fail, aware that my deepest need had always been to give – and I knew now, more than ever, that only in that way could I approach life again – I began to read to him on Thursday afternoons.

His faithful driver, Pete, would bring him to my home. For the next two hours, while the doctor sipped two glasses of sherry, Pete would sit on the terrace in the door-yard garden and watch the birds, or if it were winter, would sit in the kitchen. I urged him to sit in the den where the TV was, but, of the old school, he would decline, saying that he would rather sit in the kitchen and nod. Thoroughly appreciative of the care that Pete continually gave him, Claiborne would often say to me, quietly, "Pete is a gentleman."

Pete, himself, had been a patient of Dr. Smith's for a long time. The doctor would still say to him everyday, or sometimes when Pete appeared short of breath, "Pete, are you taking your digitalis?" And Pete would often admit that he'd grown careless.

Knowing how much Claiborne enjoyed sitting on his porch in summer, with the old "drug-store" or ceiling-fan creaking, watching his birds, the two of us came to spend our Thursday afternoons in summer there. Pete would be at the other end of the porch, "listening-out."

Sometimes I would go back on Friday afternoons for the pleasure of seeing Claiborne's plump benign figure, with his silver hair and pink cheeks, sitting in a chair on the lawn surrounded by the children from the kindergarten next door. Throughout the week, the children would have looked forward to accepting their standing invitation to come through the opening in the hedge for lemonade on Friday, for what Claiborne termed "a lawn party." Pete, and Mary, the cook, would be in attendance.

Claiborne had continued to live in the bungalow in which he and his wife, Bertha, had started out. Until the hospital moved to its new site, three miles from town, Claiborne had been just two blocks from his work. After that, their neighborhood became an assortment of small enterprises, but fortunately, the public library, which had always meant so much to the doctor, was still there, a short walk away. The house to the right of the Smiths had become the nursery school, and the voices there, of what I came to think of as "the little squealers," were constant.

On those afternoons when we decided to have our weekly readings on the Smith porch, the creak of the drug-store fan and the screaming children would, in themselves, have been enough of a complication to make reading aloud difficult had there been nothing else, but a busy thoroughfare at the bottom of the hill, and three blocks away, the railroad, made it next to impossible to be heard. With the train whistle, and the loud motors of the trucks, the fan, and the children, it was uphill all the way. As amusing as it all seems now, I would not for anything forfeit the memory, for those afternoons expressed the span of time in an unforgettable way.

Not all our time was spent in reading, however. For in graphic detail, Claiborne could tell how his forebears had suffered not only the privations of the Civil War and the years that came after, but it was approximately thirty years after the end of the war that his father's tragic death would leave his mother with nine children to bring up; Claiborne, himself, as yet unborn.

It was at their plantation home, "Woodstock," that his father was killed. In the way of the times, in order to get his crops to market, his father had had a railroad built through his fields. Cotton and other products would be sent this way to Norfolk's port or to Petersburg, and then on. But one day, the train backed over the young father and he lost his life. I suppose that it was to reduce expenses that Mrs. Smith, who had come as a bride from Petersburg, and her large family of ten moved down the road to another part of the original Smith land grant to live with Claiborne's paternal widowed Grandmother. This, too, was a lovely old house, "Magnolia." It was there that Claiborne's earliest memories began. We can only imagine what the adjustment of an aging grandmother must have been to the sound of twenty growing feet tramping up and down the beautiful wishbone, but carpetless, stairway. For her own bedroom was on the first floor. It was there, at the age of four, Claiborne remembered, that he slept at the foot of his grandmother's bed, and that late at night, the fire burning low, since her eyesight was poor, when the clock struck twelve-thirty, his grandmother would waken him to have him give her the exact position of the clock's hands, and again when it struck one, and again at one-thirty, for until she knew just what time it was, she could not get back to sleep.

He remembered that his grandmother gave him a love for the *Book of Common Prayer*, and that, in the afternoon, when the cook would not yet have started the preparations for supper, his grandmother would call out pitiably, but facetiously, "Nervy!" for her cook's name was Minerva, "Hurry up, Nervy, I'm feeling mighty weak!"

When the little grandson was ten, he began to plough, and to make the job less dull, he memorized and recited poetry. The recalling of poetry was to become a lifetime habit.

That, at some point, through a certain Arthur Smith Bryan, the Smiths genealogical line and that of my mother's crossed, came to light for me only a few years ago when Claiborne's son, another Claiborne, published his informative and well-documented book, *Planters on the Roanoke*. And to find that both families had had some connection with a tract of land that, because of its having a pond, was given the enchanting name, "Looking Glass Farm," was my great delight.

Knowing that I would arrive promptly at three for our reading, and that I would come in through the back door, I would find the doctor sitting in the corner of the porch, ready and waiting. He would be flanked by two styrofoam coolers sitting on the floor, their tops long gone. These had become the receptacles for his favorite books of poetry. He would have spent the week going through them, slowly, with his magnifying glass, selecting things he would want me to read. He would have placed innumerable bookmarks in the 1911 poetry book which he had studied at Chapel Hill.

Pete would already have brought him his first glass of sherry. Mary, the cook, would have made a pitcher of lemonade for me. This would be sitting on a round wicker table, the size and shape that had earlier been spoken of in our part of the world as a "center table." In the middle of the table would be the most endearing thing of all. Mary would have gone into the garden, and at random, have selected a few flowers. The container mattered little; it might even have been a soft drink bottle. You could tell that the flowers had been wedged into the neck of the bottle all at one time. But that little floral note was especially significant to the old Doctor.

With all her good qualities, however, Mary developed a taste for alcohol. Only one of the doctor's children lived in town, the daughter, who, because of having been the first daughter, is called "Sister," Mrs. Flake Chipley, who has been spoken of by our whole town throughout her life, as "Sister Smith." Visiting her father everyday, Sister saw that Mary had grown slack in the ways of housekeeping. The other two children, Claiborne Jr., a psychologist, of Philadelphia, and Elizabeth, since her marriage to Dr. Milton Miller, in Roanoke, Virginia, recognized this in Mary as well. The three of them approached their father about making a change.

"I will not," he declared, "Mary's had a hard life, she's had no advantages, and she loves flowers. I don't want to hear anymore about it." So things went on in the way they were, until changes came into Mary's own life that made her have to give up the job.

The Smith house needed so many repairs that the doctor's banker told the Smith children it would be in their father's interest not to remain there. For it was indicative of the doctor's generosity that although his skill had been widely recognized, and although he was sought by thousands as a doctor of internal medicine, he had not accumulated much of a "back-log." By this time, however, a beautiful, well-run retirement center had been built in Tarboro, sixteen miles away from our own. And that is where Claiborne went for the few remaining years of his life.

With his great store of common sense and his positive attitude toward life, Claiborne was perfectly happy there. He laughingly referred to it as a "luxury hotel." What seems to me the most beautiful thing in this condensed version of a good man's life, who's philosophy was, "Let me live in deeds that bless other men's lives," is knowing that when Pete was told that the doctor's finances were dwindling, and that once in the retirement center, he might not be able to continue to have his services, Pete said, "Well, then, I will go for nothing." Fortunately, that was not necessary. These two fine men, in their respect and affection for each other, would spend the daylight hours together until the end of the doctor's life. Pete is still alive and continuing his life of service to those who are incapacitated.

No two ever had a happier marriage than Claiborne and Bertha Smith, formerly Bertha Albertson, a young girl on a neighboring plantation. Claiborne liked to tell how he had fallen in love with Bertha when she was fifteen, and he was just entering medical school. Kemp Battle, who's already appeared in this story, used to say, admiringly, "Claiborne Smith is the only man I've ever known who lives with a mother-in-law and *her* mother-in-law!"

It had been only after Bertha's death, and Tom's, that Claiborne's love of books and mine came to be shared. The by-product of this was that when I told Claiborne that I was finding a certain escape from sadness in writing, and that I might someday do my memoirs, he began to bring to me some of the things he, himself, had written. Often, between our visits, he would mail me a little note, and after I mentioned doing my autobiography, he wrote to encourage me, saying at the end, "Never forget that the word "auto" means "self." Even your nearest and dearest will not understand why the inclusion of certain things is important to you." In these years of my writing, I have sensed the truth of that.

≈ ≈ ≈

During that first year of my having to make a new life for myself, being able to share my love of books with Claiborne and others was to be a constant help. One of these was Tom's first cousin, Eleanor Pearsall.

Eleanor's mother, Tom's aunt by marriage to his Uncle Dave Pearsall, was a woman of intelligence, and except for one understandable pocket of her mind, Aunt Addie was a person of breadth.

The daughter of a doctor who was also a landowner in the coastal section of Eastern Carolina around Warsaw, Aunt "Addie," for Adelaide, had been a young child during the years of the Civil War. Her family had known all its privations, including having to wear pasteboard in their shoes. They had lived in a fine old house. Because there was no longer anybody to till the land, the house and the other property were lost.

Naturally these things had carried over in Aunt Addie's approach to the Civil War. She became an ardent member of the Daughters of the Confederacy, with regular attendance at its meetings, frequently writing papers for its other members on the subject of Confederate heroes. The town was informed of these meetings in detail in our local newspaper, *The Evening Telegram*. Regularly we were being told about Confederate generals, colonels, majors, corporals, and not only about Lee's Traveler, but of other horses that had played a part in the conduct of the war, as well.

At the time, Emily Thigpen was the Society Editor for the *Telegram*. Emily wrote with a flair; we the people lapped it up. Next to Aunt Addie's informative columns about the UDC meetings, there would be long write-ups of the town's social activities. Hostesses were made happy, rewarded for their labors by having the most minute items of their patriotic meetings and their social functions described in colorful detail. One afternoon we had the heady news that – and here I substitute a fictitious name – Miss Sallie Sharpe, at her luncheon the day before, in harmony with her color scheme of pink roses and cosmos, had served a delicious pink potato salad!

These things were going on in those busy years, when, in my own life, I was trying to be all things to all men. By nature, not much of a joiner, I regret something I said one day as I was driving Aunt Addie to one of her UDC meetings. She had suggested that I join that group, which I came to know later, was, and is doing worthwhile things in the way of scholarships. Then uniformed, however, I gave Aunt Addie something of a short and unbecoming answer. In that way of youth that sees everything in black or white, I replied, "Oh Aunt Addie, I like to belong to things that look forward, rather than backward. I'm giving my energies to World Peace Through World Government. If you could tell me one concrete thing that your organization does, I might feel differently."

Aunt Addie all but lost her breath before she could reply. "Oh my poor child," she gasped. "Don't you know that but for us, the history books would be so distorted that it would be criminal?" Her last sentence was a classic:

"As it is, they make Abraham Lincoln out a hero!"

Naturally, Aunt Addie's much revered hero was Robert E. Lee. Since, during my growing up, our family had spent so much time in Richmond, the statue at the heart of the city, with one word on it – "Lee" – was familiar. Not so many years ago, when the biography mentioned earlier, *Lee: The Last Years* came out, I was so impressed with it that I gave a dozen copies at Christmas. I found there a little incident that was as amusing as it is to be hoped, was effective. It tells of a time when a Mrs. Norris, grandniece of General Lee, driven to the point of desperation by her quarreling children, said to her little son, "If your Uncle Robert could bring himself to offer his sword to General Grant, surely you can beg your sister's pardon!"

Aunt Addie had two children. Leon, the older, was to go to the Naval Academy at Annapolis, Eleanor, to receive her college education at Goucher in Baltimore, and at Columbia University. In that way, brother and sister were often paying visits to each other at their schools. Among midshipmen, Eleanor – the attractive person that she still is – had many beaux. There was to be one serious romance. Whether it was that he was to have a Naval career with no roots anywhere, or for some other reason, Eleanor chose to go on to study art, for which she has a very real talent, and to obtain her degree in Library Science at Columbia to qualify her for her life's work and to remain single. Those four years in New York gave her a great love for the theater, and as long as she was physically active, she spent at least one week in New York a year, seeing new plays.

She was to become our high-school librarian, and her life influenced many students who became her life-long friends. Eleanor now lives a few blocks away from me, and I am aware of how many of these faithful students return year after year for the pleasure of still enjoying her keen mind. I, myself, find Eleanor a source of ready information at the other end of the telephone. As this writing goes on, whenever I'm stumped for something that needs to be placed chronologically, or for some literary source that I very much want but which has escaped me, I call Eleanor, since she has an extensive library, and though confined to a wheelchair, knows her bookshelves so well that she can direct her attendant to within a few inches of the volume she wants. Eleanor has a keen sense of humor. Occasionally, during our visits, she will produce from her collection of limericks, a favorite, one of which, goes like this:

> There was an old artist named Phidias,
> who had a distaste for the hideous,
> So he sculpted Aphrodite
> without any nightie,

> *which startled the ultra-fastidious!*

Another from her collection is the one of the "Goosegirl," of which the rhymester says:

> *See the geese beneath the tree,*
> *gathered 'round the goose-girl's knee*
> *while she reads them, by the hour,*
> *from the works of Schopenhaur.*
> *But do they really comprehend?*
> *Nor does she, nor, for that*
> *matter, does he?*

But I think my favorite is this one:

> *I want to know a butcher paints,*
> *a baker rhymes for his pursuit,*
> *a candlestick-maker much acquaints*
> *his soul with song, or happily mute,*
> *Blows out his brains upon the flute.*

Claiborne enjoyed limericks as well, and from his early life at Magnolia and plantation days, gave me this one:

> *Tears fell from the*
> *potato's eyes.*
> *The cabbage hung*
> *its head.*
> *It was a sad day in*
> *the kitchen.*
> *For the vinegar's mother*
> *was dead.*

Younger readers may be puzzled by the use of the word "mother" in this context. Applied to vinegar, it is the cloudy substance that forms when the liquid is no longer any good.

Through her study of art, Eleanor developed her own style, which she calls, "dry watercolor," a technique in which, through the use of a semi-dry brush and watercolors, she is able to get the detail she loves so much. Because of her failing eyesight, she no longer paints, but as she sits all day by the fireplace in her living room, she faces a wall of her own paintings, those that in their clear bright colors, depict seated Oriental figures that fill the room with life.

It was this love of detail in art that led her to another long-held interest: a collection of first edition reproductions of fairy tales, which include the works of two outstanding illustrators of their time: the Frenchman, Edmund Dulac, and the Englishman, Arthur Rackman. It is that these reproductions were first editions that makes them so desirable, so sharp in detail. Although the illustrations are stimulating to the imaginations of children, they may not be to everyone's taste; Arthur Rackman's, with a low-limbed, black and gray tree and a multiplicity of gnarled branches, each branch ending in a face, might possibly appear frightening. These and others in Eleanor's collection, among which are some beautifully reproduced Persian miniatures – my favorites – are all carefully preserved, and have been accepted by the University of North Carolina for its rare books collection, where they will go at Eleanor's death.

A common interest in books and in writing has been the thread that has, in part, made the little circle of friendship which was to include Claiborne, Eleanor, Marion and me; I have been the connector. The four of us were to meet as a group only once. It was during the first year of my being alone; Marion was my houseguest at the time. It was on a Thursday, my day to read to Claiborne, and I invited Eleanor and Marion to join us in our reading session. We sat together in my living room having tea or sherry, according to preference, stopping for discussion as I read. There was less reading than conversation that day, however; it was delightful in a different way. As we said goodbye in the front hall, laughing and joking among ourselves, Marion furnished us the best laugh of the afternoon when she said, "This must, indeed, be the world's smallest literary society."

It was a cold day, and Dr. Smith never wore an overcoat. Standing in the hall with Pete ready to help him out to the car, I said, "Oh, Claiborne, you need a woolen scarf!" and ran upstairs to get him one of my own.

He walked with a stick, and as he stood, not having a free hand, I put the scarf around his neck. As I did, Eleanor said, wittily, "The patient doctors the Doctor!"

This black and white woolen scarf went everywhere with Claiborne in winter ever after. Through the three years of his being in the retirement center, sixteen miles away, whenever I visited him there in his room, I would find him seated at his desk, with the help of a magnifying glass, writing his daily letters, the black and white woolen scarf hanging on the back of his chair.

Toward the end of his life, he wrote, in a letter to me, "Although I am going blind, that I can continue to make the adjustments necessary to life, makes me feel God."

How could you not have enjoyed opening a letter on an average morning to find from this wonderful and patient man, in his uphill, downhill writing, these beautiful lines to greet the sun, nothing else on the page: "Good morning, good morning, pride of the East, glorious star!"

Those who knew the Doctor, knew that, correspondence being the vital thing to him that it was, when he ran out of stamps there was a temporary crisis while Pete made a hurried trip to the post office. For the life of the mind was, for Claiborne, ever present; it held this wonderful man up to the very last.

Claiborne's *spirit* lives on in his great-granddaughter, as expressed in her prize-winning essay written when she was in the second grade:

> *My great-grandfather is an important person. He was a very good doctor. Now he is retired and lives in a retirement home. On each visit, Granddaddy has a tea party of cheeseballs and a diet drink. He tells stories about when he was a little boy. He never knew his father. He died before Granddaddy was born. The old folks said he would be a doctor when he grew up. He was.*
>
> *Another story that Granddaddy tells is when his mother put his only shoes by the fireplace to dry and they shrank. The next day he had to wear his sister's button shoes to school. He was embarrassed. He tells poems and sings songs.*
>
> *He gives us books to start a library in my house. He writes letters with old good sayings.*
>
> *He has given my brothers money for college, and he gives me money for college, too. School is important to Granddaddy. I love my Granddaddy a whole lot.*
>
> Claire Smith
> Grade Two
> Greenfield School

The arrival of this tiny girl's delightful description of her grandfather, which her mother was kind enough to send to me after Claiborne's death, brings me the most pleasant of feelings. In a roundabout way, it spurs me to endeavor.

I never made a visit to Claiborne without coming away with the thought which I now bring away from each visit I make to Eleanor, now that she is housebound, that "Stone walls do not a prison make, nor iron bars a cage." At ninety-four, Eleanor's comment on age comes in something she readily quotes: "As much as worthy friends add to the enjoyment and pleasure of life, in the end we are *our own* best friend, and *our own* worst enemy."

≈ ≈ ≈

Charlotte Timberlake "Timmie" Battle is my cousin by marriage. Recently returned from Boca Grande, she came by my house to relay a conversation she'd had with my dear friend Marne Donnelly while on the island. When Marne inquired more specifically, "What is Elizabeth's book about?" Timmie had the perfect reply: "It's about Elizabeth's world," she said, with characteristic grace. Following the example of the women in her own background, Timmie's talent for leadership is widely recognized. At present, Timmie has the distinction of serving as a regent on the Board of Directors of Mount Vernon. There are thirty-two of these regents, the unvarying rule being that there always be one from each of the original thirteen states, terms of office now limited to fifteen years. This is a working board; twice a year, spring and fall, the regents come from their respective states to spend a week in simple cottages on the estate, where they make plans for supplementing the funds allotted by the government, and those from the tourists, sources that are not enough to cover the expense of preserving this national shrine in the way that the patriotic woman from South Carolina – as far back as 1852 – envisioned, when she had the inspiration to enlist the help of a handful of like-minded woman in so significant an undertaking.

Sallie Southhall Cotton, Timmie's great-grandmother, was, herself a remarkable woman. While living the plantation life of Eastern Carolina three generations ago, this ancestor of Timmie's made it a point to keep a journal and to write long letters. In some of these letters she often became philosophical. The fact that she led a well-rounded plantation life would cause William Stephenson, now professor at East Carolina University, to choose her as a subject for his study entitled *A Woman's Life in North Carolina*. It was Timmie who lent me her copy of that book, from which I drew this lovely thought. Among the many things that have been written on the virtues of solitude, a thought that Sallie expressed in a letter to a friend is one I find meaningful: "Days of solitude hold no terror for me," she wrote, "I find it means leisure and time to think, and introspection often brings new thoughts to gladden life and to make its duty clearer."

Sometimes on those days when I have hours alone, with no obligation to the human race, especially if it's a rainy day, I take a cup of tea to a window, and looking out, think of Sallie.

≈ ≈ ≈

Alone as I am for so much of the time now, I am grateful that in solitude I am able to find some of the things which Sallie found. Among the things that gladden life for me is the daily awareness of how fortunate I have been, and still am, in having the dedication of two fine women as my housekeepers. Nannie and Laura keep me regularly informed of what goes

on in the lives of their children and grandchildren. Nannie Silver, a widow, has one son, Joey. Joey is a young man who knew from the time he was in high school that he wanted to study criminology. After four years of college, Joey went for six months to the Federal Law Enforcement Training Center in Glencoe, Georgia. As part of his training, he had to live in the city of Washington where he did six months of guard duty at our Capitol. No matter, his eight-hour shift had to be filled. That was followed by a tour of duty on guard at the White House. His training finished, Joey returned to his hometown, Rocky Mount, and joined the police force. In a short while he was given an award for being the best groomed of all the officers. After perhaps two years he was persuaded to join the police force of Charleston, South Carolina, and it is there that Joey now lives happily, a young man under thirty, with his fine, intelligent wife, Debbie, who, immediately after their having moved to Charleston, became manager of a shoe store.

Laura's eight children have all done well. Those who wanted college educations have been able to have them. Each of them now has a good job. One of Laura's grandchildren, Michelle, has a superior mind. Now a sophomore at East Carolina University, partly on scholarship, she is working toward a career in business administration. In summer she earns money to help toward the next year's tuition by working for the state school system training cheerleaders.

Nannie and Laura, who for so long have been a part of my life, have become as much my friends as my housekeepers. We understand each other's personalities, and day to day, share our thoughts on life and all its ups and downs, not only in the lives of those around us, but in the lives of those about whom we hear and about those whom we read in the newspapers. I'm constantly aware of the tolerant attitude in Nannie's and Laura's natures, for they hold very close to their Christian tenets.

With them I can be completely frank about questions of race. And recently, when I asked them, singly, what their response would be to being called "African Americans" they each reacted favorably. "I would be proud to be called an African-American."

From Laura, "It didn't take us long to get used to saying 'Black,' but I think this is even better."

That was a thought that had occurred to me. In a classroom with a quotient of Japanese-Americans, Italian-Americans, Vietnamese-Americans, and Korean-Americans, the designation "African-American" would be one in which a child could have pride.

≈ ≈ ≈

When I felt that as best I could, I had tried in the five years since Tom's death, to go ahead with my chin up in the way that he would have wanted, so much so, that even my sisters and my closest friends would say, from the beginning, "Isn't Elizabeth remarkable?", I had an illness that resulted in depression, a kind called "situational depression." From having had a serious and prolonged viral infection, against which, a series of antibiotics had proven ineffective, but to which, one after another, I had an adverse reaction, I became a shadow of myself. Having gone from my usual weight of 116 pounds to a hundred, I became, in every way, discouraged.

This had gone on for several months, when my local doctor recommended a stay at Duke, where I went for three weeks. My symptoms suggested cancer, and everyday there were tests connected with the search for that. The search was gradually narrowed to the area of the pancreas, which was suspected, but happily, in the end, that possibility was ruled out.

At that point, an interval of psychoanalysis was finally suggested, and from the beginning of these sessions, and the recounting of what had gone before in my life, I was gradually being given insight into my illness. For Dr. Gianturco would say to me, somewhere along the line, "From the time you were a year old, from your having lived so closely with your sister's illness, where illness in general is concerned, you were being conditioned to anxiety."

Only vaguely had I been aware of that in myself. I'd always felt myself to be an optimist, seeing the funny side of things, and had always enjoyed finding a sense of humor in others. But thinking it over, I understood what he meant. The major anxieties in my life have, indeed, been those connected with illness in my loved ones.

In a country way of life, where there is so much tale-telling, everything of consequence is dramatized, even the Sunday afternoon trips to the cemetery with Miss Ruth Hobgood where she wove into drama the lives of many who were buried there. Although in the way that children love ghost stories, these tales were exciting, perhaps on some of us they were making an impression of another kind. Many of the graves were those of children. At home, even the domestics – to relieve the dullness of their circumscribed lives – with their inborn gift for the dramatic, were always providing gripping accounts of things that had gone on in their own lives and among those they knew. Each tale could be spun out for hours and returned to, day after day, until some other startling episode in the community sprang up to claim their attention. Some of these had to do with terrible fires, with runaway horses, fist-fights that had gone on to the point of knives-drawn and the landing in jail of one or another of the fighters. Often Father would have had to intervene as a character witness to get the culprit freed.

The tales that went on in my family from generation to generation held all the interest of a novel. Running through them was the frequent highlighting of illnessess, for these, even if they had not brought death, had changed the course of lives. Somehow, they did not seem to give a gloomy outlook either to the teller of the tale, or the listener. I, myself, was enthralled. Some of the tales did, indeed, involve death, and one of the most tragic of these was the awful story of Grandma Bryan's sister, our Aunt Nancy's inadvertently giving her sick husband tablets of morphine instead of the prescribed calomel, the doses for which was a tablet every half hour. During this great uncle's illness, the identical pillboxes sat on the mantelpiece in the sickroom. Soon after the patient fell into a deep sleep, the mistake was discovered. The horsefeeder was sent at breakneck speed to Mount Mariah for Dr. Phillips. On arrival, Dr. Phillips prescribed having the sick man "walked." This meant walking incessantly from the house down the long avenue to the gate, supported on either side by a fieldhand, while another fieldhand whipped the poor sick man with the tip of wet towels. All to no avail. I can't imagine what Great Aunt Nancy was doing other than wringing her hands.

The oral passing on of these tragedies was, I suppose, to teach us about life and to help us place things in perspective. Coupled with my own observations, I was being given a firm belief – where illness was concerned – in cause-and-effect.

Further, there was the story of my Grandmother Braswell's sudden death. Grandpa had died a year earlier, and the family had decided that Grandma would be happier if she gave up living in the country and came to live near Mother and Father in the village. The cottage in which Mother and Father had started out their marriage and which had been moved to a spot near our newer and larger home then became Grandma's, and there she lived, with Miss Cornelia, her housekeeper, and their domestics.

Then one night Grandma took a hot bath immediately after supper. For this she would have used something called a hip-bath, a long slender pear-shaped tub made of white enamel that all my life sat in our attic among several Victorian beds, the bedsteads made ornamental with carved apples and pears and grapes on the headboards, the bedsteads, themselves, piled high with featherbeds no longer in use, their feathers being saved to make pillows. The hip-bath also sat near Sister's handsome wicker baby carriage, its parasol now too rusty to go up and down. Nearby sat the cradle in which we had all been rocked, a tall dark wooden one, with carved spindles. In this enormous attic, which covered the main body of the house, there was a wealth of large old trunks – a fascinating "other world" for a child.

The last night of Grandma's life, the hip-bath would have been brought into her bedroom and placed in front of the fire. Immediately after her bath, Grandma had a stroke, and in a few hours, was gone. So that, forever thereafter in our family, hot baths after meals were not recommended.

Although I was not even born then, I felt that I had been there during that crisis. That was my first large lesson in illness, and in cause-and-effect. The second lesson was Alice Bryan's osteomyelitis, which had come from scratching a mosquito bite, and which had gone into blood poisoning. Another came from the fact that a classmate of mine, when I was in my teens, did what you were not by any means supposed to do, and had died. Violet had washed her hair and had gone to bed with it wet, in a cold room. The cold she "caught" had gone into meningitis.

Surprisingly, half a century later, three thousand miles away, across the Atlantic, I was to find that word "caught" in use in connection with illness. It even extended beyond the way we used it. When Tom and I were visiting our English friends, the Gore-Lloyds, they spoke of having lost their son to cancer, which he had "caught" while at Oxford. Incidentally, the Gore-Lloyds had then adopted their son's university roommate, an orphan from Australia. This young man, who had then become John Gore-Lloyd, had gone on to work with the Milbank Travel Agency on Bond Street in London. Tom and I had come to know him well, and would always have him plan our trips over the British Isles.

With these kinds of threads, the "catching" of illnesses, running through my early life, I can now see that when my own children were small, whenever those childhood illnesses came, I was probably more apprehensive about complications than the average, and since these were the years when Tom was in politics, I can remember often having being torn between leaving the children when they were sick, which I felt I must, and being at my post, with Tom. Yet, knowing that I could call back by telephone, there was, for me, lurking somewhere in my makeup, once we had driven out through the gate, the ability to leave my worries at home, to enter into the spirit of whatever was underway, for I've always believed firmly in living in the moment; not to seems, to me, a waste.

I could now see that Dr. Gianturco's perceptions about me were correct. Under his guidance, I began to recover quickly from the depression.

This period of analysis which had gone on for six months, with longer and longer intervals between visits, had begun in my hospital room. Before mentioning analysis to me, Dr. Cory, my physician, had first suggested the possibility to my two sons. The next time they arrived for a visit, they came, mentally tip-toeing around the recommendation. Ever so gently they began, "Mother," said one, "you know, Duke is making a great study of geriatrics."

"Yes, I know," I answered.

"Sometimes it's found that as people get older, they benefit from a special kind of therapy."

With that I leaped into the situation, "If you're talking about my seeing a psychoanalyst, bring me twenty!" I meant it. And they relaxed.

No time was lost in getting the word to Dr. Cory. And when this dedicated man, who rarely left the hospital to go home for dinner until nine at night, next came by my room, he said, "I've talked to your sons, and with your permission, I've chosen an analyst for you. Dr. Gianturco, whom you'll like, has agreed to see you here in your room tomorrow evening."

"Does this mean that I will have shock treatment?" I asked quickly, trying to make it halfway light, for I had a horror, perhaps as most women do, of being considered neurasthenic, and not having been born yesterday, had gathered unto myself a marvelous smattering of ignorance.

"Indeed, no," he replied. "There are eight degrees of depression. Yours is number one. You are far from needing anything like that." Then he went on to finish making his rounds.

As scheduled, the next night at seven, Dr. Gianturco appeared. I was glad that he took the easy chair in my room; it established a mood of informality, and, I suppose, in that I felt he was a guest in my room, I felt a sense of responsibility, something of a hostess, so I began the conversation. Again this was on a light note. I explained my surprise at being told that I was depressed, that my illness had now gone from the physical to the emotional, but that I was sorely in need of help, and welcomed his presence. Then it seemed in order to get down to the nitty gritty. "But Doctor, this is all new to me. How do we begin? Do I talk, or do you?" I didn't want us to flounder before we even got started.

This kind, gentle, perceptive man, must have thought, *What type of creature do I have on my hands?* At any rate, we liked each other from the start. Just as Dr. Cory had done, he knew how to help me.

Nothing of consequence from that first visit stands out, except that Dr. Gianturco made this observation, partly from his conversation with Dr. Cory, "I can tell that you don't give up easily. Dr. Cory tells me that several times a day you get up and walk around the loop in your hall, encouraging the other patients to join you. You're going to be all right.

It will just take a little time."

At the end of a few days, I was at home, beginning on a schedule of going back to see Dr. Gianturco every two weeks. Knowing how expensive an hour with a psychoanalyst is, and afraid that I would ramble and not say anything of importance, I began to sift my thoughts in advance, on legal pads. With my addiction to the pen, by the time of the visit, I had an epistle. Both the doctor and I came to laugh at this, for instead of our sessions becoming entirely dismal, they were in part, usually the reverse. For those who have never undergone analysis, I must say, that regardless of cartoons, I assume that few couches are now used. True, Dr. Gianturco's office had a sofa, but he sat behind a large desk which had photographs of his wife and children; I sat at a right angle on the sofa. There was a wall of books, apparently medical. The atmosphere was friendly, not overly professional. During our easy conversations there were often long pauses given to his taking notes. Naturally, there were sadnesses in my life to be recounted; tears to fall without embarrassment. These were mainly concerned with Tom's illness and his death, and the other family heartache that was to follow in two years; Mack and Cecile's separation.

Tom and I had always hoped that our sons would wait until after college to be married. Yet, when Mack and the lovely and artistically talented Cecile Martin of Jacksonville, Florida, and Chapel Hill by way of Sweetbriar had met, and both families had been approached on the subject of marriage, each family gave its blessing.

But, regrettably, there was not to be long-range happiness. In temperament, that aspect of life which in youth is apt to go unexamined, they were different. As the years went by, they grew apart, and in the third year following Tom's death, they went through that tragic experience which Mack describes as a "little death": divorce.

Yet, in recounting these things to Dr. Gianturco that day, I could say with thankfulness, and some pride, that Mack and Cecile's son, my grandson, Brad, who had been fifteen at the time of the separation, had gone on to graduate Cum Laude from Washington and Lee University in Lexington, Virginia and to obtain a Law Degree from the University of Florida. A few years later I would have been able to add that Brad has begun the practice of law in Florida, at the same time, maintaining a keen interest in musical composition, and that, in time, his parents would have each found a second happiness. After a few years, Mack remarried. Cecile is now back in Jacksonville among her old friends, and has become a successful realtor. I, who for so long had *no* daughter, now in my heart have two. Each of them has always been introduced as "my daughter," not the less-warm term, "daughter-in-law." For that is the way I feel.

My new daughter, Janice, and Mack have now been married for eight years. Janice is a dedicated environmentalist, an interest that Mack is catching. They have built a simple home on the side of a mountain near Ashville; Mack continues to come back to Rocky Mount often on business. Before that afternoon session with the Doctor was over, I could see, as he had said it would, my depression was lifting. I could even say to him, when Mack and Janice come to see me, they good-naturedly chide me about not using Saran Wrap a second time. I replied that I had a hard enough time with it on the first go-round, and we jokingly agreed that a life of seventy decades – going on eight – should allow some margin for error.

But no one session was without the introduction of the philosophical. When I expressed having been surprised at the diagnosis of situational depression, with, "Especially since you have said that you find me lively. Aren't the two contradictory?" the doctor answered, "No, not necessarily. In fact, bringing levity into life is a natural defense against life's sorrows."

"Then, isn't that provision of nature something like Byron's line: "If I laugh at any mortal thing, it is in order that I not weep?" For you certainly don't have to live to be very old to know that in one form or another, nobody escapes adversity and sorrow."

"Oh, yes. It's been said in many different ways down the ages," the Doctor replied.

"So that obviously humor is our saving grace," I began. "After all, aren't humans the only creatures who have the ability to laugh, Dr. Gianturco? I've never heard a laughing hyena, but I should think the noise would be called a laugh only because of its rhythm, something like a 'Ho! Ho! Ho!'. For certainly the laughing gulls at Captiva never sounded happy, even though I loved to hear them shatter the warm, languid stillness of a afternoon with their three rapid nasal, 'Hank! Hank! Hanks!'. Their reverberations lingering against the equally toneless caw of the fish crow made the repetitious coo of the dove the more beautiful. But you can see that I'm a romantic, Doctor. I tend to be fanciful, and to jump to conclusions; to over simplify, and as I've told you, I've always been considered impulsive by my friends and my family, a sort of mish-mash personality."

I could soon see that an analyst has to be a philosopher, a teacher, and has to have the patience of Job. By mutual but silent consent, however, our interviews always ended on a positive note, and I felt that progress was being made. Of the telling things that I remember verbatim from this succession of visits, was the comment which Dr. Gianturco made somewhere in one of our discussions about the human condition, "Oh, life is a struggle!" he said.

Yet we each knew that that was a point of view not to be sustained. And the session over, the secretary would give me another appointment two weeks away.

For the second interview with the doctor, I went into my adulthood. "Dr. Gianturco," I began, "I had one of the happiest marriages in the world."

Then I shared with the doctor one of my most treasured memories, one with which nothing could compare. For, to me, it conveys some of the best things that go with a good marriage: honesty, fairness, and the wisdom that comes with maturity; all of it bound in never-failing affection. It was a day when Tom had some commitment, either in Raleigh or Chapel Hill; I was going along for a day of a different kind; perhaps there would be lunch with a friend. Although at the appointed time for our starting out, Tom was back at home and ready to leave, I was still involved turning those "taps" which come to a woman's mind before she leaves her house for the day. Against the possibility of my having an unpredicted long wait for Tom before starting home, my final preoccupation was the gathering of several books, a legal pad, and some ball-points to go into an approximation of a shopping bag.

Poor Tom sat in the car, patiently waiting. When I finally made it into my seat, I was filled with remorse. As we drove out through the gate, I recovered enough breath to say apologetically, "There must have been many things about me over the years that you would have changed if you'd been able to."

His answer was one that gave me that most treasured of memories, for he said, quietly, "No. For to have changed those would have been to change others."

I felt that this little incident was one which the analyst might find pleasant. And he did, indeed, smile in appreciation as his answer came, understandingly, "He saw you as a whole person."

I can't imagine what my life would have been without Tom. Although I suppose it's naive to think that there's only one man in the world for every woman or vice versa, it was what we believed about our marriage. And although there had been five years since Tom's death when I began seeing Dr. Gianturco, in that from the very beginning I had tried to be strong in every way, I suppose I might just have tried too hard.

There was something that had happened when Tom was perfectly well that had made me know how he would have felt about the death of one or the other of us. We had gone for a visit to our friend Frank Wilkinson, who was slowly dying at home, of emphysema. Dot had cheerfully met us at the door, and during our visit in Frank's room, we could see that those two were meeting the situation with composure. When we left and were on the way home, Tom said, "If something like that," meaning terminal illness, "should happen to me, I hope you will be as sensible as Dot is being." For Tom always believed in doing the sensible thing.

It was February when I returned home from Duke after Dr. Cory discharged me from the hospital stay that had carried me over to the beginning of analysis. At home the next day there came one of our rare snowstorms. For a few days the community lived in a white frozen world under six inches of snow, every limb and every twig covered in ice. Even my domestics couldn't come, and impulsively, I began to write the story of my illness. I wrote almost without volition, without any sense of direction. With the thaw a few days later, I took what I had written to a printer, and as a surprise for Dr. Cory, had it made into a booklet. By the time I was due back for my first office visit with Dr. Gianturco, two weeks later, the booklet for Dr. Cory was ready. Its dedication read:

To
Dr. Ralph Cory
of
Duke Hospital
and
to
The Memory of Tom,
who over the fifty-two years of our
marriage would often say, patiently,
and wisely, of a given situation,
Things have to evolve.

At the end of that second interview with Dr. Gianturco, I went to another part of the hospital to find Dr. Cory's office. I was not expected, yet a kindly receptionist allowed me two minutes of the Doctor's time between a large number of waiting patients. Surprised to see me, but seemingly glad, there was just time enough for me to take from behind my back the small blue booklet of twenty-five pages, its title: *From a Southern Way of Life,* and to hand it to him, saying one word, "Goals!"

For this had been his parting admonition when I was being dismissed from the hospital. He had led into it this way, "You think that because you've reached eighty, life is over. For a woman of your health and interests, and with your liking of people, there should be many good years ahead. Isn't there something you've always wanted to do and haven't?"

Though startled, my reply came swiftly, "Yes, I've always wanted to write a book."

"Then write it," he clipped.

The conversation was taking place in my hospital room. There had been an intern along, and as the two men were leaving, I said to them, "I don't know what I'll write about, but I'll write." And the younger man replied, "Write about life. What better subject?"

Then, on a wave of all-round harmony and good will, and on my part, good, but vague intentions, we said goodbye. I felt much pleased to have so soon given Dr. Cory such a surprise; among his patients, to be "Exhibit A" for what a firm little lecture can do.

But then Dr. Cory said, to my surprise, "I'm going to want to see you again."

"You are," I asked. "When?"

And he answered, "When you have written the second volume."

≈ ≈ ≈

Three years passed. In a more limited way, I was endeavoring to keep up an active interest in some of the things for which Tom and I had felt a responsibility. Our local college, North Carolina Wesleyan, was high on this list. As such, I continued each year to drive the three miles out for its Founder's Day celebration which comes in late October.

There had been nothing in the customary invitation that year to make me think that this anniversary program would be different from the others, when Mack, who, at the time, was still living in Rocky Mount, had suggested that we attend together. He had added, casually, that his brother, Tom, would, at that time, be in town for several days of business, and that he had indicated an interest in going as well.

When that morning came, we set out. Since the college does not, as yet, have an auditorium, these ceremonies are held in the gym. The faculty and the students are adept at making the conversion, however, and except for the use of folding chairs in front of the bleachers, you can forget your surroundings. Being ushered to front seats was, to me, not unexpected; because of Tom's having been a Trustee, we'd always been seated there. In addition, local people, knowing that I have a hearing loss, are always taking care of me.

The loss of my hearing had begun when I was in my fifties. Consultations with specialists had brought an agreement among them that since there was nerve damage, there was nothing to be done. With the comforting prognosis that it was doubtful that I would ever completely lose all hearing, as is sometimes the case with nerve damage, for several subsequent years I had resisted resorting to any kind of hearing aid. Perhaps I was afraid of becoming dependent on that kind of help.

Finally it dawned on me that I was being unfair to my family not to try, and I went through those first months of wondering whether I was better equipped with or without. For while it was true that it was lovely to hear the birds sing again, the amplification of the garble of small noises that filled the air was maddening. With time and perseverance, however, and with continuous improvements being made for the modulation of noises in those wonderful instruments, this annoyance became negligible. And with that first morning prayer of thanksgiving which has long been my habit as I lie in bed, "Oh Lord, I thank you for morning light, and that I have eyes to see," I began to add, "and thank-you for Alexander Graham Bell." And I would be thinking of the story of this man's interesting life.

Born in Scotland, the young Alexander had begun to work closely with his father, and had travelled with him to give lectures on the science of speech in Edinburgh, London, Washington, and Boston. Soon the young Alexander began lecturing on his own in Boston, on the side working on projects that would lead to inventions in the transmitting of sound. Among his more well-known achievements was an invention for the deaf, and he engaged in numerous studies that would ultimately mean the triumph of almost restored hearing.

As a child, I had known one old man who, because of his deafness, used an "ear trumpet," one of those long curved horns that was somehow always amusing to see, especially if you were a child. To think that now that we have, through a tiny battery in a nearly invisible instrument, the ability to be open to life on all fronts, is, to me, one of the miracles.

In my case, the hearing aid, per se, has been so successful that strangers are unaware that I have a hearing difficulty. Its major drawback is that in large social gatherings – wedding receptions or cocktail parties – the combination of the hum of voices and music becomes deadly. But since much of life is spent learning to cope, I have found a way. Arriving at one of those large social gatherings, and realizing that there is music, I unobtrusively, as though I were touching my hair, manage to pocket the hearing aid in my purse. And since very little is said at large cocktail parties that couldn't be done without, I find that my own combination of a broad smile and a bright, "Really?" usually takes care of the situation.

Church is a different matter. I'm rarely able to follow the sermon, but the prayers and the music and the meditation are enough. I find myself more and more, however, attending the earliest of the morning services, at eight o'clock. There is no music then, and no sermon, but being there when the air is fresh and the morning light streams through the stained glass – those things conducive to meditation – is a beautiful way to start the day.

The morning of that particular Founder's Day, to which I've referred, opened with numbers from the glee club and was followed by a talk from President Leslie Garner. This led to an address from Judge Phil Carlton, long a Chairman of the Board of Trustees. As always, it was inspiring to be informed of where the college stood at the moment. That over, the speaker's remarks took on another aspect. As I sat, comfortably relaxed, I suddenly heard my name being mentioned, and of all things, in connection with an award, the Algernon Sydney Sullivan, given by the college once a year. Not only that, but Phil was saying, "I should like first to read to you a letter that came from Mrs. Pearsall to me as Chairman of the Trustees a few months ago, with the information that she was planning a contribution to the college library." And he read:

December 13, 1988

Dear Phil:

After considering the possible areas for contributions to Wesleyan I have decided on the library.

This letter contains a few thoughts that I should like to express in that connection, my reasons for having selected Wesleyan, and specifically, the library, for the largest single donation of my life, reasons why, to me, it is the rounding out of something meaningful and personal.

My thoughts have run along the paragraphs attached which I hope you will share with the other Trustees.

Very sincerely,

Elizabeth Pearsall

Thoughts From Elizabeth Braswell Pearsall

My life, from the beginning, has been blessed with economic security. This security has come about through the land and the fruits thereof, the agricultural products of Eastern Carolina.

My father was a rather large land owner, and in a system of share-cropping, which was the prevailing way at the time, we had a great many tenants.

Doing their best for themselves and for us, the days for these workers went from dawn to dusk, with back breaking toil; often their children were kept out of school to help in the fields. In spite of everything, weather conditions sometimes led to crop failure, or some blight would come for which there was no known remedy. Yet the tenants worked cheerfully, they asked little of life, and – with rare exceptions – were honorable in every way.

Living in the center of our farms, our family, my mother, my father, and my three sisters, the three much older than I – and there were to be no sons – our lives and those of the tenants were twined and intertwined in a thousand-and-one ways. We saw, at close range, that they had a strength of character to match their physical strength, and, I suppose this was my first insight into that greatest of the imponderables, the inequities of life.

With the coming of automation to Eastern Carolina, farm work became less hard, science stepped in with the control of blights, but alas, through no fault of their own a great mass of the people in our area were and are without jobs. For although industry has come, these people know only one kind of work, and in factories, where skilled labor is required, industry can absorb only so many.

This places Eastern Carolina in a period of transition. Not to believe that our problem has a solution is not to believe in ourselves and in this the part of the world that we all love best and want most to see achieve economic security for all.

During the meantime there must be leadership, and leadership-training, and collective thinking, and collective effort.

Fate, as you know, has sent us – in the President of Wesleyan College – a young man, an Eastern Carolinian himself, a man with a vision, a vision for the betterment of Eastern Carolina. He is in a key position. And it gives me pleasure to feel that in this gift to the Wesleyan College Library I may, in some measure, be providing impetus to the endeavor, that I may – in some way – be returning something to where it belongs.

With the elevating surprise of that honor, I was escorted to the dais to receive a framed citation explaining the origin of the medal and of the award – 1925 – and a mounted bronze medal which holds a quotation from Lowell: "He reached out both hands in constant helpfulness to his fellow men. As one lamp lights another, nor grows less, so nobleness enkindleth nobleness." My own name was on the base.

As the medal and the citation were handed to me there rose a wave of applause. When it had subsided, Judge Carlton asked me, in a whisper, if I would like to say something, and, swept along – dreamlike – I moved to the podium. And from somewhere on high, was able to utter a few sentences of gratitude, of pride in our college, and faith in its future. By this time I was being given a standing ovation, and was being escorted back to my seat and a row of embracing arms. I had never felt more humbled.

As though that were not enough, a year later, a few months ahead of the following Founder's Day, I was informed that the name of the college library would, on that day in late October, be given my name. *How could all this be true?* I wondered.

When the day came, it was unseasonably cold for October in Eastern Carolina. I hurriedly let go the idea of wearing my silk suit, to substitute one of wool, because the program was to be held outside.

When I arrived, I found that my local friends of all ages had loyally attended. I worried a little that they seemed lightly clad, had not been aware of the sudden change in temperature, and hoped that none of them would develop colds. But I worried only briefly, for the beautiful one-story building that is the library had been brought to a peak of loveliness with a wealth of potted yellow chrysanthemums on each side of its broad steps. With the scheduled choral numbers from the glee club and Dr. Garner's address from a platform that had been erected to one side of the steps over, he came down the steps to escort me up the library steps where I was joined by my two sons – "*our sons*" I thought, with a lump in my throat – who were standing on a lower step. At my side, Dr. Garner lifted the black cloth from the plaque which, when unveiled, read, *Elizabeth Braswell Pearsall*. Not knowing what else to do, I waved, and smiled to the whole of the cheering section.

Hardly aware of the photographers – they were kneeling on the steps below and snapping away – a collective joy seemed to carry the day. The next day, the photographs appeared, in color, on the front page of our local paper. As the papers were delivered that afternoon, my telephone began to ring. Friends were asking, "Have you seen your picture?" Not having brought my own paper in, I had not. "Well, run out and get your paper!" said one friend of longstanding. "You'll be surprised at how young you look in that sassy white beret and scarf." Two woolen items I had ferreted out of moth balls that morning at the last minute.

From another friend, "That old red plaid suit of yours came out fine in the picture. It blended so well with the shade of the President's red robe." Leave it to women! We don't miss much.

From a third, "We're all carried away with that picture of you waving and smiling. You did our generation proud."

These are the joys of small town life. That Founder's Day celebration came several years ago. The time in between has been spent with almost daily writing on the story of my life. Now it is early spring of 1995, and that writing nearing the end. Soon after that honor, I began to look in another direction. I was making plans to attend the coming reunion of my class at Salem College, in the city of Winston-Salem, two-hundred-miles to the west. A form letter was sent out by the alumni secretary, announcing those classes that had been selected for reunions in the spring of '92. My own was among them. As usual, there was an appeal for attendance, and in a surge of awareness of the continuity in my life in regard to Salem – Mother, my sisters, my aunts, my cousins, and even as far back as Grandma Bryan – I wrote that I would be there.

A few weeks later, a second letter came. This one was from the president of my own class, the Anna Pauline Schaffner who to our class had been "A.P.," and who has since become Anna Pauline Schaffner Slye. A.P. is our perennial alumni class president, and her letter was a reminder of the classes having their reunions. The list began with the Class of 1924; it was followed by a biographical capsule of news items which those planning to attend had earlier sent in about themselves. My own capsule of information came under *Class of 1927.* It read:

> *Elizabeth Braswell Pearsall writes that she's coming for the reunion, that she has had a happy, and relatively useful life as wife and mother. That she is now at work on her memoirs. By hand. And finding it a pleasurable pastime.*

And a pleasurable pastime it has continued to be. For, as the novelist Madeleine L'Engle says in that lovely book of hers, *A Circle of Quiet:*

"Although we write in isolation, we are not alone. It is our reaction to the world in which we live."

Slowly, this becomes the attitude of the amateur, and we cannot write enough.

Tom was right. Things do have to evolve.

Afterword

Although I am not now, and never have been, other than indirectly and informally at occasional small meetings, involved in family business affairs, in a nebulous way – willy-nilly –I seem to get involved. I'm always getting messages to have planes met, and although I use only one car, I have to see that there are always three on the premises at the ready, for my sons are always flying in and out for one reason or another.

Mack and Janice still make their home three-hundred miles away near Asheville. Although the home they built is simple, their mountaintop property was carefully chosen for its proximity to Asheville and to the local airport, a twenty-five minute drive from each. In Mack's office, a short walk from the house, where, more than likely, their two retrievers keep him company, he is involved in a challenge of another kind. Having two years ago co-chaired the successful campaign for Governor Jim Hunt, he has been asked to co-chair, with Julianne Thrift, President of Salem College, a commission for a continually competitive North Carolina, more specifically, to work in a collaborative effort, with forty state leaders to devise and to help implement a plan for a new economic and human resource development strategy for North Carolina for the remainder of the 1990s and into the 21st century.

Mack says that with the arrival of 1996 he will retire. To that end, he and Janice have recently bought a sailboat, one which they themselves will crew. It is being berthed at Wrightsville Beach. To tease me, as my menfolk have always done, he adds that they "plan to sail uncharted seas, and land on barbarous coasts."

My answer is a light one, "Couldn't you postpone that until I've gone to dwell among the angels?"

"Oh, No!" he says. "We're planning to take you with us!"

"I was only fishing for an invitation. For I bid to man the crow's nest."

My son, Tom, continues his work in New York as an architectural consultant, where he has been studying and teaching Interior Design while pursuing his doctorate in that field. This sometimes takes him to Paris for a month in summer. In recognition of their interest in the arts, Tom and Mack have endowed the conversion of a building at North Carolina Wesleyan College, formerly known as the Power Plant, to house academic classrooms for studies supporting music and the visual arts. The renovated building will be known as the Thomas J. Pearsall II Center for the Fine Arts.

Something else of significance to our family, and yet, not one to command public attention, came about recently. It was in connection with

"Head Start," the federally funded movement for giving children a better future than might otherwise be theirs.

Head Start, when it began some twenty years ago, became one of Tom's major interests. With the coming of automation, cultivation of farm land required fewer tenants. State and federal organizations providing instruction in infant care, homemaking, and nutrition were at work, making our central cannery that had served in those capacities for our farm families no longer necessary. Those services had been formerly dispensed from an old store in the village that had been attractively converted for the purpose. The building now stood empty, and we offered it to the leaders in the black community for a community center. Seeing how successful this had become, we soon offered to build something more modern in an area where there would be room for playgrounds. The building was to be theirs, a nominal sum required for the lease of the land.

It was gratifying to find that many of those who accepted responsibility for leadership in this and subsequent community endeavors were, had been, or were the children or grandchildren of those who had been our tenants. And when the national movement called "Head Start" came into being, everything for that additional profoundly important step was in place.

But sad to say, over the years, the building suffered damage by fire, not once, but six times. In each case, arson was suspected. As discouraging as it was among those who were trying so hard to give their children a better life, there was never any feeling of recrimination; repairs were made quietly and the work went on. With the seventh fire, the building was burned to the ground. Since most of the leaders of the Head Start organization continued to be our tenants, the morning after the building had been reduced to ashes, Tom called the fathers and grandfathers together, and offered to furnish the materials for rebuilding if they would agree to work on weekends toward that end. The cooperation was enthusiastic. Reconstruction began, and with their commitment to working almost around the clock, the work was done, a very real triumph of the spirit.

It was natural, however, that with time, those who, from the beginning had so gladly assumed leadership in this community project should consider it desirable to have their organization own the land. Approached on the subject of selling it to them, our family gladly made it a gift.

On the day appointed for the transfer of the deed – to a group of people whom, in every way, we held in respect – three of their leaders met Mack at the office of our family's attorney, Bob Wiley, who, incidentally, is a favorite person of ours in his own right, as is his wife, Margaret, daughter of the afore affectionately mentioned Frank and Nimi Winslow, something

560

which I bring into the story purely for the satisfaction it gives me, the sense of the carryover that has run through my life. The spokesman for the three representatives of their organization announced their appreciation at a dinner in honor of the Braswell family, for "the many ways in which, from far back, our family had helped to lift up those who needed it," dates to be worked out later, and that was done.

So it was, that in the late afternoon of a summer day, through fields that on each side of the road were at their most lush, Tom and Mack and I drove to that branch of Head Start near the village of Battleboro, where the whole year round, children from the community gather, and where, between instruction and play, they are being molded into citizens for a world which they will, in turn, help to make. There were speakers, the food was delicious, the fellowship wonderful. To see how up-to-date their equipment is was to have high hopes for the future. I was particularly happy to see that for the toddlers' corner, there were dolls with different colored skins. And when we came out under the stars from what they have given my father's name, "M.C. Braswell Cultural and Educational Development Center, Inc.", I looked up, and the stars seemed bright.

To add to this family diversity, in a spirit of "What next?" which, I suppose, helps to keep me on my toes, there is my daughter, Janice's, dedication to the environment and to all avenues of promoting its awareness. At the moment, she is making summer plans to visit Mexico and Costa Rica to brush up on her language skills. From a friendship formed earlier, through the Big Sisters branch of Youth Improvement, she will be accompanied by a young twelve-year-old girl from Rocky Mount, Jennifer May.

At Christmas, there came the happy news from Florida that my grandson, Brad, is married. All we know at the moment, is that his bride has a lovely name, Sarah Duran, that she happens to be a lawyer, and that she comes from the state of Michigan. Brad and Sarah will be setting up a law practice together, as Duran & Pearsall, where they will specialize in Immigration Law. Sarah's first note to us is lovely and warm, and our family is excited over getting to know her.

As for myself, when the time for my aforementioned class reunion at Salem drew near, I decided not to attend, mainly, because it had gradually come to me that to enjoy it in all its aspects would have meant being on foot, uphill and down, among those beautiful hills that, from a distance, give the college the appeal of a lovely well-kept German village. For, in this, as in a thousand other ways, the Moravians have left their mark. Even so, it was better for me to enjoy the reunion at a remove.

In the general whirlwind of family activity, of which I get the backwash,

I go along with my quieter pursuits. As always, I continue to enjoy what Timmie Battle speaks of as "playing house," for shifting furniture and objects of art to enhance the pleasure they give me has always been second nature, so much so, that although I'm not given to changing fabrics and the colors of walls often, I've recently done something that to a person of twenty or thirty or forty might seem more than odd: at eighty-seven, I've just had the seats of my dining room chairs re-covered, replacing the subdued champagne shade they'd long worn with the freshness of white, a pleasing contrast to the dark wood of the Chippendale design of the chairs. As I came downstairs into the hall the morning after the chairs had come back from the upholsterer, I could see them through the opening of the double doors into the dining room, and was enraptured. For now I've completed the Captiva-look I'd set out to achieve twelve years ago when we sold our island home. The process has been gradual. A decorator could never have done it for me, for it had to have a certain hit-or-miss quality, the Captiva way. The display of some of the things I've collected, especially the largest of my tiles, which, sitting on their teakwood stands, take me back to my travels, and my trademark random piles of books and bowls of fruit make it unmistakably my own. Having it accrue was part and parcel of the satisfaction. The white of the chairs in harmony with the use of white throughout the house, seems to have brought things full circle. I now have, here, the atmosphere of "our island," a daily reminder of those charmed years.

That at such a great age I should be making aesthetic changes in the house has made me think of something that Uncle Jim once said. When he had reached eighty, and was living quietly at home with domestics and Miss Bertha, the nurse, to take care of his health, he suddenly decided to have a door cut from a side hall into the living room. He explained that while it would rarely be used in this solitary life he lived, for he sat altogether in the library, the oversight of not having a door in that strategic spot had been inconvenient for a long time, and might as well be changed. Then he added, sagaciously, "Don't ever get too old to cut a door in your house if the spirit moves you."

Concurrent with my writing I am up to my elbows in a new interest, that of making starter bread, sharing the treat with friends and relatives, dropping by to see them with a loaf or two which I make important by having them nestled in a small, handpainted basket under an attractive cloth. I've hardly enjoyed anything so much, and as my plaudits grow louder and my reputation spreads, my loaves grow smaller, the more to enlarge my clientele. For, as my friend, Jay, used to say of all those years at Vassar where, while reading the *New York Times* on Sunday afternoon, she would

562

be baking four large, lovely brown loaves, "When I knead bread I'm always conscious of early woman. Although the first of her needs must have been to get animal skins on the family, surely the second must have been to provide them with the staff of life." I, too, as I mix and let rise and bake – the aroma spreading over the house – feel a bond, not only with early woman, but with all women over time, and am glad.

Appendix

Data on the Braswell family as taken from *Rocky Mount: The Peer of Any City in the Good Ol' North State, and the Rapidity of its Growth and Development*, published around 1910.

Mr. M. C. Braswell

Proprietor of Largest Supply Business in State. Farms on
Immense Scale.
Interested in Many Enterprises

The general supply business conducted by Mr. M.C. Braswell at Battleboro is one of the largest, if not the largest, in volume of business transacted, in Carolina. The business was until a few years ago conducted under the firm name of T.P. Braswell & Son, being composed of two partners, the late loved and lamented father of the present proprietor being the senior member. However, at that time Mr. M.C. Braswell was the active manager of the business. At the death of the senior member, the business passed under the sole proprietorship of the latter and he has continued to conduct it in the same capable manner. The volume of business done annually will amount to a quarter million dollars. As a supply house, it ranks second to none in Eastern North Carolina, and is one of the largest retail dealers in fertilizers in the State, selling more than 3500 tons annually.

No man in this section of the State is held in higher esteem than Mr. M.C. Braswell. He has not made his worldly goods by grinding down his fellow man, but by dint of hard, persistent work, combined with a mind that is acutely fitted to handle business problems. In fact, Mr. Braswell has been successful in practically all that he has undertaken, and has not only accumulated wealth, but his lines of endeavor have always been broad gauged, and he has been ready and willing to join in any enterprise that would help build larger or better the community in which he has lived. Though living in Battleboro, eight miles from Rocky Mount, he owns considerable property in the latter city, is a director in a large number of business institutions in this city and a stockholder in practically every corporation gotten up for the advancement of the city. Mr. Braswell is also a large planter. He is one of the largest land owners in Nash and Edgecombe counties and plants cotton, tobacco and peanuts on a large scale.

Mr. Braswell has two brothers living in Rocky Mount, Mr. J.C. Braswell, president of The Planters Bank and Dr. M. R. Braswell, both of

564

whom have been mentioned in several places in this book, as they also have been identified in a very large measure with the wonderful development and growth of Rocky Mount. In fact, the three brothers have been of incalculable benefit to this section of the State. They have what is seldom found combined, the means, the ability and the inclination for progress and by bringing these combined elements into operation it can be said without question that they have exerted by far the largest influence in the growth of Rocky Mount of any one family.

Mr. M.C. Braswell was married in 1894 to Miss Alice Bryan, a charming and cultured woman, and a member of one of the most highly respected families in the county. They live in truly a palatial home, a picture of which is shown in these pages. They have four children.

T. P. Braswell & Son

This firm is decidedly the most prominent one in Nash County, and fills a distinguished place among the leading mercantile concerns of Eastern North Carolina. Composed of two partners, each of whom is so prominent in the financial world, the concern cannot easily fail being what it is. T. P. Braswell & Son do an annual business of $150,000.00. As supply people they rank second to none and are among the largest retail dealer in fertilizers, selling annually more than 2,000 tons. The firm owns more than 4,000 acres of land situated in Nash and Edgecombe Counties. In an individual way, Mr. T. P. Braswell, the senior member of the firm, owns 5,000 acres of land. Leaving out of consideration the many other minor crops, he plants every year 250 acres of tobacco, 350 acres in cotton, and 75 in peanuts. Mr. M.C. Braswell plants annually 150 acres of tobacco, 500 in cotton and 150 in peanuts. Combining the individual interest of the two partners, with that of their partnership interest, they rank as the largest farmers in North Carolina. The firm, as well as the individual members of it, are singularly free from debts or obligations of any character except current ones. The acquisition of so much wealth by men who had all to gain by their own talent, activity and enterprise in the financial world, requires that some attention be paid to the two remarkable men who compose the firm.

Thos. P. Braswell was born in Edgecombe County in 1832, now being 74 years of age. Since his early manhood he has been conspicuous in the affairs of Nash County. While yet young his countymen recognized him to be honest, reliable and of unusual force and ability, elected him to represent the county in the Legislature. The duties of the office he discharged in a manner creditable to himself and constituency. He has also served as chairman of the county commissioners and also chairman of the Democratic Executive Committee of Nash County. In many other ways he has been a strong vital force in shaping the good government and healthy public sentiment that prevails so largely in his county. Broad gauged, of perfect mental balance and equipoise, with a vast fund of human kindliness in his composition, he has the respect of every one so fortunate as to know him well. The "Old Squire," as his many friends love to call him, occupies a place in their esteem that nothing can eradicate. He is a philosopher of that kindly school who reason that there is something of good in every man, and it is something of frequent virtue more or less bright that goes to palliate. Cool and never disturbed, with a brain superlative in its strength and unerring in judgment, he stands unexcelled by any business man of this section. Neither has his success in life been peculiar to himself any more than that of many of his sterling qualities. He has raised a family of three boys, M.C. Braswell before mentioned, Dr. M.R. Braswell and J.C. Braswell. To each of them he has imparted in a large measure the same splendid judgment, perfect mental composition and undefinable quality that wins success in everything all the time.

Dr. M.R. Braswell is a prominent physician of Rocky Mount and, besides other large and varied interests, occupies a conspicuous place in the insurance world as president of the Underwriters Fire Insurance Co. of Rocky Mount.

Mr. J.C. Braswell has achieved both distinction and success as banker, tobacconist, merchant, mill man and farmer. It seldom falls to the lots of one in life to have the happy fortune of transmitting to his children whatever of good quality he possesses and of knowing that all of them deservedly command the respect and confidence of all.

Mr. M.C. Braswell, whom we have before alluded to as the junior member of the firm of T. P. Braswell & Son, has entitled him to political preferments, but every time he has been offered the glittering prize of public office his multitudinous private business cares and innate good sense led him to decline. He is of that superior mental build in connection with perfect habits, energy and enterprise that will give prominence in whatever field of endeavor he may embark.

He, too, is a man of large and varied talents with the quality of concentrating his splendid mental force upon whatever undertaking he has in hand. NO interest of concern is too large for him to manage successfully and neither is any detail too small for him to see that it is properly looked after and adjusted to its right place. To him belongs the encomium of having dealt with all manner of men in almost every legitimate business in the country without having upon his character and business reputation the slightest blemish.

He has a beautiful home in Battleboro, presided over by one of the most charming and accomplished women in North Carolina. He was married some years ago to Miss Alice Bryan, a member of the distinguished Edgecombe family of that name. They have an interesting family. His whole life might be summed up as ideal.

Though Messrs. T. P. and M.C. Braswell live at Battleboro, 8 miles from Rocky Mount, they are the largest real estate owners in Rocky Mount and are the largest stockholders in The Planters Bank, Mr. M.C. Braswell being one of its directors. They are also identified largely with a great many other enterprises in Rocky Mount, and can always be counted in the lead for the upbuilding of the town.

Supplemental note on Robert Bracewell, the original Braswell American ancestor:

Oxford University and colonial Virginia's records show that, in his eagerness for the challenges of the new world, the young ministerial student, Robert Bracewell, left the university for the Jamestown colony before getting his degree, but that, in 1631, he went back for it, returning then to continue his work for the church, and to live out his life in Tidewater Virginia.